HANDBOOK OF RESEARCH NEGOTIATION

Handbook of Research on Negotiation

Edited by

Mara Olekalns

Professor of Management (Negotiation), Melbourne Business School, Australia

Wendi L. Adair

Associate Professor of Organizational Psychology, University of Waterloo, Canada

Edward Elgar
Cheltenham, UK • Northampton, MA, USA

© Mara Olekalns and Wendi L. Adair 2013

All rights reserved. No part of this publication may be reproduced, stored in a retrieval system or transmitted in any form or by any means, electronic, mechanical or photocopying, recording, or otherwise without the prior permission of the publisher.

Published by
Edward Elgar Publishing Limited
The Lypiatts
15 Lansdown Road
Cheltenham
Glos GL50 2JA
UK

Edward Elgar Publishing, Inc.
William Pratt House
9 Dewey Court
Northampton
Massachusetts 01060
USA

A catalogue record for this book
is available from the British Library

Library of Congress Control Number: 2013930510

This book is available electronically in the ElgarOnline.com Business Subject Collection, E-ISBN 978 1 78100 590 3

ISBN 978 1 78100 589 7 (cased)

Typeset by Servis Filmsetting Ltd, Stockport, Cheshire
Printed and bound in Great Britain by T.J. International Ltd, Padstow

Contents

List of figures	vii
List of tables	viii
List of contributors	ix

PART I INTRODUCTION

1 The complexity of negotiating: from the individual to the context, and what lies between — *Mara Olekalns and Wendi L. Adair* ... 3

PART II THE INDIVIDUAL NEGOTIATOR

2 Individual differences in negotiation — *Hillary Anger Elfenbein* ... 25

3 Motivated cognition in negotiation — *Lukas Koning and Eric van Dijk* ... 46

4 Shared cognition and identity in negotiation — *Leigh Anne Liu and Wei Cai* ... 75

5 The demise of the 'rational' negotiator: emotional forces in conflict and negotiation — *Gerben A. Van Kleef and Marwan Sinaceur* ... 103

PART III SOCIAL-PSYCHOLOGICAL PROCESSES

6 Power, status, and influence in negotiation — *Jennifer R. Overbeck and Yoo Kyoung Kim* ... 133

7 Trust and negotiation — *Roy J. Lewicki and Beth Polin* ... 161

8 Fairness and ethics in bargaining and negotiation — *Kristina A. Diekmann, Andrew T. Soderberg and Ann E. Tenbrunsel* ... 191

9 Gender and negotiation: a social role analysis — *Alice F. Stuhlmacher and Eileen Linnabery* ... 221

10 Dignity, Face, and Honor cultures: implications for negotiation and conflict management — *Soroush Aslani, Jimena Ramirez-Marin, Zhaleh Semnani-Azad, Jeanne M. Brett and Catherine Tinsley* ... 249

11 Managing uncertainty in multiparty negotiations 283
   Harris Sondak, Margaret A. Neale and Elizabeth A. Mannix

PART IV   COMMUNICATION PROCESSES

12 Talking it through: communication sequences in negotiation 311
   Wendi L. Adair and Jeffrey Loewenstein
13 Punctuated negotiations: transitions, interruptions, and
   turning points 332
   Daniel Druckman and Mara Olekalns
14 The costs and benefits of e-negotiations 357
   Raymond Friedman and Liuba Y. Belkin

PART V   COMPLEX NEGOTIATIONS

15 International trade negotiations 387
   Larry Crump
16 Making peace through negotiation 416
   Kristine Höglund and Daniel Druckman
17 Environmental disputes: negotiating over risks, values and
   the future 445
   Barbara Gray and Julia Wondolleck
18 Crisis negotiation: from suicide to terrorism intervention 473
   Simon Wells, Paul J. Taylor and Ellen Giebels

PART VI   CONCLUSION

19 Guiding new directions in negotiation research: a negotiation
   context levels framework 499
   Wendi L. Adair and Mara Olekalns

Index 519

Figures

1.1	Four perspectives on the negotiation process	4
3.1	Social motivations categorized by weight assigned to own (vertical axis) and other's outcomes (horizontal axis)	49
4.1	Conceptual model on shared cognition and identity in negotiation	78
4.2	Relationship of mental models and outcomes in negotiation in Liu et al. (2012a)	81
8.1	Amount of research in fairness/ethics (construct) × actor/recipient (role) × bargaining/negotiation (context)	210
9.1	Examples of factors that increase negotiator role and gender role congruity for women	235
13.1	Framework for analyzing turning points	335
13.2	Turning point sequence for conflicts of interest	344
13.3	Turning point sequences for cognitive conflicts	344
13.4	Turning point sequence for value-based conflicts	344
13.5	An expanded model of turning point sequences	352
14.1	Into-the-wind strategy	377
17.1	Factors shaping the framing and outcomes of environmental negotiations	452
18.1	A schematic overview of the interpersonal skills relevant to communicating with antagonistic individuals	474

Tables

3.1	Example item of the Triple Dominance Measure of social value orientation	51
3.2	Example of a multi-issue negotiation with integrative potential	55
3.3	Example payoff structure of the Motivated Deception Game	65
10.1	Cultural logics of Dignity, Face, and Honor for conflict management	255
10.2	Cultural factors that influence negotiation strategy	267
12.1	Negotiation content analysis coding schemes	313
14.1	Summary of empirical findings on computer mediated communication	361
14.2	Summary of findings of effects of CMC on negotiations	366
18.1	The Table of Ten influence tactics	485
19.1	Negotiation context levels framework	506

Contributors

Wendi L. Adair (Ph.D., Northwestern University) is Associate Professor of Organizational Psychology at the University of Waterloo (Ontario, Canada). Her research focuses on communication processes in the multicultural workplace, specifically in the contexts of negotiation, conflict management, and teamwork. She teaches these topics and other topics including multiculturalism and managing diversity to university, executive, and industry audiences. Her award-winning research appears in journals including *Journal of Applied Psychology*, *Organization Science*, and *Negotiation and Conflict Management Research*, and in multiple edited volumes.

Soroush Aslani is a Ph.D. Candidate in Management and Organizations at the Kellogg School of Management at Northwestern University. His research is primarily in the area of negotiation and conflict management. In particular, he studies the motives, attitudes, emotions and strategies of people in honor cultures when they engage in bargaining and disputes. He is also interested in the micro-foundations of the problem of collective action and examines how different frames and discourses resonate with different audiences of a movement or a social cause.

Liuba Y. Belkin is an Assistant Professor in the Department of Management, College of Business and Economics, Lehigh University. She received her Ph.D. at Rutgers University. Professor Belkin conducts her research in the areas of Organizational Behavior and Negotiations, with interests in emotions and affect, communication media, trust and ethical decision-making. Her work has been published in a variety of academic journals, including *Journal of Applied Psychology*, *Organizational Behavior and Human Decision Processes*, and *Journal of International Business Studies*, among others.

Jeanne M. Brett is the DeWitt W. Buchanan, Jr., Professor of Dispute Resolution and Organizations at the Kellogg School of Management, Northwestern University. She received a Ph.D. degree in psychology from the University of Illinois. Her research focuses on culture and negotiation strategy.

Wei Cai is an MBA student at Georgia State University's Robinson College of Business, Atlanta. Her research interests are broadly focused on cross-cultural cognition, negotiation and conflict resolution. She received her doctorate in Chinese language and linguistics from Fudan University, China.

Larry Crump specializes in the study of complex negotiations and developing methodology to conceptualize such phenomena. Over the past ten years Larry has focused on bilateral, regional and multilateral trade treaty negotiations between nations to advance negotiation linkage theory, temporal theory, framing theory, and turning points theory. He has won awards for his teaching and research – most recently the 2010 Outstanding Book Award presented by the International Association for Conflict Management for *Multiparty Negotiation* (Sage, 2008), co-edited with Lawrence E. Susskind (MIT). Larry serves on the International Advisory Board of *International Negotiation*, the Editorial Advisory Board of the *Negotiation Journal*, and the Editorial Board of the journal *Negotiation and Conflict Management Research*. He has a tenured appointment with the Department of International Business, Griffith University, Brisbane, Australia.

Kristina A. Diekmann is the Bill Daniels Professor of Business Ethics in the David Eccles School of Business at the University of Utah. She received M.S. and Ph.D. degrees in Organizational Behavior from the Kellogg Graduate School of Management at Northwestern University and an A.B. degree in Psychology from Harvard College. Her research focuses on fairness and ethics, negotiation, intrapersonal and interpersonal perception, cognitive biases, and impression management.

Daniel Druckman is Professor of Public and International Affairs at George Mason University, and has been a distinguished scholar at several universities in Australia. He has published widely on topics ranging from international negotiation to electronic mediation and nonverbal communication. Two recent books – *Doing Research: Methods of Inquiry for Conflict Analysis* (Sage, 2005) and, with Paul F. Diehl, *Evaluating Peace Operations* (Lynne Reinner, 2010) – received the outstanding book award from the International Association for Conflict Management (IACM). He also received a lifetime achievement award from the IACM.

Hillary Anger Elfenbein is a Professor at the Olin School of Business at Washington University in St. Louis. She holds a Ph.D. in Organizational Behavior, a Master's degree in Statistics, and undergraduate degrees in Physics and Sanskrit, all from Harvard University. Her research focuses on interpersonal behavior and systematic differences across individuals in interpersonal functioning. Her work has appeared in the *Academy of Management Annals*, *Academy of Management Journal*, *Journal of Applied*

Psychology, Journal of Personality and Social Psychology, Psychological Bulletin, and *Psychological Science.* She is currently an Associate Editor at *Management Science.*

Raymond Friedman is the Brownlee O. Currey Professor of Management at the Owen Graduate School of Management, Vanderbilt University. He received his Ph.D. from the University of Chicago, and his B.A. from Yale University. Professor Friedman's research interests include negotiation, dispute resolution, labor relations, and the management of diversity. His recent work has focused on US–Chinese differences in conflict management. He is the author of *Front Stage, Backstage: The Dramatic Structure of Labor Negotiations* (MIT Press, 1994), as well as numerous journal articles. Professor Friedman has served as Chair of the Conflict Management Division of the Academy of Management, and president of the International Association for Conflict Management.

Ellen Giebels, Ph.D., is Professor of Psychology at the University of Twente, the Netherlands, and head of the department of Psychology of Conflict, Risk and Safety. In her research, teaching and consulting work, Ellen focuses on conflict management interventions that are conducive to behavioral change and information gathering in domains such as crisis/hostage negotiations, police interviews, witness protection, and work-related abuse.

Barbara Gray is a Professor and Executive Programs Faculty Fellow in the Smeal College of Business at Penn State University. She also serves as Director of the Center for Research in Conflict and Negotiation. She has studied organizational and environmental conflict, collaboration and institutional processes for over 35 years and has served as an organizational consultant, mediator and trainer for many private, public and non-governmental organizations worldwide. She has published three books and over 90 other publications and holds a B.S. in Chemistry from University of Dayton and a Ph.D. in Organizational Sociology from Case Western Reserve University.

Kristine Höglund is Associate Professor at the Department of Peace and Conflict Research, Uppsala University, Sweden. Her research has covered issues such as violence and peace negotiations, mediation and other third parties, and the causes and consequences of electoral violence. Her work has been published in journals such as *Democratization, Review of International Studies, Negotiation Journal, International Negotiation* and *International Peacekeeping.* She is the author of *Peace Negotiations in the Shadow of Violence* (Martinus Nijhoff, 2008) and is the co-editor of *Understanding Peace Research: Methods and Challenges* (Routledge, 2011).

Yoo Kyoung Kim is a Ph.D. student in the Department of Management and Organization at the Marshall School of Business, University of Southern California. Her research interests include power and negotiation.

Lukas Koning graduated in psychology at Leiden University. After graduating, he wrote his dissertation at Leiden University on the use of deception in bargaining. Currently, Lukas works as a post-doctoral researcher at the University of Amsterdam, studying the interpersonal effects of emotions.

Roy J. Lewicki is the Irving Abramowitz Professor Emeritus at the Max M. Fisher College of Business, The Ohio State University. Professor Lewicki maintains research and teaching interests in the fields of negotiation, conflict management and dispute resolution, trust development, managerial leadership, organizational justice and ethical decision making, and has published many research articles and book chapters on these topics. He is the author/editor of 36 books, including *Negotiation, 6E* (Lewicki, Barry and Saunders, 2010), the leading academic textbook on negotiation.

Eileen Linnabery is a doctoral candidate in Industrial/Organizational Psychology at DePaul University in Chicago. Her research interests revolve around gender issues in organizations, focusing on organizational justice and well-being of employees. She received her master's degree from the University of West Florida and her bachelor's degree from Tulane University.

Leigh Anne Liu is an Associate Professor of International Business at Georgia State University's Robinson College of Business, Atlanta. She received her doctorate in Organizational Behavior from Vanderbilt University. Leigh Anne's research explores culture's dynamic influence on negotiation, conflict, relationship, and identity.

Jeffrey Loewenstein is a faculty member in the Department of Business Administration at the University of Illinois at Urbana-Champaign's College of Business. His research examines how people generate, learn and apply knowledge, primarily through studying analogy, categories, and vocabularies. His work provides guidance for how to negotiate, make decisions, communicate and work together more effectively. He received his Ph.D. from Northwestern University, and taught previously at the Kellogg School of Management, Columbia Business School and The University of Texas at Austin.

Elizabeth A. Mannix is Professor of Management and Organizations at the Samuel Curtis Johnson Graduate School of Management at Cornell University. Professor Mannix's research and teaching interests include effective performance in managerial teams, diversity, power and alliances, negotiation and conflict, and organizational change and renewal.

Margaret A. Neale is the Adams Distinguished Professor of Management at the Graduate School of Business at Stanford University. Professor Neale's major research interests include bargaining and negotiation, distributed work groups, and team composition, learning, and performance.

Mara Olekalns is Professor of Management (Negotiations) at the Melbourne Business School. Her recent research has investigated the role of trust in shaping the use of deception, and on the conditions under which trust buffers negotiators against unexpected events. She also investigates gender stereotype violations in negotiation. Mara's research is published in journals including *Human Communication Research, Journal of Applied Psychology, Journal of Business Ethics,* and *Journal of Management,* as well as in multiple edited volumes.

Jennifer R. Overbeck is a visiting Associate Professor of Management at the University of Utah. Her research focuses on the individual psychology and group dynamics associated with power and status, and on power and emotion effects in negotiation. Her work has been published in the *Journal of Personality and Social Psychology,* the *Journal of Experimental Social Psychology, Negotiation and Conflict Management Research,* and *Organizational Behavior and Human Decision Processes.*

Beth Polin is a graduating doctoral candidate in the Management and Human Resources Department at the Max M. Fisher College of Business, The Ohio State University. She will continue her career with the School of Business at Eastern Kentucky University. Her research and teaching interests include conflict management, interpersonal trust development and repair, empowerment, and socialization.

Jimena Ramirez-Marin obtained her Ph.D. (cum laude) at the University of Seville, Spain. She is an active young scholar committed to negotiation teaching and research focusing on the influences of culture and relationships on negotiation and conflict resolution. She has been collaborating internationally with European research teams at the University of Amsterdam, Leiden University, and in the US at the Kellogg School of Management and the McDonough School of Business at Georgetown University. Her research has been awarded by the *International Association for Conflict Management* and the *Academy of Management.* She is currently Lecturer of Management and Organizations at the Kellogg School of Management, Northwestern University.

Zhaleh Semnani-Azad is a Ph.D. student in Industrial Organizational Psychology at the University of Waterloo. Her main line of research is on nonverbal communication in cross-cultural negotiation. She is also interested in the influence of cultural ideologies and values on decision-making and problem solving in cross-cultural negotiation.

Marwan Sinaceur is Assistant Professor of Organisational Behaviour at INSEAD. He received his Ph.D. in Organizational Behavior from the Graduate School of Business, Stanford University. His research focuses on negotiations, emotions, and group decision-making. He has published papers in leading journals, such as the *Journal of Applied Psychology*, *Psychological Science*, the *Journal of Experimental Social Psychology*, *Personality and Social Psychology Bulletin*, and *Group Decision and Negotiation*.

Andrew T. Soderberg is a Ph.D. student of Organizational Behavior in the David Eccles School of Business at the University of Utah. He received his B.S. degree in physiology from Brigham Young University. His research interests focus on issues related to fairness and ethics, groups and teams, leadership and followership, and negotiations.

Harris Sondak is Professor of Business Administration at the David Eccles School of Business at the University of Utah. Professor Sondak's research investigates the psychology of allocation decisions including two-party and multi-party negotiations and in market contexts, group process and decisions, and procedural justice and ethics.

Alice F. Stuhlmacher is a Professor of Psychology at DePaul University, Chicago. Her research interests include negotiation and conflict in organizations, particularly relating to gender, training, labor mediators, and virtual communication. She has been active in applying meta-analyses to summarize existing research and has also published research relating to personality, workplace safety, and decision making. She received her Ph.D. in Industrial/Organizational Psychology from Purdue University.

Paul J. Taylor, Ph.D., uses experimental, archival and field research to better understand why certain people are uniquely effective at gaining cooperation from those who are mistrusting or hostile. Paul is Professor of Psychology at Lancaster University, UK, and Professor of Human Interaction at the University of Twente, the Netherlands. At Lancaster, Paul directs Security Lancaster, a university-wide center of excellence for security research that houses 45 staff and the latest in research and training facilities.

Ann E. Tenbrunsel is the Rex and Alice A. Martin Professor of Business Ethics in the Mendoza College of Business at The University of Notre

Dame. She received her Ph.D. and M.B.A. from the Kellogg Graduate School of Management at Northwestern University and her B.S.I.O.E from the University of Michigan. Her recent research interests focus on the psychology of ethical decision-making, examining the situational and organizational contributors to unethical behavior.

Catherine Tinsley is a Professor of Management and head of the Management group at the McDonough School of Business at Georgetown University. She studies how factors such as culture, reputations, and gender influence negotiation and conflict resolution. She also studies how people make decisions under risk, applying decision analytic frameworks to understand organizational disasters, and individual and expert responses to natural disasters (such as hurricanes) and man-made disasters (terrorist attacks). Her work has been published in several peer-reviewed journals and she is currently on the editorial board of *Organization Behavior and Human Decision Processes*, among others.

Eric van Dijk graduated in economics and psychology at Groningen University, and then went to Leiden to write his dissertation on social dilemmas. He is a Professor at Leiden University, and his research concentrates on the understanding of economic and social decision making.

Gerben A. Van Kleef is Professor of Social Psychology at the University of Amsterdam, the Netherlands. His main research interests revolve around emotion, power, social influence, conflict, negotiation, and group processes. His work has appeared in leadings journals in the field of social and organizational psychology, including the *Journal of Personality and Social Psychology*, *Psychological Science*, *Advances in Experimental Social Psychology*, *Social Psychological and Personality Science*, *Journal of Applied Psychology*, and *Academy of Management Journal*. He is currently Associate Editor of *Social Psychological and Personality Science*.

Simon Wells is currently researching communicating with antagonistic people. He is particularly interested in how research can be translated into practice, as Simon is a Crisis Negotiator and was the United Kingdom Course Director for Hostage and Crisis Negotiation. Recently, Simon has been using research and research methods to further our understanding of communicating with individuals involved in terrorist activity, in particular kidnapping and hostage taking.

Julia Wondolleck is on the faculty of the University of Michigan's School of Natural Resources and Environment where she teaches courses in Environmental Conflict Management, Negotiation Skills for Resolving Environmental Disputes, and Environmental Mediation. Her research examines innovation in the management of environmental conflicts involving public lands and marine ecosystems. She is the author of *Making Collaboration Work: Lessons from Innovation in Natural Resource Management* (with Steven Yaffee, Island Press, 2000); *Environmental Disputes: Community Involvement in Conflict Resolution* (with James Crowfoot, Island Press, 1990); and *Public Lands Conflict & Resolution: Managing National Forest Disputes* (Plenum, 1988).

PART I

INTRODUCTION

1. The complexity of negotiating: from the individual to the context, and what lies between
Mara Olekalns and Wendi L. Adair

Does negotiation research have an ancestral tree? If we were to trace the negotiation tree back to its origins, what would they be? No doubt each negotiation scholar has her own answer, but three books stand out to us as laying out the foundations from which negotiation research was launched. Published in 1965, Walton and McKersie's *A Behavioural Theory of Labour Negotiations: An Analysis of Social Interaction Systems* set out two approaches to negotiation, integrative and distributive, that continue to underpin scholarship in the field. In the early 1970s, two books began to explore these concepts in greater depth, and foreshadowed many of the topics that negotiation researchers have since returned to. The *Social Psychology of Bargaining and Negotiation*, by Rubin and Brown (1975), provides a comprehensive review of research drawing on experimental games such as Acme Trucking and Prisoner's Dilemma. Their analysis provides an in-depth discussion of how structural variables such as the number of parties, the number and types of issues, and the physical setup shape negotiations. They go on to consider how individual differences, power, motivational orientation, and influence impact on negotiations. These latter themes are developed in Morton Deutsch's (1977) *The Resolution of Conflict: Constructive and Destructive Processes*, which explored the factors that direct negotiators to either compete or cooperate in greater depth. Among these factors are the context within which negotiations takes place, the content of communication (threats and promises), as well as the nature of the relationship (trust or suspicion).

These books set out the themes, shown in Figure 1.1, that continue to shape negotiation research today. But those themes have expanded and become more nuanced as subsequent generations of researchers strive to gain deeper insight into the factors that influence negotiators' actions at and away from the negotiating table. Our goal, in editing this Handbook, was to both look backwards at what we have learned about the negotiation process and to look forwards to the challenges that we have yet to tackle. Consequently, we asked our authors to provide a comprehensive review of their topics and to highlight the important questions they believe

4 *Handbook of research on negotiation*

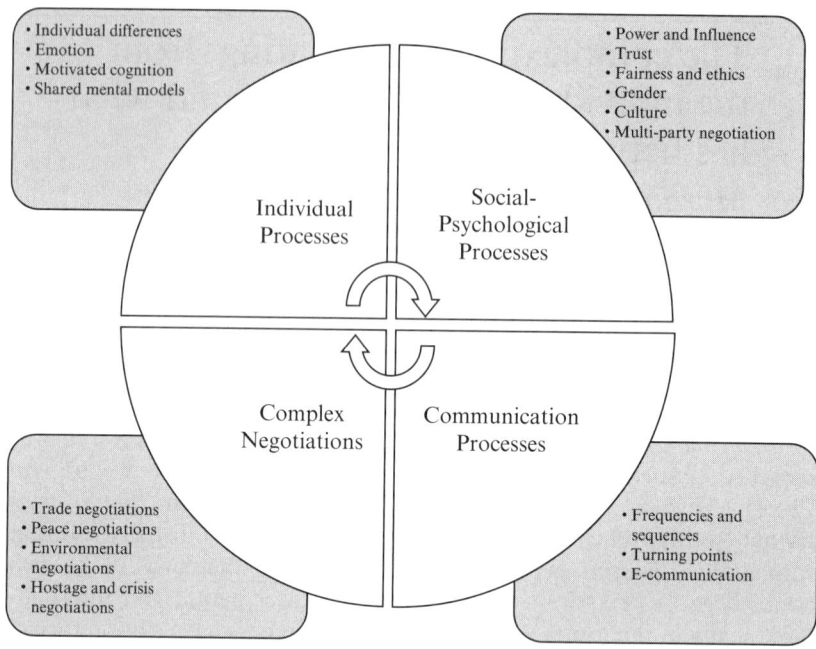

Figure 1.1 Four perspectives on the negotiation process

are yet to be answered. In structuring chapters in this way, we aspired to provide readers with state-of-the-art reviews, and also to enthuse and motivate future generations of negotiation scholars to continue exploring what for us is a fascinating study of human behavior. We have edited this book at a time when many large-scale negotiations, critical to our survival, continue to stall or fail and the daily news is dominated by seemingly intractable social conflicts. Grappling with the complexities of these negotiations, understanding the factors that continue to cause negotiators to prefer self-interest over mutual collaboration and problem-solving, and the factors that stall negotiations rather than move them forward, continues to be fertile ground for research.

NEGOTIATION IN CONTEXT

It is not our goal, in this section, to provide a comprehensive review of negotiation research. There are many excellent reviews already available (e.g., Bazerman et al., 2000; Carnevale and Pruitt, 1992; Thompson et al., 2010). Rather, it is our intention to give you a taste of the influences that have shaped negotiation research over past decades. We believe this taste is important because it sets the scene for understanding where negotiation research is today, and provides the context for the chapters in this book. And, in one way or another, context is the theme that binds those chapters.

The Prisoner's Dilemma Game (PDG), which provided the first experimental paradigm for exploring negotiators' behavior, stripped the negotiation process down to its most fundamental aspect. It highlighted the tension that continues to be at the heart of negotiation research, that between self-interest and mutual benefit. The idea of a mixed-motive task, one in which individuals strive to balance individual and joint gain, has been one of the most enduring concepts of negotiation theory. The PDG paradigm, even as it served as a tool for better understanding how negotiators manage this tension, served to highlight the shortcomings of such a pared down experimental approach. As negotiation theory evolved, it became increasingly clear that the more complex and informationally-rich environment within which everyday negotiations take place has a profound influence on how negotiations unfold. This realization, together with the emerging models described in the next paragraph, was the catalyst for new and more complex experimental investigations of negotiation.

Two models, converging from different disciplines, both consolidated and elaborated our understanding of this tension. A pivotal theoretical advance came with the introduction of the Dual Concern Model. In this model, Pruitt (1981) proposed that negotiators' strategy preferences are shaped by the relative emphasis that negotiators place on achieving their own and the other party's goals. Of particular interest to negotiation scholars – then and now – were the factors that encourage negotiators to assign importance to both goals, consequently approaching the negotiation with a problem-solving orientation. In a parallel development, Fisher and Ury (1981) identified the importance of understanding underlying interests rather than focusing on negotiators' positions and demands. Together, these models highlighted the importance of gaining a deeper understanding of opponents' motivations as a means for effective problem-solving. They also hinted at the future of negotiation research, because implicit in the discussion of problem-solving was the quality of the relationship between negotiators.

FROM INDIVIDUALS TO CONTEXT, AND BEYOND

When we started planning this book, we had a clear idea of how our chapters would fit together. Very loosely, we started with the individual and moved through increasingly more complex levels of interaction. In this section we continue our historical overview of negotiation research, integrating with it an overview of the parts and chapters of this Handbook.

Individual Deal-makers

The first wave of negotiation research built our understanding of how the limits that negotiators set, as well as the pattern of demands and concessions, shape a negotiation. This research showed that high limits (reservation points) or high goals increased negotiators' demands at the start of a negotiation. It also delivered a cautionary message for negotiators inclined to be tough: high demands combined with slow concessions at best slowed a negotiation, but could trigger an impasse. Being soft was not necessarily the answer, as negotiators who made low opening demands and more rapid concessions ended with poorer outcomes than their opponents (Carnevale and Pruitt, 1992; Pruitt and Carnevale, 1993). These patterns suggested that the management of demands and concessions was critical to negotiators' outcomes. Building on these findings, researchers have shown negotiators can protect their outcomes if they ensure that their concessions are reciprocated and if, in multi-issue negotiations, they make concessions on their low importance issues in return for gaining maximum benefits on their high importance issues (Carnevale and Pruitt, 1992; Pruitt and Carnevale, 1993). They have also shown that negotiators who set high and specific goals obtain better outcomes than those who start negotiations with general "do your best" goals (Huber and Neale, 1997; Northcraft et al., 1994).

This period of research was also characterized by investigations of the role that contextual variables played in shaping negotiators' broad approach and outcomes. The central goal in this stream of research was to determine which contextual variables pushed negotiators to a competitive approach, and which pushed them to a cooperative approach. Perhaps the first, and most pervasive, variable to be explored was motivational orientation: whether negotiators' goals motivated them to maximize their individual outcomes or to maximize both their own and their opponents' outcomes. It is perhaps one of the most enduring findings of negotiation research that an individualistic goal encourages competition whereas a cooperative goal encourages problem-solving (De Dreu et al., 2000). Motivational orientation is not, however, the only contextual variable to be investigated. Negotiators are also more likely to behave competitively when they have power, when they do not anticipate future interactions, and when they are accountable to constituents (Ben-Yoav and Pruitt, 1984; Mosterd and Rutte, 2000). Conversely, negotiators become more conciliatory as deadlines approach, and more recent research has focused on how negotiators can release themselves from deadline pressure (Gino and Moore, 2008; Moore, 2004; 2005).

The next wave of research focused on the role of individuals' attributes and cognitions in shaping the negotiation process. One component of this research explored the extent to which individual differences affected negotiators' behaviors and outcomes. As part of this stream, researchers attempted to find personality variables that predicted negotiators' success. To a large extent, this endeavor was unsuccessful. As Bazerman et al. (2000) pointed out, not only did personality account for very little variance in negotiators' behavior, but personality effects were rapidly washed out by situational factors (for an exception see Barry and Friedman, 1998). A more fruitful line of research focused on negotiators' Social Value Orientations (SVO), that is, negotiators' preferences for resource allocation. A dispositional parallel to motivational orientation, SVO influences negotiators' concession patterns and outcomes, as well as their preferred strategies (De Dreu and Van Lange, 1995; Olekalns et al., 1996). Early research also counted gender as an individual difference variable. Like personality effects, gender effects proved elusive. Nonetheless, meta-analyses showed small but reliable gender differences in negotiation outcomes and strategies (Stuhlmacher and Walters, 1999; Walters et al., 1998). The small effect sizes may occur because gender influences negotiation in relatively subtle ways, and cannot be considered independent of the context within which women and men are negotiating (Kolb and McGinn, 2009; Sondak and Stuhlmacher, 2009).

A second component of this research integrated negotiation theory and behavioral decision theory. Bazerman et al.'s (1985) seminal work demonstrated that, like other decision-makers, negotiators respond differently to outcomes framed as losses or as gains (see also Neale and Bazerman, 1991). They demonstrated that loss-framed negotiators are risk-seeking, making higher opening demands and fewer concessions than gain-framed negotiators. Subsequent research from a behavioral decision perspective demonstrated overconfidence on the part of negotiators, leading to the belief that negotiations would end favorably for them. Finally, this research also showed that negotiators are anchored by the first offer placed on the table, in a way that gives the first mover an advantage.

Paralleling these decision-making biases, negotiation researchers also demonstrated that the social perception biases that color our everyday interactions also shape negotiators' behavior. Two of these biases relate to negotiators' assumptions about their opponents' preferences: the fixed-pie bias describes negotiators' assumption that interests are necessarily mutually opposed (fixed-sum), and the incompatibility bias described negotiators' failure to recognize that they both want the same thing

(Thompson and Hastie, 1990a). Negotiators are also prone to the egocentric bias, overweighting outcomes favorable to themselves, and reactive devaluation, underweighting the costs of an opponent's concessions, offers and willingness to problem solve (Thompson and Hastie, 1990b).

Broadly, this body of research can be described as focusing on how the underlying goals and motives of negotiators shape their reasoning about negotiations, and the motives that underpin their strategic thinking (Carnevale and De Dreu, 2006; De Dreu and Carnevale, 2003). This view of negotiators does not, however, present a complete picture. Even though our understanding of negotiators' actions was significantly increased by the identification of the cognitive and social perception biases that shape their interpretation of a negotiation, this research did not fully capture the factors that influence individual negotiators. To further deepen our understanding of the factors that drive negotiators' actions, researchers turned to emotion (e.g., Morris and Keltner, 2000). This research showed that the emotions that negotiators express affect their opponents' willingness to concede, the offers that they make, as well as their willingness to problem-solve. Research moved rapidly from comparing positive versus negative emotions (especially happiness versus anger), to a more nuanced view of emotions (Olekalns and Druckman, in press). As research progressed, researchers distinguished different kinds of emotions (for example, anger versus disappointment), and also started to explore how emotional transitions might affect negotiations (Filipowicz et al., 2011).

Part II of this Handbook, "The Individual Negotiator", focuses on how individual-level processes shape negotiations. The chapters in this section take up the story of deal-making and negotiators' cognition. In her chapter on individual differences, Elfenbein considers what is new in our understanding of individual differences in negotiation. Citing research that shows negotiators' performance is remarkably consistent across time, she argues for better understanding how individual differences – broadly interpreted – contribute to negotiators' performance. This understanding needs to go beyond an analysis of enduring dispositions, to a consideration of how motivational styles, negotiators' expectancies, demographic characteristics and abilities shape their negotiation performance.

Koning and van Dijk, in their chapter on motivated cognition, broaden the theme of decision biases to consider the role of cognition in shaping how negotiators' interpret their outcomes, process information about the task, and the strategies that they choose. As well as demonstrating the link between individual differences and information processing, they highlight the ways in which negotiators reduce cognitive load by relying on a range of heuristics to simplify information processing. Building on the theme of cognition, Liu and Cai argue that to understand the value creation process we need to understand how negotiators develop a shared understanding of the negotiation. These authors present a complex multi-level model that incorporates three broad categories of variables: affective, informational and relational, and consider how the alignment of these variables, among negotiators, assists in the development of shared mental models. Finally, they link the development of a shared mental model and a shared identity to negotiators' ability to create value.

In the final chapter of Part II, Van Kleef and Sinaceur remind us that understanding cognition only tells part of the negotiation story. To fully understand negotiators' actions at the bargaining table, we need to understand both how their emotions shape their own cognitions and behaviors, and how their emotional expressions shape the cognitions and behaviors of other negotiators. A central theme in this chapter is that, to understand how emotions shape negotiators' actions, we need to move from a focus on positive versus negative affective to a focus on more specific emotions. Their discussion of the interpersonal effects of emotion provides a link between emotion and cognition by establishing that individuals' emotions affect the extent and depth of negotiators' information processing.

Social Context

Even as negotiation researchers were exploring individuals' cognition and emotion, a parallel research track explored the role of social context in negotiations. This wave of negotiation research takes up the idea that negotiators' relationships, as well as the broader social context within which negotiations occur, are critical to how negotiations develop. It highlights the interdependency between negotiators, and emphasizes that their actions are influenced not just by their individual characteristics but also by the social context within which negotiations are conducted. One piece of the social context puzzle focuses on the idea that negotiators accrue not just economic capital but also social capital (Curhan et al., 2006; Olekalns and Brett, 2008). The Subjective Values Inventory (SVI) (Curhan et al., 2006) identifies four dimensions on which negotiators assess their outcomes: satisfaction with their economic outcome, self-esteem, fairness of the process, and satisfaction with the underlying relationship. The SVI highlights the importance of understanding how justice and fairness judgments shape negotiators' perceptions of their experiences, and also hints at the role played by judgments of an opponent's intentions and ethicality in shaping social outcomes.

A parallel research stream focuses on how negotiators' impressions of their opponents shape their experiences. Not only does this research show that negotiators engage in thin-slicing – the formation of impressions based on very small samples of behavior – it links this rapid impression formation to negotiators' strategy choices, including the use of deception, and their final outcomes (Curhan and Pentland, 2007; Olekalns and Smith, 2007; 2009). In recent years, considerable attention has been given to the role of trust in negotiation, showing that trust influences negotiators' strategy choices including the use of deception, their interpretations of unexpected events in negotiation, as well as their ability to find joint gain (Druckman and Olekalns, in press; Druckman et al., 2009; Dunn and Schweitzer, 2005; Giebels et al., 2008; Gunia, Brett et al., 2011; Olekalns and Smith, 2005).

Social context also shapes what we expect from our opponents and how we react to their negotiation tactics. This is because the context conveys norms about appropriate behaviors, and violations of those norms trigger apprehension and suspicion about others' intentions. Reputation and past history provide one mechanism for establishing what is normative (O'Connor et al., 2005; Tinsley et al., 2002). When behaviors fall short of expectations they are evaluated negatively, whereas when they exceed expectations they are evaluated positively (Hilty and Carnevale, 1992). Social stereotypes provide a second mechanism for establishing behavioral norms. One such set of stereotypes, prescriptive gender stereotypes, has proven useful in furthering our understanding of the social costs (and possibly economic costs) that women incur when they negotiate (Bowles, in press; Kulik and Olekalns, 2012). Similarly, cultural norms shape the strategies that negotiators use and that they expect to characterize negotiations (Brett, 2007). When these norms are violated, as may be the case in cross-cultural negotiations, there is potential for misinterpretation of an opponent's intentions at best and considerable social costs at worst.

Part III, "Social-Psychological Processes", explores how social context shapes negotiation processes and outcomes. Starting from the traditional view of power as available alternatives, Overbeck and Kim consider how power may change as a negotiation progresses based on negotiators' comparisons not only of the relative power of each negotiator but also the relationship between negotiators; and discuss the ways in which power affects negotiators' behavior including the propensity for unethical actions. The authors contrast power with status, or the esteem accorded to an individual, and in doing so shift focus to how the attribution of status might affect negotiation processes and outcomes.

The next two chapters focus on the intangible factors that shape negotiators' actions at the bargaining table. Continuing the theme that impressions of an opponent play an important role in negotiations, Lewicki and Polin elaborate on how trust and trust violations affect the negotiation process. As well as identifying the fundamental dilemma faced by negotiators, that is, the trade-off between trusting and not trusting an opponent, these authors explore how trust is built and eroded in negotiations. They introduce the important concept of trust congruence, or the extent to which both negotiators have the same level of trust in each other. Closely related to trust are the issues of fairness and ethics. In Chapter 8, Diekmann, Soderberg and Tenbrunsel explore the personal and situational characteristics that motivate negotiators to make more or less fair offers to their opponents. Considering the view from the other side, they also discuss how these factors affect a recipient's reaction to an unfair offer. Mirroring this discussion, they also consider the characteristics of negotiators and their opponents that elicit unethical behavior in negotiation.

A third dimension is added to our understanding of the social psychological context when we consider the behavioral norms conveyed by social roles. Stuhlmacher and Linnabery provide a new perspective on our understanding of gender by focusing on how underlying social roles shape both differences in how women and men approach negotiation, and in the reactions they evoke when they do negotiate. They provide a nuanced analysis of gender in negotiation by considering how the negotiating context, including differences such as communication mode, negotiation tasks, and ambiguity, amplifies or attenuates gender differences. Finally, they contrast gender differences in workplace negotiations with negotiations at home, with family, in political settings, and in negotiation ethics. A second set of behavioral expectations may be created through culture. In Chapter 10, Aslani and his co-authors take us beyond the traditional dimensions of individualism-collectivism to build a new perspective for interpreting and understanding cultural differences in negotiation. These authors differentiate three cultural prototypes – honor, dignity, and face – and discuss the implications of each culture for negotiators' preferred strategies. They argue that a preference for a question-and-answer approach versus a substantiation-and-offer approach is underpinned by cultural differences in the level of trust, whether negotiators approach reasoning systematically or holistically, and how negotiators react to emotional expression.

The final chapter in Part III shifts levels again, from dyadic to multiparty negotiations. Sondak, Neale and Mannix, in their analysis of multiparty negotiations, focus on the uncertainty inherent in these more complex negotiations. This complexity starts with the need to identify the parties in the negotiation, understand the needs of multiple parties, and manage relationships, including emerging alliances between parties. The need to manage relationships is highlighted in their discussion of intra-team negotiations, that is, the negotiations that take place within a team of negotiators who must first uncover and then align the interests of team members, in order to present a united face to their opponents. Finally,

Sondak and his co-authors draw attention to the uncertainty inherent in marketplace negotiations, where negotiators search for the best match among many available counterparties.

Social Interaction

At the same time that organizational behavior and social psychology scholars were focused on the ways in which biased information processing affects negotiations, communication scholars took negotiation research in a different direction. A critical point of difference between Prisoner's Dilemma Games and negotiations is that there is considerably more communication between individuals in negotiation. This means that what negotiators say to each other, and how communication flows and unfolds over time, also influences negotiation outcomes (Carroll and Payne, 1991; Putnam, 1990).

Communication theory and research encouraged negotiation scholars to focus on the "black box" of negotiation, that is, on what negotiators say to each other, and how these communication patterns shape negotiators' outcomes (Weingart and Olekalns, 2004; Putnam, 1990). The focus on communication took researchers in several directions. Researchers working within a communication framework have analyzed how the relative frequency with which negotiators use cooperative and competitive strategies shapes outcomes. They have built more nuanced perspectives by incorporating time into their analyses, either by considering short sequences of strategies or by considering how dominant strategies change over time (phases) as negotiators work towards agreement. This research has shown the role that strategy matching plays in establishing a dominant strategy orientation, as well as the role of strategy mismatching in disrupting established routines (see Weingart and Olekalns, 2004, Olekalns and Weingart, 2008 for reviews). Negotiation researchers are now drawing on the broader constructs of behavioral synchrony, mimicry and contagion to further develop our understanding of the subtle ways that communication shapes negotiators' outcomes. For example research shows that negotiators are most satisfied when their nonverbal displays of submissiveness and dominance are complementary (Tiedens and Fragale, 2003). Taking this idea in a slightly different direction, Fragale (2006) shows that paralinguistic cues signaling powerlessness increase perceived communality.

Within this communication framework, negotiation researchers have also focused on the role that context plays in shaping strategies. One aspect of context goes back to the structural variables that have long held researchers' interests: motivational orientation, social value orientation, and power. Findings here show that not only do these variables affect the strategies that negotiators favor, they also affect the strategies that are best suited to creating value (Weingart and Olekalns, 2004). A second aspect of context addresses negotiators' choice of communication medium. This growing topic has documented the particular challenges that negotiators face when they engage with each other via electronic means rather than face-to-face (Moore et al., 1999; Morris et al., 2002; Nadler and Shestowksy, 2006). Finally, a third aspect of context is the number of parties in a negotiation. Communication in multi-party negotiations continues to be an under-investigated topic (see Weingart et al., 2007 for an exception), but one that opens the possibility of linking emergent communication networks to coalition building, influence and negotiators' outcomes.

Part IV, "Communication Processes", shifts perspective from characteristics of the individual negotiator and the social context within which negotiations take place to the interplay between negotiators. In Chapter 12, Adair and Loewenstein focus on micro-level communication patterns, exploring how both verbal and nonverbal communication patterns shape the negotiation process. One aspect of communication is how negotiators respond to each other, that is, how they sequence strategies. The way that negotiators respond to each other is context sensitive, determining the strategies that negotiators choose to match (reciprocate) as well as affecting which strategy sequences are most effective for reaching mutually beneficial outcomes. However, as this chapter highlights, there is more to communication than negotiators' verbal behavior. The extent to which individuals establish rapport through nonverbal behaviors, the ways in which they signal power and status, and the media through which they communicate also influence the success of their negotiations. Taking a more macro-level perspective, Druckman and Olekalns focus on how communication accumulates over time to build phases of coherent activity within negotiations. Central to their exploration of phases is the question of what triggers shifts from one phase to another, that is, the question of how negotiators adapt their communication patterns and strategies to advance negotiations to settlement. They discuss, in depth, the role of turning points: either internal or external events that disrupt the negotiation process and alter the dynamic. Finally, Friedman and Belkin explore how communication between negotiators is affected when it takes place via email, rather than taking place face-to-face. Drawing on traditional theories of media richness, and more recent theories such as Construal Level Theory (Trope and Liberman, 2003; 2010), these authors highlight both the costs and benefits of e-negotiation. An interesting pattern emerges from this discussion. The social distance that comes with e-negotiation appears to help with the substantive aspects of the task: it improves decision-making because it reduces normative and social pressure, it encourages more equal participation, and it reduces emotional intensity. At the same time, social distance harms relationships: it establishes lower trust at the outset of negotiations, increases the likelihood that contention will breach trust, and lowers negotiators' ethical thresholds. To conclude, these authors outline an "into-the-wind" strategy that captures the benefits of both social distance and social closeness.

Complex Negotiations

The individual negotiations that have been the focus of this Handbook, so far, are embedded in a broader context. For example, gender researchers argue that to fully understand the impact of gender on the negotiation process we need to consider not just "the woman" but the context within which negotiations take place (Kolb and McGinn, 2009; Sondak and Stuhlmacher, 2009). More generally, many negotiations are embedded in a broader societal context. Negotiations about climate change measures cannot be divorced from the relative wealth of the countries involved, or the ability to sell agreements to stakeholders outside of the formal negotiations. Peace negotiations cannot be understood without placing them in context, and understanding the history within which conflicts are embedded. And we cannot negotiate through crises without considering the emotionally charged environment within which negotiations are taking place. In this final part of the Handbook, we consider how negotiators navigate real-world negotiations.

Part V, "Complex Negotiations", shifts the level of analysis to explore the dynamics of more complex real-world negotiations. This section starts with an analysis, by Crump, of the variables that shape trade negotiations. The chapter continues many of the themes that were evident in earlier parts of the book. Unsurprisingly, parties' past history and reputations have a strong influence on how trade negotiations progress. Beyond these issues, trade negotiations take place in a simultaneously more structured and more ambiguous environment. Such negotiations play out in the context of the regulatory and political environments that shape how each party approaches the negotiation. They are shaped not just by the parties at the table, but the networks to which they belong, meaning that negotiators are mindful of how any given trade negotiation will affect other ongoing negotiations, how they will affect subsequent negotiations with the same countries, and the kinds of precedents that might be set by a trade agreement.

Trade negotiations, in which parties are willing participants, contrast dramatically with the subject of Höglund and Druckman's chapter on peace negotiations. In these negotiations, a key challenge is getting parties to the negotiating table. To do so requires a frame shift on the part of warring parties, that is, a shift from viewing the situation as a conflict to viewing it as a negotiation. This in turn might require warring parties to make themselves vulnerable by agreeing to disarm before talks begin. Importantly, this chapter highlights the possibility that parties are not always working towards agreement: spoilers and veto players may perceive that maintaining a conflict is their best interests. Finally, this chapter identifies a critical variable in successful peace negotiations, that is, whether agreements are forward-looking or backward-looking.

Uncertainty increases even further when environmental issues are the focus of negotiations. As Gray and Wondolleck outline in Chapter 17, this uncertainty results from a lack of clear boundaries for the negotiation that makes it challenging to identify participants, issues and stakeholders: it is difficult to disentangle any one environmental conflict from the social and ecological systems to which it is connected, thus making the boundaries of the conflict unclear. A second layer of complexity is added to negotiations because the science that underpins environmental disputes is both complex and uncertain. A third layer of complexity comes into play because many environmental conflicts are also conflicts of value systems and ideologies. Despite these many levels of uncertainty, negotiations about environmental issues are also embedded within an institutional context that, because of existing norms, policies and procedures, tightly constrains the negotiations.

A different kind of complexity characterizes high stakes crisis and terrorism negotiations. Several of the topics covered earlier in this Handbook are integrated in Wells, Taylor and Giebels' final chapter. In discussing crisis and terrorism negotiations, these authors highlight the critical role of opening moments in shaping how such negotiations unfold. It is critical, at this stage, for negotiators to establish a relationship with perpetrators and to prevent escalating the situation. By using language that focuses on observable behaviors rather than on values and ideologies, they are implementing Fisher and Ury's injunction to "focus on the problem, not the person". These authors further highlight the importance of assessing the frame that perpetrators are using, and to build rapport by ensuring that frames and other aspects of communication are in-sync. Communication, in this context, is time sensitive: for strategies to be effective, they need to be used at the right moment in a negotiation. What sets these negotiations apart, making them more complex and uncertain, is that they are underpinned by extreme emotion and arousal on the part of the perpetrator.

THE THEMES THAT BIND

As we started to read the chapters in this book, we realized that several themes ran through our levels of analysis: temporal horizons, uncertainty and sense-making, and context and subjectivity. These themes connect ideas across levels, identify points of commonality and enable us to start thinking about cross-level of models of negotiation.

Temporal Horizons

One of the recurrent themes in this Handbook is the role of time in negotiation. First explored in the idea of deadlines and negotiators' expectations of future interactions, we can trace the role of time through several of the chapters in this book. The communication chapters, in particular, draw attention to negotiation as a dynamic rather than a static process. An emphasis on time highlights the role of adaptability and flexibility in negotiation, emphasizing the need for negotiators to manage the negotiation process on a moment-to-moment basis. In this more dynamic view of negotiation, the impact of negotiators' strategies cannot be understood without considering where in the negotiation process they are placed. Strategies that are effective early in a negotiation may be ineffective in the end game, and vice versa. This point is most clearly highlighted in the discussion of crisis negotiations, in which the effectiveness of strategies is time-sensitive. Events that punctuate negotiations place a temporal marker in the process, and redirect it to a new phase.

It is not, however, just communication processes that are dynamic. Negotiators' cognitions also change over time, in light of new information. This is evident in the evolution of negotiators' shared identities and shared mental models of the negotiation process. The temporal horizons that are salient to negotiators also shape negotiators' cognitions: whether negotiators focus on a near or far temporal horizon shifts their level of analysis. Near horizons make negotiators more prone to systematic processing, whereas far horizons encourage a more abstract level of information processing (Henderson, 2011; Henderson et al., 2006). They may also be salient to negotiators' ethical judgments. The theory of multiple selves suggests that individuals' ethicality is affected by the extent to which they perceive their past, present and future selves to be overlapping. As the degree of overlap increases, so does the ability to simulate future consequences with a resultant increase in ethicality (Hershfield et al., 2012)

Time also shapes negotiators' relationships with their counterparts. Although trust can be established early in a negotiation, it is updated as negotiators observe their opponents' behaviors. Actions that stand out from the flow of the negotiation attract attention, and trigger a reassessment of opponents' trustworthiness. In the longer-term, experiences with an opponent build that person's reputation. Information and experience from one negotiation spills over to shape subsequent negotiations with the same opponent. As the chapter on international trade negotiations demonstrates (Chapter 15), issues of reputation and temporal spillover shape not just everyday negotiations, but also complex multilateral negotiations. This chapter also alerts us to a different kind of spillover: outcomes from one negotiation may shape similar, simultaneous negotiations and may also set precedent for future negotiations with the same parties.

Uncertainty and Sense-making

A second recurrent theme is that of uncertainty and the ways in which negotiators' attempt to reduce uncertainty. Negotiations are by their very nature uncertain and this uncertainty is evident at several levels. At the individual level, negotiators face a complex information processing task. To reduce this complexity, they utilize a range of decision-making heuristics that offer the benefit of reducing complexity while carrying the risk that negotiators will overlook unique and critical information. Negotiators may also reduce uncertainty by drawing on their own emotional states, as well as the expressed emotions of their opponents, to draw inferences about their opponents' intentions and to provide an interpretive filter for ambiguous behaviors.

At the interpersonal level, negotiators strive to reduce uncertainty by gathering information about their opponents. At least some of their effort is directed towards assessing whether opponents will negotiate in good faith, that is, whether opponents will be fair and ethical. Negotiators may draw on several sources of information in order to reduce uncertainty about their opponents' intentions. First impressions of trustworthiness, longer-term reputations, and opponents' power and status all create expectations about how opponents will behave. Negotiators may also draw on more widely held behavioral norms, such as those implied by gender or culture, to track opponents' behavior. Negotiators will form impressions of opponents' intentions based on the degree to which behaviors match pre-existing behavioral expectations. These impressions play a critical role in shaping the tone of negotiations as disparate as everyday negotiations conducted via email (Morris et al., 2002), and those conducted in crisis or hostage situations.

The level of uncertainty increases when we move from two-party to multi-party negotiations. In addition to determining the intentions of an opponent, negotiators now need to determine who is involved in the negotiation, to assess where alliances are likely to form, and how actions at and away from the negotiating table shape the final deal. If they are part of a negotiating team, individuals need to consider not just how well aligned interests are within the team but also to manage uncertainty about team members' intentions and actions. This uncertainty increases as we move to even more complex negotiations. Here, the political environment, the very boundaries of environmental conflicts, the scientific uncertainty associated with environmentalists' claims, and the social and ecological systems within which environmental conflicts are embedded add several layers of uncertainty to the negotiation process.

Context and Subjectivity

A final theme highlights the role that context plays in shaping how negotiators interpret, respond to and manage their negotiations. At the intrapersonal level, this context is created by individual characteristics. The chapters on individual differences and negotiators' cognition demonstrated that, at a very fundamental level, individuals differ in how they interpret the world around them. For example, individuals with a proself orientation scan outcomes for self-gain whereas those with a prosocial orientation scan outcomes for mutual benefit. These different orientations flow on to shape the ways in which individuals approach negotiations, their decisions about strategies, their moral judgments, and their perceptions of fairness. The same theme informs the discussion of more complex negotiations, such as peace, environmental, and terrorist negotiations, all of which are shaped to some extent by individuals' ideologies.

Context also shapes the way in which individuals perceive and interpret others' actions. As Chapter 9 on gender highlighted, social roles establish expectations about how individuals should behave, and actual behavior is evaluated against these expectations. To the extent that actions violate social role-based expectations, they can disrupt if not damage underlying relationships. A similar theme emerges in Chapter 10 on culture, which highlights how different cultural values shape negotiators' strategy preferences, because it shapes the underlying process of reasoning, emotional expression and trust-building. Negotiators' strategy preferences cannot be understood without understanding the different frames that culture imposes on the same "objective" context. Continuing this theme into even more complex negotiations, Chapter 18 on crisis and terrorism highlights the difficulties faced by crisis negotiators because the perpetrators lack a negotiations script. This means that negotiators start without the common assumptions shared by individuals in business negotiations and must endeavor to build a shared frame from which to conduct the negotiation.

Complex negotiations add a further dimension to the role played by context in shaping how negotiations are interpreted. The success of peace negotiations depends, in part, in the ability to reframe the situation from a conflict to negotiation. Whether and how this is accomplished can be understood only if we understand the context within which the negotiation plays out: internal politics, the support or lack of support from negotiators' constituents, a predisposition to distrust others and to escalate the conflict, and the primary role of survival in driving negotiations all contribute to the broader context within which peacemakers conduct negotiations. The theme of survival plays out not only in peace negotiations but also in environmental conflicts. These conflicts are often embedded in opposing value systems, and associated with strong emotions. Consequently, like crisis negotiations, they are conducted in a more volatile environment. Ideology, values, and emotions add a subjective dimension to the negotiating context that changes the impact and effectiveness of specific strategies.

IN CONCLUSION

Each of these themes highlights the extent to which negotiations, in all their facets, are a dynamic and evolving process. For negotiators to be successful, they need to establish a shared understanding of the context within which the negotiation takes place, as well as of how their conflict of interests will be resolved. This may require negotiators to reframe both the problem they are solving and their approach as they work towards a shared script for the negotiation. Their definition and redefinition of the negotiation is shaped by external factors ranging from the political context within which negotiations take place to the social roles that shape our expectations of others' behaviors. On the road to disambiguating those behaviors, negotiators use a range of shortcuts – cognitive heuristics, their emotions, and their first impressions – to predict their opponents' behavior and to select their own strategies. Where negotiations start, strategically, informs opponents' actions and triggers a feedback loop in which negotiators reassess their perceptions of the context, their impressions of their opponents, and their own strategic choices.

ACKNOWLEDGEMENTS

We would like to thank our authors for the thoughtful way in which they approached their chapters. We hope that you, as readers, agree that each chapter provides an innovative perspective on a current topic in negotiation. Our authors benefited from each other's feedback, and from the opportunity to hear about and discuss the chapters during a book authors' conference. We are indebted to Jeanne Brett, DeWitt W. Buchanan, Jr. Professor of Dispute Resolution and Organizations and Director of Dispute Resolution Research Center at Kellogg School of Management, Northwestern University, whose sponsorship made the conference possible.

REFERENCES

Barry, B. and Friedman, R. (1998). Bargainer characteristics in distributive and integrative negotiation, *Journal of Personality and Social Psychology*, 74, 345–359.
Bazerman, M.H., Curhan, J., Moore, D., and Valley, K. (2000). Negotiation, *Annual Review of Psychology*, 50, 279–315.
Bazerman, M.H., Magliozzi, T., and Neale, M.A. (1985). Integrative bargaining in a competitive market, *Organizational Behavior and Human Decision Processes*, 35, 294–313.
Ben-Yoav, O. and Pruitt, D.G. (1984). Resistance to yielding and the expectation of cooperative future interaction, *Journal of Experimental Social Psychology*, 20, 323–335.
Bowles, H.R. (in press). Psychological perspectives on gender in negotiation. In M.K. Ryan and N.R. Branscombe (eds), *The Sage Handbook of Gender and Psychology*.
Brett, J. (2007). *Negotiating Globally: How to Negotiate Deals, Resolve Disputes, and Make Decisions Across Cultural Boundaries* (second edition). San Francisco: Jossey Bass.
Carnevale, P.J. and De Dreu, C.K.W. (2006). Motive: The negotiator's raison d'être. In Leigh Thompson (ed.), *Frontiers of Social Psychology: Negotiation theory and research* (pp. 55–76). New York: Psychology Press.
Carnevale, P.J. and Pruitt, D.G. (1992). Negotiation and mediation, *Annual Review of Psychology*, 43, 531–582.
Carroll, J.S. and Payne, J.W. (1991). An information processing approach to two-party negotiations, *Research on Negotiation in Organizations*, 3, 3–34.
Curhan, J. and Pentland, A. (2007). Thin slices of negotiation: Predicting outcomes from conversational dynamics within the first 5 minutes, *Journal of Applied Psychology*, 92, 802–811.
Curhan, J.R., Elfenbein, H.A., and Xu, H. (2006). What do people value when they negotiate? Mapping the domain of subjective value in negotiation, *Journal of Personality and Social Psychology*, 91, 493–512.
De Dreu, C.K.W. and Carnevale, P.J. (2003). Motivational bases of information processing and strategy in negotiation and social conflict, *Advances in Experimental Social Psychology*, 35, 235–291.
De Dreu, C.K.W. and Van Lange, P.A.M. (1995). The impact of social value orientations on negotiator cognition and behavior, *Personality and Social Psychology Bulletin*, 21, 1178–1188.
De Dreu, C.K.W., Weingart, L.R. and Kwon, S. (2000). Influence of social motives on integrative negotiations: A meta-analytic review and test of two theories, *Journal of Personality and Social Psychology*, 78, 889–905.
Druckman, D. and Olekalns, M. (in press). Motivational primes, trust and negotiators' reactions to a crisis, *Journal of Conflict Resolution*.
Druckman, D., Olekalns, M., and Smith, P. (2009). Interpretive filters: Social cognition and the impact of turning points in negotiation, *Negotiation Journal*, 25, 13–40.
Dunn, J.R. and Schweitzer, M.E (2005). Feeling and believing: The influence of emotion on trust, *Journal of Personality and Social Psychology*, 88, 736–748.
Filipowicz, A.S., Barsade, S., and Melwani, S. (2011). Understanding emotional transi-

tions: The interpersonal consequences of changing emotions in negotiations, *Journal of Personality and Social Psychology*, 101, 541–556.

Fisher, R. and Ury, W.L. (1981). *Getting to Yes: Negotiating Agreement Without Giving In*. London: Penguin.

Fragale, A.R. (2006). The power of powerless speech: The effects of speech style and task interdependence on status conferral, *Organizational Behavior and Human Decision Processes*, 101, 243–261.

Giebels, E., De Dreu, C., and Van de Vliert, E. (1998). Social motives and trust in negotiation: The disruptive effects of punitive capability, *Journal of Applied Psychology*, 83, 408–422.

Gino, F. and Moore, D.A. (2008). Why negotiators should reveal their deadlines: Disclosing weaknesses can make you stronger, *Negotiation and Conflict Management Research*, 1, 77–96.

Gunia, B.C., Brett, J.M., Nandkeolyar, A.K., and Kamdar, D. (2011). Paying a price: Culture, trust, and negotiation consequences, *Journal of Applied Psychology*, 96, 774–789.

Henderson, M.D. (2011). Mere physical distance and integrative agreements: When more space improves negotiation outcomes, *Journal of Experimental Social Psychology*, 47, 7–15.

Henderson, M.D., Trope, Y., and Carnevale, P.J. (2006). Negotiation from a near and distant time perspective, *Journal of Personality and Social Psychology*, 91, 712–729.

Hershfield, H.E., Cohen, T.R., and Thompson, L. (2012). Short horizons and tempting situations: Lack of continuity to our future selves leads to unethical decision making and behavior, *Organizational Behavior and Human Decision Processes*, 117, 298–310.

Hilty, J. and Carnevale, P.J. (1992). Black-hat/white-hat strategy in bilateral negotiation, *Organizational Behaviour and Human Decision Processes*, 55, 444–469.

Huber, V.L. and Neale, M.A. (1987). The effects of self and competitor goals on performance of an interdependent bargaining task, *Journal of Applied Psychology*, 72, 197–203.

Kolb, D. and McGinn, K. (2009). Beyond gender and negotiation to gendered negotiations, *Negotiation and Conflict Management Research*, 2, 1–16.

Kulik, C. and Olekalns, M. (2012). Negotiating the gender divide: Lessons from the negotiation and organizational behavior literatures, *Journal of Management*, 38, 1387–1415.

Malhotra, D. and Bazerman, M.H. (2008). Psychological influence in negotiation: An introduction long overdue, *Journal of Management*, 34, 509–531.

Moore, D.A. (2004). Myopic prediction, self-destructive secrecy, and the unexpected benefits of revealing final deadlines in negotiation, *Organizational Behavior and Human Decision Processes*, 94, 125–139.

Moore, D.A. (2005). Myopic biases in strategic social prediction: Why deadlines put everyone under more pressure than everyone else, *Personality and Social Psychology Bulletin*, 31, 668–679.

Moore D.A., Kurtzberg T.R., Thompson L.L., and Morris M.W. (1999). Long and short routes to success in electronically mediated negotiations: Group affiliations and good vibrations, *Organizational Behavior and Human Decision Processes*, 77, 22–43.

Morris, M.W. and Keltner, D. (2000). How emotions work: The social functions of emotional expression in negotiations, *Research in Organizational Behavior*, 22, 1–50.

Morris, M.W., Nadler, J., Kurtzberg, T.R., and Thompson, L.L. (2002). Schmooze or lose: Social friction and lubrication in e-mail negotiations, *Group Dynamics*, 6, 89–100.

Mosterd, I. and Rutte, C.G. (2000). Effects of time pressure and accountability to constituents on negotiation, *International Journal of Conflict Management*, 11, 227–247.

Nadler, J. and Shestowsky, D. (2006). Negotiation, information technology and the problem of the faceless other. In L. Thompson (ed.), *Negotiation Theory and Research*. New York: Psychology Press.

Neale, M.A. and Bazerman, M.H. (1991). *Cognition and Rationality in Negotiation*. New York: Free Press.

Northcraft, G.B., Neale, M.A., and Earley, P.C. (1994). Joint effects of assigned goals and training on negotiator performance, *Human Performance*, 7, 257–272.

O'Connor, K.M., Arnold, J.A., and Burris, E.R. (2005). Negotiators' bargaining histories and their effects on future negotiation performance, *Journal of Applied Psychology*, 90, 350–362.

Olekalns, M. and Brett, J. (2008). Beyond the deal: Next generation negotiation skills (Introduction to Special Issue), *Negotiation and Conflict Management Research*, 1, 309–314.

Olekalns, M. and Druckman, D. (forthcoming). With feeling: How emotions shape negotiation. In B. Martinovksi (ed.), Emotion in Group Decision and Negotiation. Vol. 5, *Advances in Group Decision and Negotiation*. Dordrecht, the Netherlands: Springer.

Olekalns, M. and Smith, P. (2005). Moments in time: Metacognition, trust and outcomes in negotiation, *Personality & Social Psychology Bulletin*, 31, 1696–1707.

Olekalns, M. and Smith, P. (2007). Loose with the truth: Predicting deception in negotiation, *Journal of Business Ethics*, 76, 225–238.

Olekalns, M. and Smith, P. (2009). Mutually dependent: Power, trust, affect and the use of deception in negotiation, *Journal of Business Ethics*, 85, 347–365.

Olekalns, M. and Weingart, L. (2008). Emergent negotiations: Stability and shifts in process dynamics, *Negotiation and Conflict Management Research*, 1, 135–160.

Olekalns, M., Smith, P.L., and Kibby, R. (1996). Social value orientations, negotiator strategies and outcomes, *European Journal of Social Psychology*, 26, 299–313.

Pruitt, D.G. (1981). *Negotiation Behavior*. New York: Academic Press.

Pruitt, D.G. and Carnevale, P.J. (1993). *Negotiation in Social Conflict*. Oxford: Oxford University Press.

Putnam, L.L. (1990). Reframing integrative and distributive bargaining: A process perspective, *Research on Negotiation in Organizations*, 2, 3–30.

Sondak, H. and Stuhlmacher, A. (2009). Gendered organizational order and negotiations research, *Negotiation and Conflict Management Research*, 2, 107–120.

Stuhlmacher, A.F. and Walters, A.E. (1999). Gender differences in negotiation outcome: A meta-analysis, *Personnel Psychology*, 52, 653–677.

Thompson, L., Wang, J., and Gunia, B. (2010). Negotiation, *Annual Review of Psychology*, 61, 491–515.

Thompson, L. and Hastie, R. (1990a). Social perception in negotiation, *Organizational Behavior and Human Decision Processes*, 47, 98–123.

Thompson, L. and Hastie, R. (1990b). Judgment tasks and biases in negotiation. In B.H. Sheppard, M.H. Bazerman, and R.J. Lewicki (eds), *Research in Negotiation in Organizations*, Vol. 2, pp. 31–54. JAI.

Tiedens, L. and Fragale, A. (2003). Power moves: Complementarity in dominant and submissive nonverbal behavior, *Journal of Personality and Social Psychology*, 84, 558–568.

Tinsley, C.H., O'Connor, K.M., and Sullivan, B.A. (2002). Tough guys finish last: The perils of a distributive reputation, *Organizational Behavior and Human Decision Processes*, 88, 621–642.

Trope, Y. and Liberman, N. (2003). Temporal construal, *Psychological Review*, 110, 403–421.

Trope, Y. and Liberman, N. (2010). Construal-level theory of psychological distance, *Psychological Review*, 117, 440–463.

Walters, A.E., Stuhlmacher, A.F., and Meyer, L.L. (1998). Gender and negotiator competitiveness: A meta-analysis. *Organizational Behavior and Human Decision Processes*, 76, 1–29.

Weingart, L. and Olekalns, M. (2004). Communication processes in negotiation. In M. Gelfand and J. Brett (eds), *Handbook of Culture and Negotiation*. Stanford: Stanford University Press.

Weingart, L., Brett, J., Olekalns, M., and Smith, P.L. (2007). Conflicting social motives in negotiating groups, *Journal of Personality and Social Psychology*, 93, 994–1010.

PART II

THE INDIVIDUAL NEGOTIATOR

2. Individual differences in negotiation
*Hillary Anger Elfenbein**

For this chapter to be included in a research handbook on negotiation involves a certain leap of faith. After all, large-scale reviews have long concluded that individual differences are unreliable predictors of negotiation outcomes, with a preponderance of null and inconsistent results (Lewicki et al., 1994; Terhune, 1970; Thompson, 1990). Previous authors have gone so far as to conclude, "from what is known now, it does not appear that there is any single personality type or characteristic that is directly and clearly linked to success in negotiation" (Lewicki and Litterer, 1985, p. 276); "personality and individual differences appear to play a minimal role in determining bargaining behavior" (Thompson, 1990, p. 515); and "few findings have proven replicable, and contradictory findings are not uncommon" (Barry and Friedman, 1998, p. 345).

And yet the chapter appears, largely due to the persistent intuition many of us share about the important role of enduring traits in the bargaining process. Some negotiators simply seem well suited for the task of extracting a good deal for themselves, some seem well suited to manage a sticky situation with everyone feeling good in the end, and others seem ill suited for either. Although researchers' focus on individual differences in negotiation tended to decrease in the wake of the pessimistic reviews quoted above (Neale and Northcraft, 1991), it never disappeared entirely. After reviewing the existing body of work, this chapter discusses new approaches that my colleagues and I have taken in the hope of reconciling the mystery whereby intuition and conventional wisdom have tended to clash with inconsistent empirical findings (Elfenbein et al., 2008; Elfenbein et al., 2010; Sharma et al., 2012). The chapter concludes with a research agenda for the field to move forward.

EMPIRICAL FINDINGS ON INDIVIDUAL DIFFERENCES IN NEGOTIATION

It is a tall order in one chapter to review all negotiations research that includes factors differing from person to person. Not only has there been a half-century of work focused on this topic; the majority of negotiations research includes at least some individual factors as control variables.

Below is a necessarily brief review of the wide range of individual differences studied, capturing five distinct categories: (a) enduring dispositions, (b) motivational styles, (c) expectancies and beliefs, (d) demographic and work background, and (e) abilities. In each case, the review describes existing work predicting objective outcomes—namely, the terms of the deal—as well as subjective value (Curhan et al., 2006)—namely, satisfaction with the deal.

Enduring Dispositions

The theoretical construct of personality has been defined as consistency over time in an individual's behaviors when that individual is placed in the same situation (Fleeson, 2004; Magnusson and Endler, 1977; Mischel and Shoda, 1995). This definition emphasizes the importance of situations, and yet it also emphasizes that the individual crafts a unique signature of responses to those situations. At the top of the list of enduring dispositions studied in negotiation is the comprehensive "big five"-factor personality model that resulted from an exhaustive analysis and validation based on colloquial personality terms (Costa and McCrae, 1992). The five factors are extraversion, agreeableness, conscientiousness, neuroticism, and openness.

Extraversion refers to an individual's level of sociability, assertiveness, activity, optimism, and talkativeness. Findings suggest it can be a liability in distributive bargaining, potentially due to excessive information sharing and concern for social interactions, but these same sociable traits may be an asset for integrative bargaining, which requires more communication and social interaction to reveal hidden trade-offs and compatibilities (Barry and Friedman, 1998). Even so, the assertiveness subcomponent could help negotiators to stand their ground (Elfenbein et al., 2010).

Agreeableness is a measure of courteousness, flexibility, sympathy, trust, cooperation, and tolerance. In the case of objective negotiation outcomes, agreeableness predicts slightly lower outcomes for distributive negotiations—likely, as with extraversion, due to greater social concerns—but it has no apparent effect on integrative negotiation performance (Amanatullah et al., 2008; Barry and Friedman, 1998; Morris et al., 1999). Negotiators and their counterparts may benefit subjectively from agreeableness (Barry and Friedman, 1998), particularly given that it is associated with lesser use of quarrelsome and assertive negotiation tactics (Graziano et al., 1996).

Conscientiousness is a measure of self-discipline, indicating that individuals are well organized, careful, responsible, and motivated to achieve. Of the five traits, conscientiousness is the best predictor of overall job performance (Barrick and Mount, 1991). One might expect conscientious negotiators to outperform their less conscientious peers, given their general task achievement and likely greater preparation, although empirical results have not supported such an association (Barry and Friedman, 1998). It is worth speculating this null finding is an artifact of laboratory studies in which more conscientious participants have no greater opportunity to prepare than less conscientious participants.

Neuroticism refers to an individual's general level of anxiety, depression, worry, and insecurity. Although Barry and Friedman (1998) found no influence of neuroticism on economic outcomes, subjectively those who are high on neuroticism tend to report more negative experiences in their negotiations (Elfenbein et al., 2008). Neuroticism is related to face threat sensitivity, which predicts greater likelihood of impasses and lesser joint value when the negotiation is self-threatening, for example when playing a job candidate versus recruiter (White et al., 2004).

Openness is a measure of imaginativeness, broad-mindedness and divergent thinking. People who are high on openness are said to be intellectually curious and willing to consider unconventional ideas. Openness predicts greater mutual gain in integrative settings—resulting from negotiators' ability to craft solutions that benefit their counterparts as well as themselves—but has no clear relationship with distributive negotiation (Barry and Friedman, 1998). Research has yet to document what, in particular, negotiators high in openness do differently to create greater value.

Another perspective on enduring dispositions is to examine systematic differences in the chronic experience of emotional states (for a detailed review, see Van Kleef and Sinaceur, Chapter 5 this volume). Watson et al.'s (1998) circumplex model classifies individuals according to their frequency of experiencing *positive affect* and *negative affect*, which appear to be independent of each other both theoretically and empirically. A substantial and growing body of research has examined the influence of affect on objective negotiation performance. Forgas (1998) argued for mood-congruent influences—leading to greater cooperation versus competition when negotiators or counterparts are in positive versus negative moods, respectively—as well as more flexible problem solving, confidence, and ambition among those in positive moods. Those high in positive affect—including both chronic traits and temporary states—tend to achieve higher individual and joint outcomes, due to greater use of cooperative strategies, fewer contentious strategies, higher goals, greater development of trust, more effective exchange of information, and greater confidence (Anderson and Thompson, 2004; Barry et al., 2004; Carnevale and Isen, 1986; Forgas, 1998). Barry and Oliver (1996) also argued that positive affect tends to benefit negotiators by increasing post-settlement compliance and the continuation of working relationships. Indeed, counterparts appear to be able to judge cooperative tendencies visually through facial expressions of positive affect (Carnevale and De Dreu, 2006).

In contrast with positive mood, negative mood appears to harm negotiation performance. Negotiators induced with negative moods are less accurate in reading their counterparts' interests (Allred et al., 1997), are more likely to reject offers that are economically superior to their alternatives (Pillutla and Murnighan, 1996), and tend to retaliate against counterparts' competitive behavior—even at their own expense (Brown, 1968). Although it is possible to use expressions of negative mood strategically to convince a counterpart that further concessions are necessary, this tends to create ill will for further interactions (Carnevale and De Dreu, 2006). However, in a highly complex negotiation setting, negative moods may be helpful for enhancing an information processing style that is bottom-up, more systematic and detailed, more narrow and vigilant in attention, and more externally focused towards changing one's existing situation (for reviews, see Clore et al., 1994; Forgas, 2003). Because negative mood signals that we are in an unsatisfactory or even dangerous situation, we need to process information more deeply and with greater causal reasoning in order to address the underlying concern (Clore et al., 1994).

Related to work on trait affect, research on *regulatory focus* also examines tendencies to focus on positive stimuli (i.e., promotion focus) versus negative stimuli (i.e., prevention focus; Brockner and Higgins, 2001).

Machiavellianism is a personality construct developed by Christie and Geis (1970) to measure agreement with ideas espoused by the sixteenth-century political philosopher Nicolo Machiavelli. High-Machs tend to be pragmatic, opportunistic, maintain emotional distance from others, and believe that the ends justify means. Empirical evidence is inconsistent as to whether Machiavellianism increases or decreases objective negotiation performance, as this varies across studies (Barry and Friedman, 1998; (Thompson, 1990), which suggests value in a systematic investigation of contextual variables that can moderate its effect.

Maximizing versus *satisficing* is a recently developed personality construct (Schwartz et al., 2002) with important implications for negotiation. High-maximizers seek optimal outcomes and are generally less satisfied with their choices than low-maximizers, that is, satisficers, and they are more prone to regret. Although maximizing students tend to outperform their satisficing classmates in employment negotiations with higher starting salaries, because they spend more time examining alternatives, they are less satisfied with their jobs and the job hunting process (Iyengar et al., 2006). Taken together, this suggests that maximization—and its counterpart, *regret*—is a positive influence on objective scores but deleterious for subjectively experienced performance.

Self-esteem is a matter of holding oneself in highly positive regard (Rosenberg, 1965). It may help objective performance in distributive settings, in that those high in self-esteem believe that they are more deserving and act competitively to gain valued resources (Hermann and Kogan, 1977). However, it may be a hindrance in integrative settings, in that negotiators high in self-esteem may overestimate their performance and foreclose prematurely on further potential gains (Kramer et al., 1993). Subjectively, individuals with high self-esteem are more prone to self-enhancing biases and tend to judge their negotiation outcomes as more favorable than do those with low self-esteem, even in the absence of objective differences (Kramer et al., 1993).

Motivational Styles

"Social psychologists", Carnevale and De Dreu (2006) argued, "consider goals and motives as central elements of negotiation, indeed as the raison d'être, its reason for being" (p. 55). This focus echoes theoretical perspectives on individual differences in terms of the goals that people bring to different situations (Mischel and Shoda, 1995). Negotiators' goals, motives, and prior expectations influence their behaviors as well as their perceptions—the very way that negotiators construe the settings in which they find themselves (Carnevale and De Dreu, 2006). Although any individual's motivations will vary over time and across situations, there are also chronic trends from person to person, such that any of these styles can also be studied as an individual difference.

At the core of models of motivation in the negotiation context is a tension between having concern for oneself versus concern for the other (e.g., Pruitt and Rubin, 1986). Indeed, outside of negotiations, the balance between focusing on relationships versus personal agency is a core human concern (Bakan, 1966). In spite of the complexity of human social interaction, Interpersonal Theory suggests that interpersonal behaviors can be described in terms of just two dimensions, or dominance and affiliation (Kiesler, 1983; Wiggins, 1979). These two dimensions are theorized to be orthogonal such that they form the axes of a two-dimensional space which, Wiggins (1979) argued, defines the entire range of meaningful interpersonal events and judgments. Dominance and affiliation have appeared under many different labels that essentially map onto each other, such as agency and communion, competence and warmth, and status and love (Cuddy et al., 2008; Osgood, 1970; Wiggins, 1979). In the case of integrative bargaining, these concerns map onto negotiators' mixed-motives both to cooperate and to compete.

The classic Dual Concern Model argues that negotiators vary along these two separate dimensions (Blake and Mouton, 1964; Rubin and Brown, 1975), and empirical findings support the notion that the two dimensions are independent (De Dreu et al., 2000). Although Dual Concern theory argues for the impact of situational cues on strategic choices, it can also be used a model of individual differences in that people can vary in their chronic styles of approaching conflict (De Dreu et al., 2000). The construct of *social value orientation* (SVO) refers to positions within this two-dimensional grid of concern for the self versus other (Carnevale and De Dreu, 2006; De Dreu et al., 2000). A *pro-social* orientation represents concern for total gains (the upward-sloping 45-degree diagonal line), a *competitive* orientation represents concern for the discrepancy between one's own gain and that of the counterpart (the downward-sloping 45-degree diagonal line), and an *egoistic* or *individualist* orientation represents concern for one's own gains, with indifference towards the gains of one's counterpart. In a meta-analysis, De Dreu et al. (2000) found that pro-social negotiators achieved higher joint outcomes and were less contentious than egoistic negotiators, but only when their goals were ambitious enough that it was not easy to reach an agreement by accommodating or compromising without the need for active collaboration or problem solving.

To the extent that the balance between concern for relationships versus personal agency is a core human concern, great imbalance in either direction becomes problematic (Bakan, 1966). Concern for the self versus other can have different effects on negotiation performance at extreme levels. Individuals high in *unmitigated communion*—who have extreme concern for others, even at their own expense—tend to perceive greater relationship costs to asserting their own interests in negotiations, and consequently set lower aspirations and claim less value for themselves (Amanatullah et al., 2008). They do not necessarily differ from others in their perception that negotiation has instrumental rewards, but they have heightened concerns for the potential costs to relationships, and report greater relationship satisfaction when paired with others who are also high in unmitigated communion (Amanatullah et al., 2008). Outside of negotiation, research shows poor health outcomes for such individuals when they become ill, due to neglect of their own welfare in favor of attending to the needs of others (Hegelson, 2003). By contrast, individuals high in *unmitigated agency* fall at the other end of the balance between relationships and personal agency (Hegelson and Fritz, 1999), and pursue objective negotiation outcomes at the expense of a positive relationship.

EXPECTANCIES AND BELIEFS

An exciting and relatively newer perspective on individual differences in negotiation relates to negotiators' expectancies and beliefs. Expectancies are predictions about behavioral consequences—for example, which actions are likely to be rewarded versus punished—and these expectancies operate independently from negotiators' motivations to achieve certain end states (Ames, 2008). After all, negotiators base their actions not only on their desired goals, but also on their idiosyncratic perceptions about what they expect their actions to accomplish (Ames, 2008; Mischel and Shoda, 1995). Mischel and Shoda (1995) argued that individual differences can be manifested in consistent patterns of situation-behavior relationships, driven in part by "if . . . then contingencies" (p. 248).

Making a distinction between expectancies and motivations is not to argue the two do not overlap substantially—given that we tend to be motivated by positive consequences, and we tend to expect more positive consequences in pursuing our desired ends. The relationship appears mutually reinforcing. For example, De Dreu et al. (2000) argued that social value orientations are learned over time as individuals are exposed to the costs and benefits of competitive and cooperative behavior and develop expectations accordingly. Likewise, the fixed-pie bias (Thompson and Hastie, 1990) is a belief that both parties at a negotiation have diametrically opposed interests—rather than some interests that overlap and other interests with possible trade-offs. Any particular belief can be influenced by contextual factors, and yet can be subject to chronic individual differences.

A key expectancy relevant in this setting is *negotiation self-efficacy*, or a sense of confidence in being able to use specific tactics successfully (Sullivan et al., 2006). Distributive self-efficacy involves confidence in using tactics such as gaining the upper hand, preventing the other negotiator from exploiting weaknesses, and convincing the other party to make most of the concessions. Integrative self-efficacy involves confidence in exchanging concessions, finding trade-offs that benefit both parties, establishing a high level of rapport, and looking for agreements that maximize both parties' interests. Such beliefs matter because negotiators base their choices of tactics on their perceived chances of success that, in turn, can guide negotiation process and outcomes (Sullivan et al., 2006). Confidence feeds into higher aspirations and, consequently, negotiation outcomes (Galinsky et al., 2002; Stevens et al., 1993). Further, confidence can reflect past negotiation success, and may represent negotiators' intuitions about their general levels of objective performance (Curhan et al., 2006).

Appropriateness of negotiation is another relevant expectancy (Curhan, 2005)—that is, the subjective perception of whether it is appropriate to negotiate in a particular setting. Although perceptions of appropriateness vary naturally from setting to setting, individuals also vary in their chronic report that entering into a negotiation is appropriate. Indeed, a survey that spans domains as diverse as flea markets, gas stations, and department stores achieves conventional levels of inter-item reliability (Curhan, 2005). Negotiators are likely to experience greater comfort and confidence if they believe that it is normative and worthwhile to seek out opportunities to negotiate. As with self-efficacy, high feelings of negotiation appropriateness are associated with better performance and subjective satisfaction (Elfenbein et al., 2008).

A further type of belief—beyond confidence and comfort—is a negotiator's *implicit belief* regarding the extent to which negotiation skills are malleable (incremental theorists) versus fixed (entity theorists). Kray and Haselhuhn (2007) found that incremental theorists outperformed entity theorists across a range of distributive and integrative negotiation tasks, and even in negotiation classroom assignments that were independent of performance in role-playing exercises. They argued that those who believe skills are malleable are more likely to persist in the face of challenge and to enjoy learning experiences rather than believe that challenges are diagnostic of low ability and prefer opportunities that demonstrate existing mastery. Examining relationship conflicts, Kammrath and Dweck (2006) found that those who believe personality is malleable were more likely to voice dissatisfaction with their relationship partner and to attempt to resolve conflicts, whereas those who believe personality is fixed felt such attempts would be futile and either resigned themselves to flaws or withdrew from the relationship. Further, they found that the more active steps taken by incremental theorists predicted greater relationship satisfaction, as they served to repair the underlying conflict. This suggests that incremental theorists—in addition to achieving better objective outcomes—are likely to work towards a more subjectively satisfying negotiation experience.

The final type of belief that we examine concerns *negotiation ethics*. Given that negotiation involves, at least to some extent, a clash in the interests and desires of two or more parties, the question of selfish and opportunistic behavior looms large. Based on previous theoretical perspectives on lying and deception, case studies, and interviews with students and executives, Robinson et al. (2000) developed and validated a five-factor model of ethical and marginally ethical tactics in negotiation: (a) *traditional bargaining tactics*, such as making highly optimistic opening offers and pretending not to be in a hurry; (b) *attacking a counterpart's network*, such as attempts to make a counterpart look weak or foolish in front of their colleagues, or even trying to get them fired; (c) *making false promises* that the negotiator knows will not be honored; (d) *misrepresenting information*, by presenting false information, denying the validity of truthful information, or misrepresenting the progress of a negotiation; and (e) *inappropriate information gathering*, such as paying those who are in a knowledgeable position to reveal information, or cultivating an insincere friendship with the counterpart (see also Diekmann et al., Chapter 8 this volume). As with other forms of expectancies, these beliefs about what is appropriate do overlap to some extent with motivations—in particular when individuals who report more competitive versus cooperative orientations also endorse more strongly the tactics listed in the SINS scale (Robinson et al., 2000). Robinson et al. (2000) found no reliable performance differences, although Elfenbein et al. (2008) found greater performance for those endorsing traditional bargaining tactics.

Taken together, expectancies and beliefs form the most consistently reliable set of individual difference measures in predicting negotiation performance. This is not surprising, perhaps, because these measures have been developed specifically for the negotiation setting. The empirical success of this class of variables provides optimism for training programs in negotiation—in that it is more accessible to influence a person's beliefs about negotiation activities than it is to influence a person's enduring disposition.

DEMOGRAPHIC AND WORK BACKGROUND

Gender is perhaps the most widely studied individual difference in negotiation, and is reviewed at length as a topic in its own right in this volume (Stuhlmacher and Linnabery, Chapter 9 this volume). Likewise, cultural background has been a fruitful topic of research in negotiation (Aslani et al., Chapter 10 this volume).

Less often studied are other aspects of demographic background that can be relevant to the negotiation process, such as socio-economic background and education level. Individuals' degree of formal experience with negotiation has been a powerful predictor of better negotiation performance, particularly for a single-item measure (Elfenbein et al., 2008). Presumably, people who are more successful negotiators tend to seek out relevant experiences, just as learning from these experiences reinforces success. Note that economic and work-related factors can interact with traditional demographic factors, for example when gender influences negotiation performance indirectly via differences in exposure to negotiation experience across men versus women (Kray and Thompson, 2005).

ABILITIES

The ability to negotiate effectively may relate to an individual's abilities. Starting with *cognitive intelligence*, general mental ability—also known as "*g*"—is a broad ability to learn, catch on and make sense of familiar and unfamiliar surroundings, to think abstractly, and to think ahead to devise strategies—which also includes such factors as memory encoding and retrieval, cognitive speed, sensory perception, and specific abilities such as math and spelling (Fulmer and Barry, 2004). Given that negotiation is a complex decision-making task with a range of alternative sources of action, cognitive skills factor prominently in information-processing approaches to negotiation (Bazerman and Carroll, 1987). Thus, it is natural to expect such skills to help negotiators—particularly in situations that are novel and/or complex (Fulmer and Barry, 2004). Highly intelligent individuals are better able to approach problem-solving tasks, to process and analyse information, and to perform well across a wide variety of occupations (Barry and Friedman, 1998; Thompson, 1990). In spite of the robust association between cognitive ability and performance across a wide range of occupations, its role in negotiation has been explored relatively rarely, due in part to several early null results (Fulmer and Barry, 2004). In a recent meta-analysis, cognitive ability is a reliable predictor of value creating across a number of studies (Sharma et al., 2012).

Cognitive complexity—also known as integrative complexity—is a cognitive style in analysing information and making decisions that is defined by two steps: evaluative differentiation, which is the recognition of multiple perspectives and dimensions, and conceptual integration, which is the integration and recognition of the interrelatedness of these multiple dimensions (Suedfeld et al., 1992; Tetlock, 1988). As a chronic tendency rather than a capability, cognitive complexity appears to be uncorrelated with traditional measures of cognitive intelligence (Fulmer and Barry, 2004; Streufert et al., 1968). Individuals who are cognitively complex tend to engage in a wide range of activities relating to approaching negotiations in a sophisticated manner. This includes using a broader range of information for decision making, generating more alternatives, being more accurate in their predictions, engaging in more flexible trial-and-error activity, and acting comfortably in unstructured tasks (Pruitt and Lewis, 1975; Tetlock, 1988; Streufert et al., 1968). As a consequence, they are suited to achieve more beneficial agreements in mixed-motive bargaining games.

By contrast with cognitive intelligence, *emotional intelligence* (EI) refers to an individual's ability to appraise and express emotions, to use information generated by emotions, and to regulate their own emotions effectively (Mayer et al., 1990). EI has been a controversial area of research, garnering detailed critiques (e.g., Matthews et al., 2002) covering topics as diverse as conceptual clarity, divergent validity from existing constructs, and scoring difficulties—particularly psychometric shortcomings, the questionable validity of pencil-and-paper measures, and the theoretical quandary about how to define correct performance. That said, there is provocative new evidence that the best existing tests of emotional intelligence do predict workplace performance, above and beyond the role of cognitive intelligence (Mayer et al., 2008). The Mayer, Salovey, and Caruso (2000) model of emotional intelligence has become the dominant standard in academic research, due to its larger body of evidence for scientific validation, and its greater distinction than other models from existing personality traits (Fulmer and Barry, 2004). This model includes four factors: (a) *perceiving emotion*, the ability to recognize the emotional content in nonverbal behavior and abstract stimuli—which can assist negotiators in deciphering their counterparts' overt and hidden feelings (Elfenbein et al., 2007; Fulmer and Barry, 2004); (b) *facilitating emotion*, the ability to access, generate, and harness emotions so as to assist thought—which can assist negotiators in using their moods as a source of information and to derive tangible value from their gut instincts (Schwarz and Clore, 2003); (c) *understanding emotion*, the ability to understand emotional concepts and general knowledge such as emotion lexicons—which can help negotiators to monitor, predict, and shift the emotional state of their counterparts (Fulmer and Barry, 2004); and (d) *managing emotion*, the ability to control one's own and others' emotions towards desired ends—which can help negotiators to maintain the composure of both parties during emotionally charged situations (Fulmer and Barry, 2004; Mueller and Curhan, 2006). EI is clearly a valuable set of capabilities for the negotiator (Fulmer and Barry, 2004) although, like other individual differences, the body of replicable empirical findings for EI lags behind theory-building—particularly for studies using validated measures of ability, rather than self-report scales.

Another social ability that has been attracting recent attention is *Cultural Intelligence* (CQ; Earley and Ang, 2003), which is defined as an individual's capability to adapt effectively to situations that involve cultural diversity. The model of CQ includes four factors: (a) *metacognitive*—awareness about cultural differences during cross-cultural interactions (b) *cognitive*—having information about how cultures differ (c) *motivational*—intrinsic motivation and self-efficacy related to intercultural interaction, and (d) *behavioral*—having a repertoire of behaviors that are successful for cross-cultural interactions (Earley and Ang, 2003). High CQ negotiators tend to achieve greater integrativeness in their settlements, due to more effective information sharing behaviors (Imai and Gelfand, 2010).

Creativity has also been established as an ability that varies meaningfully from person to person, and is defined as ideas or solutions that are both new and useful (Amabile, 1983). Mary Parker Follett's (1940) classic writings on negotiation emphasize the importance of creativity and thinking outside of the box: "Integration involves invention" (p. 33). Creativity involves novel ways to solve problems as well as new combinations of familiar ideas and concepts, which can be an asset in integrative negotiations to generate possible alternatives with mutual benefit, and to encourage questions to reveal unanticipated interests (Kurtzberg, 1998). Kurtzberg (1998) found that greater creativity in both the dyad and the individual increased the integrative potential of the negotiation without influencing distributive outcomes, a finding replicated by Elfenbein et al. (2008).

QUESTIONING THE IMPORTANCE OF INDIVIDUAL DIFFERENCES IN NEGOTIATION

Although the results reviewed above include an array of findings, the lack of a uniform theoretical framework and lack of consistent replication lie at the center of the critiques quoted in the opening paragraph of this chapter (Thompson, 1990). Should we give up on individual differences in negotiation?

Answering "yes" include those who argue that research on individual differences in negotiation is of limited use because individuals can do little or nothing to change their dispositional or demographic characteristics—and, indeed, for this reason it can be almost unethical to study the topic (Bazerman and Carroll, 1987). However, I argue that research findings have the potential to encourage fit by allowing organizations and teams to select individuals mindfully when a role involves negotiation, and help steer individuals towards roles that are consistent with their natural strengths. Further, research findings can alert individuals to domains where they will need to adjust their default behavior. After all, "personality" refers to our preferred ways of being (Costa and McCrae, 1992; Mischel and Shoda, 1995), and we always have the option to choose a non-preferred way of being on a temporary basis when the stakes are high enough. Acting against one's default behavioral signature can be feasible for brief periods of time, but it should be noted that this counter-normative behavior comes at a cost of consuming limited cognitive resources and should be used sparingly. Further, research into personality and negotiation that tests mechanisms has applied value if it can reveal concrete behaviors and processes that can be incorporated more easily into negotiators' repertoires than a personality intervention (Fulmer and Barry, 2004).

Others who answer "yes" advocate for examining personality strictly in the context of situations as moderating factors—that is, interactions of Person x Situation (PxS). Indeed, work on PxS interactions has been very fruitful—negotiation researchers have found that individual differences are more influential in situations that are less constrained, such as gender in the case of greater situational ambiguity about being able to negotiate (Bowles et al., 2005), positive affect in the case of greater power (Anderson and Thompson, 2004), and extraversion or agreeableness in the absence of high aspirations (Barry and Friedman, 1998). Interestingly, research on personality x situation interactions tends to be more replicable than research on personality alone, and this approach is clearly worthwhile. Nevertheless, many of us believe that main effects are still worthwhile to examine alongside interaction terms.

I propose that there are a number of reasons why past research may have been conservative and may not fully capture the potential power of individual differences. First, on a methodological note, studies in which participants take part in one negotiation exercise use the equivalent of single-item measures for performance. This makes findings highly conservative, due simply to the lower reliability of the dependent measure. By contrast, in research examining the association between personality and general job performance, such performance is measured by ratings or other outcomes that represent the result of extensive experience over time (Barrick and Mount, 1991). Second, on an analytical note, statistical concerns arise when negotiations are inherently dyadic and yet personality is inherently at the level of the individual. Researchers have typically addressed this mismatch in levels of analysis by examining one role at a time, examining dyad-level averages (e.g., Barry and Friedman, 1998), or using multilevel modeling to examine individuals and dyads simultaneously (e.g., Mueller and Curhan, 2006). These methods also reduce statistical power, to the detriment of finding positive results. Third, researchers have tended to start with personality traits that are imported from elsewhere in psychology, rather than to start by developing new traits that may be specific to the behavioral tendencies of a great negotiator. Fourth and finally, methodology differs enough across studies that attempting to reconcile them together is a matter of comparing apples and oranges—which suggests that the field may already "know" more than it thinks.

My colleagues and I are among those holding out hope that new approaches to studying personality traits in negotiation can produce clear and replicable findings. We attempted to address all of the concerns above in a recent paper (Elfenbein et al., 2008). Rather than starting—as most studies do—with one or more specific traits, we stepped back and asked the more general question of whether individuals are even consistent in their own performance from one negotiation to the next. That is, does negotiation performance even "live" at the individual level? If not, then the lack of associations with individual-level traits is veridical and the long-standing search can end because there is no variance to explain. Asking this question, we used Kenny's (1994) Social Relations Model (SRM) to examine cross-negotiation consistency. Participants were assigned to round-robin groups of five people, within which each person took part in a one-on-one negotiation with each other person. This provided four different measures of negotiation performance—rather than the typical single-item measure—and also provided us with the opportunity to see how consistent negotiators were in their performance from interaction to interaction. Accounting for order effects controlled for the possible influence of learning. Indeed, we found that a substantial 49 percent of the variance in performance "lived" at the level of the individual—a value that can be interpreted akin to an R^2 coefficient.

With the finding in hand that individual differences at the most abstract are highly predictive of negotiation outcomes, we looked at correlations between these outcomes and a large battery of trait measures. The SRM allowed us to address both the first and second concerns above. The first concern was about the typical use of single-item measures, and by contrast the SRM round-robin design provided four measures of performance. The second concern was matching the level of analysis of dyadic negotiation outcomes with individual differences, whereas the algorithms of the SRM use the repeated nature of measures to disentangle for each individual the equivalent of an average score. We also attempted to address the third concern, namely that researchers often use existing traits rather than traits specific to negotiation. In doing so, we supplemented the standard items in the battery with several negotiation-specific traits that had recently been developed—that is, negotiation self-efficacy (Sullivan et al., 2006) and implicit negotiation beliefs (Kray and Haselhuhn, 2007)—as well as Curhan's (2005) "Appropriateness of Price Negotiation" scale under development, which addresses the extent to which people believe that they are behaving appropriately if they initiate negotiations in various real-world settings. Overall, we found cause for optimism in a $r = .30$ ($p < .01$) association of performance with "positive negotiation expectation and beliefs"—that is, a composite consisting of these and several other related factors: self-efficacy, appropriateness of price negotiation, implicit negotiation beliefs, endorsement of traditional bargaining tactics (from Robinson et al.'s 2000 SINS scale), and self-rated formal negotiation experience. The only other significant associations with objective performance were for the motivational style of concern for one's own outcome ($r = .21, p < .01$) and positive affect ($r = .17, p < .05$). However, consistent with the subjective intuitions that personality plays an important role, there were strong associations between a variety of traits and subjective value—that is, one's satisfaction with the negotiation experience (Curhan et al., 2006). In general, traits that were associated with better objective performance also predicted greater satisfaction for oneself and lesser satisfaction for one's counterpart. However, beyond this trend, there was a strong pattern in which enduring dispositions predicted negotiators' own satisfaction—with a positive association for positive-valence traits such as agreeableness, openness, and self-esteem, and a negative association for negative-valence traits such as neuroticism and Machiavellianism. In the case of what we termed "visible personal characteristics"—that is, gender, age, non-native English, and attractiveness, there were no effects on performance or negotiator's subjective value, but there were negative effects on counterparts' subjective value in each case.

In our subsequent work in progress (Elfenbein et al., 2010), we attempt to take this approach one step further by examining at a micro level what makes some negotiators better than others. Using detailed coding systems, we open the "black box" to examine what behaviors lead to individual negotiators' consistent performance across their various encounters. In doing so, we take as a starting point the theoretical foundation that defines personality as consistency over time in an individual's behaviors when that individual is placed in the same situation (e.g., Mischel and Shoda, 1995). In this case, determining the behaviors that are both consistent across encounters and predictive of outcomes can lead us to identify new or potentially untapped traits to examine in the negotiation setting. This type of approach can allow researchers to come full circle, and to end with a list of traits that predict performance—grounded in personality theory, rather than the other way around. We hope that such work can respond to (Thompson, 1990) the call for research on personality in negotiation to move from a disparate collection of predictions to a comprehensive theory.

MOVING THE FIELD FORWARD

In setting an agenda for this work, a first step is to address to the extent possible the methodological, analytical, and conceptual concerns listed above—so that we do not pursue our best work with the proverbial arm tied behind our back. Another step is to allow for flexibility whenever possible, by studying "weak" situations in which individual differences are most free to emerge. A major critique of research on individual differences in negotiation outcomes has been that heavy situational constraints may have limited the role of stable dispositions (Barry and Friedman, 1998; Thompson, 1990). After all, personality has more room to influence behavior when such behavior is not already constrained (Mischel, 1977). Given theories of personality that emphasize its importance in predicting how individuals self-select into their social environments (Mischel and Shoda, 1995), ideally there can be room for participants to decide even whether to initiate versus bypass an opportunity to negotiate (Babcock et al., 2006). Flexibility can also include allowing participants to choose their own market partners. Looking outside of potential classroom exercises, underlying individual differences may manifest not only in overall frequencies of behaviors, but also in patterns of where and when those behaviors take place (Mischel and Shoda, 1995)—which suggests the need to study individual differences in negotiation in a richer and wider array of real-world organizational contexts.

Settings with bona fide stakes for participants are ideal, such as real world field settings rather than laboratory protocols. For example, colleagues and I have begun to examine negotiations for new cars at a dealership willing to share data on their actual profit, as well as electronics shops in India at which price negotiation is common (Elfenbein et al., 2011).

It is also important to examine the personality of both individuals in the negotiation dyad—in that negotiators' traits may influence not only their own performance, but also the performance that they typically evoke in counterparts. These *counterpart effects* are theoretically rich, and empirically appear with some regularity—for example, where abilities such as greater cognitive intelligence or creativity appear to increase a counterpart's score without increasing the negotiator's own (Elfenbein et al., 2008).

Another important piece of an agenda for the future is to emphasize subjective value (Curhan et al., 2006). In our large-scale project (Elfenbein et al., 2008) existing trait measures appeared to be better at predicting subjective versus objective performance. That is, a number of factors influenced negotiators' subjective experience without necessarily translating into better objective performance. We have argued that, even so, SV can still benefit negotiators as a good in itself, as an intuition about performance that may drive persistence and learning, and as a possible predictor of future value in the long term due to healthy working relationships (Curhan et al., 2006). Recent longitudinal research demonstrates that higher subjective value can predict higher objective value in the future (Curhan et al., 2010; Curhan et al., 2009). Taken together, these findings suggest the importance of including subjective outcome measures in research on individual differences in negotiation, and also the likelihood that conventional personality measures may play a stronger role in predicting objective outcomes in longitudinal designs—as mediated through subjective value.

Finally, testing causal mechanisms that can account for the influence of personality on negotiation performance is a necessary component of more comprehensive theoretical treatment. Elucidating the underlying processes is necessary—given that personality does not act directly on performance, but rather on behaviors that themselves have performance implications (Fulmer and Barry, 2004; Thompson, 1990).

Almost two decades ago, even while reporting pessimistically about the existing body of work, Lewicki et al. (1994) argued that "researchers may have closed the book on the effects of individual differences on negotiation prematurely" (p. 348). With the blossoming of research since that time, and its increasing precision and theoretical richness, one can hope that future literature reviews will make qualitatively different concluding statements.

NOTE

* For their inspiration and thoughtful contributions, I thank collaborators Jared Curhan, Noah Eisenkraft, Aiwa Shirako, Ashley Brown, Sudeep Sharma, and Bill Bottom, handbook editors Wendi Adair and Mara Olekalns, as well as fellow contributors Dan Druckman, Jeff Loewenstein, Alice Stuhlmacher, and Gerben Van Kleef.

REFERENCES

Allred, K.G., Mallozzi, J.S., Matsui, F., and Raia, C.P. (1997). The influence of anger and compassion on negotiation performance. *Organizational Behavior and Human Decision Processes*, 70, 175–187.

Amabile, T.M. (1983). The social psychology of creativity: A componential conceptualization. *Journal of Personality and Social Psychology*, 45, 357–376.

Amanatullah, E.T., Morris, M.W., and Curhan, J.R. (2008). Negotiators who give too much: Unmitigated communion, relational anxieties, and economic costs in distributive and integrative bargaining. *Journal of Personality and Social Psychology*, 95, 723–738.

Ames, D.R. (2008). Assertiveness expectancies: How hard people push depends on the consequences they predict. *Journal of Personality and Social Psychology*, 95, 1541–1557.

Anderson, C. and Thompson, L. (2004). Affect from the top down: How powerful individuals' positive affect shapes negotiations. *Organizational Behavior and Human Decision Processes*, 95, 125–139.

Babcock, L., Gelfand, M.J., Small, D.A., and Stayn, H. (2006). Gender differences in the propensity to initiate negotiations. In D. De Cremer, M. Zeelenberg, and J.K. Murnighan (eds), *Social Psychology and Economics*. Mahwah, NJ: Lawrence Erlbaum.

Bakan, D. (1966). *The Duality of Human Existence*. Chicago, IL: Rand McNally.
Barrick, M.R. and Mount, M.K. (1991). The Big Five personality dimensions and job performance: A meta-analysis. *Personnel Psychology*, 44, 1–26.
Barry, B. and Friedman, R.A. (1998). Bargainer characteristics in distributive and integrative negotiation. *Journal of Personality and Social Psychology*, 74, 345–359.
Barry, B. and Oliver, R. (1996). Affect in dyadic negotiation: A model and propositions. *Organizational Behavior and Human Decision Processes*, 67, 127–143.
Barry, B., Fulmer, I.S., and Van Kleef, G. (2004). I laughed, I cried, I settled: The role of emotion in negotiation. In M.J. Gelfand and J.M. Brett (eds), *The Handbook of Negotiation and Culture: Theoretical Advances and Cross-cultural Perspectives* (pp. 71–94). Palo Alto, CA: Stanford University Press.
Bazerman, M.H. and Carroll, J. (1987). Negotiator cognition. *Research in Organizational Behavior*, 9, 247–288.
Blake, R.R. and Mouton, J.S. (1964). *The Managerial Grid*. Houston, TX: Gulf Publishing.
Bowles, H.R., Babcock, L., and McGinn, K.L. (2005). Constraints and triggers: Situational mechanics of gender in negotiation. *Journal of Personality and Social Psychology*, 89, 951–965.
Brockner, J. and Higgins, E.T. (2001). Regulatory focus theory: Implications for the study of emotions at work. *Organizational Behavior and Human Decision Processes*, 86, 35–66.
Brown, B.R. (1968). The effects of need to maintain face on interpersonal bargaining. *Journal of Experimental Social Psychology*, 4, 107–122.
Carnevale, P.J. and De Dreu, C.K.W. (2006). Motive: The negotiator's raison d'être. In L. Thompson (ed.), *Frontiers of Social Psychology: Negotiation Theory and Research* (pp. 55–76). New York: Psychology Press.
Carnevale, P.J.D. and Isen, A.M. (1986). The influence of positive affect and visual access on the discovery of integrative solutions in bilateral negotiation. *Organizational Behavior and Human Decision Processes*, 37, 1–13.
Cherulnik, P.D., Way, J.H., Ames, S., and Hutto, D.B. (1981). Impressions of high and low Machiavellian men. *Journal of Personality*, 49, 388–400.
Christie, R. and Geis, F. (1970). *Studies in Machiavellianism*. New York: Academic Press.
Clore, G.L., Schwartz, N., and Conway, M. (1994). Affective causes and consequences of social information processing. In R.S. Wyer and T.K. Srull (eds), *Handbook of Social Cognition* (2nd edn, Vol. 1, pp. 323–417). Hillside, NJ: Erlbaum.
Costa, P.T., Jr. and McCrae, R.R. (1992). *Revised NEO Personality Inventory (NEO-PI-R) and NEO Five-Factor Inventory (NEO-FFI) Professional Manual*. Odessa, FL: Psychological Assessment Resources.
Cuddy, A.J.C., Fiske, S.T., and Glick, P. (2008). Warmth and competence as universal dimensions of social perception: The stereotype content model and the BIAS map. *Advances in Experimental Social Psychology*, 40, 61–149.
Curhan, J.R. (2005). *The Appropriateness of Price Negotiation Scale*. Unpublished survey instrument. Massachusetts Institute of Technology, Cambridge, MA.
Curhan, J.R., Elfenbein, H.A., and Eisenkraft, N. (2010). The objective value of subjective value: A multi-round negotiation study. *Journal of Applied Social Psychology*, in press.
Curhan, J.R., Elfenbein, H.A., and Kilduff, G.J. (2009). Getting off on the right foot: Subjective value versus economic value in predicting longitudinal job outcomes from job offer negotiations. *Journal of Applied Psychology*, 94, 524–534.
Curhan, J.R., Elfenbein, H.A., and Xu, H. (2006). What do people value when they negotiate? Mapping the domain of subjective value in negotiation. *Journal of Personality and Social Psychology*, 91, 493–512.
De Dreu, C.K., Weingart, L.R., and Kwon, S. (2000). Influence of social motives on integrative negotiation: A meta-analytic review and test of two theories. *Journal of Personality and Social Psychology*, 78, 889–905.
Earley, P.C. and Ang, S. (2003). *Cultural Intelligence: Individual Interactions Across Cultures*. Palo Alto, CA: Stanford University Press.
Elfenbein, H.A., Curhan, J.R., Eisenkraft, N., Shirako, A., and Baccaro, L. (2008). Are some

negotiators better than others? Individual differences in bargaining outcomes. *Journal of Research in Personality*, 42, 1463–1475.

Elfenbein, H.A., Curhan, J.R., Eisenkraft, N., Shirako, A., and Brown, A. (2010). Why are some negotiators better than others? Opening the black box of bargaining behaviors. Paper presented at the 23rd Annual Meeting of the International Association for Conflict Management. Cambridge, MA.

Elfenbein, H.A., Eisenkraft, N., DiLalla, L.F., Curhan, J.R., and Perlis, R. (2012). Person × environment interactions when the environment is another person: Twins in negotiations. Paper presented at the 72nd meeting of the Academy of Management, Boston, MA.

Elfenbein, H.A., Foo, M.D., White, J.B., Tan, H.H, and Aik, V.C. (2007). Reading your counterpart: The benefit of emotion recognition ability for effectiveness in negotiation. *Journal of Nonverbal Behavior*, 31, 205–223.

Elfenbein, H.A., Sharma, S., Kopelman, S., Eisenkraft, N., and Curhan, J.R. (2011). Individual differences and negotiation outcomes: A cross-cultural field study. Paper presented at the 71st meeting of the Academy of Management, San Antonio, Texas.

Fleeson, W. (2001). Towards a structure- and process-integrated view of personality: Traits as density distributions of states. *Journal of Personality and Social Psychology*, 80, 1011–1027.

Fleeson, W. (2004). Moving personality beyond the person-situation debate: The challenge and the opportunity of within-person variability. *Current Directions in Psychological Science*, 13, 83–87.

Follett, M.P. (1940). Constructive conflict. In H.C. Metcalf and L. Urwick (eds), *Dynamic Administration: The Collected Papers of Mary Parker Follett*. New York: Harper.

Forgas, J.P. (1998). On feeling good and getting your way: Mood effects on negotiation strategies and outcomes. *Journal of Personality and Social Psychology*, 74, 565–577.

Forgas, J.P (2003). Affective influences on attitudes and judgments. In R.J. Davidson, K.R. Scherer, and H.H. Goldsmith (eds), *Handbook of Affective Sciences* (pp. 596–618). Oxford: Oxford University Press.

Fulmer, I.S. and Barry, B. (2004). The smart negotiator: Cognitive ability and emotional intelligence in negotiation. *International Journal of Conflict Management*, 15, 245–272.

Galinsky, A.D., Mussweiler, T., and Medvec, V.H. (2002). Disconnecting outcomes and evaluations in negotiations: The role of negotiator focus. *Journal of Personality and Social Psychology*, 83, 1131–1140.

Graziano, W.G., Jensen-Campbell, L.A., and Hair, E.C. (1996). Perceiving interpersonal conflict and reacting to it: The case for agreeableness. *Journal of Personality and Social Psychology*, 70, 820–835.

Hegelson, V.S. (2003). Unmitigated communion and adjustment to breast cancer: Associations and explanations. *Journal of Applied Social Psychology*, 33, 1643–1661.

Hegelson, V.S. and Fritz, H.L. (1999). Unmitigated agency and unmitigated communion: Distinctions from agency and communion. *Journal of Research in Personality*, 33, 131–158.

Hermann, M.G. and Kogan, N. (1977). Effects of negotiators' personalities on negotiating behavior. In D. Druckman (ed.), *Negotiations: Social-psychological Perspectives* (pp. 247–274). Beverly Hills, CA: Sage.

Imai, L. and Gelfand, M.J. (2010). The culturally intelligent negotiator: The impact of cultural intelligence (CQ) on negotiation sequences and outcomes. *Organizational Behavior and Human Decision Processes*, 112, 83–98.

Iyengar, S.S., Wells, R.E., and Schwartz, B. (2006). Doing better but feeling worse: Looking for the "best" job undermines satisfaction. *Psychological Science*, 17, 143–150.

Kammrath, L.K. and Dweck, C. (2006). Voicing conflict: Preferred conflict strategies among incremental and entity theorists. *Personality and Social Psychology Bulletin*, 32, 1497–1508.

Kenny, D.A. (1994). *Interpersonal Perception: A Social Relations Analysis*. New York: Guilford Press.

Kiesler, D.J. (1983). The 1982 interpersonal circle: A taxonomy for complementarity in human transactions. *Psychological Review*, 90, 185–214.

Kramer, R.M., Newton, E., and Pommerenke, P.L. (1993). Self-enhancement biases and negotiator judgment: Effects of self-esteem and mood. *Organizational Behavior and Human Decision Processes*, 56, 110–133.

Kray, L.J. and Haselhuhn, M.P. (2007). Implicit negotiation beliefs and performance: Experimental and longitudinal evidence. *Journal of Personality and Social Psychology*, 93, 49–64.

Kray, L.J. and Thompson, L. (2005). Gender stereotypes and negotiation performance: An examination of theory and research. *Research in Organizational Behavior*, 26, 103–182.

Kurtzberg, T.R. (1998). Creative thinking, cognitive aptitude, and integrative joint gain: A study of negotiator creativity. *Creativity Research Journal*, 11, 283–293.

Lewicki, R.J. and Litterer, J.A. (1985). *Negotiation*. Homewood, IL: R.D. Irwin.

Lewicki, R.J., Litterer, J.A., Minton, J.W., and Saunders, D.M. (1994). *Negotiation* (2nd edn). Burr Ridge, IL: Irwin.

Magnusson, D. and Endler, N.S. (1977). *Personality at the Crossroads: Current Issues in Interactional Psychology*. Hillsdale, NJ: Erlbaum.

Matthews, G., Zeidner, M., and Roberts, R.D. (2002). *Emotional Intelligence: Science and Myth*. Cambridge, MA: The MIT Press.

Mayer, J.D., DiPaolo, M., and Salovey, P. (1990). Perceiving affective content in ambiguous visual stimuli: A component of emotional intelligence. *Journal of Personality Assessment*, 54, 772–781.

Mayer, J.D., Roberts, R.D., and Barsade, S.G. (2008). Human abilities: Emotional intelligence. *Annual Review of Psychology*, 58, 507–536.

Mayer, J.D., Salovey, P., and Caruso, D.R. (2000). Models of emotional intelligence. In R.J. Sternberg (ed.), *Handbook of Intelligence* (pp. 396–420). Cambridge, UK: Cambridge University Press.

Mischel, W. (1977). The interaction of person and situation. In D. Magnusson and N.S. Endler (eds), *Personality at the Crossroads: Current Issues in Interactional Psychology* (pp. 333–352). Hillsdale, NJ: Erlbaum.

Mischel, W. and Shoda, Y. (1995). A cognitive-affective system theory of personality: Reconceptualizing situations, dispositions, dynamics, and invariance in personality structure. *Psychological Review*, 102, 246–268.

Morris, M.W., Larrick, R.P., and Su, S.K. (1999). Misperceiving negotiation counterparts: When situationally determined bargaining behaviors are attributed to personality traits. *Journal of Personality and Social Psychology*, 77, 52–67.

Mueller, J.S. and Curhan, J.R. (2006). Emotional intelligence and counterpart mood induction in a negotiation. *International Journal of Conflict Management*, 17, 110–128.

Neale, M.A. and Northcraft, G.B. (1991). Behavioral negotiation theory: A framework for conceptualizing dyadic bargaining. *Research in Organizational Behavior*, 13, 147–190.

Osgood, C.E. (1970). Speculation on the structure of interpersonal intentions. *Behavioral Science*, 15, 237–254.

Pillutla, M.M. and Murnighan, J.K. (1996). Unfairness, anger, and spite: Emotional rejections of ultimatum offers. *Organizational Behavior and Human Decision Processes*, 68, 208–224.

Pruitt, D.G. and Lewis, S.A. (1975). Development of integrative solutions in bilateral negotiation. *Journal of Personality and Social Psychology*, 31, 621–630.

Pruitt, D.G. and Rubin, J.Z. (1986). *Social conflict: Escalation, Stalemate, and Settlement*. New York: McGraw-Hill.

Robinson, R.J., Lewicki, R.J., and Donahue, E.M. (2000). Extending and testing a five factor model of ethical and unethical bargaining tactics: Introducing the SINS scale. *Journal of Organizational Behavior*, 21, 649–664.

Rosenberg, M. (1965). *Society and the Adolescent Self-image*. Princeton, NJ: Princeton University Press.

Rubin, J.Z. and Brown, B.R. (1975). *The Social Psychology of Bargaining and Negotiation*. New York: Academic Press.

Schwarz, N. and Clore, G.L. (2003). Mood as Information: 20 Years Later. *Psychological Inquiry*, 14, 296–303.
Schwartz, B., Ward, A., Monterosso, J., Lyubomirsky, S., White, K., and Lehman, D.R. (2002). Maximizing versus satisficing: Happiness is a matter of choice. *Journal of Personality and Social Psychology*, 83, 1178–1197.
Sharma, S., Bottom, W., and Elfenbein, H.A. (2012). Cognitive intelligence, emotional intelligence, and negotiation outcomes: A meta-analysis. Paper to be presented at the 72nd meeting of the Academy of Management, Boston, MA.
Stevens, C.K., Bavetta, A.G., and Gist, M.E. (1993). Gender differences in the acquisition of salary negotiation skills: The role of goals, self-efficacy, and perceived control. *Journal of Applied Psychology*, 78, 723–735.
Streufert, S., Streufert, S.C., and Castore, C.H. (1968). Leadership in negotiations and the complexity of conceptual structure. *Journal of Applied Psychology*, 52, 218–223.
Suedfeld, P., Tetlock, P.E., and Streufert, S. (1992). Conceptual/integrative complexity. In C.P. Smith, J.W. Atkinson, D.C. McClelland, and J. Veroff (eds), *Motivation and Personality: Handbook of Thematic Content Analysis* (pp. 393–400). New York: Cambridge University Press.
Sullivan, B.A., O'Connor, K.M., and Burris E.R. (2006). Negotiator confidence: The impact of self-efficacy on tactics and outcomes. *Journal of Experimental Social Psychology*, 42, 567–581.
Terhune, K. (1970). The effects of personality in cooperation and conflict. In P. Swingle (ed.), *The Structure of Conflict* (pp. 193–234). Beverly Hills: Sage.
Tetlock, P.E. (1988). Monitoring the integrative complexity of American and Soviet policy rhetoric: What can be learned? *Journal of Social Issues*, 44, 101–131.
Thompson, L. (1990). Negotiation behavior and outcomes: Empirical evidence and theoretical issues. *Psychological Bulletin*, 108, 515–532.
Thompson, L. and Hastie, R. (1990). Judgment tasks and biases in negotiations. In B.H. Sheppard, M.H. Bazerman, and R.J. Lewicki (eds), *Research in Negotiation in Organizations* (Vol. 2, pp. 31–54). Greenwich, CT: JAI Press.
Watson, D., Clark, L.A., and Tellegen, A. (1988). Development and validation of brief measures of positive and negative affect: The PANAS scales. *Journal of Personality and Social Psychology*, 54, 1063–1070.
White, J.B., Tynan, R., Galinsky, A.D., and Thompson, L.L. (2004). Face threat sensitivity in negotiation: Roadblock to agreement and joint gain. *Organizational Behavior and Human Decision Processes*, 94, 102–124.
Wiggins, J.S. (1979). A psychological taxonomy of trait-descriptive terms: The interpersonal domain. *Journal of Personality and Social Psychology*, 37, 395–412.
Wilson, D.S., Near, D., and Miller, R.R. (1996). Machiavellianism: A synthesis of the evolutionary and psychological literatures. *Psychological Bulletin*, 119, 285–299.

3. Motivated cognition in negotiation
Lukas Koning and Eric van Dijk

As people live side by side in ever-growing societies, conflicts of interests seem almost inevitable. Conflicts may appear at a large scale involving many people (for example, a conflict between nations) or at a small scale involving just two people (for example, two partners bickering over the daily chores). Inherent to all conflicts is their potential to escalate. Conflicts between nations can escalate into wars and conflicts between partners can turn into fights. Such escalations are often costly to all parties involved. A war, for example, may result in a large loss of lives. It is clear that escalation of a conflict is something one wants to avoid. Negotiations offer a more constructive way to solve conflicts. Given the potential benefits, it should be no surprise that negotiations have been a focal topic in economic and psychological research.

Negotiating can be described as a social interaction in which two or more parties in conflict seek a better outcome through joint action than they could realize independently (Lax and Sebenius, 1986). It is important to note that this definition stresses both a conflict of interests and interdependency. Parties will only be likely to resolve their conflict through negotiations when they perceive a common interest. Interests in negotiations are therefore not merely opposed, but must also converge to some degree. As a result, negotiators cannot solely focus on their own interests and ignore the interests of the other party. In this regard, negotiations can be considered mixed-motive situations (for an overview, see Komorita and Parks, 1995; Pruitt and Carnevale, 1993). It should therefore not come as a surprise that motives play an important role in negotiations. Motivation has a strong impact on how negotiators evaluate outcomes, select strategies and process information during a negotiation. This chapter focuses on how social and cognitive motives influence the negotiation process. We note that much of the research cited in this chapter uses bargaining paradigms. In this chapter no further distinction is made between bargaining and negotiating.

In Section 3.1 we discuss social motives and review different motives that have been identified in the literature. The mixed-motive nature of negotiations is reflected in the two motives that are generally considered of key importance in such settings: self-interest and other-regarding motives. We first discuss the role of social motives in simple zero-sum negotiation settings such as the ultimatum game. We follow this with a discussion of social motives in more complex negotiations involving multiple issues. Such negotiations often offer a way to integrate interests. However, such integration can only be achieved when parties have information about the preferences and priorities of other parties; the next two sections of this chapter focus on information search and information provision during negotiations.

In Section 3.2 we discuss information processing and the role cognitive motivation plays during this process. At the outset of a negotiation, negotiators often have little information about the preferences or intentions of the other parties involved in the negotiation. It may take some cognitive effort to get an accurate understanding of the way preferences and priorities align or converge. We discuss how heuristics and biases may influence information processing by negotiators. Furthermore, we discuss individual differences between negotiators in cognitive motivation.

In Section 3.3 we focus on information provision during negotiation. Negotiations pose an information dilemma, as negotiators have to decide which information they will share with other parties. We therefore also discuss the prominence of deception and investigate the acceptability and ethics of such practices. However, information may also be inferred from other sources than verbal communication. Nonverbal communication and prior interactions may provide opponents with information about someone's preferences and intentions. We therefore also briefly focus on reputation and impression management.

3.1 SOCIAL MOTIVES AND MIXED-MOTIVE SETTINGS

Economists and psychologists have long studied the behavior of people in mixed-motive settings. The traditional economic perspective on how people behave in such settings is based on two principles, rationality and self-interest (e.g., Thaler, 1992). According to this perspective, people are self-interested and try to maximize their own outcomes. Moreover, the principle of rationality dictates that people are quite clever in finding ways to accomplish this goal. Failure to maximize their own outcomes is often attributed to people's limited cognitive capacities. That is, people perhaps do not always comprehend the nature of the situation or fail to understand how they could maximize their payoffs. The view of self-interested rationality dictates that people should pay no regard to the outcomes of others.

Cooperation between people is explained in terms of self-interest in the longer term. In long-term relations people may forfeit short-term gain, but only when doing so provides them with a greater benefit later on. Cooperative relations are built through reciprocity: cooperative behavior is met with cooperative responses, while competitive behavior is met with competitive responses. Axelrod (1980a; 1980b) demonstrated neatly that reciprocity can be very effective in instilling cooperation in repeated social dilemmas. In such dilemmas, mutual competition leads to worse outcomes than mutual cooperation. Therefore, when actors strictly reciprocate each other's behavior, even self-interested actors end up being better off by cooperating than by competing.

Through reciprocity, cooperative behavior may be explained in terms of rational self-interest. However, other behavior may be harder to explain through such mechanisms. For example, it is hard to imagine how self-interest and reciprocity could play a role in anonymous donations to charities. Yet many people make such donations and this behavior raises the question whether self-interested rationality suffices to subscribe actual economic behavior. Opposing the idea that people are *rational economic people* acting purely out of rational self-interest, other theories began to emerge that considered motives besides self-interest.

One such alternative is interdependence theory (Kelley and Thibaut, 1978; see also Van Lange et al., 2007). Interdependence theory describes how social motives can "transform" objective outcomes into subjective utility. The core assumption underlying interdependence theory is that subjective evaluations do not necessarily correspond with objective outcomes. In evaluating outcomes, people may care about their own outcomes but they also care about the outcomes of others. Suppose one has to choose between two distributions of outcomes: the first option grants you $10 and another person $0 the second option grants you $6 and the other person $5. From the perspective of rational self-interest, people would always pick the first option as $10 is more than $6. However, this preference will be different if one attaches as much weight to the outcomes of the other as to own outcomes. In that case, the second option yields better outcomes ($11 in total) than the first option ($10 in total). The objective pattern of outcomes is thus transformed into a subjective evaluation according to someone's social motivation.

Many motivations can be identified that differ in the weight they assign to both own outcomes and those of others. Figure 3.1 depicts these motivations in relation to the concern for own outcomes (horizontal axis) and others' outcomes (vertical axis) (see Griesinger and Livingston, 1973). Individualists are on the right-hand side of the horizontal axis as they are motivated purely by self-interest. However, this motivation is only one out of eight possible motivations. Opposed to the individualists are the masochists, who also only consider their own outcomes but attach a negative

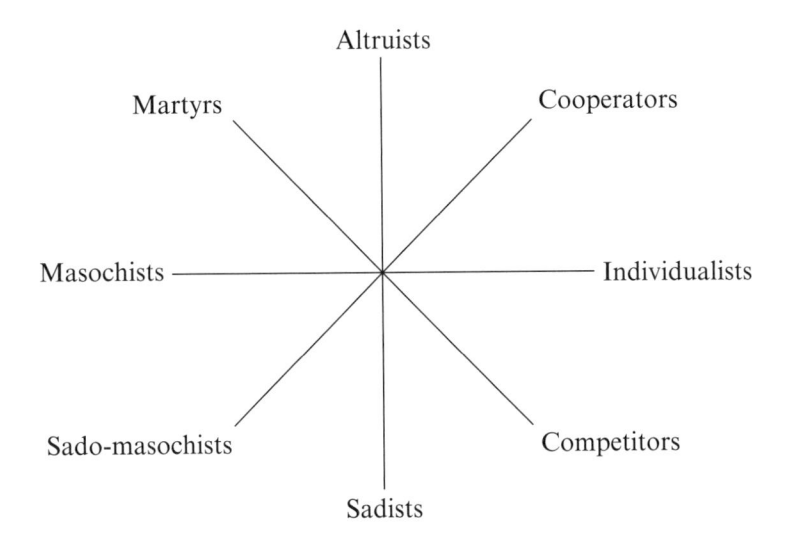

```
            Altruists
Martyrs   |   Cooperators
      \   |   /
       \  |  /
        \ | /
Masochists ——————●—————— Individualists
        / | \
       /  |  \
      /   |   \
Sado-masochists | Competitors
            Sadists
```

Source: Based on work by Griesinger & Livingston (1973).

Figure 3.1 Social motivations categorized by weight assigned to own (vertical axis) and other's outcomes (horizontal axis)

weight to these outcomes. On the vertical axis the motivations are depicted that assign weight only to the outcomes of others and not to their own outcomes. Altruists assign a positive weight to the outcomes of others, while sadists assign a negative weight to these outcomes. The four remaining motivations on the diagonals assign weight to both own outcomes and those of others. For competitors the weight for own outcomes is positive, while the weight for the outcomes of others is negative. On the other end of the diagonal we find martyrs for whom this pattern is reversed. The other diagonal shows sado-masochists who assign a negative weight to both own outcomes and those of others. Opposed to the sado-masochists are cooperators, who assign a positive weight to both their own outcomes and those of others.

So far we have considered the weights people may assign to their own outcomes and those of others. These weights can be positive, negative or even zero. Moreover, the weight can be either congruent (i.e., both positive) or incongruent (i.e., one negative and one positive). Apart from the weight assigned to the own and others' outcomes, one may also focus on how the two relate to each other. That is, one may also consider the relative difference between two outcomes with people often striving for equality when distributing outcomes (see e.g., Deutsch and Krauss, 1965).

People may thus be motived to minimize the difference between their own outcomes and those of others. The opposite is also possible, as some people may want to maximize the difference between their outcomes and those of others. For example, competitors may want to increase their advantage over an opponent even if this means putting in more effort themselves. Competitors may thus lower their own outcomes if by doing so they decrease the outcomes of their opponent even more. The relative difference between own and others' outcomes thus adds another dimension to the subjective evaluation of outcome patterns.

Although it is clear from the above discussion that many different motives may play a role in the evaluation of outcomes, not all motivations are equally common. A rather parsimonious framework can be extracted from the empirical literature using only four unique motivations. The individualistic motivation (MaxOwn) emphasizes own outcomes with little or no regard for the outcomes of others. The competitive motivation (MaxRel) emphasizes the difference between own outcomes and those of others. Competitively motivated bargainers try to maximize their outcome advantage over others. The cooperative motivation (MaxJoint) emphasizes maximizing the outcomes for both the self and others. Finally, the egalitarian motivation (MinDiff) minimizes differences between own outcomes and those of others. Of these four motivations, the first two can be described as proself motivations as they place greater emphasis on the outcomes for the self. The latter two motivations can be described as prosocial motivations as they emphasize both own outcomes and those of others.

Social motivation can be influenced by both contextual factors and personality traits. Negotiating instructions, payoff structures and framing of the negotiation setting have been found to influence social motivation. However, social motivation also stems from personality traits. A personality trait strongly related to social motivation is social value orientation. Social value orientation can be described as a relatively stable preference for a certain distribution of outcomes (Messick and McClintock, 1968). A widely used method for measuring social value orientation is the decomposed games approach (see e.g., Liebrand and McClintock, 1988; Roch and Samuelson, 1997). For example, the Triple Dominance Measure pits cooperative, competitive and individualistic motivations against each other (Van Lange et al., 1997). The measure lets people choose between combinations of outcomes for themselves and an anonymous other. Outcomes are represented by points, and people are instructed to imagine that these points have value for both parties. Each distribution of outcomes represents a particular motivation. Table 3.1 shows an example item offering a choice between 500 points for self and 500 points for other (option

Table 3.1 Example item of the Triple Dominance Measure of social value orientation

	Option A	Option B	Option C
Points to self	500	560	500
Points to other	500	300	100

Source: Van Lange et al. (1997).

A), 560 points for self and 300 for other (option B) and 500 points for self and 100 for other (option C). Option A represents the prosocial motivation, because it provides an equal distribution of outcomes (i.e., 500 points for both self and other), and generates the highest collective outcome (i.e., 1000 points versus option B: 860 points or option C: 600 points). Option B represents the individualistic motivation because own outcomes are maximized (i.e., option B: 560 points versus option A and C: 500 points) irrespective of other's outcomes. Option C represents the competitive motivation because this distribution maximizes the difference between own outcomes and other's outcomes (i.e., option C: 500 − 100 = 400, versus option A: 500 − 500 = 0, and option B: 560 − 300 = 260). When people consistently pick the option that is associated with either a prosocial, individualistic or competitive motivation they are classified as having that orientation (e.g., McClintock and Allison, 1989; Van Lange and Kuhlman, 1994). Finally, the individualistic- and competitive orientations are often combined into a proself orientation (see also Messick and McClintock, 1968; Van Lange, 1999).

Although the effects of social value orientation on bargaining have received considerable attention in research, much less is known about the development of the different orientations. A notable exception is work by Van Lange et al. (1997) who argued and showed that social value orientations stem from social interactions in early childhood and are further shaped throughout adulthood. Their results show that people with a prosocial orientation have greater levels of secure attachment than people with a proself orientation. Furthermore, the number of siblings and their genders seem to affect social value orientation. People with a prosocial orientation reported having more siblings than people with a proself orientation. Remarkably, the number of sisters one has seems to correlate with a prosocial orientation while no such effect is found for the number of brothers. Finally, the prevalence of a prosocial orientation increases with age, while the prevalence of proself orientations decreases with age. Together these findings suggest that value orientations are formed and shaped through interactions with others, especially at an early age. However, more research on how social value orientations are shaped would certainly be helpful.

Social Motives In Negotiation

Social motives have been found to have a large impact on behavior in negotiations. To study social motives in bargaining, researchers have often focused on ultimatum bargaining. Ultimatums are an essential part of bargaining and often form the final stage in the bargaining process (Handgraaf et al., 2003; Thaler, 1992). A game that captures this process in a simple and elegant manner is the ultimatum game (Güth et al., 1982). In the ultimatum game two parties have to come to an agreement on the distribution of a resource, for example, a sum of money. One party – often called the allocator – starts the bargaining process by making an offer to the other party on how to split the resource. The other party – often called the responder – is then allowed to react to this offer, but only in two discrete ways; the responder has to choose between either accepting or rejecting the offer. If the responder accepts the offer, the resource is divided as proposed by the allocator. However, if the responder rejects the offer both parties end up getting nothing. After the responder has made a decision, the bargaining process ends.

The ultimatum game is a very popular paradigm to study the motives of bargainers: The simple structure of the game makes it easy to understand and emphasizes the choice between own interests and those of another party. Based on the perspective that people are purely motivated by self-interest and will always try to maximize their own outcomes, it is easy to make clear-cut predictions about how people should behave in the ultimatum game. If people are purely driven by self-interest, one would predict that allocators offer the smallest amount possible to the responder. Arguing that anything is better than nothing, responders should accept any offer above zero.

Research using the ultimatum game does not support these predictions. Results show that responders frequently reject offers lower than 20 percent of the resource and that allocators typically offer 30 percent to 40 percent of the resource, with a 50/50 split being the mode (see e.g., Camerer and Thaler, 1995; Güth and Tietz, 1990; Handgraaf et al., 2003; Komorita and Parks, 1995; Pillutla and Murnighan, 2003). It thus seems that responders prefer both parties getting nothing over accepting an unequal split of the resource. These findings seem to support the idea that bargainers may not act purely out of self-interest and that other motives may play a role.

However, it has been argued that the behavior of the allocator may be driven partly by strategic considerations rather than a true concern for fairness. Knowing that responders reject low offers, it is in the interest of the allocator to slightly increase the offer. In the end, it is better for the allocator to have a slightly less profitable offer accepted than to face rejection and receive nothing. To disentangle this "strategic fairness" from "true fairness", researchers have introduced information asymmetries into the ultimatum game. For example, Kagel et al. (1996) had bargainers divide 100 chips which were worth more to the allocator than to the responder. In addition, they manipulated the distribution of information. Allocators were informed that the responder either did know (symmetric information) or did not know (asymmetric information) about the differential value. In the symmetric information condition, allocators often compensated for the differential value, by allocating more chips to the responder than to themselves. In contrast, many allocators in the asymmetric condition did not compensate for the differential value and offered an equal split of the chips. Similar findings have been obtained by other researchers (e.g., Croson, 1996; Pillutla and Murnighan, 1995; Van Dijk and Vermunt, 2000). Note that by offering an equal split, allocators made an offer that seemed fair to the responder and therefore allocators did not have to fear rejection. However, due to the differential values allocators ended up earning more than responders.

The above results show that the importance of self-interest may not be so easily dismissed in the ultimatum game. The generous offers of allocators can be partially attributed to strategic self-interest rather than other-regarding motives. However, people may differ from one another in the weight they assign to these motives. Therefore, Van Dijk et al. (2004) conducted a similar experiment but included social value orientation to study individual differences in social motivation. The results showed that proself bargainers utilized their information advantage while prosocial bargainers did not. Proself bargainers did not compensate for the differential value when the opponent was unaware of this difference. Prosocial bargainers on the other hand did compensate for the differential values regardless of whether the opponent was aware of this difference or not. Thus, proself bargainers acted out of strategic self-interest while prosocial bargainers showed a genuine concern for the outcomes of the other party.

Although these findings provide insight into the motives of bargainers, one could argue that the ultimatum game does not provide a very rich bargaining context. The setup of the game is rather limiting in terms of the behavioral choices it offers. Especially the responder's options are quite limited, being allowed only to choose between accepting or rejecting an offer. The ultimatum game thus captures only the final stage of bargaining, where a take-it-or-leave-it offer is put on the table. In contrast, many realistic negotiations are characterized by an exchange of offers until an agreement is reached or parties withdraw from the bargaining table.

Furthermore, the ultimatum game is a typical zero-sum bargaining setting as it offers a fixed amount of resources to be divided by the two parties. Bargainers cannot change the amount of resources available to them in any way. The zero-sum nature of the ultimatum game therefore further limits the behavioral options bargainers have. To combat some of these limitations, more complex multi-issue negotiation paradigms have been developed.

Negotiations with Integrative Potential

Zero-sum negotiations offer a fixed amount of resources for bargainers to divide and are therefore said to have a "fixed pie". However, interests are not always directly opposed and ways can be found to integrate the interests of bargaining parties. Follett (1940) offers a nice illustration by describing a conflict about an orange. Two sisters quarrel about an orange and finally decide to split it in half. Next, one sister squeezes her half and throws the peel away. The other sister uses only the peel of her half for baking a cake. Clearly splitting the orange in half was not the most optimal solution. Both sisters would have gained more if one had taken all the juice while the other had taken the entire peel. When there are ways to increase joint outcomes by integrating diverging interests, the negotiation is said to have *integrative potential*.

To study how bargainers behave in negotiations with integrative potential, research typically uses multi-issue bargaining paradigms (for an overview, see De Dreu et al., 2000). Table 3.2 shows a typical example of such a paradigm in which two parties (X and Y) bargain over three issues (A, B and C) that have five levels that can be agreed upon. Issue A is more important to party X while issue B is more important to party Y. Issue C is equally important to both parties and their interests on this issue are directly opposed. Simply compromising on level 3 for all issues would yield 820 points for both parties. However, parties can achieve higher joint outcomes through other solutions. For example, picking level 1 for issue A, level 5 for issue B and level 3 for issue C would yield both parties 900 points. Note that this solution maximizes joint outcomes while it also results in an equal distribution of the outcomes between both parties. Personal gains could go up even higher in unequal distributions. For example, picking level 1 for all the issues would yield party X 1040 points and party Y 600 points. This solution maximizes the inequality in outcomes between both parties in favor of party X.

Table 3.2 *Example of a multi-issue negotiation with integrative potential*

	Party X			Party Y		
	A	B	C	A	B	C
1	400	240	400	200	200	200
2	350	230	350	210	250	250
3	300	220	300	220	300	300
4	250	210	250	230	350	350
5	200	200	200	240	400	400

Multi-issue negotiations allow for many solutions resulting in more or less desirable outcomes for the parties involved. Bargainers may try to arrive at their preferred outcomes by using different bargaining strategies. The literature on bargaining strategies often organizes these strategies in three categories: contending, yielding and problem solving (Pruitt, 1983). Contending involves forcing one's will onto others. Contentious strategies are used to claim personal value at the expense of others. Making excessively high demands or threatening the other party to exit the negotiation are both examples of contending. These strategies put pressure on another party to yield.

Yielding involves a reduction in one's aspirations and means lowering personal outcomes to benefit others. Yielding is a unilateral decision that does not require consent from the other party. Although yielding typically lowers one's outcomes, it can be a good way to quickly end the negotiation.

Finally, problem solving is employed to find a solution to the negotiation that is acceptable to all negotiation parties. Problem solving involves identifying mutual interests and strategies for creating joint value. A typical example is yielding on a less important issue while claiming value on a more important issue. This strategy is often referred to as *logrolling* (e.g., Lewicki et al., 1994; Pruitt and Carnevale, 1993). A central question in negotiation research is which strategies are employed and how they influence bargaining outcomes.

Social Motives in Integrative Negotiations

From the perspective of rational self-interest, one would expect bargainers to be primarily focused on contentious strategies to increase their own outcomes. However, given that such strategies may result in an impasse, even self-interested bargainers may sometimes need to switch to problem-solving or yielding. One would thus predict that bargainers will only use the integrative potential in a negotiation when it is required to avoid impasse. While the traditional perspective could thus explain the use of multiple strategies, its focus on self-interest as the main motive may be somewhat narrow and inconsistent with actual negotiation behavior. Theories on bargaining strategies have emerged that include motives other than self-interest.

The most prominent of these theories is the dual concern model by Pruitt (1983). The dual concern model states that the selection of bargaining strategies depends on both a concern for the own outcomes and a concern for the outcomes of others. If one has strong concern for the own outcomes but little or no concern for the outcomes of others, one will most likely opt for contentious strategies. However, overuse of such contentious strategies may lead to an impasse or simple compromises. Overuse of contentious strategies may thus lead to suboptimal outcomes and prevent realizing integrative potential. The same may be true when bargainers have a strong concern for the outcomes of others, but little concern for their own outcomes. In such cases, bargainers may resort to yielding too easily and (quickly) reach an agreement without searching for better ways to integrate their interests. Thus according to the dual concern model bargainers need to have both a strong concern for their own outcomes and for the outcomes of others to arrive at integrative solutions. Only then will bargainers engage in problem solving and find ways to integrate their interests.

Concerns for the own outcomes and those of others are frequently related to the social motives described earlier. Bargainers with a proself motivation have a strong concern for their own outcomes and a weak (or even negative in the case of competitors) concern for the outcomes of others. Compared to proself bargainers, prosocial bargainers have a stronger concern for the outcomes of others. In addition, prosocial bargainers might have a weaker concern for their own outcomes compared to proself bargainers. Given these relations between the two concerns and social motives, one would expect that social motives also influence the selection of bargaining strategies.

A meta-analysis including 28 studies on bargaining by De Dreu et al. (2000) found strong support for the dual concern model and the impact of social motives. Results showed that bargainers with a prosocial motive engaged in more problem-solving behavior and less contentious behavior than bargainers with a proself motive. However, prosocial bargainers only attained higher joint outcomes when they had a high resistance to yielding. As predicted by the dual concern model, high joint outcomes were only attained when bargainers had both a strong concern for their own outcomes as well as a strong concern for the outcomes of others.

However, one's selection of strategies is not only determined by one's own motivation. The interaction with the opponent during the bargaining process may also shape one's selection of strategies. For example, consistently pursuing a contentious strategy may result in an impasse when the opponent also persists in such strategies. Therefore even proself bargainers may eventually switch to problem solving or even yielding. Bargaining strategies may thus be influenced by the actions and orientation of the opponent. This interplay between bargainers makes it considerably harder to predict which strategies will be selected.

Kelley and Stahelski (1970; see also Van Lange and Visser, 1999) describe how different social motivations interact in social dilemmas. According to their findings, prosocials will act competitively when facing a competitive opponent but not when facing another prosocial negotiator. A prosocial motivation can thus transform into a competitive one, and this transformation has been labeled *behavioral assimilation*. As a result of behavioral assimilation, a competitive opponent may mistake a prosocial negotiator for a competitor. Competitors will not be aware that behavioral assimilation has taken place. Consequently, competitors will always expect their opponent to be competitive as well, while prosocials may hold more heterogeneous expectations of their opponents. Although these findings may hold for social dilemmas, one may wonder how they translate to bargaining and the selection of bargaining strategies. One might expect that prosocial bargainers will be more flexible in their selection of strategies than competitive bargainers. That is, prosocial bargainers may also be more prone to switching between contentious strategies and problem-solving strategies depending on the (expected) orientation of their opponent. Competitively oriented bargainers on the other hand may be more stable in their use of bargaining strategies and focus on contentious strategies.

Olekalns and Smith (2003, but see also Olekalns and Smith, 1999; Weingart et al., 2007) studied the relation between social motives, bargaining strategies and bargaining outcomes in dyadic negotiations. The influence of social motives was assessed by creating prosocial, proself and mixed-motive dyads. For each type of dyad, the authors identified sequences of strategies that lead to either high or low joint outcomes. For prosocial dyads, process management and relationship building were more important than in other dyad types. Especially when process management focused on problem-solving strategies and reciprocating such strategies, prosocial dyads achieved high joint outcomes. Low joint outcomes were attained when contentious strategies were reciprocated. For proself dyads, contentious strategies were associated with low joint gain, especially when such strategies were reciprocated. It was less clear which sequences of strategies were associated with high joint gain in proself dyads. Finally, mixed dyads resembled prosocial dyads in their use of strategies when they achieved high joint outcomes. Mixed dyads that achieved low joint outcomes did not resemble prosocial or proself dyads and developed their own unique set of strategies.

Although the results showed that dyads differed in their use of strategies, there was strong support across dyad types that a common set of strategies lead to either high or low joint outcomes. Low joint outcomes were associated with high levels of contention and with reciprocating such contentious strategies. High joint outcomes on the other hand were associated with sharing priority information and reciprocating such problem-solving strategies. Moreover, these two pathways were mutually exclusive in the sense that strategies that were frequent at low joint gain were infrequent at high joint gain and vice versa. Gaining insight into the preferences and priorities of other parties thus seems key in attaining high joint outcomes. These findings stress that information plays a key role in negotiations.

3.2 INFORMATION SEARCH AND INFORMATION PROCESSING

As pointed out above, information about the preferences and priorities of other parties is of key importance for realizing integrative potential and thereby increasing joint outcomes. Precise information about such topics, however, typically lacks at the beginning of a negotiation. Therefore negotiators have to search for and process such information. However, people may process information in different ways. They may process information rather quickly and effortlessly by relying on heuristics and well-learned prior associations. Alternatively, people may engage in more deliberate and systematic information processing that involves rule-based inferences (see e.g., Chaiken and Trope, 1999). This deliberate form of information processing is more effortful, and people may not always be able or motivated to engage in it. Negotiators may differ from one another in their motivation to engage in effortful information processing and may instead rely on "cognitive shortcuts" such as heuristics or stereotypes. Moreover, biases may further hinder gaining an accurate understanding of the negotiation and the underlying pattern of interests.

Epistemic Motivation

People differ in their motivation to obtain and maintain an accurate understanding of their surroundings. This motivation is often referred to as "epistemic motivation" (see e.g., De Dreu and Carnevale, 2003; Kruglanski and Webster, 1996; Webster and Kruglanski, 1994; Kruglanski, 1989). People high in epistemic motivation often feel less certain and experience lower confidence in their knowledge than people low in epistemic motivation. As a result, people high in epistemic motivation engage in more deliberate and systematic information processing. The extent to which people are motivated to process and search for information is influenced by both personality and situational factors. Below we will discuss the most prominent of these factors.

Epistemic motivation has been linked to a number of personality traits, such as the need for cognition (Cacioppo and Petty, 1982), the personal need for structure (Thompson et al., 1989) and the need for cognitive closure (Webster and Kruglanski, 1994). Individuals scoring high on need for cognition, low on personal need for structure or low on need for cognitive closure have increased epistemic motivation compared to people who score on the opposite end of these scales. These people will generally process information more thoroughly and are less likely to draw conclusions quickly. In negotiation settings, such people are likely to put more effort into processing information about preferences and priorities and are therefore likely to reach better integrative solutions.

However, epistemic motivation not only depends on personality; it is also influenced by situational factors. The way a situation is framed or perceived, for example, may influence epistemic motivation. Epistemic motivation is increased when a situation is perceived as competitive rather than cooperative (e.g., Van Kleef et al., 2010). Moreover, epistemic motivation is increased when people deal with losses rather than gains (e.g., De Dreu et al., 1994).

Structural features of a negotiation may also affect epistemic motivation. For example, power differences between bargaining parties can affect epistemic motivation (e.g., De Dreu and Van Kleef, 2004; Fiske and Dépret, 1996; Keltner et al., 2008). Bargainers having a relatively low power position tend to have a higher epistemic motivation than bargainers in a relatively high power position. Furthermore, if negotiators are held accountable for their actions during the negotiation they also have higher epistemic motivation (see e.g., Lerner and Tetlock, 1999; Van der Schalk et al., 2009). When negotiators are representatives of a larger group, their epistemic motivation is increased and they tend to process information more thoroughly.

Finally, epistemic motivation tends to go down when people are mentally fatigued (Webster et al., 1996), put in a situation with environmental noise (Kruglanski and Webster, 1991) or put under time pressure (Van Kleef et al., 2004). Thus when people lack the energy or time to process information thoroughly, they tend to rely more on cognitive shortcuts such as heuristics. Epistemic motivation may be raised, however, when people find a task personally involving and show high levels of engagement in a task (Eagly and Chaiken, 1993; Petty and Cacioppo, 1986).

From the above it is clear that numerous factors impact the epistemic motivation of negotiators. Epistemic motivation seems highly related to negotiators' goals and motives. When goals are expected to be hard to reach, for example due to the competitive nature of the negotiation or a relatively low power position, negotiators tend to process information more thoroughly. In a similar vein, a task that is personally involving may also motivate negotiators to process more thoroughly. Finally, one may expect social motivation and epistemic motivation to interact. Unfortunately, there is only limited research in this area (for exceptions, see De Dreu et al., 2006; De Dreu and Boles, 1998) and it would be worthwhile to further investigate the relation between both types of motivation.

Other factors that influence epistemic motivation seem to relate more directly to cognitive capacity. Environmental noise or mental fatigue seems to limit the cognitive capacity available to process information. Additionally, impasses or unexpected events may change the way negotiators process information (see e.g., Harinck and De Dreu, 2004; 2008; Galinsky et al., 2002). There seems to be limited research on how events during the course of a negotiation impact epistemic motivation. This is unfortunate, given the relevance to negotiation practices. For example, it is not uncommon to continue important negotiations well into the night. Although one may attempt to force an opponent into yielding this way, the mental fatigue and resulting lower epistemic motivation may hinder finding a more optimal, integrative solutions.

Heuristics and Biases

When bargainers are not able or motivated to process information thoroughly, they may use heuristics to speed up and simplify information processing. In addition, they may fall prey to cognitive biases distorting information processing. In this section we discuss such heuristics and biases related to negotiations. Following De Dreu et al. (2007), we will discuss cognitive heuristics, naïve realism and ego defensiveness.

Cognitive heuristics. Cognitive shortcuts or heuristics make processing information less effortful and faster, however, they are also more prone to bias and error. Therefore, heuristics may prevent negotiators from finding solutions that integrate their interest in the best possible way. In line with work from Kahneman and Tversky (1973), we now discuss three categories of cognitive heuristics that are related to negotiation, namely anchoring and adjustment, availability and representativeness.

Expectations play an important role in negotiations and are often used by negotiators to evaluate offers and outcomes. Offers or outcomes that fall short of expectations are often coded as losses, while offers or outcomes above expectations are viewed as gains. According to prospect theory (Kahneman and Tversky, 1979), losses and gains are perceived differently in such a way that "losses loom larger than equivalent gains". Negotiators find a loss more important than an equivalent gain. Framing a negotiation in terms of losses makes people less willing to make concessions and may also cause them to select more risky contentious strategies (see e.g., De Dreu et al., 1994). Expectations thus strongly impact the negotiation process and the strategies negotiators select.

However, initial expectations may not always be based on solid information and research has shown that expectations are not always adjusted sufficiently when new information becomes available (Kahneman and Tversky, 1973). This effect has been labeled the anchoring effect, as the initial evaluation functions as an anchor on which all further evaluations are based. The anchoring effect has been demonstrated by Northcraft and Neale (1987) in a study on real-estate agents. Real-estate agents were confronted with an inaccurate price estimate for a property and this estimate was either too low or too high. The inaccurate estimate influenced the agent's final estimates even when they had accurate information about the characteristics of the property. The agents were unable to dismiss the inaccurate initial estimate and let it cloud their final judgments of the price of a property. Inaccurate or irrelevant information can thus easily influence the course of a negotiation process.

In addition to anchoring, negotiators may also take other cognitive shortcuts, for example, by relying on information that is easily available in memory. Negotiators may focus on so-called *prominent solutions* (Pruitt, 1981) to a negotiation. These prominent solutions are often related to fairness norms such as equality or equity. In zero-sum negotiations, splitting the resources in half is often considered the most fair solution and the solution that is also most acceptable to all parties. Therefore, an equal split has become a very prominent solution in this type of negotiations. Because the equal split is so well-known, negotiators may also apply it to other types of negotiations. In multi-issue negotiations, however, an equal split on all issues is almost never the best way to integrate interests. The salience of the equal division rule may thus cause negotiators to forego opportunities to find integrative solutions that maximize joint gains.

Finally, negotiators may resort to stereotypes when they are unable or unwilling to process information thoroughly. Negotiators may rely, for example, on stereotypes to predict the preferences or intentions of their opponent. When an opponent is seen as a representative of a group, stereotypes about the group may be used to generate predictions about what the opponent wants and how he or she will behave. De Dreu et al. (1995), for example, demonstrated that negotiators expected students majoring in business to be more competitive than those majoring in religion. As a result, participants in their study choose a more competitive course of action when facing an opponent majoring in business rather than religion. It is easy to see how relying on stereotypes in such a manner can lead to self-fulfilling prophecies. By choosing a more competitive course of action, negotiators may in turn evoke a more competitive response thereby confirming their stereotypical expectations (see also Morris et al., 1999). In this manner, relying on stereotypes can be a threat to reaching an integrative solution to a negotiation.

Naïve realism. Negotiations are uncertain and complex settings in which interests may both align and conflict. People often hold their own views on the negotiation process to deal with these complexities and uncertainties. It has been remarked that people are naïve realists who assume that they are rational and reasonable. They therefore assume that the world is as they perceive it themselves. When confronted with others who may hold different views, people are quick to attribute these differences to the ignorance or lack of intelligence of those others (Ross and Ward, 1995). Obviously, such ideas may magnify the perceived differences between people and demotivate people to try and solve the differences between them (see e.g., Robinson et al., 1995). This problem is further exacerbated by the fact that people tend to search for information that confirms (rather than disconfirms) their current beliefs. Such confirmatory information search ensures that people stick to their original beliefs and increases the chance that negotiation strategies are based on such inadequate beliefs (Neale and Bazerman, 1991; Rubin et al., 1994).

One belief many people hold about negotiations, is that they assume negotiations to have a fixed pie (Thompson and Hastie, 1990). People thus often focus on how their interests conflict with those of others rather than on how they align. This in turn may cause people to overlook the integrative potential present in a negotiation. These so-called "fixed-pie perceptions" may cause people to put little or no effort into searching for ways to integrate their interests and lead to suboptimal negotiation outcomes (for a review see Thompson and Hrebec, 1996).

Finally, negotiators may be overly optimistic about the timeframe of a negotiation or their ability to be successful during a negotiation. Negotiators may believe that they have unlimited time and that a complete, unilateral victory is just around the corner (Pronin et al., 2004; Ross and Ward, 1995). Obviously, such (false) beliefs may hamper concession making, again leading to suboptimal outcomes.

Ego defensiveness. People prefer to evaluate themselves in a favorable manner and are motivated to develop, maintain and defend a positive self-evaluation (Taylor and Brown, 1988; 1994; Campbell and Sedikides, 1999). In negotiation, such biased self-evaluation and the willingness to defend it may hinder successful conflict resolution. People may consider themselves to be fairer, more honest and more cooperative than their opponents (see e.g., Messick et al., 1985). Such perceptions may cause negotiators to be less critical about their own behavior. Moreover, it has been demonstrated that negotiators tend to be more critical about the behavior of their opponents. Research by Ross and Stillinger (1991), for example, shows that negotiators evaluate the same offer completely differently depending on whether it was presented as coming from an ally or from the opponent. Biased perceptions of the self and the opponent may enlarge perceived differences between parties, thereby making an escalation of the conflict more likely.

3.3 INFORMATION PROVISION

In the previous section we discussed negotiators' motivation to acquire and process information and how biases and heuristics may interfere with information processing. During negotiations, however, negotiators also provide information to others about their preferences and intentions. This information can be communicated either through verbal or nonverbal communication. This section focuses on information provision during the negotiation process.

Information can help parties identify mutual interests and explore what the most profitable compromise is between their own interests and those of others. It should be noted, however, that parties typically do not have exactly the same information at the outset of a negotiation. For example, sellers know the lowest price they are willing to sell for, but this information is typically not available to potential buyers. In similar vein, buyers know the maximum price they are willing to pay, but this information is often not available to sellers. Informational asymmetries thus exist between parties and parties have to exchange information to overcome these asymmetries.

However, bargainers may face a dilemma whether they should share information about their preferences and whether they should do so truthfully. In the above example, sellers may not want to reveal the lowest price they are willing to sell for, arguing that buyers will then offer their lowest price. It should not come as a surprise that negotiators are often reluctant to share (accurate) information. For this reason, research on information exchange during negotiation has often focused on deception; that is, withholding information or providing inaccurate information.

The Role of Deception

Deception is a common tactic in bargaining (e.g., Lewicki, 1983; Tenbrunsel, 1998) and research has confirmed that bargainers often use deception to benefit themselves. For example, Croson et al. (2003; see also Boles et al., 2000) found that responders in the ultimatum game could elicit higher offers by using deception. Responders were allowed to lie about the amount of money they would receive upon rejecting the offer. In response to such lies, allocators slightly increased their offers to avoid rejection. In turn, allocators also used deception to benefit themselves. Allocators were allowed to lie about the amount of resources that was to be divided. By stating that this amount was lower than it actually was, allocators could get lower offers accepted. For both allocators and responders deception thus was a means to increase the own outcomes. In similar vein, Gneezy (2005) found that deception occurred more frequently when it yielded larger benefits to the self. Deception thus has frequently been related to self-interest and can be considered a contentious bargaining strategy. Given the emphasis on self-interest, one might expect that proself bargainers are more willing to use deception than prosocial bargainers.

Research by Steinel and De Dreu (2004) set out to test how social motives influence the use of deception in negotiations. In their experiments, participants had full knowledge about the payoffs in a negotiation setting. In contrast, the opponent was unaware of the participant's payoffs. Participants were then given the option to inform the opponent about their payoffs. The social motivation of the participant was measured and participants were given bogus feedback on the motivation of the opponent. Results showed that participants were more likely to deceive an opponent with a proself motivation than an opponent with a prosocial motivation. More interestingly, this effect was stronger for participants with a prosocial motivation than for participants with a proself motivation. Prosocial bargainers thus were more deceptive towards proself opponents than towards prosocial opponents. For proself bargainers, this effect was less pronounced. Proself bargainers did not differentiate between proself and prosocial opponents. Again, also at the information level it seems that prosocial bargainers are more flexible in their use of strategies than proself bargainers (compare with Kelley and Stahelski, 1970; Van Lange, 1992; Van Lange and Visser, 1999).

Table 3.3 Example payoff structure of the Motivated Deception Game

	Distribution 1	Distribution 2	Distribution 3
Participant	500	200	400
Opponent	200	500	400

In addition to deception, Steinel and De Dreu (2004) also studied the self-reported motives related to such behavior. Their results showed that both greed and fear of exploitation were motives to engage in deception. Greed is obviously highly related to a concern for their own outcomes. Fear of exploitation is also related to a concern for receiving low outcomes, but may also be related to a concern for fairness. Fear of exploitation could also be seen as a concern for receiving less than a fair share. To some extent, fear of exploitation may therefore also be related to a prosocial motivation.

To provide a more direct test whether prosocial motives may play a role in deception, Koning et al. (2010) developed the *motivated deception game*. In this game, an allocator and responder split an amount of resources. The allocator was allowed to choose between three distributions of outcomes. The first distribution favored the allocator, while the second favored the responder. The third distribution yielded equal outcomes and maximized joint outcomes (see Table 3.3 for an example). Responders had no direct influence over the outcomes, but could influence the allocator's decision by using deception. Prior to the allocator's decision, responders were allowed to (mis)inform the allocator about the payoff structure. Note that deception could persuade the allocator to select the distribution that maximized the responder's outcomes or that maximized joint outcomes. Social value orientation of the participants was measured and participants were provided with bogus feedback about the orientation of their opponent.

Results showed that both proself and prosocial responders used deception. However, proself responders mainly used deception to maximize their own outcomes, while prosocial responders used a multitude of strategies depending on the orientation of their opponent. Prosocial responders often used deception to maximize joint outcomes when they believed that their opponent had a proself orientation. Against a prosocial opponent, however, prosocial responders most frequently refrained from using deception.

The finding that people are often reluctant to use deception is frequently replicated in research. Typically, a substantial proportion of the participants do not use deception even when there are incentives for using deception. One explanation for these findings is that the unethical nature of deception deters people from using it. This raises the question which practices are deemed acceptable in negotiation and which are not.

Deception and Ethics

Negotiations, with their mixed-motive nature and central role for information exchange, may pose an ethical dilemma to negotiators; although lying is generally considered unethical (e.g., Dees and Cramton, 1991), it is also not feasible to be entirely honest in negotiation. Negotiations can thus easily evoke unethical behavior and this has often been noted (see e.g., Tenbrunsel, 1998). Several authors even suggest that some dishonest behavior is appropriate or even required to be an effective negotiator (see e.g., Lewicki, 1983; Lewicki and Robinson, 1998; Lewicki and Stark, 1996). The issue of what is ethically appropriate in negotiations and what is not, is very much alive (see also Diekmann et al., Chapter 8 this volume).

Lewicki and Robinson (1998; see also Lewicki and Stark, 1996) provide a first answer to this question. They investigated the perceived ethicality of a range of negotiation tactics, including the use of promises and threats, but also misrepresentation of information. The authors concluded that "negotiation tactics are not seen as moral absolutes" (p. 676). The considerable variability in judgments suggested that not all bargaining tactics were seen as equally unethical even when they involved some degree of dishonesty. For example, lying about one's bottom line or making excessively high opening demands were considered acceptable negotiation tactics. Making false promises and threats or misrepresenting factual information on the other hand were considered far more unethical. Although these findings describe which tactics are considered ethical and which ones are not, the question remains why certain tactics are more unethical than others.

A major factor in determining the ethicality of an action is the consequences the action brings about. Ethicality has often been related to the negative consequences an action may have for others (see e.g., Gino et al., 2009; Jones, 1991). When an action has larger negative consequences for others, it is often considered more unethical. Gneezy (2005), for example, demonstrated that the use of deception was influenced not only by benefits to the self, but also by losses for others. Participants were more tempted to use deception when it yielded them larger benefits. More importantly, participants were more reluctant to use deception when it had larger negative consequences for another participant. This finding confirms that people take the negative consequences for others into account when making ethical decisions. This is especially relevant for negotiations where interests are often opposed at least to some degree. The temptation to increase the own outcomes may therefore harm the outcomes of others. From an ethical point of view, contentious strategies could therefore be regarded as problematic. However, a certain level of empathy may be required for caring about the consequences for others (Batson, 1991; 1998; 2011). For example, research on the ultimatum game has demonstrated that offers increase with the level of empathy allocators have for responders. Empathy has been manipulated by giving allocators information about the responder's hobbies (Bohnet and Frey, 1999) or family name (Charness and Gneezy, 2008) thereby decreasing social distance between the two parties. These results show that situational factors may affect empathy, but personality traits may have similar effects.

Most relevant for the current purpose is social value orientation, which has been linked to empathy. Declerck and Bogaert (2008) found that a prosocial motivation is associated with higher levels of empathy than a proself motivation. People with a prosocial motivation were better at taking the perspective of another person than people with a proself motivation. These differences in empathy may also translate into differences in moral judgments. Indeed, it has been argued that different social motivations may hold different views on morality (see e.g., Deutsch, 1982; Liebrand et al., 1986; Sattler and Kerr, 1991; Van Lange and Kuhlman, 1994). People with a proself motivation are more focused on power or dominance, while people with a prosocial motivation are more focused on moral judgment and evaluation. In addition, Emonds et al. (2011) showed that both motivations differ in their adherence to norms. Based on fMRI research, the authors conclude that proselfs are calculative and incentive driven, while prosocials are more focused on compliance with internalized norms.

Future research could further investigate how (adherence to) norms differ between proself and prosocial bargainers and how this affects bargaining behavior. Especially prosocial bargainers may feel reluctant to use bargaining strategies that go against norms of fairness or honesty. Moreover, prosocial bargainers may also respond more fiercely when an opponent uses such strategies against them. Negotiators not only judge their own actions, but also those of their opponents. Reputations and impressions therefore play an important role in negotiations.

Reputation and Impression Management

Impressions matter, especially in negotiations. Negotiators will try to form an impression of their opponent and will determine their course of action based on such impressions. For negotiators, it is therefore important to manage such impressions. Often negotiators are motivated to create a tough, competitive impression of themselves (e.g., Chaiken et al., 2001). Negotiators may want to signal to their opponent that they have high limits and are not easily willing to give in. Such impression management not only involves verbal communication, but may also include nonverbal communication. Negotiators may use their emotions to convey information about their intentions and limits (e.g., Sinaceur and Tiedens, 2006; Van Kleef et al., 2004). For example, displaying anger signals that one has high limits and ambitious goals in a negotiation. Of course, positive emotions also play a role and showing happiness, for example, may signal more cooperative intentions.

If negotiators are representatives of a group, their impression management may also be extended to this group. Negotiators may worry whether the group they represent will positively evaluate their performance during the negotiation. As a result, representatives often tend to be more competitive in negotiations (Brown, 1977; Carnevale et al., 1979; Mosterd and Rutte, 2000). This competitive attitude has been interpreted as the representatives signaling to their group that they are not squandering the groups' interests. However, more recent research shows that the motivational composition of the constituents may also play a role. Aaldering and De Dreu (2012), for example, demonstrated that representatives acted more cooperatively when a high status majority of their constituents had a cooperative motivation. Being accountable to a group of constituents may thus have strong implications for how the negotiation unfolds. Representatives are in an especially difficult position as they have to manage their image towards both their constituents and the opponent.

CONCLUSIONS

In this chapter we discussed the role of social and cognitive motivation in negotiation. First, we explored which social motives are identified in the literature. Most notably, we distinguished between proself and prosocial motivations. We then explored the role of social motives in zero-sum negotiations, such as ultimatum bargaining. Research in this area shows that prosocial bargainers have a genuine concern for the welfare of others and make fair offers because of this concern. Proself bargainers on the other hand do not share this concern and will only make fair offers based on strategic considerations. In more complex, multi-issue bargaining settings, social motives affect the choice of negotiation strategies. Although there are clear links between different social motives and negotiation strategies, the findings are not entirely parsimonious. Future research should further explore how different social motives interact during bargaining and how they affect the selection of bargaining strategies and outcomes. Research on bargaining often focuses on outcomes, but the process by which these outcomes are realized may be even more interesting. Studying such processes, however, is complex as many different combinations and sequences can emerge. Limiting the number of strategic options may help structure the process, albeit at the cost of external validity.

One thing that clearly emerges from research on bargaining is that information is of key importance. Bargainers need information about the preferences of other parties to find ways to integrate their own interest with those of the other parties. However, bargainers do not always process such information thoroughly; individual differences and situational factors may limit the ability or motivation to process information and cognitive biases may further distort information processing. Such obstacles in information processing can be partially attributed to motivation, including social motivation. There is, however, only scarce research on how social motives impact information processing. A more comprehensive picture of the interaction between social and cognitive motivation in negotiation settings would be most welcome.

During negotiation, parties also often provide others with information about their own preferences. Negotiations often pose an information dilemma: disclosure of such preferences may help identify mutual interests, but such information may also be exploited by opponents. This raises the question how open and honest negotiators should be about their preferences. For this reason, it is no surprise that deception is a common tactic in bargaining. Deception has often been linked to self-interest, but recent research shows that deception may also be used for other goals. Social motives may also affect which information bargainers share and with whom. Furthermore, social motives may affect the perceived ethicality of bargaining tactics such as deception. There is limited evidence that prosocial bargainers may be guided more strongly by norms than proself bargainers. Much of this area remains to be explored by future research.

REFERENCES

Aaldering, H. and De Dreu, C.K.W. (2012). Why hawks fly higher than doves: Intragroup conflict in representative negotiation. *Group Processes & Intergroup Relations*, 15, 713–724.

Axelrod, R. (1980a). Effective choice in the prisoner's dilemma. *Journal of Conflict Resolution*, 24, 3–25.

Axelrod, R. (1980b). More effective choice in the prisoner's dilemma. *Journal of Conflict Resolution*, 24, 379–403.

Batson, C.D. (1991). *The altruism question: Toward a social psychological answer*. Hillsdale, NJ: Erlbaum.

Batson, C.D. (1998). Altruism and prosocial behavior. In D.T. Gilbert, S.T. Fiske, and G. Lindzey (eds), *The handbook of social psychology* (pp. 282–316). New York: McGraw-Hill.

Batson, C.D. (2011). *Altruism in humans.* Oxford: Oxford University Press.

Bohnet, I. and Frey, B. (1999). Social distance and other-regarding behavior in dictator games: Comment. *American Economic Review*, 89, 335–339.

Boles, T.L., Croson, R.T.A., and Murnighan, J. (2000). Deception and retribution in repeated ultimatum bargaining. *Organizational Behavior and Human Decision Processes*, 83, 235–259.

Brown, B.R. (1977). Face-saving and face-restoration in negotiation. In D. Druckman (ed.), *Negotiations* (pp. 275–300). Beverly Hills: Sage.

Cacioppo, J.T. and Petty, R.E. (1982). The need for cognition. *Journal of Personality and Social Psychology*, 42, 116–131.

Camerer, C. and Thaler, R.H. (1995). Anomalies: Ultimatums, dictators and manners. *Journal of Economic Perspectives*, 9, 209–219.

Campbell, W.K. and Sedikides, C. (1999). Self-threat magnifies the self-serving bias: A meta-analytic integration. *Review of General Psychology*, 3, 23–43.

Carnevale, P.J.D., Pruitt, D.G., and Britton, S.D. (1979). Looking tough: The negotiator under constituent surveillance. *Personality and Social Psychology Bulletin*, 5, 118–121.

Chaiken, S., Gruenfeld, D.H., and Judd, C.M. (2001). Persuasion in negotiations and conflict situations. In M. Deutsch and P. Colemand (eds), *Conflict resolution* (pp. 67–89). New York: Guilford Press.

Chaiken, S. and Trope, Y. (1999). *Dual-process theories in social psychology.* New York: Guilford Press.

Charness, G. and Gneezy, Y. (2008). What's in a name? Anonymity and social distance in dictator and ultimatum games. *Journal of Economic Behavior & Organization*, 68, 29–35.

Croson, R.T.A. (1996). Information in ultimatum games: An experimental study. *Journal of Economic Behavior & Organization*, 30, 197–212.

Croson, R.T.A., Boles, T.L., and Murnighan, J. (2003). Cheap talk in bargaining experiments: lying and threats in ultimatum games. *Journal of Economic Behavior & Organization*, 51, 143–159.

Declerck, C.H. and Bogaert, S. (2008). Social value orientation: Related to empathy and the ability to read the mind in the eyes. *Journal of Social Psychology*, 148, 711–726.

De Dreu, C.K.W and Boles, T. (1998). Share and share alike or winner takes all? Impact of social value orientation on the choice and recall of decision heuristics in negotiation. *Organizational Behavior and Human Decision Processes*, 76, 253–267.

De Dreu, C.K.W and Carnevale, P.J.D. (2003). Motivational bases of information processing and strategy in conflict and negotiation. *Advances in Experimental Social Psychology*, 35, 235–291.

De Dreu, C.K.W and Van Kleef, G.A. (2004). The influence of power on the information search, impression formation, and demands in negotiation. *Journal of Experimental Social Psychology*, 40, 303–319.

De Dreu, C.K.W., Weingart, L.R., and Kwon, S. (2000). Influence of social motives on integrative negotiation: A meta-analytic review and test of two theories. *Journal of Personality and Social Psychology*, 78, 889–905.

De Dreu, C.K.W., Yzerbyt, V., and Leyens, J-Ph. (1995). Dilution of stereotype-based cooperation in mixed-motive interdependence. *Journal of Experimental Social Psychology*, 21, 575–593.

De Dreu, C.K.W, Beersma, B., Steinel, W., and Van Kleef, G.A. (2007). The psychology of negotiation: Principles and basic processes. In A.W. Kruglanski and E.T. Higgins (eds), *Social psychology: Handbook of basic principles* (2nd edn, pp. 608–629). New York: Guilford Press.

De Dreu, C.K.W, Beersma, B., Stroebe, K., and Euwema, M.C. (2006). Motivated information processing, strategic choice, and the quality of negotiated agreement. *Journal of Personality and Social Psychology*, 90, 927–943.

De Dreu, C.K.W, Carnevale, P.J.D., Emans, B.J.M., and Van de Vliert, E. (1994). Effects

of gain-loss frames in negotiation: Loss aversion, mismatching, and frame adoption. *Organizational Behavior and Human Decision Processes*, 60, 90–107.
Dees, J.G. and Cramton, P.C. (1991). Shrewd bargaining on the moral frontier: Toward a theory of morality in practice. *Business Ethics Quarterly*, 1, 135–167.
Deutsch, M. (1982). Interdependence and psychological orientation. In V. Derlega and J. Gezelak (eds), *Cooperation and helping behavior* (pp. 15–42). Cambridge: Cambridge University Press.
Deutsch, M. and Krauss, R.M. (1965). *Theories in social psychology*. New York, NY: Basic Books.
Eagly, A.H. and Chaiken, S. (1993). *The psychology of attitudes*. Harcourt Brace Jovanovich College Publishers.
Emonds, G., Declerck, C.H., Boone, C., Vandervliet, E.J.M., and Parizel, P.M. (2011). Comparing the neural basis of decision making in social dilemmas of people with different social value orientations, a fMRI study. *Journal of Neuroscience, Psychology, and Economics*, 4, 11–24.
Fiske, S.T. and Dépret, E. (1996). Control, interdependence and power: Understanding social cognition in its social context. *European Review of Social Psychology*, 7, 31–61.
Follett, M.P. (1940). Constructive conflict. In H.C. Metcalf and L. Urwick (eds), *Dynamic Administration: The collected papers of Mary Parker Follett*. New York: Harper.
Galinsky, A.D., Seiden, V.L., Kim, P.H., and Medvec, V.H. (2002). The dissatisfaction of having your first offer accepted: The role of counterfactual thinking in negotiations. *Personality and Social Psychology Bulletin*, 28, 271–283.
Gino, F., Moore, D.A., and Bazerman, M.H. (2009). No harm, no foul: The outcome bias in ethical judgments. Working paper. Accessed from http://ssrn.com/abstract=1099464.
Gneezy, U. (2005). Deception: The role of consequences. *The American Economic Review*, 95, 384–394.
Griesinger, D. W., and Livingston, J. W. (1973). Toward a model of interpersonal motivation in experimental games. *Behavioral Science 18*, 173–188.
Güth, W. and Tietz, R. (1990). Ultimatum bargaining behavior: A survey and comparison of experimental results. *Journal of Economic Psychology*, 11, 417–449.
Güth, W., Schmittberger, R., and Schwarze, B. (1982). An experimental-analysis of ultimatum bargaining. *Journal of Economic Behavior & Organization*, 3, 367–388.
Handgraaf, M.J.J., Van Dijk, E., and De Cremer, D. (2003). Social utility in ultimatum bargaining. *Social Justice Research*, 16, 263–283.
Harinck, F. and De Dreu, C.K.W. (2004). Negotiating interests or values and reaching integrative agreements: The importance of time pressure and temporary impasses. *European Journal of Social Psychology*, 34, 595–611.
Harinck, F. and De Dreu, C.K.W. (2008). Take a break! Or not? The impact of mindsets during breaks on negotiation processes and outcomes. *Journal of Experimental Social Psychology*, 44, 397–404.
Jones, T.M. (1991). Ethical decision making by individuals in organizations: an issue-contingent model. *Academy of Management Review*, 16, 366–395.
Kagel, J.H., Kim, C., and Moser, D. (1996). Fairness in ultimatum games with asymmetric information and asymmetric payoffs. *Games and Economic Behavior*, 13, 100–110.
Kahneman, D. and Tversky, A. (1973). On the psychology of prediction. *Psychological Review*, 80, 237–251.
Kahneman, D. and Tversky, A. (1979). Prospect theory: An analysis of decision under risk. *Econometrica*, 47, 263–291.
Kelley, H.H. and Stahelski, A.J. (1970). Social interaction basis of cooperators' and competitors' beliefs about others. *Journal of Personality and Social Psychology*, 16, 66–91.
Kelley, H.H. and Thibaut, J.W. (1978). *Interpersonal relations. A theory of interdependence*. New York: Wiley-Interscience.
Keltner, D., Van Kleef, G.A., Chen, S., and Kraus, M.W. (2008). A reciprocal influence model of social power: Emerging principles and lines of inquiry. *Advances in Experimental Social Psychology*, 40, 151–192.

Komorita, S.S. and Parks, C.D. (1995). Interpersonal relations: Mixed-motive interaction. *Annual Review of Psychology*, 46, 183–207.

Koning, L., Steinel, W., Van Beest, I., and Van Dijk, E. (2010). Goals and the use of deception. Manuscript in preparation for publication.

Kruglanski, A.W. (1989). *Lay epistemics and human knowledge: Cognitive and motivational bases*. New York: Plenum Press.

Kruglanski, A.W. and Ajzen, I. (1983). Bias and error in human judgment. *European Journal of Social Psychology*, 13, 1–44.

Kruglanski, A.W. and Webster, D.M. (1991). Group members' reactions to opinion deviates and conformists at varying degrees of proximity to decision deadline and of environmental noise. *Journal of Personality and Social Psychology*, 61, 212–225.

Kruglanski, A.W. and Webster, D.M. (1996). Motivated closing of the mind: "Seizing" and "freezing". *Psychological Review*, 103(2), 263–283.

Lax, D.A. and Sebenius, J.K. (1986). *The manager as negotiator: Bargaining for cooperation and competitive gain*. New York: Free Press.

Lerner, J.S. and Tetlock, P.E. (1999). Accounting for the effects of accountability. *Psychological Bulletin*, 125, 255–275.

Lewicki, R.J. (1983). Lying and deception: A behavioral model. In M.H. Bazerman and R.J. Lewicki (eds), *Negotiating in organization* (pp. 68–90). California: Sage.

Lewicki, R.J. and Robinson, R.J. (1998). Ethical and unethical bargaining tactics: An empirical study. *Journal of Business Ethics*, 17, 665–682.

Lewicki, R.J. and Stark, N. (1996). What is ethically appropriate in negotiations: An empirical examination of bargaining tactics. *Social Justice Research*, 9, 69–95.

Lewicki, R.J., Litterer, J.A., Minton, J.W., and Saunders, D.M. (1994). *Negotiation* (2nd edn). Boston: Irwin.

Liebrand, W.B.G. and McClintock, C.G. (1988). Role of interdependence structure, individual value orientation, and another's strategy in social decision making: A transformational analysis. *Journal of Personality and Social Psychology*, 55, 396–409.

Liebrand, W.B.G., Jansen, R.W.T.L., Rijken, V.M., and Suhre, C.J.M. (1986). Might over morality: Social values and the perception of other players in experimental games. *Journal of Experimental Social Psychology*, 22, 203–215.

McClintock, C.G. and Allison, S. (1989). Social value orientation and helping behavior. *Journal of Applied Social Psychology*, 19, 353–362.

Messick, D.M. and McClintock, C.G. (1968). Motivational basis of choice in experimental games. *Journal of Experimental Social Psychology*, 4, 1–25.

Messick, D.M., Bloom, S., Boldizar, J.P. and Samuelson, C.D. (1985). Why we are fairer than others. *Journal of Experimental Social Psychology*, 21, 480–500.

Mosterd, I. and Rutte, C.G. (2000). Effects of time pressure and accountability to constituents on negotiation. *International Journal of Conflict Management*, 11, 227–247.

Morris, M.W., Larrick, R.P., and Su, S.K. (1999). Misperceiving negotiation counterparts: When situationally determined bargaining behaviors are attributed to personality traits. *Journal of Personality and Social Psychology*, 77, 52–67.

Neale, M.A. and Bazerman, M.H. (1991). *Cognition and rationality in negotiation*. New York: Free Press.

Northcraft, G.B. and Neale, M.A. (1987). Experts, amateurs, and real estate: An anchoring-and-adjustment perspective on property pricing decisions. *Organizational Behavior and Human Decision Processes*, 39, 84–97.

Olekalns, M. and Smith, P.L. (1999). Social value orientations and strategy choices in competitive negotiations. *Personality & Social Psychology Bulletin*, 25, 657–668.

Olekalns, M. and Smith, P.L. (2003). Social motives in negotiation: The relationship between dyad composition, negotiation processes and outcomes. *The International Journal of Conflict Management*, 14, 233–254.

Petty, R.E. and Cacioppo, J.T. (1986). The elaboration likelihood model of persuasion. *Advances in Experimental Social Psychology*, 19, 123–205.

Pillutla, M.M. and Murnighan, J.K. (1995). Being fair or appearing fair: Strategic behavior in ultimatum bargaining. *Academy of Management Journal, 38,* 1408–1426.
Pillutla, M.M. and Murnighan, J.K. (2003). Fairness in bargaining. *Social Justice Research, 16,* 241–262.
Pronin, E., Gilovich, T., and Ross, L. (2004). Objectivity in the eye of the beholder: Divergent perceptions of bias in self versus others. *Psychological Review, 111,* 781–799.
Pruitt, D.G. (1981). *Negotiation behavior* (Vol. 47). New York: Academic Press.
Pruitt, D.G. (1983). Strategic choice in negotiation. *American Behavioral Scientist, 27,* 167–194.
Pruitt, D.G. and Carnevale, P.J. (1993). *Negotiation in social conflict.* Oxford: Oxford University Press.
Robinson, R.J., Keltner, D., Ward, A., and Ross, L. (1995). Actual versus assumed differences in construal: "Naive realism" in intergroup perception and conflict. *Journal of Personality and Social Psychology, 68,* 404–417.
Roch, S.G. and Samuelson, C.D. (1997). Effects of environmental uncertainty and social value orientation in resource dilemmas. *Organizational Behavior and Human Decision Processes, 70,* 221–235.
Ross, L. and Stillinger, C. (1991). Barriers to conflict resolution. *Negotiation Journal, 7,* 389–404.
Ross, L. and Ward, A. (1995). Psychological barriers to dispute resolution. *Advances in Experimental Social Psychology, 27,* 255–304.
Rubin, J.Z., Pruitt, D.G., and Kim, S.H. (1994). *Social conflict: Escalation, stalemate, and settlement.* New York: McGraw-Hill.
Sattler, D.N. and Kerr, N.L. (1991). Might versus morality explored: Motivational and cognitive bases for social motives. *Journal of Personality and Social Psychology, 60,* 756–765.
Sinaceur, M. and Tiedens, L.Z. (2006). Get mad and get more than even: When and why anger expression is effective in negotiations. *Journal of Experimental Social Psychology, 42,* 314–322.
Steinel, W. and De Dreu, C.K.W. (2004). Social motives and strategic misrepresentation in social decision making. *Journal of Personality and Social Psychology, 86,* 419–434.
Taylor, S.E. and Brown, J.D. (1988). Illusion and well-being: a social psychological perspective on mental health. *Psychological Bulletin, 103,* 193–210.
Taylor, S.E. and Brown, J.D. (1994). Positive illusions and well-being revisited: Separating fact from fiction. *Psychological Bulletin, 116,* 21–27.
Tenbrunsel, A.E. (1998). Misrepresentation and expectations of misrepresentation in an ethical dilemma: The role of incentives and temptation. *Academy of Management Journal, 41,* 330–339.
Thaler, R.H. (1992). *The winner's curse: Paradoxes and anomalies of economic life.* Princeton, NJ: Princeton University Press.
Thompson, L. and Hastie, R. (1990). Social perception in negotiation. *Organizational Behavior and Human Decision Processes, 47,* 98–123.
Thompson, L. and Hrebec, D. (1996). Lose–lose agreements in interdependent decision making. *Psychological Bulletin, 120,* 396–409.
Thompson, M.M., Naccarato, M.E., and Parker, K.E. (1989, June). Assessing cognitive need: The development of the personal need for structure and personal fear of invalidity scales. Paper presented at the annual meeting of the Canadian Psychological Association, Halifax, Canada.
Van der Schalk, J., Beersma, B., van Kleef, G.A., and De Dreu, C.K. (2009). The more (complex), the better? The influence of epistemic motivation on integrative bargaining in complex negotiation. *European Journal of Social Psychology, 40,* 355–365.
Van Dijk, E. and Vermunt, R. (2000). Strategy and fairness in social decision making: Sometimes it pays to be powerless. *Journal of Experimental Social Psychology, 36,* 1–25.
Van Dijk, E., De Cremer, D., and Handgraaf, M.J.J. (2004). Social value orientations and the strategic use of fairness in ultimatum bargaining. *Journal of Experimental Social Psychology, 40,* 697–707.

Van Kleef, G.A., De Dreu, C.K., and Manstead, A.S. (2004). The interpersonal effects of emotions in negotiations: a motivated information processing approach. *Journal of Personality and Social Psychology*, 87, 510–528.

Van Kleef, G.A., De Dreu, C.K., and Manstead, A.S. (2010). An interpersonal approach to emotion in social decision making: The emotions as social information model. *Advances in Experimental Social Psychology*, 42, 45–96.

Van Lange, P.A.M. (1992). Confidence in expectations: A test of the triangle hypothesis. *European Journal of Personality*, 6, 371–379.

Van Lange, P.A.M. (1999). The pursuit of joint outcomes and equality in outcomes: An integrative model of social value orientations. *Journal of Personality and Social Psychology*, 77, 337–349.

Van Lange, P.A.M. and Kuhlman, D.M. (1994). Social value orientations and impressions of partner's honesty and intelligence: A test of the morality effect. *Journal of Personality and Social Psychology*, 67, 126–141.

Van Lange, P.A.M. and Visser, K. (1999). Locomotion in social dilemmas: How people adapt to cooperative, tit-for-tat, and noncooperative partners. *Journal of Personality and Social Psychology*, 77, 762–773.

Van Lange, P.A.M., De Bruin, E.M.N., Otten, W., and Joireman, J.A. (1997). Development of prosocial, individualistic, and competitive orientations: Theory and preliminary evidence. *Journal of Personality and Social Psychology*, 73, 733–746.

Van Lange, P.A.M., De Cremer, D., Van Dijk, E., and Van Vugt, M. (2007). Self-interest and beyond: Basic principles of social interaction. In A.W. Kruglanski and E.T. Higgins (eds), *Social psychology: Handbook of basic principles* (2nd edn, pp. 540–561). New York: Guilford.

Webster, D.M. and Kruglanski, A.W. (1994). Individual differences in need for cognitive closure. *Journal of Personality and Social Psychology*, 67, 1049–1062.

Webster, D.M., Richter, L. and Kruglanski, A.W. (1996). On leaping to conclusions when feeling tired: Mental fatigue effects on impressional primacy. *Journal of Experimental Social Psychology*, 32, 181–195.

Weingart, L.R., Brett, J.M., Olekalns, M., and Smith, P.L. (2007). Conflicting social motives in negotiating groups. *Journal of Personality and Social Psychology*, 93, 994–1010.

4. Shared cognition and identity in negotiation
Leigh Anne Liu and Wei Cai

> The U.S.–China relationship was of crucial importance, said [Chinese diplomat] Dai. China would do its best to cooperate with the United States wherever possible. "If we expand the pie for the common interest, the pie will be larger and more delicious." Together, the two sides should work collaboratively for the good of the world, especially since the two countries were "passengers in the same boat". Dai urged careful management of the relationship and respect for each other's core interests and concerns.
>
> Wikileaks, 18 (S)

The above quote shows how a Chinese diplomat understands Sino–American relationships and hopes for the understanding and metaphors to be shared by both parties. A shared mental model, or a common understanding of some situation or phenomenon among a dyad of individuals, has been an important goal for negotiators to pursue. Negotiation is a social exchange where individuals perceive themselves as having opposing interests regarding scarce resources (Bazerman et al., 2000). To be effective, each negotiation party needs to seek to claim as much of the resources as possible. At the same time, they need to establish agreements on not leaving resources on the bargaining table (Swaab et al., 2007). Thus, a key challenge for most negotiators is to align individual and group interests, which requires individual negotiators to recognize some overarching commonalities leading them to pursue outcomes that benefit themselves as well as others (Swaab et al., 2007). This is precisely what a shared mental model and identity may offer: They positively influence each other and group outcomes because they give rise to an understanding of underlying interests as well as a willingness to make trade-offs. Our purpose in this chapter is to propose an integrative input-output framework that organizes current literature and future directions on the study of shared cognition and identity in negotiation. We maintain that the input factors reflect negotiators' perceptions of various antecedents to a dynamic process that cultivates shared cognition and identity. The output factors convey the expressed manifestation or outcomes of such dynamic processes.

SHARED MENTAL MODELS IN NEGOTIATIONS

With few exceptions (Liu et al., 2012a; Olekalns and Smith, 2005; Van Boven and Thompson, 2003), previous works about shared mental models are concerned overwhelmingly with the domain of teamwork. Researchers who study teamwork generally define shared mental models as the commonality and similarity of individually held mental models, or the consensus with which team members interpret and categorize strategic issues such as team task and team relationship (Mathieu et al., 2000; Mohammed and Dumville, 2001). Scholars of team mental models also acknowledge the formation process of shared mental models as being dynamic and ongoing as team members share more experiences.

From the perspective of social interaction, negotiation can be regarded as a type of teamwork. Like members of a team, negotiators share a common goal of reaching an agreement. During the process of achieving the common goal, both team members and negotiators are interdependent. But negotiation differs from teamwork by the open recognition of the different preferences held by the negotiation parties. In the process of reaching shared mental models, multiparty negotiations differ from typical teamwork. In negotiation, the differences held by each party are generally made explicit, whereas in teamwork, while each member may interpret the common goal differently, the difference may or may not be explicitly acknowledged. The open acknowledgement of differences makes the mental model sharing process in negotiation unique from that among team members. In definition, "a shared mental model can be described as the extent to which a dyad of individuals possesses a similar cognitive representation of some situation or phenomenon" while "the notion of team mental model is distinct from that of a shared mental model in that it refers to shared cognition in a team as a collectivity, not shared cognition among dyads of individuals" (Langan-Fox et al., 2001, p. 99).

SHARED IDENTITIES IN NEGOTIATIONS

In a separate literature, individuals may also construct a sense of shared identity in negotiation when they readily interact and observe each other's actions and reconcile differences to establish interpersonal relations (Postmes et al., 2005a; Postmes et al., 2005b). Social identity theory (Doosje et al., 1999) suggests that people's reaction to group memberships and their willingness to engage group norms depend upon the salience of the group membership and the relative importance they attach to such membership. For example, group members who identify strongly with the group will support collective improvements even at the expense of their own personal interests (Ellemers et al., 1993; Ellemers et al., 1997). In the same situation, group members who do not identify with the group will focus on personal risks and benefits (Smith et al., 2003). Social identity researchers have concluded that group activities are more productive to the extent that individuals identify with their group (Tajfel and Turner, 1979; Turner et al., 1987). Further, empirical evidence shows that group identification affects work motivation (Ellemers and Rink, in press; Ouwerkerk et al., 2000) and performance (Van Leeuwen et al., 2003). The impact of inductively formed identities is significant to groups in a variety of decision-making settings, ranging from collaborative decision making (Postmes et al., 2001) to negotiations and dispute resolution (Swaab et al., 2002) and social dilemmas. The overall conclusion from this research is that shared identity positively affects groups because it promotes pro-social behavior, trust, and commitment (De Dreu and Carnevale, 2003).

SHARED MENTAL MODELS AND IDENTITIES IN NEGOTIATIONS

In this chapter, we seek to integrate these literatures by introducing a theoretical framework about shared mental models and shared identity in negotiation, by examining antecedents and the interactive process of cultivating shared cognition and identity, by explaining relationships between shared mental models and group identification, and by depicting consequences of shared mental models and shared identities, including learning, satisfaction, and economic gains on both individual and collective levels. Figure 4.1 illustrates our integrative input-output framework that organizes the antecedents, interactive processes, consequences, and moderating factors of shared mental models and shared identity in negotiation. In this figure, we delineate the individual, collective, and contextual levels of analysis as well as the affective, informational, and relational factors in the content of negotiator mental models. In order to focus on the dynamic interactions in the process of cultivating shared cognition and identity, we structure the following text first by using the category of affective, informational, and relational variables, and then discuss the moderating effects of contextual variables.

INPUT PROCESS OUTCOME

Affective variables (individual differences)
- Personality
- Gender
- Unmitigated communion
- Mood
- Self-motivation
- Team spirit
- Affinity

Affective variables
- Hostility
- Fear
- Shame
- Self-blame
- Disappointment
- Anger
- Sympathy
- Liking
- Social motive
- Egoistic motive
- Need for closure
- Face-concern triggered emotions

Informational variables
- Task-related knowledge
- Individual knowledge structure
- Group-level common understanding of the task

Informational variables
- Reflexivity
- Knowledge of others' capability
- Strategic knowledge

Relational variables
- Pre-existing relationship
- Power
- Self-identity

Relational variables
- Level of engagement
- Assimilation
- Reciprocity
- Rapport
- Trust
- Social perspective exchange
- Communication

Contextual variables
- Time
- Task type
- Similarity of organizational structure
- Effective preplanning
- Closeness of cultures
- Group climate
- Task procedural complexity
- Task coordination

shared mental model + shared identity = joint economic/relational gains

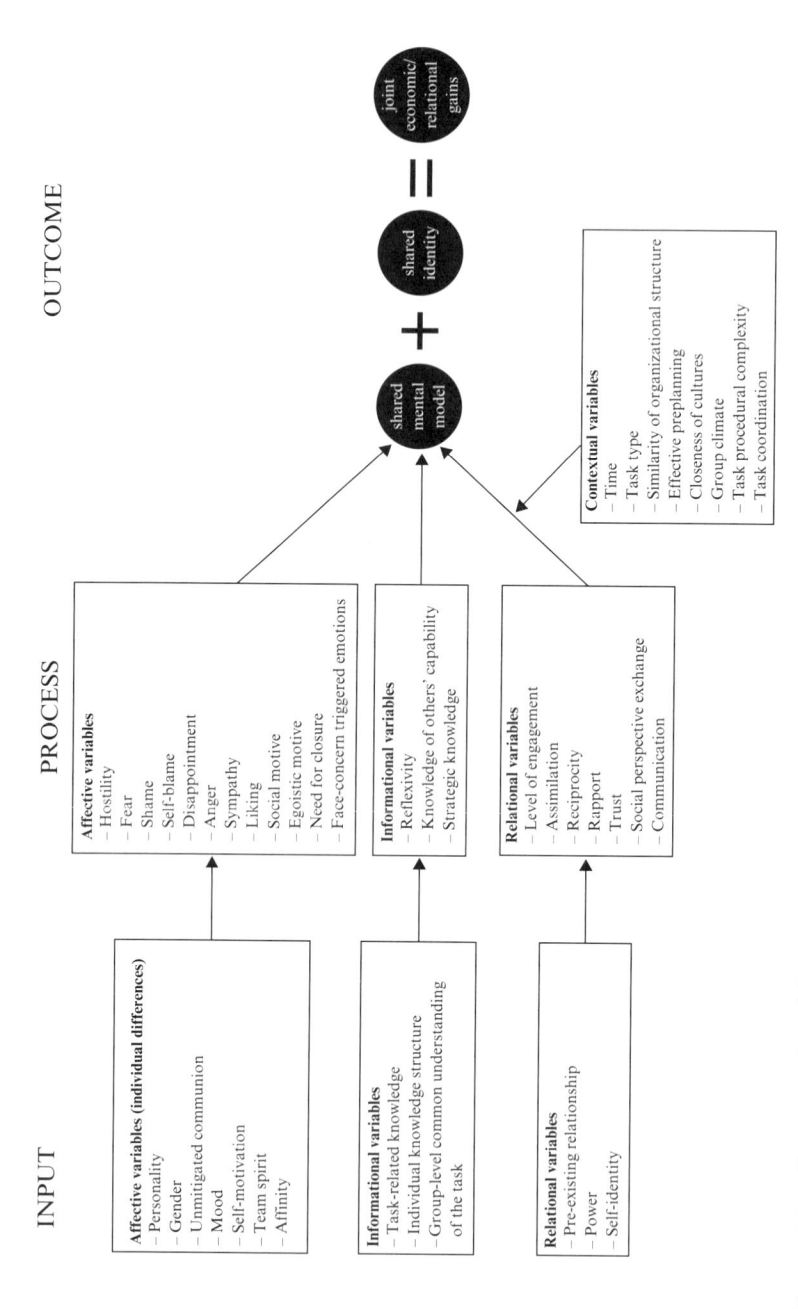

Figure 4.1 Conceptual model on shared cognition and identity in negotiation

AN INTEGRATIVE FRAMEWORK OF SHARED MENTAL MODELS

Negotiations have been characterized as a three-stage process (Neale and Bazerman, 1991): pre-negotiation planning (e.g., preferred position); negotiations (e.g., strategies used); and outcomes (e.g., final resolution, commitment). In the process of cultivating shared cognition and identity, we identify categorical input, dynamic process, critical triggers, and consequences. Based on previous research that has concentrated on three types of variables influencing negotiation behavior and outcome (Beersma and De Dreu, 1999; Liu et al., 2012a; Mannix et al., 1989; Polzer et al., 1998; Thompson et al., 1988; Weingart et al., 1993; Weingart and Brett, 1998), we propose a negotiator's mental model is more than a collection of independent processes operating in a modular cognitive system (Barsalou et al., 2007). Instead, we propose that a negotiator's mental model is a network comprised of interrelated affective, informational, and relational components of knowledge that allows an individual negotiator to make sense of specific situations, and to predict future states (Gentner, 2002).

There are four common characteristics of mental models in social interaction. First, mental models are affective. Affective mechanisms play central roles in cognition, and optimal cognitive performance occurs when affective information is included in decision-making. In other words, cognition divorced from affect is not rational, and a full understanding of cognition without taking affective factors into account is impossible. For instance, emotion, reward, and motivation tightly intertwine with each and with the cognitive system (Barrett, 1995; Barrett et al., 2007). Furthermore, when negotiators recognize the similarities among important elements of individuals' mental models, it creates a pro-social climate, which is a strong precursor to mutually satisfactory negotiation and decision-making (Swaab et al., 2002). Second, mental models are informational. A negotiator's mental model stands for pre-existing knowledge structures people use to understand the task and situation, anticipate counterparties' actions and coordinate their own behaviors especially when there is a time constraint or special circumstance (Marks et al., 2000). Third, mental models are relational. A mental model shares common features but can be distinguished from other cognitive structures such as cognitive maps (Axelrod, 1976), scripts, schemas (Fiske and Taylor, 1991), frames (Minsky, 1975), and belief or knowledge structures (Fiske and Taylor, 1991) because it yields an integrated network of relations among perceived elements at a given point in time (Liu et al., 2012a) and considers the interrelationship of different elements in a situation. As information is accumulated through interactions in negotiations, a mental model reflects a holistic and specific cognitive experience, and a shared mental model or identity is thought to converge over time (Johnson-Laird, 1989; Klimoski and Mohammed, 1994; Mathieu et al., 2005). Finally, mental models are situation specific and contextual. Shared mental models are not the simple sum of individual mental models but include the synergistic effect of the communication process between individual models. In other words, in social interaction, people's individual mental models influence and are influenced by the social context, the people they communicate with, and the type of communication experienced (Liu and Dale, 2009).

In this chapter, we adopted Ren and Argote's method (2011) and searched for research articles in the Web of Science database with the keywords "shared mental model", "shared identity", and "negotiation" in the title in three citation databases: Science Citation Index Expanded, Social Sciences Citation Index, and Arts and Humanities Citation Index. We found 52 papers that were published between January 2000 and October 2012. We included papers with a primary focus on the relationship between variables and shared mental models or identities. To inform our review, we also reviewed all stage papers on shared mental models and identities in the literature. Only one paper is a review on the relationship between shared mental models and identities, published by Swaab et al. (2007) while other papers focus on investigating the impact of individual variables on negotiation outcomes (e.g., Gunia, et al., 2011) emphasize the effects that shared mental models (Cannon-Bowers et al., 1993; Choi, 2010; Thompson and Fine, 1999) or shared identities have on integrative negotiations (De Dreu and Carnevale, 2003; Postmes et al., 2001), or explain why the same processes that predict joint gains in negotiation should also predict shared mental models and shared identity. For instance, drawing on previous research on mental models and joint gains in negotiation (e.g., Olekalns and Smith, 2005; Van Boven and Thompson, 2003), Liu and colleagues (Liu, et al., 2012a) created the following figure (see Figure 4.2) supporting the argument that humans are unusual in establishing joint attention and good at representing other minds (Barsalou et al., 2007), particularly to illustrate how two negotiation parties reach an integrative agreement and maximize joint gains because of mental model convergence.

Although individual factors concerning negotiation consequences and the impact of shared mental models and shared identity on negotiation are well-documented, few works present a comprehensive framework to explain the development of shared mental models and identities in negotiations. Below we elucidate how previous research found each category of variables were related to integrative outcomes in negotiations with the purpose of developing a framework to examine how shared mental models and identities come into play and lead to consensus (Liu et al., 2012a). We

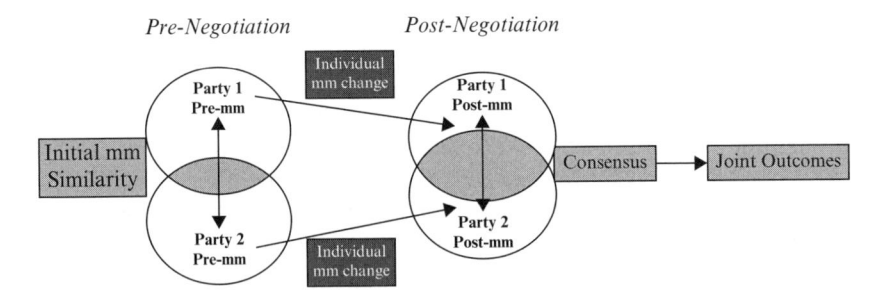

Note: mm refers to mental model.

Figure 4.2 Relationship of mental models and outcomes in negotiation in Liu et al. (2012a)

also propose potential relationships between shared mental models and identities.

ANTECEDENTS TO THE DEVELOPMENT OF SHARED MENTAL MODELS AND IDENTITIES

Individual Differences

A shared mental model is a construct derived from individual mental models. Individual differences in characteristics and motivations are influential for the development of a shared mental model and identity, especially at the beginning of a negotiation (Yang et al., 2008). A dominant assumption is that similarities in individual differences are the foundation for a shared mental model and group identification. Individuals identify with groups on the basis of shared characteristics such as skin color, gender, personality or attitudes. The more within-group similarities there are, the higher possibility shared mental models will form or the stronger the social identity will be (Jans et al., 2011). The results of previous studies consistently indicate that individual characteristics such as agreeableness (Yang et al., 2008) and extraversion (Barry and Friedman, 1998; Wood and Bell, 2008) can be a potent cause of integrative outcomes. In general, gender similarity can make a significant influence on the development of shared mental models and identities. The presence and proportion of women at the negotiation table may facilitate the development of shared cognition and identity. Female negotiators are more concerned about relationships (Gelfand et al., 2006; Kray and Gelfand, 2009), have less assertive negotiation styles (Amanatullah, 2007), lack propensity to initiate negotiations (Bowles et al., 2007; Babcock and Laschever, 2003; Small et al., 2007), and more frequently adopt an accommodating style (Kray and Thompson, 2005). As a result women may be more open and accommodating to new ideas and perspectives from the other parties than men, though they are not perceived as effective negotiators (Kray et al., 2001). While these findings suggest gender similarity should aid the formation of shared mental models, there is other mixed evidence for the idea that individual differences explain the degree to which negotiators develop a shared mental model and group identification.

Recent research suggests that the outcomes of similarities in negotiators' individual differences are mixed and can be negative. Indeed, Amanatullah and colleagues (2008) find that joint economic gain in an integrative negotiation is reduced when individuals on both sides of the bargaining table score high on Unmitigated Communion (UC) although there may exist a high relational satisfaction (Curhan et al., 2008). Scholars (Jans et al., 2011; Savelkoul et al., 2011) argue that diversity does not necessarily undermine the formation of a shared mental model or social identity.

Proposition 1: Composition patterns and the match among negotiators in gender, personality, and unmitigated communion, and individual capabilities will significantly influence the dynamic process of cultivating shared mental models and identity in negotiation, but the influence is complex.

Informational Input

A shared mental model among multiple-party negotiators is achieved when negotiators have group-wide consensus on the payoff structure and the same understanding of task related information (Cooke et al., 2003; Lewis, 2004; Rentsch and Woehr, 2004). In this sense a shared mental model refers to the network in which negotiation parties process and use information (He et al., 2007; MacMillan et al., 2004). During negotiation, shared information such as shared understanding of task-related knowledge, relationships, and emotions can guide behavior and decision-making and thus enhance the quality of performance in negotiations (Cooke et al., 2003; Fiore et al., 2001; Liu et al., 2012a). In other words, negotiation, a process of communicative exchange, would proceed more smoothly and yield more positive outcomes when negotiators share a common understanding of tasks (Tindale and Kameda, 2000).

When negotiators engage in an integrative negotiation, they are likely to have a more accurate understanding of their negotiation task and of the possibility for trade-offs that lead to mutual gain (Van Boven and Thompson, 2003). When team members share similar views of the collective task and how to coordinate, they are likely to perform better (Kerr and Tindale, 2004; Mathieu et al., 2000; Swaab et al., 2007; Tindale and Kameda, 2000). For instance, Mathieu et al. (2000) found that similarity among team members' knowledge of an F-16 flight simulation and function was positively associated with increased performance. When negotiators are given opportunities to think or discuss among themselves how they would conduct a negotiation, a shared understanding of the negotiation task among the negotiators is more likely to emerge, and it is more likely to lead to a successful negotiation involving maximized mutual gains (Bouas and Komorita, 1996; Swaab et al., 2007; Liu et al., 2012a; Van Boven and Thompson, 2003). Therefore we propose that the degree and extent of common knowledge among negotiators will be impactful to the development of shared cognition and identity.

Proposition 2: The degree of common understanding of the negotiation task among negotiators will positively influence the dynamic process of cultivating a shared mental model and identity in negotiation.

Relational Input

Negotiation is an inherently relational activity, and "so an individual negotiator's performance is affected not only by his or her own aspirations, motivations, and behaviors, but also by those of his or her opponent" (Chen et al., 2003, p. 1). Burnham and colleagues (2000) find that referring to another party as a "partner" rather than an "opponent" seriously improves trust and trustworthiness behavior. An amicable relationship encourages cooperation and triggers a more integrative approach to the problem solving aspect of negotiation, although sometimes by avoiding conflict (Lewicki et al., 2003; Thompson, 2005). We therefore expect that congenial relationships will enhance the likelihood of developing shared cognition and identity in negotiation.

Proposition 3: Amicable relationships among negotiators will positively influence the dynamic process of cultivating shared cognition and identity in negotiation.

In this section, we described individual, informational, and relational factors that are input antecedents for the dynamic process of developing shared cognition and identity, and we proposed potential questions to be tested in future research. Empirically, we note that individual characters, cognitive information, and perceptions of relationships can be studied at both the individual and collective levels, as well as being tested in moderating interactions. Next, we turn to the dynamic process of developing shared cognition and identity and explicate the affective and motivational, informational, and relational processes that contribute to a later stage of shared cognition and identity in negotiation.

THE DYNAMIC PROCESS OF THE DEVELOPMENT OF SHARED MENTAL MODELS AND IDENTITIES

Affective and Motivational Processes

A negotiation is a concentration of human emotions. Most conflicts in negotiation occur because emotions are not well controlled. Affect regulation and motivation play substantial roles in human activities (Barsalou et al., 2007), and cognition divorced from affect is not rational (Damasio, 1994). We review and propose affective and motivational factors that can significantly influence the process of developing shared cognition and identity in negotiation.

Emotion. To develop a negotiated agreement, people need to have a good control of their emotions (Boonstra, 1998). Scholars (e.g., Bell and Song, 2005) have proved that emotions influence the conflict process by motivating or predisposing a person towards specific behaviors. Indeed, emotions are critical elements of conflict that can influence an individual's subjective experience and response to the conflict situation (Forgas and George, 2001). In general, positive relational emotions such as sympathy, respect and liking for the other party are usually associated with pro-social cognition and behavior, cooperative or integrative strategies, and thus lead to cooperation (Batson and Moran, 1999), integrating or compromising strategies. Negative relational emotions such as anger, anxiety, and frustration are related to aggressive thoughts and impulses (Harmon-Jones, 2003; Roseman et al., 1994), which may impede the development of shared cognition and identities. Self-conscious emotions including shame, guilt, embarrassment and humiliation are more likely to be associated with compliant behaviors (Barrett, et al., 2007; Fischer and Tangney, 1995), which will predict an obliging strategy, and thus lead to agreements. Other-focused emotions such as withdrawal or fear are related to a readiness to avoid, avert or protect, which will predict an avoiding strategy.

However, if negotiators are self-concerned, negative affect such as fear, hostility, disappointment, frustration, or anger may occur due to an anticipation of personal loss. Therefore, it is difficult to offer clear-cut predictions. Different from self-concern, other-concern is always associated with empathy or feelings of affection, which will predict positive relational emotions. In particular, we predict that the shared mental models of negotiators who reach optimal settlements (thereby solving the negotiation problem) would be more likely to display (1) positive relational emotions; (2) self-conscious emotions; and (3) other-concern emotions.

Proposition 4:   The relationships between emotions and expressed behaviors during negotiations are divergent and complex. Positive relational, self-conscious, and other-concern emotions are usually associated with integrative or problem-solving strategies, which lead to the development of shared cognition and identity in negotiation.

Motivation. In the negotiation context, motivational orientation has been defined as a negotiator's preference for a particular outcome distribution between him/herself and his/her opponent in a given situation (De Dreu et al., 2000). Negotiation research typically distinguishes between a pro-social motive, aimed at seeking optimal outcomes for oneself as well as for others, and an egoistic motive, aimed at maximizing outcomes for oneself only (De Dreu et al., 2000). In a negotiation, both types of motives necessarily exist (Pruitt and Carnevale, 1993), but they vary in salience due to individual differences, situational variations, or both (De Dreu and Van Lange, 1995). Negotiators with an egoistic motive try to maximize their own outcome with no regard for their opponents' outcome. In contrast, negotiators with a pro-social motive try to maximize their own as well as others' outcome (Zhang and Han, 2007). In the literature, a key theoretical assumption is that there is a positive relationship between a pro-social motive and joint gains in negotiations. Indeed, scholars (De Dreu et al., 1998; Weingart et al., 1993) have verified that pro-social groups engage in more problem-solving and less contentious behaviors and achieve higher joint outcomes than egoistic negotiators. This finding is important, but incomplete. It leaves the impression that if negotiators are from relationally focused cultures such as China, Japan or India, being more concerned about others will lead to harmonious interactions and joint gains in negotiations. Yet there is evidence showing that negotiators from pro-social cultures may not achieve optimal outcomes from negotiation because they place too much emphasis on relationships (Amanatullah et al., 2008; Curhan et al., 2008). Indeed, negotiators from Asian cultures are cooperative only when their counter party has similar social motives (Liu et al., 2012b). For instance, Chen and Li (2005) reported that Chinese are more likely to cooperate with in-group members than with out-group members. Thus, we predict that when there is a similarity between negotiators' social motives, a shared mental model and identity is more likely to take place.

Among these motivations, researchers have found that two specific motivations, Need for Closure (Fu et al., 2007; Liu et al., 2012a) and Concern for Face (Liu et al., 2012a), are particularly relevant to the development of shared cognition, especially in cross-cultural negotiations. Findings from Fu et al. (2007) and Liu et al. (2012a) show that Need for Closure can be detrimental to building shared cognition while Concern for Face can facilitate shared cognition, especially during intercultural interactions. Their reasoning is that while the Need for Closure leads to close-mindedness (De Dreu et al., 2000; De Grada et al., 1999), Concern for Face reflects a pro-social orientation (Cheung et al., 1996; Oetzel and Ting-Toomey, 2003; Ting-Toomey, 2005).

Besides emotions and motivations at the individual level, we believe such factors at the collective level, such as an uplifting team spirit and rapport among negotiators, could provide cumulative support for developing shared cognition and identity. Therefore, emotions and motivations can have a complicated impact on the dynamic process leading to shared cognition and identity, with some emotions and motivations being constructive (such as higher need for closure) and others being counterproductive (such as anger and face threat). Future research needs to further investigate such mechanisms. In particular, we predict that it is less likely to have a shared mental model and identity when negotiators feel (1) higher need for closure or (2) face threat in a negotiation. This is particularly true with pro-social negotiators.

Proposition 5: When there is similarity between negotiators' social motives, shared mental models and identity are most likely to develop. However, motivational processes during negotiations can have divergent and complex influences on the development of shared mental models and identity in negotiation.

Informational Processes

Shared mental models have been described as "knowledge structures held by members of a team that enable them to form accurate explanations and expectations of the task" (Cannon-Bowers et al., 1993, p. 288). For negotiation tasks, performance and outcomes not only depend on whether or not negotiators actually share the information, but it also depends on the extent to which good strategies are developed and implemented (Salas et al., 2005). If negotiators "overtly reflect upon the negotiation objectives, strategies, and processes and adapt them to current or anticipated endogenous or environmental circumstances" (West, 1996, p. 559), high performance or shared cognition is most likely. This link between reflexivity and group performance has been replicated in some recent studies (Schippers et al., 2003). In other words, if negotiators have difficulties developing task adaptive strategies, and rethinking and revising strategies adopted earlier, they are less likely to build similarities of individual mental models (Gurtner et al., 2007).

Reflexivity can be conceived as a group discussion, which has an advantage of leading to more cooperation and less contention. It is a trend towards taking the opponent's perspectives and thus brings a higher degree of satisfaction for negotiators. Although reflexivity did not directly affect joint gains in some studies, greater post-negotiation judgment accuracy regarding the opponent's point values was found to significantly correlate with greater joint gains and with greater rates of information exchange, which are both important for successful integrative negotiation (e.g., De Dreu et al., 2000). Therefore, we predict that reflexivity should enable negotiators to revise and develop effective strategies that facilitate offer trading, and promote coordination. As a result, we expect negotiators with more degrees of reflexivity to engage in more cooperative and problem-solving processes that ultimately lead to a larger extent of shared cognition and identity.

Proposition 6: Reflexivity in the dynamic negotiation process positively promotes the development of shared mental models and identity in negotiation.

Relational Processes

Interpersonal relationships
Negotiation scholars have acknowledged that establishing interpersonal relationships and appreciating mutual differences facilitate the development of shared mental models and identities. For example, Loewenstein and colleagues show that negotiators who were attracted to the other party displayed more pro-social behavior and chose mutually beneficial alternatives (Loewenstein et al., 1989). In a study on multiparty negotiations, Swaab et al. (2008) note that researchers (Gillespie et al., 2000) believe that interpersonal relations between group members significantly predict whether a shared mental model and identity will be developed. Recent studies (Gaertner et al., 2006; Rognes and Schei, 2010) confirm that good interpersonal relations among all group members can create the conditions under which they are willing to assimilate behaviorally, and thus facilitate the integrative solution of complex tasks. In other words, negotiators without such relationships will have to exert more efforts to act integratively towards each other in order to build shared mental models and shared identities.

Trust
Economic outcomes are best advanced through accommodating behavior such as liking, trust and reputation (Kulik and Olekalns, 2012). Trust leads to constructive dialogues and compromises in negotiations because trusting negotiators usually behave more cooperatively (Rubin and Brown 1975), less competitively, and use less inappropriate information gathering (Elahee et al., 2002). Butler (1995) has shown that trusting negotiators feel confident that their counterpart will not use shared information to take advantage of the situation, and those with high trust propensity are more likely to share information and less likely to behave competitively (Mintu-Wimsatt et al., 2005). Thus trust could facilitate cooperative behaviors during negotiations and help negotiators build shared cognition and identity, as well as achieve better outcomes.

Perspective exchange and good communication skills
When people occupy different social positions within a cooperative task they experience discrepant role and situation demands and they have divergent perspectives (Gillespie and Richardson, 2011). Experiments have shown that even getting participants to imagine the perspective of the other, and how the other might react to one's own actions, can reduce intergroup competition (Wolf et al., 2009). This is called perspective or social position exchange. Researchers (Gillespie and Richardson, 2011) have become increasingly convinced that perspective exchange within a cooperative task can help negotiators move out of their own social situation and into the social situation of the other, thus overcoming divergences of perspective and experiencing the situation of the other directly. In negotiations, effective negotiators have the ability to use their unusually good communication skills that allow them to coordinate shared mental states and cooperation to resolve complex tasks and reach optimal settlements (Barsalou et al., 2007). Both perspective exchange and good communication skills function as vehicles through which group members' interpersonal differences, commonalties, and relations flow, which can facilitate shared cognition and identity formation. For example, Postmes et al. (2000) found that email messages among group members converged in both content and form over time so that intra-group interaction facilitated the emergence of unique attributes of the group. Gillespie and Richardson (2011) show that position exchange increased the likelihood of dyads solving a communication conflict based on discrepant perspectives. Postmes and colleagues (Postmes et al., 2005a; 2005b) describe pathways to the emergence shared identity and especially address the role that communicative exchange plays in the process. These findings indicate that negotiators are more likely to

"create value" by working with one another to exchange information and maximize joint gains than others if they are willing to exchange their social positions or have good communication skills (Van Boven and Thompson, 2003).

Power
Power is defined as the capacity that one group has to influence the behavior of another (Smith et al., 2003). It is linked to the extent that the group controls important, scarce, or non-substitutable resources (Greenberg and Baron, 2000). Pozzebon and Pinsonneault (2012) suggest that individuals or groups base power and knowledge on resources that can be owned or controlled, which are relational in nature and intertwined in action. In three case studies to investigate the dynamics of client-consultant relationships, Pozzebon and Pinsonneault (2012) demonstrate how knowing and powering mechanisms can reinforce or change implementation trajectories, which, in turn, can affect performance outcomes. Giebels et al. (2000) found that in a group decision-making task, imbalances in the power positions of group members led them to focus on their individual outcomes instead of on group outcomes, because it is more likely for a group with power to form a coalition, and engage in more distributive and less integrative behavior in order to claim a large part of the negotiation pie for themselves (Beersma and De Dreu, 2002). This behavior is viewed as defection at the group level, which will ultimately prevent negotiators from reaching higher joint outcomes. Hence we expect the existence of asymmetrical power would be detrimental to the development of shared cognition and identity.

Reciprocation wariness
Negotiation is a process of interpersonal interaction in which two or more parties attempt to reach an agreement and produce consensus in perceptions through reciprocation (Carnevale and Pruitt, 1992). In the context of negotiation, reciprocation wariness refers to a general belief of caution in offering and rewarding help to avoid exploitation in interpersonal interactions (Eisenberger et al., 1987). Reciprocation wariness is modestly related to actual reciprocal behavior (Perugini et al. 2003). In other words, a negotiator's reciprocation wariness could influence negotiators' actual reciprocation behavior in negotiations. Zhang and Han (2007) note that reciprocation wariness may also influence the information sharing between negotiators. High-wary negotiators fear that their opponents would take advantage of them and expect the opponents will not return truthful information when they disclose truthful information first. Put differently, high-wary negotiators are more likely to see information sharing

as a risk instead of an opportunity to find trade-offs. Consequently they tend to refuse information reciprocity and behave uncooperatively, which is detrimental to the construction of shared cognition. In contrast, negotiators with low reciprocation wariness believe their opponents will reciprocate with truthful information as long as they disclose information about themselves; they regard the opponents' such behaviors as cooperative and are more likely to build trust between each other and reach agreement in negotiation. But overall, reciprocation wariness inhibits the development of trust among negotiators and reduces negotiators' cooperative orientation and behavior, and is detrimental to building shared cognition among negotiators.

To summarize, the relational processes in building shared cognition and identity can be complex. It would be helpful for negotiators to have amicable relationships, high levels of trust, and effective communication, but lower levels of power asymmetry and reciprocity wariness.

Proposition 7: Among the relational processes in negotiation, interpersonal relationships, trust, and communication are constructive, while power and reciprocity wariness can be detrimental to building shared cognition and identity among negotiators.

Contextual Factors

Whether and how much negotiators act communally also depends on contextual factors such as task complexity (Akgun et al., 2005), task structure (Beersma and Dreu, 2002), past negotiation relationship (Gibbins et al., 2001), time pressure, differences along negotiators' occupational lines (Gelfand et al., 2006), relative bargaining power (Gruder, 1971; Kahan, 1968; Savage et al., 1989) and expectations from negotiations (Ng and Tan, 2003) and cultural differences in negotiation strategy (Gunia et al., 2011). In other words, the processes leading to shared mental models, shared identities and high joint gain are context dependent (Olekalns and Smith, 2003).

Task structure
Studies (e.g., Beersma and De Dreu, 2002) show the importance of symmetric task structure or conversely the detrimental effects of asymmetric task structure of shared mental models and group identities. In a three-party negotiation, if two parties (the majority) share identical preferences while the remaining party (the minority) has opposite preferences, this asymmetrical task structure will lead majority parties to join forces and focus on their individual outcomes instead of on group outcomes,

thus excluding the minority. To answer the question whether asymmetry of the task structure influences the likelihood of the group reaching high joint outcomes, Beersma and De Dreu (2001) directly compared symmetrical with asymmetrical task structures and found that groups in an asymmetrical task structure engaged in more distributive and less integrative behavior, reached lower joint outcomes, and experienced a less positive group climate especially when they had an egoistic rather than pro-social motivation and applied unanimity rather than majority rules.

Cultural difference in behavior and strategies
Socially shared knowledge of history, concepts of identity, values and norms, stereotypes and prejudices, and behavior are usually formed in long socialization processes and become part of a cultural memory (Erll and Nünning, 2008). In a same-culture encounter, negotiators have been socialized to communicate in similar behavioral patterns naturally (Adair, 2003), which may facilitate the development of shared cognition and identity. Conversely, negotiators from different cultural backgrounds may exhibit different behaviors and expectations, which may delay shared cognition and identity formation. Particularly, the influence of cultural difference in negotiation behavior or strategy becomes stronger in situations that do not provide specific guidance or explicit rules on how to deal with cultural differences, as well as those that require close collaboration among people, such as mixed motive and multi-issue negotiations (Gibson et al., 2008). Numerous studies have shown that negotiators sharing cultural values and native languages are more likely to match each other's behaviors (Patterson, 1983), and generate joint gains (Olekalns and Smith, 2000).

To summarize, the configuration of the negotiation task, the relationship, power structure, and cultural compositions among the negotiators could influence directly or indirectly, independently or simultaneously, the degree of sharedness in cognition that they build during the negotiation process. Besides these factors, external factors such as time pressure or location could also have such effects. For example, individuals under time pressure are less likely to revise inaccurate preexisting cognitive structures during negotiation and consequently reach agreements of lower quality (De Dreu, 2003), which are hallmarks of less shared cognition. Therefore we propose:

Proposition 8: Contextual factors during the process of developing shared cognition among negotiators can have main effects or moderating effects on the degree of sharedness in shared cognition at the end of the negotiation.

OUTCOMES OF SHARED COGNITION IN NEGOTIATION

The theoretical model in Figure 4.1 ends with the consequences of shared cognition in negotiation. Compared with the antecedents to shared cognition, findings are much more consistent about the impact of shared mental models and shared cognition on outcomes in social interactions such as teamwork and negotiation. Numerous empirical studies have shown that shared mental models increase coordination and thus have a positive impact on group performance (e.g., Marks et al., 2002; Mathieu et al., 2000). In negotiation, Van Boven and Thompson (2003) and Liu et al. (2012a) found a positive association between the quality of negotiated agreements and the extent to which negotiators had similar conceptualizations of their tasks in both intra- and intercultural negotiation. Moreover, Swaab and colleagues (2002) demonstrated a causal link by showing that the presence of shared mental models about a problem facilitated settlement in a subsequent phase of dispute resolution. Similar to these findings showing the beneficial effects of shared mental models on collaborative performance and negotiation (Mathieu, et al., 2000; Swaab et al., 2007; Van Boven and Thompson, 2003), shared mental models seem to be beneficial in increasing cooperation in ultimatum bargaining (Schelling, 1960).

According to Thompson (1990), the outcomes of negotiation can be classified into two categories: economic and social-psychological measures. While economic measures focus on the gains that negotiators get from the negotiation, including joint gains, social-psychological measures are negotiators' perceptions of the negotiation situation, the self, and the other party (Thompson, 1990), including shared identity, satisfaction of economic gains and process, and expectation of future relationship. Negotiation is a joint decision-making process, and the goal is the allocation of resources under conditions in which the negotiators have different preferences and utilities for the resources (Neal and Northcraft, 1991).

Chronologically, the end state of shared mental models and joint economic gains might emerge concurrently. However, as mentioned earlier, the process of mental model sharing continues during the whole negotiation, starting from the beginning of the interpersonal interaction. Therefore, shared mental models are formed throughout the whole negotiation process. In other words, shared mental models establish the social psychological foundation for joint economic gains, as well as social psychological outcomes such as subjective values (Curhan et al., 2006) and shared identity. Social identity-based group goal setting brings into play additional processes of social influence, cooperation and organic coordination, which also helps us understand why shared mental model and identity can lead to even more positive outcomes. At the same time, researchers point to the fact that goals do not have a universal, context-independent impact. Instead their impact is mediated by engagement of the self. Depending on the nature of the negotiation, including duration, consequences, and contingencies as a result of the negotiation, negotiators may bond and develop shared identity as a result. For instance, in cross-border merger and acquisition cases, the participants of those negotiations become colleagues as a result of the merger or acquisition, therefore fostering shared identity.

The process of cultivating shared cognition and shared identity can increase the likelihood of joint economic gains. This process has several advantages: increase the resources each party can claim, produce satisfaction and strengthen long-term relationships, decrease the possibility that future conflicts will arise, and benefit the larger community of which the negotiating group is a part, such as the overall organization (Brett, 1991; De Dreu et al., 2000; Mannix, 1993). A well-documented relationship would be: opportunities for joint gains arise when negotiators have a more accurate insight into the opponent's point values and developed a similarity between individual mental models (Brett and Okumura, 1998; Olekalns and Smith, 2003). The process of mental model and identity sharing would aid negotiators to see each other's perspective better. The higher the sharedness in shared cognition, the more smoothly negotiators reach consensus. The process of mental model sharing requires coordination, accurate interpretation of each other's messages, and a thorough sharing of important issues during the decision-making to achieve the optimal outcome for all parties. We acknowledge the possibility of generating joint gains as an important objective in negotiation (Brett, 2007; Requejo and Graham, 2008), can also facilitate the development of shared cognition and identity. Therefore the process of developing shared cognition is embedded in the whole exchange process of negotiating, directly or indirectly influencing the both social psychological and economic outcomes at the individual, collective, and contextual levels.

Proposition 9: Shared cognition developed throughout the negotiation process can have a positive impact on both social psychological and economic outcomes at the individual and collective levels.

DISCUSSION

In this chapter, we proposed a multilevel framework of shared cognition and identity in negotiation that integrates input antecedents, the dynamic development process, and output consequences from affective, informational, and relational factors. The variables we review and discuss here are by no means exclusive; we do however hope this framework might stimulate more comprehensive inquiries on these topics. We believe negotiation can provide a dynamic context to study shared cognition and identity. With few exceptions (Van Boven and Thompson, 2003; Olekalns and Smith, 2005; Liu et al., 2012a), we still know little about the comprehensive process of developing shared cognition in a multicultural world. Swaab et al. (2008) believed that social identity theorists have largely ignored processes of emergent shared mental models, and the relationship between shared mental models and group identification. They pointed out that negotiation provides an ideal context to examine the interactive process by which shared mental and group identities develop and subsequently influence negotiation outcome.

Although a few studies have examined the effects of integration on more than one outcome measures (e.g., De Dreu et al., 2000; Liu et al., 2012a), existing research typically only includes one economic outcome and some subjective outcomes (Curhan et al., 2006), without assessing a broader spectrum of outcome dimensions. Galinsky et al. (2002) show that objective and subjective outcome measures do not always converge. We believe that the shared cognition and identity developed during the process of negotiation influence both outcome quality and different aspects of perceptions (Rognes and Schei, 2010). Further empirical research could investigate the complex process and interactive patterns on the antecedents, development, and consequences of shared cognition and identity in various negotiation settings.

We feel an important direction for future research is to explore the dynamic interactive processes involving shared cognition and identity with multiple methods and sources of data. Qualitative research methods such as observations, journals, event recordings and concept maps could offer rich data and insights into how people construct and adjust their cognitive representations and identities. Such studies could shed light on the direct and immediate experience and perspectives of individual and groups of negotiators. Converging results from multiple theoretical perspectives and empirical methods will also help clarify relationships among the negotiators, the context, and the interactive processes.

REFERENCES

Adair, W.L. (2003). Integrative sequences and negotiation outcome in same- and mixed-culture. *International Journal of Conflict Management*, 14, 273–296.

Adair, W.L. and Brett, J.M. (2001). Negotiation behavior when cultures collide: The U.S. and Japan. *Journal of Applied Psychology*, 86(3), 371–385.
Akgun, A., Byrne, J., and Keskin, H. (2005). Knowledge networks in new product development projects: A transactive memory perspective. *Information and Management*, 42(8), 1105–1120.
Amanatullah, E.T. (2007). Negotiating too assertively: The unique social consequences of assertive behavior in self-representing female negotiators. Unpublished manuscript.
Amanatullah, E.T., Morris, M.W., and Curhan, J.R. (2008). Negotiators who give too much: Unmitigated communion, relational anxieties, and economic costs in distributive and integrative bargaining. *Journal of Personality and Social Psychology*, 95(3), 723–738.
Axelrod, R. (1976): *Structure of Decision – The cognitive maps of political elites*. Princeton, NJ: Princeton University Press.
Babcock, L. and Laschever, S. (2003). *Women don't ask: Negotiation and the gender divide*. Princeton, NJ: Princeton University Press.
Barrett, K.C. (1995). A functionalist approach to shame and guilt. In J.P. Tangney and K.W. Fischer (eds), *Self-conscious emotions: The psychology of shame, guilt, embarrassment, and pride* (pp. 25–63). New York: Guilford Press.
Barrett L.F., Mesquita B., Ochsner K.N., and Gross J.J. (2007). The experience of emotion. *Annual Review of Psychology*, 58, 373–403.
Barry, B. and Friedman, R. (1998). Bargainer characteristics in distributive and integrative negotiation: The role of personality and cognitive ability. *Journal of Personality and Social Psychology*, 74, 345–359.
Barsalou, L.W., Breazeal, C., and Smith, L.B. (2007). Cognition as coordinated non-cognition. *Cognitive Processing*, 8, 79–91.
Batson, C.D. and Moran, T. (1999). Empathy-induced altruism in a prisoner's dilemma. *European Journal of Social Psychology*, 29, 909–924.
Bazerman, M.H., Curhan, J.R., Moore, D.A., and Valley, K.L. (2000). Negotiation. *Annual Review of Psychology*, 51, 279–314.
Beersma, B. and De Dreu, C.K.W. (1999). Negotiation processes and outcomes in prosocially and egoistically motivated groups. *International Journal of Conflict Management*, 10, 385–402.
Beersma, B. and De Dreu, C.K.W. (2002). Integrative and distributive negotiation in small groups: Effects of task structure, decision rule, and social motive. *Organizational Behavior and Human Decision Processes*, 87, 227–252.
Bell, C. and Song, F. (2005). Emotions in the conflict process: An application of the cognitive appraisal model of emotions to conflict management. *International Journal of Conflict Management*, 16(1), 30–54.
Boonstra, J.J. (1998). Team working. The effects on the quality of working life, organizational climate and productivity. International Conference on Work and Work organization. University of Sheffield, 1–3 July, http://www.jaapboonstra.nl/publicaties/engelstalig/team%20working.pdf.
Bouas, K. and Komorita, S. (1996). Group discussion and cooperation in social dilemmas. *Personality and Social Psychology Bulletin*, 22, 1144–1150.
Bowles, H.R., Babcock, L., and Lai, L. (2007). Social incentives for gender differences in the propensity to initiate negotiations: Sometimes it does hurt to ask. *Organizational Behavior and Human Decision Processes*, 103, 84–103.
Brett, J.M. (1991). Negotiating group decisions. *Negotiation Journal*, 7(3), 291–310.
Brett, J.M. (2007). *Negotiating globally: How to negotiate deals, resolve disputes, and make decisions across cultural boundaries* (2nd edn). San Francisco, CA: Jossey-Bass.
Brett, J.M. and Okumura, T. (1998). Inter-and intracultural negotiation: U.S. and Japanese negotiators. *Academy of Management Journal*, 41(5), 495–510.
Brett, J.M., Shapiro, D.L., and Lytle, A.L. (1998). Breaking, bangles, and beads: Modeling the evolution of negotiating groups over time. In M.A. Neale, E.A. Mannix, and S. Blount-Lyons (eds), *Research on managing groups and teams: Time in groups* (Vol. 6, pp. 39–64). New York: Elsevier Science Press.

Burnham, T., McCabe, K., and Smith, V.L. (2000). Friend-or-foe? Intentionality priming in an extensive trust game. *Journal of Economic Behavior and Organization*, *43*(1), 57–73.

Butler, J.K. (1995). Behaviors, trust, and goal achievement in a win-win negotiating role-play. *Group and Organization Management*, *20*, 486–502.

Cannon-Bowers, J.A., Salas, E., and Converse, S. (1993). Shared mental models in expert team decision making. In J. Castellan Jr. (ed.), *Current issues in individual and group decision making* (pp. 221–246). Hillsdale, NJ: Erlbaum.

Carnevale, P.J. and Pruitt, D.G. (1992). Negotiation and mediation. *Annual Review of Psychology*, *43*, 531–582.

Chen, X.P. and Li, S. (2005). Cross-national differences in cooperative decision-making in mixed-motive business contexts: The mediating effect of vertical and horizontal individualism. *Journal of International Business Studies*, *36*(6), 622–636.

Chen, Y, Mannix, E., and Okumura, T. (2003). The importance of who you meet: The importance of self versus other concerns among negotiators in the United States, the People's Republic of China, and Japan. *Journal of Experimental Social Psychology*, *39*(1), 1–15.

Cheung, F.M., Leung, K., Fan, R.M., Song, W.Z., Zhang, J.X., and Zhang, J.P. (1996). Development of the Chinese Personality Assessment Inventory. *Journal of Cross Cultural Psychology*, *27*, 181–199.

Choi, D.W. (2010). Shared metacognition in integrative negotiation. *International Journal of Conflict Management*, *21*(3), 309–333.

Cooke, N.J., Kiekel, P.A., Salas, E., Stout, R.J., Bowers, C., and Cannon-Bowers, J. (2003). Measuring team knowledge: A window to the cognitive underpinnings of team performance. *Group Dynamics: Theory, Research and Practice*, *7*, 179–199.

Curhan, J.R., Elfenbein, H.A., and Xu, H. (2006). What do people value when they negotiate? Mapping the domain of subjective value in negotiation. *Journal of Personality and Social Psychology*, *91*, 493–512.

Curhan, J.R., Neale, M.A., Ross, L., and Rosencranz-Engelmann, J. (2008). Relational accommodation in negotiation: Effects of egalitarianism and gender on economic efficiency and relational capital. *Organizational Behavior and Human Decision Processes*, *107*, 192–205.

Damasio, A.R. (1994). *Descartes' error: Emotion, reason, and the human brain*. New York: Avon.

De Dreu, C.K.W. (2003). Time pressure and closing of the mind in negotiation. *Organizational Behavior and Human Decision Processes*, *91*, 280–295.

De Dreu, C.K.W. and Carnevale, P. (2003). Motivational bases for information processing and strategy in negotiation and conflict. In M.P. Zanna (ed.), *Advances in experimental social psychology* (Vol. 35). New York: Academic Press.

De Dreu, C.K.W. and Van Lange, P.A.M. (1995). The impact of social value orientations on negotiator cognition and behavior. *Personality and Social Psychology Bulletin*, *21*, 1178–1188.

De Dreu, C.K.W., Giebels, E. and Van de Vliert, E. (1998). Social motives and trust in integrative negotiation: The disruptive effects of punitive capability. *Journal of Applied Psychology*, *83*, 408–422.

De Dreu, C.K.W., Koole, S., and Steinel, W. (2000). Unfixing the fixed pie: A motivated information-processing approach to integrative negotiation. *Journal of Personality and Social Psychology*, *79*, 975–987.

De Dreu, C.K.W., Weingart, L.R., and Kwon, S. (2000). Influence of social motives on integrative negotiation: a meta-analytic review and test of two theories. *Journal of Personality and Social Psychology*, *78*(5), 889–905.

De Grada, E., Kruglanski, A.W., Mannetti, L., and Pierro, A. (1999). Motivated cognition and group interaction: need for closure and the contents and processes of collective negotiations. *Journal of Experimental Social Psychology*, *35*, 346–365.

Doosje, B., Ellemers, N., and Spears, R. (1999). Commitment and intergroup behavior. In N. Ellemers, R. Spears, and B. Doosje (eds), *Social identity: Context, commitment, content* (pp. 84–106). Oxford: Blackwell.

Earley, P.C. (1997). *Face, harmony, and social structure: an analysis of organizational behavior across cultures*. New York: Oxford University Press.

Eisenberger, R., Cotterell, N., and Marvel, J. (1987). Reciprocation ideology. *Journal of Personality Social Psychology*, 53, 743–750.

Elahee, M.N., Kirby, S.L., and Nasif, E. (2002). National culture, trust and perceptions about ethical behavior in intra- and cross-cultural negotiations: An analysis of the NAFTA Countries. *Thunderbird International Business Review*, 44(6), 799–818.

Ellemers, N. and Rink, F. (in press). Identity in work groups: The beneficial and detrimental consequences of multiple identities and group norms for collaboration and group performance. In S.R. Thye and E.J. Lawler (eds), *Advances in group processes* (Vol. 22). New York: Elsevier Science.

Ellemers, N., Spears, R., and Doosje, B. (1997). Sticking together or falling apart: Group identification as a psychological determinant of group commitment versus individual mobility. *Journal of Personality and Social Psychology*, 72, 123–140.

Ellemers, N., Wilke, H., and van Knippenberg, A. (1993). Effects of the legitimacy of low group or individual status on individual and collective status-enhancement strategies. *Journal of Personality and Social Psychology*, 64, 766–778.

Erll, A. and Nünning, A. (eds) (2008). *Cultural memory studies. An international and interdisciplinary handbook*. Berlin: De Gruyter.

Fiore, S.M., Salas, E., and Cannon-Bowers, J.A. (2001). Group dynamics and shared mental model development. In M. London (ed.), *How people evaluate others in organizations: Person perception and interpersonal judgment in industrial/organizational psychology* (pp. 309–336). Mahwah, NJ: Erlbaum.

Fischer, K.W. and Tangney, J.P. (1995). Self-conscious emotions and the affect revolution: Framework and overview. In J.P. Tangney and K.W. Fischer (eds), *Self-conscious emotions: The psychology of shame, guilt, embarrassment, and pride* (pp. 3–24). New York: Guilford.

Fiske, S.T. and Taylor, S.E. (1991). *Social cognition*. New York and UK: Mcgraw-Hill.

Forgas, J.P. and George, J.M. (2001). Affective influences on judgments and behavior in organizations: An information processing perspective. *Organizational Behavior and Human Decision Processes*, 86, 3–34.

Fu, H., Morris, M.W., Lee, S., Chao, M., Chiu, C., and Hong, H. (2007). Epistemic motives and cultural conformity: Need for closure, culture, and context as determinants of conflict judgments. *Journal of Personality and Social Psychology*, 92(2), 191–207.

Gaertner, L., Iuzzini, J., Guerrero Witt, M., and Oriña, M.M. (2006). Us without them: Evidence for an intragroup origin of positive ingroup regard. *Journal of Personality and Social Psychology*, 90, 426–439.

Galinsky, A.D., Seiden, V., Kim, P.H., and Medvec, V.H. (2002). The dissatisfaction of having your first offer accepted: The role of counterfactual thinking in negotiations. *Personality and Social Psychology Bulletin*, 28, 271–283.

Gelfand, M.J., Major, V., Raver, J.L., Nishii, L.H., and O'Brien, K. (2006). Negotiating relationally: The dynamics of relational self in negotiations. *Academy of Management Review*, 31, 427–451.

Gentner, D. (2002). Mental models, psychology of. In N.J. Smelser and P.B. Bates (eds), *International encyclopedia of the social and behavioral sciences* (pp. 9683–9687). Amsterdam, Netherlands: Elsevier.

Gibbins, M., Salterio, S., and Webb, A. (2001). Evidence about auditor-client management negotiation concerning the client's financial reporting. *Journal of Accounting Research*, 39(3), 535–563.

Gibson, C.B., Maznevski, M., and Kirkman, B.L. (2008). When does culture matter? In R.S. Bhagat and R.M. Steers (eds), *Handbook of Culture, Organizations, and Work*. Cambridge: Cambridge University Press.

Giebels, E., De Dreu, C.K.W., and Van de Vliert, E. (2000). Interdependence in negotiation: Effects of social motive and exit options on distributive and integrative negotiation. *European Journal of Social Psychology*, 30, 255–272.

Gillespie, A. and Richardson, B. (2011). Exchanging social positions: Enhancing intersubjective coordination within a joint task. *European Journal of Social Psychology*, 41, 608–616.
Gillespie, J.J., Brett, J.M., and Weingart, L.R. (2000). Interdependence, social motives, and outcome satisfaction in multiparty negotiation. *European Journal of Social Psychology*, 30(6), 779–797.
Graham, J., Mintu, A., and Rodgers, W. (1994). Explorations of negotiation behaviors in ten foreign cultures using a model developed in the United States. *Management Science*, 40, 72–95.
Greenberg, G. and Baron, R. (2000). *Behavior in organizations*. Upper Saddle River, NJ: Prentice Hall.
Gruder, C.L. (1971). Relationships with opponent and partner in mixed-motive bargaining. *Journal of Conflict Resolution*, 15(3), 403–416.
Gunia, B.C., Brett, J.M., Nandkeolyar, A., and Kamdar, D. (2011). Paying a price: Culture, trust, and negotiation consequences. *Journal of Applied Psychology*, 96(4), 774–789.
Gurtner, A., Tschan, F., Semmer, N.K., and Nägele, C. (2007). Getting groups to develop good strategies: Effects of reflexivity interventions on team process, team performance, and shared mental models. *Organizational Behavior and Human Decision Processes*, 102, 127–142.
Harmon-Jones E. (2003). Anger and the behavioral approach system. *Personality and Individual Differences*, 35(5), 995–1005.
He, J., Butler, B.S., and King, W.R. (2007). Team cognition: Development and evolution in software project teams. *Journal of Management Information Systems*, 24(2), 261–292.
Jans, L., Postmes, T., and Van der Zee, K. (2011). The induction of shared identity: The positive role of individual distinctiveness for groups. *Personality and Social Psychology Bulletin*, 37(8), 1130–1141.
Johnson-Laird, P.N. (1989). Mental models. In M.I. Posner (ed.), *Foundations of cognitive science*. Cambridge: The MIT Press.
Kahan, J.P. (1968). Effects of level of aspiration in an experimental bargaining situation. *Journal of Personality and Social Psychology*, 8, 154–159.
Kerr, N.L. and Tindale, R.S. (2004). Group performance and decision making. *Annual Review of Psychology*, 55, 623–655.
Klimoski, R., and Mohammed, S. (1994). Team mental model: Construct or metaphor? *Journal of Management*, 20, 403–437.
Kray, L.J. and Gelfand, M. (2009). Relief versus regret: The impact of gender and negotiating norm ambiguity on reactions to having one's first offer accepted. *Social Cognition*, 27, 418–436.
Kray, L.J. and Thompson, L. (2005). Gender and negotiation. *Research in Organizational Behavior*, 26, 102–182.
Kray, L.J., Thompson, L., and Galinsky, A. (2001). Battle of the sexes: Gender stereotype confirmation and reactance in negotiations. *Journal of Personality and Social Psychology*, 80, 942–958.
Kray, L.J., Reb, J., Galinsky, A.D., and Thompson, L. (2004). Stereotype reactance at the bargaining table: The effect of stereotype activation and power on claiming and creating value. *Personality and Social Psychology Bulletin*, 30, 399–411.
Kruglanski, A.W. and Webster, D.M. (1996). Motivated closing of the mind: "seizing" and "freezing". *Psychological Review*, 103, 263–283.
Kruglanski, A.W., Webster, D.M., and Klem, A. (1993). Motivated resistance and openness to persuasion in the presence or absence of prior information. *Journal of Personality and Social Psychology*, 65(5), 861–876.
Kulik, C.T. and Olekalns, M. (2012). Negotiating the gender divide: Lessons from the negotiation and organizational behavior literatures. *Journal of Management*, 38, 1387–1415.
Langan-Fox, J., Wirth, A., Code, S., Langfield-Smith, K., and Wirth, A. (2001). Analyzing shared and team mental models. *International Journal of Industrial Ergonomics*, 28, 99–112.
Lewicki, R.J., Barry, B., Saunders, D.M., and Minton, J.W. (2003), *Negotiation*. New York: McGraw-Hill.

Lewis, K. (2004). Knowledge and performance in knowledge-worker teams: A longitudinal study of transactive memory systems. *Management Science, 50*(11), 1519–1533.

Loewenstein, G.F., Thompson, L., and Bazerman, M.H. (1989). Social utility and decision making in interpersonal contexts. *Journal of Personality and Social Psychology, 57*(3), 426–441.

Liu, L.A. and Dale, C. (2009). Using mental models to study cross-cultural interactions. In C. Nakata (ed.), *Beyond Hofstede: Culture frameworks for convergence marketing and management* (pp. 222–246). Hampshire, UK: Palgrave Macmillan.

Liu, L.A., Friedman, R.A., Barry, B., Gelfand, M.J., and Zhang, Z-X. (2012a). The dynamics of consensus building in intracultural and intercultural negotiations. *Administrative Science Quarterly, 57*(2), 269–304.

Liu, W., Friedman, R., and Hong, Y-Y. (2012b). Culture and accountability in negotiation: Recognizing the importance of in-group relations, *Organizational Behavior and Human Decision Processes, 117*, 221–234.

MacMillan, J., Entin, E.E., and Serfaty, D. (2004). Communication overhead: The hidden cost of team cognition. In E. Salas and S.M. Fiore (eds), *Team Cognition: Understanding the factors that drive process and performance* (pp. 61–82). Washington, DC: American Psychological Association.

Mannix, E.A. (1993). Organizations as resource dilemmas: The effects of power balance on group decision making. *Organizational Behavior and Human Decision Processes, 55*, 1–22.

Marks, M.A., Sabella, M.J., Burke, C.S., and Zaccaro, S.J. (2002). The impact of cross-training on team effectiveness. *Journal of Applied Psychology, 87*, 3–13.

Marks, M.A., Zaccaro, S.J., and Mathieu, J.E. (2000). Performance implications of leader briefings and team-interaction training for team adaptation to novel environments. *Journal of Applied Psychology, 85*, 971–986.

Mathieu, J.E., Heffner, T.S., Goodwin, G.F., Cannon-Bowers, J.A., and Salas, E. (2005). Scaling the quality of teammates' mental models: Equifinality and normative comparisons. *Journal of Organizational Behavior, 26*(1), 37–56.

Mathieu, J.E., Heffner, T.S., Goodwin, G.F., Salas, E., and Cannon-Bowers, J.A. (2000). The influence of shared mental models on team process and performance. *Journal of Applied Psychology, 85*(2), 273–283.

Minsky, M. (1975): A framework for representing knowledge. In P.H. Winston (ed.), *The psychology of computer vision*. New York: McGraw-Hill.

Mintu-Wimsatt, A., Rosanna G. and Calantone, R. (2005). Risk, trust and the problem solving approach: A cross cultural negotiation study. *Journal of Marketing Theory and Practice, 13*(1), 52–61.

Mohammed, S. and Dumville, B.C. (2001). Team mental models in a team knowledge framework: expanding theory and measurement across disciplinary boundaries. *Journal of Organizational Behavior, 22*, 89–106.

Neale, M.A. and Bazerman, M.H. (1991). *Cognition and rationality in negotiation*. New York: Free Press.

Neale, M.A. and Northcraft, G.B. (1991). Behavioral negotiation theory: A framework for conceptualizing dyadic bargaining. In L. Cummings and B. Straw (eds), *Research in organizational behavior*, Connecticut: Jai Press.

Ng, T.B.P. and Tan, H.T. (2003). Effects of authoritative guidance availability and audit committee effectiveness on auditors' judgments in an auditor-client negotiation context. *Accounting Review, 78*(3), 801–818.

Oetzel, J.G. and Ting-Toomey, S. (2003). Face concerns in interpersonal conflict: A cross-cultural empirical test of the face negotiation theory. *Communication Research, 30*, 599–624.

Olekalns, M. and Smith, P.L. (2000). Understanding optimal outcomes: The role of strategic sequences in competitive negotiations. *Human Communication Research, 26*(4), 527–557.

Olekalns, M. and Smith, P.L. (2003). Social motives in negotiation: The relationship between dyad composition, negotiation processes and outcomes. *International Journal of Conflict Management: Special Issue on Processes in Negotiation, 14*, 233–254.

Olekalns, M. and Smith, P.L. (2005). Cognitive representations of negotiation. *Australian Journal of Management*, 30, 57–76.

Ouwerkerk, J., de Gilder, D., and de Vries, N.K. (2000). When the going gets tough, the tough get going: Social identification and individual effort in intergroup competition. *Personality and Social Psychology Bulletin*, 26, 1550–1559.

Patterson, M.L. (1983). *Nonverbal behavior: A functional perspective*. New York: Springer-Verlag.

Perugini, M., Gallucci, M., Presaghi, F., and Ercolani, A.P. (2003). The personal norm of reciprocity. *European Journal of Personality*, 17, 251–283.

Polzer, J.T., Mannix, E.A., and Neale, M.A. (1998). Interest alignment and coalitions in multiparty negotiation. *Academy of Management Journal*, 41, 42–54.

Postmes, T., Haslam, S.A., and Swaab, R.I. (2005a). Social influence in small groups: An interactive model of social identity formation. *European Review of Social Psychology*, 16, 1–42.

Postmes, T., Spears, R., and Cihangir, S. (2001). Quality of decision making and group norms. *Journal of Personality and Social Psychology*, 80(6), 918–930.

Postmes, T., Spears, R., and Lea, M. (2000). The formation of group norms in computer-mediated communication. *Human Communication Research*, 26, 341–371.

Postmes, T., Spears, R., Novak, R., and Lee, T. (2005b). Individuality and social influence in groups: Inductive and deductive routes to group identity. *Journal of Personality and Social Psychology*, 89, 747–763.

Pozzebon, M. and Pinsonneault, A. (2012). The dynamics of client-consultant relationships: exploring the interplay of power and knowledge. *Journal of Information Technology*, 27(1), 35–56.

Pruitt, D.G. and Carnevale, P.J. (1993), *Negotiation in social conflict*. Pacific Grove, CA: Brooks/Cole.

Ren, Y. and Argote, L. (2011). Transactive memory systems 1985–2010: An integrative framework of key dimensions, antecedents, and consequences. *The Academy of Management Annals*, 5(1), 189–229.

Rentsch, J.R. and Woehr, D.J. (2004). Quantifying congruence in cognitions: Social relations modeling and team member schema similarity. In E. Salas and S.M. Fiore (eds), *Team cognition: Understanding the factors that drive process and performance* (pp. 11–31). Washington, DC: American Psychological Association.

Requejo, W.H. and Graham, J.H. (2008). *Global negotiation: The new rules*. New York: Palgrave Macmillan.

Rognes, J.K., and Schei, V. (2010). Understanding the integrative approach to conflict management. *Journal of Managerial Psychology*, 25, 82–97.

Roseman, I.J., Wiest, C., and Swartz, T.S. (1994). Phenomenology, behaviors, and goals differentiate discrete emotions. *Journal of Personality and Social Psychology*, 67, 206–221.

Rubin, J.Z. and Brown, B. (1975). *The social psychology of bargaining and negotiation*. New York: Academic Press.

Salas, E., Sims, D.E., and Burke, C.S. (2005). Is there a big five in teamwork? *Small Group Research*, 36 (5), 555–599.

Savage, G.T., Blair, J.D., and Sorenson, R.L. (1989). Consider both relationships and substance when negotiating strategically. *The Academy of Management Executive*, 3(1), 37–48.

Savelkoul, M., Gesthuizen, M., and Scheepers, P. (2011). Explaining relationships between ethnic diversity and informal social capital across European countries and regions: Test of constrict, conflict and contact theory. *Social Science Research*, 40, 1091–1107.

Schelling, T.C. (1960). *The strategy of conflict*. Cambridge, MA: Harvard University Press.

Schippers, M.C., Den Hartog, D.N., Koopman, P.L., and Wienk, J.A. (2003). Diversity and team outcomes: The moderating effects of outcome interdependence and group longevity and the mediating effect of reflexivity. *Journal of Organizational Behavior*, 24, 779–802.

Small, D.A., Gelfand, M., Babcock, L., and Gettman, H. (2007). Who goes to the bargaining table? The influence of gender and framing on the initiation of negotiation. *Journal of Personality and Social Psychology*, 93, 600–613.

Smith, H.J., Tyler, T.R., and Huo, Y.J. (2003). Interpersonal treatment, social identity and organizational behavior. In S.A. Haslam, D. van Knippenberg, M.J. Platow, and N. Ellemers (eds), *Social identity at work: Developing theory for organizational practice* (pp. 155–171). Philadelphia, PA: Psychology Press.

Swaab, R., Postmes, T., and Spears, R. (2008). Identity formation in multiparty negotiations. *British Journal of Social Psychology*, 47, 167–187.

Swaab, R.I., Postmes, T., Van Beest, I., and Spears, R. (2007). Shared cognition as a product of, and precursor to, shared social identity: The role of communication in negotiations. *Personality and Social Psychology Bulletin*, 33(2), 187–199.

Swaab, R.I., Postmes, T., Neijens, P., Kiers, M.H., and Dumay, A.C.M. (2002). Multi-party negotiation support: The role of visualization's influence on the development of shared mental models. *Journal of Management Information Systems*, 19, 129–150.

Tajfel, H. and Turner, J.C. (1979). An integrative theory of intergroup conflict. In W.G. Austin and S. Worchel (eds), *The social psychology of intergroup relations* (pp. 33–48). Monterey, CA: Brooks/Cole.

Thompson, L. (1990). Negotiation behavior and outcomes: Empirical evidence and theoretical issues. *Psychological Bulletin*, 108, 515–532.

Thompson, L. (2005). *The Mind and Heart of the Negotiator* (3rd edn). Upper Saddle River, NJ: Pearson Prentice Hall.

Thompson, L. and Fine, G. (1999). Socially shared cognition, affect and behavior: A review and integration. *Personality and Social Psychology Review*, 3(4), 278–302.

Thompson, L.L., Mannix, E.A., and Bazerman, M.H. (1988). Negotiation: Effects of decision rule, agenda and aspiration. *Journal of Personality and Social Psychology*, 54, 86–95.

Tindale, R.S. and Kameda, T. (2000). Social sharedness as a unifying theme for information processing in groups. *Group Processes and Intergroup Relations*, 3, 123–140.

Ting-Toomey, S. (2005). The matrix of face: An updated face-negotiation theory. In W.B. Gudykunst (ed.), *Theorizing about intercultural communication* (pp. 71–92). Thousand Oaks, CA: Sage.

Turner, J.C., Hogg, M.A., Oakes, P.J., Reicher, S.D., and Wetherell, M.S. (1987). *Rediscovering the social group: A self-categorization theory*. Oxford, UK: Blackwell.

Valley, K.L., Neale, M.A., and Mannix, E.A. (1995). Friends, lovers, colleagues, strangers: the effects of relationships on the process and outcome of dyadic negotiation. *Research on Negotiation in Organizations*, 5, 65–93.

Van Boven, L. and Thompson, L. (2003). A look into the mind of the negotiator: Mental models in negotiation. *Group Processes and Intergroup Relations*, 6(4), 387–404.

Van Leeuwen, E., van Knippenberg, D., and Ellemers, N. (2003). Continuing and changing group identities: The effects of merging on social identification and ingroup bias. *Personality and Social Psychology Bulletin*, 29, 679–690.

Webster, D.M., and Kruglanski, A.W. (1994). Individual differences in need for cognitive closure. *Journal of Personality and Social Psychology*, 67(6), 1049–1062.

Weingart, L.R. and Brett, J.M. (1998). *Mixed motive orientations in negotiating groups: Convergence and reaching agreement*. Evanston, IL: Dispute Resolution Research Center, Northwestern University.

Weingart, L.R., Bennett, R.J., and Brett, J.M. (1993). The impact of consideration of issues and motivational orientation on group negotiation process and outcome. *Journal of Applied Psychology*, 78, 504–517.

Weingart, L.R., Hyder, E.H., and Prietula, M.J. (1996). Knowledge matters: The effect of tactical descriptions on negotiation behavior and outcome. *Journal of Personality and Social Psychology*, 70, 1205–1217.

Weingart, L.R., Simons, T., Robinson, S., and Brett, J. (1990). Towers II coding manual. Unpublished manuscript, Carnegie Mellon University.

Weingart, L.R., Thompson, L., Bazerman, M.H., and Carroll, J.S. (1999). Tactical behavior and negotiation outcomes. *International Journal of Conflict Management*, 1, 7–31.

West, M.A. (1996). Reflexivity and work group effectiveness: A conceptual integration. In M.A. West (ed.), *Handbook of work group psychology* (pp. 525–579). London: Wiley.

Wolf, S.T., Cohen, T.R., Kirchner, J.L., Rea, A., Montoya, R.M., and Insko, C.A. (2009). Reducing intergroup conflict through the consideration of future consequences. *European Journal of Social Psychology*, *39*(5), 831–841.

Wood, V.F. and Bell, P.A. (2008). Predicting interpersonal conflict resolution styles from personality characteristics. *Personality and Individual Differences*, *45*, 126–131.

Yang, H.D., Kang, H.R., and Mason, R.M. (2008). An exploratory study on meta skills in software development teams: Antecedent cooperation skills and personality for shared mental models. *European Journal of Information Systems*, *17*, 47–61.

Zhang, Z.X. and Han, Y.L. (2007). The effects of reciprocation wariness on negotiation behavior and outcomes. *Group Decision and Negotiation*, *16*(6), 507–525.

5. The demise of the 'rational' negotiator: emotional forces in conflict and negotiation
Gerben A. Van Kleef and Marwan Sinaceur

Conflict is a natural fact of life. Whether we focus on interactions between individuals, groups, organizations, or nations—conflicts are omnipresent (Pruitt and Carnevale, 1993). Often, the divergent interests that lie at the heart of conflict give rise to intense emotions, which may in turn strongly influence conflict development (Barry and Oliver, 1996; Morris and Keltner, 2000; Van Kleef et al., 2008). This means that attempts at reconciling such divergent interests through negotiation are also likely to be pervaded by emotions. In this chapter we review the state of the art of theory and research on the role of emotions in negotiation. The first part of the chapter is devoted to a review of influential theorizing and research, which is organized according to a distinction between intrapersonal effects of emotional experiences and interpersonal effects of emotional expressions. In the second part of the chapter we identify important caveats in the current knowledge and outline several avenues for future research.

Before diving into the literature, let us consider some conceptual issues. Various terms are used in reference to emotional phenomena, the most common being affect, mood, and emotion. Affect is the most general term, referring to a subjective feeling that can range from diffuse moods such as cheerfulness or depression to specific and acute emotions such as happiness or anger. The word affect is also used to refer to relatively stable individual dispositions (i.e., trait positive and negative affect; Watson et al., 1988). Emotion and mood are generally seen as subtypes of affect. They are differentiated by the degree to which they are directed toward a specific stimulus—be it a person, an object, or an event (Ekman and Davidson, 1994). Most emotion theories hold that discrete emotions arise as a result of an individual's conscious or unconscious evaluation (appraisal) of some event as positively or negatively relevant to a particular concern or goal (Frijda, 1986; Lazarus, 1991). Accordingly, emotions are directed toward something, or, more typically, someone (e.g., a colleague, a customer, a negotiation partner), whereas moods are not directed at anything in particular—one can feel cheerful or grumpy for no apparent reason. Emotions are also comparatively short-lived and intense, whereas moods tend to be more enduring and mild. Furthermore, unlike moods, emotions are characterized by distinct subjective experiences, physiological reactions, expressions, and action tendencies (Ekman and Davidson, 1994).

In conceptualizing the role of affect in negotiation, it is useful to make a distinction between *intra*personal effects and *inter*personal effects (Morris and Keltner, 2000; Van Kleef et al., 2004a). Intrapersonal effects refer to the influence of an individual's affective state on his or her own cognitions, strategies, perceptions, and behaviors. Interpersonal effects, on the other hand, refer to the influence of one individual's emotional expressions on one or more other individuals in the social context. Such emotional expressions may or may not reflect the privately experienced feelings of the individual. Some emotional expressions are involuntary and spontaneous, whereas others may be strategic in that they are voluntary and premeditated. For example, emotions may be strategically feigned, exaggerated, or suppressed in a calculated attempt to influence others (Côté and Hideg, 2011; Kopelman et al., 2006; Sinaceur and Tiedens, 2006; Van Kleef et al., 2011). We discuss the intrapersonal and interpersonal effects of emotions in turn.

INTRAPERSONAL EFFECTS OF EMOTIONS

Theoretical Developments

Since the late 1970s, several theoretical perspectives on the intrapersonal consequences of affective states have emerged. Three of these perspectives are particularly relevant to the role of emotion in negotiation. First, the affect-as-information model (Schwarz and Clore, 1983) posits that people use their affect as information when deciding how to respond to social situations. The model posits that when evaluating objects or belief statements, people often act as though they ask themselves, "How do I feel about it?" and then use their feelings directly as input to their judgment. Thus, according to the affect-as-information model, individuals may "misattribute" their pre-existing, unrelated mood state as pertaining to the target of their judgment (see Schachter and Singer, 1962). Accordingly, only moods that have not (yet) been attributed to a source (e.g., the weather) should have judgmental consequences. For example, an ill-tempered negotiator who is unaware of the cause of his or her bad temper may attribute the bad mood to the counterpart's latest offer, resulting in a negative impression of the other and a bad feeling about the other's proposal. Likewise, a negotiator who is in a good mood may infer that s/he is satisfied with the counterpart's offer. However, a negotiator who is aware that his or her mood was caused by the weather should be less likely to use this mood as input in the negotiation.

Second, according to affect priming models, moods and emotions influence social thinking and behavior by selectively priming related ideas and memories that are part of an associative network, thereby facilitating their use when planning and executing behavior (Bower, 1981; Bower and Forgas, 2001; Isen et al., 1978). In other words, these models assume that mood effects on judgment are mediated by positive or negative associations with the object of judgment. A good mood is hypothesized to function as a cue that temporarily activates positive cognitions that influence the evaluation of subsequent stimuli. Conversely, a bad mood increases the accessibility of negative cognitions. Specifically, mood effects may occur through selective attention, selective encoding, and/or selective retrieval of affect-congruent information. For example, a negotiator in a positive mood may see his or her partner's offer through rose-tinted glasses and focus on its favorable aspects, whereas a negotiator in a bad mood may focus on the unfavorable aspects of the other's proposal.

Third, the affect infusion model (AIM; Forgas, 1995) offers a way of integrating the affect-as-information and affect priming perspectives. According to the AIM, the two models suggest complementary processes of affect infusion that operate under different circumstances. Which process dominates is assumed to depend on the decision maker's information processing strategy. Four such strategies are distinguished: direct access, motivated, heuristic, and substantive processing. The first two are relatively closed to affective influences, because individuals either rely on prior evaluations (direct access) or have a strong motivational goal that guides their decision (motivated processing). The latter two processes, by contrast, are relatively open to affect infusion. When a heuristic processing style is adopted (e.g., when the judgment is of low personal relevance or little cognitive capacity is available), individuals may directly infer their judgments from their prevailing mood state (as specified by the affect-as-information model). In situations that promote substantive processing (e.g., high personal relevance and sufficient cognitive capacity), affect infusion is more likely to occur through the selective priming of information used in computing a judgment (as specified in the affect priming model). In sum, the AIM maintains that affective influences on judgments vary as a function of the processing strategy used. It suggests that our negotiator's good or bad mood should have a stronger impact on his or her decisions and behavior when a heuristic or substantive rather than a direct access or motivated processing style is adopted.

Although different in their outlook—especially with regard to the underlying processes—the predictions that can be derived from these models are largely complementary. At the most general level, these models predict affect-congruent influences on social judgments and behavior, such that experienced positive affect (both moods and emotions) inspires cooperative behavior, and experienced negative affect fuels competitive behavior. Thus, negotiators in a positive affective state should be expected to make more generous offers and adopt more cooperative strategies than those in a negative affective state.

The Empirical Record

The first study on the intrapersonal effects of positive affect on negotiation behavior was conducted by Carnevale and Isen (1986). They manipulated negotiators' moods by means of humorous cartoons and a small gift, and found that participants in a positive mood exhibited more cooperation and problem solving than did negotiators in a neutral mood. Compatible findings have been obtained in subsequent research using a variety of affect manipulations (Baron, 1990; Baron et al., 1990; Forgas, 1998; Kramer et al., 1993) as well as measures of state affect (Anderson and Thompson, 2004). For example, Forgas (1998) used a false-feedback technique to manipulate participants' moods. He found that participants who were led to believe that they had performed well on a verbal ability test (and who were therefore in a good mood) planned and reported more cooperative and fewer competitive bargaining strategies than did those who received no feedback (neutral mood) or negative feedback (sad mood) on their performance. The link between negative affect and competition seems to be quite robust, as it has also been observed in various types of experimental games, including resource dilemmas (Knapp and Clark, 1991) and prisoner's dilemma games (Kassinove et al., 2002).

In another classic study, Pillutla and Murnighan (1996) manipulated the extent to which recipients of an ultimatum offer could evaluate the fairness of the offer by providing either complete or incomplete information about the amount of money that was to be divided. They found that participants were more likely to reject an offer if they were able to assess its unfairness and, more important, that this effect could be explained by higher levels of experienced anger. Although this represents an intrapersonal effect of anger (i.e., an effect of the participant's own anger on his or her own behavior), the emotion in this study is more social than the emotions in the studies described above, in the sense that the anger was felt towards the opponent (as opposed to feeling good or bad due to bogus feedback or a gift from the experimenter).

Later studies have shown that increased rejection occurs for anger (as in Pillutla and Murnighan's 1996 study) but not for sadness, and that the effect is attenuated when the recipient misattributes his or her anger to an unrelated cause (Srivastava et al., 2009)—a finding that is in line with the affect-as-information model. Interestingly, other work has shown that rejection rates of unfair offers are reduced when recipients can convey their negative feelings to the proposer by sending an (angry) message, which presumably reduces the desire to engage in costly punishment (Xiao and Houser, 2005). Other studies have found compatible effects. For instance, Allred et al. (1997) found that negotiators with high levels of anger and low levels of compassion had less concern for their counterpart's interests, achieved lower joint gains, and had less desire to work with the other in the future than did negotiators who had more positive emotional regard for the other party.

Switching to a different class of emotions, Ketelaar and Au (2003) examined the effects of guilt in repeated social bargaining games. In one experiment they showed that participants who had been experimentally induced to feel guilty about their previous (uncooperative) behavior in a prisoner's dilemma game displayed higher levels of cooperation in the subsequent round of the game than did those who had not been induced to feel guilty, a finding that is in line with the idea that people keep track of their good and bad deeds (Monin and Miller, 2001). In a second experiment they demonstrated that self-reported feelings of guilt were also related to increased cooperation in an ultimatum game. These findings are consistent with theorizing by Frank (1988), who emphasized the important role that emotions serve in solving problems of commitment. The idea is that the experience of certain emotions (such as guilt) promotes the adoption of behavioral strategies that fare well in repeated social bargaining games. More specifically, Frank's commitment model proposes that emotion helps to solve the problem of overcoming the attraction of immediate rewards, leading individuals to make binding commitments to forego their short-term self-interests in order to pursue a more effective long-term strategy. In Frank's analysis this functionality is primarily located at the intrapersonal level of analysis (e.g., a person's feelings of guilt lead that person to behave more cooperatively towards someone else), but guilt may also have beneficial interpersonal effects, as we shall see below.

Brooks and Schweitzer (2011) recently focused attention on another previously neglected emotional state: anxiety. In a series of experiments, they experimentally induced feelings of anxiety or neutral affect in participants. Their experiments revealed that, compared to participants in an affectively neutral state, those who felt anxious expected lower outcomes, made lower first offers, responded more quickly to their counterpart's offers, exited the bargaining situation earlier, and ultimately obtained worse outcomes. Brooks and Schweitzer further found that the effects of anxiety are buffered by self-efficacy. In a related vein, O'Connor et al. (2010) showed that stress decreases negotiators' performance, but that the negotiator's appraisal of the looming negotiation moderates this effect. When a negotiation is appraised as a threat, negotiators experience stress, behave passively, develop inaccurate perceptions of their counterpart, and reach low-quality outcomes. These effects are attenuated when the negotiation is appraised as a challenge.

This overview of studies on the intrapersonal effects of moods and emotions in negotiations shows that emotional states have pervasive effects on negotiators' cognitions and behaviors. The effects of general positive versus negative affect are straightforward and consistent with the predictions of the affect-as-information, affect priming, and affect infusion models: Negotiators who experience positive affect are generally more cooperative than those who experience negative affect. More recent studies on the effects of discrete emotions in negotiations paint a somewhat more complicated picture, however, which cannot be fully explained in terms of the various models of affect infusion. It seems that negative emotions such as anger inspire competitive negotiation behavior, whereas negative emotions such as guilt and anxiety fuel more cooperative behavior. These apparent inconsistencies can be accounted for by appraisal theories of emotion (e.g., Frijda, 1986; Roseman, 1984; Scherer et al., 2001; Smith et al., 1993), which hold that each emotion arises as a result of a unique combination of appraisals (or evaluations) of the situation (e.g., whether the situation is favorable or unfavorable, who is to blame or credit for the situation), and that each emotion is associated with a particular pattern of action tendencies (e.g., anger is associated with a tendency towards aggression and hostility, whereas guilt is associated with a tendency to remedy harm inflicted upon another person). This points to the importance of examining discrete emotions instead of diffuse positive versus negative affect, an issue to which we return below.

INTERPERSONAL EFFECTS OF EMOTIONS

Theoretical Developments

Inspired by the early writings of Darwin (1872), researchers have increasingly come to emphasize that emotions do not occur merely *within* individuals, but also *between* individuals. Although emotions can be privately experienced, they are often expressed in one way or another. People may be unaware that their inner feelings are reflected on their faces, in their voices, in their bodily postures, or in their choice of words (Ekman and O'Sullivan, 1991; Manstead et al., 1984; Scherer et al., 1985); they may actively share their emotional experiences with others (Rimé et al., 1991); or they may purposefully express emotions to influence others (Clark et al., 1996; Fitness, 2000; Sinaceur and Tiedens, 2006; Van Kleef et al., 2011). Regardless of whether they are spontaneous or premeditated, emotional expressions are often observed by others, who in turn respond to them. This idea is at the heart of social-functional approaches to emotion, which maintain that emotions not only influence those who experience them, but also those who observe them (Fischer and Manstead, 2008; Frijda and Mesquita, 1994; Hareli and Rafaeli, 2008; Keltner and Haidt, 1999; Oatley and Jenkins, 1992; Parkinson, 1996; Van Kleef, 2009).

Emotions as Social Information (EASI) theory (Van Kleef, 2009; 2010; Van Kleef et al., 2010; 2011) integrates theoretical notions of various social-functional approaches in a unifying theory of the interpersonal effects of emotional expressions. EASI theory posits that the interpersonal effects of emotions come about via two distinct processes—affective reactions and inferential processes—the relative importance of which depends on the information processing depth of the perceiver of the emotional expression and on social-contextual factors that influence the perceived appropriateness of the emotional expression.

One type of affective reaction is produced by emotional contagion, the tendency to catch other people's emotions (Hatfield et al., 1994). "Primitive" emotional contagion occurs when individuals mimic others' nonverbal displays of emotion (e.g., facial, vocal, and postural expressions) and come to feel the accompanying emotional state via afferent feedback (i.e., physiological feedback from facial, vocal, and postural movements; e.g., Hawk et al., 2012; Hess and Blairy, 2001; Neumann and Strack, 2000). In addition, "non-primitive" emotional contagion can occur via processes that do *not* require mimicry, such as classical conditioning and perspective taking. Thus, emotional contagion can occur even in the absence of face-to-face interaction and mimicry, for instance through computer-mediated interaction (e.g., Cheshin et al., 2011; Friedman et al., 2004; Van Kleef et al., 2004a), perspective taking (Hawk et al., 2011), or social appraisal processes (Parkinson and Simons, 2009). As a result of these processes, individuals tend to catch others' emotions on a moment-to-moment basis, not just from their facial displays, but also from vocal, postural, and verbal expressions. The resulting feeling states may in turn influence judgments and decisions via the various types of affect infusion discussed above. In addition to emotional contagion, affective reactions may take the form of favorable or unfavorable impressions (Knutson, 1996; Van Kleef, 2009). Expressions of positive emotions tend to inspire positive impressions, and negative emotions negative impressions (Clark and Taraban, 1991). Such impressions may in turn shape behavior. For instance, individuals tend to help others whom they like and to deny help to others whom they do not like (Clark et al., 1996).

Another way in which emotional expressions exert interpersonal effects is by triggering inferential processes in observers (Van Kleef, 2009). Specific emotions arise in response to appraisals (interpretations) of specific situations (Frijda, 1986; Lazarus, 1991). For instance, sadness arises when one faces irrevocable loss and experiences low coping potential, and guilt arises when one feels that one has transgressed some social norm or moral imperative (Scherer et al., 2001; Smith et al., 1993). Because discrete emotions have such distinct appraisal patterns, they potentially provide a wealth of information to observers (Van Kleef, 2010). For instance, emotional expressions convey information about the expresser's feelings (Ekman, 1993), social intentions (Fridlund, 1994), and orientation toward other people (Hess et al., 2000; Knutson, 1996). In addition, observers may make inferences about the expresser's appraisal of the situation (Manstead and Fischer, 2001; Van Doorn et al., 2012). This is illustrated by classic work on social referencing, which revealed that infants are more likely to cross a visual cliff when their mother smiles at them than when she looks fearful (e.g., Klinnert et al., 1983). Presumably the mother's emotional display signals that the environment is safe (happiness) or unsafe (fear), which informs the infant's behavior. Individuals can thus distill useful pieces of information from others' emotional expressions, which may inform their behavior (Van Kleef, 2009). These inferences may influence negotiators' reactions to a greater extent than do other pieces of information (Thompson et al., 1995).

Building on the idea that emotional expressions provide information about the expresser, EASI theory further posits that the interpersonal effects of emotional expressions depend on the observer's motivation and ability to process the information conveyed by these expressions. Such information processing is jointly determined by personality factors (e.g., need for cognition, need for cognitive closure) and situational influences (e.g., accountability, time pressure; De Dreu and Carnevale, 2003; Kruglanski and Webster, 1996; Van Kleef et al., 2010). EASI theory postulates that the deeper the information processing, the more likely individuals are to draw inferences based on other people's emotional expressions; the shallower the information processing, the more likely individuals are to respond to others' emotional expressions based on their own affective reactions (Van Kleef, 2009).

The relative predictive strength of affective reactions and inferential processes further depends on social-contextual factors that influence the perceived appropriateness of the emotional expression (Van Kleef, 2010). Such factors include cultural or organizational norms regarding emotion expression, the way the emotion is expressed (e.g., its target, intensity, and authenticity), relative status, and dispositional preferences for social harmony (Van Kleef et al., 2011). Individuals are more likely to use the emotions of others as information to guide their own behavior to the degree that they perceive these expressions as appropriate for the context. When they perceive others' emotional expressions as inappropriate, people are more likely to respond based on their (negative) affective reactions.

In sum, EASI theory distinguishes two mechanisms of interpersonal emotional influence: inferential processes and affective reactions. The theory posits that the relative predictive strength of inferential processes (compared to affective reactions) increases to the extent that the focal person is motivated and able to engage in thorough information processing and/or perceives the emotional expression as appropriate; the predictive strength of affective reactions (compared to inferential processes) increases to the extent that the focal person's information processing is reduced and/or s/he perceives the emotional expression as inappropriate. This general theory of the social effects of emotions helps to make sense of the growing body of empirical research on the interpersonal effects of emotions in negotiation.

The Empirical Record

In an initial investigation of the interpersonal effects of emotions in negotiation, Van Kleef and colleagues (2004a) examined the effects of anger and happiness using a computer-mediated negotiation task. In the course of the negotiation, participants received emotional messages from their (simulated) opponent (e.g., "This negotiation pisses me off"; "I feel good about this negotiation"). Negotiators who received angry messages inferred that the opponent's limit was high, and to avoid costly impasse they made relatively large concessions. Conversely, negotiators who received happy messages inferred that the opponent's limit was low, felt no need to concede to avoid impasse, and therefore made smaller concessions. Additional experiments revealed that behavioral responses to the emotional expressions of the counterpart were mediated by inferences regarding the counterpart's limits.

Compatible findings were obtained in two experiments by Sinaceur and Tiedens (2006). In a scenario study and in a face-to-face negotiation experiment in which one of the negotiators was instructed to display either anger or no emotion (i.e., keeping a "poker face"), they found that participants conceded more to angry as opposed to non-emotional counterparts.

Furthermore, and in line with Van Kleef et al.'s (2004a) finding that negotiators use their opponent's emotions to infer the other's limit, Sinaceur and Tiedens demonstrated that the effect of anger was mediated by the focal negotiator's appraisal of the opponent's toughness, with angry opponents appearing tougher and therefore eliciting larger concessions than non-emotional counterparts. A more recent study by Sinaceur and colleagues further revealed that the effects of anger expressions on concession making are also mediated by threat perceptions (Sinaceur et al., 2011). Expressions of anger were construed by participants as conveying an implied threat, which explained why they conceded more to angry as opposed to non-emotional opponents (see also Averill, 1982; Sinaceur and Neale, 2005).

Another study revealed that the inferences that negotiators draw from their counterpart's emotions can result in better joint outcomes in an integrative negotiation task. In a computer-mediated negotiation simulation, negotiators inferred from their counterpart's verbal and nonverbal expressions of happiness (versus anger) that the other attached relatively low (rather than high) value to a particular issue. These inferences led them to stand firm on their own high-value issue and to give in on the issue that appeared more important for the counterpart, thereby exploiting the integrative potential of the task (Pietroni et al., 2008). This result is important because it suggests that different emotional expressions can be targeted at different issues in a negotiation, and that such differentiation can improve joint negotiation outcomes.

As is the case for studies on the intrapersonal effects of emotions, most interpersonal effects research has focused on the effects of anger and happiness. Only a few studies have examined the interpersonal effects of other emotions. In one of these studies, Thompson and colleagues (1995) investigated how an opponent's signs of disappointment versus happiness affect a focal negotiator's judgments regarding negotiation success. They found that, independent of objective negotiation performance, negotiators felt more successful when the opponent was disappointed rather than happy. This finding indicates that negotiators take the other's disappointment as a signal that the other was hoping for more, suggesting that they themselves did a good job in extracting concessions from the other. It also indicates how powerful others' emotional expressions can be in influencing perceptions about negotiated outcomes.

In another study using the aforementioned computer-mediated negotiation paradigm, Van Kleef et al. (2006a) addressed emotions that may arise as a result of the appraisal that one has taken too much or received too little from one's opponent. Specifically, the authors focused on the interpersonal effects of disappointment, worry, guilt, and regret on demands and concessions in negotiations. In a first experiment they showed that participants whose opponents expressed emotions of appeasement (guilt or regret) developed a positive impression of their opponents, yet were non-conciliatory in the level of their demands. By contrast, participants whose opponents showed supplication emotions (disappointment or worry) rated their opponents less positively, yet they made larger concessions in the course of the negotiation. Additional experiments revealed that another's expressions of guilt were interpreted as a sign that the expresser had claimed too much, whereas disappointment was taken as a signal that the expresser had received too little. In line with EASI theory, these studies indicate that negotiators draw inferences from opponents' discrete emotional expressions, which in turn shape their behavior.

With regard to the other key mechanism of EASI theory, there is also ample evidence that emotional expressions trigger affective reactions in negotiators. For instance, negotiators dealing with an angry (as opposed to a happy or non-emotional) opponent have been found to feel more angry themselves (Friedman et al., 2004; Van Dijk et al., 2008), to develop a more negative impression of the other (Van Kleef et al., 2004a), to be less satisfied with the negotiation afterward, and to be less willing to engage in future interaction with the same party (Kopelman et al., 2006; Van Kleef et al., 2004b). Several studies further indicate that such negative affective reactions to expressions of anger can, in turn, shape behavior by undermining cooperation in negotiations and reducing the likelihood of a settlement. For instance, Friedman and colleagues' (2004) study demonstrated that negotiations are more likely to break down when negotiators express anger toward an opponent with a strong negotiation position. Furthermore, Kopelman et al. (2006) showed that negotiators who expressed negative affect at the bargaining table were less likely to secure a deal in the first place than were those who expressed positive affect.

Given that emotional expressions can trigger both inferential processes and affective reactions, which often motivate opposite behaviors, it is important to understand when one process takes precedence over the other, and vice versa. In this respect there is growing evidence for EASI's proposition that responses to emotional expressions are more likely to be driven by inferential processes to the degree that observers are motivated to engage in thorough information processing. In a series of studies by Van Kleef and colleagues, negotiators with a low need for cognitive closure, those who were under low time pressure, and those who depended strongly on their counterpart were more likely to infer from their counterpart's expressions of anger versus happiness that the counterpart was tough or lenient, respectively, and to adjust their behavior accordingly by making larger or smaller concessions. In contrast, negotiators with a high need for closure, those who were under high time pressure, and those who did not depend on their counterpart did not draw such inferences and were therefore uninfluenced by the counterpart's emotional expressions (Van Kleef et al., 2004b). Other studies indicate that the interpersonal effects of anger and happiness are similarly moderated by power, with low-power negotiators being more strongly affected by their counterpart's emotions than high-power negotiators (e.g., Overbeck et al., 2010; Sinaceur and Tiedens, 2006; Van Dijk et al., 2008; Van Kleef et al., 2006b; also see Friedman et al., 2004). In addition, Overbeck and colleagues (2010) showed that low-power negotiators were more strongly affected by their counterpart's emotions than by their own emotions.

Other studies point to the role of the perceived appropriateness of emotional expressions in determining the relative predictive strength of inferential processes and affective reactions on negotiation behavior. For instance, Steinel et al. (2008) differentiated between emotions that are directed toward a negotiator's offer and emotions that are directed toward the negotiator as a person. When emotional statements were directed at the participant's offer, participants used the opponent's emotion to assess his or her limits, and consequently they conceded more to an angry opponent than to a happy one. In other words, participants' behavior in this condition was mediated by inferential processes. However, when the emotions were directed at the negotiator as a person (and anger was therefore presumably perceived as less appropriate), negotiators conceded *less* to an angry opponent than to a happy one. In this case, participants did not find useful information in their opponent's emotions, but instead felt affronted by the opponent's inappropriate angry remarks. These findings speak to the idea that a negotiators' effectiveness relies on being tough on the issues, while remaining soft on the person (Fisher and Ury, 1981). Relatedly, Sinaceur and colleagues (2011) found that, although both anger and threats are tough tactics, threats are generally perceived as less aggressive and coercive than anger. Thus, negotiators need to be mindful of the potential limitations associated with expressing anger.

Research by Van Kleef and Côté (2007) provides further support for the role of appropriateness. They examined the effects of anger in the presence or absence of an explicit display rule that prohibited expressions of anger. When there was an explicit norm prohibiting expressions of anger, high-power negotiators made *smaller* concessions to an angry counterpart than to a neutral one (but low-power negotiators did not, due to lack of behavioral leeway). Additional measures revealed that participants developed strong negative affective reactions (i.e., feelings of revenge) in response to the opponent's anger because they perceived the anger as inappropriate, and this in turn fueled competitive behavior among participants who felt sufficiently powerful to act on their retaliatory desires.

Compatible evidence comes from a study by Adam et al. (2010), who examined the effects of verbal expressions of anger across cultures. They found that European American participants conceded more to angry than to neutral opponents, whereas Asian American participants conceded *less* to angry than to neutral opponents. Asian American participants deemed expressions of anger inappropriate, and this explained why they responded negatively to such expressions. Similarly, Kopelman and Rosette (2008) found that East Asian negotiators, who generally value humility and deference, were more likely to accept an offer from a counterpart who displayed positive emotions and less likely to accept an offer from a counterpart who expressed negative emotions, compared to Israeli negotiators who did not hold humility and deference in such high regard.

This review reveals that discrete emotional expressions have pervasive effects on negotiation behavior. Consistent with EASI theory (Van Kleef, 2009; 2010; Van Kleef et al., 2010; 2011), these interpersonal effects are driven by both affective reactions and inferential processes. The relative predictive strength of these two mechanisms depends on the target's information processing depth, on his or her power, and on social-contextual factors that determine the perceived appropriateness of the emotional expressions, such as display rules, cultural norms, and the way in which emotions are expressed.

IMPLICATIONS AND DIRECTIONS FOR FUTURE RESEARCH

Our overview of research on intrapersonal and interpersonal affective influences in negotiation and related conflict resolution settings reveals that a lot of progress has been made in the last 25 years or so. We now know a lot more about the effects of our own and other people's emotions on our thinking and behavior. Nevertheless, there is still a lot of work to be done, both conceptually and empirically. In this section we identify ten issues that we believe are especially important to consider in future research.

We Need to Let Go of the Misleading Distinction between Emotion and Rationality

Historically, many thinkers have juxtaposed emotion and rationality, arguing that emotions cloud our reasoning and distract from rational argumentation. This view dates back at least to the philosophy of Plato, and it has since been voiced by many other great thinkers (e.g., Seneca, Descartes). The preceding overview of theorizing and research on emotion in negotiation suggests that this dominant view of the relation between emotion and rationality needs to be reconsidered (see also Damasio, 1994). Instead of repressing emotions to allow for "unclouded" reasoning, successful negotiators manage their emotions in such a way that they obtain better outcomes, either for themselves or at the dyadic level. Recent research indicates that successful negotiators do not always want to feel positive emotions; rather, they strategically upregulate negative emotions such as anger to claim a larger share of the pie, or put themselves in a sad mood to be more effective at soliciting help (Tamir, 2009). Given that we have seen above that feeling such emotions can indeed help negotiators to claim more value, one could argue that this instrumental perspective on emotion is much more "rational" than the traditional view that emotions must be kept at bay if we want to be successful. Likewise, given that we know that being in a positive affective state facilitates flexibility, creativity, and the discovery of integrative negotiation solutions (e.g., Carnevale and Isen, 1986), it would seem much more rational to nurture positive emotions rather than suppressing them if one desires to craft a mutually satisfying deal.

A similar argument can be made for the rationality of emotion at the interpersonal level of analysis. Instead of hiding how they feel, negotiators should try to develop an understanding of how their emotions influence their counterpart, and, vice versa, how their own behavior is affected by the emotions of the opponent. Simply suppressing emotions in order to be "rational" is not the path to negotiation success, or success in life more generally. Expressing anger can be very effective if one wants to claim value or signal a problem that needs to be resolved (e.g., unfairness), and this anger may be directed specifically at those issues that are essential to the expresser, as opposed to expressing generalized anger (Pietroni et al., 2008). On the other hand, expressing happiness can be very functional if one desires to build rapport and maintain a fruitful long-term negotiation relationship. Further, expressing disappointment can be very helpful in extracting concessions, without triggering the negative affective reactions that we often see in response to displays of anger. In short, it is about time that we rid ourselves of the simplistic distinction between emotion and rationality. Using emotions to reach our goals can be highly rational.

We Need to Incorporate the Role of Emotional Intelligence

It will be apparent from the preceding argument that using emotions rationally requires a certain level of emotional intelligence. Two of the central skills that are featured in the so-called four-branch ability model of emotional intelligence relate to the accurate recognition and adequate regulation of one's own and others' emotions (Mayer et al., 2004). Clearly, many of the interpersonal effects reviewed here rest on the assumption that individuals perceive their partner's emotional state. However, people vary in their ability to accurately recognize emotions in others (Salovey and Mayer, 1990). There is some evidence that successful decoding of emotion is an important factor in negotiation (Elfenbein et al., 2007). In a similar vein, it has been suggested that emotional expressivity, which arguably enhances the recognizability of one's emotions by others, facilitates trust and cooperation (Boone and Buck, 2003). These notions point to the importance of studying the social consequences of emotion recognition.

Our review also points to the importance of emotion *regulation*. For instance, the finding that expressions of positive emotion are conducive to good relations but not to high individual outcomes, whereas expressions of negative emotions such as anger may damage relationships but also produce better individual outcomes points to the advantages of adaptive emotion regulation (Côté, 2005; Elfenbein, 2007). Individuals who successfully navigate social conflict and negotiation are likely to be those who understand when and how to show particular emotions, and who are able to regulate their emotions accordingly.

Importantly, successful emotion regulation requires not just showing the right emotion at the right time, but also showing the right emotion in the right way. Research by Krumhuber and colleagues (2007; 2009) shows that, in cooperative situations, authentic displays of happiness are more likely than inauthentic displays to elicit cooperation from others. Along similar lines, Côté et al. (2013) found that, in a negotiation situation, "deep acted" displays of anger made a target more conciliatory, whereas "surface acted" anger displays had the reverse effect. This difference was explained in terms of lower levels of authenticity and trust in the latter condition. Future research is needed to develop a fuller understanding of the role of emotion regulation and authenticity in negotiation.

We Need to Study Discrete Emotions

It is still common to conceptualize emotions in terms of their positive or negative valence. The findings reviewed above challenge this practice. They reveal, among other things, that expressions of anger, disappointment, and worry in negotiation often elicit cooperation, whereas expressions of guilt and regret elicit competition. Thus it appears that the effects of appeasement emotions such as guilt, embarrassment, shame, and regret are opposite to the effects of dominance-related emotions such as anger and supplication emotions such as worry and disappointment, even though all are negatively valenced (for a more extensive discussion, see Van Kleef et al., 2010).

Together with a growing body of research outside of social decision making documenting distinct effects of discrete negative emotions (e.g., Bodenhausen et al., 1994; DeSteno et al., 2000; Keltner et al., 1993; Lerner and Keltner, 2000; 2001; Tiedens and Linton, 2001) the present review suggests that there is more promise in conceptualizing emotions in terms of their unique appraisal patterns and action tendencies than in terms of their valence. For instance, the "core relational themes" of anger and guilt are other-blame and self-blame, respectively (Smith et al., 1993), which helps to explain why they have opposite effects. Accordingly, future research would do well to measure or manipulate discrete emotions, rather than diffuse mood states. The predictive validity of affect can be expected to increase as a function of the level of specificity, because more specific emotions carry more clear-cut behavioral implications (Weiner, 1986). In short, considering the cognitive appraisals behind emotions—that is, how emotions are defined in terms of blame orientation, uncertainty, control, power, and so on (e.g., Smith et al., 1993)—might help us better understand both the intrapersonal and the interpersonal effects of emotions (Hareli and Hess, 2010; Van Kleef et al., 2010).

We Need to Expand Our Repertoire of Emotions

When it comes to discrete emotions, our review highlights important gaps in our knowledge. Although we are beginning to understand the effects of anger, happiness, anxiety, disappointment, worry, guilt, and regret, the effects of many other emotions have yet to be explored. A focus on other discrete emotions is needed to gain a more complete understanding of the role of emotion in negotiation. As our review shows, researchers have developed quite a nuanced picture of the effects of anger (versus happiness), the conditions under which anger is effective and those under which anger is ineffective, and the associated causal mechanisms. Yet, our understanding of the moderating conditions that shape the effectiveness of emotions other than anger and happiness (and the associated causal mechanisms) remains quite incomplete. In addition, few studies have compared the effectiveness of anger to that of other *negative* emotions (but see Lelieveld et al., 2012, for an exception).

Besides comparing the relative effectiveness of anger compared to other negative emotions, future research could address whether different positive emotions (e.g., happiness, pride, gratitude, relief, hope, compassion) have differential effects on negotiation behavior, as is the case for negative emotions such as guilt versus disappointment (Van Kleef et al., 2006a). It could be, for example, that positive emotions with an "other" focus (e.g., gratitude, compassion) have very different effects than positive emotions with a "self" focus (e.g., pride, relief).

We Need to Study More Intricate Patterns of Emotion

Without exception, the studies reviewed in this chapter have examined the effects of unidimensional affective states (e.g., relatively "pure" anger, happiness, guilt, or disappointment). However, in everyday life individuals often experience "blends" of emotions (Scherer and Tannenbaum, 1986). These blends may even comprise emotions with a different valence. For instance, individuals reported that they simultaneously experienced happiness and sadness on graduation day (Larsen et al., 2001) and after a "disappointing win" or a "relieving loss", where one respectively wins less or loses less than expected (Larsen et al., 2004). To date, very little is known about how such "mixed emotions" influence negotiation behavior. There is some evidence, however, that the simultaneous experience of positive and negative emotions may enhance individual creativity (Fong, 2006), suggesting that emotion blends might affect problem solving at the intrapersonal level of analysis. In addition, qualitative research on emotional contrast effects indicates that the alternating or simultaneous expression of positive and negative emotions can be an effective instrument of social influence (Rafaeli and Sutton, 1991), suggesting that patterns of mixed emotions may also affect negotiation behavior at the interpersonal level.

Recent studies have started to explore the effects of changing or mixed emotions in negotiations. Filipowicz et al. (2011) showed that negotiators who started by expressing happiness and then moved to expressing anger over the course of a negotiation elicited both better relational impressions and greater concessions in comparison to negotiators who expressed steady-state anger. This "becoming angry" (happy to angry) emotional transition effect was explained by attributional processes and emotional contagion processes. Specifically, the emotional transition from happiness to anger elicited greater situational attributions (i.e., observers became more convinced that the expressed emotion was due to something in the negotiation, that is, their own actions) and less dispositional attributions, whereas steady-state anger elicited greater dispositional attributions (i.e., observers became more convinced that the expressed emotion was a result of the displayer's own personality), and less situational attributions. In addition, there was evidence of emotional contagion, such that the initial happiness of the expresser was caught by observers and carried over into the later anger period. In other words, initial expressions of happiness carried over as a positive emotional buffer for subsequent expressions of anger.

In a related vein, Sinaceur et al. (2013) explored the effects of emotional inconsistency and unpredictability in negotiations. They found that emotional inconsistency and unpredictability (i.e., alternating several times between expressing anger and happiness) increased value-claiming in both face-to-face, integrative negotiations and computer-mediated, distributive negotiations in comparison to consistent expressions of anger or happiness. Emotional inconsistency had benefits for expressers because it made recipients feel less in control over their outcomes. This finding speaks to the theory that projecting an aura of mystery through one's reactions elicits compliance from recipients (Schelling, 1960). It also supports the theory that inconsistency in emotions has, in itself, a signaling function (Frijda, 1986; Scherer, 2009)—emotions "have meaning because they change" (Kuppens et al., 2010, p. 1042).

It is important to note that both these initial investigations into mixed emotions addressed main effects. Therefore, future research could investigate moderators of the basic effects of emotional change. For example, both Filipowicz and colleagues (2011) and Sinaceur and colleagues (2013) considered change of emotions across valence, but is possible that emotional change within valence (e.g., moving from sadness to anger) would lead to different results. Thus, changes across other dimensions than valence might be considered, for example, changes in intensity and/or in appraisals such as blame, control, power, and uncertainty. The recipients' power might also moderate the effects of emotional change insofar as it might generally impact the effect of emotions (Overbeck et al., 2010; Sinaceur and Tiedens, 2006; Van Kleef et al., 2006b). Perhaps having low power can be compensated for by expressing changing emotions. Alternatively, communicating changing emotions may backfire, leading to punishment for not following the typical expression of low-power emotions of sadness, fear, and gratitude (Overbeck et al., 2010; Tiedens, 2001). Clearly, future research is needed to shed more light on the boundary conditions and the mechanics of intricate configurations of emotion.

We Need to Consider Temporal Effects

Another avenue for future study concerns the long-term consequences of emotional expressions in negotiation. For instance, how does anger influence the relationship between parties in conflict over time? Do the beneficial effects of anger persist over time, or do they diminish or even backfire in the long run? Research has shown that negotiators with an angry opponent become angry themselves, are less satisfied with the negotiation, and are less willing to engage in future interaction with the same opponent (Friedman et al., 2004; Kopelman et al., 2006; Van Kleef et al., 2004a; 2004b) than are negotiators with non-angry counterparts. This notion points to an interesting dilemma facing negotiators who anticipate future interaction. On the one hand, negotiators may be motivated to strategically suppress anger in order to make a good impression and to induce or maintain a positive interpersonal relationship. On the other hand, they may choose to use anger to get their opponents to go along with their preferences. Interestingly, a recent study indicates that the effects of anger expressions can transfer from one negotiation to the next (Van Kleef and De Dreu, 2010). This study revealed that negotiators tend to make larger concessions in negotiations with counterparts who had previously expressed anger during an earlier negotiation, even if the counterpart remained emotionally neutral during the later negotiation. More research is needed to clarify the boundary conditions of this spillover effect and to establish whether it is limited to anger or generalizes to other emotions.

We Need to Compare Different Conflict Issues and Settings

Still another avenue for future research concerns the role of conflict issues in negotiations. Negotiations may involve interests, factual issues and normative issues (Harinck et al., 2000). The conflict issue at hand influences the extent to which parties reach win-win agreements, and how they communicate with each other. More specifically, negotiators are less likely to yield to the other party or to engage in logrolling when normative issues rather than interests are at stake. Given that moral values are central to personal identity (Rokeach, 1973), people are motivated to affirm their sense of self by endorsing self-expressive moral positions or "moral mandates" (Skitka, 2002). Individuals' concomitant attachment to their norms and values renders trade-offs on moral dimensions inappropriate, hence making some issues "taboo" (Tetlock et al., 2000; Wade-Benzoni et al., 2002). Extending this line of reasoning, Harinck and Van Kleef (2012) recently found that expressing anger is less effective and even harmful when the negotiation centers around normative issues rather than interests, due to parties' unwillingness to give in on normative issues. This effect might apply in particular to those political and social conflicts widely reported in the media, which, in turn, helps to explain lay people's ordinary intuition that anger seems counterproductive in negotiations. Perhaps anger is especially effective in business-like negotiations from which normative issues are usually absent, but plainly ineffective in social and political negotiations in which normative issues are typically present.

More research is needed to develop a more complete picture of the interplay between emotional expressions and conflict issues. Along related lines, it would be interesting to explore whether the effects of emotional expressions are similar in different types of negotiation settings, such as deal-making versus dispute resolution, or whether these effects differ across settings (see Friedman et al., 2004).

We Need to Distinguish between Integral and Incidental Emotions

The question of whether moods and emotions arise during negotiation (i.e., integral affect) or are "imported" from other situations (i.e., incidental affect; see e.g., Lerner et al., 2004) seems highly relevant, yet is largely unexplored. Knowing where affective states come from may enable better predictions as to their effects. For example, as noted by Schwarz and Clore (1983), if ambiguity regarding the source of one's mood enables one to misattribute one's mood to the behavior of one's interaction partner (as opposed to the weather, for instance), stronger affective influences can be expected. In contrast, at the interpersonal level stronger effects may be expected when the other's emotion clearly arises from the social interaction, because in this case the emotion carries more diagnostic and readily useful information that observers can use to inform their behavior (Van Kleef, 2010). Indeed, Filipowicz and colleagues' (2011) study highlights that anger that seems to arise from the social interaction (thus eliciting a situational attribution; e.g., that the expressed emotion is due to something in the negotiation) is more effective. Exploring possible differential processes and effects of integral versus incidental affect appears to be a promising area of inquiry.

We Need to Explore the Role of Intensity

Another aspect that has been largely overlooked so far is the intensity of emotional expressions. It seems intuitively plausible that emotional expressions have different effects depending on the intensity of the expression (Gibson et al., 2009), but it is currently unknown exactly how intensity moderates the effects of emotional expressions. There might be a linear relationship between the intensity of emotional expressions and the magnitude of their effects. Alternatively, the relationship might be curvilinear, so that the effectiveness of emotional expressions peaks at a certain level but emotional expressions become ineffective when they are too extreme. It is also conceivable that some emotions would show a linear pattern whereas others would exhibit a curvilinear relationship. Future research is needed to shed light on these issues.

We Need to Study Emotions in Multi-party Negotiation

A final question that we believe is in need of further investigation is the role of emotions in multi-party negotiation. Almost without exception, the research reviewed here has examined the effects of emotional expressions in dyadic negotiations (but see Friedman et al., 2004, for situations involving a mediator). Additional dynamics are at play in multi-party negotiations, in which the question is not merely what type of agreement one will reach, but also with whom one will reach an agreement (Bolton et al., 2003). In some cases it is possible to switch to a different negotiation partner in case of a looming stalemate with one's current partner. In addition, multi-party negotiations often allow for the formation of coalitions, which may or may not include all the parties involved (Bazerman et al., 2000). The question then becomes who will end up being part of the coalition, and whether this is determined in part by the emotions of the negotiating parties.

Preliminary findings indicate that even though coalition partners are more likely to concede to an angry partner if they have nowhere else to go, they tend to exclude angry partners from a profitable coalition if they have the chance to negotiate with other potential partners (Van Beest et al., 2008). This finding is consistent with the idea that only those recipients who have poor alternatives make concessions to angry expressers (Sinaceur and Tiedens, 2006). Nonetheless, it suggests that expressing anger in multi-party negotiation, where more alternatives might be available in the form of various potential partners, may be even more risky than expressing anger in dyadic negotiation. Further, acting tough in a multi-party situation might be even more detrimental because enjoying a tough reputation can backfire by eliciting negative expectations (Tinsley et al., 2002). More work is needed to establish whether and how the effects of other emotional expressions (e.g., of worry, disappointment, or guilt) also differ between dyadic and multi-party negotiations.

CONCLUSION

Emotions have pervasive effects in negotiations, both within and between negotiation partners. Much research has accumulated on the effects of pure emotions, particularly anger versus happiness, in relatively short-lived, two-party business-like negotiations about interests. Thanks to this research we now have a thorough understanding of when anger is effective in such negotiations and when it is not. Future research can make important new contributions by exploring conditions under which emotions other than anger and happiness may be effective in obtaining concessions (in isolation or in combination), by exploring changes in emotions over time, and by exploring other contexts beyond short-lived, two-party business-like negotiations, such as dispute resolution and value conflicts. Awaiting such endeavors, we conclude that the distinction between rationality and emotion is simplistic and misguided, and should be abandoned from our theorizing. Negotiating rationally does not mean suppressing one's emotions; it means being aware of the role emotions play in negotiations, and using this knowledge wisely to develop a successful negotiation strategy.

REFERENCES

Adam, H., Shirako, A., and Maddux, W.W. (2010). Cultural variance in the interpersonal effects of anger in negotiations. *Psychological Science*, *21*, 882–889.
Allred, K.G., Mallozzi, J.S., Matsui, F., and Raia, C.P. (1997). The influence of anger and compassion on negotiation performance. *Organizational Behavior and Human Decision Processes*, *70*, 175–187.
Anderson, C., and Thompson, L.L. (2004). Affect from the top down: How powerful individuals' positive affect shapes negotiations. *Organizational Behavior and Human Decision Processes*, *95*, 125–139.
Averill, J.R. (1982). *Anger and aggression*. New York: Springer.
Baron, R.A. (1990). Environmentally induced positive affect: Its impact on self-efficacy, task performance, negotiation, and conflict. *Journal of Applied Social Psychology*, *20*, 368–384.
Baron, R.A., Fortin, S.P., Frei, R.L., Hauver, L.A., and Shack, M.L. (1990). Reducing organizational conflict: The role of socially-induced positive affect. *International Journal of Conflict Management*, *1*, 133–152.
Barry, B. and Oliver, R.L. (1996). Affect in dyadic negotiation: A model and propositions. *Organizational Behavior and Human Decision Processes*, *67*, 127–143.
Bazerman, M.H., Curhan, J.R., Moore, D.A., and Valley, K.L. (2000). Negotiation. *Annual Review of Psychology*, *51*, 279–314.
Bodenhausen, G.V., Sheppard, L.A., and Kramer, G.P. (1994). Negative affect and social judgment: The differential impact of anger and sadness. *European Journal of Social Psychology*, *24*, 45–62.
Bolton, G.E., Chatterjee, K., and McGinn, K.L. (2003). How communication links influence coalition bargaining: A laboratory investigation. *Management Science*, *49*, 583–598.
Boone, R.T. and Buck, R. (2003). Emotional expressivity and trustworthiness: The role of nonverbal behavior in the evolution of cooperation. *Journal of Nonverbal Behavior*, *27*, 163–182.
Bower, G.H. (1981). Mood and memory. *American Psychologist*, *36*, 129–148.
Bower, G.H. and Forgas, J.P. (2001). Mood and social memory. In J.P. Forgas (ed.), *Handbook of affect and social cognition* (pp. 95–120). Mahwah, NJ: Erlbaum.
Brooks, A.W. and Schweitzer, M.E. (2011). Can Nervous Nelly negotiate? How anxiety causes negotiators to make low first offers, exit early, and earn less profit. *Organizational Behavior and Human Decision Processes*, *115*, 43–54.
Carnevale, P.J. and Isen, A.M. (1986). The influence of positive affect and visual access on the discovery of integrative solutions in bilateral negotiation. *Organizational Behavior and Human Decision Processes*, *37*, 1–13.
Cheshin, A., Rafaeli, A., and Bos, N. (2011). Anger and happiness in virtual teams:

Emotional influences of text and behavior on others' affect in the absence of non-verbal cues. *Organizational Behavior and Human Decision Processes*, *116*, 2–16.

Clark, M.S. and Taraban, C.B. (1991). Reactions to and willingness to express emotion in two types of relationships. *Journal of Experimental Social Psychology*, *27*, 324–336.

Clark, M.S., Pataki, S.P., and Carver, V.H. (1996). Some thoughts and findings on self-presentation of emotions in relationships. In G.J.O. Fletcher and J. Fitness (eds), *Knowledge structures in close relationships: A social psychological approach* (pp. 247–274). Mahwah, NJ: Erlbaum.

Côté, S. (2005). A social interaction model of the effects of emotion regulation on work strain. *Academy of Management Review*, *30*, 509–530.

Côté, S. and Hideg, I. (2011). The ability to influence others via emotion displays: A new dimension of emotional intelligence. *Organizational Psychology Review*, *1*, 53–71.

Côté, S., Hideg, I., and Van Kleef, G.A. (2013). The consequences of faking anger in negotiations. *Journal of Experimental Social Psychology*, *49*, 453–463.

Damasio, A.R. (1994). *Descartes' error: Emotion, reason, and the human brain*. London: Penguin.

Darwin, C. (1872). *The expression of the emotions in man and animals* (3rd edn). London: HarperCollins.

De Dreu, C.K.W. and Carnevale, P.J.D. (2003). Motivational bases of information processing and strategy in conflict and negotiation. *Advances in Experimental Social Psychology*, *35*, 235–291.

DeSteno, D., Petty, R., Wegener, D.T., and Rucker, D.D. (2000). Beyond valence in the perception of likelihood: The role of emotion specificity. *Journal of Personality and Social Psychology*, *78*, 397–416.

Ekman, P. (1993). Facial expression and emotion. *American Psychologist*, *48*, 384–392.

Ekman, P. and Davidson, R.J. (eds) (1994). *The nature of emotion: Fundamental questions*. New York: Oxford University Press.

Ekman, P. and O'Sullivan, M. (1991). Who can catch a liar? *American Psychologist*, *46*, 913–920.

Elfenbein, H.A. (2007). Emotion in organizations: A review and theoretical integration. *Academy of Management Annals*, *1*, 315–386.

Elfenbein, H.A., Foo, M.D., White, J., Tan, H.H., and Aik, V.C. (2007). Reading your counterpart: The benefit of emotion recognition accuracy for effectiveness in negotiation. *Journal of Nonverbal Behavior*, *31*, 205–223.

Filipowicz, A., Barsade, S., and Melwani, S. (2011). Understanding emotional transitions: The interpersonal consequences of changing emotions in negotiations. *Journal of Personality and Social Psychology*, *101*, 541–556.

Fischer, A.H. and Manstead, A.S.R. (2008). Social functions of emotion. In M. Lewis, J. Haviland, and L. Feldman Barrett (eds), *Handbook of emotion* (3rd edn.). New York: Guilford.

Fitness, J. (2000). Anger in the workplace: An emotion script approach to anger episodes between workers and their superiors, co-workers and subordinates. *Journal of Organizational Behavior*, *21*, 147–162.

Fong, C.T. (2006). The effects of emotional ambivalence on creativity. *Academy of Management Journal*, *49*, 1016–1030.

Forgas, J.P. (1995). Mood and judgment: The affect infusion model (AIM). *Psychological Bulletin*, *117*, 39–66.

Forgas, J.P. (1998). On feeling good and getting your way: Mood effects on negotiator cognition and behavior. *Journal of Personality and Social Psychology*, *74*, 565–577.

Frank, R.H. (1988). *Passions within reason: The strategic role of the emotions*. New York: Norton.

Fridlund, A.J. (1994). *Human facial expression: An evolutionary view*. San Diego, CA: Academic Press.

Friedman, R., Anderson, C., Brett, J., Olekalns, M., Goates, N., and Lisco, C.C. (2004). The positive and negative effects of anger on dispute resolution: Evidence from electronically mediated disputes. *Journal of Applied Psychology*, *89*, 369–376.

Fisher, R. and Ury, W. (1981). *Getting to yes*. London: Penguin.
Frijda, N.H. (1986). *The emotions*. Cambridge: Cambridge University Press.
Frijda, N.H. and Mesquita, B. (1994). The social roles and functions of emotions. In S. Kitayama and H.S. Markus (eds), *Emotion and culture: Empirical studies of mutual influence* (pp. 51–87). Washington, DC: American Psychological Association.
Gibson, D.E., Schweitzer, M., Callister, R.R., and Gray, B. (2009). The influence of anger expressions on outcomes in organizations. *Negotiation and Conflict Management Research*, 2, 236–262.
Hareli, S. and Hess, U. (2010). What emotional reactions can tell us about the nature of others: An appraisal perspective on person perception. *Cognition and Emotion*, 24, 128–140.
Hareli, S. and Rafaeli, A. (2008). Emotion cycles: On the social influence of emotion. *Research in Organizational Behavior*, 28, 35–59.
Harinck, F., and Van Kleef, G.A. (2012). Be hard on the interests and soft on the values: Conflict issue moderates the interpersonal effects of anger in negotiations. *British Journal of Social Psychology*, 51, 741–752.
Harinck, F., De Dreu, C.K.W., and Van Vianen, A.E.M (2000). The impact of conflict issue on fixed-pie perceptions, problem solving, and integrative outcomes in negotiation. *Organizational Behavior and Human Decision Processes*, 81, 329–358.
Hatfield, E., Cacioppo, J.T., and Rapson, R.L. (1994). *Emotional contagion*. New York: Cambridge University Press.
Hawk, S.T., Fischer, A.H., and Van Kleef, G.A. (2011). Taking your place or matching your face: Two routes to empathic embarrassment. *Emotion*, 11, 502–513.
Hawk, S.T., Fischer, A.H., and Van Kleef, G.A. (2012). Face the noise: Embodied responses to nonverbal vocalizations of discrete emotions. *Journal of Personality and Social Psychology*, 102, 796–814.
Hess, U. and Blairy, S. (2001). Facial mimicry and emotional contagion to dynamic emotional facial expressions and their influence on decoding accuracy. *International Journal of Psychophysiology*, 40, 129–141.
Hess, U., Blairy, S., and Kleck, R.E. (2000). The influence of facial emotion displays, gender, and ethnicity on judgements of dominance and affiliation. *Journal of Nonverbal Behaviour*, 24, 265–283.
Isen, A.M., Shalker, T.E., Clark, M., and Karp, L. (1978). Affect, accessibility of material in memory, and behavior: A cognitive loop? *Journal of Personality and Social Psychology*, 36, 1–12.
Kassinove, H., Roth, D., Owens, S.G., and Fuller, J.R. (2002). Effects of trait anger and anger expression style on competitive attack responses in a wartime prisoner's dilemma game. *Aggressive Behavior*, 28, 117–125.
Keltner, D. and Haidt, J. (1999). Social functions of emotions at four levels of analysis. *Cognition and Emotion*, 13, 505–521.
Keltner, D., Ellsworth, P.C., and Edwards, K. (1993). Beyond simple pessimism: Effects of sadness and anger on social perception. *Journal of Personality and Social Psychology*, 64, 740–752.
Ketelaar, T. and Au, W.T. (2003). The effects of feelings of guilt on the behaviour of uncooperative individuals in repeated social bargaining games: An affect-as-information interpretation of the role of emotion in social interaction. *Cognition and Emotion*, 17, 429–453.
Klinnert, M., Campos, J., Sorce, J., Emde, R., and Svejda, M. (1983). Emotions as behavior regulators: Social referencing in infants. In R. Plutchik and H. Kellerman (eds), *Emotion theory, research, and experience* (Vol. 2, pp. 57–68). New York: Academic Press.
Knapp, A. and Clark, M. (1991). Some detrimental effects of negative mood on individuals' ability to solve resource dilemmas. *Personality and Social Psychology Bulletin*, 17, 678–688.
Knutson, B. (1996). Facial expressions of emotion influence interpersonal trait inferences. *Journal of Nonverbal Behavior*, 20, 165–182.
Kopelman, S. and Rosette, A.S. (2008). Cultural variation in response to strategic emotions in negotiations. *Group Decision and Negotiation*, 17, 65–77.

Kopelman, S., Rosette, A.S., and Thompson, L. (2006). The three faces of Eve: An examination of the strategic display of positive, negative, and neutral emotions in negotiations. *Organizational Behavior and Human Decision Processes, 99,* 81–101.

Kramer, R.M., Newton, E., and Pommerenke, P.L. (1993). Self-enhancement biases and negotiator judgment: Effects of self-esteem and mood. *Organizational Behavior and Human Decision Processes, 56,* 110–133.

Kruglanski, A.W. and Webster, D.M. (1996). Motivated closing of the mind: "Seizing" and "freezing". *Psychological Review, 103,* 263–283.

Krumhuber, E., Manstead, A.S.R., Cosker, D., Marshall, D., and Rosin, P.L. (2009). Effects of dynamic attributes of smiles in human and synthetic faces: A simulated job interview setting. *Journal of Nonverbal Behavior, 33,* 1–15.

Krumhuber, E., Manstead, A.S.R., Cosker, D., Marshall, D., Rosin, P.L., and Kappas, A. (2007). Facial dynamics as indicators of trustworthiness and cooperative behavior. *Emotion, 7,* 730–735.

Kuppens, P., Oravecz, Z., and Tuerlinckx, F. (2010). Feelings change: Accounting for individual differences in the temporal dynamics of affect. *Journal of Personality and Social Psychology, 99,* 1042–1060.

Larsen, J.T., McGraw, A.P., and Cacioppo, J. (2001). Can people feel happy and sad at the same time? *Journal of Personality and Social Psychology, 81,* 684–696.

Larsen, J.T., McGraw, A.P., Mellers, B., and Cacioppo, J. (2004). The agony of victory and the thrill of defeat: Mixed emotional reactions to disappointing wins and relieving losses. *Psychological Science, 15,* 325–330.

Lazarus, R.S. (1991). *Emotion and adaptation.* New York: Oxford University Press.

Lelieveld, G.-J., Van Dijk, E., Van Beest, I., and Van Kleef, G.A. (2012). Why anger and disappointment affect bargaining behavior differently: The moderating role of power and the mediating role of reciprocal and complementary emotions. *Personality and Social Psychology Bulletin, 38,* 1209–1221.

Lerner, J.S., and Keltner, D. (2000). Beyond valence: Toward a model of emotion-specific influences on judgment and choice. *Cognition and Emotion, 14,* 473–493.

Lerner, J.S. and Keltner, D. (2001). Fear, anger, and risk. *Journal of Personality and Social Psychology, 81,* 146–159.

Lerner, J.S., Small, D.A., and Loewenstein, G. (2004). Heart strings and purse strings: Carryover effects of emotions on economic decisions. *Psychological Science, 15,* 337–341.

Manstead, A.S.R. and Fischer, A.H. (2001). Social appraisal: The social world as object of and influence on appraisal processes. In K.R. Scherer, A. Schorr, and T. Johnstone (eds), *Appraisal processes in emotion: Theory, research, application* (pp. 221–232). New York: Oxford University Press.

Manstead, A.S.R., Wagner, H.L., and MacDonald, C.J. (1984). Face, body, and speech as channels of communication in the detection of deception. *Basic and Applied Social Psychology, 5,* 317–332.

Mayer, J.D., Salovey, P., and Caruso, D.R. (2004). Emotional intelligence: Theory, findings, and implications. *Psychological Inquiry, 15,* 197–215.

Monin, B. and Miller, D.T. (2001). Moral credentials and the expression of prejudice. *Journal of Personality and Social Psychology, 81,* 33–43.

Morris, M.W. and Keltner, D. (2000). How emotions work: An analysis of the social functions of emotional expression in negotiations. *Research in Organizational Behavior, 22,* 1–50.

Neumann, R. and Strack, F. (2000). "Mood contagion": The automatic transfer of mood between persons. *Journal of Personality and Social Psychology, 79,* 211–223.

Oatley, K., and Jenkins, J.M. (1992). Human emotions: Function and dysfunction. *Annual Review of Psychology, 43,* 55–85.

O'Connor, K., Arnold, J. and Maurizio, A. (2010). The prospect of negotiating: Stress, cognitive appraisal, and performance. *Journal of Experimental Social Psychology, 46,* 729–735.

Overbeck, J.R., Neale, M.A., and Govan, C.L. (2010). I feel, therefore you act: Intrapersonal

and interpersonal effects of emotion on negotiation as a function of social power. *Organizational Behavior and Human Decision Processes*, *112*, 126–139.
Parkinson, B. (1996). Emotions are social. *British Journal of Psychology*, *87*, 663–683.
Parkinson, B. and Simons, G. (2009). Affecting others: Social appraisal and emotion contagion in everyday decision making. *Personality and Social Psychology Bulletin*, *35*, 1071–1084.
Pietroni, D., Van Kleef, G.A., De Dreu, C.K.W., and Pagliaro, S. (2008). Emotions as strategic information: Effects of other's emotions on fixed-pie perception, demands and integrative behavior in negotiation. *Journal of Experimental Social Psychology*, *44*, 1444–1454.
Pillutla, M.M. and Murnighan, J.K. (1996). Unfairness, anger, and spite: Emotional rejections of ultimatum offers. *Organizational Behavior and Human Decision Processes*, *68*, 208–224.
Pruitt, D.G. and Carnevale, P.J. (1993). *Negotiation in social conflict*. Buckingham, UK: Open University Press.
Rafaeli, A. and Sutton, R.I. (1991). Emotional contrast strategies as means of social influence: Lessons from criminal interrogators and bill collectors. *Academy of Management Journal*, *34*, 749–775.
Rimé, B., Mesquita, B., Philippot, P., and Boca, S. (1991). Beyond the emotional event: Six studies on the social sharing of emotion. *Cognition and Emotion*, *5*, 435–465.
Rokeach, M. (1973). *The nature of human values*. New York: Free Press.
Roseman, I.J. (1984). Cognitive determinants of emotion: A structural theory. *Review of Personality & Social Psychology*, *5*, 11–36.
Salovey, P., and Mayer, J.D. (1990). Emotional intelligence. *Imagination, Cognition, and Personality*, *9*, 185–211.
Schachter, S. and Singer, J.E. (1962). Cognitive, social, and physiological determinants of emotional state. *Psychological Review*, *69*, 379–399.
Schelling, T.C. (1960). *The strategy of conflict*. Cambridge, MA: Harvard University Press.
Scherer, K.R. (2009). The dynamic architecture of emotion: Evidence for the component process model. *Cognition and Emotion*, *23*, 1307–1351.
Scherer, K.R. and Tannenbaum, P.H. (1986). Emotional experiences in everyday life: A survey approach. *Motivation and Emotion*, *10*, 295–314.
Scherer, K.R., Schorr, A., and Johnstone, T. (eds) (2001). *Appraisal processes in emotion: Theory, methods, research*. Oxford: Oxford University Press.
Scherer, K.R., Feldstein, S., Bond, R.N., and Rosenthal, R. (1985). Vocal cues to deception: A comparative channel approach. *Journal of Psycholinguistic Research*, *14*, 409–425.
Schwarz, N. and Clore, G.L. (1983). Mood, misattribution, and judgments of well-being: Informative and directive functions of affective states. *Journal of Personality and Social Psychology*, *45*, 513–523.
Sinaceur, M. and Neale, M.A. (2005). Not all threats are created equal: How implicitness and timing affect the effectiveness of threats in negotiations. *Group Decision and Negotiation*, *14*, 63–85.
Sinaceur, M. and Tiedens, L.Z. (2006). Get mad and get more than even: When and why anger expression is effective in negotiations. *Journal of Experimental Social Psychology*, *42*, 314–322.
Sinaceur, M., Adam, H., Van Kleef, G.A., and Galinsky, A.D. (2013). The advantages of being unpredictable: How emotional inconsistency extracts concessions in negotiation. *Journal of Experimental Social Psychology*, *49*, 498–508.
Sinaceur, M., Van Kleef, G.A., Neale, M.A., Adam, H., and Haag, C. (2011). Hot or cold: Is communicating anger or threats more effective in negotiation? *Journal of Applied Psychology*, *96*, 1018–1032.
Skitka, L.J. (2002). Do the means always justify the ends, or do the ends sometimes justify the means? A value protection model of justice reasoning. *Personality and Social Psychology Bulletin*, *28*, 588–697.
Smith, C.A., Haynes, K.N., Lazarus, R.S., and Pope, L.K. (1993). In search of the "hot"

cognitions: Attributions, appraisals, and their relation to emotion. *Journal of Personality and Social Psychology, 65*, 916–929.

Srivastava, J., Fedorikhin, A., and Espinoza, F. (2009). Coupling and decoupling of unfairness and anger in ultimatum bargaining. *Journal of Behavioral Decision Making, 22*, 475–489.

Steinel, W., Van Kleef, G.A., and Harinck, F. (2008). Are you talking to me?! Separating the people from the problem when expressing emotions in negotiation. *Journal of Experimental Social Psychology, 44*, 362–369.

Tamir, M. (2009). What do people want to feel and why? Pleasure and utility in emotion regulation. *Current Directions in Psychological Science, 18*, 101–105.

Tetlock, P.E., Kristel, O.V., Elson, S.B., Green, M.C., and Lerner, J.S. (2000). The psychology of the unthinkable: Taboo trade-offs, forbidden base-rates, and heretical counterfactuals. *Journal of Personality and Social Psychology, 78*, 853–870.

Thompson, L., Valley, K.L., and Kramer, R.M. (1995). The bittersweet feeling of success: An examination of social perception in negotiation. *Journal of Experimental Social Psychology, 31*, 467–492.

Tiedens, L.Z. (2001). Anger and advancement versus sadness and subjugation: The effect of negative emotion expressions on social status conferral. *Journal of Personality and Social Psychology, 80*, 86–94.

Tiedens, L.Z. and Linton, S. (2001). Judgment under emotional certainty and uncertainty: The effects of specific emotions on information processing. *Journal of Personality and Social Psychology, 81*, 973–988.

Tinsley, C.H., O'Connor, K.M., and Sullivan, B.A. (2002). Tough guys finish last: The perils of a distributive reputation. *Organizational Behavior and Human Decision Processes, 88*, 621–645.

Van Beest, I., Van Kleef, G.A., and Van Dijk, E. (2008). Get angry, get out: The interpersonal effects of anger communication in multiparty negotiation. *Journal of Experimental Social Psychology, 44*, 993–1002.

Van Dijk, E., Van Kleef, G.A., Steinel, W., and Van Beest, I. (2008). A social functional approach to emotions in bargaining: When communicating anger pays and when it backfires. *Journal of Personality and Social Psychology, 94*, 600–614.

Van Doorn, E.A., Heerdink, M.W., and Van Kleef, G.A. (2012). Emotion and the construal of social situations: Inferences of cooperation versus competition from expressions of anger, happiness, and disappointment. *Cognition and Emotion, 12*, 442–461.

Van Kleef, G.A. (2009). How emotions regulate social life: The emotions as social information (EASI) model. *Current Directions in Psychological Science, 18*, 184–188.

Van Kleef, G.A. (2010). The emerging view of emotion as social information. *Social and Personality Psychology Compass, 4/5*, 331–343.

Van Kleef, G.A., and Côté, S. (2007). Expressing anger in conflict: When it helps and when it hurts. *Journal of Applied Psychology, 92*, 1557–1569.

Van Kleef, G.A., and De Dreu, C.K.W. (2010). Longer-term consequences of anger expression in negotiation: Retaliation or spill-over? *Journal of Experimental Social Psychology, 46*, 753–760.

Van Kleef, G.A., De Dreu, C.K.W., and Manstead, A.S.R. (2004a). The interpersonal effects of anger and happiness in negotiations. *Journal of Personality and Social Psychology, 86*, 57–76.

Van Kleef, G.A., De Dreu, C.K.W., and Manstead, A.S.R. (2004b). The interpersonal effects of emotions in negotiations: A motivated information processing approach. *Journal of Personality and Social Psychology, 87*, 510–528.

Van Kleef, G.A., De Dreu, C.K.W., and Manstead, A.S.R. (2006a). Supplication and appeasement in conflict and negotiation: The interpersonal effects of disappointment, worry, guilt, and regret. *Journal of Personality and Social Psychology, 91*, 124–142.

Van Kleef, G.A., De Dreu, C.K.W., and Manstead, A.S.R. (2010). An interpersonal approach to emotion in social decision making: The emotions as social information model. *Advances in Experimental Social Psychology, 42*, 45–96.

Van Kleef, G.A., De Dreu, C.K.W., Pietroni, D., and Manstead, A.S.R. (2006b). Power and emotion in negotiations: Power moderates the interpersonal effects of anger and happiness on concession making. *European Journal of Social Psychology, 36*, 557–581.

Van Kleef, G.A., Van Doorn, E.A., Heerdink, M.W., and Koning, L.F. (2011). Emotion is for influence. *European Review of Social Psychology, 22*, 114–163.

Van Kleef, G.A., Van Dijk, E., Steinel, W., Harinck, F., and Van Beest, I. (2008). Anger in social conflict: Cross-situational comparisons and suggestions for the future. *Group Decision and Negotiation [Special Issue on Emotions in Negotiation], 17*, 13–30.

Wade-Benzoni, K.A., Hoffman, A.J., Thompson, L.L., Moore, D.A., Gillespie, J.J., and Bazerman, M.H. (2002). Barriers to resolution in ideologically based negotiations: The role of values and institutions. *Academy of Management Review, 27*, 41–57.

Watson, D., Clark, L.A., and Tellegen, A. (1988). Development and validation of brief measures of positive and negative affect: The PANAS scales. *Journal of Personality and Social Psychology, 54*, 1063–1070.

Weiner, B. (1986). *An attributional theory of motivation and emotion.* New York: Springer-Verlag.

Xiao, E. and Houser, D. (2005). Emotion expression in human punishment behavior. *Proceedings of the National Academy of Sciences, 102*, 7398–7401.

PART III

SOCIAL-PSYCHOLOGICAL PROCESSES

6. Power, status, and influence in negotiation
Jennifer R. Overbeck and Yoo Kyoung Kim

Negotiation is a process in which two or more people must reach agreement on how to divide some resource, when they have different preferences for how to do so. Given this, it is no surprise that *influence* is a fundamental element of negotiation, nor that both parties tend to want and seek influence over the counterpart in negotiation. This chapter will focus on two primary sources of influence: *power* and *status*. Power is a source of influence from objective, structural sources such as possession of resources or position in networks of relationships; status is a source of influence stemming from others' consensual judgments (Fiske and Berdahl, 2007; Fragale et al., 2011). Though power has (and will be) the focus of work on influence in negotiation, both are important and both are considered here. We turn first to power.

One of the earliest definitions of power was, in essence, *the ability to get what you want* (Russell, 1938). Russell noted that the most basic form of power is physical force: using the threat or imposition of pain, even death, to compel compliance. Because this "naked power" is costly to maintain, and because modern societies generally frown on its use, softer forms of power are used instead. For example, instead of deploying the army to suppress every disagreement, modern governments use political processes and negotiations to reach mutually acceptable outcomes. As such, negotiation is both a softer power channel in itself, and a context in which both softer and harder (e.g., use of threats) power plays out.

Popular press articles and paid workshops extol the benefits of, and offer coaching for, increasing power in negotiations ("Seven strategies to build 'Negotiating Power'", James, 2009; "Women's negotiation 'Problem' may be power, not gender", Pynchon, 2011; "How to tap into more power than you think you have", Karrass Institute, 2012; "The secrets of power negotiating", Dawson, 1987). Most scholarly work on power and negotiation has examined the ways in which power affects negotiation outcomes, often through interaction with other constructs such as emotion (Anderson and Thompson, 2004; Overbeck et al., 2010; Sinaceur and Tiedens, 2006; Van Kleef et al., 2006), gender (Kray et al., 2004; Kopelman et al., 2006; Miles and Clenney, 2010), and personality

(Mohammed et al., 2008; Velden et al., 2007); the emerging conclusions from this work are reviewed below. Before focusing tightly on power and negotiation, however, it may be helpful to consider how power is viewed and studied outside the bargaining room.

POWER

Definitions and Perspectives

Power has fascinated philosophers, political scientists, and—more recently—psychologists, because of both its pervasive and universal presence ("Power is everywhere", Foucault, 1995) and the significant consequences that result from power dynamics. Weber (1946) argued that power was "the probability that one actor within a social relationship will be in a position to carry out his own will despite resistance, regardless of the basis on which this probability rests", making explicit the notion that power cannot exist without both a high-power party (HPP), to wield power, and a low-power party (LPP), to be subject to it. Relative power can also reflect how much an LPP is *asymmetrically* dependent on an HPP for resources (Pfeffer and Salancik, 1978; Thibaut and Kelley, 1959) or subject to behavioral or outcome control by the HPP (Fiske, 1993; Overbeck and Park, 2001; Thibaut and Kelley, 1959); it is possible for two parties to both have relatively high (or low) power, but the difference between them could be small or large depending on the degree of asymmetry in dependence.

French and Raven (1959; Raven, 1964) argued that power is properly seen as the *potential* for influence; that is, rather than being the actual act of influencing, it is one's capacity to do so, regardless of whether that capacity is exercised. In a negotiation context, for example, obtaining a concession from the other side because that side was simply happy to concede would not constitute power. However, the ability to wrest that concession from the other side, despite its objections, would reflect an underlying capacity to influence that party, and thus would constitute power. Power can also lie in the ability to control the agenda for discussion and decision-making (Bachrach and Baratz, 1962) or the ability to control whether LPPs can even distinguish their own interests from those of the powerful (Lukes, 1974).

In the context of negotiations, the social nature of power is focused less on the kind of outcome, resource, and agenda control studied in much of the social psychological literature, and more on one's ability to press one's case, emerging with a settlement that reflects desired outcomes and claims disproportionate value for the self. Negotiation is essentially formalized reciprocity, and reciprocity is a particular form of exchange. As such, negotiation inherently involves and enacts exchange-based power (compare Bacharach and Lawler, 1981; Emerson, 1962). This view holds that power consists in the degree to which Party A's counterpart, Party B, is dependent on A while A is not (or, is not as) dependent on B. More precisely, Bacharach and Lawler's (1981) *Dependence Theory of Bargaining Power* argued that power in negotiations is a function of B's dependence on A as well as the degree of B's commitment to alternatives that A controls. Power may be considered *absolute* (one party's power is defined by the other party's dependence and commitment), *relative* (defined by the ratio of one party's dependence and commitment to the other's), and *total* (the sum of both parties' power); regardless, the effects of power rely both on objective states of affairs and on the parties' subjective perceptions of those states.

Following from these perspectives, the most common operational definition of power in most experimental studies of negotiation and power is the BATNA—the Best Alternative to a Negotiated Agreement (Fisher and Ury, 1981). As its name states, the BATNA represents the most positive, desirable, and valuable alternative that a negotiator may choose if the current negotiation does not result in agreement. For example, consider a job candidate negotiating an offer package worth $150,000. The job candidate has two other offers on the table, one worth $145,000 and one worth $155,000. All else equal (a key assumption), the candidate's BATNA is the more-valuable $155,000 offer. In fact, because the BATNA is worth more than the offer being negotiated, the candidate is unlikely to accept that offer unless it is raised to equal or exceed the BATNA. As generations of MBA student negotiators can attest, lay negotiators typically assume that hiring officers always have more power than do candidates. However, the concept of BATNA makes clear that the role does not determine power. A candidate with a superior BATNA may be more powerful than the hiring officer; it depends on that officer's BATNA. If the hiring officer has no other attractive applicants, then the candidate is more powerful. If the hiring officer also has good alternatives, then she is less so.

In short, the BATNA is a parsimonious and tractable way to conceptualize power in negotiations, one that disambiguates the factors likely to drive agreement or nonagreement (primarily, the value of the prospective deal) and those that are less proximal in their effects on agreement (e.g., roles, prestige, and interpersonal manner). Research has shown that better BATNAs are associated with greater value claiming (compare Galinsky and Mussweiler, 2001; Magee et al., 2007; Mussweiler and Strack, 1999; Overbeck et al., 2010), though important boundaries may limit this effect. For example, once the current deal offers value equivalent to one's BATNA, the BATNA becomes less potent in determining one's ability to claim value (Thompson et al., 2010). BATNA is likely to continue to be the primary operational definition of power in the domain of negotiation.

Perhaps the most comprehensive, compelling recent account of power and negotiation was developed by Kim et al. (2005). They argued that power in negotiation is not a simple matter of dependence. Rather, the term "power" can refer to any of four distinct states. Each party has some degree of *potential* power, the prospective ability to gain value in an agreement—for example, a negotiator with a strong BATNA facing a counterpart with a weak BATNA has strong potential power. However, this may be different from the mutual *perceived* power in the negotiation—that is, the parties' beliefs about their own and their counterpart's power. A small vendor facing a Walmart buyer may perceive a vast power difference, regardless of reality. Perceived power can be manipulated through power-change and power-use *tactics* whereby each party may strive to project a more (or less) powerful image. In the end, the final, *realized* power reflects not only the objective potential that each party started with, but also the perceptions and tactics that manipulate how this potential is enacted.

Of importance, the model specifies that not only does the BATNA determine a negotiator's potential power, but so too does each party's contribution to the negotiated agreement. That is, the BATNA determines a minimum threshold for agreement; however, contributions delineate how negotiators will divide the surplus that remains after both parties' BATNAs have been reached. The model analyses perceived power as a function of the evaluation and weighting of own and counterpart's BATNA and contributions.

This model is based almost exclusively in the exchange tradition of power theory (Blau, 1964; Emerson, 1962), but to some extent it offers a bridge from that focus in negotiation to more recent work outside negotiation. For one thing, the authors explicitly consider how relational properties such as trust affect perceptions of power in the negotiation (Kim et al., 2005). Likewise, the model is strongly social in its focus: Every stage is posited to reflect comparisons of the potential, perceptions, and actions of both parties.

Further afield, though, perceived power could also be affected by more distal negotiator characteristics such as organizational affiliation, gender, and many others. Here, a negotiator's practiced ability to control others' behaviors and outcomes may translate into behaviors that convey power even without superior potential power. That is, we might conceive of this model as postulating an initial stage (potential power) defined by the exchange-based ratio of dependence between the two parties, defined by their relative BATNA and contributions. The parties' potential power is then perceived and interpreted, not only through evaluation of the structural elements of potential power, but also through social and personal dynamics that signal dominance and privilege. For example, a young female vendor negotiating a sales contract with a physically imposing, older, male buyer may have a far superior BATNA and be able to provide more contributions to the deal. However, she may perceive the power balance as being less in her own favor due to characteristics often related to, but—in this case—irrelevant to, potential power.

Likewise, negotiators' efforts to change the power balance through power-change tactics, or their efforts to preserve it through power-use tactics, are likely to reflect the power-related behaviors studied by social psychologists and sociologists. Finally, the realized power outcome appears to reflect not only the structural balance of dependence between the parties determined by the agreement, but also the construal of the parties' actions during the negotiation process. That is, much of the final balance of power reflects belief, in addition to structure.

Indeed, although most treatments of power and negotiation share a focus on power as exchange, it should not be overlooked that less exchange-oriented views of power are relevant to negotiation, as well—particularly insofar as they shape the subtle behavioral and interpersonal dynamics of the negotiation, the way negotiators position themselves and communicate with one another, and the sense of inhibition or license that affects their motivation and goals. For example, consider a corporate manager entering a negotiation on behalf of his employer. At work, the manager enjoys substantial control over resources. Imagine further that this manager's company is larger and more prominent than the counterpart's company. Even if the two parties' BATNAs were equivalent—meaning that neither negotiator has more exchange-based power—the first manager is likely to exhibit several power-related tendencies that confer advantage in the negotiation. For example, he may commandeer a desirable seat and spread out to occupy a lot of physical space, thus signaling dominance (DePaulo and Friedman, 1998; Tiedens and Fragale, 2003). He may take early control of the conversation and make the first offer in the negotiation (Galinsky and Mussweiler, 2001), feeling entitled to direct the interaction. He may be very decisive (Magee et al., 2005) and even be more comfortable feeling and expressing anger than his counterpart, whose lack of chronic experience with power may create feelings of timidity and loss of focus in response (Overbeck et al., 2010). He may even manipulate the physical environment, moving furniture or changing the thermostat for his own comfort, in ways that signal his right to have his preferences satisfied (Galinsky et al., 2003). Because others tend to defer to expansive, dominant behaviors by subconsciously ceding space and adopting more deferential postures (compare Tiedens and Fragale, 2003), the counterpart is likely to feel more submissive, hesitate to counter strongly, and acquiesce more to the dominant negotiator, creating a significant difference in ability to claim value (and perhaps to create it—more on this below) even though the dominant negotiator may have no actual power at all.

Effects of Power on Cognition, Attitudes, and Behavior

Power produces a number of psychological responses that may affect negotiation processes and outcomes. For example, power is associated with more goal-oriented thinking, and HPPs tend to be more flexible in attending to goal-relevant alternatives than are LPPs (Guinote, 2007; Overbeck and Park, 2001; 2006; Slabu and Guinote, 2010). Research has shown that aspirations—a negotiator's goal or target point—are strong predictors of final value claiming: Those who set the most aggressive aspirations are the ones who tend to claim the most value (Hamner and Harnett, 1975, cited in Thompson, 1990). This suggests that one reason why HPPs tend to claim more value in negotiations is not only their superior BATNA, but also the fact that they may be better able to stay focused on their aspirations (goals), to pursue possible agreements that would fulfill those aspirations, and to avoid proposals that threaten their aspirations. Indeed, some work has shown that HPPs set higher aspirations than do LPPs (e.g., Mannix and Neale, 1993; Overbeck et al., 2010); more important, and not yet demonstrated in empirical research, is the idea that HPPs use these aspirations as a guide to their negotiation choices.

Power may also be associated with better self-regulatory control, at least in the short term. Researchers recently established that HPPs can delay gratification and exert more self-control, provided that the activity requiring self-control is both expected, and consistent with their hierarchical standing (DeWall et al., 2010). That is, powerful people were able to persevere at a difficult task longer, and perform better, when it reflected a higher degree of skill and professionalism than when it reflected rote, mundane production. Although HPPs showed this advantage even when they were ego-depleted (a condition that often limits people's ability to exert self-control), it persisted only as long as they were forewarned that they would need to self-regulate. When surprised by an unexpected activity requiring self-control, HPPs actually showed a rebound effect whereby their persistence and performance dipped far below those of LPPs. Again, this pattern has implications for power and negotiation. Negotiation can be a taxing activity, and to make the best deal negotiators are often required to feign or suppress emotion (compare Allred, 1999), to think hard and creatively to find integrative options (Thompson, 2011), and to continue interacting with the counterpart even when the negotiation induces fatigue or has dragged on for a long time. If HPPs are better able to monitor and control their responses, maintain focus, and perform strongly, they are likely to reach better deals. Indeed, Overbeck and colleagues (2010) found that HPPs who were made angry at their counterparts actually felt more cognitively focused than those who were happy, whereas for LPPs this pattern reversed.

Perhaps the strongest picture of powerholders to emerge from recent psychological work on power is of people who are predisposed to action and approach, oriented toward rewards, implemental, risk-taking, and decisive. Keltner et al. (2003) argued that power activates the *behavioral approach system*, whereas low power activates the *behavioral inhibition system*. Approach activation fosters attention to opportunities and rewards in the environment, gives rise to positive feelings, prompts people to take action rather than being passive, and reduces time-consuming, systematic thought. Inhibition, on the other hand, elicits caution and hesitancy as people try to avoid making costly or painful errors, directs attention toward potential threats, heightens negative feelings, and engenders systematic thought. Although these patterns might suggest that power leads to impulsivity and carelessness, research has shown HPPs to be able to maintain high levels of attention and performance even while processing their environment rapidly (Overbeck and Park, 2001).

Indeed, even when powerholders' behaviors seem potentially counterproductive, they may serve beneficial ends. For example, Anderson and Galinsky (2006) showed that high power negotiators take more risks by revealing more information about their own interests and preferences. Though this is a risky behavior, it also facilitates better negotiated agreements. Similarly, Inesi (2010) showed that power reduces the pain associated with losses—possibly one reason why HPPs find risks more acceptable. Though loss aversion may provide a useful signal to negotiators to avoid negative deals, being overly concerned with that pain can also stop them from accepting deals that could be of benefit. Power may thus inoculate negotiators from failing to make deals that, though risky, could be good for them.

At the same time, recent work has also shown powerholders to have sometimes shaky relationships with morality. Though they have high standards for others' behaviors—advocating strong sanctions against dishonesty (Lammers et al., 2010) and punishing others for transgressions (Wiltermuth and Flynn, in press)—they are sometimes lax themselves, allowing themselves more latitude to violate social norms (Brauer and

Chekroun, 2005) and moral strictures (Lammers and Stapel, 2009). Because powerholders actually tend to be given the benefit of the doubt, and seen as *more* moral than others (Overbeck et al., 2012), this can be a problematic issue. Several studies have shown that certain circumstances can elicit deception among powerful negotiators. For example, in asymmetrically-powerful dyads characterized by mistrust or negative affect, deception increased (Olekalns and Smith, 2009). Likewise, powerful proposers in a bargaining game were more likely than the non-powerful respondents to engage in blatant deception (lying; Rabin, 1997; see also Diekmann, Soderberg, and Tenbrunsel, Chapter 8, this volume; but see Koning et al., 2009, for an opposite finding). Relatedly, Haselhuhn and Wong (2012) recently demonstrated that male, but not female, negotiators with a higher facial width-to-height ratio (a measure previously found to predict aggression) also engaged in more dishonesty in negotiation; a second study, involving cheating on a dice roll rather than negotiation, established that the relationship between the facial ratio and dishonesty was mediated by the men's subjective sense of power (using a measure created by Anderson and Galinsky, 2006). Paired with the recent findings of the psychological literature on power, these findings suggest that counterparts of powerful negotiators may wish to be cautious.

STATUS

Definitions and Perspectives

Status has been studied in diverse academic fields including sociology, anthropology, and social psychology (Chen et al., 2012). Most commonly defined as the esteem and regard with which someone is held (Anderson et al., 2001; but see Frank, 1985, for an alternative view), status reflects the degree to which they are valued, sought after, and accorded greater opportunities and privileges (Merten, 1997). Recently, Chen and her colleagues (2012) suggested that status can be obtained through two routes—dominance and prestige (see also Cheng et al., 2010; Halevy et al., 2012). Status orders exist in both human and nonhuman society; from an evolutionary standpoint, humans are thought to gain high status in hierarchical groups and organizations either by force—the method corresponding to dominance—or persuasion—the method corresponding to prestige (Henrich and Gil-White, 2001). The former does not require consensus from group/organization members, but the latter can be obtained only through voluntary compliance or even endorsement (Fragale et al., 2011). In human societies, it appears that status more often comes from one's accomplishment in respected domains (Henrich and Gil-White, 2001): Others defer to the status-holder because of their sense that that person deserves deference, whether due to personal characteristics or formal standing. Because of its prevalence, in this chapter, status is discussed in terms of prestige.

Much of the aforementioned work on power may, when applied to a negotiation context, actually shed light on dynamics of *status* in negotiations. That is, once the fundamentally exchange-based nature of power in negotiations (via BATNA and contributions) is removed, the effect of power from outside the negotiation context can be argued to represent an effect of status.

In a negotiation, a person who has great power outside the negotiation, but an inferior BATNA and contributions relative to the counterpart, actually has low power. However, her high external power may engender respect and deference from the counterpart, thus endowing her with high status that may be a source of influence in the negotiation (compare Thye, 2000). Likewise, if she chronically occupies positions of power, and thus retains power-related behaviors and cognitive and affective styles in the negotiation, then these tendencies may create a sense of presence that also conveys status.

Reputation may be an important source of status in negotiations. Anderson and Shirako (2008) showed that both past negotiating behaviors and a negotiator's social connectedness contribute to forming a reputation, whether positive or negative, that influences counterparts' expectations for interacting with that negotiator. Once a negotiator acquires a reputation for selfish, aggressive negotiating behavior, counterparts are likely to respond with precautionary resistance, using fewer integrative and more distributive strategies and even engaging in greater deception (Fulmer et al., 2009; Glick and Croson, 2001; Tinsley et al., 2002). Though reputation differs from status (*reputation* is others' set of beliefs about the character and behaviors of the negotiator, see Anderson and Shirako, 2008; whereas *status* refers to a value-laden ranking of the negotiator relative to some comparison other, such as the counterpart), it is clear that one's reputation has implications for one's status in a negotiation. The selfish negotiator may not be very esteemed or respected; thus, even with other strong markers of status present, he may not be as influential as if his reputation were more positive.

Effects of Status on Cognition, Attitudes, and Behavior

Unlike power, status is generally examined in terms of how people perceive the status-holder, rather than how that person's own psychology changes as a function of holding status. For example, much of the basic psychological and sociological research on status focuses on how and why people gain status within groups, and the reciprocal relationship between high-status group members who are given privileges in anticipation of the contributions they are expected to make to the group (Blau, 1964; Frank, 1985; Lenski, 1966); and lower-status group members who benefit from those contributions but must sacrifice and accept fewer advantages in exchange for having less responsibility for the group. In fact, one conceptualization of status holds that it is assigned to those who are seen as competent, whether based on high-fidelity cues such as performance, or *diffuse* cues only heuristically related to competence, such as gender or age (Berger et al., 1972; Carli and Eagly, 1999; Ridgeway and Diekema, 1992). Once status is assigned, an important benefit accorded to high-status group members is greater latitude to violate group norms; in essence, they accrue *idiosyncrasy credits* by conforming to the group on important dimensions, and once enough credits are accrued, they can metaphorically cash them in for the freedom to be nonconformist (Hollander, 1958).

Recent research on status has shown that high-status parties can tend to be highly confident, and that their confidence may persist even after it is shown to be overblown (Anderson et al., 2012; Anderson and Kilduff, 2009). In part, this may result from different characteristics that drive someone to pursue status: Those who want status to enjoy its benefits, and who gain status based on their extraversion (Bendersky and Shah, in press) or the display of *hubristic pride*, reflecting excessive ego (Cheng et al., 2010), may gain status due to their strong public claim, in spite of poor actual ability. This kind of status may be brittle, requiring greater vigilance and defense. A status-holder in this vein may use negotiations as a way to reify his or her position of esteem. On the other hand, those who are more neurotic and thus concerned with not alienating the group (Bendersky and Shah, in press), or who gain status based on *authentic pride* from a record of past accomplishment, may be granted a more stable, enduring status by the group, and may face fewer threats to their status. As such, in negotiations their demeanor may better elicit the kind of deferential behavior that high status tends to attract.

Regardless of its origins, status appears to make status-holders believe that they enjoy others' approval. Pettit and Sivanathan (2012) showed that inducing feelings of high status caused participants to perceive approving facial expressions more rapidly than could those without status. Likewise, high-status participants heard tape-recordings of applause as louder than did those without status. These findings suggest that status causes status-holders, at a basic perceptual level, to sense greater approval coming from others. Such feelings in a negotiation context could lead a high-status negotiator to sense more receptiveness to her proposals.

Most of the above models presuppose that both the high- and lower-status parties are part of the same group, with aligned goals and common fate. In negotiations, of course, the parties commonly belong to different groups, and are competing to divide some resource (even if they are cooperatively doing so). Both their goals and their fate may differ. As such, status may manifest differently in negotiation contexts, where relative status is important as a source of influence—a resource in itself that can be used to gain advantage in bargaining. For example, individuals have been shown to perceive exchangeable objects controlled by high-status individuals as more valuable than those controlled by low-status individuals (Thye, 2000), which implies that high-status negotiators may get more return on their resources simply due to differences in valuation. In short, the negotiator seeking to influence the counterpart toward desired agreements, and particularly toward a deal that preserves the relationship and offers ripe future opportunities, would be well served by emphasizing his status in the negotiation.

Relatedly, Flynn and Amanatullah (2012) proposed the effect of perceived status with a task including solving anagrams and playing video games. They argued that competing with a strong performer evokes high anxiety and leads to decreased performance. But, when an individual independently performs alongside an outstanding performer, that individual's performance improves. This study suggests that an individual's perception of the high-status individual significantly affects her performance. Likewise, a counterpart's perceived status relative to the negotiator may be critical: The low-status negotiator may be less likely to perform well when paired with a high-status counterpart because of the low-status party's concern that she will not gain much from that counterpart.

Status versus Power

Indeed, influence derived from status may have a very different character from power-based influence. The latter depends only on the relatively objective balance of dependence between the negotiating parties. However, status-based influence relies on the continued consent and deference of the lower-status party. Status attainment is costly and distracts people from focusing on the main task (Bendersky and Shah, in press). Furthermore, it is controversial whether high-status holders achieve greater performance in a group. It can be advantageous because status allows better chances to earn resources, but it can be disadvantageous because of the complacency and lack of focus (Bothner et al., 2012). As such, the high-status negotiator may be more constrained in his ability to impose his will and extract concessions. The process may be slower and more reciprocal.

On the other hand, there may be advantages for a high-status negotiator even in the absence of power. Fragale and colleagues (2011) examined judgments of individuals at varying levels of power and status, and found that judgments were particularly negative when the target had high power but low status (HPLS). Observers typically assumed that HPLS targets were likely to be cold and dominant, that they were trying to obstruct the perceiver's goals, and that interacting with them would be aversive (Fragale et al., 2011). The authors argued that such perceptions create anticipatory hostility in interactions, such that simple statements and requests may be filtered through negative expectations and interpreted as hostile or overbearing. In a negotiation context, this may manifest as interpreting a powerful, low-status counterparts offers as excessively aggressive or insulting—interpretations likely to lead to resistant counteroffers or even a breakdown in negotiations altogether.

Power and Status in Negotiation

Past work on influence in negotiations has produced a large and diverse body of findings; because influence is such a key element of negotiation, this is not surprising. We argue that the literature can be grouped into a few broad findings, which we now outline.

First, *power fosters value claiming in negotiations*. To some extent this is a tautological statement, given that power is typically defined in terms of the BATNA and research has shown that negotiators tend to claim their BATNAs in any deal, as prerequisite for reaching agreement, and then divide the surplus roughly evenly between them. As such, the party with the higher BATNA should by definition claim more value (Kim and Fragale, 2005; Thompson et al., 2010). Further, recall that Kim et al. (2005) established the role of both BATNA and contributions in constituting a negotiator's power. Even if BATNAs are equal, the party who can offer greater benefits to the counterpart can reap greater rewards from the negotiated agreement. Perhaps because of the circularity of this relationship between power and value claiming, researchers have tended to focus on moderators of the effect, as cited earlier in this chapter; nonetheless, the main effect has been confirmed repeatedly as well (Dwyer, 1984; Olekalns, 1991; Overbeck et al., 2010).

More interesting is the fact that HPPs not only claim more value, but seem satisfied with merely claiming value from the initial (fixed) pie, rather than trying to expand the amount of value available to be claimed. Mannix and Neale (1993) argued that it is the LPP who drives integrative bargaining, perhaps because the alternative is to accept a very disadvantageous outcome. Obversely, HPPs appear to assume a fixed pie and not even seek opportunities for value creation (De Dreu, 2005; also see Olekalns and Smith, in press).

Second, *power imbalances foster a range of suboptimal assumptions and behaviors in negotiations*. Negotiations in an equal-power context—or at least, a relatively balanced-power context—generally reflect better processes and outcomes. Negotiators with equal power produce more integrative agreements than do those with power asymmetry (Mannix and Neale, 1993; Wolfe and McGinn, 2005; but see Rubin and Zartman, 1995). To the extent that power balance and level of power can be disentangled (for example, two negotiators may both be low-level clerks or high-power executives, but still differ in BATNAs; see also Olekalns and Smith, 2010, who manipulated each party's power separately but allowed for negotiations between two HPPs or two LPPs), it appears that these negative effects of asymmetry are driven by the HPPs. Greer and Van Kleef (2010) found that pairs of low-power negotiators were *more* effective at resolving conflicts when their power was unbalanced, whereas for pairs of high-power negotiators, imbalance impeded conflict resolution. The study examined conflicts within top management teams, all of whom had high power but who varied in power from person to person, and compared those with conflicts within lower-level teams, all of whom had relatively low power but again varied from person to person. Because the powerful are highly competitive and motivated to maintain power, relatively less powerful member in pairs of high-power negotiators made efforts to become powerful again. This power conflict can thus escalate conflicts for pairs of high-power negotiators.

In a similar vein, Mannix and Neale (1993) showed that unequal-power dyads can create value when the *low*-power negotiator sets high aspirations and pursues them. The problems may stem, in part, from faulty assumptions held by the powerful: power imbalance seems to prompt them to regard coercive threats as a useful bargaining strategy (De Dreu, 1995), and power tends to foster a fixed-pie assumption about bargaining (De Dreu, 2005). Both of these effects diminish as power differences diminish.

Third, and relatedly, *powerful negotiators tend to try to rely on "brute force" to compel counterparts to comply with their demands, whereas low-power negotiators work to preserve their choice and their interests*. Powerful parties' dominance is based on their perception that they have more important things to do but their less powerful counterparts have trivial and narrow interests (Rubin and Zartman, 1995). Such self-justifying beliefs and behaviors become intensified in a competitive context, as high and low power negotiators adopt a lack of trust and a negative attitude toward each other (Tjosvold, 1981). Given such competitive, zero-sum framing of the negotiating context, higher-power negotiators tend not to take the other's perspective but threaten the other side to get what they want (Tjosvold et al., 1984). Lower-power negotiators, on the other hand, ask more diagnostic questions and work to understand their counterpart and achieve positive relations (De Dreu and Van Kleef, 2004). When these strategies fail, though, in the face of a threatening and powerful counterpart, LPPs do seem to stand their ground, using tactics such as threatening to withdraw or even walking out of negotiations to protect themselves (Tjosvold et al., 1984).

Fourth, *power and anger work synergistically in negotiation contexts.* If power leads to greater value claiming, then power plus anger leads to even more. Many studies have examined the relationship between power and emotion in negotiation; these invariably find that angry HPPs claim more value, whether because the LPP concedes more out of feelings of intimidation (Sinaceur and Tiedens, 2006) or pressure (Van Kleef et al., 2004) or because the HPP feels more focused and aggressive (Overbeck et al., 2010; also see Van Kleef and Sinaceur, Chapter 5, this volume). A powerful negotiator's anger provides both a social signal to the counterpart ("I am tough and demanding, and you will have to sacrifice in order to satisfy me!") and intrapersonal effects on the self (cognitive focus, sense of toughness). Through both pathways, it appears to improve HPPs' value claiming (Overbeck et al., 2010). Surprisingly, there is some evidence that HPPs' anger—and greater anger in the dyad, overall—may even help in value creation. Overbeck and colleagues (2010) found that value creation increased as the number of angry parties in the dyad increased, and that HPP anger was particularly helpful for value creation. Few other studies have examined anger and value creation, so the robustness of this finding cannot be evaluated. However, it is reasonable to think that angry negotiators may be stubborn and refuse to give in, and that—assuming they do not simply walk away from the table—they may thus generate creative solutions in an effort to wrest value from the deal.

Fifth, *power and status dynamics are often moderated by gender.* As discussed earlier, Haselhuhn and Wong (2012) showed that greater facial width-to-height ratios (which appear to correspond to greater subjective sense of power) are associated with dishonesty in negotiations, but only among men. Salter et al. (2005) argued that responses to powerful negotiators depend on gender: Men tend to be avoidant and try to exit negotiations with a powerful male counterpart, whereas women tend to use appeasement strategies and cues of affiliation and even courtship to secure better outcomes. Kray et al., 2001, examined not gender, but gender stereotypes, finding that activation of masculine stereotypes helped powerful negotiators claim more value whereas activation of feminine stereotypes led to more integrative agreements.

Status dynamics may be affected by gender, as well. Curhan and Overbeck (2008) showed that high-status negotiators respond differently to impression motivation based on their gender. Female negotiators, assigned to a high-status role and told to make a good impression on a low-status counterpart, adopted tougher behaviors; male negotiators in the same position actually became softer and more accommodating. The authors suggested that each gender believed that "making a good impression" would be facilitated by deviating from the usual behavior expected of their gender. In contrast, Kulik and Olekalns (2012) showed that women, at least, are actually seen more negatively and gain fewer advantages in negotiation when they violate gender norms; to succeed, the authors argue, women must carefully balance agentic and warm behaviors.

Of course, it is important to note that gender is itself a form of endowed status—that is, maleness is typically more prized than is femaleness (Ridgeway and Bourg, 2004) and stereotypically masculine qualities are often seen as more desirable than stereotypically feminine qualities (compare Eagly and Steffen, 1984; Kray, et al., 2001). This suggests that gender may not only interact with status, but in fact represent a source of status. Indeed, Miles and Clenney (2010) showed that male negotiators were better able to balance cooperation and competitiveness in negotiations than were female negotiators, precisely because men are seen as higher in status than women—they are perceived as more competent and legitimate, which allows them to engage in a range of actions without sanction. It seems possible that the common tendency of male negotiators to engage in tougher bargaining behavior (compare Kray et al., 2001) is tempered among high-status men, who recognize the need to maintain others' consent and approval for status maintenance, and use cooperativeness as a strategy to do so. Though the association of gender and status may provide this advantage to men, of course, it may work to the detriment of women. Being perceived as lower status the moment she walks into a negotiation, simply on the basis of gender, is likely to cause the devaluing of a woman's contributions (compare Bowles et al. 2007; see also Hogue and Yoder, 2003) and to lower the counterpart's motivation to please her (also see Stuhlmacher and Linnabery, Chapter 9, this volume).

Finally, perhaps one of the most prominent perspectives on power and negotiation has not yet been addressed in this chapter because it extends beyond the dyadic perspective on which we have focused. *One of the most robust sources of power in negotiation is the coalitions and alliances that negotiators build with other parties in group negotiation settings.* To get a sense for why coalitions are so important for power relations, consider the situation of employees negotiating with a large corporate employer over issues such as wages, benefits, and working conditions. Each individual employee, confronting a one-on-one negotiation with the employer, is likely to be in a state of severely restricted power: He or she is easily replaceable (especially in the modern, post-economic-crisis age of job scarcity), has a poor BATNA relative to the company's, and offers contributions that, regardless of their importance, are likely regarded by the company in terms of labor costs—unfortunate, unavoidable perhaps, and certainly to be minimized.

So what is a worker to do? Well, for decades an attractive option has been to band together with other workers and negotiate collectively with the employer—that is, to form (or join) a union. The union offers power that individual workers cannot enjoy, largely through its ability to create a very unpleasant BATNA for the employer: loss of production and profitability should workers decide to go on strike. In general, groups can offer strength, and even safety, that individuals cannot achieve; and coalitions of groups—think of neighbors, environmental organizations, and urban justice advocates opposing the introduction of a large, polluting power plant—can achieve what one group alone cannot (Cohen and Thompson, 2011; Morgan and Tindale, 2002; Polzer, 1996; Thompson et al., 1996).

In coalitions and with allies, negotiators can divide tasks to maximize strengths, pool resources, and create a more credible opposition to the counterpart. Groups offer certain reliable tendencies that confer advantage, such as setting higher aspirations, refusing to settle until high value is obtained, and using more strategic offer patterns—even misrepresentation—to drive more favorable deals (Cho et al., 2012; Cohen et al., 2010; Polzer, 1996). Unlike other forms of power, group-based power even seems to improve negotiators' ability to create value, due to the team's superior problem-solving capacity (Thompson et al., 1996). Though teams do not always produce outcomes superior to those of individuals (compare Cohen and Thompson, 2011), they do clearly confer power, particularly to those who enter the negotiation at a disadvantage.

SUMMARY

The extant literature on power in negotiations seems to support the popular notion that power is a good thing to have: Powerful people can claim more value; compel others to concede, even through use of unpleasant behaviors; and feel invigorated even when the negotiation makes them angry. At the same time, they may sacrifice opportunities to gain even more value through value creation; they probably damage relationships through their more destructive behaviors; and they may lazily fall back on using their power rather than working more collaboratively with the counterpart.

Though we know much less about status in negotiations, it appears that these negative effects occur less when the negotiator's potential for influence is based on status, rather than power. Because (prestige-based) status, by definition, requires others' deference and consent—responses that must be earned by the status-holder—a high-status negotiator can ill afford to rely on force, threats, and one-sided behaviors. Rather, she is likely to adopt a more conciliatory stance and to rely on integrative bargaining, not simply aggressive value claiming, to maximize the economic value derived from the negotiation. Of course, it helps that counterparts tend to value the contributions of the high-status party more (Thye, 2000) and make more favorable offers to that party (Ball and Eckel, 1996). That is, the high-status negotiator may not *need* to rely on coercive strategies because the counterpart has internalized the idea that someone with high status deserves more value from the negotiation.

FUTURE DIRECTIONS IN NEGOTIATION RESEARCH INVOLVING POWER, STATUS, AND INFLUENCE

Though the construct of influence suffuses negotiation research and practice—at the very least, negotiation training consistently emphasizes the BATNA and ways of countering power moves by the opposing party—there has been a surprising narrowness to the scope of the overall literature focusing on power, status, and negotiation. This may be a natural consequence of the negotiation literature's focus on issues that affect value claiming and creation, but it leaves many questions to be answered. For example, at this point we know little about the mutual causation of influence dynamics in dyadic (or group) negotiations—that is, how the interaction between negotiators affects influence dynamics, and how those in turn can affect negotiation outcomes. Most study designs assign high and low power to each party, have them negotiate, and then use power as a dichotomous predictor in some outcome such as claimed value. Richer, more interactive designs—perhaps using new multilevel statistical methods such as the Actor-Partner Interaction Model (APIM; Kenny et al., 2006; see also Overbeck et al., 2010)—could provide deeper insight into influence in negotiations.

For example, as discussed above, the research consensus holds that power imbalances create suboptimal negotiation processes and outcomes. But we do not have a great deal of insight into the interpersonal dynamics that create these effects. For example, work by Mannix and Neale (1993) suggests that power-imbalanced negotiations go poorly when the LPP is not responding as constructively as possible, whether by setting insufficient aspirations or by exhibiting resistance. Anecdotally, this chapter's authors have observed students in negotiation classes engage in power struggles whereby the LPP tries mightily to resist being dominated or disadvantaged by the powerful counterpart. It's not surprising that such an interaction would go poorly and produce a poor agreement. Likewise, if the LPP should simply give up in the face of the HPP's aggressive approach, that appears unlikely to produce optimal outcomes. Students in low-power negotiating roles often bemoan their disadvantage in trying to procure a beneficial arrangement from someone who does not need to accommodate. Much of the current state of research would imply that they are in a no-win (or not-much-win) situation.

However, some recent research indicates that, for LPPs, embracing their hierarchical weakness can actually work to their advantage (Wiltermuth et al., 2008). When one person assumes a dominant posture—expansive, erect or leaning back, with limbs held at a distance from the body—then a counterpart tends, automatically and unconsciously, to take on a submissive posture—constricted, hunched forward, with limbs drawn close to the body or crossed (Tiedens and Fragale, 2003). Not only does this postural complementarity send a clear visual signal of who is in charge and who is dependent, but it has even been shown to alter basic body chemistry in ways that reify the hierarchy. That is, dominant postures tend to elevate testosterone (associated with aggression) and depress cortisol (associated with stress), whereas submissive postures do the opposite (Carney et al., 2010). Further, both interaction participants report greater mutual liking and satisfaction for the task when postures are complementary than when they are either both dominant or both submissive (Tiedens and Fragale, 2003).

The existing research (Tiedens and Fragale, 2003) suggests a "first-mover" advantage whereby the first person to adopt a dominant posture seems to "own" that posture, and the counterpart is expected to become posturally submissive. If a negotiator finds that his counterpart is the first to become posturally dominant, he faces a difficult choice between becoming dominant himself, to resist acquiescing to a subordinate role, or acquiescing in order to maintain harmony and goodwill in the interaction. That is, becoming posturally submissive will make him more liked and satisfy the dominant counterpart more, but the implied power differences could foster expectations that he will concede more and accept less value. Becoming posturally dominant could help protect against those damaging expectations, but at cost of a rougher negotiation and more resistance from the counterpart.

Wiltermuth et al. (2008) examined this question, and found that it is better to adopt a submissive posture in the face of a first-mover dominant negotiator. Counter-intuitively, it turns out, though submissive negotiators do claim a smaller share of the pie than their dominant counterparts, they claim much more than do those who try to counter dominance with dominance. Submissive negotiators tend to ask more probing questions, fostering a more productive exchange of information in the negotiation and thus greater value creation. This expansion of value is how these negotiators ultimately claim more value than those who are not complementary: They claim the same proportion as any other submissive negotiator, but that proportion comes from a larger pie.

Along similar lines, Olekalns and Smith (in press) conducted an even more complex and detailed analysis, examining dyads in which power was symmetrically high, symmetrically low, or asymmetric (high and low). They showed that asymmetrical power fosters complementarity in behaviors, allowing both parties to use strategies that provide good fit to their power standing and their goals and to balance dominant and affiliative behaviors. Among the key findings was that neither the high- nor the low-power member of asymmetric dyads unilaterally controls the bargaining process; instead, their strategy develops in a manner distinct from how symmetrically high- or low-power dyads negotiate. Though specific consequences for the low-power party are not addressed, this is consistent with the notion that low-power negotiators, by participating in the negotiation and not merely adopting a stance of resistance toward the powerful counterpart, may find their disadvantage less severe than expected.

These studies offer two examples of how looking not only at the static, dichotomous variable of assigned power but more broadly at how interactions between negotiating counterparts—and how the two parties' behavior is mutually causative—can enrich our understanding of influence in negotiations. Of course, interactional designs pose additional challenges for data analysis, and perhaps this has been one of the key impediments to the field's adopting such designs more widely. New techniques such as the APIM (Kenny et al., 2006) should help. Even more sophisticated analyses of interactions and behavioral sequences over time can be conducted through the use of advanced methods such as Markov modeling (compare Olekalns et al., 2012; Smith et al., 2005; Weingart et al., 1999; Turan et al., 2011) and even machine learning models (Turan et al., 2011). As these methods are embraced by more and more negotiation scholars, our knowledge of influence and negotiations should expand considerably.

Finally, as noted above, there has been relatively little study of the effects of *status* in negotiation. In particular, we suggest that it may be fruitful to examine how the effects of power and status on negotiations differ. As noted earlier, Fragale and colleagues (2011) distinguished status from power and found that perceivers regard those with high power but low status quite negatively. This work did not examine a negotiation context, but could usefully be applied to negotiations. Recently, Blader and Chen (2012) demonstrated that perceivers have a negative association between power and justice but a positive association between status and justice. Applying this to a negotiation context, future research may investigate whether status leads negotiators to behave more fairly during negotiation, or to perceive a high-status counterpart as being more fair, and whether high status negotiators may achieve more fair agreements compared with powerful negotiators. On the other hand, a high status negotiator's enhanced justice may well inhibit value claiming. Such investigations would enrich our understanding of influence processes, broadly speaking, in negotiation.

Power and Status as Outcomes of Negotiation

A final ripe area for development in the literature on influence and negotiation is the examination not of how power and status influence negotiation outcomes, but how negotiation can create and alter power and status dynamics. That is, influence can also be an *outcome* of negotiation. Consider Menachem Begin and Anwar Sadat, the Israeli and Egyptian leaders who negotiated the original peace accords. Certainly each man's status and power influenced the outcome of the negotiation. But the negotiation also changed their futures in a fundamental way, cementing their places in history and offering each man political strength through his demonstrated ability to secure important concessions for his own nation. A successful negotiation can change one's role in the eyes of fellow group members—and so can an unsuccessful negotiation. Through negotiation, one can gain resources that elevate one's power globally, or bargain effectively in a way that changes one's power balance with the counterpart. Having succeeded may impart status and improved future ability to claim value; having failed may reduce status and impair that future ability. In fact, because power and status tend to be awarded to those seen as likely to bring benefits to the group in the future (compare Lenski, 1966), then negotiations on behalf of the group may be a key channel through which fitness to maintain a position of influence is evaluated. Keltner et al. (2008) noted that powerholders need the approval of others, and must consistently deliver what the group expects, to retain power. As such, success at negotiating on the group's behalf may sometimes be a way not of advancing power so much as just holding onto it.

Recently, some investigators have begun to examine these issues. For example, Halevy and colleagues (Halevy et al., 2012) demonstrated that benefitting the ingroup by harming an outgroup increased the perceived influence of a person performing value-claiming actions similar to negotiation. The kind of influence depended on features of the context: When harming the outgroup was the only way to benefit the ingroup, then the actor gained prestige (akin to status) but not dominance (akin to power). When the actor had a choice of whether to harm the outgroup or not, choosing to do so led to greater perceived dominance and lower prestige. Finally, actors were penalized for being too conciliatory with the outgroup; those who shared outside their own group were judged lower on both sources of influence. This suggests that not only the outcomes, but merely the conduct of negotiation can have consequences for one's subsequent power and status.

Similarly, Carnevale and Gonzalez (2010) showed that, within teams of negotiators, individuals who want to boost their own within-team status negotiate more aggressively with the opposing team: They accept fewer deals and claim higher value in their negotiations. Carnevale and Gonzalez argued that this reflects an effort to demonstrate their own, individual value to the group—that by bargaining hard, they are well suited to advance the group's interests, and thus deserve higher status. Indeed, Cho et al. (2011) showed that groups with unsettled hierarchy may prompt members to adopt such status-enhancing strategies. Further, the presence of these negotiators seems to make the group both more strategic—they tend to manipulate information asymmetry to elicit greater concessions—and more aggressive—they tend to avoid accepting their counterparts' settlement agreements. This suggests that individuals may even be placing more priority on how the negotiation will affect their own status than on securing the best outcome possible for the group.

Curhan et al. (2006) pointed out that there are multiple sources of subjective value in negotiation beyond instrumental value, including feelings about the self, the negotiation process, and the relationship. Given the apparently universal concern that people have for their status and their group standing (Frank, 1985; Leary et al., 1995), it is important to continue to examine how individuals may weight their own status outcomes versus group value.

CONCLUSIONS

This chapter opened by saying that influence is a fundamental aspect of negotiation. Though popular press and workshop instructors tend to focus on how to gain more power in negotiation, and how to deal with the counterpart's power, it is also clear that power is not the entire story. In fact, as much of the past literature makes clear, relying on power in a negotiation may be a significantly suboptimal strategy: You can get more if you are powerful, but only more than the other party, and not necessarily as much as you could be getting if you did not rely on power to get it. It may be much more productive to rely on status as a source of influence, given that it seems to prompt the counterpart to *volunteer* more concessions, and to value the status-holder's contributions more highly—all without the need to coerce or engage in relationship-damaging tactics in order to secure those concessions. Ideally, of course, one would have a great BATNA, solid contributions, a sterling reputation, and many characteristics associated with high status; but negotiators are rarely that lucky, at least not all the time.

What we know about power, status, and influence in negotiations is still limited. To borrow terminology from Katz and Kahn's (1978) classic *Social Psychology of Organizations*, our current knowledge focuses on power and status as inputs to negotiation. We have much yet to learn about the throughputs (the detailed processes of power, status, and influence during negotiation interactions) and outputs (how power, status, and influence are formed and affected by negotiations). Fortunately, it is also a time of enormous scholarly interest in these topics, and so we can look forward to new knowledge on the topic emerging soon and often.

REFERENCES

Allred, K.G. (1999). Anger and retaliation: Toward an understanding of impassioned conflict in organizations. In R.J. Bies, R.J. Lewicki, and B.H. Sheppard (eds), *Research on negotiations in organizations* (Vol. 7). Greenwich, CT: JAI Press.

Anderson, C. and Galinsky, A.D. (2006). Power, optimism, and risk-taking. *European Journal of Social Psychology*, 36, 511–536.

Anderson, C. and Kilduff, G.J. (2009). Why do dominant personalities attain influence in face-to-face groups? The competence-signaling effects of trait dominance. *Journal of Personality and Social Psychology*, 96(2), 491.

Anderson, C. and Shirako, A. (2008). Are individuals' reputations related to their history of behavior? *Journal of Personality and Social Psychology*, 94, 320–333.

Anderson, C. and Thompson, L.L. (2004). Affect from the top down: How powerful individuals' positive affect shapes negotiations. *Organizational Behavior and Human Decision Processes*, 95, 125–139.

Anderson, C., Brion, S., Moore, D.A., and Kennedy, J.A. (2012). A status-enhancement account of overconfidence. *Journal of Personality and Social Psychology*, 103(4), 718–735.

Anderson, C., John, O.P., Keltner, D., and Kring, A.M. (2001). Who attains social status? Effects of personality and physical attractiveness in social groups. *Journal of Personality and Social Psychology*, 81, 116–132.

Bacharach, S.B. and Lawler, E.J. (1981). *Bargaining: Power, tactics and outcomes*, San Francisco: Jossey-Bass.

Bachrach, P. and Baratz, M.S. (1962). Two faces of power. *The American Political Science Review*, 56, 947–952.
Ball, S.B. and Eckel, C.C. (1996). Buying status: Experimental evidence on status in negotiation. *Psychology and Marketing*, 13, 381–405.
Bendersky, C. and Hays, N.A. (2012). Status conflict in groups. *Organization Science*, 23, 323–340.
Bendersky, C. and Shah, N. (in press). The downfall of extraverts and rise of neurotics: The dynamic process of status allocation in task groups. *The Academy of Management Journal*.
Berger, J., Cohen, B.P., and Zelditch, N. (1972). Status characteristics and social interaction. *American Sociological Review*, 37, 241–255.
Blader, S.L. and Chen, Y.-R. (2012). Differentiating the effects of status and power: A justice perspective. *Journal of Personality and Social Psychology*. Advance online publication, January 9. doi: 10.1037/a0026651
Blau, P.M. (1964). *Exchange and power in social life*. New York: Wiley.
Bothner, M.S., Kim, Y.-K., and Smith, E.B. (2012). How does status affect performance? Status as an asset vs. status as a liability in the PGA and NASCAR. *Organization Science*, 23, 416–433.
Bowles, H.R., Babcock, L., and Lai, L. (2007). Social incentives for gender differences in the propensity to initiate negotiations: Sometimes it does hurt to ask. *Organizational Behavior and Human Decision Processes*, 103, 84–103.
Brauer, M. and Chekroun, P. (2005). The relationship between perceived violation of social norms and social control: Situational factors influencing the reaction to deviance. *Journal of Applied Social Psychology*, 35, 1519–1539.
Carnevale, P.J. and Gonzalez, C. (2010). Within-group status processes and between-group negotiation. University of Southern California (unpublished data).
Carli, L.L. and Eagly, A.H. (1999). Gender effects on social influence and emergent leadership. In G. Powell (ed.), *Handbook of gender in organizations* (pp. 203–222). Thousand Oaks, CA: Sage.
Carney, D.R., Cuddy, A.J.C., and Yap, A.J. (2010). Power posing. *Psychological Science*, 21, 1363–1368.
Chen, Y.-R., Peterson, R.S., Phillips, D.J., Podolny, J.M., and Ridgeway, C.L. (2012). Introduction to the Special Issue: bringing status to the table—attaining, maintaining, and experiencing status in organizations and markets. *Organization Science*, 23, 299–307.
Cheng, J.T., Tracy, J.L., and Henrich, J. (2010). Pride, personality, and the evolutionary foundations of human social status. *Evolution and Human Behavior*, 31(5), 334–347.
Cho, Y., Overbeck, J.R., and Carnevale, P.J. (2011). Status conflict in negotiation. In E.A. Mannix, M.A. Neale, and J.R. Overbeck (eds), *Research on Managing Groups and Teams: Negotiation and Groups* (pp. 111–136). New York: Emerald Group Publishing Limited.
Cho, Y., Overbeck, J.R., and Carnevale, P.J. (2012). *The effects of group structure on intergroup negotiation*. Unpublished manuscript, University of Southern California.
Cohen, T.R. and Thompson, L. (2011). When are teams an asset in negotiations and when are they a liability? In E.A. Mannix, M.A. Neale, and J.R. Overbeck (eds), *Research on Managing Groups and Teams: Negotiation and Groups* (pp. 3–34). New York: Emerald Group Publishing Limited.
Cohen, T., Leonardelli, G., and Thompson, L. (2010). The agreement bias in negotiation: Teams facilitate impasse. In IACM 23rd Annual Conference Paper, May.
Curhan, J.R. and Overbeck, J.R. (2008). Making a positive impression in a negotiation: Gender differences in response to impression motivation. *Negotiation and Conflict Management Research*, 1, 179–193.
Curhan, J.R., Elfenbein, H.A., and Xu, H. (2006). What do people value when they negotiate? Mapping the domain of subjective value in negotiation. *Journal of Personality and Social Psychology*, 91, 493–512.
Dawson, R. (1987). *Secrets of power negotiating: You can get anything you want*.

Audio/CD training. Retrieved 10 September 2012 from http://www.amazon.com/The-Secrets-Power-Negotiating-anything/dp/B000BTBDWO/ref=tmm_abk_title_0?ie=UTF8&qid=1347309165&sr=8-1.

De Dreu, C.K.W. (1995). Coercive power and concession making in bilateral negotiation. *Journal of Conflict Resolution, 39*, 646–670.

De Dreu, C.K.W. (2005). A PACT against conflict escalation in negotiation and dispute resolution. *Current Directions in Psychological Science, 14*, 149–152.

De Dreu, C.K.W. and Van Kleef, G.A. (2004). The influence of power on the information search, impression formation, and demands in negotiation. *Journal of Experimental Social Psychology, 40*, 303–319.

DePaulo, B.M. and Friedman, H.S. (1998). Nonverbal communication. In DePaulo, B.M. and H.S. Friedman (eds), *The handbook of social psychology, Vols. 1 and 2* (4th edn) (pp. 3–40). New York: McGraw-Hill.

DeWall, C.N., Baumeister, R.F., Mead, N.L., and Vohs, K.D. (2010). How leaders self-regulate their task performance: Evidence that power promotes diligence, depletion, and disdain. *Journal of Personality and Social Psychology, 100*, 47–65.

Dwyer, F.R. (1984). Are two better than one? Bargaining behavior and outcomes in an asymmetrical power relationship. *Journal of Consumer Research, 11*, 680–693.

Eagly, A.H. and Steffen, V.J. (1984). Gender stereotypes stem from the distribution of women and men into social roles. *Journal of Personality and Social Psychology, 46*, 735–754.

Emerson, R.M. (1962). Power-dependence relations. *American Sociological Review, 27*, 31–41.

Fisher, R. and Ury, W. (1981). *Getting to yes*. Boston: Houghton Mifflin.

Fiske, S.T. (1993). Controlling other people: The impact of power on stereotyping. *American Psychologist, 48*, 621–628.

Fiske, S.T. and Berdahl, J. (2007). Social power. In A.W. Kruglansk and E.T. Higgins (eds), *Social psychology: Handbook of basic principles* (pp. 678–692). New York: Guilford Press.

Flynn, F.J. and Amanatullah, E.T. (2012). Psyched up or psyched out? The influence of coactor status on individual performance. *Organization Science, 23*(2), 402–415.

Foucault, M. (1995). *Discipline and punish: The birth of the prison*. New York: Vintage.

Fragale, A.R., Overbeck, J.R., and Neale, M.A. (2011). Resources versus respect: Social judgments based on targets' power and status positions. *Journal of Experimental Social Psychology, 47*, 767–775.

Frank, R.H. (1985). *Choosing the right pond: Human behavior and the quest for status*. New York: Oxford University Press.

French, J.R.P. and Raven, B. (2001). The bases of social power. In D. Cartwright (ed.), *Studies of social power* (pp. 118–149). Ann Arbor, MI: Institute for Social Research.

Fulmer, I.S., Barry, B., and Long, A. (2009). Lying and smiling: Informational and emotional deception in negotiation. *Journal of Business Ethics, 88*(4), 691–709.

Galinsky, A.D. and Mussweiler, T. (2001). First offers as anchors: The role of perspective-taking and negotiator focus. *Journal of Personality and Social Psychology, 81*, 657–669.

Galinsky, A.D., Gruenfeld, D.H., and Magee, J.C. (2003). From power to action. *Journal of Personality and Social Psychology, 85*, 453–466.

Glick, S. and Croson, R. (2001). Reputations in negotiation. In S. Hoch and H. Kunreuther (eds), *Wharton on making decisions* (pp. 177–186). New York: Wiley.

Greer, L.L. and Van Kleef, G.A. (2010). Equality versus differentiation: The effects of power dispersion on group interaction. *Journal of Applied Psychology, 95*, 1032–1044.

Guinote, A. (2007). Power and goal pursuit. *Personality and Social Psychology Bulletin, 33*, 1076–1087.

Halevy, N., Chou, E.Y., Cohen, T.R., and Livingston, R.W. (2012). Status conferral in intergroup social dilemmas: Behavioral antecedents and consequences of prestige and dominance. *Journal of Personality and Social Psychology, 102*, 351–366.

Hamner, W.C. and Harnett, D.L. (1975). The effects of information and aspiration level on bargaining behavior. *Journal of Experimental Social Psychology, 11*, 329–342, doi: 10.1016/0022-1031(75)90014-1.

Haselhuhn, M.P. and Wong, E.M. (2012). Bad to the bone: facial structure predicts unethical behaviour. *Proceedings of the Royal Society B: Biological Sciences, 279*, 571–576.

Henrich, J. and Gil-White, F.J. (2001). The evolution of prestige: Freely conferred deference as a mechanism for enhancing the benefits of cultural transmission. *Evolution and Human Behavior, 22*, 165–196.

Hogue, M. and Yoder, J.D. (2003). The role of status in producing depressed entitlement in women's and men's pay allocations. *Psychology of Women Quarterly, 27*, 330–337, doi: 10.1111/1471-6402.00113.

Hollander, E.P. (1958). Conformity, status, and idiosyncrasy credit. *Psychological Review, 65*, 117–127.

Inesi, M.E. (2010). Power and loss aversion. *Organizational Behavior and Human Decision Processes, 112*, 58–69.

James, G. (2009). 7 Strategies to build "negotiating power", *CBS News*, 30 June. Retrieved 10 September 2012 from http://www.cbsnews.com/8301-505183_162-28543726-10391735/7-strategies-to-build-negotiating-power/.

Karrass (2012). http://www.karrass.com/effective-negotiating-two-day-seminar.

Katz, D. and Kahn, R. (1978). *The social psychology of organizations*. New York: Wiley.

Keltner, D., Gruenfeld, D.H., and Anderson, C. (2003). Power, approach, and inhibition. *Psychological Review, 110*, 265–284.

Keltner, D., Van Kleef, G.A., Chen, S., and Kraus, M.W. (2008). A reciprocal influence model of social power: Emerging principles and lines of inquiry. *Advances in Experimental Social Psychology, 40*, 151–192.

Kenny, D.A., Kashy, D.A., and Cook, W.L. (2006). *Dyadic data analysis*. New York: Guilford Press.

Kim, P.H. and Fragale, A.R. (2005). Choosing the path to bargaining power: an empirical comparison of BATNAs and contributions in negotiation. *Journal of Applied Psychology, 90*, 373–381.

Kim, P.H., Pinkley, R.L., and Fragale, A.R. (2005). Power dynamics in negotiation. *The Academy of Management Review*, 799–822.

Koning, L., Van Dijk, E., Van Beest, I., and Steinel, W. (2009). An instrumental account of deception and reactions to deceit in bargaining. *Business Ethics Quarterly, 20*, 57–73.

Kopelman, S., Rosette, A., and Thompson, L. (2006). The three faces of Eve: Strategic displays of positive neutral and negative emotions in negotiations. *Organization Behavior and Human Decision Processes, 99*(1), 81–101.

Kray, L.J., Thompson, L.L., and Galinsky, A.D. (2001). Battle of the sexes: Gender stereotype confirmation and reactance in negotiations. *Journal of Personality and Social Psychology, 80*, 942–958.

Kray, L.J., Reb, J., Galinsky, A.D., and Thompson, L. (2004). Stereotype reactance at the bargaining table: The effect of stereotype activation and power on claiming and creating value. *Personality and Social Psychology Bulletin, 30*, 399–411.

Kulik, C.T. and Olekalns, M. (2012). Negotiating the gender divide: lessons from the negotiation and organizational behavior literatures. *Journal of Management, 38*, 1387–1415.

Lammers, J. and Stapel, D.A. (2009). How power influences moral thinking. *Journal of Personality and Social Psychology, 97*, 279–289.

Lammers, J., Stapel, D.A., and Galinsky, A.D. (2010). Power increases hypocrisy. *Psychological Science, 21*, 737–744.

Leary, M.R., Tambor, E.S., Terdal, S.K., and Downs, D.L. (1995). Self-esteem as an interpersonal monitor: The sociometer hypothesis. In: R.F. Baumeister (ed.), *The self in social psychology* (pp. 87–104).

Lenski, G.E. (1966). *Power and privilege: A theory of social stratification*. New York: McGraw-Hill.

Lukes, S. (1974). *Power: A radical view*. London: Macmillan.

Magee, J.C., Galinsky, A.D., and Gruenfeld, D.H. (2007). Power, propensity to negotiate, and moving first in competitive interactions. *Personality and Social Psychology Bulletin, 33*, 200–212.

Magee, J.C., Gruenfeld, D.H., Keltner, D., and Galinsky, A.D. (2005). Leadership and the psychology of power. In D.M. Messick and R.M. Kramer (eds), *The psychology of leadership: New perspectives and research* (pp. 275–293). Mahwah, NJ: Lawrence Erlbaum Associates.

Mannix, E.A. and Neale, M.A. (1993). Power imbalance and the pattern of exchange in dyadic negotiation. *Group Decision and Negotiation, 2*, 119–133.

Merten, J.R. (1997). Facial-affective behavior, mutual gaze, and emotional experience in dyadic interactions. *Journal of Nonverbal Behavior. Special Issue: The communicative function of facial expressions: I. Empirical challenges, 21*, 179–201.

Miles, E.W. and Clenney, E.F. (2010). Gender differences in negotiation: A status characteristics theory view. *Negotiation and Conflict Management Research, 3*, 130–144.

Mohammed, S., Rizzuto, T., Hiller, N.J., Newman, D.A., and Chen, T. (2008). Individual differences and group negotiation: The role of polychronicity, dominance, and decision rule. *Negotiation and Conflict Management Research, 1*, 282–307.

Morgan, P.M. and Tindale, R.S. (2002). Group vs individual performance in mixed-motive situations: Exploring an inconsistency. *Organizational Behavior and Human Decision Processes, 87*, 44–65.

Mussweiler, T. and Strack, F. (1999). Comparing is believing: a selective accessibility model of judgmental anchoring. In W. Stroebe and M. Hewstone (eds), *European Review of Social Psychology*, Vol. 10 (pp. 135–168). Chichester, UK: Wiley.

Olekalns, M. (1991). The balance of power: effects of role and market forces on negotiated outcomes. *Journal of Applied Social Psychology, 21*, 1012–1033.

Olekalns, M. and Smith, P.L. (in press). Dyadic power profiles: Power-contingent strategies for value creation in negotiation. *Human Communication Research*.

Olekalns, M., Smith, P.L., and Weingart, L.R. (2012). Markov chain models of negotiators' communication. In D.J. Christie (ed.), *Encyclopedia of Peace Psychology*. Chichester, UK: Wiley-Blackwell.

Overbeck, J.R. (2010). Concepts and historical perspectives on power. *The Social Psychology of Power*, 19–45.

Overbeck, J.R. and Park, B. (2001). When power does not corrupt: superior individuation processes among powerful perceivers. *Journal of Personality and Social Psychology, 81*, 549–565.

Overbeck, J.R. and Park, B. (2006). Powerful perceivers, powerless objects: Flexibility of powerholders' social attention. *Organizational Behavior and Human Decision Processes, 99*, 227–243.

Overbeck, J.R., Neale, M.A., and Govan, C.L. (2010). I feel, therefore you act: Intrapersonal and interpersonal effects of emotion on negotiation as a function of social power. *Organizational Behavior and Human Decision Processes, 112*, 126–139.

Overbeck, J.R., Tost, L.P., and Wazlawek, A. (2012). What is powerful is good: Viewing powerful authorities as high in moral character. Unpublished manuscript, University of Utah.

Pettit, N.C. and Sivanathan, N. (2012). The eyes and ears of status: how status colors perceptual judgment. *Personality and Social Psychology Bulletin, 38*(5), 570–582.

Pfeffer, J. and Salancik, G.R. (1978). *The external control of organizations*. New York: Harper and Row.

Polzer, J.T. (1996). Intergroup negotiations the effects of negotiating teams. *Journal of Conflict Resolution, 40*, 678–698.

Pynchon, V. (2011). Women's negotiation "problem" may be power, not gender. *Forbes Magazine*, 21 August. Retrieved 10 September 2012 from http://news.yahoo.com/womens-negotiation-problem-may-power-not-gender-083036302.html.

Rabin, M. (1997). *Bargaining Structure, Fairness and Efficiency*. Unpublished Manuscript, University of California.

Raven, B.H. (1964). *Social influence and power*. In I.D. Steiner and M. Fishbein (eds), *Current studies in social psychology* (pp. 371–381). New York: Holt Rinehart and Winston.

Ridgeway, C.L. and Bourg, C. (2004). Gender as status: An expectation states theory approach. In A.H. Eagly, A.E. Beall, and R.J. Sternberg (eds), *The psychology of gender* (pp. 217–241). New York: Guilford Press.

Ridgeway, C.L. and Diekema, D. (1992). Are gender differences status differences? In C.L. Ridgeway (ed.), *Gender, interaction, and inequality* (pp. 157–180). New York: Springer-Verlag.

Rubin, J.Z. and Zartman, I.W. (1995). Asymmetrical negotiations: Some survey results that may surprise. *Negotiation Journal*, *11*, 349–364.

Russell, B. (1938). *Power: A social analysis*. London: Allen and Unwin.

Salter, F., Grammer, K., and Rikowski, A. (2005). Sex differences in negotiating with powerful males. *Human Nature*, *16*, 306–321.

Sinaceur, M. and Tiedens, L.Z. (2006). Get mad and get more than even: When and why anger expression is effective in negotiations. *Journal of Experimental Social Psychology*, *42*, 314–322.

Slabu, L. and Guinote, A. (2010). Getting what you want: Power increases the accessibility of active goals. *Journal of Experimental Social Psychology*, *46*, 344–349, doi: 10.1016/j.jesp.2009.10.013.

Smith, P.L., Olekalns, M., and Weingart, L. (2005). Markov chain analyses of communication processes in negotiation. *International Negotiation*, *10*, 97–113.

Thibaut, J.W. and Kelley, H.H. (1959). *The social psychology of groups*. Oxford, UK: Wiley.

Tiedens, L.Z. and Fragale, A.R. (2003). Power moves: Complementarity in dominant and submissive nonverbal behavior. *Journal of Personality and Social Psychology*, *84*, 558–568, doi:10.1037/0022-3514.84.3.558.

Thompson, L. (1990). The influence of experience on negotiation performance. *Journal of Experimental Social Psychology*, *26*, 528–544, doi: 10.1016/0022-1031(90)90054-P.

Thompson, L. (2011). *The mind and heart of the negotiator* (5th edn). Upper Saddle River, NJ: Prentice Hall.

Thompson, L., Peterson, E., and Brodt, S.E. (1996). Team negotiation: An examination of integrative and distributive bargaining. *Journal of Personality and Social Psychology*, *70*, 66–78.

Thompson, L.L., Wang, J., and Gunia, B.C. (2010). Negotiation. *Annual Review of Psychology*, *61*, 491–515.

Thye, S.R. (2000). A status value theory of power in exchange relations. *American Sociological Review*, *65*, 407–432.

Tiedens, L.Z. and Fragale, A.R. (2003). Power moves: complementarity in dominant and submissive nonverbal behavior. *Journal of Personality and Social Psychology*, *84*, 558–568.

Tinsley, C.H., O'Connor, K.M., and Sullivan, B.A. (2002). Tough guys finish last: The perils of a distributive reputation. *Organizational Behavior and Human Decision Processes*, *88*, 621–642.

Tjosvold, D. (1981). Unequal power relationships within a cooperative or competitive context. *Journal of Applied Social Psychology*, *11*, 137–150.

Tjosvold, D., Johnson, D.W., and Johnson, R. (1984). Influence strategy, perspective-taking, and relationships between high-and low-power individuals in cooperative and competitive contexts. *Journal of Psychology*, *116*, 187–202.

Turan, N., Dudik, M., Gordon, G., and Weingart, L.R. (2011). Modeling group negotiation: Three computational approaches that can inform behavioral sciences. In E.A. Mannix, M.A. Neale, and J.R. Overbeck (eds), *Negotiation and Groups (Research on Managing Groups and Teams*, pp. 189–205). London: Emerald Group Publishing.

Van Kleef, G.A., De Dreu, C.K.W., and Manstead, A.S.R. (2004). The interpersonal effects of emotions in negotiations: A motivated information processing approach. *Journal of Personality and Social Psychology*, *87*, 57–76.

Van Kleef, G.A., De Dreu, C.K.W., Pietroni, D., and Manstead, A.S.R. (2006). Power and emotion in negotiation: Power moderates the interpersonal effects of anger and happiness on concession making. *European Journal of Social Psychology*, *36*, 557–581.

Velden, F.S.T., Beersma, B., and De Dreu, C.K.W. (2007). Majority and minority influence in group negotiation: The moderating effects of social motivation and decision rules. *Journal of Applied Psychology*, 92, 259–268.

Weber, M. (1946). Structures of power. In H.H. Gerth and C. Wright Mills (eds), *From Max Weber* (pp. 159–179). New York: Oxford University Press.

Weingart, L.R., Prietula, M.J., Hyder, E.B., and Genovese, C.R. (1999). Knowledge and the sequential processes of negotiation: A Markov chain analysis of response-in-kind. *Journal of Experimental Social Psychology*, 35, 366–393.

Wiltermuth, S.S. and Flynn, F. (in press). Power, moral clarity, and punishment in the workplace. *Academy of Management Journal*.

Wiltermuth, S.S., Tiedens, L.Z., and Neale, M.A. (2008). The benefits of dominant behaviors in cooperative negotiations. Paper presented at Transatlantic Doctoral Conference, London, UK.

Wolfe, R.J. and McGinn, K.L. (2005). Perceived relative power and its influence on negotiations. *Group Decision and Negotiation*, 14, 3–20.

7. Trust and negotiation
Roy J. Lewicki and Beth Polin

INTRODUCTION

Trust is an inherent part of the negotiation context. Parties engage in a negotiation because they have each decided that they are dependent on the other to provide something—particularly the exchange of accurate information and the willingness to implement their agreement—that will improve their current situation and enable them to negotiate successfully. It is because of this very interdependence that trust—which is about risk in and of itself—or distrust will develop between negotiating parties. Therefore, trust, distrust, interdependence, and information sharing are integral to the negotiation process itself and to its ultimate success or failure. The ubiquitous nature of trust in the negotiation context makes this chapter a necessity in a negotiation handbook such as this.

We have taken a unique approach to the design of this chapter by summarizing research around ten commonly asked questions about trust in the context of negotiation. We believe this is a simple, direct way of presenting a comprehensive overview of how and why trust is important to include in any discussion about negotiation. Some answers allow for a straightforward 'yes' or 'no' response followed by support of that answer, and others involve a more complex discussion and analysis in order to reach a conclusion. In the pages of this chapter, you will find answers to the basic and advanced questions in the following list:

1. What is trust?
2. Why is trust integral to negotiation?
3. What is the trust/honesty dilemma in negotiation?
4. What affects the development of trust in negotiation transactions?
5. How does culture affect trust and negotiation transactions?
6. What are the ways that trust can be broken in a negotiation?
7. What are the consequences of broken trust for negotiators?
8. Can broken trust be repaired?
9. If parties believe that trust can be repaired, then what are the ways this can happen?
10. What have we learned and what do we still need to learn about trust and negotiation?

The first three questions define the basic conceptual domains of this chapter: trust, negotiation, and the challenges of managing trust in a negotiation. With this foundation established, Question 4 addresses more complex issues surrounding the characteristics of negotiating parties or the negotiation context that affect trust. Question 5 assesses how parties from various national cultures may be differently disposed to trust issues in negotiation. Questions 6 through 9 discuss broken trust in negotiation, including how trust can be broken and how broken trust can be repaired. The last question summarizes the chapter and also recommends future research directions concerning trust and negotiation. After reading this chapter, you should have a comprehensive understanding of trust in the negotiation context.

QUESTION 1: WHAT IS TRUST?

A number of definitions of trust exist, each differing in the target of the emphasis. Some definitions explain trust in terms of the trustor's motives and intentions. Lewicki et al. (1998) define trust in such terms, saying it is the "confident positive expectations regarding another's conduct" (p. 439). Similarly, Mayer et al. (1995) define trust as "the willingness of a party to be vulnerable to the actions of another party based on the expectation that the other party will perform a particular action important to the trustor, irrespective of the ability to monitor or control that other party" (p. 712). Other definitions identify trust through behaviors, such as those that can be seen in simple experimental games (e.g., Berg et al., 1995). Gillespie (2003) proposed a behavioral trust inventory that operationalized trusting intentions into behaviors within specific organizational contexts. Yet other authors present trust as a unique internal state of an individual; for example, Rousseau et al. (1998) state that trust is "a psychological state comprising the intention to accept vulnerability based upon positive expectations of the intentions or behavior of another" (p. 395). This final definition has improved upon previous conceptualizations of trust, and as such is one of the most commonly used definitions in the building research literature.

Several authors have suggested that there are different types of trust. These different types of trust are representative of the stage of development in which the trust resides, indicating that trust has a dynamic and transformational nature and changes as it develops. Shapiro et al. (1992) called the most basic form of trust—the type of trust required by any negotiating parties—*deterrence-based trust*. As explained by the authors, "a minimal condition for many business relationships is that individuals' actions follow their words" (p. 366). Particularly in a negotiation context, parties must trust that the other will follow through with promises made during the negotiation; for example, if a seller promises to deliver goods to a buyer, that promise must be kept and the goods must indeed be delivered. It includes the word "deterrence" because the authors argue that the primary motivator for complying with the trust is deterrence, that is, strong negative consequences for not complying with the trust. Following up on this work, Lewicki and Bunker (1995; 1996) discuss the evolutionary nature of trust, but suggest that deterrence is not the only motivator behind keeping one's word. Trust can also be motivated by positive rewards for complying with the agreement. As such, Lewicki and Bunker argue for this type of trust to be termed *calculus-based trust*; the trustor should rationally decide to trust the other party not because they are afraid of negative consequences, but because they want to achieve positive consequences. Returning to our example, a seller should want to follow through and deliver a good to a buyer not only because they are afraid of losing the buyer as a client, being sued, or losing money, but also because they want the relationship to continue, the agreement to be fulfilled, and the buyer to continue to make purchases from them in the future.

As a negotiating relationship advances due to either positive repeated interactions or the length of a single transaction, calculus-based trust has the opportunity to evolve into a deeper-rooted form of trust called *knowledge-based trust*. Both Shapiro et al. (1992) and Lewicki and Bunker (1995; 1996) agree that this form of trust goes beyond trusting that the other party will keep their word; it resides in the ability of one party to come to know and understand the other so as to accurately predict what the other party wants and how the other party will behave. The predicted behavior can be either positive or negative (e.g. the other party can cooperate or be uncooperative); the key is that the behavior is predictable (Shapiro et al., 1992). This leaves the trustor with a certain degree of control over the situation, which reduces the negative feelings (fear and anxiety) that might be associated with the risk that is being taken by trusting the other party. Graduating to a point of being able to predict each other's behavior takes effort, which may come in the form of learning more about the other party's tendencies and behavior prior to engaging in the negotiation and communicating regularly throughout the negotiation (Shapiro et al., 1992), as well as by continually monitoring the other party through verification of information offered (Lewicki and Polin, in press). Thus, if a negotiator knows that the other party will frequently agree to things but then forget to implement them and follow up, the negotiator can periodically monitor the agreement or take other safeguards to protect against the other's failure to follow through.

As the relationship between the negotiating parties continues to develop even further, knowledge-based trust has the opportunity to advance and morph into *identification-based trust* (Lewicki and Bunker, 1995; 1996; Shapiro et al., 1992). Identification-based trust is the strongest form of trust, the "highest order of trust" (Shapiro et al., 1992, p. 371) in which parties "effectively understand and appreciate the other's wants" (Lewicki and Stevenson, 1998, p. 107). This form of trust is characterized by an identification with the other and an effort to help the other realize their goals. This type of trust is often seen in integrative negotiations, and particularly between parties who know each other very well, where the parties not only have individual goals to achieve but also define and work to accomplish joint goals. After all, as explained by Lewicki and Bunker (1996), identification-based trust allows for each party to act as an agent for the other party if need be. While some business relationships actually evolve to this level, most negotiation agreements—and most business relationships in general—rarely reach the level of claiming identification-based trust.

In addition to the different types of trust that might be operative in a negotiated relationship, other researchers have suggested that it is important to distinguish trust from distrust. While trust is "confident positive expectations regarding another's conduct," distrust can be defined as "confident negative expectations regarding another's conduct" (Lewicki et al., 1998, p. 439). These authors explore a number of implications of separating trust and distrust, but probably the most important implication for a chapter on negotiation is that trust and distrust can co-exist in a negotiated relationship, and that they need to be managed differently. Negotiators should be focused on building trust with the other but also on 'managing' distrust by taking precautions that protect the negotiator from the negative consequences if trust is broken. Actions that build trust—ones that we will discuss later in this chapter—are different from actions that 'manage distrust', and the wise negotiator attends to both.

Up to this point, we have explained the general definitions of trust, the different types of trust that exist based on the stage of development of the relationship, and the difference between trust and distrust. As we have attempted to answer *What is trust?* we may also define the construct in terms of *what trust is not*. Research has shown that trust is not the same as cooperation, confidence, or a lack of suspicion. Regarding the first, while cooperative behavior may lead to trust and trust may lead to cooperative behavior, cooperation does not necessarily involve risk as trust does (Mayer et al., 1995). Furthermore, one party can cooperate with another party and not trust them, or they can trust them but decide to not cooperate with them. A negotiator may choose to use cooperation as a strategy (e.g., a negotiator may cooperate in order to appear friendly while really taking advantage of the other party), or a negotiator may not want to cooperate but they must do so because their superiors are instructing them to act cooperatively. Trust is also not necessarily synonymous with confidence. One can have confidence in another party, but that confidence does not necessarily relate to positive behavior; for example, a negotiator may think that they can be confident that the other party will take advantage of them, or that they will ignore their gestures of cooperation. This confidence can be on the basis of previous experience with another party, knowing about the other party through their reputation, or on the basis of nonverbal signals that they may be sending even before one has established a reputation with them (compare Luhmann, 1988). Finally, distrust is different from suspicion, which is defined as perceiving ambiguity about another's motives (Sinaceur, 2010). Having suspicion can actually provide greater benefits to a negotiator than simply having trust, since suspicion motivates the negotiator to more extensively search for cues about the other's trustworthiness. In a series of research studies, pairs of negotiators in which one party was suspicious actually achieved more successful integrative agreements than when both parties 'automatically' trusted the other (Sinaceur, 2010).

Finally, trust is not the same as trustworthiness. Whereas trust was defined earlier in terms of the judgment that one person (the trustor) makes about another in a trust judgment, trustworthiness can be defined as a characteristic or a quality of the other party (the trustee). Trustworthiness, then, enables one party to make a judgment about how 'trustable' the other party is based on the characteristics of the other party. Let us elaborate on the importance of this understanding of trustworthiness as distinct from trust.

There are three dimensions of trustworthiness to look for in an opposing party: ability, benevolence, and integrity. Perceived ability is defined as "that group of skills, competencies, and characteristics that enable a party to have influence within some specific domain" (Mayer et al., 1995, p. 717). In a negotiation, we can observe that the other negotiator has appropriately prepared for the negotiation by gathering background data on the specific issues, working to understand the context of the negotiation, and educating themselves on proper and effective negotiation proceedings. Perceived benevolence is defined as "the extent to which a trustee is believed to want to do good to the trustor, aside from an egocentric profit motive" (Mayer et al., 1995, p. 718). Specific to a negotiation, benevolence is seen in the way that the other party treats us. We must trust that the other is, of course, going to try to achieve their goals in the negotiation, but that in doing so, they will not purposely try to harm us.

Signs of benevolence include showing courtesy and respect. For example, a negotiator may kindly explain their position, and then listen attentively as we explain our position. Negotiators may also actively refrain from using ethically ambiguous negotiation tactics (discussed in Questions 6 and 7). A demonstration of benevolence can be most easily seen when the negotiation is integrative and/or when an identification-based level of trust has been reached: each party seeks to help the other achieve their goals. Finally, perceived integrity is defined as "the trustor's perception that the trustee adheres to a set of principles that the trustor finds acceptable" (Mayer et al., 1995, p. 719). Whereas benevolence is defined by how nicely the opponent treats us (and vice versa, in their eyes), integrity judgments are made about the other based on their broader patterns of behavior, not just the way they specifically treat us. Integrity gets at the fundamental ethical character of the other party: do they follow through with promises made, do they tell the truth (credibility), are they professional, and do others speak about them as having integrity?

In answering Question 1, we have presented several general definitions of trust and indicated which is the most commonly used definition. We have explained the evolutionary nature of trust and how different levels of trust exist. We have also introduced the idea that trust, distrust, cooperation, confidence, and suspicion are different, and that distrust and suspicion may actually be advantageous in a negotiation. Finally, we have clarified that trust is not the same as trustworthiness, the latter of which is one characteristic of the trustee and understood by the trustor based on the other's ability, benevolence, and integrity. Trusting the other, and being trustworthy in one's own actions, jointly exhibited by both sides, are critical for a maximally effective negotiation.

QUESTION 2: WHY IS TRUST INTEGRAL TO NEGOTIATION?

Since this is a handbook on negotiation, many other chapters in this volume have extensively defined negotiation and elaborated on the core components of the negotiation process. We will outline only the basics here, highlighting why trust (or distrust) will naturally exist, even if effort is not put toward the development (or reduction) of trust. First, negotiation is a process by which "two or more parties attempt to resolve their opposing interests" (Lewicki et al., 2010, p. 6). In attempting to resolve these opposing interests, the need for trust in negotiation arises because of each party's interdependence with the other in achieving this resolution. Negotiators depend on each other to help them achieve their goals and objectives, primarily by depending on the amount and accuracy of the information presented by the other party, on the outcomes to which the parties commit throughout the negotiation process, and on the other party delivering on those commitments. As noted elsewhere (Kelley, 1966; Lewicki and Polin, in press), navigating this dependence on the other requires a negotiator to continually evaluate how much he can trust what the other party says, as well as how honest (and hence vulnerable) the negotiator himself can be about what he discloses to the other party. An effective negotiator cannot afford to be too trusting of the other party and run the risk of being fooled, tricked, or taken advantage of; at the same time, if he does not trust enough, it may be impossible to accept anything the other party says at face value or reach a viable agreement. Similarly, if a negotiator is too honest with the other party, she risks becoming too vulnerable by giving away her bargaining position; but if she is not honest enough, she may not be able to give the other party enough information to make an agreement possible. (This challenge is discussed further in Question 3.)

Recent research has confirmed how problematic these dilemmas can be for parties in social and economic interactions, the reason being that each party tends to view the situation from their own unique perspective and hence not understand their impact on others or how others are judging them. Trustors focus primarily on the risk associated with being vulnerable, while trusted parties evaluate the relationship based on the amount of benefit they expect to receive. For example, suppose a job candidate is negotiating a job offer with a potential employer. The candidate has no other job offers, but she is hesitant to reveal this because she knows that the recruiter could abuse the situation by making a very low salary offer. The recruiter asks the candidate, 'So what other job offers do you have?' The candidate decides to be honest and tell the recruiter that she has none, hoping that her honesty will be rewarded with a viable market-competitive salary. In this situation, the candidate (the trustor) is fearful about how much she has made herself vulnerable by answering truthfully, while the recruiter is privately enjoying the fact that he now realizes he can probably get the candidate to accept a reasonably skimpy offer.

Malhotra (2004) proposes that in such situations, trustors trust more when risk is low but tend to ignore the benefit that is received by trusted parties, while trustees are more likely to reciprocate when the benefit is high but tend to ignore the amount of risk the trustor faces when engaging in trusting actions. Moreover, each party is not highly sensitive to the factors that tend to govern the other's decisions, suggesting that even as the parties attempt to coordinate actions in the design and execution of a negotiated agreement, they may be quite 'out of sync' with each other in how their attention is focused in creating an effective transaction. For example, Weber et al. (2005) argue that the decision to trust another party is often made as a result of a need to minimize the risk associated with one's own dependence on the other party, hence leading the actor to initiate 'irrationally' less cautious behavior (from a risk-minimization point of view) but which may nevertheless initiate reciprocally trusting gestures from the other party.

To summarize our answer to Question 2, we have provided a basic definition of negotiation and explained that trust is an inherent part of negotiation because of negotiation's interdependent nature. Parties negotiate because they believe that they are better off negotiating than not negotiating. In any interdependent relationship, levels of trust or distrust will naturally exist. Of course, trust in a negotiation is more efficacious than a situation with distrust, as will be discussed further later in the chapter.

QUESTION 3: WHAT IS THE TRUST/HONESTY DILEMMA IN NEGOTIATION?

What are the consequences—both benefits and liabilities—of trusting in a negotiation? There are several ways that trust can simplify negotiation. First, one of the primary purposes of negotiation is the exchange of information between parties in order to persuade the other to 'see it your way'. Trust is integral to this exchange of information. Each party has to be able to believe what the other is saying, since they often cannot verify or confirm all statements, claims, and charges. Thus, ultimately, trust between negotiators can minimize transaction costs in closing a deal. Deals can be completed and verified 'on a handshake' because the established trust between the parties creates the expectation that all parties will follow through and keep their promises and commitments. Secondly, in the exchange of information, the other's trustworthiness becomes as important as trust. To be trustworthy, a negotiator must work to establish and maintain his credibility. One's credibility is grounded in the perception that the information being conveyed is accurate and verifiable. (Credibility is often one of the components of 'integrity' we described in Question 1, and we discuss trustworthiness in more detail again later in this chapter.) Finally, then, once credibility is established, a negotiator develops a reputation. Reputations are how other people speak about their experiences of trustworthiness in another party. For example, merchants develop a reputation for honesty, a reputation that is conveyed to others in the marketplace. A reputation for credibility and honesty is integral for a merchant to maintain positive working relationships in all strategic affiliations; deals can be struck efficiently and without a great deal of time and effort being invested in verification. Similarly, maintaining a reputation for trustworthiness is critical to negotiators, and negotiators should frequently monitor whether their reputation is as good as they would like it to be. Finally, although we pointed out earlier that they are not identical, research shows that trustworthiness and cooperation can spiral and create dynamic interdependence. Trust feeds cooperation, cooperation feeds trust, and the two can stimulate each other in a dynamic spiral that greatly enhances the give and take of negotiation (Ferrin et al., 2008).

Yet, as we noted earlier, a negotiator can be too trusting, leading to an internal struggle for any negotiator. Take, for example, the two fundamental, conflicting dilemmas of a negotiation: the dilemma of honesty and the dilemma of trust (Kelley, 1966). The dilemma of honesty concerns how honest each party should be with the other. Recall that a condition that makes negotiation possible is that parties do not have complete information about one another and should not share complete information with one another. Moreover, there are certain ethically ambiguous tactics often used in a negotiation. Each party can assume that other parties are not being completely honest with them just as they are not being completely honest with other parties. This ushers in the dilemma of trust, which concerns how much each party should trust what is being said, and whether they will keep their promises. The only way to deal with the dilemma of honesty and the dilemma of trust is to work to maintain a balance in a negotiation. For example, it is true that one party would be a fool to completely trust another party and/or reveal all information to the other party, as this would allow the other party to easily exploit this information and use deception to their advantage. Yet, if that same party does not trust anything the other is telling them and chooses not to reveal any information to the other party, then how will an agreement ever be reached? Finding a balance between these two dilemmas suggests that parties should trust with caution and cautiously be honest with one another.

Just as too little trust can bring the negotiation to a stalemate, too much trust can lead to too much disclosure to the other. In at least one recent study, researchers demonstrated that excessive straightforwardness (candor) and trust can lead a negotiator to be too concerned with the other's interests, which can result in greater concession-making toward the other and perhaps poorer outcomes for oneself (DeRue et al., 2009). Similar research showed that high trust can make members of a work team reluctant to monitor one another's behavior in task performance. If team members are reluctant to monitor each other, and team members can function autonomously in the task, performance can suffer. Monitoring and autonomy are critical variables to pay attention to in team dynamics, again striking an appropriate balance between trust and distrust (Langfred, 2004). In negotiation, too much trust can lead parties to disclose too much information to the other, while insufficiently monitoring the commitments being made by the other party so that they can be held accountable to follow through or protecting oneself from having the other party use that information to take advantage. Similarly, too much distrust might lead a negotiator to not disclose critical facts that might make an agreement viable, while also leading a distruster to create complex ways to manage the distrust of the other.

If the logic for the importance of trust in establishing and sustaining effective negotiation is not clear, consider the alternative, or the ways that low or nonexistent trust can make a negotiation more difficult. Information is still the primary currency of exchange. However, the negotiator does not have reason to believe that they can trust the accuracy of what the other party is saying. This doubt in the other's veracity may result from what the negotiator has learned about the other's reputation, or it may come about through verbal and nonverbal cues transmitted by the negotiator that suggest exaggeration, bluffing, or outright deception. As a result, much of what the other says must be independently confirmed and verified. Such verification may or may not be possible, and if it is possible, it may require significant delays in establishing the accuracy of the information on which the agreement is based. Moreover, even if the information can be verified, low trust between negotiators often necessitates the creation of elaborately written, formalized, complex contracts and other documents. While these documents remind people as to what they have agreed and are often useful in minimizing some of the miscommunication that may occur if a deal is based only on verbalization and a handshake, creating them can also add significant time delay and cost to the deal itself.

Finally, creation of such agreements then, requires elaborate consequences and penalties for violating the terms of the agreement. Complex penalties for violation, mechanisms for enforcing those penalties, the employment of 'monitors' and 'policeman' to conduct the enforcement, and appeal systems and grievance procedures for wrongful accusations or penalization all become part of this system of enforcement. When we recognize that entire professions are built and sustained around managing anticipated or actual distrust—attorneys, inspectors, judges, referees, auditors, monitors, and regulators, for example—one can appreciate the power that effective trust can create in minimizing these costs.

We are not so naïve as to believe that distrust in negotiation can be eliminated, nor that all deals could be consummated (and/or revised) with a simple handshake and without backup documentation and specification of consequences for noncompliance. We recognize, in fact, that a certain amount of distrust can be very healthy in a negotiation. Checking on the reputation of a new or unfamiliar opponent can clearly be a valuable action. Beyond this, written 'memoranda of understanding', formalized agreements, and ways of monitoring the other's compliance can play an extremely important role in cementing a negotiated agreement. But we draw these extremes in order to reinforce how integral strong trust is to effective negotiation, and to reiterate that negotiators must pay attention to ways they can create and manage solid trust in the negotiations themselves.

Our conclusion, then, to answer Question 3 is that the dilemma of trust and dilemma of honesty are two of the most fundamental, contradicting challenges facing any negotiator. The key to overcoming these challenges is to manage a balance between being too trusting and being too honest with the other party. The characteristics of that specific balance, however, differ in each negotiation context.

QUESTION 4: WHAT AFFECTS THE DEVELOPMENT OF TRUST IN NEGOTIATION TRANSACTIONS?

In answering the first three questions, we have laid out what we hope is a solid foundation for the basic principles of trust and negotiation. In this question, we seek to investigate the more complex ways that trust is developed and/or affected in a negotiation context. The research findings presented in response to this question center on what is communicated and how it is communicated, and ultimately how trust and negotiation feed each other and interact to yield either successful or unsuccessful outcomes.

To begin, the communication medium can affect both truth telling and trusting behavior in a negotiation. Face-to-face communication is more likely to develop trust than telephone (audio only) communication or written communication because of more personal rapport. As a result, parties in a face-to-face negotiation are more likely than parties in audio-only or written-only communication negotiation contexts to disclose information truthfully, hence increasing their ability to attain mutual gain. In contrast, negotiation through written channels is more likely to end in impasse than negotiation either face-to-face or by telephone (Valley et al., 1998). The importance of both verbal and nonverbal cues is closely connected to the reasoning behind the consequences of communication medium because these cues can be a signal of trust. When a negotiator signals emotionally that they want to be cooperative, the nonverbal cues themselves are sufficient to create a foundation for trust. Thus, a negotiator who wants to signal trustworthiness should not only do it verbally, but also express it in their emotional tone of voice (positive and upbeat) (Boone and Buck, 2003). Moreover, nonverbal cues through facial dynamics can significantly influence a negotiator's decision as to with whom to engage in a cooperative exchange, and the decision to cooperate oneself (Krumhuber et al., 2007). Opponents who displayed an authentic smile and 'positive emotions' were perceived as more likeable, attractive, trustworthy and a person whom we would like to work with again in the future, compared to those opponents whose smile was perceived as 'fake' or whose face was nonexpressive (for nonverbal cues, see also Adair, Chapter 12 this volume).

Different emotions can trigger different negotiation dynamics. When parties have competitively-oriented goals in a negotiation, anger increases distrust; when the parties have cooperatively-oriented goals, compassion increases trust (Liu and Wang, 2010; see also Van Kleef and Sinaceur, Chapter 5 this volume). Prenegotiation affective trust can also lead to important 'turning points' in negotiation, which improves negotiation outcomes (Olekalns and Smith, 2005; see also Druckman and Olekalns, Chapter 13 this volume). Note, however, that one does not necessarily have to be 'nice' (benevolent) to create trustworthiness and better agreements. Trustworthiness and bargaining toughness can work together to create higher levels of cooperation and negotiated agreements, as well as higher levels of concession making. A negotiator can be trustworthy simply by being clear and explicit about what is expected, and being willing to deliver on the commitments she makes (Schurr and Ozanne, 1985). At the same time, a negotiator does not necessarily 'lose' trustworthiness by also being 'tough' about their bargaining position (i.e., making a high initial demand and small concessions toward a preferred agreement).

Different types of communication messages can influence trust dynamics, too. Srivastava and Chakravarti (2009) examined the impact of three different types of messages (informational, relational, coercive) versus no communication, and how these interacted with the reputational trustworthiness (high versus low) of the other party in a sequential bargaining communication study. In one study, the explicit use of informational and relational messages greatly enhanced the ability of the parties to reach negotiated agreements, compared to those pairs who merely traded offers and counteroffers or who did not communicate with the other. When the parties shared mutual reputations of trustworthiness, the effects were even more dramatic. Finally, when mutual reputations of trustworthiness were high, relational messages elicited the most positive outcomes, compared to no communication; informational messages had a small but still positive impact on trust and trustworthiness, and the trading of offers and counteroffers had an even smaller impact on trust and trustworthiness, again compared to no communication between parties.

Events at the beginning and end of a negotiation sequence play an important role in building and maintaining trust. Management literature emphasizes the importance of a good first impression, and achieving this in negotiation carries no less weight. Lount et al. (2008) present competing hypotheses in a study about the timing of a trust breach during a negotiation. They find that a trust violation earlier in a relationship is more detrimental than one occurring later in a relationship, meaning that initial impressions and early cooperation are important. Looking now to the end of a negotiation, the follow through of an agreement is just as important as the first impression. The successful implementation of a negotiated agreement, which is an indicator of trust, can be enhanced both by verbalization and by emotional expression. In several studies, Mislin et al. (2011) showed that promises and relationship building, strengthened by a strong 'contingent' agreement (in which the consequences for compliance and noncompliance were spelled out), considerably enhanced the quality of contract implementation. Positive emotions also motivated implementation behavior, but the effect of these positive emotions depended on the form of the contract. Binding contracts can be detrimental to a relationship if the negotiators plan to continue their relationship and work together again the future. Contracts, in general, control behavior and reduce risk, but binding contracts have also been shown to reduce cooperation. In their study, Malhotra and Murnighan (2002) found that an individual's trust will increase as the number of positive interactions between parties increases. Furthermore, binding contracts influenced individuals to think that cooperative behaviors were due to the contract and not to personal choices, and thus binding contracts were not as effective at building trusting relationships. Non-binding contracts, or "informal promises that communicate an intent to cooperate" (p. 551), were more effective at building trust and increased the frequency of trusting behaviors. Another study by Pillutla et al. (2003) supports the idea that trusting behaviors are especially important earlier in a relationship, and that although trusting early is a risk, it may be a risk well worth taking.

Finally, an aspect of trust in the negotiation context that is perhaps more important than the trust level between parties is the trust congruence between parties; trust congruence does not mean that the parties necessarily have mutual or reciprocal trust, but instead it means that there is a "degree of symmetry" between the trust levels of the parties (Tomlinson et al., 2009). As explained by Tomlinson et al. (2009), level of trust in the other party affects the behaviors enacted by a negotiator, and if trust congruence does not exist, then behaviors toward one another will be different and run the risk of being misinterpreted. If two parties share a high trust congruence at the high trust level, the authors propose that joint-behavioral outcomes will be highest; on the other hand, these outcomes will be the lowest when two parties share a high trust-congruence at the low level of trust. When parties are different in their initial level of trust, the situation is likely to be unstable as trust and mistrust 'duel' for dominance in the ensuing relationship.

Our answer to Question 4, then, is that many variables affect trust and the interaction of trust and the negotiation context including, but not limited to, the communication medium, verbal and nonverbal cues, emotions, bargaining toughness, the type of communication messages, first impressions, outcome implementation, the presence of contracts, and trust congruence. Trust is not developed and maintained in only one manner, but multiple characteristics of a negotiator and his approach to the negotiation must be managed in a consistent manner such that behaviors reinforce trust development and maintenance as opposed to behaviors contradicting each other in regards to trust efforts.

QUESTION 5: HOW DOES CULTURE AFFECT TRUST AND NEGOTIATION TRANSACTIONS?

While there are a number of important moderators in the relationship between trust and negotiation, one that is currently drawing a great deal of attention is that of culture. How do cultural differences in trust and trustworthiness affect a negotiation? First, a number of studies have examined the degree to which individuals from different national cultures tend to vary in their willingness to trust each other (see Ferrin and Gillespie, 2010 for one excellent review). Westerners (e.g., those from Western Europe and North America) tend to trust others more quickly, and to assume others can be trusted unless they demonstrate that they are untrustworthy (Meyerson et al., 1996); those from Asia tend to initially trust less and depend more heavily on situational cues about whether they can be trusted. These differences may result from different ways that cultures control behavior. Thus, culture can moderate the level of trust with which parties enter a negotiation. Across many cultures, some (e.g., Westerners) tend to trust quickly and presume that the other will be trustworthy; other cultures (e.g., East and South Asians) tend to initially trust less, and specifically condition their trust based on the situation. Underlying these differences is the mechanism by which some countries are 'tight' (in which social norms are clearly defined and systematically imposed), while others are 'loose' (in which social norms are relatively flexible and only occasionally imposed) (Gelfand et al., 2006). In tight cultures (e.g., Asian), strong social norms govern how negotiation proceeds, and levels of interpersonal trust between negotiators play a lesser role; in loose cultures (e.g., Western), individual skills in reading and exhibiting interpersonal trust become far more critical (see also Takahashi et al., 2008; Gunia et al., 2011; Aslani et al., Chapter 10 this volume). These cultural differences in initial presumptive trust and trustworthiness may also impact how the dilemmas of honesty and trust are judged, leading to greater willingness to use certain deceptive tactics in some cultures relative to others, and this question requires further research attention.

A number of studies have explored the impact of trust on negotiation behaviors and outcome (compare Ferrin and Gillespie, 2010, for a review), but the most extensive work has pursued the impact of the 'tightness-looseness' cultural dimension on trust and culture. Following pioneering work by Adair and Brett (2005) and others, researchers have examined the use of two different negotiating strategies: ones which are dominantly asking questions and giving answers (Q&A) and others which are dominantly making single offers and substantiating them through more competitive tactics (S&O). These authors found that the use of Q&A strategies were more likely to lead to higher joint payoff. Trust was proposed to be positively related to the use of Q&A strategies, while distrust was proposed to be negatively related to the use of S&O strategies. Hence, cultures which were more culturally 'tight' and less trusting (Indian) were more likely to use S&O strategies and achieved lower joint gain than cultures which were more culturally 'loose' and more trusting (U.S. American) were more likely to use Q&A strategies and achieve higher joint gain (Gunia et al., 2011).

While these studies are provocative, much work remains to be done on the relationship between trust and culture. Trust has been differentially conceptualized in cross-cultural negotiations, and a number of cognitive biases and social barriers can impact the way negotiators perceive each other and enact trust dynamics (compare Kramer, 2010). Given that both negotiation dynamics and trust/trustworthiness can vary significantly across cultural boundaries, this is a ripe area for further research.

QUESTION 6: WHAT ARE THE WAYS THAT TRUST CAN BE BROKEN IN A NEGOTIATION?

Answering this question requires us to consider the uniqueness of the negotiation context, and why some behaviors that would absolutely break trust outside of a negotiation context are considered acceptable within the negotiation context. Think of some commonly used negotiation tactics: good cop/bad cop, bogey, lowball/highball, chicken, snow job, the nibble, intimidation, and different forms of aggressive behavior just to name a few (compare Lewicki et al., 2010). Outside of a negotiation context, intimidating or threatening another person may be considered unkind, unethical, and even unlawful (see also, Diekmann et al., Chapter 8 this volume). Yet, the rules of the game change when one steps into a negotiation context. Lewicki and Robinson (1998) state that negotiation tactics must be considered along a continuum of *ethically inappropriate* to *ethically appropriate*, with many tactics falling somewhere between the two extremes, rendering them *ethically ambiguous*. These tactics vary in the degree to which they are viewed as appropriate based on ethical standards (does the tactic meet some standard of appropriate moral conduct), legal standards (what the law permits), or standards of 'prudence' (what might be smart to do based on their impact on the negotiation outcome and/or the relationship between the parties) (Missner, 1980). Assuming that the use of ethically appropriate behaviors within a negotiation will not break trust, and that the use of ethically inappropriate behaviors will almost certainly break trust, the remaining question is, *What are the ethically ambiguous tactics that will break trust in a negotiation?* In other words, negotiators know that they can get away with a certain amount of ethically ambiguous behavior and still maintain trust, but where do the negotiators need to draw the line?

Recall that we described negotiation as the process of managing information in order to resolve conflicts of interest. One of the most common ethically ambiguous behaviors is for one or both parties to use deception in their management of information. As summarized by Lewicki and Hanke (2012), negotiators use deception in order to enhance their power, that is, to gain some advantage by manipulating information to persuade the other party that something is true when in reality it is not. In other words, negotiators may engage an inappropriate resolution of the dilemma of honesty. Negotiators confront the dilemma of honesty differently; one assumes that it is possible to risk honesty and be trustworthy, while the other believes that one should not risk honesty and/or that it is smarter to exploit the other's honesty by being dishonest and deceptive themselves. Hence, the less honest negotiator employs tactics which vary in their degree of truth-distortion, but which are perceived as viable within the normative expectations of negotiating give and take.

Another area of ethically ambiguous tactics is that of truth telling. Various versions of truth telling—lying, bluffing, exaggeration, manipulation, or concealment—are common behaviors in negotiation, especially since the possession of information unknown to the other party is crucial to achieving one's interests. This may be because, again, information is an important source of power in a negotiation (Lewicki and Robinson, 1998). As such, lying serves a number of social functions to help the negotiator maintain power, as explained by Lewicki (1983, p. 75):

- Lies may misinform the opponent so as to obscure some objective that was originally desired by the deceived;
- Lies may eliminate or obscure relevant choice alternatives for the target person;
- Lies may be used to manipulate the perceived costs and benefits of choice alternatives for the target;
- Lies change the degree of uncertainty in the target's choices.

Lying can be useful and be considered ethical and acceptable in a negotiation as long as the party engaging in such tactics is willing to accept the consequences of such an action. The consequences could lead to a tarnished reputation, a loss of credibility, and a loss of power, even though the initial use of the lie was to gain power. If the consequences are willing to be accepted, however, then lies can be effective and arguably necessary. For example, Carr (1968) suggests that "the ethical standards of the business game . . . are a far cry from those of private life" (p. 144). Business leaders must engage in ethically ambiguous tactics sometimes in order to capitalize on advantageous business dealings. Expanding this to negotiators, he argues that negotiators should abide by the same rules as a poker player: various forms of truth telling are acceptable in the game of negotiation.

Besides deception and truth telling, there are other ethically ambiguous tactics to consider, and Lewicki and Robinson (1998) studied a number of such tactics to try and discover which are seen as ethically appropriate and which are seen as ethically inappropriate. They found that tactics such as gaining information by questioning members of the opponent's network, making an initial demand much greater than what one is hoping to achieve, hiding one's bottom line, and trying to get the opponent to concede quickly are considered ethically appropriate. Tactics such as intentionally misrepresenting factual information to your opponent in order to support your position, gaining information about an opponent by bribing your opponent or attempting to recruit one of your opponent's key subordinates, threatening to harm your opponent if they do not give in to your demands or promising your opponent good things if they give in to your demands, or threatening to make your opponent look weak are all considered ethically inappropriate. Robinson et al. (2000) built upon this earlier work by refining the categories of tactics available to negotiators: traditional competitive bargaining, attacking an opponent's network, false promises, misrepresentation, and inappropriate information gathering. Negotiators judged the category of traditional competitive bargaining to be the most appropriate type of tactic, followed, in order, by attacking an opponent's network, inappropriate information gathering, false promises, and misrepresentation. And Barry et al. (2000) showed how tactics that included emotional manipulation should be added to these categories.

As noted by Barry, Robinson, and other researchers working in this area, because manipulation of information can be an effective negotiating tactic, many negotiators see some of these tactics as ethically and prudently appropriate—particularly the first two categories (traditional competitive bargaining and emotional manipulation)—even though they are less than fully honest. In contrast, the other four tactics are generally seen as ethically (but perhaps not prudently) inappropriate. Thus, there is informal consensus among many negotiators that it is acceptable to 'draw a line' between appropriate dishonest tactics and inappropriate dishonest tactics. And, not surprisingly, the willingness to use those tactics varies considerably based on personality and situational variables. The type of lies told (Carson et al., 1982), the negotiator's need for and use of power (Shapiro and Bies, 1994; Olekalns and Smith, 2008), expectations of the other party's trustworthiness (Graebner, 2009), the type of the negotiation problems (e.g., distributive versus integrative), situational norms governing the negotiation context (i.e., a negotiation with a used car dealer versus a negotiation with a long term business partner) (O'Connor and Carnevale, 1997), and the magnitude of incentives at stake (Tenbrunsel, 1998) can all affect the willingness and likelihood of using deceptive tactics in a negotiation (see also Lewicki et al., 2010; Lewicki and Hanke, 2012 for more complete reviews).

To return to our initial question, there are many ways that trust can be broken in a negotiation, including using deception, intentionally misrepresenting factual information, bribing others, or threatening harm. But because the negotiation context allows for behaviors to be judged under a different set of assumptions about right and wrong, there are many behaviors that could potentially break trust, and it is the victim of the trust violation who decides what behaviors do and do not break trust.

QUESTION 7: WHAT ARE THE CONSEQUENCES OF BROKEN TRUST FOR NEGOTIATORS?

The net effects of using deceptive tactics in negotiation can have short-term and long-term consequences. In the short term, the research appears to show that if negotiators use deception carefully and work to avoid detection, significant short-term rewards can be gained. A number of studies have shown that negotiators who use deception achieve better outcomes than their opponents: these tactics include lies by omitting information or by making explicitly false statements (Schweitzer and Croson, 1999), and using emotional manipulation tactics (Fulmer et al., 2009). Better outcomes could also be achieved through deception when there were high stakes to be achieved and the negotiator knew that the other party had a weak alterative if a deal was not met (Boles et al., 2000).

Not unsurprisingly, however, if this deception is *not* done carefully or is detected, the long-term consequences are far less positive to the negotiator's future. Research demonstrated that when one party discovers that the other has been deceptive, the deceived negotiator is far more likely to act retributively in an attempt to punish the other than if the other has not been deceptive. Both negotiators tended to use deception in the future, and the consequences were mutually destructive in terms of joint payoff (Boles et al., 2000; Shapiro and Bies, 1994). In addition, discovering that a party is using deceptive tactics also has consequences for a negotiator's reputation. Negotiators who used deception were rated by their opponents as less trustworthy and less trustful, and the opponents were much less willing to work with that other party in the future (Boles et al., 2000; Tinsley et al., 2002).

Thus, the short- and long-term consequences of using deception and engaging in other trust-breaking behaviors are much like those predicted by studies of simple games like the prisoner's dilemma: while short-term defection can lead to enhanced payoffs, the long-term consequences are a significant decline in trust and poor individual and joint gain in the future. Our answer to Question 6 is similar to that of Question 7, in that we must state again that the consequences of a trust violation are decided by the victim of the trust violation. Any ethically questionable tactic, even if it is something as simple as making an initial offer greater than where one is willing to settle, misleads the other party and encourages negative affect (e.g., anger, embarrassment). One can never predict with perfect certainty how the other party may react in such a situation. A negotiator can get away with maintaining trust even in the face of unethical tactics only so far as the victim will allow it. And the wise negotiator should be attuned to what the other negotiator is doing, occasionally monitor the other, and question any words or behavior which may appear to be less than truthful (see Lewicki et al., 2010, for ways that a negotiator can challenge and confront inappropriate behavior in the other).

QUESTION 8: CAN BROKEN TRUST BE REPAIRED?

Yes, it is possible to repair broken trust, but it is not always an easy or quick process. A number of variables play a role in determining (a) if trust repair is possible, and (b) how difficult the trust repair may be. Before we discuss such variables, however, we must address the nature of and define repaired trust, that is, whether repaired trust is the same as never-broken trust.

It is debatable as to whether repaired trust is the same as never-broken trust (see Dirks et al., 2009). In our view, trust repair depends upon the stage of development in which the trust is broken. Recall that trust development is a complex process: the type of trust that exists between two parties—calculus-based, knowledge-based or identification-based—can be characterized based on the depth of that trust. Part of the challenge of repairing trust lies in what type of trust was broken. Because calculus-based trust is a more surface-based trust, characteristic of newly formed relationships or arms-length market transactions, a trust violation at this level of trust may not be too detrimental (unless the cost of the trust violation to the trustee was very high). The parties do not have a great deal invested in the relationship yet, and removing themselves from the relationship may not be difficult. Trust repair after a violation of this type of trust is often not desired; it may be easier to find another party with which to deal, and hence keeping one's 'options open' is highly desirable. (In negotiation terms, if the trustee has a viable BATNA, trust may not be repaired.) If trust repair is desired, it may be easier to achieve if the parties are willing to explicitly state their intent to repair, explicitly spell out their intentions for their own behavior as well as their expectations of the other's behavior, and clarify what sanctions may be invoked in case of subsequent violations. A violation of knowledge-based trust is more difficult to address because a breach at this level causes the victim to not only assess the violator but also themselves and their abilities to be a good judge of how well they know, understand, and can predict the other. As explained by Lewicki and Bunker (1996), "If the event can be dismissed as a simple temporary episode, or as situationally caused, then it may be ignored. If not, the individual will revise his or her perception of the other" (p. 127). This revisitation of one's perceptions is what controls whether trust repair is possible: if the victim judges their new perception of the violator to be too distant from their original perception and thus too disconcerting, trust repair may not be possible. Finally, a violation of identification-based trust is the most difficult with which to deal because it is not the victim's perception that is called into question but instead their identity and self-image. Fundamentals of the psychological contract between the parties are called into question. Moreover, this type of trust is so strong and unquestioned that parties often do not build any control mechanisms into the agreement (Lewicki and Stevenson, 1998). As such, this is the most challenging type of trust to repair. Additional research is required to address this question, beginning with the important question of when negotiators might attempt to repair trust as opposed to believing that trust repair is neither possible or worth the effort. Clearly, the availability of a viable BATNA is one factor which would determine this decision, but much additional research is needed on this issue, since little research has attempted to understand *when* negotiators will or will not attempt to repair trust.

Whether or not trust repair is possible and how difficult that trust repair may be also depends on the type of violation that occurred. That is, was the violation intentional? If the intent of the negotiator was to deceive the victim, then they most likely engaged in questionable actions including lying. A violator may also choose to purposely not follow through with promises made. In this case, the character of the violator is called into question. If a victim views these actions to be a natural part of the character of the violator and fears they may occur again in the future despite any discussions about curbing such behaviors, then trust repair may not be possible and thus not desired. If the victim views these actions to be characteristic only of the unique circumstances of the current situation, then trust repair may be possible and would need to focus on a restatement of expectations and/or a change in the victim's perception of the violator. As Kim et al. (2004) show, trust repair may be different based on the perceived intent of the violation and how the trustee attributes that intent to the violator.

Finally, trust repair is not possible unless both the violator and the victim are willing to engage in the bilateral trust repair process. It is true that more work needs to be put in by the violator (which often includes providing a verbal account, offering reparations, or instituting structural arrangements as discussed in the next section), but just as trust repair is offered by the violator, it must be accepted by the victim. The victim must first be able to and willing to recognize when trust repair is being initiated. Once this is recognized, the victim must be willing to outwardly acknowledge the offer of trust repair by forgiving the violator. Finally, victims must be willing to forgive themselves if the trust violation shed light on their own shortcomings such as in their judgment of whom to trust.

In conclusion of our answer to Question 8, debates exist on whether repaired trust is the same as never broken trust, and further research is required. Trust repair itself is contingent upon a number of variables including the stage of development of the trust when it was broken as well as the willingness of the violator and the victim to engage in the trust repair process. However, it should be pointed out that much of the review in this section is drawn from several broad studies of trust repair across a variety of contexts, and still needs significant empirical verification in negotiation situations.

QUESTION 9: IF PARTIES BELIEVE THAT TRUST CAN BE REPAIRED, THEN WHAT ARE THE WAYS THIS CAN HAPPEN?

If the parties agree that trust repair is possible and both parties are willing to put in the effort needed to make the trust repair efforts a success, then there are three fundamental trust repair strategies that can be utilized: verbal accounts, payment of reparations, and structural solutions.

A verbal account is any outward statement in which the party who violated trust attempts to acknowledge that a violation has occurred, explain why the violation occurred, and/or offer an apology to the victim. The reason a verbal account can be effective is that it allows the victim to try and discern the intent of the violator. There are many different forms of verbal accounts: accounts, recounts, explanations, justifications, or apologies (Kramer and Lewicki, 2010).

The most common type of verbal account is the apology. Based on recent work by Lewicki and Polin (2012) and Polin et al. (2012), effective apologies can contain a combination of other forms of verbal accounts, such as explanations and justifications. Lewicki and Polin (2012) suggest that there are actually six critical components of an effective apology: an expression of regret for the offense; an explanation of why the violation occurred; an acknowledgement of responsibility; a declaration of repentance; an offer of repair; and a request for forgiveness. An apology including all of these components is thought to be more effective than an apology that only includes a few of these components. Although this component-based approach to understanding apologies in trust repair is still in its infancy, there is established research, such as that by Tomlinson et al. (2004), that shows that victims are more willing to participate in trust repair efforts if they are offered an apology by a violator, particularly an apology appearing to be sincere (i.e., an expression of regret). Tomlinson et al. also found that an apology with an internal attribution (the violator explicitly accepted responsibility for causing the violation) was found to be more effective than an apology with an external attribution (indicating that the violation was caused by 'bad luck' or other causes outside the violator's control). To further show the importance of an apology, other research has shown that no apology can actually lead to anger in the victim (Thomas and Millar, 2008). Finally, mixed reviews exist regarding when apologies should be offered: Frantz and Bennigson (2005) hypothesized and found support for the idea that later apologies are more effective since it shows the victim that the violator has had time to think about their transgression; Tomlinson et al. (2004), however, found that a victim was more willing to accept trust repair efforts when they were made sooner after a trust violation.

In place of or in addition to a verbal account, payment of reparations may also be offered by the violator. Reparations (or penance) are something that has tangible economic benefit and are paid to the victim to minimize or reduce the economic cost of the violation. The reason this form of trust repair can be effective is that it allows the victim to be compensated (all or in part) for the impact of the trust violation. Verbal accounts can assuage the emotional pain from a trust violation, but they can do nothing to diminish any tangible losses the victim may incur due to the violation. This is why some have referred to verbal accounts as "cheap talk" (Farrell and Rabin, 1996), and why offers of penance have been found to be better at restoring trust (at least in the form of more positive affective reactions) than apologies (Bottom et al., 2002). Larger offers of penance (payment of financial compensation after a trust violation has taken away that financial compensation) are not necessarily more effective than smaller substantive offers, however (Bottom et al., 2002), but they are more effective when offered voluntarily versus involuntarily (Desmet et al., 2010).

Finally, structural solutions are a third form of trust repair. In this case, the parties focus less on the consequences of the current violation, and focus more on altering the relationship in some way so as to prevent trust violations from occurring again in the future. Structural solutions are effective at repairing trust because they force the parties to focus on the future, to re-evaluate their relationship for the improvement of interaction, and to establish (or re-establish) boundaries for the parties' behavior. This may require new rules or policies to be made clear to both parties, formal contracts to be signed, or ways for the parties to monitor one another to be established (see Kramer and Lewicki, 2010 for one review). As stated by Lewicki and Polin (in press), such structural solutions "are formalized mechanisms for either regulating the process by which parties negotiate, limiting undesirable behaviors, and/or specifying consequences and punishments for those undesirable behaviors". Examples are memoranda of understanding, contracts, treaties, judicial rulings, restraining orders, and so on. For example, Chou et al. (2011) have shown that less specific employment contracts enhance organizational commitment and task persistence, both in the short and long term. But legalistic remedies are not always the answer: as noted by Sitkin and Roth (1993), they are more likely to be effective when posed to address context-specific problems. And as we noted earlier in this chapter, creating structural solutions may make it more likely that mistrust is not reduced, but they are unlikely to build or rebuild trust. For example, Malhotra and Murnighan (2002) showed that the existence of a contract promoted cooperation but that the parties attributed the cooperation to the contract, and not to developing trust between them.

QUESTION 10: WHAT HAVE WE LEARNED AND WHAT DO WE STILL NEED TO LEARN ABOUT TRUST AND NEGOTIATION?

In this chapter, we have attempted to review what is known about the key role of trust in the negotiation process. We have indicated that trust plays a critical role in negotiation. First, negotiation is about the exchange of information and efforts to persuade the other, and each party must be able to trust that the other's information is accurate and verifiable. Second, negotiators must also be able to trust that the other will follow through on the commitments they make during a negotiation; while written agreements and contracts can help, it is highly inefficient (and often impossible) to specify all of the possibilities and contingencies for failing to comply. Finally, there are significant incentives for parties not to be completely honest and truthful, first because dishonesty can create a short-term power advantage, and second, given the way most people characterize a negotiation (as a more competitive, distributive process), the parties often do not expect the other to be completely honest and truthful. Establishing and maintaining trust in a negotiation is a delicately balanced dynamic process of being as honest and truthful as one can without giving away their bargaining position, while periodically 'testing' the other's honesty and truthfulness and protecting oneself against unfortunate and costly exploitation. In our review, we have also summarized much of the extant research on trust in negotiation. This research has focused on the ways that trust is communicated during the negotiation process, the various ways that trust can be breached during a negotiation and the consequences of this breach, and the various options available for trust repair. Much of this research has been conducted in explicit negotiation contexts, while in other cases, we have extrapolated the findings of trust building and rebuilding from other contexts similar to explicit negotiation dynamics.

Despite the strong body of research that is being established on the role of trust in negotiation, much remains to be done. We have answered 10 commonly asked questions about negotiation in this chapter, but many questions remain to be answered. Below we offer a brief agenda of five issues that need further investigation.

- What individual differences affect the development of trust in a negotiation (e.g., age, gender, etc.)? Much work has been done in the field of psychology on individual differences in trust and trustworthiness (e.g., Rotter, 1980). Individuals differ in their dispositional tendency to trust others and their need to be trustworthy themselves. This disposition may shift with age and with gender (compare Kulik and Olekalns, 2012 for one review), and certainly will vary as two parties with different dispositional tendencies, ages, and/or genders may interact.
- What are some possible strategies for dealing with an untrustworthy opponent? In other words, what can a negotiator do, if anything, to build trust when the opponent does not want to reciprocate? We know that many negotiation experts suggest to not negotiate when the other party "acts in bad faith" (Lewicki et al., 2010, p. 7), but what if the parties have no choice and must negotiate with one another? We noted in this chapter there were three dominant ways an opponent can demonstrate trustworthiness: first, based on their ability (are they competent?), second, based on their benevolence (are they nice?), and third, based on their integrity (do they tell the truth and do they keep their commitments?). But even if one party makes an attempt to show their trustworthiness and their desire to have a clean negotiation, the other party may choose not to reciprocate, or they may even take advantage of the opponent's show of trustworthiness. The answer to this question would involve a prescriptive answer, and while we can offer our own advice based on our expertise (e.g., verify all information, ask questions), there is little known about how to handle the trust management process when a party suspects that a trust violation will occur in the future, but a breach has not yet occurred.
- Are there advantages to not trusting the other party or having the other party not trust you? To answer the first part of this question, one advantage to not trusting the other party is that a negotiator is forced to be more vigilant during negotiation exchanges. Sometimes when parties trust their opponent, they fail to take precautionary measures, and this can lead to a failure to obtain what they desire, especially in distributive negotiation situations. On the other hand, the question of having the other party not trust you is an entirely different question. All proficient negotiators have their strategy, and

it might be to one's advantage to not be trustworthy. For example, a lawyer may decide to appear untrustworthy and be unpleasant to force an opponent into settling a case earlier rather than later, by making the opponent believe that the longer the negotiation carries on, the more untrustworthy behaviors will be exhibited. To our knowledge, there is no research on this idea of appearing untrustworthy as a strategy, but it would be an interesting avenue to explore.

- What is the minimum level of trust—either individual or reciprocal—required to successfully conduct a negotiation? We know that trust is thought to begin at a low but positive level when first encountering a stranger, and if a positive reputation precedes an individual, then trust in that individual at the start of a negotiation is even higher (Lewicki et al., 2010). But this does not mean that a positive level of trust is required for a negotiation to reach an outcome. There are many cases in which parties do not trust one another yet they manage to come to an agreed-upon negotiation. In fact, the answer to the previously posed question above—that of whether being untrustworthy can be an advantage—would affect the answer to this question. Effectively answering this question will require far more precise ways to calibrate trust levels, both at any given point in a negotiation as well as dynamic changes over time. While approaches to measuring trust have improved significantly, additional advancement in measurement is required to understand how changes in trust can be better calibrated over time. Additional research is also needed to pinpoint the particular level of trust that is required for a particular outcome to be achieved.

- Finally, what direction does trust and negotiation research need to go in the near future? One interesting area that could help us to understand these constructs better is the physiological reactions to trust and distrust during a negotiation. Paul Zak, a neuroeconomist, combines knowledge derived from neuroscience, economics, and psychology to understand what exactly is going on inside the brain when it makes certain decisions. Although not yet specifically applied to negotiation, Zak has explored the effects of the hormone oxytocin, finding it to be associated with trusting others. For example, in one study, after participating in a traditional trust game, blood was drawn from participants. Results of their study show that oxytocin levels are higher in individuals when an intention to trust is present; when "a social intention of trust" is extinguished, oxytocin levels decrease, as does trustworthiness (Zak et al., 2005, p. 526). Turning back to negotiation, research needs to begin addressing what neurochemical dynamics may be related to the many different behaviors exhibited during negotiation. What is going on in the brain when negotiators seek an integrative solution; what is going on when negotiators lie or exhibit untrustworthy behavior? The application of neuroeconomics may be an interesting next step for negotiation research.

While much has been done, there are clearly significant opportunities for additional research on the important role of trust in the negotiation process.

REFERENCES

Adair, W.L. and Brett, J.M. (2005). The negotiation dance: Time, culture, and behavioral sequences in negotiation. *Organization Science*, *16(1)*, 33–51.

Barry, B., Fulmer, I.S., and Long, A. (2000). Ethically marginal bargaining tactics: Sanction, efficacy, and performance. Presented at a meeting of the Academy of Management. Toronto, Ontario.

Berg, J., Dickhaut, J., and McCabe, K. (1995). Trust, reciprocity and social history. *Games and Economic Behavior*, *10*, 122–142.

Boles, T.L., Croson, R.T.A., and Murnighan, J.K. (2000). Deception and retribution in repeated ultimatum bargaining. *Organizational Behavior and Human Decision Processes*, *83(2)*, 235–259.

Boone, R.T. and Buck, R. (2003). Emotional expressivity and trustworthiness: The role of nonverbal behavior in the evolution of cooperation. *Journal of Nonverbal Behavior*, *27(3)*, 163–182.

Bottom, W.P., Gibson, K., Daniels, S.E., and Murnighan, J.K. (2002). When talk is not cheap: Substantive penance and expressions of intent in rebuilding cooperation. *Organization Science*, *13(5)*, 497–513.

Carr, A.Z. (1968). Is business bluffing ethical. *Harvard Business Review*, *46(1)*, 143–153.

Carson, T.L., Wokutch, R.E., and Murrmann, K.F. (1982). Bluffing in labor negotiations: Legal and ethical issues. *Journal of Business Ethics*, *1(1)*, 13–22.

Chou, E.Y., Halevy, N., and Murnighan, J.K. (2011). Less specific contracts stimulate motivation, commitment and performance. Paper presented at the Academy of Management Meetings, San Antonio, TX.

DeRue, D.S., Conlon, D.E., Moon, H., and Willaby, H.W. (2009). When is straightforwardness a liability in negotiations? The role of integrative potential and structural power. *Journal of Applied Psychology*, *94(4)*, 1032–1047.

Desmet, P.T.M., De Cremer, D., and van Dijk, E. (2010). On the psychology of financial compensations to restore fairness transgressions: When intentions determine value. *Journal of Business Ethics*, *95*, 105–115.

Dirks, K.T., Lewicki, R.J., and Zaheer, A. (2009). Repairing relationships within and between organizations: Building a conceptual foundation. *Academy of Management Review*, *34(1)*, 68–84.

Farrell, J. and Rabin, M. (1996). Cheap talk. *Journal of Economical Perspectives*, *10(3)*, 103–118.

Ferrin, D.L. and Gillespie, N. (2010). Trust differences across national-societal cultures: Much to do, or much ado about nothing? In M. Saunders, D. Skinner, G. Dietz, N. Gillespie and R.J. Lewicki (eds), *Trust across cultures: Theory and practice* (pp. 42–86). Cambridge, UK: Cambridge University Press.

Ferrin, D.L., Bligh, M.C., and Kohles, J.C. (2008). It takes two to tango: An interdependence analysis of the spiraling of perceived trustworthiness and cooperation in interpersonal and intergroup relationships. *Organizational Behavior and Human Decision Processes*, *107(2)*, 161–178.

Frantz, C.M. and Bennigson, C. (2005). Better late than early: The infuence of timing on apology effectiveness. *Journal of Experimental Social Psychology*, *41(2)*, 201–207.

Fulmer, I.S., Barry, B., and Long, D.A. (2009). Lying and smiling: Information and emotional deception in negotiation. *Journal of Business Ethics*, *88(4)*, 691–709.

Gelfand, M.J., Nishi, L.H., and Raver, J.L. (2006). On the nature and importance of cultural tightness-looseness. *Journal of Applied Psychology*, *91*, 1225–1244.

Gillespie, N. (2003). *Measuring trust in working relationships: The behavioral trust inventory*. Paper presented at the Academy of Management Conference, Seattle, WA.

Graebner, M.E. (2009). Caveat venditor: Trust asymmetries in acquisitions of entrepreneurial firms. *Academy of Management Journal*, *52(3)*, 435–472.

Gunia, B.C., Brett, J.M., Nandkeolyar, A.K., and Kamdar, D. (2011) Paying a price: Culture, trust and negotiation consequences. *Journal of Applied Psychology*, *96(4)*, 774–789.

Kelley, H.H. (1966). A classroom study of the dilemmas in interpersonal negotiation. In K. Archibald (ed.), *Strategic interaction and conflict: Original papers and discussion* (pp. 49–73). Berkeley, CA: Institute of International Studies.

Kim, P.H., Ferrin, D.L., Cooper, C.D., and Dirks, K.T. (2004). Removing the shadow of suspicion: The effects of apology vs. denial for repairing competence-based vs. integrity-based trust violation. *Journal of Applied Psychology*, *89*, 104–118.

Kramer, R.M. (2010). Trust barriers in cross-cultural negotiations: a social psychological analysis. In M. Saunders, D. Skinner, G. Dietz, N. Gillespie and R.J. Lewicki (eds), *Trust across cultures: Theory and practice* (pp. 42–86). Cambridge, UK: Cambridge University Press.

Kramer, R.M. and Lewicki, R.J. (2010). Repairing and enhancing trust: Approaches to reducing organizational trust deficits. *The Academy of Management Annals*, *4(1)*, 245–277.

Krumhuber, E., Manstead, A.S.R., Cosker, D., Marshall, D., Rosin, P.L., and Kappas, A. (2007). Facial dynamics as indicators of trustworthiness and cooperative behavior. *Emotion*, *7(4)*, 730–735.

Kulik, C. and Olekalns, M. (2012). Negotiating the gender divide: Lessons from the negotiation and organizational behavior literature. *Journal of Management*, *38(4)*, 1387–1415.

Langfred, C.W. (2004). Too much of a good thing? Negative effectives of high trust and individual autonomy in self-managing teams. *Academy of Management Journal*, *47(3)*, 385–399.

Lewicki, R.J. (1983). Lying and deception: A behavioral model. In M. Bazerman and R.J. Lewicki (eds), *Negotiating in organizations* (pp. 68–90). Beverly Hills, CA: Sage Publications.

Lewicki, R.J. and Bunker, B.B. (1995). Trust in relationships: A model of trust development and decline. In B.B. Bunker and J.Z. Rubin (eds), *Conflict, cooperation, and justice* (pp. 133–174). San Francisco: Jossey-Bass.

Lewicki, R.J. and Bunker, B.B. (1996). Developing and maintaining trust in work relationships. *Trust in Organizations: Frontiers of Theory and Research* (pp. 114–139). Thousand Oaks, CA: Sage Publications.

Lewicki, R.J. and Hanke, R. (2012). Once fooled, shame on you! Twice fooled, shame on me! What deception does to deceivers and victims: Implications for negotiators in situations where ethicality is unclear. In B. Goldman and D. Shapiro (eds), *The Psychology of Negotiations for the 21st Century* (pp. 211–244). Oxford, UK: Routledge Press.

Lewicki, R.J. and Polin, B. (2012). The art of the apology: The structure and effectiveness of apologies in trust repair. In R.M. Kramer and T.L. Pittinsky (eds), *Restoring Trust in Organizations and Leaders: Enduring Challenges and Emerging Answers* (pp. 95–128). New York: Oxford University Press.

Lewicki, R.J. and Polin, B. (in press). The role of trust in negotiation processes. In

R. Bachman and A. Zaheer (eds), *Handbook of advances in trust research*. Cheltenham, UK and Northampton, MA, USA: Edward Elgar Publishing.

Lewicki, R.J. and Robinson, R.J. (1998). Ethical and unethical bargaining tactics: An empirical study. *Journal of Business Ethics*, *17(6)*, 665–682.

Lewicki, R.J. and Stevenson, M. (1998). Trust development in negotiation: Proposed actions and a research agenda. *Journal of Business and Professional Ethics*, *16(1/3)*, 99–132.

Lewicki, R.J., Barry, B., and Saunders, D. (2010). *Negotiation* (6th edition). Burr Ridge, IL: McGraw-Hill Irwin.

Lewicki, R.J., McAllister, D.J., and Bies, R.H. (1998). Trust and distrust: New relationships and realities. *Academy of Management Review*, *23(3)*, 438–358.

Liu, M. and Wang, C. (2010). Explaining the influence of anger and compassion on negotiators' interaction goals: An assessment of trust and distrust as two mediators. *Communication Research*, *37(4)*, 443–472.

Lount, R.B. Jr., Zhong, C., Slvanathan, N., and Murnighan, J.K. (2008). Getting off on the wrong foot: The timing of a breach and the restoration of trust. *Personality and Social Psychology Bulletin*, *34(12)*, 1601–1612.

Luhmann, N. (1988). Familiarity, confidence, trust: Problems and alternatives. In D. Gambetta (ed.), *Trust: Making and breaking cooperative relations* (pp. 94–107). Oxford, UK: Basil Blackwell.

Malhotra, D. (2004). Trust and reciprocity decisions: The differing perspectives of trustors and trusted parties. *Organizational Behavior and Human Decision Processes*, *94(2)*, 61–73.

Malhotra, D. and Murnighan, J.K. (2002). The effects of contracts on interpersonal trust. *Administrative Science Quarterly*, *47*, 534–559.

Mayer, R.C., Davis, J.H., and Schoorman, F.D. (1995). An integrative model of organizational trust. *Academy of Management Review*, *20(3)*, 709–734.

Meyerson, D., Weick, K.E., and Kramer, R.M. (1996). Swift trust and temporary groups. In R.M. Kramer and T.R. Tyler (eds), *Trust in organizations: Frontiers of theory and research* (pp. 165–190). Thousand Oaks, CA: Sage Publications.

Mislin, A.A., Campagna, R.L., and Bottom, W.P. (2011). After the deal: Talk, trust building and the implementation of negotiated agreements. *Organizational Behavior and Human Decision Processes*, *115(1)*, 55–68.

Missner, M. (1980). *Ethics of the business system*. Sherman Oaks, CA: Alfred Publishing Company.

O'Connor, K.M. and Carnevale, P.J. (1997). A nasty but effective negotiation strategy: Misrepresentation of a common-value issue. *Personality and Social Psychology Bulletin*, *23(5)*, 504–515.

Olekalns, M. and Smith, P.L. (2005). Moments in time: Metacognition, trust and outcomes in dyadic negotiations. *Personality and Social Psychology Bulletin*, *31(12)*, 1696–1707.

Olekalns, M. and Smith, P.L. (2008). Mutually dependent: Power, trust, affect and the use of deception in negotiation. *Journal of Business Ethics*, *85*, 347–365.

Pillutla, M.M., Malhotra, D., and Murnighan, J.K. (2003). Attributions of trust and the calculus of reciprocity. *Journal of Experimental Social Psychology*, *39*, 448–455.

Polin, B., Lount, R.B., Jr., and Lewicki, R.J. (2012). On the importance of a full apology: How to best repair broken trust. Presented at a meeting of the Academy of Management. Boston, MA.

Robinson, R., Lewicki, R.J., and Donahue, E. (2000). Extending and testing a five factor model of ethical and unethical bargaining tactics: The SINS scale. *Journal of Organizational Behavior*, *21(6)*, 649–664.

Rotter, J.B. (1980). Interpersonal trust, trustworthiness, and gullibility. *American Psychologist*, *35*, 651–655.

Rousseau, D.M., Sitkin, S.B., Burt, R.S., and Camerer, C. (1998). Not so different after all: A cross-discipline view of trust. *Academy of Management Review*, *23(3)*, 393–404.

Schurr, P.H. and Ozanne, J.L. (1985). Influences on exchange processes: Buyer's preconceptions of a seller's trustworthiness and bargaining toughness. *Journal of Consumer Research*, *11(4)*, 939–953.

Schweitzer, M.E. and Croson, R. (1999). Curtailing deception: The impact of direct questions on lies and omissions. *International Journal of Conflict Management, 10(3)*, 225–248.

Shapiro, D.L. and Bies, R. (1994). Threats, bluffs and disclaimers in negotiations. *Organizational Behavior and Human Decision Processes, 60(1)*, 14–35.

Shapiro, D.L., Sheppard, B.H., and Cheraskin, L. (1992). Business on a handshake. *Negotiation Journal, 8(4)*, 365–377.

Sinaceur, M. (2010). Suspending judgment to create value: Suspicion and trust in negotiation. *Journal of Experimental Psychology, 46(3)*, 543–550.

Sitkin, S.B. and Roth, N.L. (1993). Explaining the limited effectiveness of legalistic "remedies" for trust/distrust. *Organization Science, 4(3)*, 367–392.

Srivastava, J. and Chakravarti, D. (2009). Channel negotiations with information asymmetries: Contingent influences of communication and trustworthiness reputations. *Journal of Marketing Research, 46(4)*, 557–572.

Takahashi, C., Yamagishi, T., Liu, J.H., Wang, F.X., Lin, Y.C., and Yu, S. (2008). The intercultural trust paradigm: Studying joint cultural interaction and social exchange in real time over the Internet. *International Journal of Intercultural Relations, 32*, 215–228.

Tenbrunsel, A.E. (1998). Misrepresentation and expectations of misrepresentation in an ethical dilemma: The role of incentives and temptation. *Academy of Management Journal, 41(3)*, 330–339.

Thomas, R.L. and Millar, M.G. (2008). The impact of failing to give an apology and the need-for-cognition on anger. *Current Psychology, 27(2)*, 126–134.

Tinsley, C.H., O'Connnor, K.M., and Sullivan, B.A. (2002). Tough guys finish last: the perils of a distributive reputation. *Organizational Behavior and Human Decision Processes, 88(2)*, 621–642.

Tomlinson, E.C., Dineen, B.R., and Lewicki, R.J. (2004). The road to reconciliation: Antecedents of victim willingness to reconcile following a broken promise. *Journal of Management, 30(2)*, 165–187.

Tomlinson, E.C., Dineen, B.R., and Lewicki, R.J. (2009). Trust congruence among integrative negotiators as a predictor of joint-behavioral outcomes. *International Journal of Conflict Management, 20(2)*, 173–187.

Valley, K.L., Moag, J., and Bazerman, M.H. (1998). 'A matter of trust': Effects of communication on the efficiency and distribution of outcomes. *Journal of Economic Behavior and Organization, 34(2)*, 211–238.

Weber, J.M., Malhotra, D., and Murnighan, J.K. (2005) Normal acts of irrational trust: motivated attributions and the trust development process. In B. Staw and R. Kramer, *Research in Organizational Behavior, 26*, 75–101.

Zak, P.J., Kurzban, R., and Matzner, W.T. (2005). Oxytocin is associated with human trustworthiness. *Hormones and Behavior, 48*, 522–527.

8. Fairness and ethics in bargaining and negotiation
Kristina A. Diekmann, Andrew T. Soderberg and Ann E. Tenbrunsel

Fairness and ethics. At a macro level, they are fundamental building blocks of our society. Translated to a more micro-level, they are essential ingredients in our interpersonal interactions. Essential? Yes. Understood? Often not. This chapter seeks to shed light on research on these topics in one of the most fundamental of human exchanges: bargaining and negotiations. In doing so, we aspire to uncover and expose what we have learned and, at the same time, direct scholars to fruitful areas for future investigations.

We organize this chapter broadly along three dimensions: construct, roles, and context. Our first dimension, *construct*, incorporates both fairness and ethics. Fairness and ethics are inevitably entwined (Cropanzano and Stein, 2009; Skitka et al., 2008), with the instrumental use of fairness, for example, asserted to have a dark connotation, one that could be described as unethical (Van Dijk et al., 2012). Although they are linked, they are not synonymous (Folger et al., 2005). Our second dimension focuses on *roles* and here we follow the distinction in reviews of the fairness literature (e.g., Brockner et al., 2009) between the focal actor enacting (un)fair behavior and the recipient who receives the (un)fair behavior by the interaction partner. We apply this same distinction to the ethics literature. In terms of our third dimension, *context*, we separately examine the research in bargaining games (ultimatum and dictator games) and research in negotiation contexts. Bargaining games and negotiation involve mixed-motive situations, described as those where two or more parties experience a motivation to cooperate and compete with each other (Shelling, 1960) and two main motives of self-interest and fairness (De Dreu et al., 2007). It has been argued that bargaining games are the ideal context to examine fairness related issues, in particular the conflict between equity and self-interest (Handgraaf et al., 2008); similarly, negotiation is an ideal context to study ethics (Tenbrunsel, 1998).

Using this fairness/ethics × actor/recipient × bargaining/negotiation organizing structure, we examine the literature on fairness and then turn to the literature on ethics. We then reflect on the research that has been done to identify the "holes" in the literature, highlighted in part by this organizing structure, and identify opportunities for future research.

WHY PEOPLE DESIRE FAIRNESS AND ETHICAL BEHAVIOR

Before we begin our review, it is important to discuss why people care about fairness and ethics, want to be fair and ethical, and want to be treated fairly and ethically. Three explanations have been provided in the organizational justice literature for why people care about fairness (see Cropanzano and Stein, 2009 for a review). First, people care about fairness for instrumental reasons (e.g., Adams, 1965). Focal actors want to be fair to get rewards and resources from others. Recipients want to be treated fairly as that signals that one's outcomes will be fair or favorable. Second, people have relational concerns and care about fairness because of its status affirming and identity enhancing processes (Lind and Tyler, 1988; Tyler and Lind, 1992). Fairness signals that one is a valued member of the group. Actors want to be fair so that others respect them and affirm their status and recipients want to be treated fairly as fair treatment affirms their status and standing in the group. The third explanation, a justice motive, reflects a concern for fairness for fairness sake (e.g., Folger, 2001; Skitka et al., 2008). People want to be fair and treated fairly because fairness is consistent with their moral convictions. This perspective contends that people have a predisposition to care about morality. These same three motivations can also explain why people care about ethics. While the instrumental explanation has been the focus of much research on ethics (see Cropanzano and Stein, 2009), relational concerns and moral convictions likely also play a role.

FAIRNESS

What is Fair?

Both distributive and procedural fairness matter in negotiation. Distributive fairness is the fairness of the outcome (e.g., offer in ultimatum bargaining game (ubg), negotiated outcome). Procedural fairness is the fairness of the process used to arrive at those outcomes and how fairly one was treated during the negotiation.

In terms of distributive fairness, while negotiators have a strong preference for outcomes with equal payoffs over outcomes with unequal payoffs

(Loewenstein et al., 1989; Messick and Sentis, 1985), when inequality is unavoidable, they prefer unequal outcomes that favor themselves versus unequal outcomes that favor the other party (e.g., Loewenstein et al., 1989). This egocentric fairness bias has been shown to be a strong tendency in bargaining and negotiation situations (e.g., Babcock et al., 1995 Loewenstein et al., 1993). For instance, Thompson and Loewenstein (1992) found negotiators playing the role of a union representative in a wage negotiation perceived a higher wage to be fairer while those playing the role of management perceived a lower wage to be fairer. Such egocentric fairness perceptions have been argued to be a major cause of conflict, rejection of offers, and impasse in negotiation (e.g., Babcock and Loewenstein, 1997; Loewenstein et al., 1993).

While distributive fairness focuses on the distribution of outcomes among the interdependent parties, procedural fairness focuses on the process by which those outcomes are achieved. Several factors have been identified as affecting individuals' perceptions of procedural fairness in negotiation. Hollander-Blumoff and Tyler (2008) provide evidence that four components of procedural fairness – input or voice, neutrality, respect/politeness, and trust – affect negotiators' perceptions of how fairly they are treated. When negotiators thought they were listened to, treated with courtesy, had their rights respected by the other party, and felt that the other party was trustworthy, they perceived greater fairness. In contrast, how well they did in the negotiation did not affect perceptions of procedural fairness.

The Focal Actor – Bargaining Games

Making fair offers

For many years researchers have used bargaining games as a useful context within which to study the concept of fairness. Two bargaining games that have been utilized extensively are ultimatum bargaining games (ubgs) and dictator games. In its simplest form, the ubg involves the distribution of resources between the proposer, who decides how much of a fixed amount to offer and how much to keep for the self, and a recipient who decides whether or not to accept or reject the offer (Güth et al., 1982). An acceptance results in a division of resources as proposed by the proposer, whereas a rejection results in both parties receiving nothing. The simple dictator game utilizes the same structure as the ubg but does not allow the recipient a choice in the allocation; all resources are divided between both parties as stated by the proposer. Over the years fairness has been one of the most frequently studied topics in bargaining games research.

One of the fundamental questions of this research involves understanding why proposers in ultimatum and dictator games do not always behave as game theory would predict. Game theory typically assumes that all participants will act in a self-interested manner: proposers should offer as little as possible so they can keep as much as possible for themselves; recipients should accept any positive amount offered as even a small amount is better than nothing (Camerer, 2003; Handgraaf et al., 2003a). However, the modal offer in most ubg experiments is an even 50–50 split, with average offers often ranging between 30–40 percent of the total amount (e.g., Güth et al., 1982; Murnighan and Pillutla, 1995). Results for dictator games are often more favorable for the proposer but many still exhibit a strong tendency towards more equal offers (Pillutla and Murnighan, 2003). These results show that people make offers that seem to be constrained by fairness considerations. Indeed, in the earlier stages of this research, researchers pointed to fairness to explain proposers' motivations for making these non-game-theoretic offers (Güth and Tietz, 1990). However, many began to question if proposers behaved in this way due to a truly virtuous and innate sense of fairness, or for instrumental reasons. Although from both perspectives the end result is the same, the motivations behind these "fair" offers in each case are quite different.

Motivations for making "fair" offers
Some researchers have argued and provided evidence that an innate desire for fairness, not necessarily self-interest, is the real motivation behind fair offers (Dickinson, 2000). Indeed, one study by Bethwaite and Tompkinson (1996) indicated that more than 50 percent of participants demonstrated true concern for fairness as the prime motivation for their behavior in the ubg, whereas only about 25 percent showed a self-interested motivation. Others, however, have argued in support of a more instrumental view of fairness in bargaining contexts and have shown that fair offers are motivated instead by a fear of rejection by the recipient (Kahneman et al., 1986; Weg and Zwick, 1994). Using a repeated ubg, Buchan et al. (2004) found that when participants' beliefs about fairness were aligned with self-interest, beliefs of fair behavior could predict behavior; however, when fairness beliefs were not aligned with bargainers' self-interest, these beliefs had no influence on behavior, suggesting that self-interest plays a stronger role than fairness concerns in determining proposer behavior in bargaining games.

Indeed, research has shown that proposers may exhibit a desire to appear fair, not necessarily to actually be fair, to entice the recipient to accept the proposed offer and keep as much of the money as possible (e.g., Pillutla and Murnighan, 1995; Straub and Murnighan, 1995). Thus the previously categorized "fair" behavior of proposers may be more aptly described as self-interested behavior disguised in an illusion of fairness. A variety of other studies have shown similar results using "unknown pot" ubgs (e.g., Straub and Murnighan, 1995). When recipients were unaware of the total amount, proposers made significantly smaller offers than when recipients were aware of the total, again suggesting that proposers cared more about appearing to be fair than actually being fair.

What if proposers did not need to worry about appearing to be fair to obtain larger payoffs, such as in dictator games wherein proposers know that the recipient has no choice but to accept the offer? Generally, as long as the recipient has some power, offers decline as the recipient's power declines (Blader and Chen, 2012; Forsythe et al., 1994). When proposers have reason to be less concerned about having to appear fair such as when they can label their offer as fair, they often behave in a more self-interested manner (Pillutla and Murnighan, 1995). Nevertheless, concern for fairness for fairness sake may still play a role. Forsythe and colleagues (1994) found that only 21 percent of proposers in a dictator game offered nothing and kept everything for themselves. Even when the anonymity of proposers in a dictator game increases, while proposers make lower offers, 33 percent still make offers of some positive amount (Hoffman et al., 1994). Other researchers have shown that when the recipient's power is completely eliminated and the recipient is completely powerless proposers may actually increase their offers (Handgraaf et al., 2008; van Dijk and Vermunt, 2000). When recipients become completely powerless, proposers may feel a sense of social responsibility that prompts them to make more generous offers than they might when the recipient has at least some power (Handgraaf et al., 2008). According to van Dijk and Vermunt (2000) there is a fundamental difference in the psychological processes evoked between ubgs and dictator games in that dictator games evoke a stronger concern for actual fair behavior, whereas ubgs simply evoke a concern for appearing to be fair.

Factors affecting proposer behavior
Characteristics of the proposer. Van Dijk and Tenbrunsel (2005) identified three individual factors (social value orientation or SVO, power, and information) that have direct and interactive effects on the type of behavior that proposers exhibit in ubgs. In terms of SVO, the appearance of fairness explanation may be more accurate for pro-self actors than for pro-social actors. Van Dijk et al. (2004) demonstrated that pro-self individuals made offers that varied depending on what information recipients were given and changed their offers based on varying recipient power while pro-social individuals remained consistent. Other individual-level

factors shown to affect fair behavior include the proposer's concern for their own reputation (Nowak et al., 2000), culture (e.g., Henrich et al., 2001), and emotions such as regret (e.g., Zeelenberg and Beattie, 1997).

Relationship between proposer and recipient. Other factors affecting individual's offers include characteristics of the relationship between proposer and recipient, including social distance (e.g., proposers make smaller offers to recipients who are more socially distant; Hoffman et al., 1996) and competition (e.g., when there are multiple recipients, proposers make lower offers; Fischbacher et al., 2009).

Situational factors. One important situational element that influences fairness in bargaining games pertains to how individuals view their role as proposer. For example, simply changing the manner in which participants are assigned to the role of proposer can affect their subsequent behavior. When proposers felt entitled to be in their role (either by winning it or by earning it as a reward) versus just being randomly assigned to it, they behaved much more self-interestedly by making lower offers and fewer 50–50 offers in ubgs and dictator games (e.g., Hoffman et al., 1994). Particularly in dictator games, when proposers earned the wealth that was to be distributed in the game, they made more $0 offers (self-interested offers) versus when the money used was earned by the recipients, in which case they made more allocations greater than half of the total amount (Oxoby and Spraggon, 2008).

Other structural elements, especially those which affect the way in which the game is presented to the proposer (e.g., such as whether the game is presented as a buyer-seller ubg versus a standard ubg) can have a significant effect on the offers observed (e.g., Hoffman et al., 1994). Finally, education has been shown to affect the fairness of offers. Wang et al. (2011) recently showed that economics majors and non-majors enrolled in economics courses made lower offers in a dictator game. When distributing $10 between themselves and another person, students in economic courses kept more money ($7.76) than those in education courses ($6.50).

The Focal Actor – Negotiations

Being fair
While there is copious research on engagement in fair behavior and drivers of such behavior in the bargaining games literature reviewed above, there is surprisingly little work on engagement in fair behavior in negotiation. The limited research on enacting fairness in negotiation has typically examined factors, including characteristics of the actor and the situation that may affect concern with and engagement in fairness.

Characteristics of actor. Similar to the findings in the ubg literature reviewed above, De Dreu and Van Lange (1995) showed that negotiators with a pro-social orientation have a greater concern with the other party's well-being than those with an individual and competitive orientation and that these concerns are negatively related with demand levels and positively related with concessions in negotiation. Blader and Chen (2012) examined the effect of individual's status versus power on engagement in outcome and process fairness in several different contexts (including a dictator game, distributive and integrative negotiations) and found that high status individuals were more likely to enact fair outcomes and processes while high power individuals were less likely to do so. They argue that enacting fairness is critical for high status individuals to ensure their lower status interaction partners continue to view them with respect and esteem and help maintain their current status. High power individuals on the other hand focus mostly on achieving their own self-interested goals and view interactions with others as a way to attain those goals.

Situational factors. Various situational factors affect negotiators being fair. Negotiating face-to-face places constraints on negotiators in terms of fairness compared to negotiating electronically: individuals negotiating face-to-face make more fairness-based price concessions compared to those negotiating electronically (Kachelmeier and Towry, 2002). Being primed with fairness (e.g., being asked to identify the lowest and highest fair price for a used car) prior to negotiating places constraints as well – buyers identify higher prices as being fair, make larger concessions, and reach agreement faster (Maxwell et al., 1999). Gain versus loss frame has also been shown to affect motivation to maximize own outcome versus to be fair in coalition formation, with negotiators being less likely to exclude others when negotiating losses (van Beest et al., 2005).

Though limited in scope, the negotiation literature reveals that negotiators' perceptions and behaviors often reflect a concern about being fair but the reason for this concern may vary as may the strength of this concern. We next turn to examining research on reactions to (un)fairness.

The Recipient – Bargaining Games

Reactions to unfair offers

A substantial portion of the ubg literature involves recipients' perceptions of fairness and how these perceptions help to explain why they sometimes choose to accept and other times choose to reject an offer. The ubg literature often refers to the recipients' ability to punish a proposer they perceive to be unfair. This is accomplished by simply rejecting the proposer's offer and causing him/her to receive no monetary payoff. However, by rejecting an offer, recipients also forfeit any monetary payoff for themselves as well.

From a strictly economic standpoint, it does not make sense for a recipient to reject any positive offer because any such offer increases their economic utility. However, as we will show, recipients are far from being strictly economically driven and rejections are common occurrences in ubg research.

From the first ubg experiment conducted (Güth et al., 1982), researchers have uncovered evidence that recipients do not hesitate to punish proposers who take too much. In fact, recipients are often willing to sacrifice personal monetary gain to punish proposers they perceive as unfair (e.g., Güth and Tietz, 1990; Turillo et al., 2002). In general, recipients typically reject offers that are worse (i.e., lower) than a 70–30 split between the proposer and the recipient (Camerer, 2003; Kahneman et al., 1986). Some have asserted that self-interest is one motivation driving such rejections (Kahneman et al., 1986). Others have questioned this interpretation since in most cases when offers are rejected, recipients sacrifice personal monetary gain without any potential future benefit to themselves (Ochs and Roth, 1989), suggesting a motivation of a desire for fairness for its own sake (Turillo et al., 2002).

In one study providing evidence for a motivation for fairness, recipients were observed to sometimes demonstrate "hyper-fairness" where they would reject offers that were both too low as well as too high (Bahry and Wilson, 2006). Another experiment has since provided strong support for fairness simply for its own sake (Nelissen et al., 2009). In this modified ubg, recipients had the option to obtain a higher monetary payoff if they would reject the proposer's equal (50–50) offer. A large number of recipients did not reject the offer but accepted the equal split resulting in a lower payoff for themselves. This result was not simply an indifference to the alternative option but based on the participants' concern for the outcomes of the proposers.

When ultimatum offers become low enough for recipients to judge them unfair, they often trigger emotional responses that play an important role in influencing the decision to accept or reject the offers. Murnighan and colleagues incorporated recipients' feelings of anger, spite, and wounded pride to explain why recipients reject offers (Murnighan and Pillutla, 1995; Straub and Murnighan, 1995; Pillutla and Murnighan, 1995). Unfavorable offers often result in increased perceptions of unfairness for the recipient who may experience feelings of wounded pride. When a recipient's pride has been wounded in this manner it can frequently lead to feelings of anger or spite directed towards the proposer as the source of the unfair offer (Pillutla and Murnighan, 1995). These feelings of anger and spite can then take a preeminent role in the recipient's decision to reject an offer and punish the proposer (Murnighan and Pillutla, 1995). Emotional responses of anger and spite can thus become the impetus for rejection; however people may still use fairness to justify their spiteful behavior stemming from these emotional responses to their own wounded pride (Straub and Murnighan, 1995; Pillutla and Murnighan, 2003). Neurological evidence has also shown the importance of emotions in recipients' responses to unfair offers. Simply receiving unfair ultimatum offers elicits activity in areas of the brain known to be associated with emotion (e.g., Dulebohn et al., 2009).

Intentions also seem to matter. Recipients often evaluate the fairness of an offer based on their perceptions of the proposer's underlying intentions behind the offer. Falk and colleagues (2003) demonstrated that recipients rejected low offers more when they perceived the proposer to have unfair intentions. Indeed, perceived intentions of fairness have been found to matter more to recipients than the actual outcome in rejecting an offer (Nelson, 2002). Even though intentions of the proposer are important, this is not to say that outcomes are not. Research demonstrates that intentions, actions, and outcomes all are important factors determining not only how people judge the fairness of others' behavior, but also how people will react to these judgments (Falk and Fischbacher, 2006). As described below, a large amount of research has identified other situational and relational factors that influence recipients' perceptions of fairness and affect offer acceptance.

Situational factors. It appears that an important determinant of recipients' decisions is whether they make their decision focused more on an intrapersonal (absolute) or an interpersonal (relative) comparison. For example, Handgraaf and colleagues (2004) showed that whichever one of these components was more evaluable became more important and had a stronger effect on the observed outcome (i.e., when the intrapersonal comparative component was more salient, recipients were more accepting of unfair offers) than the other component. Previous research has also identified that who/what was responsible for causing the choice to have to be made and the degree to which human agents were perceived to have an interest in the outcome affected which comparison (absolute versus relative) was more salient (Blount, 1995).

In other studies, researchers have used a more structural manipulation to activate whether individuals focused on absolute versus relative payouts. In this research, when the stakes were high, a majority of participants were still more concerned with relative (opposed to absolute) payoffs, though more unfair offers were still accepted than when stakes were low (e.g., Tompkinson and Bethwaite, 1995). In a set of sequential ubgs between a leader (proposer) and two followers (recipients), recipients exhibited stronger concerns for fairness if the amount allocated to the other recipient was greater than the amount they received (Ho and Su, 2009). Often simple structural modifications such as whether the game is real or hypothetical (see Forsythe et al., 1994) or the temporal order of events (see Boles and Messick, 1990) can influence recipients' behavior in bargaining games. Whether recipients are faced with a single choice versus a choice of two offers has also been shown to affect recipient's acceptance rates. Handgraaf and colleagues (2003b) offered recipients a straightforward choice of two offers (e.g., to receive 30 chips and the proposer receives 70 chips or to receive 0 chips and the proposer receives 0 chips) instead of just a single choice to accept or reject as in the standard ubg. When presented in this manner, recipients' acceptance levels for the 30–70 offer increased, even for offers that were considered unfair. Other research has similarly shown that recipients were less concerned for fairness in ubgs when they were given the ability to choose between multiple options compared to when they had to consider those options one at a time (Blount and Bazerman, 1996).

Another important structural element is how the decision is framed. Some research has shown that recipients are more concerned with fairness in a gain frame than in a loss frame (e.g., De Dreu, 1996). But, other research has shown the opposite, namely that offers associated with losses (versus gains) were perceived to be more unfair and had more rejections from recipients (Zhou and Wu, 2011) and fairness concerns were more important to recipients than self-interest when bargaining with negatively valenced outcomes (Leliveld et al., 2009).

Relationship between proposer and recipient. How recipients are treated by the proposer can also have a striking effect on the behavior of recipients. Under conditions of low interactional justice (i.e., when a low offer was coupled with an impolite statement), recipients were more likely to reject the offer than when there was no impolite statement (Kravitz and Gunto, 1992). Other research has shown the importance of social accounts (an aspect of interactional justice) and how they can affect recipients' perceptions, judgments and behavior. Van Dijke and De Cremer (2011) demonstrated that recipients who responded with low stress to uncertainty were more likely to accept unfair offers following a denial from the proposer, whereas those who responded with high stress tended to accept unfair offers more after an apology

The Recipient – Negotiations

Reactions to (un)fairness
While the bargaining games literature primarily focuses on how individuals respond to outcome (un)fairness, the literature on negotiations has started to examine how individuals respond to procedural fairness, though this research is still limited (Hollander-Blumoff and Tyler, 2008).

Much of the work on reactions to procedural fairness has been conducted in dispute resolution situations, which has examined individuals' reactions to third-party authorities (e.g., judges, mediators, arbitrators). While we did not include this literature in this review given space constraints, robust findings in this literature include the relationship between perceived fair treatment and outcome acceptance, such that individuals who perceive that they have been treated fairly by third-party authorities are more likely to accept the decision (Lind et al., 1993) and to comply with the outcomes of the dispute resolution (e.g., Pruitt et al., 1990; Tyler, 1990; Tyler and Blader, 2004). Similar effects are found in negotiation contexts: in general, negotiators react negatively when they perceive their outcomes to be unfair and/or that they have been treated unfairly by the other party, and react positively when they perceive their outcomes and treatment fair. This is consistent with the broader organizational justice literature, which has focused extensively on reactions to procedural fairness.

In terms of distributive fairness, research shows that negotiators respond to the fairness of offers. Maxwell et al. (2003) found that negotiators made more concessions and were more likely to reach agreement when their opponent reciprocated their concessions more (100 percent of the time) versus less (20 percent of the time). This effect was more pronounced when negotiators were primed with fairness before negotiating. Other research shows that the degree of concessions matters even if they are not experienced but simply observed as part of another negotiation (McGillicuddy et al., 1984).

Negotiators also respond very strongly to procedural fairness. Hollander-Blumoff and Tyler (2008) found when negotiators perceived the process to be fair, they perceived the negotiation to be more collaborative, were more willing to accept an agreement, and achieved higher joint gain. Perceiving that one has been treated fairly by the other party can also attenuate egocentric biases and result in quicker settlements and fewer impasses (Leung et al., 2004). Leung and colleagues (2004) argue that being treated fairly causes negotiators to view the other party's demands as more justified (because it signals that party's trustworthiness and reduced likelihood of exploiting them) and more likely to view a smaller share for themselves as fair.

Procedural fairness perceptions (e.g., whether the other party listened to one's concerns, considered one's wishes and needs, and whether the overall process was fair) have been argued to be an important aspect of negotiator's subjective value (see Curhan et al., 2006; 2010). Curhan and colleagues (2006; 2010) showed that negotiators' subjective value strongly influenced their desire for future interaction with the other party and also influenced their performance in future negotiations wherein they achieved greater individual and joint gain. In a field study, Curhan et al. (2009) found that subjective value was a significant predictor of MBA graduates' satisfaction with their compensation and their job one year after the job negotiations as well as a strong predictor of their intention to stay. The actual economic value of their negotiations, however, was not associated with these attitudes and intentions. Similarly, Ferguson et al. (2008) demonstrated that MBA graduates' perception of how fairly they were treated in their job negotiation affected their desire to stay with the company long term.

The limited research in negotiations that has been conducted on fairness and emotions reveals that fairness has strong effects on emotional responses. Allred (1999) found that negotiators who perceived their outcome to be unfair became angrier. Similarly, Hegtvedt and Killian (1999) found that negotiators who perceived the negotiation process to be fair were less likely to feel negative emotions (agitated, angry, resentful) and more likely to be pleased with the negotiation process. Carnevale and Pruitt (1992) argue that perceptions of unfairness in negotiation often result in feelings of hostility toward the other party. Though limited in scope, this research is consistent with that on emotional reactions to (un)fair offers in ubgs.

Research has shown that procedural fairness judgments have stronger effects on some people than others. Beersma and De Dreu (2003) manipulated pro-social (versus egoistic) motives of both parties in a negotiation. They found that pro-social negotiators perceived greater procedural fairness, which resulted in more integrative outcomes. Pro-socially motivated negotiators seem to be more concerned with the other party's interests and may be more likely to ask about those interests and actively listen, which in turn influences perceptions of procedural fairness by the other party. This is consistent with research we reviewed above on the focal actor's SVO in both bargaining games and negotiations, where pro-social actors had a consistent and strong concern with fairness.

In the above section, we reviewed research on fairness in bargaining games and negotiation, which reveals that fairness has important effects on the focal actor's and recipient's perceptions, attitudes, behaviors and outcomes. We now turn to a review of research on ethics.

ETHICS

What is (Un)ethical?

There exists some normative debate as to whether deception in negotiation should even be considered to be unethical at all. Carson et al. (1982), for example, argue that many forms of bluffing in labor negotiations are not only legal and economically advantageous, but that associated tactics (e.g., lying), are generally morally acceptable. Strudler (1995) asserts that in limited situations some deception in negotiations, including lying about one's reservation price, may be morally acceptable. Others disagree. Provis (2000a; 2000b) suggests that the stance that deception in negotiations is ethical and acceptable is problematic and further asserts that appeals to rationales for such behavior in the form of fairness or self-defense are unjustified. Cohen (2002), identifying respect as a foundational ethical challenge in negotiations, affirms that the other party is both a person as well as a means to one's ends and argues that this duality creates a tension which requires one to respect the fundamental dignity of the other party. Others have called for a middle ground between these two views, proposing that a judgment on the ethicality of deception depends on the situation. Along those lines, Dees and Cramton (1991) propose a "mutual trust principle" which argues that it is unreasonable for someone to abide by rules of trust (and by extension, rules of ethical behavior) when the other party is not expected to abide by those same rules.

While the above arguments have focused on normative debates as to what is ethical, others have taken a more descriptive approach, attempting to understand what affects the judgment of unethical behavior. Lewicki and his colleagues (Lewicki, 1983; Lewicki and Robinson, 1998; Lewicki and Stark, 1996) identified five underlying factors of unethical tactics in negotiation (traditional competitive bargaining, bluffing, misrepresentation, questionable information collection, and influencing the other party's professional network) each encompassing specific behaviors, and then grouped those behaviors on a continuum of ethical appropriateness. Making a "high ball" opening offer (classified as traditional competitive bargaining) was generally seen as ethically appropriate while making false threats and promises (types of bluffing) was generally seen as ethically unacceptable. Other research has shown that emotional deception (e.g., acting surprised or pretending to be angry when one is not) is generally seen as more appropriate than cognitive deception (e.g., misrepresenting information) (Fulmer et al., 2009).

The perceived ethical appropriateness of various tactics may not be consistent across all people in all situations. In fact, research has shown that it depends on factors such as gender, culture and nationality, educational focus, work experience, and personality. With regard to gender, men have been found to have more lenient ethical standards (Kray and Haselhuhn, 2012) and view ethically questionable tactics more acceptable (e.g., Lewicki and Robinson, 1998) than women. Moreover, while there is a general tendency for negotiators to interpret ethics in an egocentric manner (Kronzon and Darley, 1999), male negotiators have been shown to have stronger egocentric judgments than female negotiators (Kray and Haselhuhn, 2012).

Lewicki and Robinson, 1998; Robinson et al., 2000) were among the first to note that the perceived appropriateness of various negotiation tactics varied by culture. Robinson and colleagues (2000) found that Asian students rated certain questionable tactics as more appropriate than did Western students. Volkema (1998) identified differences between participants in the U.S. and Mexico, with respondents from Mexico rating ethically questionable tactics as less appropriate than U.S. participants. Further study by Volkema (2004) painted a more comprehensive picture, noting that in addition to cultural factors, demographic and economic considerations also affect the perceived appropriateness of negotiation tactics. And, recent research by Ma et al. (2012) demonstrated the complexity of the relationship between culture and unethical behavior and further underscored the interactive effects that culture and gender have on unethical behavior. They discovered that managers from China, a culture characterized by high power distance but low levels of uncertainty avoidance, were more likely to consider ethically questionable tactics acceptable than U.S. managers, though this relationship was qualified by gender.

Individual differences also seem to affect judgments of ethically questionable tactics. Kray and Haselhuhn (2012) recently showed that implicit negotiation beliefs (e.g., having either fixed beliefs "ability is not changeable", versus malleable beliefs "effort predicts success") affected judgments of ethicality. Negotiators, especially male negotiators, holding fixed beliefs exhibited lower ethical standards than those holding malleable beliefs. Given the known link between attitudes and behavior (Ajzen and Fishbein, 1969), the factors identified above as influencing judgments of the appropriateness of unethical tactics are also likely to influence the use of such tactics in bargaining and negotiation, to which we now turn.

THE FOCAL ACTOR – BARGAINING GAMES

A review of the literature on ethical behavior by the focal actor in bargaining games focuses on instrumental concerns as a fundamental driver of unethical behavior – unethical behavior is more likely when the net payout (i.e., benefits minus costs) is positive. Research in ubgs identifies several variables that are considered in that calculus, including direct effects, such as economic gains, and factors that have an indirect effect on payouts, such as fear of rejection, anonymity, and power.

Being (Un)ethical

The direct payout from deception is a key factor in predicting whether deception will be employed as a strategy. In a repeated ubg, Boles et al. (2000) found that financial rewards increased unethical behavior, such that proposers were most deceptive when the potential profits were the highest. Similarly, Cohen and colleagues (2009) found that groups playing a modified deception game engaged in deception when it maximized their economic outcome and, conversely, engaged in honest behavior when that tactic maximized their payoff.

Characteristics of proposer and recipient. Power seems to increase the prevalence of unethical behavior in bargaining games, perhaps because power carries with it a confidence that the offer will be accepted and hence payout will increase. Boles and colleagues (2000) found that while proposers and recipients in a repeated ubg chose deceptive strategies equally, proposers, which are granted with significant power in traditional ubgs, were more likely to tell outright lies. However, research by Koning and colleagues (2010) contradicts these findings, demonstrating that proposers low in power used deception more than those in a high power position.

Situational factors. Anonymity and privacy, which reduce the likelihood that one will suffer repercussions (i.e., rejection of one's offer) of an unethical action, is another factor that is linked to unethical behavior. Examining proposers in a dictator game, Naquin et al. (2010) found that MBA students who communicated their offer via email, which leads to increased anonymity, were more likely to lie and feel justified about their lies than those who communicated their offer via pen and paper using their campus mailbox. Boles and colleagues (2000) also found that deceptive strategies in ubgs were more prevalent when private information (for the proposer, the size of the pot; for the recipient, the size of outside option) was not revealed and proposers were most deceptive when their potential profit was highest.

It also appears that ethical behavior can be encouraged. Using a deception game, where actors could tell the truth or lie about two payoff options to another player (option A pays player 1 $10 and player 2 $5; option B pays player 1 $5 and player 2 $10), Gunia and colleagues (2012) found that having actors engage in contemplation (engaging in moral reasoning) and moral conversations (talking with a person playing the same role about an ethical issue regarding the game) led them to tell the truth more.

Relationship between proposer and recipient. Van Dijk and colleagues (2008) found that deception was more likely to be used by proposers in ubgs when they were playing against an angry versus happy recipient, and underlying this relationship was the perceived fear of rejection. In other words, anger exhibited by the recipient increased the perception that an offer would be rejected (and thus lower the proposer's payout) which in turn increased the use of deceptive strategies by the proposer to mitigate that concern. These results support the assertion made by Van Dijk and colleagues (2012) that the opponent's behavior is a "catalyst" for unethical behavior.

THE FOCAL ACTOR – NEGOTIATIONS

Behaving Unethically

In the negotiation literature, there has been substantially more research conducted on the focal actor and what factors influence use of unethical behavior. Some studies have revealed that unethical behavior occurs in more than 90 percent of negotiations (Volkema et al., 2010). As with bargaining games, research has shown that the higher the payoff for unethical behavior, the more likely negotiators engage in it (Tenbrunsel, 1998). A variety of individual, relational, and situational factors have been linked to unethical behavior in negotiation.

Characteristics of the actor. Males and younger negotiators and those from cultures characterized by uncertainty avoidance, masculinity, individualism, and low power distance are more likely to use ethically questionable tactics (Volkema, 2004). Ethical orientation has also been found to influence the use of unethical tactics in negotiation, with subjectivists (low in idealism, high in relativism) more likely to use such tactics than absolutists (high in idealism, low in relativism) (Banas and McLean Parks, 2002). Perry and Nixon (2005) found that negotiators with strong end-result and social contract ethical philosophies were more willing to use questionable ethical tactics whereas individuals with a strong rule ethical philosophy, higher levels of religiosity, and those with a cooperative attitude in negotiations were more likely to adopt higher ethical standards. Consistent with these findings, Aquino (1998) showed that when ethical standards were made more salient, negotiators were less likely to engage in deception.

Perceptions of the self are also related to unethical behaviors. Hershfield et al. (2012) found that low future self-continuity (similarity between one's present and future self) was associated with increased unethical tactics, including lies, false promises and cheating. Moreover, Cohen and colleagues (2011) found that individuals who have a tendency to think that they made a mistake (i.e., high guilt negative behavior evaluation) and those who tend to think of themselves as a bad person (i.e., shame negative self-evaluation) were less unethical; however those who have a tendency to hide or withdraw from public (i.e., high in shame-withdraw behaviors) were more likely to behave unethically. Other research has shown that receiving feedback from the negotiation opponent that one was unethical leads to greater honesty in a subsequent negotiation, though receiving feedback that one was ethical leads to greater intended cooperation (Kim et al., 2003).

Emotions have been shown to influence use of unethical tactics. Negotiators who exhibit high anxiety and anger (Olekalns and Smith, 2009) or feel greater envy (Moran and Schweitzer, 2008) are more likely to use unethical tactics. Though, those who perceive the situation as less threatening (greater tolerance of ambiguity) are less likely to misrepresent information (Yurtsever, 2001).

Characteristics of the counterpart. Perceived and actual characteristics of the other party have been shown to influence deception by the focal negotiator. If the other party has a reputation as a good negotiator, individuals report they would be less likely to misrepresent facts to them; conversely, if the other has a reputation as an unethical negotiator, the focal negotiator is more likely to reciprocate with unethical behavior of their own, including bluffing (i.e., misleading intentions) and misrepresentation (i.e., misleading arguments) (Volkema and Leme Fleury, 2002). Olekalns and Smith (2007) extended these results by showing that positive perception of one's counterpart's integrity and trustworthiness led to increased likelihood of sins of omission whereas perception that the other party was powerful increased the likely use of sins of commission; perceptions that the other party was benevolent increased both sins of omission and commission. Actual behavior of the other party also influences unethical behavior by the focal negotiator, with cooperative partners reducing the likelihood that the focal negotiator engages in sins of omission (O'Connor and Carnevale, 1997; Steinel and De Dreu, 2004).

The relationship between the actor and the recipient. When negotiators anticipate a future relationship with their opponent, they are less likely to use unethical tactics (Volkema and Leme Fleury, 2002). And, the greater the asymmetry in power between parties, the greater the use of unethical tactics (Crott et al., 1980; Tenbrunsel and Messick, 2001). In an extension of the research on power, Olekalns and Smith (2009) examined different dimensions of power and different types of unethical behavior and found that mutuality of dependence (extent to which negotiators are equally dependent on one another) was more strongly tied to the use of sins of commission than to the use of sins of omission but the level of dependence (extent to which negotiators rely upon one another) was more strongly tied to sins of omission.

The Situation. Other research demonstrates the important role of the situation on unethical behavior in negotiation. For instance, Halevy et al. (2012) found that perceptions of the negotiation as a game of chicken (where highest payoff occurs when focal negotiator competes and opponent cooperates and best move is to do the opposite of one's opponent) led to more deception than when the negotiation was perceived to be one of maximizing differences, assurance, or a traditional prisoner's dilemma. Negotiators primed with an individualistic motivation have also been shown to use misrepresentation more than those primed with a cooperative motivation (O'Connor and Carnevale, 1997). Moreover, whether the negotiators have a gain or loss frame seems to play a role. Kern and Chugh (2009) found that negotiators were more likely to engage in unethical behavior when they were presented with a loss versus gain frame, replicating the finding by Van Beest and colleagues (2005) with regard to negotiators engaging in (un)fairness.

Communication medium has also been shown to influence unethical behavior, with email negotiations (Paulson and Naquin, 2004) and written negotiations (Valley et al. 1998) encouraging the use of deception compared with face-to-face negotiations, though Schweitzer et al. (2002) found that negotiating via video-conferencing versus telephone led to greater use of deception, they argue, because visual access allows the deceiver to monitor the target's receipt of the deception and adjust the deception appropriately.

The Role of Interactions. Research has looked at the interactions between the focal negotiator, the target, and/or the situation and in doing so, provide a more complicated understanding of why and how unethical behavior is perpetuated. Volkema and colleagues (2010) found that the best predictor of competitive-unethical behavior was the interaction between the attitude of a focal negotiator toward competitive-unethical behavior and the behavior of the other party: the more appropriate the focal negotiator perceived the tactics and the more the other party used these tactics, the more likely it was that the focal negotiator employed these tactics. And, Olekalns and Smith (2009) found that the use of deception was influenced by the interaction between the power distribution among the negotiators and the affect of those negotiators.

The bargaining games and negotiation literatures shed significant light on why and when focal actors might initiate unethical behavior. While the bargaining games literature focuses primarily on an instrumental model, suggesting that unethical behavior is elicited when benefits outweigh the costs, the negotiation literature highlights that the picture may be more complex and that other factors (e.g., the counterpart, the relationship, the situation and also the interaction between these factors) need to be considered.

THE RECIPIENT – BARGAINING GAMES

Though unethical behavior in bargaining games and negotiation affects both the focal negotiator and the target of unethical behavior, nearly all of the research in this area has focused on the former while very little research has examined how people respond to unethical behavior. To our surprise, we found only a few studies in the bargaining games literature that examined recipient's responses to the unethical behavior of the proposer. For instance, Croson et al. (2003) found that in the short term, when proposers lied about the size of the pie (and recipients were unaware of these lies), recipient's acceptance rates were unaffected. But in the long term, when proposer's lies were revealed, recipients were more likely to reject subsequent offers. Similarly, Boles and colleagues (2000) showed that when proposer's deception was revealed, recipients rejected their subsequent offers in a repeated ubg more than offers from honest proposers or proposers whose deception was not revealed. Recipients who knew they had been deceived also viewed the proposers as less believable and desirable counterparts in the future. And, even when recipients did not know they were deceived, they were less satisfied with the outcome, evaluated the proposer as less truthful, and had less interest in interacting with the proposer in the future than when the proposer was honest.

THE RECIPIENT – NEGOTIATIONS

What impact does unethical behavior have in negotiations? Again, the research on reactions to (un)ethical behavior in negotiations is sparse. The limited empirical research reveals that negotiators react strongly to the perceived unethical behaviors of the other party. Schweitzer and colleagues (2002) found that negotiators who were lied to were overall less likely to trust the other party who lied to them. From a behavioral perspective, Volkema and colleagues (2010) found that the more the focal actor used unethical tactics, the more recipients used such tactics as well.

Though the research on recipient's reactions to unethical behavior in bargaining and negotiation is sparse, the research that exists provides interesting insights. From the bargaining games research, we know that having knowledge that the other party behaves unethically results in negative reactions from the recipient. Similarly, in negotiation, the

210 *Handbook of research on negotiation*

actor's deception influences reciprocity in the recipient, with perceptions of honesty significant in driving perceptions of the negotiator, desire for future interaction, and perceptions of the outcome (Volkema et al., 2010). However, we also know that negotiators often misperceive their counterparts' use of unethical behavior: Volkema and colleagues (2010) found no significant relationship between the opponent's actual use of unethical behaviors and negotiator's perceptions of the opponent's honesty. Thus, a negotiator may be judged more by the perceptions of their behavior than their actual behavior.

DISCUSSION

Having reviewed the literature on fairness and ethics in bargaining and negotiation, we want to reflect now on what has been done and identify the "holes" and areas ripe for future research. Utilizing the fairness/ethics × actor/recipient × bargaining/negotiation structure reveals very quickly where the holes are (see Figure 8.1). The focus of the research has been on the focal actor making fair offers and recipients' reactions to unfair offers in bargaining game contexts and on the focal actor being unethical in negotiation contexts. In bargaining games, a significant amount of attention has focused on why proposers make fair offers and when they are likely to do so and why recipients reject unfair offers and when they are more likely to do so. With regard to ethics, there is ample research on when actors will be unethical, particularly in negotiation contexts.

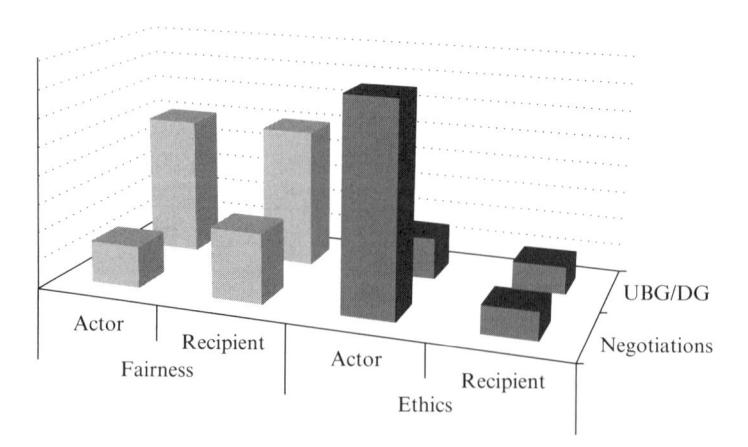

Figure 8.1 *Amount of research in fairness/ethics (construct) × actor/ recipient (role) × bargaining/negotiation (context)*

One question for which there is not much empirical research is why and when negotiators enact fairness. And, given that most of the research on focal actor's engagement in fairness has been conducted in bargaining games, and most of that research has focused almost exclusively on outcome fairness, there is little understanding of why and when people behave fairly in contexts that involve both distributive and procedural fairness. Indeed these questions of why and when people behave fairly have not only been ignored in the negotiation literature but in the organizational justice literature more broadly, as recently noted by a number of scholars (e.g., Blader and Chen, 2012; Brief, 2012; Brockner et al., 2009). This is curious given the attention this issue has received in the bargaining games literature with regard to distributive fairness, investigating why and when proposers make fair offers, and even more curious given all the research in the negotiation literature on why and when negotiators behave unethically. Clearly there is a need, and therefore opportunity, to examine empirically why negotiators treat their opponents with respect, allow them input, or actively listen to them. Is it primarily to maximize self-interest, as suggested by research on distributive fairness in the bargaining games literature? Or is it because of relational concerns or the motive to be fair for fairness sake, as suggested by research in the organizational justice literature? Examining when negotiators enact fairness can shed light on the question of why they do so. Negotiation researchers interested in fairness should follow the example set by those studying fairness in the bargaining games literature and those studying ethics in the negotiation literature to examine this important question, thus contributing to the broader organizational justice literature where scholars have been clamoring recently for exactly such research.

While there has been more attention on how individuals react to unfairness in bargaining games and negotiation, the focus has been mostly on distributive fairness given the extensive research in bargaining games that has examined recipients' reactions to unfair offers. Indeed, Hollander-Blumoff and Tyler (2008) recognized that "fairness research relating to negotiated conflict has focused predominantly on outcome fairness, or distributive fairness (Welsh, 2004), with only limited attention given to the role of fairness of process, or procedural justice, in negotiations." (p. 476). Most of the work that has been done has examined procedural fairness issues in third-party dispute resolution situations (e.g., Tyler and Blader, 2004; Lind et al., 1993; Pruitt et al., 1990). It is clear from this literature and the vast organizational justice literature that individuals care about being treated fairly, at times even more than whether they perceive an offer or outcome to be fair (e.g., Folger and Konovsky, 1989; Lind and Tyler, 1988). We encourage researchers to examine negotiators' reactions to both outcome and process fairness, further examining factors which might lead to stronger responses to unfairness. With regard to ethics, it is even more surprising how little research has examined reactions to (un)ethical behavior. In the bargaining games literature, this is more understandable given that ethics may be difficult to discern as offers and the total amount available are typically all that are communicated and there often is no face-to-face interaction. But, in the negotiation literature, there are so many opportunities to be ethical or unethical, as evidenced by the large amount of research we reviewed on why and when negotiators are unethical. Clearly it is important to understand how negotiators respond to the opponent's bluffing or exaggerated first offers. But, it is also important to differentiate among these different types of unethical behaviors to determine whether they lead to similar or different responses. As Brief (2012) recently decried about the behavioral ethics literature, only certain types of unethical behavior are examined and there may be very different reactions to different types of unethical behavior. So, in terms of negotiation, how do negotiators respond to misrepresentation, bluffing, versus exaggerated first offers, not just in terms of their perceptions, but also in terms of their affective and behavioral responses?

As may be evident by the above discussion, some research focuses on the "good" (fair/ethical behavior), while most research focuses on the "bad" (unfair/unethical). With regard to the recipient, both in terms of fairness and ethics, the predominant focus of the research has been on the bad (unfair/unethical). Brockner (2010, p. 62) defends this in the fairness literature by arguing that "the causal attribution process that draws people's attention to process fairness information is more strongly instantiated when outcomes are relatively unfavorable" and "people generally are more likely to initiate a process of sense-making, in which they seek to understand the meaning of their outcomes by assigning causality for them, in response to outcomes that are unfavorable rather than favorable". But, why does this need to be the case for the focal actor? Much of the literature on ethics focuses on factors affecting engagement in unethical behavior. Shouldn't we be turning our focus to ethical behavior and how people can become more ethical? Indeed, the recent research by Gunia and colleagues (2012), showing that people become more honest when they are asked to engage in individual contemplation or moral conversations with another person facing a similar situation, is a step in that direction. But, much more is needed.

Finally, while we have been avoiding the issue of what is the relationship between fairness and ethics (and indeed wrote separate sections on fairness and ethics because of the current segmentation in the two literatures we reviewed), we feel we cannot end our review without at least raising this thorny issue. Previous scholars have commented on the lack of integration among the organizational justice and behavioral ethics literatures. In a recent chapter on the behavioral ethics literature, Brief (2012) commented on the role of organizational justice research and stated that "with few exceptions, it did not explicitly concern itself with ethics; rather, it principally has been focused on the linkage between perceived justice and outcomes deemed relevant to the economic performance of firms." (p. 21). Schminke et al. (1997) similarly note that there is hardly any research that integrates these two literatures despite similarities in focus, such as the distinction between process and outcome concerns. Indeed, Cropanzano and Stein (2009) highlight that "workplace fairness researchers in the social sciences may be equally surprised to discover that much of what they study could properly fall within the domain of behavioral ethics research" (p. 193). The organizational justice and ethics literatures have for the most part ignored the other related literature, resulting in a chasm between the two. This has led some organizational justice researchers to integrate fairness and ethics in their theorizing by identifying fairness as a motive (Lerner, 1975), moral duty (Folger, 2001), or moral conviction (Skitka et al., 2005) and not merely a by-product of instrumental or relational concerns. A few have even started to examine empirically the relationship between ethics and fairness and the individual and combined effects on reactions and behaviors (e.g., Schminke et al., 1997).

And yet, it is important to not conflate the constructs of fairness and ethics as is often done in the two literatures, where the constructs of fairness, justice, and ethics are often used interchangeably. As Folger and colleagues (2005) argue, fairness and ethics are not synonymous and fairness is just one aspect of morality, albeit an important one. We see a tremendous need to better understand how fairness and ethics are related. Do people view what has been argued to be a fairness violation in bargaining game contexts (e.g., receiving only 30 percent of a resource when the proposer keeps 70 percent) also to be unethical? For that matter, do people view what has been argued to be an ethical violation in negotiation (e.g., being lied to) as unfair? What factors influence these perceptions and why? When are fairness and ethical perceptions the same and when are they different? Clearly, there is much more we need to understand regarding fairness and ethics and their relationship, providing ample opportunity for future research.

CONCLUSION

In our attempt to provide a comprehensive review of the research on fairness and ethics in bargaining games and negotiation, we have identified areas where we still do not have sufficient understanding of what happens and why. We have also identified a consistent theme, namely one of myopia, where scholars in one literature often ignore what is being done in the other literatures. Given the number of scholars who have already identified this lack of integration among highly related literatures and those who are already making linkages empirically, we are hopeful the field is on the right track and will quickly move towards integration and knowledge creation. We offer this review with the hope that it will provide additional impetus to help the field move even faster.

REFERENCES

Adams, J.S. (1965). Inequity in social exchange. In L. Berkowitz (ed.), *Advances in experimental social psychology* (267–299). New York: Academic Press.

Ajzen, I. and Fishbein, M. (1969). The prediction of behavioral intentions in a choice situation. *Journal of Experimental Social Psychology*, 5, 400–416.

Allred, K.G. (1999). Anger driven retaliation: Toward an understanding of impassioned conflict in organizations. In R.J. Bies, R.J. Lewicki, and B.H. Sheppard (eds), *Research on negotiations in organizations* (27–58). Greenwich, CT: JAI Press.

Aquino, K. (1998). The effects of ethical climate and the availability of alternatives on the use of deception during negotiation. *International Journal of Conflict Management*, 9, 195–217.

Babcock, L. and Loewenstein, G. (1997). explaining bargaining impasse: the role of self-serving biases. *Journal of Economic Perspectives*, 11, 109–126.

Babcock, L., Loewenstein, G., Issacharoff, S., and Camerer, C. (1995). Biased judgments of fairness in bargaining. *The American Economic Review*, 85, 1337–1343.

Bahry, D.L. and Wilson, R.K. (2006). Confusion or fairness in the field? Rejections in the ultimatum game under the strategy method. *Journal of Economic Behavior and Organization*, 60, 37–54.

Banas, J.T. and McLean Parks, J.M. (2002). Lambs among lions? The impact of ethical ideology on negotiation behaviors and outcomes. *International Negotiation*, 7, 235–260.

Beersma, B. and De Dreu, C.K.W. (2003). Social motives in integrative negotiation: The mediating influence of procedural fairness. *Social Justice Research*, 16, 217–239.

Bethwaite, J. and Tompkinson, P. (1996). The ultimatum game and non-selfish utility functions. *Journal of Economic Psychology*, 17, 259–271.

Blader, S.L. and Chen, Y. (2012). Differentiating the effects of status and power: A justice perspective. *Journal of Personality and Social Psychology*, 102, 994–1014.

Blount, S. (1995). When social outcomes aren't fair: the effect of causal attributions on preferences. *Organizational Behavior and Human Decision Processes*, 63, 131–144.

Blount, S. and Bazerman, M.H. (1996). The inconsistent evaluation of absolute versus comparative payoffs in labor supply and bargaining. *Journal of Economic Behavior and Organization*, 30, 227–240.

Boles, T.L. and Messick, D.M. (1990). Accepting unfairness: Temporal influence on choice. In K. Borcherding, O.I. Larichev, and D.M. Messick (eds), *Contemporary Issues in Decision Making* (375–389). North-Holland: Elsevier Science Publishers.

Boles, T.L., Croson, R.T.A., and Murnighan, J.K. (2000). Deception and retribution in repeated ultimatum bargaining. *Organizational Behavior and Human Decision Processes*, 83, 235–259.

Brief, A.P. (2012). The good, the bad, and the ugly: What behavioral business ethics researchers ought to be studying. In D. De Cremer, and A.E. Tenbrunsel (eds), *Behavioral Business Ethics: Shaping an Emerging Field* (17–44). New York: Routledge.

Brockner, J. (2010). *A contemporary look at organizational justice: Multiplying insult times injury*. New York: Routledge/Taylor & Francis Group.

Brockner, J., Wiesenfeld, B.M., and Diekmann, K.A. (2009). Towards a "fairer" conception of process fairness: Why, when and how more may not always be better than less. *The Academy of Management Annals, 3*, 183–216.

Buchan, N.R., Croson, R.T.A., and Johnson, E.J. (2004). When do fair beliefs influence bargaining behavior? Experimental bargaining in Japan and the United States. *Journal of Consumer Research, 31*, 181–190.

Camerer, C.F. (2003). *Behavioral game theory: Experiments in strategic interaction*. Princeton, NJ: Princeton University Press.

Carnevale, P.J. and Pruitt, D.G. (1992). Negotiation and mediation. *Annual Review of Psychology, 43*, 531–582.

Carson, T.L., Wokutch, R.E., and Murrmann, K.F. (1982). Bluffing in labor negotiations: Legal and ethical issues. *Journal of Business Ethics, 1*, 13–22.

Cohen, J.R. (2002). The ethics of respect in negotiation. *Negotiation Journal, 18*, 115–120.

Cohen, T.R., Gunia, B.C., Kim-Jun, S.Y., and Murnighan, J.K. (2009). Do groups lie more than individuals? Honesty and deception as a function of strategic self-interest. *Journal of Experimental Social Psychology, 45*, 1321–1324.

Cohen, T.R., Wolf, S.T., Panter, A.T., and Insko, C.A. (2011). Introducing the GASP scale: A new measure of guilt and shame proneness. *Journal of Personality and Social Psychology, 100*, 947–966.

Cropanzano, R. and Stein, J.H. (2009). Organizational justice and behavioral ethics: Promises and prospects. *Business Ethics Quarterly, 19*, 193–233.

Croson, R., Boles, T., and Murnighan, J.K. (2003). Cheap talk in bargaining experiments: lying and threats in ultimatum games. *Journal of Economic Behavior and Organization, 51*, 143–159.

Crott, H., Kayser, E., and Lamm, H. (1980). The effects of information exchange and communication in an asymmetrical negotiation situation. *European Journal of Social Psychology, 10*, 149–163.

Curhan, J.R., Elfenbein, H.A., and Eisenkraft, N. (2010). The objective value of subjective value: A multi-round negotiation study. *Journal of Applied Social Psychology, 40*, 690–709.

Curhan, J.R., Elfenbein, H.A., and Kilduff, G.J. (2009). Getting off on the right foot: Subjective value versus economic value in predicting longitudinal job outcomes from job offer negotiations. *Journal of Applied Psychology, 94*, 524–534.

Curhan, J.R., Elfenbein, H.A., and Xu, H. (2006). What do people value when they negotiate? Mapping the domain of subjective value in negotiation. *Journal of Personality and Social Psychology, 91*, 493–512.

De Dreu, C.K.W. (1996). Gain-loss-frame in outcome-interdependence: Does it influence equality or equity considerations? *European Journal of Social Psychology, 26*, 315–324.

De Dreu, C.K.W. and van Lange, P.A.M. (1995). The impact of social value orientations on negotiator cognition and behavior. *Personality and Social Psychology Bulletin, 21*, 1178–1188.

De Dreu, C.K.W., Beersma, B., Steinel, W., and van Kleef, G.A. (2007). The psychology of negotiation: Principles and basic processes. In A.W. Kruglanski, and E.T. Higgins (eds), *Social psychology: Handbook of basic principles* (608–629). New York: Guilford.

Dees, J.G. and Cramton, P.C. (1991). Shrewd bargaining on the moral frontier: Toward a theory of morality in practice. *Business Ethics Quarterly, 1*, 135–167.

Dickinson, D.L. (2000). Ultimatum decision-making: A test of reciprocal kindness. *Theory and Decision, 48*, 151–177.

Dulebohn, J.H., Conlon, D.E., Sarinopoulos, I., Davison, R.B., and McNamara, G. (2009). The biological bases of unfairness: Neuroimaging evidence for the distinctiveness of procedural and distributive justice. *Organizational Behavior and Human Decision Processes, 110*, 140–151.

Falk, A. and Fischbacher, U. (2006). A theory of reciprocity. *Games and Economic Behavior, 54*, 293–315.

Falk, A., Fehr, E., and Fischbacher, U. (2003). On the nature of fair behavior. *Economic Inquiry*, 41, 20–26.
Ferguson, M., Moye, N., and Friedman, R. (2008). The lingering effects of the recruitment experience on the long-term employment relationship. *Negotiation and Conflict Management Research*, 1, 246–262.
Fischbacher, U., Fong, C.M., and Fehr, E. (2009). Fairness, errors and the power of competition. *Journal of Economic Behavior and Organization*, 72, 527–545.
Folger, R. (2001). Fairness as dissonance. In S. Gilliland, D.D. Steiner, and D.P. Skarlicki (eds), *Theoretical and Cultural Perspectives on Organizational Justice* (3–31). Greenwich, CT: Information Age.
Folger, R. and Konovsky, M. (1989). Effects of procedural and distributive justice on reactions to pay raise decisions. *Academy of Management Journal*, 32, 115–130.
Folger, R., Cropanzano, R., and Goldman, B. (2005). What is the relationship between justice and morality? In J. Greenberg, and J. Colquitt (eds), *The Handbook of Organizational Justice* (215–245). Mahwah, NJ: Lawrence Erlbaum Associates.
Forsythe, R., Horowitz, J.L., Savin, N.E., and Sefton, M. (1994). Fairness in simple bargaining experiments. *Games and Economic Behavior*, 6, 347–369.
Fulmer, I.S., Barry, B., and Long, D.A. (2009). Lying and smiling: Informational and emotional deception in negotiation. *Journal of Business Ethics*, 88, 691–709.
Gunia, B.C., Wang, L., Huang, L., Wang, J., and Murnighan, J.K. (2012). Contemplation and conversation: Subtle influences on moral decision making. *Academy of Management Journal*, 55, 13–33.
Güth, W. and Tietz, R. (1990). Ultimatum bargaining behavior: A survey and comparison of experimental results. *Journal of Economic Psychology*, 11, 417–449.
Güth, W., Schmittberger, R., and Schwarze, B. (1982). An experimental analysis of ultimatum bargaining. *Journal of Economic Behavior and Organization*, 3, 367–388.
Halevy, N., Chou, E.Y., and Murnighan, J.K. (2012). Mind games: The mental representation of conflict. *Journal of Personality and Social Psychology*, 102, 132–148.
Handgraaf, M.J.J., van Dijk, E., and De Cremer, D. (2003a). Social utility in ultimatum bargaining. *Social Justice Research*, 16, 263–283.
Handgraaf, M.J.J., van Dijk, E., Wilke, H.A.M., and Vermunt, R.C. (2003b). The salience of a recipient's alternatives: Inter- and intrapersonal comparison in ultimatum games. *Organizational Behavior and Human Decision Processes*, 90, 165–177.
Handgraaf, M.J.J., van Dijk, E., Wilke, H.A.M., and Vermunt, R.C. (2004). Evaluability of outcomes in ultimatum bargaining. *Organizational Behavior and Human Decision Processes*, 95, 97–106.
Handgraaf, M.J.J., van Dijk, E., Vermunt, R.C., Wilke, H.A.M., and De Dreu, C.K.W. (2008). Less power or powerless? Egocentric empathy gaps and the irony of having little versus no power in social decision making. *Journal of Personality and Social Psychology*, 95, 1136–1149.
Hegtvedt, K.A. and Killian, C. (1999). Fairness and emotions: Reactions to the process and outcomes of negotiations. *Social Forces*, 78, 269–302.
Henrich, J., Boyd, R., Bowles, S., Camerer, C., Fehr, E., Gintis, H., and McElreath, R. (2001). In search of homo economicus: Behavioral experiments in 15 small-scale societies. *The American Economic Review*, 91, 73–78.
Hershfield, H.E., Cohen, T.R., and Thompson, L. (2012). Short horizons and tempting situations: Lack of continuity to our future selves leads to unethical decision making and behavior. *Organizational Behavior and Human Decision Processes*, 117, 298–310.
Ho, T.H. and Su, X. (2009). Peer-induced fairness in games. *The American Economic Review*, 99, 2022–2049.
Hoffman, E., McCabe, K., and Smith, V.L. (1996). Social distance and other-regarding behavior in dictator games. *The American Economic Review*, 86, 653–660.
Hoffman, E., McCabe, K., Shachat, K., and Smith, V. (1994). Preferences, property rights, and anonymity in bargaining games. *Games and Economic Behavior*, 7, 346–380.
Hollander-Blumoff, R. and Tyler, T.R. (2008). Procedural justice in negotiation: Procedural

fairness, outcome acceptance, and integrative potential. *Law and Social Inquiry*, *33*, 473–500.
Kachelmeier, S.J. and Towry, K.L. (2002). Negotiated transfer pricing: Is fairness easier said than done? *The Accounting Review*, *77*, 571–593.
Kahneman, D., Knetsch, J.L., and Thaler, R.H. (1986). Fairness and the assumptions of economics. *Journal of Business*, *59*, 285–300.
Kern, M.C. and Chugh, D. (2009). Bounded ethicality: The perils of loss framing. *Psychological Science*, *20*, 378–384.
Kim, P.H., Diekmann, K.A., and Tenbrunsel, A.E. (2003). Flattery may get you somewhere: The strategic implications of providing positive vs. negative feedback about ability vs. ethicality in negotiation. *Organizational Behavior and Human Decision Processes*, *90*, 225–243.
Koning, L., van Dijk, E., van Beest, I., and Steinel, W. (2010). An instrumental account of deception and reactions to deceit in bargaining. *Business Ethics Quarterly*, *20*, 57–73.
Kravitz, D.A. and Gunto, S. (1992). Decisions and perceptions of recipients in ultimatum bargaining games. *Journal of Socio-Economics*, *21*, 65–84.
Kray, L.J. and Haselhuhn, M.P. (2012). Male pragmatism in negotiators' ethical reasoning. *Journal of Experimental Social Psychology*, *48*, 1124–1131.
Kronzon, S. and Darley, J. (1999). Is this tactic ethical? Biased judgments of ethics in negotiation. *Basic and Applied Social Psychology*, *21*, 49–60.
Leliveld, M.C., van Beest, I., van Dijk, E., and Tenbrunsel, A.E. (2009). Understanding the influence of outcome valence in bargaining: A study on fairness accessibility, norms, and behavior. *Journal of Experimental Social Psychology*, *45*, 505–514.
Lerner, M. (1975). The justice motive in social behavior: Introduction. *Journal of Social Issues*, *31*, 1–19.
Leung, K., Tong, K., and Ho, S.S. (2004). Effects of interactional justice on egocentric bias in resource allocation decisions. *Journal of Applied Psychology*, *89*, 405–415.
Lewicki, R.J. (1983). Lying and deception: A behavioral model. In M.H. Bazerman, and R.J. Lewicki (eds), *Negotiating in Organizations* (68–90). Beverly Hills, CA: Sage Publications.
Lewicki, R.J. and Robinson, R.J. (1998). Ethical and unethical bargaining tactics: An empirical study. *Journal of Business Ethics*, *17*, 665–682.
Lewicki, R.J. and Stark, N. (1996). What is ethically appropriate in negotiations: An empirical examination of bargaining tactics. *Social Justice Research*, *9*, 69–95.
Lind, E.A. and Tyler, T.R. (1988). *The social psychology of procedural justice*. New York: Plenum Press.
Lind, E.A., Kulik, C.T., Ambrose, M., and de Vera Park, M.V. (1993). Individual and corporate dispute resolution: using procedural fairness as a decision heuristic. *Administrative Science Quarterly*, *38*, 224–251.
Loewenstein, G.F., Thompson, L., and Bazerman, M.H. (1989). Social utility and decision making in interpersonal contexts. *Journal of Personality and Social Psychology*, *57*, 426–441.
Loewenstein, G.F., Issacharoff, S., Camerer, C., and Babcock, L. (1993). Self-serving assessments of fairness and pretrial bargaining. *Journal of Legal Studies*, *22*, 135–159.
Ma, Z., Liang, D., and Chen, H. (2012). Negotiating with the Chinese: Are they more likely to use unethical strategies? *Group Decision and Negotiation*, 1–15.
Maxwell, S., Nye, P., and Maxwell, N. (1999). Less pain, same gain: The effects of priming fairness in price negotiations. *Psychology and Marketing*, *16*, 545–562.
Maxwell, S., Nye, P., and Maxwell, N. (2003). The wrath of the fairness-primed negotiator when the reciprocity norm is violated. *Journal of Business Research*, *56*, 399–409.
McGillicuddy, N.B., Pruitt, D.G., and Syna, H. (1984). Perceptions of firmness and strength in negotiation. *Personality and Social Psychology Bulletin*, *10*, 402–409.
Messick, D.M. and Sentis, K.P. (1985). Estimating social and nonsocial utility functions from ordinal data. *European Journal of Social Psychology*, *15*, 389–399.
Moran, S., and Schweitzer, M.E. (2008). When better is worse: Envy and the use of deception. *Negotiation and Conflict Management Research*, *1*, 3–29.

Murnighan, J.K. and Pillutla, M.M. (1995). Fairness versus self-interest: Asymmetric moral imperatives in ultimatum bargaining. In R.M. Kramer and D.M. Messick (eds), *Negotiation as a Social Process* (240–267). Thousand Oaks, CA: Sage Publications.

Naquin, C.E., Kurtzberg, T.R., and Belkin, L.Y. (2010). The finer points of lying online: E-mail versus pen and paper. *Journal of Applied Psychology*, 95, 387–394.

Nelissen, R.M.A., van Someren, D.S.I., and Zeelenberg, M. (2009). Take it or leave it for something better? Responses to fair offers in ultimatum bargaining. *Journal of Experimental Social Psychology*, 45, 1227–1231.

Nelson, W.R. (2002). Equity or intention: it is the thought that counts. *Journal of Economic Behavior and Organization*, 48, 423–430.

Nowak, M.A., Page, K.M., and Sigmund, K. (2000). Fairness versus reason in the ultimatum game. *Science*, 289, 1773–1775.

Ochs, J. and Roth, A.E. (1989). An experimental study of sequential bargaining. *The American Economic Review*, 79, 355–384.

O'Connor, K.M. and Carnevale, P.J. (1997). A nasty but effective negotiation strategy: Misrepresentation of a common-value issue. *Personality and Social Psychology Bulletin*, 23, 504–515.

Olekalns, M. and Smith, P.L. (2007). Loose with the truth: Predicting deception in negotiation. *Journal of Business Ethics*, 76, 225–238.

Olekalns, M. and Smith, P.L. (2009). Mutually dependent: power, trust, affect and the use of deception in negotiation. *Journal of Business Ethics*, 85, 347–365.

Oxoby, R.J. and Spraggon, J. (2008). Mine and yours: Property rights in dictator games. *Journal of Economic Behavior and Organization*, 65, 703–713.

Paulson, G.D. and Naquin, C.E. (2004). Establishing trust via technology: Long distance practices and pitfalls. *International Negotiation*, 9, 229–244.

Perry, G.M. and Nixon, C.J. (2005). The influence of role models on negotiation ethics of college students. *Journal of Business Ethics*, 62, 25–40.

Pillutla, M.M. and Murnighan, J.K. (1995). Being fair or appearing fair: Strategic behavior in ultimatum bargaining. *The Academy of Management Journal*, 38, 1408–1426.

Pillutla, M.M. and Murnighan, J.K. (2003). Fairness in bargaining. *Social Justice Research*, 16, 241–262.

Provis, C. (2000a). Ethics, deception and labor negotiation. *Journal of Business Ethics*, 28, 145–158.

Provis, C. (2000b). Honesty in negotiation. *Business Ethics: A European Review*, 9, 3–12.

Pruitt, D.G., Peirce, R.S., Zubek, J.M., Welton, G.L., and Nochajski, T.H. (1990). Goal achievement, procedural justice and the success of mediation. *International Journal of Conflict Management*, 1, 33–45.

Robinson, R.J., Lewicki, R.J., and Donahue, E.M. (2000). Extending and testing a five factor model of ethical and unethical bargaining tactics: introducing the SINS scale. *Journal of Organizational Behavior*, 21, 649–664.

Schminke, M., Ambrose, M.L., and Noel, T.W. (1997). The effect of ethical frameworks on perceptions of organizational justice. *The Academy of Management Journal*, 40, 1190–1207.

Schweitzer, M.E., Brodt, S.E., and Croson, R.T.A. (2002). Seeing and believing: Visual access and the strategic use of deception. *International Journal of Conflict Management*, 13, 258–275.

Shelling, T. (1960). *The Strategy of Conflict*. Cambridge, MA: Harvard University Press.

Skitka, L.J., Bauman, C.W., and Mullen, E. (2008). Morality and justice: An expanded theoretical perspective and empirical review. *Advances in Group Processes*, 25, 1–27.

Skitka, L.J., Bauman, C.W., and Sargis, E.G. (2005). Moral conviction: Another contributor to attitude strength or something more? *Journal of Personality and Social Psychology*, 88, 895–917.

Steinel, W. and De Dreu, C.K.W. (2004). Social motives and strategic misrepresentation in social decision making. *Journal of Personality and Social Psychology*, 86, 419–434.

Straub, P.G. and Murnighan, J.K. (1995). An experimental investigation of ultimatum games: Information, fairness, expectations, and lowest acceptable offers. *Journal of Economic Behavior and Organization, 27*, 345–364.

Strudler, A. (1995). On the ethics of deception in negotiation. *Business Ethics Quarterly, 5*, 805–822.

Tenbrunsel, A.E. (1998). Misrepresentation and expectations of misrepresentation in an ethical dilemma: The role of incentives and temptation. *The Academy of Management Journal, 41*, 330–339.

Tenbrunsel, A.E. and Messick, D.M. (2001). Power asymmetries and the ethical atmosphere in negotiations. In J.M. Darley, D.M. Messick, and T.R. Tyler (eds), *Social Influences on Ethical Behavior in Organizations* (201–216). Mahwah, NJ: Lawrence Erlbaum Associates.

Thompson, L. and Loewenstein, G. (1992). Egocentric interpretations of fairness and interpersonal conflict. *Organizational Behavior and Human Decision Processes, 51*, 176–197.

Tompkinson, P. and Bethwaite, J. (1995). The ultimatum game: raising the stakes. *Journal of Economic Behavior and Organization, 27*, 439–451.

Turillo, C.J., Folger, R., Lavelle, J.J., Umphress, E.E., and Gee, J.O. (2002). Is virtue its own reward? Self-sacrificial decisions for the sake of fairness. *Organizational Behavior and Human Decision Processes, 89*, 839–865.

Tyler, T.R. (1990). A psychological perspective on the settlement of mass tort claims. *Law and Contemporary Problems, 53*, 199–205.

Tyler, T.R. and Blader, S.L. (2004). Justice and negotiation. In M.J. Gelfand, and J.M. Brett (eds), *The handbook of negotiation and culture* (295–312). Stanford, CA: Stanford University Press.

Tyler, T.R. and Lind, E.A. (1992). A relational model of authority in groups. *Advances in Experimental Social Psychology, 25*, 115–191.

Valley, K.L., Moag, J., and Bazerman, M.H. (1998). A matter of trust: Effects of communication on the efficiency and distribution of outcomes. *Journal of Economic Behavior and Organization, 34*, 211–238.

van Beest, I., van Dijk, E., De Dreu, C.K.W., and Wilke, H.A.M. (2005). Do-no-harm in coalition formation: Why losses inhibit exclusion and promote fairness cognitions. *Journal of Experimental Social Psychology, 41*, 609–617.

van Dijk, E. and Tenbrunsel, A. (2005). The battle between self-interest and fairness: Evidence from ultimatum, dictator, and delta games. In S.W. Gilliland, D.D. Steiner, D.P. Skarlicki, and K. van den Bos (eds), *What motivates fairness in organizations?* (31–48). Greenwich, CT: Information Age Publishing.

van Dijk, E. and Vermunt, R. (2000). Strategy and fairness in social decision making: Sometimes it pays to be powerless. *Journal of Experimental Social Psychology, 36*, 1–25.

van Dijk, E., De Cremer, D., and Handgraaf, M.J.J. (2004). Social value orientations and the strategic use of fairness in ultimatum bargaining. *Journal of Experimental Social Psychology, 40*, 697–707.

van Dijk, E., de Kwaadsteniet, E.W., and Koning, L. (2012). About behaving (un)ethically: Self-interest, deception, and fairness. In D. De Cremer and A.E. Tenbrunsel (eds), *Behavioral Business Ethics: Shaping an Emerging Field* (105–121). New York: Routledge.

van Dijk, E., van Kleef, G.A., Steinel, W., and van Beest, I. (2008). A social functional approach to emotions in bargaining: When communicating anger pays and when it backfires. *Journal of Personality and Social Psychology, 94*, 600–614.

van Dijke, M. and De Cremer, D. (2011). When social accounts promote acceptance of unfair ultimatum offers: The role of the victim's stress responses to uncertainty and power position. *Journal of Economic Psychology, 32*, 468–479.

Volkema, R.J. (1998). A comparison of perceptions of ethical negotiation behavior in Mexico and the United States. *International Journal of Conflict Management, 9*, 218–233.

Volkema, R.J. (2004). Demographic, cultural, and economic predictors of perceived ethicality of negotiation behavior: A nine-country analysis. *Journal of Business Research, 57*, 69–78.

Volkema, R.J. and Leme Fleury, M.T.L. (2002). Alternative negotiating conditions and the

choice of negotiation tactics: A cross-cultural comparison. *Journal of Business Ethics*, *36*, 381–398.
Volkema, R., Fleck, D., and Hofmeister, A. (2010). Predicting competitive-unethical negotiating behavior and its consequences. *Negotiation Journal*, *26*, 263–286.
Wang, L., Malhotra, D., and Murnighan, J.K. (2011). Economics education and greed. *Academy of Management Learning and Education*, *10*, 643–660.
Weg, E. and Zwick, R. (1994). Toward the settlement of the fairness issues in ultimatum games: A bargaining approach. *Journal of Economic Behavior and Organization*, *24*, 19–34.
Yurtsever, G. (2001). Tolerance of ambiguity, information, and negotiation. *Psychological Reports*, *89*, 57–64.
Zeelenberg, M. and Beattie, J. (1997). Consequences of regret aversion 2: Additional evidence for effects of feedback on decision making. *Organizational Behavior and Human Decision Processes*, *72*, 63–78.
Zhou, X. and Wu, Y. (2011). Sharing losses and sharing gains: Increased demand for fairness under adversity. *Journal of Experimental Social Psychology*, *47*, 582–588.

9. Gender and negotiation: a social role analysis
*Alice F. Stuhlmacher and Eileen Linnabery**

Individual differences in negotiation and conflict attract attention, and gender, one of these differences, has emerged as an area of particular importance. The significance of gender in negotiation is due to the salience of male and female roles in society as well as the concern that negotiation gaps foster inequities between men and women in the workplace and other social spheres (Bowles and McGinn, 2008a). Our chapter overviews major research findings relating to how and why women, on average, experience negotiation differently than men. We use social role theories as an organizing framework to summarize findings.

We also review contextual and environmental factors to consider in interpreting these findings. Social role theories clarify areas that enhance or ameliorate gender differences. Through this lens we review work on communication mode, negotiation tasks, framing, stereotype threat, advocacy roles, and ambiguity. In addition to considering workplace negotiations, we incorporate discussions of gendered negotiations at home, with family, in political settings, and in negotiation ethics. We conclude with ideas relating to future research. Although many thoughtful reviews have emerged relating to gender and negotiation (e.g., Bowles, in press; Bowles and McGinn, 2008a; 2008b; Kolb, 2009; Kray and Babcock, 2006; Kray and Thompson, 2005; Rubin and Brown, 1975; Stuhlmacher and Winkler, 2006), we see the analysis of social roles as offering a unifying framework.

THEORETICAL FRAMEWORK

Various explanations have been applied to gender effects in negotiation, such as status characteristics theory (e.g., Miles and Clenney, 2010), power (e.g., Watson, 1994; Watson and Hoffman, 1996), and stereotype threat models (e.g., Kray et al., 2001: Kray et al., 2002; Kray et al., 2004) in addition to social role theories (e.g., Amanatullah and Morris, 2010; Miles and LaSalle, 2008; 2009; Stuhlmacher et al., 2007). We find that social role theories (e.g., Eagly, 1987; Eagly and Karau, 2002; Eagly and Wood, 2012; Katz and Kahn, 1978) offer intriguing explanations and predictions for men's and women's behavior in negotiation, and we offer our analysis of how social roles are linked to negotiation antecedents, processes, and outcomes.

First, we must describe what, exactly, is a social role. In general, roles consist of behavioral expectations individuals hold for themselves and others based on one's social positions (Katz and Kahn, 1978). Social roles (e.g., man, woman, negotiator, manager, car salesperson, student, job applicant) have both descriptive aspects (inferences about what people in that role actually do, or *not* do) and injunctive aspects (expectations on what they ought or ideally should do, think, or believe; Eagly, 1987; Eagly and Karau, 2002; Wood and Eagly, 2012). People develop perceptions about their own and others' behavior based on their role beliefs. These role beliefs and expectations can be communicated with varying specificity, direction, strength, and intensity to influence another's behavior and fit within a role (Katz and Kahn, 1978). A role "event" involves *expectations* about a person in a certain role, *sent-role* messages from others to a person in the role, *received-role* messages relating to what the person in the role perceives, and the response of *role behavior* (Katz and Kahn, 1978). The role event exists in an ongoing system of feedback loops and is influenced by interpersonal factors and attributes of the people involved.

According to role congruity theory (Eagly and Karau, 2002), when a role and a person's attributes match (or are congruent), that person is more likely to be seen as successful in that role. When there are inconsistencies between one's characteristics and a given social role, the person will be seen as less successful and prejudice may result. As people gain experience in a particular role, they may also develop skills and abilities that strengthen role alignment (Eagly and Wood, 1999), so there is a dynamic aspect to social roles and alignment.

Gender Roles and Negotiation Roles

While people occupy multiple social roles at the same time, gender roles and negotiator roles are the primary focus of this review. A gender role carries expectations about characteristics of men and women and provides reinforcement for role consistent behavior (see Eagly, 1987; Eagly and Carli, 2007). Gender roles are formed from the gender role beliefs or stereotypes that arise from observing sex differences and similarities (Eagly and Wood, 2012). Sex difference beliefs originate in part from the evolutionary division of labor relating to physical differences such as women's tie to childbearing and men's greater physical strength. Roles are formed, when, for example, childcare activities become associated with expected behaviors like caring, concern, and support and physical strength becomes associated with expected behaviors like assertiveness, dominance, and control (Eagly and Wood, 2012). According to Eagly and Wood's biosocial model (2012; Wood and Eagly, 2012), roles are also shaped by proximal influences such as hormonal regulation, social regulation, and self-regulation as well as more distal factors like culture and social structure.

The self and social aspects of roles involve interacting with the environment and relating to the world. Of significance is Bakan's (1966) discussion of two styles of relating to the world: agency and communion. An *agentic* approach is concerned with acting as an individual, mastering the environment, and experiencing power and achievement while a *communal* approach is related to the connection with others, relationships, and cooperation with others. Central to our analysis is how agency and communion approaches relate to gender roles. The typical male gender role is generally associated with agentic characteristics (e.g., assertiveness, competitive, dominance) while the typical female social role is often associated with communal characteristics such as concern for others, friendliness, helpfulness, warmth, emotional expression, and unselfishness (Eagly and Wood, 2012). Gender role expectations are often automatically activated in social interactions as gender is one of the most salient roles that individuals occupy (Cook, 1994). However, certain situations can make gender roles, and these related characteristics, more or less salient (Eagly and Karau, 2002). For example, the saliency of gender roles may be influenced by such things as the negotiation group's composition (e.g., minority or majority gender), communication form (e.g., face-to-face or not), communication style (e.g., directive versus participative), and type of task (e.g., leadership versus caretaking).

While less researched than gender roles, negotiator roles also influence the inferences and expectations about appropriate characteristics for an individual in that situation or job. Research suggests that a negotiator is expected to have agentic characteristics. Kray et al. (2002) report that negotiator traits are laden with masculine gender stereotypes. The adjectives of *assertive, good problem solver, high regard for own interests,* and *knowledgeable* were associated with men, adjectives of *emotional, insightful, good listening, verbally expressive* were associated with women, and adjectives of *rational, good judgment, sense of humor, prepared,* and *patient* as more gender neutral. Agentic or stereotypically masculine traits (e.g., strong, dominant, assertive, rational) are seen as more important for negotiation success than communal or stereotypical feminine traits (weak, submissive, intuitive, emotional), and as a result men are often perceived to have the advantage in negotiations (Kray et al., 2001, Kray and Thompson, 2005). Evidence suggests "that the term *negotiation* is not gender neutral" (Small et al., 2007, p. 610) and that these stereotypes help shape the negotiator role.

Role congruity theory (Eagly and Karau, 2002) would then suggest that characteristics consistent with that negotiation role would be seen as most successful, hence men would be expected to be successful in traditional negotiation situations. Role congruity theory was first applied as an explanation for prejudice against women in leader roles (Eagly and Karau, 2002). We suggest that being a negotiator, like being a leader, is a role where agentic qualities like assertiveness, confidence, and dominance are traditionally expected as part of the role and these agentic qualities are incongruous with the traditional female gender role. This does not mean that women are not good negotiators, or that communal attributes are not important in negotiation, rather that there are particular challenges for women in negotiation.

It is also the case, however, that research has focused almost exclusively on negotiation areas that may be more congruent for men than women (Walters et al., 1998). Miles and LaSalle (2008) reported that existing negotiation tasks are masculine stereotyped (e.g., negotiating turbo engine parts) with only a couple of research tasks seen as gender neutral (e.g., hiring for an unspecified job). They could find no examples of negotiation studies involving feminine gendered context (e.g., caretaking). They addressed this with some research on a feminine stereotyped topic: negotiating for a babysitter (Miles and LaSalle, 2008). Other research has also expanded negotiation tasks by looking at negotiation for workplace lactation rooms (Bear, 2011) and jewelry beads (Bear and Babcock, 2012). As discussed later, social role theories suggest that task stereotypes could moderate gender differences in negotiation, as could the particular gendered social role (e.g., son, mother, father, grandmother).

The actual job or work itself influences the salience of the gender role. As an example, the social role of a labor mediator is different from that of a negotiator. Although related, a mediator role is composed of communal as well as agentic characteristics (Stuhlmacher and Morrissett, 2008; Stuhlmacher and Poitras, 2010). In a field study of labor mediators (Stuhlmacher and Poitras, 2010), the disputant's trust in a mediator depended on evaluations of empathy and control displayed by that mediator. Higher trust was accorded to men who were perceived to display empathy (a feminine role characteristic) and women mediators who were perceived to display control (a masculine role characteristic). Consistent with role congruity theory, it appeared that mediators were assumed to hold the gender stereotypical characteristics but also had to convey the non-stereotypical dimension to be seen as trustworthy in the mediator role. This suggests that research needs to consider that congruity is influenced by the context and nuances of the particular roles.

In short, while effective negotiators may draw on behaviors that are agentic, as well as communal, there is convincing evidence that key elements of negotiating, or being seen as negotiator, are more consistent with a masculine social role. Accordingly, we start with a review the social roles present in the major variables in negotiation research and their moderators. Additionally, as a point of clarification, while almost all of the studies reviewed here study differences based on biological sex (men versus women), we use the term gender differences rather than sex differences. This is because the focus is not on the biological or stable sex characteristics but on the cultural and role based identity of gender (Publication Manual of the American Psychological Association, 2010). Future research will ideally go beyond a simple dichotomy in understanding gender.

NEGOTIATION BEHAVIORS

One common question is if men and women actually act differently while negotiating. To deal with this question we can consider what happens before, during, and after negotiation.

Initiating Negotiations

A negotiation starts with a decision to negotiate. Many negotiation studies assign participants the task of negotiating, but, in actuality, most of the time people must choose to negotiate rather than being instructed to do so; in other words, negotiators must decide to come to the table (Babcock et al., 2006; Gerhart and Rynes, 1991). Given the role of negotiation in securing organizational and societal resources, it is disquieting if women are less likely to initiate, or start, negotiations than men. The topic of gender differences in initiating negotiation was brought to wider audiences in books by Babcock and Laschever (2003; 2008) with coverage of some striking findings. For example, a field study (Babcock et al., 2006) found that 51 percent of male MBA graduates initiated a job negotiation compared to 12 percent of female MBA students. Men also reported initiating a negotiation more recently and expected to initiate another negotiation sooner in the future than women. The expectation that a woman would be less likely to speak up for resources for herself is consistent with gender role expectations in the assertiveness and self-interest required for entering a negotiation are incompatible with the female gender role. Similarly, in the field of workplace dispute resolution (Gwartney-Gibbs and Lach, 1994), women acted less often on workplace disputes than men, with men using formal workplace dispute resolution forums more often than women, and those who were the "gatekeepers" of dispute resolution forums pursuing women's complaints *less* often than men's.

In another example, after completing a survey on negotiation experience, Greig (2008) allowed investment bankers to request an amount on a gift card as a reward for participation. Only 76 percent of women entered a request compared to 90 percent of men, a significant difference even controlling for race, age, and nationality. Additionally, the behavior of initiating a request was related to a pattern of faster promotions and involvement in other negotiations.

Interestingly, when tasks are gender incongruent, higher aversion to negotiation exists and a higher likelihood to avoid a negotiation by passing it along to a colleague has been found (Bear, 2011). Across two studies, Bear found women more likely to avoid a negotiation about job compensation and men more likely to avoid a negotiation about access to a lactation room. Associated with the idea of initiating negotiation is the fact that women sometimes self-select out of career directions or fields. If anticipation of career difficulties (e.g., expected work–life conflict, opportunity barriers) leads women to avoid certain career paths or job opportunities, then this "opting-out" is another example of avoiding negotiations that has implications for a woman personally and society more broadly.

Even though an initial study (Gerhart and Rynes, 1991) is often cited as evidence *against* gender differences in initiating salary negotiations, among the MBA students in the study 23 percent of 153 male MBA students initiated salary negotiations while 15 percent of 52 female MBA students initiated negotiations. Despite the fact this difference is not statistically significant, it may be practically significant, with its effect size of about $d = .18$ ($r = .09$). Small effect sizes are common in gender research, and unfortunately, small sample size issues confound some existing research, with many studies lacking sufficient statistical power to detect small differences being used as evidence (see Stuhlmacher and Walters, 1999), thus adding to potential confusion in interpreting findings.

However, one compelling moderator of coming to the table is based on task instructions. Framing the task as "asking" rather than "negotiating" increased the likelihood of women's involvement (Small et al., 2007). This makes sense from a role congruity framework in that asking is more congruent with the female gender role in that it involves putting women in a less assertive position. Small et al. (2007) found that labeling the task as asking or negotiating, as well as cueing people about the possibility of negotiation, reduced the gender difference in initiating a negotiation. Thus, it appears that the question of initiating a negotiation has important moderators that remain to be uncovered.

Behaviors During and After Negotiation

An early review by Rubin and Brown (1975) suggested that men and women behave differently during negotiation because they are sensitive to different cues. Specifically, Rubin and Brown proposed that differences in interpersonal orientation (IO) can explain differences in negotiation behaviors. Current thinking has moved away from models like Rubin and Brown's that look at behaviors as driven by stable individual differences to consider gender-in-context models that recognize situational influences in gender differences (Bowles and McGinn, 2008a).

Much attention has been focused within actual negotiations on behaviors such as initial offers, counteroffers, exchanging information, as well as more deceptive behaviors like lies, threats, or bluffing. Social role theory would predict that women in general show more cooperation than men in negotiation, but also suggest potential moderators that run throughout the interaction. Walters et al.'s (1998) meta-analysis addressed part of the behavior question, comparing men and women on cooperativeness and competitiveness of negotiation offers and language (e.g., threats, putdowns, bottom line statements). A small but significant difference was found with women displaying more cooperative behavior than men (the most conservative estimate yielded a significant effect size of $r = .04$). However, along with the summary of the overall pattern of findings, a number of potential moderators emerged. First, the results for matrix games (i.e., game theory tasks involving interdependent payoff matrices but with limited interaction and communication) were very different from face-to-face negotiations, with women being more cooperative face-to-face. Some matrix game studies even found women acting more competitively than men. More opportunity for communication resulted in more gender stereotypical patterns, as did opponents whose strategy was not contingent on the negotiator's behavior. This would be consistent with role theory analysis in that the negotiator role would be more salient than gender role under a constrained task with no face-to-face interaction (Stuhlmacher et al., 2007).

It is worthwhile to note that there are difficulties associated with labeling behaviors as cooperative or competitive, and in assigning a clear value on the desirability of each of these behaviors. While competitive and assertive behaviors (e.g., high initial offers or limited concessions) might indicate a high concern for self-interests, they could be a part of a competitive, collaborating, or even avoiding strategy. Competitive behavior may or may not be beneficial, depending on the context. Likewise, cooperative behaviors (e.g., information exchange) might indicate a concern for the other party but could be part of an accommodating, compromising, or overly yielding strategy. Strategy and behaviors are not the same; judgments about cooperation and competition depend on the outcome or criteria of interest as well as task characteristics. It would be useful to study gender and the constellation of behaviors (i.e., cooperation alongside competitiveness) rather than the either-or dichotomies. As Walters et al. (1998) suggest, focusing on a single behavior does not reveal the drivers of that behavior or outcome differences, that is, the extent that social motives (e.g., accommodative, collaborative) and behaviors work together. Additionally, the behaviors could be interpreted differently depending on the social roles that are involved as well.

In teasing out where gender differences in behavior may arise in the negotiation process, Miles (2010) compared men's and women's aspiration levels, expected opening offers, and actual offers (first offers and counteroffers). Intriguingly, no gender differences in aspiration level or expected opening were found but differences appeared after the negotiation started, with women's actual opening offers less consistent (and lower) than their initial intentions than men's. Women's initial offers did not predict their final outcomes very well, while men's initial offers strongly predicted men's final outcomes. Thus, Miles suggests that the beginning of the negotiation conversation is a critical point for behavioral gender differences, and a particular point where social roles may come into play. This also suggests that role behavior exists in an ongoing environment and single snapshots of negotiation behavior are deficient in furthering our understanding.

Behaviors of the negotiation partner are also part of the ongoing puzzle. When women negotiate, one of the more troubling aspects is the backlash that women may experience (or expect to experience) for negotiating or being competitive in traditional negotiations (Amanatullah and Morris, 2010; Bowles et al., 2007). Similar to work on backlash for agentic behavior by female leaders (see Rudman and Fairchild, 2004; Rudman and Glick, 1999; Rudman and Phelan, 2008), there is the concern that women who negotiate for themselves are often liked less and are seen as less competent than men who enact the same behaviors. Thus, failure to initiate a negotiation may have some rational roots for women. Bowles et al. (2007) found that people were less interested in working with women who had attempted to negotiate as compared to women who did not attempt to negotiate. Similar backlash reactions may be found in workplaces where women are in the extreme minority (i.e., tokens); tokens have few promotions, poorer performance reviews, and higher job turnover than non-tokens following a workplace dispute settlement (Gwartney-Gibbs and Lach, 1994).

Consistent with predictions from social role theory, backlash may be reduced when women are negotiating on behalf of another rather than themselves (Amanatullah and Morris, 2010). Negotiating for another as an advocate or representative is consistent with the female gender role of caring for others. Whereas women are not expected to ask for things for themselves, it is expected that they speak up for others, particularly others who are in their care. When women negotiate as a representative or an advocate for another, gender differences have been found to disappear or reverse (Amanatullah and Morris, 2010; Bowles et al., 2005). Negotiating on the behalf of others also reduced the backlash that was expected. Strikingly, other than backlash behaviors, little research has systematically considered how negotiation behaviors differ following a negotiation.

ATTITUDES AND PERCEPTIONS: AFFECT, COGNITIONS, INTENTIONS

Because expectations vary by gender roles, this has implications for what people perceive and report in negotiation. Perceptions have long been collected in negotiation research but gender effects are not clear due to different measures, vague constructs, and little systematic consideration of how gender would be involved. However, gender roles are potentially linked to how one perceives oneself, and others, as well as how one reports on activities and events, and future interactions.

More negative reactions to negotiation from women than men, even some of the time, could lead to avoiding negotiation and represent lost opportunities and resources. Findings suggest that men report more opportunities to negotiate, are less apprehensive, and feel more entitled than women (Babcock et al., 2006), as well as report higher negotiation confidence (Watson and Hoffman, 1996), more relief at having first offer accepted (Kray and Gelfand, 2009), and higher expected outcomes (Calhoun and Smith, 1999). Additionally there are gender differences in perceptions of likability and competence of men and women in negotiation (e.g., Bowles et al., 2007). Further exploration is needed to determine how men's and women's perceptions relate to actions and outcomes in negotiation, and as suggested, perception measures vary in timing, construct, source, as well as target, which may make comparing results more complicated.

PROFIT AND ECONOMIC OUTCOMES

Of particular importance is the difference in *outcomes* between men and women in negotiation (Ayres, 1991; Dalton and Todor, 1985; Dalton et al., 1987; Gerhart, 1990; Gerhart and Rynes, 1991; Halpern and Parks,

1996; Stevens et al., 1993). Stuhlmacher and Walters' (1998) meta-analysis offered a comprehensive summary of the existing research regarding the difference in the objective outcomes between men and women in negotiation. Consistent with role congruity theory, but counter to the prevailing expectation at the time, a consistent pattern of men achieving higher negotiation outcomes than women was found (the most conservative estimate being $r = .04$). The effect size was extremely small but significant, and it was recognized that the cumulative effects over time of a negotiation differences could be substantial. Importantly, this meta-analysis stimulated exploration into the contextual moderators and constraints on women in negotiation.

One important moderator is the ambiguity about the bargaining zone or area of potential agreement. Bowles et al. (2005) compared men's and women's outcomes when the range of likely settlements was known (low structural ambiguity) or ambiguous (high structural ambiguity). Data across two studies suggested that low ambiguity minimized gender differences, but men found more success than women in higher ambiguity situations. This is consistent with social role theory in that highly ambiguous situations create a context where individual differences can have a larger effect (Bowles et al., 2005). Ambiguity also offers an explanation for the finding that larger gender differences exist in less formalized compensation categories, such as bonuses and other benefits (Elvira and Graham, 2002; Lyness and Thompson, 1997).

Relatedly, men are found to have better negotiation outcomes with masculine stereotyped issues (halogen headlights) but not feminine stereotyped issues (jewelry beads; Bear and Babcock, 2012). Bear and Babcock make the important point that men and women may be receiving different feedback on their negotiation skills, which may be biased by the type of negotiation tasks they experience. Similarly, the research on stereotype threat in negotiation suggests other moderators of negotiation outcomes that are consistent with a social role analysis. When negotiation is presented as a task requiring masculine traits, men are more successful, and when the importance of feminine stereotyped traits is highlighted, women's success increases (Kray et al., 2002). Notably, explicitly activating a gender stereotype has been found to lead to women's actively resisting this stereotype in negotiation. Certain kinds of information (for example, women being told that women's style is a hindrance) may cause counter responses (or stereotype reactance) where negotiators move in opposite directions to refute the stereotype or information given (Kray et al., 2001; Kray et al., 2004).

Since the publication of the Stuhlmacher and Walters (1999) meta-analysis, many more studies now exist which examine gender differences in negotiation outcomes. In an updated and expanded meta-analysis on this topic, Mazei et al. (working paper) likewise found men achieving better outcomes than women, but also report extremely important moderators that reduced gender differences including negotiator experience, advocacy, and when negotiators chose to negotiate rather than being assigned. These suggest critical context effects to be considered in interpreting gender differences in negotiation outcomes.

MODERATORS, CONTEXTUAL FACTORS AND GENDER TRIGGERS

So far, this review points to a several moderators of the strength and direction of the impact gender in negotiation. Bowles et al. (2005) have called these types of variables "gender triggers" in that they influence gender differences in negotiation. The moderators are consistent with role congruity explanations. Gender differences decrease as role congruence increases for women—that is, when the negotiation role is aligned with the female gender role. We see this in the findings relating to congruence of negotiation topic, framing the task as "asking" rather than "negotiating", and negotiating on behalf of others as a representative or advocate. In other cases, gender differences arise as role congruence is increased for men rather than women such as when the negotiation role requires more masculine characteristics. We see this in the stereotype threat research where men perform better in situations that label negotiation as requiring masculine characteristics, and when there is ambiguity in the task. In these ambiguous situations, agentic behaviors of being dominant and assertive in pursuing one's own interests can be an advantage.

In this section of the chapter we expand on other gender triggers that influence the saliency of gender roles. When gender is less salient, the negotiation role itself (or other roles) can become more salient than gender. For men, this would not necessarily result in any behavior change since traditional negotiation is consistent with the male gender role. However, for female negotiators, reduced attention to their gender may allow a greater focus on the social role of a negotiator, with less attention on women's social roles. In particular, we consider the saliency of a negotiator's gender based on communication mode, gender composition of the negotiation dyad, and power differences.

Virtual Negotiation

Email and written communication have less transmission of verbal, oral, and visual cues. The richness of the communication medium determines the number of channels available for the transmission of cues. Gender roles appear to weaken when negotiation occurs virtually (or not face-to-face but through email, telephone, messages) because there are fewer cues. Recipients of virtual communication are often unable to guess the gender of their partner if this information is not provided (Nowak, 2003). Virtual negotiation decreases transmission of interpersonal and social cues during the negotiation that reduce the saliency of gender roles, making the negotiation role more salient (Stuhlmacher et al., 2007).

A meta-analysis of these studies discovered women displaying more hostility in virtual negotiation (i.e., email, phone, notes) than they did during face-to-face negotiations (Stuhlmacher et al., 2007). Men, however, showed no behavioral differences in hostility regardless of the communication medium used during negotiation. Women also seemed to profit more in virtual than face-to-face negotiations. The authors proposed that the female gender role was less salient in virtual negotiations, while the negotiator role was more salient, which meant that women were more likely to attend to the negotiation role. This also explains why men did not differ between communication media—there was role congruity for men in both the virtual and face-to-face conditions. Of course, the strength of the effects may also depend on any pre-existing relationship or knowledge about the opponent, which may trigger gender role expectations.

Gender Composition

Another intriguing question concerns the impact of gender composition (all men, all women, or men and women) of the negotiator-opponent dyad: Is there an impact if the opponent is the same sex? On one hand, there may be a similarity effect for same gender dyads resulting in more in-group cooperation (Sherif, 1966; Tajfel and Turner, 1986). However, some research finds more competition and retaliation in same-gender dyads than in mixed-gender dyads (Sutter et al., 2009).

A role congruity perspective might suggest that the gender composition of the negotiation dyad can influence the salience of a gender role (Eagly and Karau, 2002; Stuhlmacher et al., 2012). The salience of the female gender role (the role most incongruent with negotiation) is expected to be stronger in mixed-gender dyads, than in same-gender dyads. In same-gender dyads, attention is not drawn to gender, but to the task at hand (and the strength and instructions of that task). In same-gender dyads (both male–male and female–female), the negotiator role (and the resulting expectation of toughness and competition) will be more salient than the expectation of cooperation and niceness. Negotiators might expect less cooperation when a strong traditional negotiation role is present and the female gender role is not salient. The actual behaviors (e.g., cooperative, competitive) and outcomes would, however, likely depend on the instructions, design of the task, and actions by the partner.

The negotiation partner adds an interesting complexity, in that each party in the interaction has role expectations about the other negotiators, which influences the unfolding interaction. Negotiators would be expected to be aware, at some level, of the negotiation partner's characteristics and roles. For example, being told the opponent was a competitive negotiator led to more demanding negotiations than when the party was not labeled with a tough reputation (Tinsley et al., 2002). A mixed-gender dyad may lead women to expect one type of interaction and men to expect a different type. A better understanding of how negotiation is influenced by the gender of the negotiation partner is needed (Kray and Thompson, 2005). Thus we suggest that, in addition to the gender of the negotiator, the gender composition of the negotiation dyad affects the saliency of gender roles and negotiation roles, and could serve as a moderator, but it seems clear from a role congruity analysis that both men's and women's expectations and behaviors could be affected by group composition. Carli (2001) suggests that men show more communal behavior toward females when there are more females in the group. This is consistent with ideas of chivalry, in that the social role for men includes the expectation that they are to be nice to women (Glick and Fiske, 1996). Thus, in a mixed-sex dyad, it is not just the female negotiators who initially hold expectations of communal behaviors, but both men's and women's perceptions and behaviors will be influenced by a mixed-gender dyad composition. Men might expect more communal behaviors in the mixed-gender context than in same-gender dyads. Women may accommodate with communal behaviors given the role incongruity. Thus, both sides may accommodate to the presence of the feminine gender role, which is more salient in mixed than same-gender dyads, and minimizes the influence of the more masculine negotiation roles (Stuhlmacher et al., 2012). However, deviations from these expectations may arise, for example if a highly competitive opponent (male or female) makes the negotiation role more salient during the interaction. In this case, expectations of niceness and cooperation could very well dissipate.

In addition to sent and received role messages, the effect of group composition depends on the task, instructions, and processes that shape what is expected in the negotiator role. For example, when negotiators were told that masculine characteristics were a negotiation advantage, payoffs increased for men (Kray et al., 2001). This only occurred in the mixed gender pairs, suggesting that the gender roles were more salient in mixed than same-gender pairs. In a traditional negotiation, male dyads might achieve higher outcomes due to the consistently agentic approach. Miles and LaSalle (2009) found that male–male dyads created more value than female–female dyads in both a masculine stereotyped and neutral task. They suggested that men were more focused on maximizing one's earnings than women, and all male dyads fostered this competition.

Social role theory suggests there are complex forces at play depending on what roles are salient. For example, when faced with a more competitive male partner, women increase persistence but this persistence can take gendered forms (Bowles and Flynn, 2010). From a social role perspective, while there may be initial expectations of a communally oriented negotiation in the mixed-sex negotiation, a fierce competitor may trigger the negotiator role over the gender role. In summary, while overall these may be small effects, gender composition has the potential to impact the strength of social roles and influence negotiation processes and outcomes, with role salience shifting at various points within a negotiation.

Power

Any discussion of moderators in negotiation must consider how power and gender interact. Ragins and Sundstrom (1989) define power as "influence by one person over others, stemming from a position . . ., from an interpersonal relationship or from an individual characteristic" (p. 51). Some suggest that power trumps gender effects in negotiation (Watson, 1994; Watson and Hoffman, 1996) while noting that it is hard to separate power from gender, and the assumptions about men, women, and power. For example, characteristics related to power include need for power, motivation to manage, aggression, self-confidence, achievement orientation (Ragins and Sundstrom, 1989)—all very masculine stereotyped characteristics.

Nonetheless, ample evidence suggests that power varies by social roles, particularly with changes over time throughout one's career and life situation. Men's and women's career paths often vary in positions, status and resources (e.g., peer networks, mentors, autonomy, position power, control over assets) and these can compound over time. This is important to consider in that, in negotiation in general, high power encourages negotiators while low power inhibits negotiators (see Galinsky et al., 2003). Research finds that high power increases aspirations, overconfidence, illusion of control, and amount of opening offer, while decreasing sensitivity to others. Low power negotiators use more avoidance strategies, in that they may ignore, withdraw or suppress resolving the negotiation. And, in introducing a power prime before negotiating (i.e., a chance for negotiators to recall a past incident where they felt powerful),

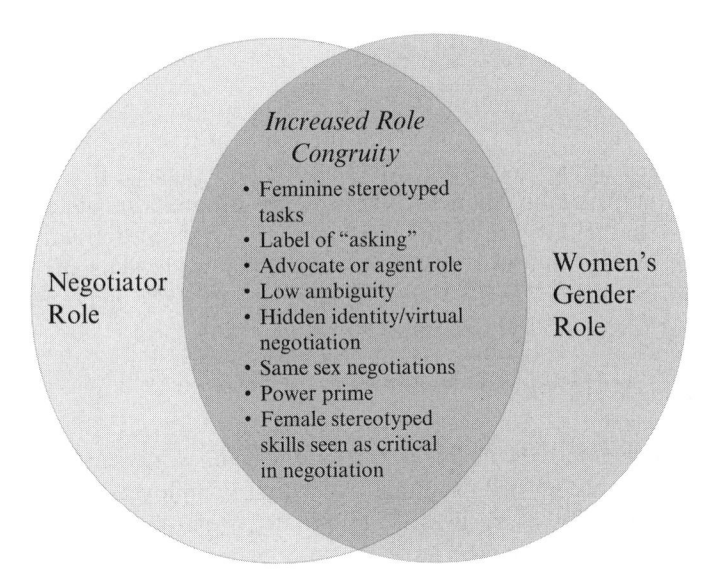

Figure 9.1 Examples of factors that increase negotiator role and gender role congruity for women

Increased Role Congruity (intersection of Negotiator Role and Women's Gender Role):
- Feminine stereotyped tasks
- Label of "asking"
- Advocate or agent role
- Low ambiguity
- Hidden identity/virtual negotiation
- Same sex negotiations
- Power prime
- Female stereotyped skills seen as critical in negotiation

women reported being less intimidated to negotiate; the power prime had no effect on men (Small et al., 2007). More evidence for the role of power as a factor relating to gender differences comes from stereotype threat negotiation studies where activating information about resource power or personal characteristics (Kray et al., 2004) increased outcomes for women.

Because power and gender are often confounded, particularly as considered in workplace activities, social role theory would encourage a closer look at the power within and outside of roles. Thus negotiation tasks that have a power difference between negotiator roles (e.g., supervisor–subordinate) or information power are important to consider in a designing research. Power can be automatically tied to particular social roles and influence gender interpretations and role congruency.

Before moving on, one message from the research reviewed is that moderators can work in concert or cancel each other out—potentially accounting for some of the mixed findings in the research. Figure 9.1 presents a summary of factors that seem to make the negotiation role more congruent for women. Our point in this chapter is that a social role perspective can assist researchers in designing research to understand and interpret gender effects by considering what roles may be activated or salient and how roles may change throughout the interaction.

GENDER AND NEGOTIATION OR GENDERED NEGOTIATION

It is important to note that much of the previous research relates to the workplace. But as Bowles and McGinn (2008b) suggest, it is useful to look beyond the labor market. Not only are negotiations outside work important in their own right, but negotiations in organizations are shaped by forces in what Bowles and McGinn discuss as two level negotiations— negotiations where "public" negotiations are directly connected with factors in "private" negotiations at home.

Negotiating Work–Life

One example of factors outside of work influencing work is in negotiating work–life balance (WLB) programs which assist employees in coordinating their home and work lives. Traditionally, work–life programs have been considered a "woman's issue" because of women's role in childcare and family. Two WLB benefits often negotiated are flextime and parental leave. Among German workers, women were more likely to ask for, and successfully negotiate, flextime arrangements and customized work schedules than were men (Hornung et al., 2008). In terms of parental leave, both men (Brandth and Kvande, 2002) and women (Greenberg et al., 2009; Ranson, 2005; Miller et al., 1996) looked for accommodations following the birth of a child or adoption. Much of the research investigating parental leave is qualitative, focusing on the description of the negotiation process rather than the prediction of negotiation outcomes. For example, Brandth and Kvande (2002) described several different strategies men used relating to parental leave including either (a) focusing on job demands first and time with the child second, (b) attempting to get as much time off as possible, (c) taking leave from work that does not require negotiation, and (d) choosing not to take parental leave. Brandth and Kvande determined that some men negotiate a long work leave for childbirth or adoption, whereas others take only take a few days off work, if any. Although there are wide differences in the time that men take for parental leave, a few commonalities were evident. Men asked their supervisor for leave and stood their ground when they faced challenges to time off as well as mentioning their job duties and tasks when determining their amount of time off. From a social role perspective, it appears that men's negotiations often integrated work roles and agentic behaviors into the processes, and it could be expected that women's negotiations in these realms would differ in terms of the centrality of work role and its perceived incongruity with motherhood. Indeed, the idea of a "motherhood" penalty, where working mothers are seen as less competent and less rewarded than working fathers (Correll et al., 2007), has critical implications for the negotiation of work-life variables. Particular gendered expectations endure about parenthood, and the roles enacted as a mother or father are very strong and interact with expectations about male and female gender roles (Fuegen et al., 2004; Güngör and Biernat, 2009).

Negotiating leave can be difficult for women, as they also wonder about backlash in their career and balancing their health and needs of the family. Qualitative data on parental leave for women in male-dominated professions suggested that even though the women worked the same hours and provided the same quality output as men following a period of leave, they no longer aligned themselves with their male coworkers and were outcast (Ranson, 2005). The literature on maternity negotiation (Liu and Buzzanell, 2004) is in line with the backlash literature, which suggests that women who negotiate for themselves are often perceived as more difficult than men who negotiate or women who choose not to negotiate.

Miller et al. (1996) provided a conceptual model suggesting that negotiating maternity leave is a type of role negotiation in which the pregnant employee must convince others that she will return from maternity leave and continue to perform at the same level as before. It seems unlikely that men are facing these kinds of issues. Factors in the maternity negotiation include the pregnant employee's career ambition, criticality of the pregnant employee's role, leader-member relationship, and bias against leave-takers (Miller et al., 1996). The timing of the pregnancy announcement constitutes one critical aspect of the maternity negotiation. Greenberg et al.'s (2009) qualitative analysis of maternity leave negotiation found that women begin informally negotiating their work role with their colleagues immediately following the pregnancy announcement. Greenberg et al. also discovered that pregnant employees negotiate more than just their maternity leave, and while at work they negotiate changing physical and psychological needs, scheduling medical appointments, and making determinations about future child care options. In approaching these negotiations, women may conceal information to avoid losing power. Because low power in negotiation inhibits the negotiator, this information concealment may benefit the pregnant employee, at least in the short term. Maternity could influence the salience of the female gender role and is often incongruent with the agentic roles of the workplace. The physical changes associated with pregnancy provide visual cues of one's gender role, increasing the saliency of the female gender role. Therefore, as a woman's pregnancy becomes more obvious, she may be perceived as less competent because of the incongruence between the negotiation role and female gender role. Thus, it is important to keep in mind the mix of gendered roles that are brought to a negotiation and consider their relevance.

Negotiating at Home

Gender roles and negotiation roles also are relevant in household negotiations. Couples or roommates negotiate the division of household labor, parents negotiate childcare, lovers negotiate condom use (Wingood and DiClemente, 1997), shoppers negotiate at garage sales (Herrmann, 2004), students negotiate grades (Medved and Heisler, 2002), and unhappy spouses negotiate divorce settlements (Sheets and Braver, 1996). All these areas of negotiations have implications for fundamental life activities like satisfaction, access to resources, health, as well as work life.

Although some qualitative studies have examined negotiating at home (e.g., Bialeschki and Pearce 1997), there is limited experimental literature in this area. The majority of studies focus on qualitative descriptions of women's experiences in these negotiation situations. Mannino and Deutsch (2007) investigated wives' attempts to negotiate the division of household labor and childcare with their husbands. Although the majority of the women interviewed were not satisfied with the division of labor in the home, few women actually planned to initiate change. Social role theory would suggest that the gender role would be particularly salient in negotiations between husbands and wives, because gender is confounded with the marital role. Role congruity theory also suggests that it could be difficult for women to initiate negotiation around labor division. Despite being unhappy with current conditions, the agentic behaviors necessary would be incompatible with not only the female gender role and their marital role that expect women to handle household and child related matters.

Non-traditional families are increasingly prevalent, and social roles offer perspective on how these families negotiate the division of labor in the home. Bialeschki and Pearce (1997) qualitatively investigated lesbian couples' role negotiations for childcare responsibilities and leisure activities. Participants determined who would fulfill duties based on each person's interest in the activity and who had time to complete it, but if neither party was interested in the task, negotiations were necessary. The participants stressed the need for equity and fairness in the negotiation of completing these undesirable tasks. Although not a part of that research, we suggest that by considering the context, beliefs, and expectations for each member in the negotiation, social role theory can be brought to analyse gender issues of non-traditional as well as traditional families.

Additionally, divorcing couples often negotiate the division of assets and child custody. The majority of divorce negotiations occur between couples with unequal levels of economic resources and power (Seltzer and Garfinkel, 1990). Often women suffer from a decline in their standard of living following a divorce, whereas men experience an increase (Braver et al., 1989). Despite these inequities, women report higher satisfaction in divorce negotiations than men (Sheets and Braver, 1996). Sheets and Braver (1996) found that women were more satisfied with custody, visitation, financial, and property settlements in divorce than were men. Women reported being more "in control" of the settlement process than did men. Because divorce settlement negotiation often includes the negotiation of childcare and custody, the negotiation may be more consistent with situations where women advocate for others (their children) than situations in which women are asked to advocate for themselves. Therefore, because negotiation for others is consistent with the female gender role (e.g., caring for others), social role theory predicts that women would find some congruence in negotiating in divorce settlements than in other types of negotiations. Further research is needed to understand how men and women frame the negotiation task during divorce settlements and the objective differences in settlement outcomes between men and women.

Gender, Peace and Ethics

In realms outside the home and workplace, researchers have contemplated if women are "natural" peacemakers (d'Estrée and Babbitt, 1998) and hence may facilitate negotiations in politically difficult situations by bringing particular skills, interests, risk attitudes, and relational orientations. In a qualitative analysis comparing approaches of men and women involved in Israeli-Palestinian workshops, d'Estrée and Babbitt report that groups of women were more open to sharing, empathy, and receptivity than men, and noted that women, through this expression and sharing of personal experiences, seemed more successful in the important political efforts for fostering relationships, networking and coalition building. Others have discussed the 'women as peacemaker' perspective in negotiation simulations with girls as young as middle school. Florea et al (2003), in an email simulation of global political policy negotiations, found that all-female groups behaved more collaboratively and engaged in less conflict than all-male groups or mixed-gender groups. These expectations are consistent with role congruity theory.

Likewise, gender differences in negotiation ethics have been suggested. When MBA students, executives, and male clergy were given negotiation scenarios, both men and women found false statements as highly unethical but women saw bluffing in negotiation as significantly more unethical than men (Anton, 1990). Interestingly the responses indicated that the context of negotiation matters—participants saw it more ethical to deceive an experienced business man than a naïve young mother, or to deceive a stranger than a friend. Again, social roles can offer some insight into these dynamics. In another multi-part scenario study, Kray and Haselhuhn (2012) also found ethical standards in negotiation differed by gender, with men endorsing more ethically questionable tactics (i.e., withholding information, lies) than women. Factors like self-interest, pressure to demonstrate competence, and implicit beliefs affected men's judgments but not women's.

In brief, we highlight these areas to illustrate the variety of areas that gender and negotiation encompass, and the fact that many contexts (work, childcare, household chores, divorce, politics) have a strongly gendered current of beliefs associated with them. By thinking beyond gender and negotiation to the idea of gendered negotiations (Kolb and McGinn, 2009), we suggest that social role theories, and the moderators reviewed here, help frame the questions and can lead to future research. Social role frameworks offer several distinct advantages for understanding gender and negotiation compared with other theoretical frameworks in the literature. First, social roles have direct relationships to existing variables in field such as stereotypes, power, status, context, behaviors, and role conflict. Stereotypes are seen as shaping social roles, and roles hold information about power and status. Roles also involve behavioral expectations and the behaviors enacted, which are central variables in the study of human interaction. Social roles tie together work family conflict and quality of work life issues through variables such as role conflict, role ambiguity, and role overload which link significant areas of gendered negotiations. Second, as discussed in this chapter, social roles offer a cohesive explanation for existing findings for men and women in negotiation. For example, social roles can account for findings like advocacy or agent effects as well as the patterns of mixed gender findings in matrix game situations, which are not as easily encompassed by other theories. Figure 9.1 summarizes how role congruity can account for existing findings, and the consistency of these findings is promising. Finally, as we consider in the final section of this chapter, social roles can be brought to bear on important research questions and suggest ways to understand multiple roles and the influence of complex environments.

FUTURE RESEARCH

In addition to the work and home issues previously discussed, there are increasing opportunities for negotiation due to changes in society. In the workplace, personal negotiation becomes more important as union representation decreases and organizations become less formalized and less centralized (Small et al., 2007). And for both men and women, career patterns are changing as never before with the rise of non-linear career paths (Brousseau et al., 1996) and career switches. Women in particular are less likely than men to be employed in large firms with formal forums for workplace dispute resolution (Gwartney-Gibbs and Lach, 1994). Thus, at present, understanding gender differences in negotiation are of significant value. If women have a tendency to perceive, initiate, interact and succeed differently than men in negotiation, this could influence a wide range of personal, organizational, and societal outcomes.

System Factors

Lewin (1936) famously suggested that behavior is a function of the environment and the person. Although some investigations of the environment are evident in the negotiation literature (e.g., differences in reward structure, time pressure), the conceptualization of the environment could be more expansive. Thus we need to understand how aspects of the physical and social environment (e.g., structural designs, policies, procedures, technology) drive and constrain the behaviors of the individual. From an open systems perspective that maps the inputs, throughputs, and outcomes operating in a particular environment (Katz and Kahn, 1978), we might expect that the environmental forces (in addition to the inputs, throughputs and outcomes) differ for men and women and have implication for their social roles. The consideration of the environment and role episodes (Katz and Kahn, 1978) offers insights into the negotiation process. Relatedly, Bendersky and McGinn (2010) found that negotiation studies that incorporated more open systems features in their design had a larger impact on the field. The open system features included (1) "who" factors—going beyond studying students or strangers negotiating and studying relationships and coalition building, (2) "when" factors, studies that had a longer temporal focus—going beyond one-time interactions to ongoing or reciprocal relations, and (3) "what" factors—a variety of dependent variables and effect on others outside the target negotiation. Their analyses found that the "when" and "what" factors in particular led to a higher article citation rate, even while controlling for other influences.

Thus, consistent with previous writings (Kolb, 2012; Kolb and McGinn, 2009; Sondak and Stuhlmacher, 2009), we encourage the incorporation of belief systems and culture patterns into future work. These can be accommodated within the social role framework and would likely include broadening the negotiation context of study. For example, Putnam and

Kolb (2000) discuss that there are many ways parties may come to an agreement, but experimental negotiation tasks have focused on "trade and transaction" rather than more complex situations. There is a tradition of scorable tasks that focus on monetary outcomes perhaps to the loss of social context and less tangible outcomes (Halpern and Parks, 1996). Frequently, the experimental situation minimizes relationships and produces very strong situations, as seen in telling people to negotiate rather than seeing who or when someone might initiate a negotiation. Additionally the proportional representation of men and women in different roles may be changing and influence what is gender appropriate. Kolb (2012) argues for increased attention to tasks that are gender neutral. It is interesting to see that feminine gendered tasks influence negotiation, but these are not as critical or central to equality for women as issues of negotiating for resources and opportunities.

In addition to expanding the variables and contexts of negotiation research, it is worthwhile to involve diverse participants. Despite the fact this is hardly a novel idea, it is important to realize that individual's gender roles vary in strength and direction. Many would consider there is more to gender than a simple dichotomy. We know little of the differences for men who act in stereotypically feminine ways as well as women who act in stereotypically feminine ways. Kolb (2012) wisely cautions that current research may be overly reinforcing gender stereotypes and calls researchers to expand beyond white middle class samples. Other roles and factors interact with gender—race, parenthood, class, work roles, negotiation reputation, emotions, work history, attractiveness, and culture are all relevant to a social role analysis of gender and negotiation. Another individual difference is relational self-construal (RSC), or how one views the self in connection to other people (Cross and Madson, 1997). RSC has been connected to many social processes including negotiation and can have both chronic accessibility (arising from individual and group differences) as well as temporary accessibility arising from situational conditions in a negotiation (Gelfand et al., 2006). Gelfand et al. propose that the strength of this relational orientation influences the psychological states, tactical behavior, outcomes, and post-negotiation results and the congruence of RSC between negotiator partners is expected to moderate economic and relational outcomes. This reflects a more complex way of thinking about individual differences in that RSC be both chronically salient, or triggered by the situation. Additionally, RSC congruence with task, role, and partners is suggested to impact the negotiation process at various points (Gelfand et al., 2009). The impact of RSC in negotiation has yet to be fully explored but it could be integral in a social role analysis given the communal nature of some roles and how roles and relationship orientations become activated and have a chronic dimension.

Determine What Works

Currently, research offers preliminary advice for women in negotiation including balancing agentic and communal behaviors, conceptualizing negotiation as advocating for others, using power primes, reducing ambiguity, and making stereotypes explicit rather than implicit (Bowles and McGinn, 2008b, Bowles et al., 2005; Kray et al., 2001; Kray et al., 2004; Small et al., 2007). But more evidence-based recommendations are needed. The field needs a meaningful look at how negotiation training works for men and women. In one of the few studies to take a serious look at negotiation training and the impact on negotiation, Stevens et al. (1993) found that women initially set fewer and lower negotiation goals than men. Either self-management training or goal setting training was offered, and enhanced perceived control served as a mechanism for increased negotiation performance over self-set goals or self-efficacy. However, they used a pre-programmed pattern of concessions based on tactics used, and it is questionable if tactics may work the same for men and women in an actual negotiation. Drawing on lessons from the diversity training literature with skills/behavior based training or awareness/sensitivity training (Roberson et al., 2003; Rynes and Rosen, 1995; Sanchez and Medkik, 2004) may suggest effective methods to increase initiation, reduce backlash, and foster equitable outcomes.

CONCLUSION

Given the role of negotiation in securing resources, it is a concern if women are less likely to initiate and prosper from negotiations than men are. We have discussed a variety of factors that relate to gender differences in negotiation, and highlighted some explanations and areas for future research. We propose that gender roles, along with other social roles, help explain gender related findings concerning entering a negotiation, the behaviors displayed, the perceptions of the negotiators themselves, the reactions of the negotiation counterparts or other observers, as well as the tangible and intangible outcomes received.

Walton and McKersie (1965) famously defined negotiation as the "deliberate interactions of two or more complex social units which are attempting to define or redefine the terms of their interdependence" (p. 3). Although this definition is expansive, it captures the broad impact that negotiations have and offers a challenge for new research. We find that integrating social roles into negotiation builds a stronger nomological network (Cronbach and Meehl, 1955) to explain current findings and guide future predictions and research. In this chapter, we suggest that social roles can frame a broader conceptualization and understanding of negotiation in terms of how roles are sent by others, how they are received and perceived by the person in that role, and how this drives perceptions and behaviors in various spheres of negotiation.

NOTE

* We gratefully acknowledge helpful comments from Wendi Adair, Steve Karau, Deborah Kolb, Beth Polin, and Michelle Stuhlmacher.

REFERENCES

Amanatullah, E.T. and Morris, M.W. (2010). Negotiating gender roles: Gender differences in assertive negotiating are mediated by women's fear of backlash and attenuated when negotiating on behalf of others. *Journal of Personality and Social Psychology*, 98, 256–267.

Anton, R.J. (1990). Drawing the line: An exploratory test of ethical behavior in negotiations. *The International Journal of Conflict Management*, 1, 265–280.

Ayres, I. (1991). Fair driving: Gender and race discrimination in retail car negotiations. *Harvard Law Review*, 104, 817–872.

Ayres, I. and Siegelman, P. (1995). Race and gender discrimination in bargaining for a new car. *The American Economic Review*, 85, 304–321.

Babcock, L. and Laschever, S. (2003). *Women don't ask: Negotiation and the gender divide*. Princeton, NJ: Princeton University Press.

Babcock, L. and Laschever, S. (2008). *Ask for it: How women can use the power of negotiation to get what they really want*. New York: Bantam Dell.

Babcock, L., Gelfand, M., Small, D., and Stayn, H. (2006). Gender differences in the propensity to initiate negotiations. In D.D. Cremer, M. Zeelenberg, and J.K. Murnighan (eds), *Social Psychology and Economics* (pp. 239–262). Mahwah, NJ: Lawrence Erlbaum.

Bakan, D. (1966). *The duality of human existence: An essay on psychology and religion*. Chicago: Rand McNally.

Bear, J. (2011). "Passing the buck": Incongruence between gender role and topic leads to avoidance of negotiation. *Negotiation and Conflict Management Research*, 4, 47–72.

Bear, J.B. and Babcock, L. (2012). Negotiation topic as a moderator of gender differences in Negotiation. *Psychological Science*, 23, 743–744.

Bendersky, C. and McGinn, K.L. (2010). Open to negotiation: Phenomenological assumptions and knowledge dissemination. *Organizational Science*, 21, 781–797.

Bialeschki, M.D. and Pearce, K.D. (1997). "I don't want a lifestyle – I want a life": The effects of role negotiations on the leisure of lesbian mothers. *Journal of Leisure Research*, 29, 113–131.

Bowles, H.R. (in press). Psychological perspectives on gender in negotiation. In M.K. Ryan and N.R. Branscombe (eds), *The Sage Handbook of Gender and Psychology*. London: Sage Publications.

Bowles, H.R., Babcock, L., and Lai, L. (2007). Social incentives for gender differences in the propensity to initiate negotiations: Sometimes it does hurt to ask. *Organizational Behavior and Human Decision Processes*, *103*, 84–103.

Bowles, H.R., Babcock, L., and McGinn, K.L. (2005). Constraints and triggers: Situational mechanics of gender in negotiation. *Journal of Personality and Social Psychology*, *89*, 951–965.

Bowles, H.R. and Flynn, F. (2010). Gender and persistence in negotiation: A dyadic perspective. *Academy of Management Journal*, *53*, 769–787.

Bowles, H.R. and McGinn, K.L. (2008a). Untapped potential in the study of negotiation and gender inequality in organizations. *The Academy of Management Annals*, *2*, 99–132.

Bowles, H.R. and McGinn, K.L. (2008b). Gender in job negotiations: A two-level game. *Negotiation Journal*, *24*, 393–410.

Brandth, B. and Kvande, E. (2002). Reflexive fathers: Negotiating parental leave and working life. *Gender, Work and Organization*, *9*, 186–203.

Braver, S.L., Gonzalez, N., Wolchik, S.A., and Sandler, I.N. (1989). Economic hardship and psychological distress in custodial mothers. *Journal of Divorce and Remarriage*, *12*(4), 19–34.

Brousseau, K.R., Driver, M.J., Eneroth, K., and Larsson, R. (1996). Career pandemonium: Realigning organizations and individuals. *The Academy of Management Executive*, *10*, 52–66.

Calhoun, P. and Smith, W.P. (1999). Integrative bargaining: Does gender make a difference? *International Journal of Conflict Management*, *10*, 203–224.

Carli, L.L. (2001). Gender and social influence. *Journal of Social Issues*, *57*, 725–741.

Cook, E.P. (1994). Role salience and multiple roles: A gender perspective. *The Career Development Quarterly*, *43*, 89–95.

Correll, S.J., Benard, S., Paik, I. (2007). Getting a job: Is there a motherhood penalty? *American Journal of Sociology*, *112*, 1297–1339.

Cronbach, L.J. and Meehl, P.E. (1955). Construct validity in psychological tests. *Psychological Bulletin*, *52*, 281–302.

Cross, S.E. and Madson, L. (1997). Models of the self: Self-construals and gender. *Psychological Bulletin*, *122*, 5–37.

d'Estrée, T.P. and Babbitt, E.F. (1998). Women and the art of peacemaking: Data from Israeli-Palestinian interactive problem-solving workshops. *Political Psychology*, *19*, 185–209.

Dalton, D.R. and Todor, W.D. (1985), Gender and workplace justice: A field assessment. *Personnel Psychology*, *38*, 133–151.

Dalton, D.R., Todor, W.D., and Owen, C.L. (1987). Sex effects in workplace justice outcomes: A field assessment. *Journal of Applied Psychology*, *72*, 156–159.

Eagly, A.H. (1987). *Sex differences in social behavior: A social-role interpretation.* Hillsdale, NJ: Erlbaum.

Eagly, A.H. and Carli, L.L. (2007). *Through the labyrinth: The truth of how women become leaders.* Boston: Harvard Business School Press.

Eagly, A.H. and Johnson, B.T. (1990). Gender and leadership style: A meta-analysis. *Psychological Bulletin*, *108*, 233–256.

Eagly, A.H. and Karau, S.J. (2002). Role congruity theory of prejudice toward female leaders. *Psychological Review*, *109*, 573–598.

Eagly, A.H. and Wood, W. (1999). The origins of sex differences in human behavior: Evolved dispositions versus social roles. *American Psychologist*, *54*, 408–423.

Eagly, A.H. and Wood, W. (2012). Social role theory. In P.A.M. van Lange, A.W. Kruglanski, and E.T. Higgins (eds), *Handbook of theories in social psychology* (pp. 458–476) Thousand Oaks, CA: Sage Publications.

Elvira, M.M. and Graham, M.E. (2002). Not just a formality: Pay system formalization and sex related earnings effects. *Organization Science*, *13*, 601–617.

Florea, N.B., Boyer, M.A., Brown, S.W., Butler, M.J., Hernandez, M., Weir, K., Meng, L., Johnson, P.R., Lima, C., and Mayall, H.J. (2003). Negotiating from Mars to Venus: Gender in simulated international negotiations. *Simulation and Gaming*, *34*, 226–248.

Fuegen, K., Biernat, M., Haines, E., and Deaux, K. (2004). Mothers and fathers in the workplace: How gender and parental status influence judgments of job-related competence. *Journal of Social Issues*, 60, 737–754.

Galinsky, A.D., Gruenfeld, D.H., and Magee, J.C. (2003). From power to action. *Journal of Personality and Social Psychology*, 85, 453–466.

Gelfand, M.J., Major, V.S., Raver, J.L., Nishii, L.H., and O'Brien, K. (2006). Negotiating relationally: The dynamics of the relational self in negotiations. *The Academy of Management Review*, 31, 427–451.

Gerhart, B. (1990). Gender differences in current and starting salaries: The role of performance, college major, and job title. *Industrial and Labor Relations Review*, 43, 418–433.

Gerhart, B. and Rynes, S. (1991). Determinants and consequences of salary negotiations by male and female MBA graduates. *Journal of Applied Psychology*, 76, 256–262.

Glick, P. and Fiske, S.T. (1996). The ambivalent sexism inventory: Differentiating hostile and benevolent sexism. *Journal of Personality and Social Psychology*, 70, 491–512.

Greenberg, D., Ladge, J., and Clair, J. (2009). Negotiating pregnancy at work: Public and private conflicts. *Negotiation and Conflict Management Research*, 2, 42–56.

Greig, F. (2008). Propensity to negotiate and career advancement: Evidence from an investment bank that women are on a "slow elevator". *Negotiation Journal*, 24, 495–508.

Güngör, G. and Biernat, M. (2009). Gender bias or motherhood disadvantage? Judgments of blue collar mothers and fathers in the workplace. *Sex Roles*, 60, 232–246.

Gwartney-Gibbs, P.A. and Lach, D.H. (1994). Gender and workplace dispute resolution: A conceptual and theoretical model. *Law and Society Review*, 28, 265–296.

Halpern, J.J. and Parks, J.M. (1996). Vive la difference: Differences between males and females in process and outcomes in low-conflict negotiation. *International Journal of Conflict Management*, 7, 45–70.

Herrmann, G.M. (2004). Haggling spoken here: Gender, class, and style in US garage sale bargaining. *The Journal of Popular Culture*, 38, 55–81.

Hornung, S., Rousseau, D.M., and Glaser, J. (2008). Creating flexible work arrangements through idiosyncratic deals. *Journal of Applied Psychology*, 93, 655–664.

Katz, D. and Kahn, R.L. (1978). *The social psychology of organizations*. New York: Wiley.

Kolb D.M. (2009). Too bad for the women or does it have to be? Gender and negotiation research over the past twenty-five years. *Negotiation Journal*, 25, 515–531.

Kolb, D.M. (2012). Are we becoming part of the problem? Gender stereotypes in negotiation research. *Negotiation and Conflict Management Research*, 5, 127–135.

Kolb, D. and McGinn, K. (2009). Beyond gender and negotiation to gendered negotiations. *Negotiation and Conflict Management Research*, 2, 1–16.

Kray, L. and Babcock, L. (2006). Gender in negotiations: A motivated social cognitive analysis. In L.L. Thompson (ed.), *Negotiation theory and research* (pp. 203–224). Madison, CT: Psychosocial Press.

Kray, L.J., Galinsky, A.D., and Thompson, L. (2002). Reversing the gender gap in negotiations: An exploration of stereotype regeneration. *Organizational Behavior and Human Decision Processes*, 87, 386–409.

Kray, L.J. and Gelfand, M.J. (2009). Relief versus regret: The effect of gender and negotiating norm ambiguity on reactions to having one's first offer accepted. *Social Cognition*, 27, 418–436.

Kray, L.J. and Haselhuhn, M.P. (2012). Male pragmatism in negotiators' ethical reasoning. *Journal of Experimental Social Psychology*, 48, 1124–1131.

Kray, L.J., Reb, J., Galinsky, A.D., and Thompson, L. (2004). Stereotype reactance at the bargaining table: The effect of stereotype activation and power on claiming and creating value. *Personality and Social Psychology Bulletin*, 30, 399–411.

Kray, L.J. and Thompson, L. (2005). Gender stereotypes and negotiation performance: An examination of theory and research. In B.M. Staw and R.M. Kramer (eds), *Research in Organizational Behavior*, Vol. 26, 103–182.

Kray, L.J., Thompson, L., and Galinsky, A. (2001). Battle of the sexes: Gender stereotype confirmation and reactance in negotiations. *Journal of Personality and Social Psychology*, 80, 942–958.

Lewin, K. (1936). *Principles of topological psychology*. New York: McGraw-Hill.
Liu, M. and Buzzanell, P.M. (2004). Negotiating maternity leave expectations. *Journal of Business Communication*, 41, 323–349.
Lyness, K.S. and Thompson, D.E. (1997). Above the glass ceiling? A comparison of matched samples of female and male executives. *Journal of Applied Psychology*, 82, 359–375.
Mannino, C.A. and Deutsch, F.M. (2007). Changing the division of household labor: A negotiated process between partners. *Sex Roles*, 56, 309–324.
Mazei, J., Hüffmeier, J., Freund, P.A., Stuhlmacher, A., Bilke, L., and Hertel, G. (working paper). *Men and women as negotiators: A meta-analysis on gender differences in economic and socioemotional negotiation outcomes*. Westfälische Wilhelms-Universität Münster, Germany.
Medved, C.E. and Heisler, J. (2002). A negotiated order exploration of critical student-faculty interactions: Student-parents manage multiple roles. *Communication Education*, 51, 105–120.
Miles, E.W. (2010). Gender differences in distributive negotiation: When in the negotiation process do the differences occur? *European Journal of Social Psychology*, 40, 1200–1211.
Miles, E.W. and Clenney, E.F. (2010). Gender differences in negotiation: A status characteristics theory view. *Negotiation and Conflict Management Research*, 3, 130–144.
Miles, E.W. and LaSalle, M.M. (2008). Asymmetrical contextual ambiguity, negotiation self-efficacy, and negotiation performance. *International Journal of Conflict Management*, 19, 36–56.
Miles, E.W. and LaSalle, M.M. (2009). Gender and creation of value in mixed-motive negotiation. *International Journal of Conflict Management*, 20, 269–286.
Miller, V.D., Jablin, F.M., Casey, M.K., and Lamphear-Van Horn, M. (1996). The maternity leave as a role negotiation process. *Journal of Managerial Issues*, 8, 286–309.
Nowak, K.L. (2003). Sex categorization in computer mediated communication (CMC): Exploring the utopian promise. *Media Psychology*, 5, 83–103.
Publications Manual of the American Psychological Association, 6th edn (2010). Washington, DC: American Psychological Association.
Putnam, L.L. and Kolb, D.M. (2000). Rethinking negotiation: Feminist views of communication and exchange. In P. Buzzanell (ed.), *Rethinking organizational and managerial communication from feminist perspectives*, pp. 76–114. Thousand Oaks, CA: Sage.
Ragins, B.R. and Sundstrom, E. (1989). Gender and power in organizations: A longitudinal perspective. *Psychological Bulletin*, 105, 51–88.
Ranson, G. (2005). No longer "one of the boys": Negotiations with motherhood, as prospect or reality, among women in engineering. *Canadian Review of Sociology and Anthropology*, 42, 145–166.
Roberson, L., Kulik, C.T., and Pepper, M.B. (2003). Using needs assessment to resolve controversies in diversity training design. *Group and Organizational Management*, 28, 148–174.
Rubin, J.Z. and Brown, B.R. (1975). *The social psychology of bargaining and negotiation*. New York: Academic Press.
Rudman, L.A. and Fairchild, K. (2004). Reactions to counterstereotypic behavior: The role of backlash in cultural stereotype maintenance. *Journal of Personality and Social Psychology*, 87, 157–176.
Rudman, L.A. and Glick, P. (1999). Feminized management and backlash toward agentic women: The hidden costs to women of a kinder, gentler image of middle managers. *Journal of Personality and Social Psychology*, 77, 1004–1010.
Rudman, L.A. and Phelan, J.E. (2008). Backlash effects for disconfirming gender stereotypes in organizations. In A.P. Brief and B.M. Staw (eds), *Research in organizational behavior*, Vol. 28 (pp. 61–79), New York: Elsevier.
Rynes, S. and Rosen, B. (1995). A field survey of factors affecting the adoption and perceived success of diversity training. *Personnel Psychology*, 48, 247–270.
Sanchez, J.I. and Medkik, N. (2004). The effects of diversity awareness training on differential treatment. *Group and Organization Management*, 29, 517–536.

Seltzer, J.A. and Garfinkel, I. (1990). Inequality in divorce settlements: An investigation of property settlements and child support awards. *Social Science Research*, 19, 82–111.

Sheets, V.L. and Braver, S.L. (1996). Gender differences in satisfaction with divorce settlements. *Family Relations*, 45, 336–342.

Sherif, M. (1966). *In common predicament: Social psychology of intergroup conflict and cooperation*. Boston: Houghton-Mifflin.

Small, D.A., Gelfand, M., Babcock, L., and Gettman, H. (2007). Who goes to the bargaining table? The influence of gender and framing on the initiation of negotiation. *Journal of Personality and Social Psychology*, 93, 600–613.

Sondak, H. and Stuhlmacher, A.F. (2009). Gendered organizational order and negotiations research. *Negotiation and Conflict Management Research*, 2, 107–120.

Stevens, C.K., Bavetta, A.G., and Gist, M.E. (1993). Gender differences in the acquisition of salary negotiation skills: The role of goals, self-efficacy, and perceived control. *Journal of Applied Psychology*, 78, 723–735.

Stuhlmacher, A.F., Citera, M., and Willis, T. (2007). Gender differences in virtual negotiation: Theory and research. *Sex Roles*, 57, 329–339.

Stuhlmacher, A.F. and Morrissett, M.G. (2008). Men and women as mediators: Disputant perceptions. *International Journal of Conflict Management*, 19, 249–261.

Stuhlmacher, A.F. and Poitras, J. (2010). Gender and job role congruence: A field study of trust in labor mediators. *Sex Roles*, 63, 489–499.

Stuhlmacher, A.F., Poitras, J., and Ittner, H. (2012). *Gender composition effects in negotiation: A role congruity analysis*. Working paper, DePaul University.

Stuhlmacher, A.F. and Walters, A.E. (1999). Gender differences in negotiation outcome: A meta-analysis. *Personnel Psychology*, 52, 653–677.

Stuhlmacher, A.F. and Winkler, R.B. (2006). Negotiating while female: Research and implications. In M. Barrett and M.J. Davidson (eds), *Gender and communication issues at work* (pp. 211–223). Aldershot: Ashgate Publishing.

Sutter, M., Bosman, R., Kocher, M.G., and van Winden, F. (2009). Gender pairing and bargaining—Beware the same sex! *Experimental Economics*, 12, 318–331.

Tajfel, H. and Turner, J.C. (1986). The social identity theory of intergroup behaviour. In S. Worchel and W.G. Austin (eds), *Psychology of intergroup relations* (pp. 7–24). Chicago, IL: Nelson-Hall.

Tinsley, C.H., O'Connor, K.M., and Sullivan, B.A. (2002). Tough guys finish last: The perils of a distributive reputation. *Organizational Behavior and Human Decision Processes*, 88, 621–642.

Walters, A.E., Stuhlmacher, A.F., and Meyer, L.L. (1998). Gender and negotiation competitiveness: A meta-analysis. *Organizational Behavior and Human Decision Processes*, 76, 1–29.

Walton, R.E. and McKersie, R.B. (1965). *A behavioral theory of labor relations*. New York: McGraw-Hill.

Watson, C. (1994). Gender versus power as a predictor of negotiation behavior and outcomes. *Negotiation Journal*, 10, 117–127.

Watson, C. and Hoffman, L.R. (1996). Managers as negotiators: A test of power versus gender as predictors of feelings, behavior, and outcomes. *Leadership Quarterly*, 7, 63–85.

Wingood, G.M. and DiClemente, R.J. (1997). The effects of an abusive primary partner on the condom use and sexual negotiation practices of African-American women. *American Journal of Public Health*, 87, 1016–1018.

Wood, W. and Eagly, A.H. (2012). Biosocial construction of sex differences and similarities in behavior. In J.M. Olson, and M.P. Zanna (eds), *Advances in experimental social psychology*, Vol. 46, pp. 55–123. London, UK: Elsevier.

10. Dignity, Face, and Honor cultures: implications for negotiation and conflict management

Soroush Aslani, Jimena Ramirez-Marin, Zhaleh Semnani-Azad, Jeanne M. Brett and Catherine Tinsley

Over the past three decades, the culture and negotiation research has contrasted strategy and outcome of negotiations in Western and East Asian cultures (Brett & Gelfand, 2006). There has been little research or theorizing concerning the nature of negotiations in Latino or Middle Eastern cultures. In this chapter, we review the implications for negotiation of theory and research concerning people's behavior in three types of culture: Honor, Dignity, and Face. We begin by identifying the key elements that distinguish Honor, Dignity, and Face cultures including the historical explanations for why these three types of culture are located in different parts of the world, e.g. Dignity cultures in Western Europe and North America, Face cultures in East and Southeast Asia, and Honor cultures in the Middle East and Latin America. Next, relying on theory and empirical research, we review the implications of these cultural differences for negotiation strategy and outcomes. As there is substantially more research on negotiation in Dignity and Face cultures than in Honor cultures, the implications we draw for negotiations in Honor cultures are decidedly more speculative and therefore ripe for future research.

Research in cultural psychology, challenged to understand differences between East Asians and Westerners, has relied heavily on the theory of individualism/collectivism (Hofstede, 1980) and its co-varying elements, for example, independence/interdependence theory (Markus and Kitayama, 1991), power distance (Hofstede, 1980), high versus low context communication (Hall, 1976), holistic versus analytical mindset (Nisbett et al., 2001). In this chapter we expand the horizon for comparative cultural research from its East/West origins to two other large geographical expanses of the world: Middle East and North Africa, Southern Europe and Latin America. Our theoretical lens is describing Dignity, Face, and Honor cultures (Kim and Cohen, 2010), our context is negotiation, and the empirical settings in which we are doing research range from China to Qatar to Spain to the U.S. and Canada.

We begin by identifying the key elements that distinguish the less familiar Honor cultures from the more familiar Dignity and Face cultures. We expand upon the psychological principles that prior research and theorizing has proposed to distinguish Honor, Face, and Dignity cultures (Leung and Cohen, 2011). We identify the geographical locations of such cultures, for example, Honor cultures in the Middle East, Southern Europe and Latin America; Face cultures in East Asia, and Dignity cultures in Northern Europe, North America, and other British influenced English speaking countries like Australia and New Zealand. We also review the historical and anthropological explanations for why these different types of culture flourished in different parts of the world. We then turn to the implications of these three different types of culture for strategy and outcomes in negotiations with integrative potential, that is, negotiations that provide the opportunity to generate joint gains through insight to the other party's interests and priorities. We focus on this type of negotiation because *Pareto optimality*, a variant of joint gains maximization, has been the primary criterion for evaluating negotiation outcomes since Luce and Raiffa's (1957) *Games and Decisions*.[1] Economists and psychologists who study negotiations emphasize Pareto optimality and joint gains maximization for several reasons. Achievement of joint gains implies that value has not been left unclaimed on the table and tradeoffs satisfying both parties' interests have occurred, increasing the likelihood of harmonious and long-term relationships (Teucher et al., 2011).[2] The core of our chapter is an analysis of the implications of these three types of culture, namely, Dignity, Face, and Honor, for three factors that influence the use of strategy in negotiations; (a) trust (high versus low), (b) mindset (linear versus holistic), and (c) emotional expression (high versus low), and how the interplay among these three factors affects negotiators' strategy and outcomes.

THREE CULTURAL PROTOTYPES

What Is Culture?

Culture is the unique profile of a society, extending from easily observable behaviors and institutions, to less obvious psychological elements such as values, beliefs, and norms (Lytle et al., 1995). Culture emerges as a functional solution to the most commonly encountered dilemmas and problems of social interaction (Trompenaars, 1996). For example, different cultures have different greeting behaviors, different driving rules, and use negotiation strategy differently (Brett, 2007). Accordingly, culture provides normative behavioral scripts that when enacted in the appropriate cultural context yield effective social interaction. We propose that Honor, Face, and Dignity cultures provide very different normative behavioral scripts and ideals for social interaction in general, and for negotiations in particular.

Defining Three Cultural Prototypes

The first cultural prototype introduced in this chapter is the *Dignity* culture which follows the logic of modern Western societies (Leung and Cohen, 2011). In Dignity cultures, a person's self-worth is primarily intrinsically derived; it is not conferred by others and cannot be taken away by others – and so is relatively stable; and is, at least theoretically, equal to that of every other member of the culture (Ayers, 1984). Dignity manifests in a reputation for independence and choosing one's own goals (Schwartz, 1994).

The second prototype is the *Face* culture. It follows the logic of East Asian societies that are traditionally known as collectivist cultures in cross-cultural literature (Schwartz, 1994). *Face* represents an individual's claimed sense of positive image in the context of social interactions (Oetzel and Ting-Toomey, 2003) and manifests in a reputation for social responsibility, respect for tradition, and honoring parents and elders (Schwartz, 1994). In Face cultures, self-worth is primarily extrinsically derived and is dependent on a person's relative position in a stable social hierarchy, and on fulfillment of the person's role obligations in that hierarchy (Heine, 2001). The different bases for self-worth in Dignity and Face cultures are familiar to cultural psychology in the distinction between the independent and interdependent selves (Markus and Kitayama, 1991).

Honor culture is the third prototype and is the characteristic of Middle Eastern and North African cultures, Latin American cultures, and to some extent, Southern European cultures. Self-worth based on *honor* is an individual's estimate of his own worth, as socially claimed from and recognized by society (Pitt-Rivers, 1968). Thus, self-worth in Honor cultures has elements of self-worth, as it is defined in Dignity cultures, as well as some elements of self-worth as it is defined in Face cultures. Honor manifests in a reputation for toughness in protecting self and family and not being taken advantage of by others (Cohen and Nisbett, 1997; Nisbett and Cohen, 1996), but also in trustworthiness and maintaining one's word (Miller, 1993) as well as warmth, hospitality, and strong family ties (Nisbett and Cohen, 1996; Pitt-Rivers, 1968; Rodriguez Mosquera et al.,

2008; Triandis, 1989). Furthermore, self-worth in Honor cultures is also much more fleeting than in Face cultures, because hierarchies are less settled and stable in honor than Face cultures. Therefore, to maintain self-worth people in Honor cultures can be quite aggressive or quite warm and hospitable, depending on the social context, whether norms of honorable toughness or norms of honorable hospitality are salient. There is substantial recent research that people in Honor cultures respond to insult aggressively, defensively and directly to protect their self-worth (Beersma et al., 2003; Bourdieu, 1977; Cohen et al., 1996; Ijzerman et al., 2007; Rodriguez Mosquera et al., 2002a; 2002b). However there has been little research examining the friendly, hospitable and warm side of Honor culture (see Harinck et al., in press, for an exception).

We discuss the historical and geographical roots of these cultural prototypes in the next section.

Anthropological Explanations of the Origins of Honor, Face and Dignity Culture

Scholars who study culture have long been fascinated by the origins and correlates of cultural differences. Multiple complementary and supplementary explanations exist for historical origins of different cultures. These explanations are mostly based on geographical conditions (for example access to abundant versus scarce agricultural crops), political conditions (for example strong versus weak rule of law), and demographic conditions (for example high versus low population density) in which a culture was developed. This study of the origins of cultural differences, although fraught with alternative explanations, is nevertheless fascinating. It may also provide insight into different patterns of social inaction in modern cultures. Scholars primarily attribute the origins of Dignity, Face, and Honor cultures to (1) the historical basis of the culture's economy, and (2) population density. There is also some discussion of existence of centralized versus decentralized government and of scarcity versus abundance of natural resources. We discuss the impact of these factors in this section.

Historically, Honor cultures developed in regions with herding economies and low population density (Nisbett and Cohen, 1996). Herds are portable wealth, but also wealth that can be difficult to defend, since herds, unlike agricultural land, are very vulnerable to poaching. Under such conditions, a reputation for toughness in defending self and family, and intolerance of insult (i.e., establishing honor), could deter theft of portable wealth. Honor norms can also be reinforced in regions without a strong central state or a weak rule of law (Cohen and Nisbett, 1997; Leung and Cohen, 2011). For example in historically tribal environment in the Middle East, clans and families with rough status equivalency tried to establish their public reputations and prove their strength, courage, and status through challenge and competition (see Bourdieu, 1977; Gilmore, 1991; Pely, 2011). Historically, the Middle East has been a region with relatively low population density and economies originally based on herding, and without a strong central state, hence a weak rule of law leading people to take the law into their own hands. The American South/Southwest (compared to the American North) also provided European immigrants with relatively similar environment in almost the first three centuries after the discovery of the American continent (Cohen and Nisbett, 1997; Leung and Cohen, 2011). In such dynamic economic and political environments, social power and status are unstable and one's perceived self-worth, as viewed by society, can easily be threatened or challenged and sometimes may need to be maintained through aggression. Such social norms persist in societies long after they may have lost economic value (Vandello and Cohen, 2004), and so there remain strong manifestations of honor norms in societies which today are highly modernized. For example, although much has changed in the American Southwest – herds are branded and fenced and there is stable central government – people living in this part of the United States resist government's interference in their self-protection rights, for example, carrying guns.

Unlike Honor cultures, Face and Dignity cultures were more likely to develop in societies built on agriculture. Face cultures were more likely to evolve when population density was high, and Dignity cultures were more likely to evolve when density was low (Flannery, 1972; Service, 1962).

In Face cultures, populations became dense in particular regions capable of producing food crops. The availability of food increases populations and increasing populations require increasingly organized food production. The need to increase food production generates a collective goal that is achieved through cooperation and organization that turn into norms for social interaction and strong central governments that promote, monitor, and sanction normative behavior. For example, this combination of an agricultural economy and high population density is characteristic of both ancient China and Japan. Those countries had strong collective norms manifested in the collective bonds of Confucian ideology (Ikels, 2004) and centralized, hierarchical governance structures. In such an environment people developed interdependent self-concepts and enhanced self-worth by maintaining harmony with others and conforming to the cooperative norms embedded in the hierarchical social system.

Dignity cultures are similar to Face cultures in their historical reliance on an agricultural economy. However regions that spawned Dignity cultures did not face problems of high population density. Availability of agricultural land made production of food more of an individual than a collective effort requiring less coordination between food producers. This may be why Dignity cultures tend to generate more independent and egalitarian governance structures. In addition the market economies so characteristic of Dignity cultures can be traced to this confluence of agrarian economy and low population density. Because of the availability of abundant agricultural land, individuals were able to produce excess food. Yet, their environments did not have, because they did not need, the centralized cooperative organizational structures that were necessary for food production and sharing in Face cultures. As a result, in order to make effective use of excess food, systems of market exchange among social equals evolved in Dignity cultures (Ayers, 1984). These environments supported both ideas of *markets* and *dignity*: an egalitarian system of independent individuals, guided by conscience but also supported by an effective system of law that could protect an individual's property rights from violence (Leung and Cohen, 2011). Compared to people in Face cultures, those in Dignity cultures enjoyed the luxury of abundant environmental resources which provided them with strong external options that allowed them to opt out of cooperation[3] unless they genuinely wanted to cooperate. This luxury of resources helped actors develop an independent and internal sense of worth. Thus a strong market exchange system was needed to encourage individuals – who were not as dependent on each other as much as those in Face cultures – to accept interdependence and engage in market negotiations. Overall, this environment made the logic of dignity not only morally correct for an individual, but also rational to solve problems and prosper in a market-based society.

IMPLICATIONS OF CULTURAL LOGICS OF DIGNITY, FACE, AND HONOR FOR CONFLICT MANAGEMENT

The literature suggests that these three cultures differ on several psychological and sociological dimensions (for another typology of differences among these cultures, see Leung and Cohen, 2011). Our interest in negotiation and conflict management leads us to elaborate four key psychological concepts that we predict are manifested differently in Dignity, Face, and Honor cultures: (1) power and status, (2) sensitivity and response to insults, (3) confrontation styles, and (4) conciliation, warmth and hospitality. All of these four concepts are related to how self-worth is defined in each culture, are affected by the historical reasons underlying what norms and values developed in each culture, and have important implications for

Table 10.1 *Cultural logics of Dignity, Face, and Honor for conflict management*

Category	Dignity	Face	Honor
Self-worth	Mostly internal	Mostly external; Socially conferred and stable	Both; Socially claimed and dynamic
Power and Status	Egalitarian; Dynamic	Hierarchical; Stable	Hierarchical; Dynamic and contested
Sensitivity and Response to Insults	Low sensitivity; Ignore insult or refer to rule of law to punish	Medium sensitivity; Refer to social superiors to punish	High sensitivity; Take matters into your own hands
Confrontation Style	Direct; Rational (cost/ benefit calculations)	Indirect; Suppress negative emotions	Both direct and indirect; Express emotions
Reconciliation, Warmth and Hospitality	Rational; Express positive emotions	Short-term irrationality; Humility; Altruism to fulfill duty toward the collective	Short-term irrationality; Hospitality; Altruism to exceed the expectations of those in your close circle

conflict management. In choosing to elaborate on these four concepts, we do not mean to imply that these are the only psychological concepts that distinguish these three cultures, only that we view these four concepts as providing deep insights into how people in these cultures manage conflict and negotiate.

Table 10.1 is our summary of insights regarding the differences between these different types of cultures with respect to self-worth as well as the above four concepts. The table intentionally places Honor culture after Dignity and Face cultures, because Honor culture takes norms and values from both the independent Dignity culture and the interdependent Face culture to generate its own unique cultural prototype. In elaborating on each set of concepts, we usually discuss the cultures in the order of Dignity, Face, and Honor, unless a different order makes an argument more clear.

Following the approach suggested by Leung and Cohen (2011) and Weber (1997), we describe Dignity, Face, and Honor cultural prototypes as "ideal types". Ideal types rarely exist in the real world; most societies are a blend of different ideal types. However ideal types describe the logics of thought and action that have developed and sustained historically in that culture and still hold normative valence, even though not practiced by all people in that culture. We neither assume that, for instance, people in a specific Honor culture society homogenously follow all ideals of Honor culture, nor suggest that all Honor cultures are similar across each of the concepts. We use the "*ideal types*" framework to capture some of the essential "family resemblance" features (Wittgenstein, 2009) for understanding conflict management in these cultures, recognizing that we are not capturing a complete profile of each of these cultural types. Within an ideal type, not only several sub-cultures (e.g., different nations) with distinct features may exist, but also individual members of each culture will vary in the extent to which they internalize or endorse the cultural ideals of their society.

Power and Status

Power and status are constructed differently in each cultural prototype. In particular, each prototype has its own specific norms for how egalitarian (versus hierarchical) and how dynamic (versus static) power and status are in a society.

Societies within the Dignity culture prototype such as the U.S., Canada, or the U.K. have developed egalitarian governance structures based on market economies (Ayers, 1984). This implies independence in social interaction, and indeed these societies are known for espousing egalitarian and independent values. The ideas of *markets* and *dignity* (i.e., intrinsic sense of worth) have developed together in such egalitarian environments that historically had abundant resources, low population density, and strong governments that could protect individuals' property rights from violence (Leung and Cohen, 2011).

In contrast, societies within the Face culture prototype like China and Japan evolved in densely populated areas that developed hierarchical social structures based on collective interdependency. Such stable and hierarchical structures facilitated the cooperative systems necessary for organized food production. Several East Asian societies have now established democratic governance structures, but their social structures remain very hierarchical. These modern societies are known for norms emphasizing *collectivism* and *power distance* (Hofstede and Bond, 1988). Such norms suggest members to enhance their self-worth by fulfilling duties in the stable hierarchy in general.

Finally societies within the Honor culture prototype, like countries in the Middle East, are also characterized by hierarchical structures – as manifested in their high *power distance* scores (Carl et al., 2004; Hofstede,

1980), yet unlike Face cultures, their social hierarchies are relatively unstable (Gilmore, 1991). Honor cultures developed in competitive social environments and herding economies where different tribes, clans, or groups competed and contested each other to establish dominance and exert control over resources (Leung and Cohen, 2011). Once a group dominated the other ones, strong hierarchies could be reestablished; however those in power were frequently facing the threat of being contested and overthrown by others eager to establish their honor. The history of several Middle Eastern and Latin American countries witnesses cycles of dictatorship and repression, followed by revolutions or reforms, short-term open political spaces, and then coups or other events to establish new structures of power and politics that were strongly hierarchical. Overall, obedience to and respect for high-status people, including the rulers and elderly, which exist in Face cultures are also visible in Honor cultures; however social hierarchies are much more dynamic, shifting, and contested than in Face cultures.

Sensitivity and Response to Insults

How people perceive insults and respond to them has important implications for conflict management in each culture. Here the primary mechanism for understanding cultural differences in sensitivity and response to insults is the extent to which insults threaten self-worth.

The inalienable and independent sense of worth in a Dignity culture suggests relatively low sensitivity to insults (compared to Face and Honor cultures) and relative toleration of insults. An *ideal* individual, defined by normative principles of Dignity cultures, can maintain his/her correct behavior independent of what others do (Kim and Cohen, 2010). If insulted, people in Dignity cultures should not feel obligated to reciprocate others' insults or even respond to insults to restore their sense of worth, which at least in theory is not touched by insult: *names do not hurt them* (Ayers, 1984). Indeed by ignoring the insult, members of Dignity cultures can turn the social denigration back on the insulter. Ideal members of Dignity cultures, feeling secure about their worth, can respond to insults by implying that it is the insulter who lacks dignity: "who are you to say that to me?" (Horowitz and Schwartz, 1974). By this argument, we by no means intend to ignore the rich body of literature on interpersonal and procedural justice in Western societies (see Bies and Moag, 1986; Lind and Tyler, 1988) which suggests the degree to which the people involved in a situation are treated with respect affects their emotional responses and overall performance and satisfaction. Rather we would like to emphasize that the internal and social consequences of insult are much stronger in

Face and Honor cultures and insults should have less ability to destabilize the power and status hierarchies in Dignity than other cultures. Overall, when self-worth is relatively inalienable as in Dignity cultures, insults, although unpleasant, do not much affect social standing.

However, this logic does not hold in Honor cultures. Insults take on special importance in Honor cultures, because they attack people's status in the social hierarchy and their sense of worth in the society. Honor norms require that an honorable person (i.e., ideal person in an Honor culture) will not tolerate even small insults and furthermore, respond aggressively to maintain his status. Aggression in response to an insult is historically justified in Honor cultures because toleration of insults to self or family signaled that the person could be taken advantage of. Maintaining one's social standing was particularly important in the fragile herding economies in which Honor cultures evolved, because of the absence of strong states that could protect individuals (Cohen et al., 1996).

Finally in Face cultures, insults should be experienced as more unpleasant than in Dignity cultures due to self-worth being externally conferred. Thus, people in Face cultures should be more sensitive to insults than people in Dignity cultures, as insults threaten people's social standing. However, the central value of harmony in Face cultures is associated with a norm of preserving face. This leads to three implications of insult in Face cultures. First, insults should be less frequent than in Honor cultures as the social hierarchy is stable and less challenged, and people are very hesitant to break harmony by insulting others. Second, because of the norm of harmony people in Face cultures may tolerate insults to preserve harmony – at least up to a point without erupting aggression. Finally, we argue that the strong and stable hierarchical structure of Face societies expects insulted individuals to defer to the hierarchy and wait for the higher status others, such as the rulers or the elderly to punish the insulters.

Confrontation Style

Each of the three cultural prototypes discussed endorses a different style of confrontation for managing conflicts. In particular, we argue that each prototype may enact rational (versus emotional) and direct (versus indirect) styles of confrontation differently.

Dignity culture norms encourage *rational* and calculated handling of conflict and discourage strong emotional reactions. Western Dignity cultures have many maxims that discourage reliance on emotions when making important decisions and approve of thoughtful and rational acts, for example, "look before you leap" and "think before you act" (Lieberman, 2000). Hirschman (1970) also argues that in American culture – which is the hallmark of Dignity cultures in our framework – a unique paradigm of problem-solving was institutionalized because American settlers often had the *neat* option of *exiting* from conflict and moving further west in the continent. They thus preferred it over the *messiness and heartbreak of voicing* conflict, and this preference persisted throughout their national history. Therefore instead of engaging in emotional battles to dominate the counterpart (as was frequently the case in Honor cultures), or avoiding conflict to preserve harmony (as was frequently the case in Face cultures), people in Dignity cultures followed rational self-interest either by resolving conflict directly and unemotionally based on rights or interests (Ury et al., 1988) or by exiting. "Why raise your voice in contradiction and get yourself into trouble as long as you can always remove yourself entirely from any given environment should it become too unpleasant?" (Hirschman, 1970, p. 108). In general, Dignity cultures acknowledge the norm of self-interest (Miller, 1999; Tocqueville, 2010/1840) and tend to have well developed institutional structures, for example, rules of law, and conflict management systems, negotiation, mediation, court or arbitration to channel aggression and conflict into a logical (*rational*), yet *direct* confrontation to resolve conflicts.

Face cultures do not acknowledge the norm of self-interest to the same extent as Dignity culture. Face cultures address conflict management by deferring to the penultimate goal of preserving *harmony*. In these cultures high population density has historically obligated people to collaborate to work together. Norms of saving each other's face, following formalities, avoiding direct confrontation of conflict and deferring to authority are all highly important for preserving harmony in Face cultures (Oetzel and Ting-Toomey, 2003; Sanchez-Burks and Mor Barak, 2004; Tjosvold et al., 2004). Because overt conflict or aggression disrupt harmony, individuals who believe they have been transgressed against are still expected to avoid direct retaliation and address the conflict to higher status others. Furthermore, the norm to suppress negative emotions over openly expressing them (Matsumoto et al., 1998) is consistent with the norm for harmony preservation, although emotional appeals that indirectly remind counterparts of their status and responsibilities in the social order are common (Brett and Gelfand, 2006). Overall some famous Face cultures' maxims discourage direct and emotional confrontation that jeopardizes harmony and approve of indirect handling of conflict, for example "tooth for a tooth, lose-lose" (Chinese proverb) and "You can avoid even a murder if you try to be patient three times" (Korean proverb).

Finally in Honor cultures, direct and emotional confrontation is much more normative than in Dignity and Face cultures. Conflicts are easily viewed in these cultures as challenges to status and reputation.

The dynamic and competitive social environments of Honor cultures encourage individuals to act assertively and even aggressively in the face of conflict – to maintain self-worth and gain honor. There are famous maxims in Honor cultures of Middle East, such as Arab and Persian cultures, that appreciate and approve of direct confrontation and response to conflict to restore honor, for example, "One who throws a clod at you should be rewarded with a stone" (Iranian proverb). In a famous poem, Hafiz (fourteenth century), the most popular poet in Persian literature, describes the creation of man as God's *honorable* response to angels. When God showed a glimpse of His face to angels and found them not mature enough to experience love, He was offended and thus created man (Adam) from those flames of anger/love so that the man can appreciate His beauty appropriately. There is substantial research that people in Honor cultures respond to insult emotionally, aggressively, defensively and directly (Beersma et al., 2003; Bourdieu, 1977; Cohen et al., 1996; Ijzerman et al., 2007; Rodriguez Mosquera et al., 2002a; 2002b). As we will argue later, an actual insult does not necessarily precede such emotional responses and people in Honor cultures may easily perceive insult out of the ambiguous cues in a conflict situation.

However honor is not only manifested in low tolerance for insult or for being cheated, but also in high standards for a reputation for being a trustworthy (honorable) person who keeps his word and can be counted on to pay his debts, in the absence of a state that forces him to do so (Miller, 1993). The implication of this aspect of honor for conflict management will be discussed in the next section on conciliation, warmth and hospitality.

Conciliation, Warmth and Hospitality

The flipside of overt confrontation and aggression is warmth, hospitality, and conciliation. Each culture has different norms for conciliation and the expression of interpersonal warmth and hospitality based on how self-worth is defined, maintained, and can be enhanced by pursuing such behaviors.

Warmth and reconciliation can be explained in Dignity cultures by the ideology of independence, rationality and protecting self-interest. As discussed earlier, the egalitarian and market-based economy of Dignity cultures – which has origins in individual's independent goals and is supported by an effective system of law – makes the goal of preserving dignity both moral and rational. Warmth and conciliation in Dignity cultures tends to be expressed in "swift" interpersonal trust: others deserve to be trusted until they prove otherwise (Dirks et al., 2009; Meyerson et al.,

1996; Weber et al., 2005), and in the frequent expression of positive emotions (Butler et al., 2007; Uchida and Kitayama, 2009). Swift trust and expressions of positive emotions and warmth are consistent with Western rationality (Tocqueville, 2010/1840), self-interest (Miller, 1999), and the cooperative motive (Messick and McClintock, 1968; Offerman et al., 1996) as they serve to enhance the welfare of others so long as doing so does not hurt one's own welfare. Even prosocial or altruistic moves (e.g., charity) may be framed as contributing to one's self-interest (e.g., receiving tax deductions) and thus *rational* in American culture (Miller, 1999). Therefore in Dignity cultures it is normative to pursue trust, warmth, conciliation, or hospitality to the extent that doing so is consistent with the norm of self-interest. Consequently, self-sacrifice or a purely altruistic act to increase the welfare of others, regardless of one's own welfare (see Offerman et al., 1996) is less normative in Dignity cultures than in Face or Honor cultures. Instead, people in Dignity cultures rely on positive reciprocity – often in the form of short-run tit-for-tat exchanges – both because it is morally correct (i.e., signal integrity and trustworthiness) and because it is rational (i.e., it pursues one's self-interest) (Tocqueville, 2010/1840). Reconciliation after disputes is also justified by the same ideology of rationality and problem-solving to benefit both sides of the conflict.

Obeying hierarchy, loyalty to institutions, and showing humility to others are three of the mechanisms that help to reconcile differences in Face cultures when interests conflict (Kim and Cohen, 2010; Leung and Cohen, 2011). In Face cultures, parties are expected to control their negative emotions and follow the directives of higher status others to conciliate and avoid escalating the conflict. Despite the normative value of emotional control in Face cultures, interpersonal and emotional concerns are found to be more important in work contexts in Face cultures than in Dignity cultures (Sanchez-Burks et al., 2008). Positive emotions are expressed, though not as commonly and as intensely as in Dignity cultures, with the goal of enhancing relationships (Lin and Yamaguchi, 2011), whereas negative emotions, in particular anger, are suppressed to avoid jeopardizing harmony (Matsumoto et al., 1998). Furthermore, self-sacrifice and altruism are justified as a fulfillment of duty to benefit society, a group, or other important collectives. In Face cultures, the five bounds of Confucian ideology emphasize that harmonious relationships extend beyond family or kinship, and the duties to develop and support those relationships spread to the entire society (Axel, 1995). In other words the prototypical family structure, with its unequal hierarchical relationships, is applied to social organizations in general; people accept or tolerate hierarchical and unequal relationships – that are common inside family – in the rest of society as well (Hofstede and Bond, 1988).

In contrast in Honor cultures, people are supposed to limit warmth and hospitality toward a selected group of others (particularly family, kin, and close friends), not toward society in general, and also limit tolerance for unequal hierarchy to such groups. Evidence for these Honor culture values are found in a survey of cultural values of middle managers in 61 countries across all six continents. For example Turkish and Iranian managers ranked 42nd and 48th respectively on *societal collectivism* (i.e., the degree to which organizational and societal institutional practices encourage and reward collective distribution of resources and collective action), whereas they ranked 4th and 3rd, respectively on *in-group collectivism* (i.e., the degree to which individuals express pride, loyalty, and cohesiveness in their organizations or families) (Dastmalchian et al., 2001; Fikret Pasa et al., 2001; Gelfand et al., 2004). On the contrary, managers from Face cultures of South Korea and Japan ranked very high, respectively 2nd and 3rd, on *societal collectivism*, but not high on *in-group collectivism*, respectively 23rd and 44th (Gelfand et al., 2004).

To understand such differences, we may need to remember the basic elements of honor. Honor manifests not only in a reputation for toughness (Cohen and Nisbett, 1997; Nisbett and Cohen, 1996), but also as in trustworthiness and maintaining one's word (Miller, 1993) and warmth, hospitality, and strong family and friendship ties (Nisbett and Cohen, 1996; Pitt-Rivers, 1968; Rodriguez Mosquera et al., 2008; Triandis, 1989). An *honorable* person gains others' respect by not tolerating being cheated or affronted; however, at the same time the honorable person keeps promises and can be counted on to pay back debts even in the absence of supervision of a strong state. An honorable person may even go beyond immediate expectations by building a reputation for noticeable warmth and hospitality toward others who are not a threat to his status or position. The importance of such a reputation for warmth and hospitality in Honor cultures justifies the normative plausibility of altruistic behaviors and self-sacrifice – which may seem *irrational* at first glance – but is consistent with a longer-term rationality. These strong norms for warmth and hospitality in Honor cultures may also serve to stop conflicts from surfacing or spiraling out of control (Nisbett and Cohen, 1996). Reconciliation after disputes is also likely in Honor cultures if the norms of honorable warmth, hospitality, and strong family or friendships can be promoted in the process of settlement. For example, elders or other higher status people can facilitate the process of reconciliation by persuading disputants that their honor will be restored and enhanced if they agree to forgive and reconcile (Pely, 2011). Finally when the relational context is strong at the first place, that is, when people have conflict of interests with close friends or family members, strong face-saving concerns (similar to Face cultures) may stop them from surfacing their interests, and cause them to accommodate the interests of the other party by sacrificing their own interests (Aslani et al., 2011).

DIGNITY, FACE, AND HONOR CULTURE DIFFERENCES IN NEGOTIATORS' STRATEGIES AND OUTCOMES

In this section, we introduce the research and theorizing concerning negotiation strategy and outcomes and then propose differences in strategy and outcomes associated with Dignity, Face and Honor cultures. We first discuss two major categories of negotiation strategy examined in previous research, namely information sharing, and substantiation and offers. In the subsequent sections we discuss Dignity, Face and Honor cultural differences in the frequency of use and the effectiveness of those strategies and the potential explanations for these differences in terms of trust, mindset, and negative emotional expression.

Negotiation Strategy

A negotiation strategy is a set of goal-driven behaviors used, consciously or unconsciously, by negotiators (Weingart et al., 1990). Research has identified two major strategic goals for negotiation, variously called integrative and distributive, value creation and value claiming, and the behaviors that negotiators use when pursuing those goals (Weingart et al., 1990). A recent conceptualization discusses these strategies in behavioral terms, namely "Question and Answers", and "Offers and Substantiations" (Teucher et al., 2011). In this section we rely on those concepts to explain cultural differences in negotiation strategies and outcomes.

The integrative goal and associated strategy correspond roughly to direct information-sharing and generally involve a process of asking questions and providing answers (Kimmel et al., 1980; Pruitt and Lewis, 1975; Weingart et al., 1990). Following Gunia and colleagues we label this strategy Q&A (Question and Answers). Questions are interrogative statements to elicit information-sharing, and Answers connote information-sharing about preferences, priorities and interests (Weingart et al., 2007; also Adair and Loewenstein, Chapter 12 this volume). This information provides insight for one party into the counterpart's interests, preferences, and priorities – which negotiators can then use to make proposals the create value (Teucher et al., 2011). The distributive or value-claiming strategy focuses on offers and arguments (Pruitt, 1981; Weingart et al., 1990).

Following Gunia and colleagues we label this strategy S&O (Substantiation and Offers). Substantiation refers to all forms of justification, rational and emotional appeals, arguments, and threats to support a party's own position and reject the other party's position (Olekalns and Smith, 2000). The goal of substantiation is to motivate the counterpart to make concessions and accept the focal party's demands. Commonly, parties use substantiation in combination with their own offers, justifying their positions while translating those positions into terms on the negotiable issues (Weingart et al., 2007). Negotiators who focus on S&O frequently are less likely to maximize joint gains (Olekalns and Smith, 2000; Weingart et al., 2007).

Cultural Factors that Influence Negotiation Strategy and Outcomes

Based on recent research and theorizing we suggest that three factors – which are influenced by culture – may affect the use of Q&A versus S&O strategy in negotiation: trust, mindset, and expression of negative emotions. Trust is one party's willingness to accept vulnerability based upon favorable expectations of the other party's behavior (Mayer et al., 1995). Mindset refers to a holistic versus analytical (also called linear) cognitive approach to reasoning. Finally negative emotional expression is the strategic or genuine communication of negative affect, especially emotions such as anger, disappointment, and frustration, in social interactions.

Trust is critical in negotiation because negotiators who trust and share information with a counterpart are vulnerable to the actions of their counterpart who can exploit the information that a negotiator shares (Butler, 1999; also Lewicki and Polin, Chapter 7 this volume). Trusting negotiators accept this vulnerability at least initially, presuming that their counterparts will use shared information in a mutually-beneficial way, and reciprocate (Butler, 1999; Gunia et al., 2011). Low-trust negotiators, fearing that their counterparts will take advantage of them, are less likely to engage in reciprocal Q&A in order to reduce vulnerability (Butler, 1999). For low-trust negotiators, engaging in Q&A may seem as an irrational invitation to take advantage of them, because Q&A discloses information about their interests and priorities (Pruitt, 1981; Pruitt and Lewis, 1977; Walton and McKersie, 1965; Weingart et al., 2007). Instead, they rely on S&O to pursue their own gains. Offers give information directly about positions and only indirectly about interests and priorities (Adair and Brett, 2005) which may be why the S&O strategy is heavily utilized by low trust negotiators (Gunia et al., 2011).

A mindset is a systematic approach to attention and reasoning. Two fundamentally different types of mindset have been identified in cultural psychology: holistic and analytic (also called linear) (Nisbett et al., 2001).

People with a holistic mindset tend to focus their attention on the relationships between focal objects and their contexts (Hansen, 1983). To explain and predict the behavior of an object in its context, they use associative and dialectical reasoning. For example, they rely on metaphors and stories to cue associations, and they engage in dialectical analysis. Dialecticism recognizes the legitimacy of contradictory perspectives and searches for means of transcending contradictions (Nisbett and Miyamoto, 2005). In contrast, people with an analytic mindset primarily pay attention to the object and its attributes, as opposed to its surrounding context (Hansen, 1983). Analytic thinkers assign objects to categories based on the object's attributes and use formal logic and rules to explain and predict the object's behavior. Analytic reasoning is generally intolerant of contradictions because contradictions are inconsistent with the linear nature of formal logic. Thus, faced with contradictions, analytic thinkers prefer choosing one perspective over another (Nisbett et al., 2001).

Recent conceptual theorizing proposes holistic versus analytic mindset as a general, theoretical explanation for cultural differences in the use of negotiation strategy (Teucher et al., 2011). These scholars suggest that when utilizing a holistic mindset negotiators focus their attention on the relationships between issues, and in doing so may transform the information contained in patterns of S&O into the insights necessary for realizing joint gains (Brett, 2007; Teucher et al., 2011). In contrast, negotiators with the linear/analytic mindset need to detect possible tradeoffs from direct information exchanged via Q&A. These negotiators should be more comfortable moving sequentially through a set of issues to discover fundamental interests rather than making indirect inferences from surface-level positions (Teucher et al., 2011). Thus, according to this theorizing S&O strategy should be compatible with a holistic mindset and Q&A strategy should be compatible with an analytic mindset.

There are major cultural differences in expressing negative emotions in general, and anger in particular, at negotiations. Emotional expression refers to the positive or negative affect conveyed in interpersonal interactions. Cultural psychology documents that different cultural rules make it relatively normative to express or even exaggerate emotional expressions in Western, individualistic cultures, but to de-amplify or suppress emotional expressions in East Asian, collectivistic cultures (Matsumoto et al., 1998; Matsumoto et al., 2008; Matsumoto et al., 2005; Yuki et al., 2007). Furthermore, because anger is particularly confrontational and socially disengaging, it threatens the East Asian emphasis on social harmony and thus should be suppressed (Adam et al., 2010; Kitayama et al., 2006).

In negotiation, emotional expression can be spontaneous, but it can also be strategic (Barry et al., 2004; Thompson et al., 1999), that is, intentionally expressed by a focal negotiator to achieve a desired outcome. For example, negotiators in a positive mood may achieve more in integrative and distributive negotiations than negotiators in neutral or bad moods, because they are more trusting and engage in less S&O and more Q&A (Carnevale and Isen, 1986; Kopelman et al., 2006; Maddux et al., 2008).

The empirical research studying the impact of negative emotional expression in negotiation presents a less consistent picture than the positive emotion research (also Van Kleef and Sinaceur, Chapter 5 this volume). It appears that the effect of the expression of anger depends on the context of the negotiation. For example, in the paradigm of research that Van Kleef and colleagues have employed, that is, a computer simulated, single issue, one-time, deal making negotiation, expressing anger typically elicited larger concessions and more cooperative responses from negotiation counterparts than not expressing an emotion or expressing other emotions, such as happiness or regret (Sinaceur and Tiedens, 2006; Sinaceur et al., 2011; Van Kleef et al., 2004a; 2004b; Van Kleef et al., 2006). However, when East Asian participants engaged in this research paradigm, expressions of anger backfired and elicited smaller concessions (Adam et al., 2010; Sinaceur and Tiedens, 2006; Steinel et al., 2008). Further, anger can backfire and hurt joint gains, as evidenced in a study of disputes between eBay buyers and sellers, when expressions of anger were reciprocated and predicted impasse (Friedman et al., 2004). However it is also possible that anger facilitates more effort for creating value. In a study of value creation in dyads where power was unequally distributed, expressing anger not only helped value-claiming, but also it facilitated value creation especially when the more powerful negotiator was angry (Overbeck et al., 2010).

We propose that in general the expression of negative emotions in negotiations with integrative potential will tip negotiation strategy toward reliance on S&O and generate poor insight and low joint gains, with some cultural differences, to be discussed in subsequent sections. We argue that when faced with an angry or threatening counterpart, a negotiator who was ready to use Q&A, because of a priori trust, will largely abandon those information sharing behaviors and use S&O in order to block the counterpart's power moves and protect his/her own interests. Expression of anger in negotiation cues the counterpart's affective reactions as well as inferential processes (Van Kleef and De Dreu, 2010). The perceiver may experience negative affective reactions (e.g., the desire to retaliate) that lead to smaller concessions (Adam et al., 2010) or make inferences (e.g., the counterpart is tough and there is a real threat of an impasse) that lead to larger concessions (Sinaceur and Tiedens, 2006; Van Kleef et al., 2004a).

Table 10.2 *Cultural factors that influence negotiation strategy*

Category	Dignity	Face	Honor
Trust	High	Low	Low
Mindset	Analytic/Linear	Holistic	Moderately linear
Negative Emotions	Suppress	Suppress*	Express
Dominant Strategy	Q&A	Cold S&O	Hot S&O

Note: * We propose that, in general, negotiators from Face cultures use S&O (including emotional appeals such as reminding counterparts of their duties, or asking them for sympathy) frequently; however, they do not express negative emotions as frequently as those from Honor cultures.

Although we noted above the substantial evidence supporting Van Kleef and colleagues' conclusion within the context of his paradigm, we argue that in a negotiation that provides the potential of joint gains via information sharing, the counterpart's expression of negative emotions like anger reduces trust, thus the willingness to engage in Q&A, and increases reliance on defensive S&O. In addition, since negative emotional expression in negotiation is typically reciprocated, a focus on negative emotion in negotiation may crowd out the cognitive effort (Pinkley and Northcraft, 1994) required to draw inferences from S&O and cause poor insight and low joint gains.

Table 10.2 summarizes how these three factors play out in Dignity, Face, and Honor cultures. We elaborate on each culture in the subsequent sections.

Negotiation Strategy and Outcomes in Dignity Cultures

In Dignity cultures, trust tends to be high, mindset tends to be analytic, and rationality tends to be favored over emotionality which suggests negotiators control their negative emotions. This profile fits with the Q&A strategy, where negotiators exchange information early in the negotiation, try to generate insight into each other's priorities and interests, and then use this insight to exchange offers and obtain joint gains.

Broadly speaking, people in Dignity cultures (e.g., North Americans, Western Europeans) tend to make the "swift trust" assumption: others deserve to be trusted until they prove otherwise (Dirks et al., 2009; Meyerson et al., 1996; Weber et al., 2005). The interpersonal trust characteristic of Dignity cultures should facilitate sharing information about interests and priorities via the Q&A strategy. The analytic mindset characteristic of these cultures (Nisbett et al., 2001) should help to make good use of information about the attributes of issues, including own and counterpart's interests and priorities. Finally, the focus on rationality, as opposed to emotionality, in these cultures (Sanchez-Burks, 2002) should also facilitate the utilization of information about interests and priorities to gain insight and negotiate joint gains.

There are several empirical studies supporting the conclusion that Q&A is supported by trust, leads to joint gains via insight, and is the dominant negotiation strategy in Dignity cultures compared to Face cultures (Adair and Brett, 2005; Adair et al., 2001) or Honor cultures (Aslani et al., 2011; Gunia et al., 2011; Ramirez-Marin et al., 2012). There is also evidence from two rather different studies that when Dignity culture negotiators fail to use Q&A they frequently are unable to reach agreements that capture tradeoffs and joint gains. Adair et al. (2007) showed that when American negotiators failed to use Q&A early in their negotiations their joint gains were low. Ramirez-Marin et al. (2012) also showed that when Americans were negotiating intra-culturally with other Americans, they used Q&A, but when negotiating inter-culturally with Spanish negotiators (in the Spanish language), they switched to S&O (which was dominant in Spanish intra-cultural negotiations), and not only failed to realize joint gains but also were claimed upon.

Negotiation Strategy and Outcomes in Face Cultures

In Face cultures, trust tends to be low; mindset is holistic and negative emotions are suppressed. This profile fits with the S&O strategy, where negotiators make and substantiate offers from the outset of the negotiation, may draw inferences from patterns of offers and substantiation, and use that insight to identify joint gains.

Interpersonal trust appears to be low in Face cultures perhaps because historically, it was not needed in everyday, social relationships as much as in Dignity cultures. Social interaction in Face cultures is governed by norms that are provided by social institutions, like religion, family, community or the state. People's conformity to those norms is monitored and, if necessary, managed by institutional sanctioning (see Takahashi et al., 2008; Yamagishi et al., 1998; Yamagishi and Yamagishi, 1994). Yamagishi and colleagues suggests that the presence of institutional monitoring and sanctioning reduces the society's need for interpersonal trust by affording a reliable external guarantor of behavior. So long as institutional monitoring is in place, they argue, there is little need to rely on interpersonal trust.

The problem of course is that even in Dignity cultures, where interpersonal trust is the lubricant of social interaction, norms and sanctions only weakly govern behavior in negotiations (e.g., Brett, 2007; Fisher and Ury,

1981; Robinson et al., 2000). For example, norms about deception do not keep negotiators from bluffing about their bottom line, and the sanctions commonly associated with these norms rarely apply in negotiation (Robinson et al., 2000). Overall Yamagishi and colleagues' comparative cultural research on behavior in trust games shows that the Japanese and Chinese (Face cultures) trust less than Americans (see Kiyonari et al., 2007; Kiyonari et al., 2006). We argue that because trust is low in Face cultures and institutional monitoring and sanctioning is low in the negotiation context, Face culture negotiators are likely to rely heavily on S&O. Past research supports this proposition (Adair et al., 2004; Adair et al., 2001; Brett, 2007).

Empirical research contrasting negotiators from Dignity and Face cultures documents major differences in the use of negotiation strategy and outcomes, consistent with the proposition that Face cultures tend to have low trust and holistic mindset compared to Dignity cultures (high trust and analytic mindset). For negotiators from Japan, Hong Kong, and Thailand the dominant strategy over the course of the negotiation was S&O, and still they could generate the same level of insight and joint gains as negotiators from Germany, Sweden, and the U.S who dominantly use Q&A (Adair et al., 2001; Brett, 2007; Brett and Okumura, 1998). Furthermore, Japanese negotiators who make offers early in the negotiation are more likely to reach high joint gains than those who delay making offers (Adair et al., 2007) which provides further evidence that negotiators from Face cultures can use holistic reasoning to infer priorities and preferences from the pattern of offers in the negotiation. The holistic mindset that is dominant in Face cultures may lead negotiators to view substantiation and offers as a whole, systemic source of information in negotiation.

There is a fascinating conundrum concerning the role of negative emotional expression in Face cultures. Negative emotions are more suppressed in Face cultures than in Dignity cultures (Matsumoto et al., 1998; Matsumoto et al., 2008; Matsumoto et al., 2005; Yuki et al., 2007) perhaps because they may seem too confrontational and socially disengaging and thus threaten the emphasis on social harmony in Face cultures (Adam et al., 2010; Kitayama et al., 2006). Yet, the negotiation research suggests that Face culture negotiators rely heavily on substantiation and offers and still can negotiate joint gains at the same level as Dignity culture negotiators using Q&A (Adair and Brett, 2005; Adair et al., 2001).

We argue that such substantiation efforts do not necessarily distract Face culture negotiators from obtaining insights so long as they do not overtly express negative emotions. There is evidence that the positive effects of the expression of anger for concession making – which is common in Dignity cultures – do not hold in Face cultures. Because the expression of negative emotions is not normative in Face cultures, expressions of anger does not elicit concessions as much as it does in Dignity cultures (Adam et al., 2010). This implies that Face culture negotiators may still obtain insight despite engaging in S&O without getting intimidated, insulted, or distracted as much as Dignity or Honor culture negotiators do. Furthermore, Face culture negotiators not only *express* negative emotions less frequently than those from Dignity or Honor cultures at the negotiation table, but also probably *experience* less negative emotions. Recent data by Gallup (2012), about experiencing negative emotions on daily basis in different countries of the world shows low levels of negative emotional experiences (anger, stress, worry, sadness, and physical pain) among people from Face cultures compared to those from Dignity and Honor cultures. Among 148 countries surveyed, only one country from East or Southeast Asia (Philippines) ranked among the first 70 countries.

Overall, we argue that Face culture negotiators who use S&O to infer information may not experience the same emotional and cognitive reactions to substantiation as Dignity and Honor culture negotiators. However if they engage in expressing and experiencing negative emotions, their ability to generate insight and joint gains from S&O diminishes. The data we have collected in China, but have not yet had the opportunity to publish, shows that Chinese dyads who expressed anger could not reach high joint gains.

Negotiation Strategy and Outcomes in Honor Cultures

Past theory and research in anthropology and cultural psychology as well as recent negotiation research provide insight into negotiation strategy and outcomes in Honor cultures, though the research on Honor cultures is not as abundant as the research on Dignity and Face cultures. Therefore our arguments in this section are more conceptual and less empirical than the arguments on negotiations strategy in Dignity and Face cultures.

Overall, we suggest that trust tends to be low in Honor cultures and expression of strong negative emotions is acceptable at the negotiation table. There is little evidence on the type of mindset (linear or holistic) that people in Honor cultures hold, but we speculate that their mindset should be somewhere in the middle of the continuum from Western analytic to Eastern holistic, though roughly leaning more toward the linear mindset. This profile fits with the S&O strategy, where negotiators make and substantiate offers from the outset of the negotiation, but may easily get involved in heated arguments and thus not draw inferences from patterns of offers and substantiation, which leads to low insight and joint gains.

It seems likely that trust is lower in negotiations in Honor cultures than in Dignity cultures (see Alon and Brett, 2007 for a study on trust in Arabic-speaking Islamic culture). As discussed in the section on the origins of Honor culture, there can be severe economic, social, and self-image costs for appearing weak or being taken advantage of in Honor cultures. By trusting the counterpart a negotiator risks being taken advantage of (Butler, 1999). Thus it seems likely that in the competitive context of negotiations, people from Honor cultures exhibit low trust to avoid the social and/or emotional costs of honor loss. There is some empirical evidence supporting this assertion. For example, a six culture study, comparing people from the U.S., Brazil, China, Turkey, Switzerland, and Oman, found that Arabs (i.e., Omanis) expressed the highest level of *betrayal aversion*, that is, the tendency to avoid extending interpersonal trust (Bohnet et al., 2008). In another study negotiators from the U.S. (Dignity culture) had higher pre-negotiation trust in their counterparts than the negotiators from India (Honor culture) (Gunia et al., 2011). This tendency to extend low trust to others does not contradict the warmth and hospitality common in Honor cultures, as Ali ibn Abi Talib (the first Imam of Shia Muslims and the fourth Caliph of Sunni Muslims) said: "Give all your love, but not all your trust, to your friend" (Majlisi, 1983, Vol. 71).

As a result of low trust, Honor culture negotiators can be expected to rely more on S&O than Q&A. Recent empirical research comparing Qatari with American negotiators (Aslani et al., 2011) and Spanish with American (Ramirez-Marin et al., 2012) negotiators suggests that the Qataris and the Spanish relied more heavily on the S&O strategy than did Americans.

It also seems likely that mindset in Honor cultures will be more linear/analytic than in Face cultures, though perhaps more holistic than in Dignity cultures. Although there is a little research in cognitive or social psychology on the mindset of people in Honor cultures, several key features of the holistic mindset seem to be absent in Honor cultures. For example, using dialectical reasoning – which recognizes the legitimacy of contradictory perspectives and is common in East Asian cultures – is not common in either Middle Eastern or Latin American cultures. Instead, using formal logic and rules to explain and predict objects' behavior has been a fixture of Middle East and India for thousands of years (Gabbay and Woods, 2004). There has been little influence of Confucian thought – which strongly influenced the holistic mindset in East Asian cultures – in Middle Eastern and Latin American cultures. Indeed, just the opposite; both areas of the world were influenced by the ancient Greeks mode of thought. The Middle East (and major parts of India) was conquered by Alexander the Great, was once part of the Hellenistic civilization, and was influenced by Greek logic (O'Leary, 1957; Versteegh, 1977), and

Latin America was heavily influenced by the logic and philosophy of the Catholic Church (Gill, 1998). By this analysis, we do not mean to ignore the impressive independent intellectual and artistic heritage of Islamic culture, which spread throughout the Middle East, North Africa and Spain; yet, we point out that that heritage still appears to be grounded in analytic, not holistic reasoning. Furthermore, recent evidence from experimental research in cognitive psychology suggests that communities founded on farming exhibit greater holistic thinking tendencies than those founded on herding (Uskul et al., 2008a; 2008b) which is consistent with our note that Honor cultures are less Holistic than Face cultures. Finally, although communication in both Middle Eastern and Latin cultures appears to be more contextual than Western European and North American cultures, we are not sure that there is necessarily a one-to-one correspondence between *holistic reasoning* and *high context communication*, and *analytic reasoning* and *low context communication*. Based on definitions (Hall, 1976), communication in low context cultures is relatively explicit, with meaning clearly contained in the words or the surface of a message, whereas in high context cultures, communication is more indirect and implicit, with subtle meaning embedded behind and around the spoken or written words. These two concepts (holistic and high context cultures, linear and low context cultures) correlate strongly in the classic East–West dichotomy. However, it is possible to have a culture that is high context and linear, or low context and holistic. Researchers should avoid conflating these two concepts.

Overall, we expect the mindset in Honor cultures to be roughly in the middle of the continuum between the mindset in Dignity and Face cultures, but leaning more toward the linear mindset. Just as in Table 10.1 where we intentionally described Honor culture as more similar to Face culture on some dimensions and more similar to Dignity culture on others, we suspect that mindset in Honor culture is more likely analytic than holistic.

Relative to people in Dignity and Face cultures those in Honor cultures should display negative emotions more openly (see Ijzerman et al., 2007, for an empirical study contrasting emotional expression in Latin American Honor cultures and U.S. Dignity cultures; also see Bar, 2004 for a discussion on open expression of negative emotions in Iran which is Middle Eastern Honor culture). The goal of some emotional expression may be pragmatic as it declares to the audience that the individual is hurt, insulted, and angry, and that he must be appeased (Bar, 2004). This willingness to display negative emotions in social interactions between members of Honor cultures is consistent with the heavy use of substantiation in negotiations in these cultures (Aslani et al., 2011; Gunia et al., 2011;

Ramirez-Marin et al., 2012). It is also consistent with research showing that, upon perceiving insult, people from Honor cultures experience more intense negative emotions (Beersma et al., 2003), more anger and shame (Rodriguez Mosquera et al., 2002b), become more upset and more physiologically primed for aggression (Cohen et al., 1996) than people from non-Honor cultures. In the recent data reported by Gallup (2012) about experiencing negative emotions on a daily basis in 148 countries, 20 of the first 30 countries in the ranking belonged to either the Middle East or Latin America, the two major clusters of Honor cultures in our framework. Furthermore, if we classify African and Southern European countries in the Honor culture cluster, 27 of the first 30 countries in this ranking will be from Honor cultures.

The tendency to experience negative emotions frequently and take insult personally suggests that even if reasoning were holistic in Honor cultures, Honor culture negotiators can be easily distracted from the cognitive work of making inferences from offers to the emotional work of protecting honor. Indeed, the empirical research contrasting Honor culture Qataris (Aslani et al., 2011), Spanish (Ramirez-Marin et al., 2012), and Indians (Gunia et al., 2011) to Americans shows that in Honor cultures, emotional tactics were used much more frequently and insight about priorities and preferences was significantly lower. As we have seen in research globally when insight is low, the short term economic joint gains are limited. Therefore spending time to develop trust and manage negative emotions – which is important in all cultures – becomes more crucial in Honor cultures so that negotiators can exchange information more openly and focus their attention on the cognitive work necessary for creating joint gains.

FUTURE DIRECTIONS

In this chapter we discussed three major cultural prototypes of Dignity, Face, and Honor and the implications of this framework for understanding negotiators' strategy and outcomes. We do not mean to suggest that our three-culture model covers all of the cultural prototypes in the world. We are aware that some geographic areas in the world are not easily classified within this model. However, this provides an opportunity for future research to examine current cultural norms and values and historical background of regions of the world and national cultures for the purpose of understanding modes of social interaction. For example, future research may show that certain logics of Honor culture are salient in southern African countries as well as the northern African ones. In order to extend and enrich this categorization, we may need to understand the subtle yet important differences among cultures within each prototype, such as different Face cultures (see Lee et al., 2012) or different Honor cultures.

For example, there is a wide geographic variation among Honor cultures and it would be naïve to equate cultures as different as those in the Middle East and those in Latin America even though they share certain logics of honor. In addition to the generic notion of honor as *the reputation for toughness or not being taken advantage of by others*, at least four other dimensions have been identified for honor (Rodriguez Mosquera et al., 2002b): (1) *social interdependence* (generosity, honesty, warmth, and hospitality), (2) *family honor* (caring for social evaluations of one's family and the defense of one's family's name and reputation), (3) *masculine honor* (being concerned with one's family's well-being, the maintenance of authority over one's family, and virility), and (4) *feminine honor* (modesty in behavior and dressing, a sense of shame in women's social relations with men, and decorum in dress, and sexual shame). Considering the wide geographic variation in Honor cultures, it is likely that these four dimensions will receive different weights in different Honor cultures and thus have different implications for negotiations in different cultures.

Future research can also develop scales to measure dignity, face, and honor cultural values and norms. Such an empirical measure would allow researchers to examine the effects of different dignity, face, and honor dimensions in more detail, distinguish between different nations or sub-prototypes, and certainly go above and beyond the classic individualism/collectivism model. In fact recent research suggests that national borders are strong factors in clustering cultural values and norms (Minkov and Hofstede, 2012) and thus differences among nations within each cultural prototype demands more attention from researchers. This approach would also allow us to examine more closely how different facets of each cultural prototype interact with the negotiation context (e.g., transactional versus disputes, business versus political, personal versus not personal, solo versus group).

According to our model on the impact of three cultural factors (trust, mindset, and emotional expression) on negotiations strategies and outcomes, Honor culture negotiators are most likely to fall prey to distributive negotiation traps and leaving value on the table. This may be consistent with the cliché that some of most complicated and escalated conflicts in the world are now happening in the Middle East – the hallmark of Honor cultures.[4] However, researchers should be aware that every culture, society, and civilization that has managed to sustain itself throughout history and especially to achieve major successes must have developed effective ways to resolve conflicts and move on. (See Pely, 2011, for examples of how reconciliation could happen and how disputants' lost honor could be restored after severe honor-related conflicts happened in Arab communities in Israel.) Understanding differences between the conflict management logics of honor with those of dignity and face (Table 10.1) can be a first step in designing effective conflict management mechanisms in these cultures. For example, the strong norms for hospitality and warmth, along with the pessimism toward strangers and low trust suggest that extra time and effort should be allocated for building trusting relationships when one or both parties at the negotiation table are from Honor cultures. After building such relationships, negotiators should be willing to exchange information more openly and use their mindset, whether linear or holistic to obtain insight and joint gains.

In general, the Honor norms for warmth, hospitality, and strong family ties are among the most understudied areas of conflict research. Most of the research in cultural psychology on Honor cultures has focused squarely on reaction to insults in aggressive behaviors and strong emotions. However warmth and hospitality can also have major implications for conflict management and so demands researchers' attention. For example, whereas high levels of emotionality in Honor culture can work as a threat to making inferences and obtaining insight, it can also act to lubricate the contentious environment of negotiations with small bargaining zones and help negotiators in reaching win-win deals (see Harinck et al., in press, for "the good news about Honor culture").

Another important area for future research is the implication of Dignity, Face and Honor cultures for intercultural negotiations. When negotiators from different cultural prototypes come to the table, they do not necessarily adhere to their intra-cultural negotiation styles and may change their negotiation behavior and perceptions depending on the negotiation context (Adair et al., 2009). Studying dominant strategies and outcomes in intercultural negotiations between Dignity-Face, Dignity-Honor, and Face-Honor dyads is a fascinating area for future research. Considering the rapid growth of transactions in the global economy and the emergence of new economic and political powers such as China, India, Brazil, and Turkey, research in this area can have very important implications for both business and politics.

Finally, from the educational research perspective, negotiation pedagogy – which was basically founded on Western principles and practices of negotiations – can benefit much from understanding conflict management styles of people in other cultures. We have already learned from past research on negotiation styles of people in Face cultures that in environments of low trust, exchanging offers and substantiations, instead of directly exchanging information about priorities and preferences, may help negotiators to obtain insights. Even if a negotiator does not have a holistic mindset, s/he can draw inferences from patterns of offers received from a counterpart. Along the same line, researchers and teachers of negotiation can learn much from the conflict management styles of people in Face and Honor cultures to improve negotiation training.

SUMMARY AND CONCLUSION

Current theory and research in cultural psychology distinguish three different types of cultures: Dignity, Face, and Honor, as opposed to the dichotomy of independent/interdependent or West/East that has dominated cultural analysis for the last 25 years. These three cultural types provide a strong basis for reorganizing our thinking about culture, negotiation strategy and joint gains. In this chapter we discussed the historical and environmental origins of these cultures and the psychological concepts that shape their conflict management logics. We have proposed three cultural factors: trust, mindset, and emotional expression that vary between Dignity, Face, and Honor cultures and argued that these cultural factors provide a theoretical explanation for the pattern of current negotiation research findings contrasting negotiations in North America and Western Europe, East Asia, and the Middle East and Latin America.

Overall, we suggest that negotiators in Dignity cultures tend to have high trust, use an analytic mindset, and rely on rationality over emotion in negotiations. This pattern of cultural influences is consistent with the Q&A negotiation strategy, accurate insight and high joint gains. We also suggest that negotiators in Face cultures tend to have low trust at least in the beginning of negotiations, use a holistic mindset, and generally suppress negative emotions in negotiations. This pattern of cultural influences can be consistent with the S&O strategy, yet accurate insight and high joint gains may depend on how emotions are managed. Finally we suggest that negotiators in Honor cultures tend to have low trust in the beginning of negotiations, use a relatively linear mindset, and express negative emotions in negotiations. This pattern of cultural influences is consistent with the S&O negotiation strategy, and creates a challenging environment for obtaining insight and joint gains compared to Dignity and Face cultures. Therefore it is crucial to spend time to develop trust and manage negative emotions so that negotiators can exchange information more openly and focus their attention on creating joint gains instead of getting trapped in zero-sum honor contests. Implications of this framework for understanding past research on culture and negotiations as well some avenues for future research were discussed.

NOTES

1. Pareto optimality and joint gains are not synonymous. A Pareto optimal decision, a negotiated outcome from which one party cannot improve the outcome for itself without hurting the outcome for the other, does not necessarily optimize joint gains. However, joint gains outcomes are Pareto optimal and the strategy and insight that is needed to generate Pareto optimal outcomes are the same that are needed to generate joint gains. For the purpose of this chapter, we use the more general terms joint gains.
2. Of course, not all value can or should be quantified. For a review of subjective value in negotiations see Curhan et al. (2006).
3. This is similar to the notion of having strong BATNA (Best Alternative To a Negotiated Agreement) in negotiation literature.
4. In defining and elaborating on the meaning of the term honor, Nisbett and Cohen (1996) argue that Honor is well captured by ethnographer David Mandelbaum's characterization of the Arabic and Persian word for honor, "izzat".

REFERENCES

Adair, W.L. and Brett, J.M. (2005). The negotiation dance: Time, culture, and behavioral sequences in negotiation. *Organization Science*, 16(1), 33–51.
Adair, W.L., Okumura, T., and Brett, J.M. (2001). Negotiation behavior when cultures collide: The United States and Japan. *Journal of Applied Psychology*, 86(3), 371.
Adair, W.L., Taylor, M.S., and Tinsley, C.H. (2009). Starting out on the right foot: Negotiation schemas when cultures collide. *Negotiation and Conflict Management Research*, 2(2), 138–163.
Adair, W.L., Weingart, L., and Brett, J. (2007). The timing and function of offers in US and Japanese negotiations. *Journal of Applied Psychology*, 92(4), 1056.
Adair, W.L., Brett, J., Lempereur, A., Okumura, T., Shikhirev, P., Tinsley, C., and Lytle, A. (2004). Culture and negotiation strategy. *Negotiation Journal*, 20(1), 87–111.
Adam, H., Shirako, A., and Maddux, W.W. (2010). Cultural variance in the interpersonal effects of anger in negotiations. *Psychological Science*, 21(6), 882–889.
Alon, I. and Brett, J.M. (2007). Perceptions of time and their impact on negotiations in the Arabic-speaking Islamic world. *Negotiation Journal*, 23(1), 55–73.
Aslani, S., Brett, J.M., Ramirez-Marin, J.Y., Tinsley, C.H., and Weingart, L.R. (2011). Implications of honor and dignity culture for negotiations: A comparative study of Middle Easterners and Americans, *24th Annual International Association for Conflict Management Conference*. Istanbul, Turkey.
Axel, M. (1995). Toward an analysis of Japanese-style management: A psycho-cultural and socio-historical approach. *Management International Review*, 35, 57–73.
Ayers, E. (1984). *Vengeance and justice*. New York, NY: Oxford.
Bar, S. (2004). Iran: Cultural values, self images and negotiation behavior. *Institute for Policy and Strategy, The Lauder School of Government, Diplomacy and Strategy IDC, Herzliya, Israel*.
Barry, B., Fulmer, I.S., and Van Kleef, G.A. (2004). I laughed, I cried, I settled: The role of emotion in negotiation. In M.J. Gelfand and J.M. Brett (eds), *Handbook of culture and negotiation*. Palo Alto, CA: Stanford University Press.
Beersma, B., Harinck, F., and Gerts, M.J.J. (2003). Bound in honor: How honor values and insults affect the experience and management of conflicts. *International Journal of Conflict Management*, 14(2), 75–94.
Bies, R.J. and Moag, J.S. (1986). Interactional justice: Communication criteria of fairness. *Research on negotiation in organizations*, 1(1), 43–55.
Bohnet, I., Greig, F., Herrmann, B., and Zeckhauser, R. (2008). Betrayal aversion: Evidence

from Brazil, China, Oman, Switzerland, Turkey, and the United States. *The American Economic Review*, 98, 294–310.

Bourdieu, P. (1977). *Outline of a theory of practice*. Cambridge, UK: Cambridge University Press.

Brett, J.M. (2007). *Negotiating globally: How to negotiate deals, resolve disputes, and make decisions across cultural boundaries* (2nd edn). San Francisco, CA: Jossey-Bass.

Brett, J.M. and Gelfand, M.J. (2006). A cultural analysis of the underlying assumptions of negotiation theory. In L. Thompson (ed.), *Frontiers of Negotiation Research* (pp. 173–201). New York, NY: Psychology Press.

Brett, J.M. and Okumura, T. (1998). Inter- and intracultural negotiation: U.S. and Japanese negotiators. *The Academy of Management Journal*, 41(5), 495–510.

Butler, E.A., Lee, T.L., and Gross, J.J. (2007). Emotion regulation and culture: Are the social consequences of emotion suppression culture-specific? *Emotion*, 7(1), 30.

Butler, J.K. (1999). Trust expectations, information sharing, climate of trust, and negotiation effectiveness and efficiency. *Group and Organization Management*, 24(2), 217–238.

Carl, D., Gupta, V., and Javidan, M. (2004). Power distance. In R.J. House, P.J. Hanges, M. Javidan, P.W. Dorfman and V. Gupta (eds), *Culture, leadership, and organizations: The GLOBE study of 62 Societies* (pp. 513–563). Thousand Oaks, CA: Sage.

Carnevale, P.J.D. and Isen, A.M. (1986). The influence of positive affect and visual access on the discovery of integrative solutions in bilateral negotiation. *Organizational Behavior and Human Decision Processes*, 37(1), 1–13.

Cohen, D. and Nisbett, R.E. (1997). Field experiments examining the culture of honor: the role of institutions in perpetuating norms about violence. *Personality and Social Psychology Bulletin*, 23(11), 1188–1199.

Cohen, D., Nisbett, R.E., Bowdle, B.F., and Schwarz, N. (1996). Insult, aggression, and the southern culture of honor: An "experimental ethnography". *Journal of Personality and Social Psychology*, 70(5), 945–960.

Dastmalchian, A., Javidan, M., and Alam, K. (2001). Effective leadership and culture in Iran: An empirical study. *Applied Psychology*, 50(4), 532–558.

Dirks, K.T., Lewicki, R.J., and Zaheer, A. (2009). Repairing relationships within and between organizations: Building a conceptual foundation. *Academy of Management Review*, 34(1), 68–84.

Fikret Pasa, S., Kabasakal, H., and Bodur, M. (2001). Society, organisations, and leadership in Turkey. *Applied Psychology*, 50(4), 559–589.

Fisher, R. and Ury, W. (1981). *Getting to yes: negotiating agreement without giving in*. Boston, MA: Houghton Mifflin.

Flannery, K.V. (1972). The cultural evolution of civilizations. *Annual Review of Ecology and Systematics*, 3, 399–426.

Friedman, R., Anderson, C., Brett, J., Olekalns, M., Goates, N., and Lisco, C.C. (2004). The positive and negative effects of anger on dispute resolution: Evidence from electronically mediated disputes. *Journal of Applied Psychology*, 89(2), 369–376.

Gabbay, D.M. and Woods, J. (eds) (2004). *Greek, Indian and Arabic logic* (Vol. 1). Amsterdam, Netherlands: Elsevier.

Gallup. (2012). *Middle East Leads World in Negative Emotions*. Retrieved 15 November 2012, from http://www.gallup.com/poll/155045/middle-east-leads-world-negative-emotions.aspx#2.

Gelfand, M.J., Bhawuk, D.P.S., Nishii, L.H., and Bechtold, D.J. (2004). Individualism and collectivism. In R.J. House, P.J. Hanges, M. Javidan, P.W. Dorfman and V. Gupta (eds), *Culture, leadership, and organizations: The GLOBE study of 62 Societies* (pp. 437–512). Thousand Oaks, CA: Sage.

Gill, A. (1998). *Rendering unto Caesar: the Catholic Church and the state in Latin America*. Chicago, IL: University of Chicago Press.

Gilmore, D. (1991). *Manhood in the making*. New Haven, CT: Yale.

Gunia, B.C., Brett, J.M., Nandkeolyar, A.K., and Kamdar, D. (2011). Paying a price: Culture, trust, and negotiation consequences. *Journal of Applied Psychology*, 96(4), 774–789.

Hall, E.T. (1976). *Beyond culture*. Garden City, NY: Anchor Press.
Hansen, C. (1983). *Language and logic in ancient China*. Ann Arbor, MI: University of Michigan Press.
Harinck, F., Shafa, S., Ellemers, N., and Beersma, B. (in press). The good news about honor culture: The preference for cooperative conflict management in the absence of insults. *Negotiation and Conflict Management Research*.
Heine, S.J. (2001). Self as cultural product: An examination of East Asian and North American selves. *Journal of Personality*, 69(6), 881–906.
Hirschman, A.O. (1970). *Exit, voice, and loyalty: Responses to decline in firms, organizations, and states* (Vol. 25): Cambridge, MA: Harvard University Press.
Hofstede, G. (1980). *Culture's consequences*. Beverly Hills, CA: Sage.
Hofstede, G. and Bond, M.H. (1988). The Confucius connection: From cultural roots to economic growth. *Organizational Dynamics*, 16(4), 5–21.
Horowitz, R. and Schwartz, G. (1974). Honor, normative ambiguity and gang violence. *American Sociological Review*, 39(2), 238–251.
Ijzerman, H., van Dijk, W.W., and Gallucci, M. (2007). A bumpy train ride: A field experiment on insult, honor, and emotional reactions. *Emotion*, 7(4), 869–875.
Ikels, C. (2004). *Filial Piety: Practice and Discourse in Contemporary East Asia*. Stanford, CA: Stanford University Press.
Kim, Y.-H. and Cohen, D. (2010). Information, perspective, and judgments about the self in face and dignity cultures. *Personality and Social Psychology Bulletin*, 36(4), 537–550.
Kimmel, M.J., Pruitt, D.G., Magenau, J.M., Konar-Goldband, E., and Carnevale, P.J.D. (1980). Effects of trust, aspiration, and gender on negotiation tactics. *Journal of Personality and Social Psychology*, 38(1), 9–22.
Kitayama, S., Mesquita, B., and Karasawa, M. (2006). Cultural affordances and emotional experience: socially engaging and disengaging emotions in Japan and the United States. *Journal of Personality and Social Psychology*, 91(5), 890.
Kiyonari, T., Foddy, M., and Yamagishi, T. (2007). Effects of direct and indirect exchange on trust of ingroup members. *The Japanese Journal of Psychology*, 77(6), 519–527.
Kiyonari, T., Yamagishi, T., Cook, K.S., and Cheshire, C. (2006). Does trust beget trustworthiness? Trust and trustworthiness in two games and two cultures: A research note. *Social Psychology Quarterly*, 69(3), 270–283.
Kopelman, S., Rosette, A.S., and Thompson, L. (2006). The three faces of Eve: Strategic displays of positive, negative, and neutral emotions in negotiations. *Organizational Behavior and Human Decision Processes*, 99(1), 81–101.
Lee, S., Brett, J., and Park, J.H. (2012). East Asians' social heterogeneity: Differences in norms among Chinese, Japanese, and Korean negotiators. *Negotiation Journal*, 28(4), 429–452.
Leung, A.K.Y. and Cohen, D. (2011). Within- and between-culture variation: Individual differences and the cultural logics of honor, face, and dignity cultures. *Journal of Personality and Social Psychology*, 100(3), 507–526.
Lieberman, M.D. (2000). Intuition: A social cognitive neuroscience approach. *Psychological Bulletin*, 126(1), 109–137.
Lin, C.-C. and Yamaguchi, S. (2011). Effects of face experience on emotions and self-esteem in Japanese culture. *European Journal of Social Psychology*, 41(4), 446–455.
Lind, E.A. and Tyler, T.R. (1988). *The social psychology of procedural justice*. New York: Springer-Verlag.
Luce, R.D. and Raiffa, H. (1957). *Games and Decisions*. New York, NY: John Wiley.
Lytle, A.L., Brett, J.M., Barsness, Z.I., Tinsley, C.H., and Janssens, M. (1995). A paradigm for confirmatory cross-cultural research in organizational behavior. In L.L. Cummings and B. M. Staw (eds), *Research in Organizational Behavior* (Vol. 17, pp. 167–214). Greenwich, CT: JAI Press.
Maddux, W.W., Mullen, E., and Galinsky, A.D. (2008). Chameleons bake bigger pies and take bigger pieces: Strategic behavioral mimicry facilitates negotiation outcomes. *Journal of Experimental Social Psychology*, 44(2), 461–468.

Majlisi, M.B. (1983). *Bihar al-anwar*. Beirut, Lebanon: Al-Wafa.
Markus, H.R. and Kitayama, S. (1991). Culture and the self: Implications for cognition, emotion, and motivation. *Psychological Review*, 98(2), 224–253.
Matsumoto, D., Yoo, S.H., and Fontaine, J. (2008). Mapping expressive differences around the world: The relationship between emotional display rules and individualism versus collectivism. *Journal of Cross-Cultural Psychology*, 39(1), 55–74.
Matsumoto, D., Yoo, S.H., Hirayama, S., and Petrova, G. (2005). Development and validation of a measure of display rule knowledge: the display rule assessment inventory. *Emotion*, 5(1), 23.
Matsumoto, D., Takeuchi, S., Andayani, S., Kouznetsova, N., and Krupp, D. (1998). The contribution of individualism vs. collectivism to cross-national differences in display rules. *Asian Journal of Social Psychology*, 1(2), 147–165.
Mayer, R.C., Davis, J.H., and Schoorman, F.D. (1995). An integrative model of organizational trust. *Academy of Management Review*, 20(3), 709–734.
Messick, D.M. and McClintock, C.G. (1968). Motivational bases of choice in experimental games. *Journal of Experimental Social Psychology*, 4(1), 1–25.
Meyerson, D., Weick, K.E., and Kramer, R.M. (1996). Swift trust and temporary groups. In R.M. Kramer and T.R. Tyler (eds), *Trust in organizations: Frontiers of theory and research* (pp. 166–195). Thousand Oaks, CA: Sage.
Miller, D.T. (1999). The norm of self-interest. *American Psychologist*, 54(12), 1053–1060.
Miller, W. (1993). *Humiliation*. Ithaca, NY: Cornell University Press.
Minkov, M. and Hofstede, G. (2012). Is national culture a meaningful concept? Cultural values delineate homogeneous national clusters of in-country regions. *Cross-Cultural Research*, 46(2), 133–159.
Nisbett, R.E. and Cohen, D. (1996). *Culture of honor: The psychology of violence in the South*. Boulder, CO: Westview Press.
Nisbett, R.E. and Miyamoto, Y. (2005). The influence of culture: holistic versus analytic perception. *Trends in Cognitive Sciences*, 9(10), 467–473.
Nisbett, R.E., Peng, K., Choi, I., and Norenzayan, A. (2001). Culture and systems of thought: Holistic versus analytic cognition. *Psychological Review*, 108(2), 291–310.
O'Leary, D.L. (1957). *How Greek science passed to the Arabs*. London, UK: Routledge and Kegan.
Oetzel, J.G. and Ting-Toomey, S. (2003). Face concerns in interpersonal conflict. *Communication Research*, 30(6), 599–624.
Offerman, T., Sonnemans, J., and Schram, A. (1996). Value orientations, expectations and voluntary contributions in public goods. *Economic Journal*, 106(437), 817–845.
Olekalns, M. and Smith, P.L. (2000). Understanding optimal outcomes. *Human Communication Research*, 26(4), 527–557.
Overbeck, J.R., Neale, M.A., and Govan, C.L. (2010). I feel, therefore you act: Intrapersonal and interpersonal effects of emotion on negotiation as a function of social power. *Organizational Behavior and Human Decision Processes*, 112(2), 126–139.
Pely, D. (2011). When honor trumps basic needs: The role of honor in deadly disputes within Israel's Arab community. *Negotiation Journal*, 27(2), 205–225.
Pinkley, R.L. and Northcraft, G.B. (1994). Conflict frames of reference: Implications for dispute processes and outcomes. *Academy of Management Journal*, 37(1), 193–205.
Pitt-Rivers, J. (1968). Honor. In D. Sills (ed.), *International encyclopedia of the social sciences* (pp. 509–510). New York, NY: Macmillan.
Pruitt, D.G. (1981). *Negotiation behavior*. New York, NY: Academic Press.
Pruitt, D.G. and Lewis, S.A. (1975). Development of integrative solutions in bilateral negotiation. *Journal of Personality and Social Psychology*, 31(4), 621–633.
Pruitt, D.G. and Lewis, S.A. (1977). The psychology of integrative bargaining. In D. Druckman (ed.), *Negotiations, Social Psychological Perspectives* (pp. 161–192). Beverly Hills, CA: Sage-Halsted.
Ramirez-Marin, J.Y., Aslani, S., Brett, J.M., Tinsley, C.H., and Munduate, L. (2012). Cool

down and explain yourself: Spanish honor and anglo dignity in intercultural negotiation. *The Academy of Management 2012 Annual Meeting*. Boston, MA.

Robinson, R.J., Lewicki, R.J., and Donahue, E.M. (2000). Extending and testing a five factor model of ethical and unethical bargaining tactics: introducing the SINS scale. *Journal of Organizational Behavior*, *21*(6), 649–664.

Rodriguez Mosquera, P.M., Fischer, A.H., Manstead, A.S.R., and Zaalberg, R. (2008). Attack, disapproval, or withdrawal? The role of honour in anger and shame responses to being insulted. *Cognition and Emotion*, *22*(8), 1471–1498.

Rodriguez Mosquera, P.M., Manstead, A.S.R., and Fischer, A.H. (2002a). Honor in the Mediterranean and Northern Europe. *Journal of Cross-Cultural Psychology*, *33*(1), 16–36.

Rodriguez Mosquera, P.M., Manstead, A.S.R., and Fischer, A.H. (2002b). The role of honour concerns in emotional reactions to offences. *Cognition and Emotion*, *16*(1), 143–163.

Sanchez-Burks, J. (2002). Protestant relational ideology and (in)attention to relational cues in work settings. *Journal of Personality and Social Psychology*, *83*(4), 919–929.

Sanchez-Burks, J. and Mor Barak, M. (2004). Interpersonal relationships in a global work context. In M.M. Barak (ed.), *Managing diversity in the age of globalization: Toward a worldwide inclusive workplace* (pp. 114–168). Thousand Oaks, CA: Sage.

Sanchez-Burks, J., Neuman, E.J., Ybarra, O., Kopelman, S., Park, H., and Goh, K. (2008). Folk wisdom about the effects of relationship conflict. *Negotiation and Conflict Management Research*, *1*(1), 53–76.

Schwartz, S.H. (1994). Beyond individualism/collectivism: New cultural dimensions of values. In *Individualism and collectivism: Theory, method, and applications* (pp. 85–119), Thousand Oaks, CA: Sage Publications.

Service, E. (1962). *Primitive social organization: An evolutionary perspective*. New York, NY: Random House.

Sinaceur, M. and Tiedens, L.Z. (2006). Get mad and get more than even: When and why anger expression is effective in negotiations. *Journal of Experimental Social Psychology*, *42*(3), 314–322.

Sinaceur, M., Van Kleef, G.A., Neale, M.A., Adam, H., and Haag, C. (2011). Hot or cold: Is communicating anger or threats more effective in negotiation? *Journal of Applied Psychology*, *96*(5), 1018.

Steinel, W., Van Kleef, G.A., and Harinck, F. (2008). Are you talking to me?! Separating the people from the problem when expressing emotions in negotiation. *Journal of Experimental Social Psychology*, *44*(2), 362–369.

Takahashi, C., Yamagishi, T., Liu, J.H., Wang, F.X., Lin, Y.C., and Yu, S. (2008). The intercultural trust paradigm: Studying joint cultural interaction and social exchange in real time over the Internet. *International Journal of Intercultural Relations*, *32*(3), 215–228.

Teucher, B., Brett, J.M., and Gunia, B.C. (2011). Culture and negotiation: Three models. In K.P. Sycara, M. Gelfand and A. Abbe (eds), *Modeling Intercultural Collaboration and Negotiation*. New York, NY: Springer.

Thompson, L., Nadler, J., and Kim, P. (1999). Some like it hot: the case for the emotional negotiator. In L. Thompson, J. Levin and D. Messick (eds), *Shared Cognition in Organizations: The Management of Knowledge* (pp. 139–161). Mahwah, NJ: Erlbaum.

Tjosvold, D., Hui, C., and Sun, H.F. (2004). Can Chinese discuss conflicts openly? Field and experimental studies of face dynamics in China. *Group Decision and Negotiation*, *13*(4), 351–373.

Tocqueville, A. (2010/1840). *Democracy in America*. Chicago, IL: University of Chicago Press.

Triandis, H.C. (1989). The self and social behavior in differing cultural contexts. *Psychological Review*, *96*(3), 506–520.

Trompenaars, F. (1996). Resolving international conflict: Culture and business strategy. *Business Strategy Review*, *7*(3), 51.

Uchida, Y. and Kitayama, S. (2009). Happiness and unhappiness in east and west: themes and variations. *Emotion*, *9*(4), 441.

Ury, W.L., Brett, J.M., and Goldberg, S.B. (1988). *Getting disputes resolved: Designing systems to cut the costs of conflict.* San Francisco: Jossey-Bass.

Uskul, A.K., Kitayama, S., and Nisbett, R.E. (2008a). Ecocultural basis of cognition: Farmers and fishermen are more holistic than herders. *Proceedings of the National Academy of Sciences, 105*(25), 8552–8556.

Uskul, A.K., Nisbett, R.E., and Kitayama, S. (2008b). Ecoculture, social interdependence, and holistic cognition: Evidence from farming, fishing, and herding communities in Turkey. *Communicative and integrative biology, 1*(1), 40–41.

Van Kleef, G.A. and De Dreu, C.K.W. (2010). Longer-term consequences of anger expression in negotiation: Retaliation or spillover? *Journal of Experimental Social Psychology, 46*(5), 753–760.

Van Kleef, G.A., De Dreu, C.K.W., and Manstead, A.S.R. (2004a). The interpersonal effects of anger and happiness in negotiations. *Journal of Personality and Social Psychology, 86*(1), 57.

Van Kleef, G.A., De Dreu, C.K.W., and Manstead, A.S.R. (2004b). The interpersonal effects of emotions in negotiations: A motivated information processing approach. *Journal of Personality and Social Psychology, 87*(4), 510–528.

Van Kleef, G.A., De Dreu, C.K.W., Pietroni, D., and Manstead, A.S.R. (2006). Power and emotion in negotiation: Power moderates the interpersonal effects of anger and happiness on concession making. *European Journal of Social Psychology, 36*(4), 557–581.

Vandello, J.A. and Cohen, D. (2004). When believing is seeing: Sustaining norms of violence in cultures of honor. In M. Schaller and C. Crandall (eds), *The psychological foundations of culture* (pp. 281–304). Mahwah, NJ: Lawrence Erlbaum.

Versteegh, C.H.M. (1977). *Greek Elements in Arabic Linguistic Thinking.* Leiden, Netherlands: Brill.

Walton, R.E. and McKersie, R.B. (1965). *A Behavioral theory of labor negotiations: An analysis of a social interaction system.* New York, NY: McGraw-Hill.

Weber, J.M., Malhotra, D., and Murnighan, J.K. (2005). Normal acts of irrational trust: Motivated attributions and the trust development process. *Research in Organizational Behavior: An Annual Series of Analytical Essays and Critical Reviews, 26*, 75–101.

Weber, M. (1997). *The theory of social and economic organization.* New York, NY: Free Press.

Weingart, L.R., Brett, J.M., Olekalns, M., and Smith, P.L. (2007). Conflicting social motives in negotiating groups. *Journal of Personality and Social Psychology, 93*(6), 994–1010.

Weingart, L.R., Thompson, L.L., Bazerman, M.H., and Carroll, J.S. (1990). Tactical behavior and negotiation outcomes. *International Journal of Conflict Management, 1*(1), 7–31.

Wittgenstein, L. (2009). *Philosophical investigations.* Malden, MA: Wiley.

Yamagishi, T. and Yamagishi, M. (1994). Trust and commitment in the United States and Japan. *Motivation and Emotion, 18*(2), 129–166.

Yamagishi, T., Cook, K.S., and Watabe, M. (1998). Uncertainty, trust, and commitment formation in the United States and Japan. *American Journal of Sociology, 104*(1), 165–194.

Yuki, M., Maddux, W.W., and Masuda, T. (2007). Are the windows to the soul the same in the East and West? Cultural differences in using the eyes and mouth as cues to recognize emotions in Japan and the United States. *Journal of Experimental Social Psychology, 43*(2), 303–311.

11. Managing uncertainty in multiparty negotiations
Harris Sondak, Margaret A. Neale and Elizabeth A. Mannix

In his well-known early book on negotiations *The art and science of negotiation*, Howard Raiffa (1982) begins his analysis by distinguishing between two-party and multiparty negotiations. While perhaps not the first to make this distinction, his treatment set the stage for much of the research and teaching on negotiation that has occurred in the last several decades.

In this chapter we consider three types of multiparty negotiations – negotiations that occur within a team as it faces the potential for a negotiation with other entities, negotiations among multiple different parties each of whom has its own interests, and negotiations in marketplace contexts where there are typically many buyers and sellers. The tasks facing negotiators in these three different contexts have both commonalities and differences, as we discuss. In each context, negotiators must recognize, understand, and manage problems of gaining and dealing with relevant but sometimes hidden, vague, or perplexing information.

As reflected in Raiffa's discussion, the importance of the distinction between two-party and multiparty negotiations reflects the challenge of acquiring and managing relevant information in the multiparty context. For example, a negotiator in a multiparty context must consider not just the interests of one other person, but those of several others; a negotiator must consider the wide range of possible agreements across a constellation of potential partners; and a negotiator might not know who all the other parties are, or even how many other parties are involved.

Managing uncertainty has been discussed both as a core managerial task and as an ongoing challenge for organizational members (Gosling and Mintzberg, 2003), as well as an essential skill for negotiators' success (Kelley, 1966; Thompson, 1991; Olekalns et al., 1996; Neale and Fragale, 2006). We agree that uncertainty is an important issue in negotiation and, in this chapter, we explore three types of uncertainty in multiparty negotiations: uncertainty of identity, uncertainty of interests, and uncertainty of inclusion. Rather than uniformly assuming that uncertainty is detrimental for negotiators' performance and thus should be minimized, we explore the impact of these three types of uncertainty, both positive and negative, on negotiation processes and outcomes.

Uncertainty inherent in the negotiation process can be beneficial, and even necessary, for reaching optimal negotiation outcomes. Research on certainty and information processing has suggested that one's level of certainty affects the way that one processes information. When individuals experience a feeling of certainty, they may process information in a heuristic fashion and rely on well-developed associations, mental shortcuts, or rules of thumb to evaluate information and make decisions. In contrast, the experience of uncertainty may cause individuals to process information more deeply or more systematically. That is, when individuals experience uncertainty they may consider multiple alternatives or points of view more carefully, scrutinize information longer, and ask more probing and insightful questions (Chaiken et al., 1989; Kahneman, 2011; Tiedens and Linton, 2001; Weary and Jacobson, 1997).

Research from negotiation contexts suggests that systematic processing of information is a critical factor for achieving integrative, or mutually or collectively beneficial, negotiation agreements (e.g., Anderson and Neale, 2004; De Dreu, 2003; Thompson, 1991). When negotiators process information carefully, they are more likely to ask the right questions, listen to the answers, and uncover opportunities for mutually beneficial trade-offs. Thus, uncertainty may facilitate the formation of integrative negotiation agreements because uncertainty may enhance systematic thinking, and systematic thinking, in turn, enhances negotiation performance through increased value creation.

While recognizing this potential advantage of the experience of uncertainty, we also acknowledge that negotiators, like other decision makers, rely on their well-learned routines, practices, and heuristics when they experience too much uncertainty. When faced with revolutionary and unexpected changes in their environment, decision makers often revert to their most over-learned, dominant behaviors (Staw et al., 1981; Ocasio, 1995). A state of threat rigidity, for example, can impair negotiators' information search and creativity and lead to reliance on myths of negotiation, such as that of the fixed pie. The point when levels of uncertainty switch from being useful for motivating the search for information and creative problem solving to detrimental because they lead to succumbing to over-learned behaviors or heuristics is a function of the expectations, abilities, and cognitive resources available to the specific negotiators as well as the informational challenges they face in their particular context.

INTRA-TEAM NEGOTIATIONS

As the unit of agency moves from the individual to the team, so does the constellation of potential solutions that are available to negotiators. The overarching uncertainty as the team chooses a course of action is whose voice is heard and whose interests will be considered. More specifically, the question arises whether the team is open to and capable of integrating the disparate interests that may exist among team members into a unified strategy and roadmap for achieving its goals. As the number of individuals in a team increases, the parties face increasing levels of uncertainty in identifying and clarifying their preferences and priorities in the process of planning the negotiation. With other team members, they must contend with the uncertainty associated with who has voice and who wants what within the team's boundaries.

Uncertainty of Identity: Who Is on My Team?

As teams begin to consider the parameters over which they will negotiate, the identity of team members – exactly who is on the team and whose preferences and priorities will be considered – and the values that will comprise the shared identity are salient considerations. While the actual identity of team members is rarely considered a source of uncertainty as intra-team interactions are often face-to-face, who is on the team may become more ambiguous as communication among team members is increasingly mediated by technology (Hinds and Mortensen, 2005).

Individuals reduce ambiguity about membership by assessing the relative similarity between their colleagues and themselves (Tajfel, 1974). The first step in reducing this uncertainty is to learn the identity of the members. Once formal membership is clarified, team members can then specify the shared values and perspectives that will characterize members in good standing. With a salient shared identity, group members are more cooperative, more loyal to the perceived interests of the group, and emphasize the welfare of the group (Brewer and Miller, 1996). Without a strongly shared identity, team members are likely to view other members' behaviors through a malevolent filter when disputes arise (Jehn et al., 1999). The less the shared identity, the more diverse the team is likely to perceive itself (see Liu and Cai, Chapter 4 this volume, for details about creating shared identity). It is this first consideration of who is inside and who is outside the boundary of the team, and the definition of the characteristics that separate members from non-members, that motivates the search for alignments of interests and specifies the standards for membership.

Uncertainty of Interests: What Do We Want?

Negotiators in teams may not be aware of the extent to which their interests and preferences differ from those around them. And, even if they recognize these differences, individuals may be reluctant to express their conflicting goals and preferences about how to achieve them. How do team members fashion an agreement with their team counterparts who are on the same side of the dispute but may bring very different expectations about the issues, strategies, and outcomes that constitute an acceptable agreement?

When faced with an intra-team negotiation, teams benefit from identifying and resolving members' conflicting goals, preferences and priorities before the external negotiation begins. If these differences remain unrecognized and unresolved, team members may experience a dilemma: should they maximize their individual interests or should they submerge their individual interests in service of the team's or other team members' interests? Having this conflict remain unresolved but active during an inter-team negotiation reduces the team's ability to develop a shared identity and discourages information sharing within the team (Halevy, 2008). Further, teams that experience this internal conflict are less able to carry out organized, collective action in the form of implementing the team's strategy in the negotiation (Borenstein, 2003). When team members experience internal conflict, they are less satisfied with the outcomes as well as with their fellow team members. So, from the perspective of the team, it is important to ensure the team's interests are aligned with the individual members' interests by explicitly preparing and implementing a negotiation process within the team to achieve an internal consensus before the team turns its collective attention across the table.

Achieving internal agreement, however, may not always be straightforward. While there has been little research in the negotiation domain that explicitly examines the existence and impact of this similarity bias on the performance of negotiating teams, we can draw from a wealth of team-based research to suggest the impact of such perceptions on the problem-solving capability of negotiating teams (for a review, see Mannix and Neale, 2005).

For example, it is not at all unusual for negotiators to assume that because individuals are on the same side of the table in a dispute that their interests are aligned. People derive part of their social identity and self-esteem from the groups or teams to which they belong (Tajfel and Turner, 1986). As such, they tend to categorize themselves into social groups that are favorably distinct from other groups (Turner, 1987). This process can motivate individuals to perceive in-group members in a positive light and to assume greater similarity of viewpoints and opinions between themselves and other in-group versus out-group members (Allen and Wilder, 1979).

When individuals see members of their team as homogenous, they are likely to extend this perception of homogeneity to a similarity of views and perspectives. This biased expectation about the others' goals may diminish the perception of, or at least the willingness of group members to voice, disagreement. Classic research on groupthink (Janis, 1982) supports the more general idea that homogeneity can decrease individuals' sensitivity to disagreement – but not because there is no disagreement. Rather, there is a veneer of agreement that may simply flow from members' voluntarily suppressing dissenting viewpoints – an outcome more likely to be experienced in homogeneous as compared to diverse groups (Abrams et al., 1990).

The perception of homogeneity diverts attention away from disagreement and difference by creating an expectation of alignment that can obscure the actual level of underlying conflict. In a study examining the effects of racial diversity on group decision-making, Phillips et al. (2006) administered a "hidden profile" task to demographically homogeneous groups (composed of three white individuals) and demographically diverse groups (composed of two white and either one Asian, Black or Hispanic individual). In hidden profile tasks, group members receive some shared information that is provided to their group members as well as some unique information (that is not provided to others). In this study, both homogeneous and diverse groups received the identical distribution of shared and unshared information, but the information received was perceived as significantly more similar by individuals in demographically homogeneous groups as compared to individuals in diverse groups.

If team members have an expectation of similarity among their teammates, this expectation is strengthened the more the teams experience their interests as homogenous. Phillips and her colleagues documented a tendency for individuals in a team to believe that they are more likely to agree with an in-group as opposed to out-group member – even when the nature of the categorization is completely unrelated to the task (Phillips, 2003; Phillips and Loyd, 2006). This expectation could, in part, explain why homogeneous juries are less effective in their deliberations: they may systematically over-estimate the extent of their internal alignment (Sommers, 2006) and, by assuming a common perspective, ignore unique information that may be critical to a high quality decision. Because of the very real possibility that teams are often composed of those who share dimensions of proximity, past experience, or friendship, the impact of similarity inferred from common team membership may enhance the selective interpretation of or exposure to conflicting points of view (Mannix and Neale, 2005).

Phillips and Apfelbaum (in press) have argued that this selective, and often motivated, perception of similarity leads to what they call the *delusion of homogeneity* or the belief that team members are more similar in their beliefs, aspirations, and goals than an objective assessment would reveal. This delusion of homogeneity or similarity can be reflected in the certainty with which the team believes that it has internal consensus. The resulting consensus, itself already an illusion, can lead negotiating teams to endorse proposals and experience levels of confidence that these proposals reflect the will of the team that is inconsistent with the true constellation of preferences and priorities of the team. This mismatch could easily result in creating proposals and valuing outcomes at the level of the team in ways that are inconsistent with the preferences of team members – and which may only become evident during the external negotiation.

It is important to assess the true alignment of goals and preferences among team members. The more similar the team's members seem to be personally, the more members expect consensus in their goals and preferences. But surface level similarity (demographic category membership or professional background and expertise), or perceived commonality as a result of the mere fact of being members of the same group or team, might conceal deep divides in what teams members are trying to achieve and the outcomes they find desirable or acceptable. Individuals normally expect congruency between surface- and deep-level distinctions such that people who are similar are assumed to have the same preferences and people who are different are assumed to have different preferences. When team members extrapolate from surface-level similarity or homogeneity they have expectations of lower levels of conflict within the group because of (the assumed similarity of) opinion and perspectives, and an expectation of an increased relationship rather than task focus (Harrison and Klein, 2007).

Recent research has found that the mere presence of surface-level differences increases perceptions of uncertainty, raises the expectation of conflict, and motivates a more elaborated and systematic search for unique or discriminating information (Phillips and Loyd, 2006). Because these surface-level differences change how confident team members are in their predictions of others' views and preferences, the subsequent search for and surfacing of deep-level differences are more effective.

Researchers found that individuals who expected to interact with those who were (surface-level) different from them were more likely to engage in more systematic information processing in attempting to understand others' perspectives. In addition, such individuals focused on the task rather than the relationship more than did those who were expecting to interact with others who were (surface-level) similar (Loyd et al., in press). The extent of systematic planning was revealed when researchers analysed the informational content of the individuals' plans. Those who expected to interact with people who were different from them developed more elaborate and detailed plans of action. Indeed, additional research convincingly demonstrated that those individuals who expected to work with dissimilar others are more likely to discuss uniquely-held information about the common task with their counterparts while those who face similar others are more likely to discuss information that they knew their counterpart already possessed (Cao and Phillips, 2011). That is, in advance of working with dissimilar team members, individuals expect that other team members will disagree with them and they plan to emphasize their unique information about the issues to be addressed. This additional elaboration bolsters the depth and quality of an individual's arguments as well as the aggregate information available to the team. Team members therefore come to a meeting better prepared and more able to articulate the reasons on which their opinions were based. In addition, they are more open to differing perspectives and are more able to recognize new and potentially valuable insights.

Uncertainty of Inclusion: Am I a Part of This Deal?

The often mistaken and potentially harmful assumption of homogeneity is, in many respects, the reflection of people's longing for the guarantee of membership and influence. The more members in a team are perceived as similar along a variety of dimensions, the clearer the distinction between members and non-members. Given that the most powerful tool for control that a team has is the ability to ostracize deviant individuals, being validated as a member in good standing facilitates the expression of similar interests, whereas it censors the expression of interests that might be divergent. Thus, the criteria for inclusion and the standards for membership are clear (Mannix and Neale, 2005).

There can be considerable fluidity in the boundary that separates who is inside and who is outside the group. Perceived differences among group members can have detrimental effects on cooperation in general and negotiation in particular. Research has demonstrated that negotiators privilege the interests of insiders and discount the interests of outsiders, even when the differences between those deemed insiders and outsiders are trivial or contrived (Brewer, 1979). While these processes are generally thought of in terms of intergroup interaction, they may also occur within a group (Hogg and Terry, 2000, Gibson and Vermeulen, 2003).

Members of a group favor other members of their sub-group (in-group) and punish members of other sub-groups (out-group) even when the highest level of common good comes at a very low cost to the in-group or when the benefits to the in-group did not differ but the benefits to the out-group increased (Tajfel et al., 1971; Turner, 1981). Thus, this often-mistaken assumption of homogeneity within and differences across negotiating teams increases the perceived competitiveness of the negotiation context and negotiating teams' interactions (Kramer, 1981). This competition, in turn, further emphasizes the importance of the team's solidarity. As this process escalates, the hurdle for an individual team member to voice his or her disagreement about goals, preferences and priorities can become insurmountable. A group member who does so runs the real risk of being perceived as disloyal, resulting in reduced influence and acceptance within the group.

Because members of a team assume that common team membership means common goals, interests, preferences, and priorities and the certainty that comes with similarity, they can easily overlook or fail to recognize the existence of internal conflict within the team and miss opportunities to create the necessary internal consensus and coordination. Failing to recognize the lack of alignment among team members leaves internal conflict unexamined and unresolved. In addition, team members may self-censor the expression of their divergent preferences to maintain membership in good standing. Thus, the certainty with which team members regard their aggregate interests is enhanced by the expectations of the team and the behavior of its members. These failures to acknowledge and resolve this intra-team uncertainty can reduce members' identification with the team because of the lack of congruence of their own interests with those espoused by the team; and the team could be less creative in developing its proposals because of the inaccurate perceptions of similarity and alignment.

Teams can often be superior to individuals in analysing information and completing tasks but often fail to consider how to coordinate the pieces of their solutions into an organized whole (Stout et al., 1999). On the other hand, individuals negotiating on their own do not have the challenge of creating internal consensus prior to negotiating, but still must often find ways to assess, manage and coordinate a complex set of information, people and interactions. It is on this context that we focus next.

MULTILATERAL NEGOTIATIONS

Multilateral negotiations are interactions in which three or more individuals, representing their own interests, or perhaps more often their own interests as well as those of others (such as departments, clients or family members), attempt to resolve perceived differences of interest (Bazerman et al., 1988; Kramer, 1991). Multilateral negotiations have tremendous potential to result in strong, creative agreements, but they are also subject to a number of challenges along the way that make them difficult to manage and to resolve. Indeed, scholars have argued that multilateral negotiations are particularly subject to breakdowns if not conscientiously managed (Brett, 1991).

As the number of different parties and so the diversity of preferences and perspectives at the table increases, the demands placed on each negotiator to manage uncertainty compounds. Consider the simplest multilateral case – a three-person negotiation. The focal negotiator has a variety of tasks that involve assessing and managing relationships (to promote identity), acquiring and interpreting information (to understand interests), and controlling processes (to be sure of inclusion). For example, a negotiator must manage her relationship with her constituents outside the negotiation, as well as inside, understand and then consider the compatibility of preferences and possible trade-offs between her and two other individuals, and then negotiate with each of the parties in the group, while at the same time guarding against a possible exclusionary alliance between them. As the group size increases to four or more, so does complexity and, potentially as a result, the degree of uncertainty on each of these dimensions. For example, the sheer amount of information expands, but so does the number of possible potential trade-offs among issues and people. The number of alliances (both with and without the focal negotiator) likewise increases. In essence, as the group size increases, so does the amount of uncertainty that each negotiator must face.

Uncertainty of Identity: Who Am I in this Context?

Unlike the members of a team who are likely to assume a similarity of goals, interests, and priorities, because multilateral negotiators are not part of the same in-group they are more likely to make the reverse assumption and to expect incompatibility among negotiators. The strength with which multilateral negotiators make and persist in this assumption of incompatibility may be as damaging to effective negotiation processes and outcomes as are team members' assumptions of exaggerated homogeneity.

In addition to their assumption of incompatibility of interests, negotiators in multilateral contexts are relatively unlikely to identify with the other negotiators who represent other groups. Especially when negotiators are representing others, their social identification is more likely to be outside the group of negotiators, with their home department, client, or family.

As such, it may be difficult for the negotiators in multilateral contexts to see the group as a cooperative social entity with a common goal, or shared set of values and norms (Katzenbach and Smith, 1993). Maximizing the group's outcome and finding the best possible solution for all parties are not only more difficult in multilateral negotiation but also may not even be credible or desirable goals. The more that group members identify outside the group, and the more they focus on their own interests, the less likely they may be to work toward high quality, integrative solutions. Thus, the untested but strongly held belief about the others players' oppositional preferences and priorities may drive members of the group further apart than their underlying interests would suggest, creating an unnecessarily competitive environment. This tendency may threaten the quality of the agreement, and even create a higher likelihood of impasse – particularly if the cooperation of all parties is required to reach a final agreement.

Uncertainty of Interests: What Does Everyone Want?

As the number of individual negotiators in a multilateral context increases from three or more in a negotiation, the number of issues, the perspectives on those issues, and the sheer amount of information to be digested grows quickly. Keeping track of the factual information, as well as the values, attitudes, and perceptions of each negotiator is a major challenge. As with a dyadic negotiation, each participant is trying to discern the priorities, targets, and reservation points of the other negotiators, and gauge where trade-offs can be made with each party. Integrating this massive amount of information into an optimal solution can be a highly demanding task as the bargaining zone changes from two dimensions to three, four or five, or more, depending on the number of participants.

Thus, negotiators in a multilateral setting labor under a variety of types of information overload as well as information uncertainty. Because of negotiators' efforts to deal with this complicated information, decision-making biases that are prevalent in dyadic negotiation may be exacerbated in the multilateral setting. The simple presence of additional parties is known to make individuals more competitive, for example, as individuals compare their outcomes to others and "winning" becomes a goal in and of itself. Uncertainty about feasible negotiated outcomes can exacerbate this tendency as players may become concerned about feeling regret over accepting an agreement that they may later judge to be sub-optimal (Galinsky et al., 2002). The less negotiators know about the bargaining zone, the more second guessing and doubt they may experience, thus increasing the possibility of impasse.

Another heuristic that threatens agreement in multilateral negotiation is the endowment effect. This bias operates when buyers and sellers have differing reference points for an object, specifically when the owner of an object values it more than the potential buyer of that object (Kahneman et al., 1990). The difference between what sellers demand and what buyers are willing to pay is a reflection of loss aversion. Sellers tend to demand too much for items when they overly identify as the owners of those objects. In multilateral negotiations this problem is increased because it may be less clear how to value bargaining issues and items when there are multiple parties at the bargaining table. Because we assess the value of issues from many sources, including from the party or parties across the table, when there are multiple parties in a negotiation there may be conflicting information on the value of various issues. For example, imagine a cross-functional group negotiating over the design of a tablet computer. The parties are likely to have different values for items like overall design, functionality, price-point, and so on, and also different projections for how each of these issues will affect the quality of the product, cost, and profitability to the firm. In this case, the increased ambiguity that arises from the varying information, opinions and projections provided by the negotiators may also heighten a reluctance to make concessions and trade-offs, increasing the chances of stalemate.

Uncertainty of Inclusion: Am I in on this Deal?

Finally, potentially the most critical distinction between dyadic and multilateral negotiation is the potential for coalition formation between two or more of the players. A coalition is defined as two or more parties who cooperate to obtain a mutually desired outcome that satisfies the interests of the coalition rather than those of the entire group within which it is embedded (Murnighan, 1986; Polzer et al., 1998). The possibility of coalitions means that one or more of the individuals could be excluded from the final agreement, or if not excluded, then forced to accept a lowered outcome (see Crump, Chapter 15 this volume, for discussion of coalitions in trade negotiations). Negotiators need to concern themselves not only about the uncertainty raised by the various coalitions among negotiators, but also about the potential alliances that have not yet surfaced. For example, Cobb (1986) defines a latent coalition as an emergent interest group that has not yet formed into an operating, active coalition. An operating coalition can be established, stable, and long-lived, or it can be temporary and focused on a single issue or problem. In all cases, coalitions face a number of challenges in their formation, maintenance, and in the distribution of resources that ultimately center on issues of trust, temptation and uncertainty (Mannix and Loewenstein, 1994).

The potential for coalition formation may be a type of uncertainty that is a positive force in multilateral negotiations. It forces negotiators to engage in high levels of strategic thinking about their alternatives and how to improve them, and to do the same for the various parties to the negotiation by taking their perspectives. It also forces negotiators to be attentive and stay engaged as the active alliances can shift at any time, changing the power dynamics and the potential costs and benefits of the interaction.

Coalitions typically begin with one founder who initiates the coalition by enlisting other members. Initiating or joining a coalition early in its development involves some risk, because the initiators and early joiners of a coalition are uncertain whether the coalition will garner enough critical mass to win, but concerns about inclusion can lead group members to come on-board nonetheless. Coalitions tend to build one member at a time, through commitments and promises made to specific individuals. Research has shown that the founder typically has to offer a disproportionate share of the resources to induce potential partners to join early, at least until the coalition is well established (Murnighan and Brass, 1991).

Coalitions include members, but they also exclude them – and herein lies some of the tension between trust and temptation as players attempt to make sure they are included in deals, but also try to obtain the largest share of the resources the coalition can command as possible. It can be effective to invite weak members into a coalition because they can deliver a lot of value to coalitions, as they can put the coalition over the top but ask for less from the winning pool. On the other hand, stronger group members give added power to the coalition but they may demand disproportionate influence and shares of the resources won by the coalition. Optimally, negotiators will build the smallest and least costly winning coalition possible (Murnighan, 1978; 1986), but determining the strategy that leads to this goal is difficult.

Decisions about alternative allies are really decisions about how to mitigate risk and manage uncertainty. The more uncertainty players perceive, either about the true goals or preferences of coalition partners, or the quality of the deal they have struck with their allies, the less likely the coalition will hold. Power and uncertainty are intertwined when coalitions are possible, as group members strive to reduce uncertainty and stabilize their coalition membership, which both depends on and increases their power. One of the key issues is for group members to assess their sources of power and to use them to avoid exclusion and ensure beneficial outcomes in multilateral negotiations.

Polzer et al. (1998) identified three key types of power in multilateral negotiations with coalition potential – strategic, normative, and relational. Strategic power is the classic form of power that emerges from the availability of alternative coalition partners; those who are invited to join alternative coalitions can be more selective in the coalitions they choose to join. Normative power derives from what parties consider a just or fair allocation of the resources the coalition can command. Normative power also can serve a strategic function because the party that proposes the principle of what constitutes a fair distribution can be at least somewhat self-serving. Finally, relationship-based power comes from the compatibility of preferences between two or more parties. Parties who see each other as having compatible interests, values, or preferences are likely to begin and maintain a relationship that can influence or block other possible coalitions.

In an empirical demonstration of their relative effects, Polzer et al. (1998) examined all three types of power simultaneously. They found relationship power to be the most effective source of power for negotiators seeking to be included in final deals and to achieve large outcomes, as it affected both the formation and stability of coalitions. Resistance from parties outside the coalition tended to strengthen the bond among the coalition members, making it more likely for them to continue to identify and cooperate with each other and compete with the non-coalition members. Therefore, when coalitions initially formed because of relationship power, they were likely to be broadly effective, influencing even those issues for which the coalition members did not have compatible preferences. In essence, this sort of power allowed negotiators to develop confidence about each other's behaviors and intentions, both in the present and in the future, which in turn lowered uncertainty about future exclusion.

Negotiators in multilateral contexts face the disadvantage of uncertainty in terms of their splintered identity as a group, and the difficulty of assessing and managing an overload of interests and other information. However, the pressure to understand the complex set of relationships in the group, with the possibility for exclusion through coalitions, can keep negotiators engaged and motivated. As a result, although high levels of uncertainty have the potential to pull the negotiation off track, resulting in sub-optimal outcomes for some if not all of the individual players, it is also possible that if the negotiators recognize their situation and manage it effectively, uncertainty can encourage a proactive and creative effort.

We now consider negotiation contexts that often involve many people – sometimes many thousands. Negotiations in the marketplace are complicated because of the number of people who are participating and the ways that uncertainty is manifested and may be managed.

NEGOTIATIONS IN THE MARKETPLACE

In many negotiation contexts, buyers have a choice of potential suppliers of the goods or services that they seek to purchase and sellers have a choice of potential customers. In such cases, buyers and sellers are negotiating not only the price at which they will strike a deal, but also whether they will transact with each other at all or whether they will buy from or sell to alternative counterparties. Identifying these alternatives is an important aspect to success at negotiation – negotiators are often advised to improve their best alternatives to an agreement with one particular counterparty – but the process has been relatively little studied (Thompson et al., 2010). We refer to situations in which there are various possible parties with whom negotiators can make deals as marketplace negotiations. Negotiators in marketplaces face various issues that create uncertainty about identity, interests, and inclusion.

Uncertainty of Identity: Who is in the Market?

In some marketplace negotiations market participants know both who the possible counterparties are as well as whom else is on their side of the market. However, it is frequently the case that market participants do not know the identities of their possible counterparties nor the competitors on their side for deals with those counterparties. In many auctions, for example, the bidders are not even in the same room and never see or speak to one another. Furthermore, market participants may not know even how many other participants are in the market. Buyers on eBay or other online auction sites, for example, generally have no idea of the number of potential bidders, even if they know the number of people who have placed a bid (see Friedman and Belkin, Chapter 14 this volume, for additional considerations about e-negotiations).

The number of bidders in a market can affect likely outcomes for participants, however, so they often actively seek to manage that number. Economists have demonstrated the advisability of doing so analytically and its advantage has emerged in empirical results produced by both economists and psychologists. Parties generally seek to increase the numbers of participants on the other side of the market from themselves and lower the number on the same side.

The advantage of having additional bidders on the other side of a market has been argued to be robust even to the difference between one possible counterparty and more than one. Bulow and Klemperer (1996) compare prices in the two kinds of contexts and conclude, "A simple competitive auction with N + 1 bidders will yield a seller more expected revenue than she could expect to earn by fully exploiting her monopoly selling position against N bidders....Our analysis implies that if the board [of a company] expects at least one extra serious bidder to appear in an auction, then it should generally not negotiate and should directly begin an auction" (p. 190). This observation provides interesting advice to negotiators to avoid negotiation and instead establish a competitive market and encourage as many bidders as possible to participate (compare Subramanian and Zeckhouser, 2004). Neale and Lys (2012) argue, however, that when propriety information needs to be shared for a sale to be completed, as in the case of allowing buyers due diligence for a corporate acquisition, the fewer potential buyers who have access to this information, the better. In such cases, despite the potential gains from having alternative potential buyers bid for a property, a seller may prefer a negotiation to an auction to protect the value of the asset under consideration.

Even if an auction were better for a seller than a straightforward negotiation, some auctions are nonetheless better than others for one side or the other. The more numerous the bidders, the more difficult it is for them to cooperate in an effort to keep prices low. The risk that they will do so is often real, especially in the common repeated ascending auctions in which bidders frequently are known or even present with each other (as at, say, Sotheby's for art objects or in many government-run auctions for parts of the electromagnetic spectrum). In such contexts not only do the bidders know what the other bidders are doing, but also they can punish rivals for entry into the market as competitors. For example, one broadcaster who had to pay more than it would have otherwise had to for rights in one market later entered the auction for rights in a rival's market where it had previously shown little interest; it entered the bidding in the second market evidently in retaliation for its rival's participation in the first (Klemperer, 2002). Buyers may not know whether or not another firm will retaliate in this kind of way, but knowing that this is possible, bidders may refrain from entering some auctions. To avoid these dynamics, sellers do better in contexts in which the number of potential bidders is high so that uncertainty on the part of buyers about who is in the marketplace is increased.

Buyers, on the other hand, who are in a market, want to raise barriers to entry to limit competition and make it easier to signal their intentions to other bidders. Among other advantages, small numbers of buyers decrease uncertainty about who is in the market and their bids, thus allowing enforcement of even tacit collusive arrangements.

Uncertainty of Interests: What do Marketplace Participants Value and How Much?

Besides allowing buyers to monitor each other's compliance on bidding strategy, small numbers can affect whether buyers are induced to pay more than is in their interest. Because the high bidder wins the auction, but when there is uncertainty about the true value of the item being auctioned the mean bidder is likely to bid most accurately, buyers are subject to the winner's curse (Thaler, 1988). Small numbers make it less likely that the winning bidder pays more than the value of the good being auctioned because with few bidders the high bid may not be particularly exaggerated. There is some evidence that sellers can attract more bidders if they offer low initial starting prices, which can ironically lead to higher selling prices because low prices encourage bidders to enter the market and thus generate additional competition (Ku et al., 2006).

Ku and her colleagues (Ku et al., 2005; Ku et al., 2006) have studied how people actually behave in auctions with varying numbers of participants. Ku et al. (2005) found that bidders exceed their predetermined limits (reservation prices) more frequently when an auction has fewer rather than more bidders participating and they do so later in an auction. Ku at al. attribute these findings to the effects of competitive arousal and escalation of commitment. A bidder being in the spotlight and being aware of his or her competitors, as occurs when there are relatively few bidders, experiences competitive arousal; and escalation of commitment results from attention to sunk costs, which increases as the auction goes on. Together these two effects contribute to "auction fever", which burns hot in part because escalation of commitment can itself increase arousal and the desire to win (compare Malhotra, 2010).

The winner's curse occurs in contexts in which the value of the item is common to all potential buyers. Common value is what a good or property is inherently worth to anyone; that is, it is a good's objective market value regardless of any kind of subjective extra valuation. In many markets, however, participants have idiosyncratic preferences that lead to differences between common value and private value. Private value is what goods are worth to particular individuals, some of whom may value the good more than other individuals for personal reasons. Commodities have almost entirely common value in the sense that one instance or lot of the good is equivalent to the next. In contrast to commodities, some goods have almost entirely private value, such as sentimental value or personal aesthetic appreciation for a painting. Many goods have both common and private value, which can be quite different, of course. This difference is perhaps a source of disappointment, for example, to many whose family heirlooms, which sometimes have high private values, are appraised for low common values (say, on *Antiques Roadshow*). In such cases, negotiators may be combining (or confusing) the common value of the object, their private value for the object, and their subjective valuation of the relationship within which the good is embedded (compare Curhan et al., 2006).

The distinction between common value and private value is important in several respects for understanding how the uncertainty faced by negotiators affects their choices and outcomes in marketplace contexts. These choices and their effects quickly grow in complexity compared to the more usually studied dyadic, team, and multilateral negotiations.

For example, when one bidder's private value is slightly higher than other bidders' common value, the risk that the other bidders will succumb to the winner's curse increases. Such private value exists when a firm sees even relatively small idiosyncratic advantages of acquiring an item, as when organizational synergies can be gained from acquiring it. Even when this apparent advantage is just a bluff, a potential buyer in an auction can benefit from the perception by other potential bidders that she perceives private value in the good being sold. When a bidder bids aggressively for a good that seems to have primarily common value, other bidders may attribute this behavior to the fact that the aggressive bidder may have some source of private value (Klemperer, 1998). Such private value increases the likelihood that the other bidders will pay too much compared to the common value, if they continue to participate in the auction. Knowing this, other bidders may drop out of the bidding, benefitting the aggressive party, but to their own detriment and to the detriment of the seller.

Private value can range widely for many reasons. In some contexts this fact raises the important issue of selecting a negotiation counterpart who provides high levels of (private) value to specific parties. Most research on negotiation assigns people to dyads or teams so that negotiators not only know with whom they are negotiating, but also know that this selection has been determined before the negotiation proceeds (Thompson et al., 2010). In some typical negotiations the counterparties are indeed fixed and predetermined. Team members may be assigned to their teams, for example, and the parties with a legitimate place at the table in multilateral contexts may be defined by the organization or industry. But in many negotiations, explicit choices about whom to engage affect the value that can potentially be gained by the negotiators on both sides.

When partner selection represents a significant source of value then not only the terms of the dyadic deals that emerge in the marketplace matter, but the matching of the parties who transact is also important. Labor markets are a prime example of this kind of context because the inherent characteristics of each party provide much of the benefit that the other side gains from reaching a negotiated agreement (Roth, 1982).

Consider a familiar example: A new PhD in organizational behavior seeks a faculty position. The job candidate must weigh a number of considerations in developing her preferences for the various outcomes she can envision. Positions are associated with some things that are simply part of the match and that are not subject to much if any negotiation – examples include the hiring schools' locations and their current portfolio of faculty members. But faculty positions also are associated with some things that a job candidate can expect to negotiate, such as salary, teaching load, and course preps. Further complicating the situation, the matching problem is two-sided, because the hiring business schools have preferences that create idiosyncratic valuations, too. A potential faculty member's research expertise, something that cannot really be negotiated but is just one dimension of who she is, matters to the schools, for example. So do her salary demands and her willingness to teach particular courses at various times, however, which can be negotiated. Anyone who has been on either side of a search for faculty will have some experience with the need to consider not just the terms of the deal one strikes in these contexts, but also with whom one strikes that deal.

High value matches are those that provide more value to both sides of the deal than could other feasible matches. That is, the task for a negotiator in marketplace contexts with meaningful levels of private value generated by partner selection is to identify the parties on the other side of the market who provide high levels of value to that negotiator, who also find high value from matching with her. The economics literature framed this issue as "the marriage problem" years ago (Gale and Shapley, 1962), because the structure of finding a mate who is attractive to you, to whom you are attractive, provides a commonly experienced context for understanding this kind of matching dynamic. Making these contexts especially complex and uncertain, in most of these kinds of matching markets value also is produced by the terms of the deal, not just the match. In a labor market, for example, finding the right firm to work for is important for a job candidate, but salary and vacation time are also important. To determine a good match while negotiating the terms of the deal is a difficult process that is fraught with uncertainty.

Uncertainty of Inclusion: Will I Make a Deal?

Additional complexity is introduced into marketplace negotiations because of the presence of competing parties on each side of the market. In markets that are presumed to involve common values, others who can tolerate thinner margins and thus are willing to accept less benefit from the deal, might outbid the focal negotiator. Parties who see private value in a potential transaction are likely to be willing to pay a premium and thus outbid the focal negotiator. In either case, she is left without a deal.

In markets in which matching is an issue, negotiators face uncertainty about whether they will come to a negotiated agreement and, if they do, whether the deal will last. While a job candidate is seeking her best possible position, for example, other candidates are negotiating with the same set of firms. "Keeping your options open" and "jockeying for position" are expressions that easily apply to such situations. Anyone who has been part of an academic job search is familiar with this aspect of the problem – business schools do not want to make offers until several candidates have come for job talks and candidates are reluctant to accept offers until they have visited their full slate of schools. Each party waits anxiously for the right moment to choose; the marketplace is a game of musical chairs.

There is another aspect to negotiations in these contexts that affects the overall value for the participants in the market as well as for individual parties – the stability of the matches. It is very difficult to know at any moment whether or not a potential match is the best that one could do in the market if one could take the time to explore all opportunities. In musical chairs one cannot take her time because other parties will sit down first; in many job markets, others may form matches before one is ready to commit. Because of this uncertainty, market participants may be likely to misrepresent their true preferences so that they receive multiple offers and string along potential match partners. "I am really interested in your company", a candidate might say to all firms so that she increases her chances of receiving offers from as many firms as possible and also keeps them in the market by remaining unmatched while they wait for her decision. But those on the other side of the market may be trying to do the same thing to generate as much interest as possible. And, since parties on both sides know that this deception may be occurring, they know that they face uncertainty that may be intractable. Offers may be made and accepted to hedge against the possibility of being left with only worse alternatives (Sondak and Bazerman, 1989; 1991). The situation can come to resemble the flirting that happens in high schools before prom dates are finalized.

This hedging behavior by individuals can lead to market failure in the form of offers being made and accepted increasingly early and then falling apart. Early deals are likely to be unstable because parties who actually would have preferred each other end up matched with other partners. When such premature deals occur, the parties to them have an incentive to renege on their agreements and form new, more desirable matches. The problem of such "unraveling" markets is not just theoretical and has affected a number of real labor markets; the market for graduating medical students is one that has been extensively discussed (Roth, 1984; Kagel and Roth, 2000). The advancement of the market for new PhDs in management from the winter to the autumn over the past decade may indicate a similar trend.

An institutional solution exists to solve the problem of unstable matching. This solution is a centralized matching clearinghouse that employs an algorithm to match parties in the marketplace. Such algorithms have been used, for example, to match medical residents and fellows with positions at hospitals, clinical psychologists to postdoctoral positions, sorority pledges, and students to high schools in New York City (Roth, 1984; Roth and Xing, 1994; 1997; Featherstone and Mayefsky, 2010).

Use of an algorithm might lead to stable solutions but individual market participants may still face uncertainty. The algorithms in two-sided matching contexts depend on rank-ordered preference lists from the participants in the market. Well-designed algorithms generally offer incentives to submit true preferences (Kagel and Roth, 2000), but individual market participants may not be fully aware of these incentives. There may be some pressures to misrepresent in any case. We suspect that if one were to ask physicians about how they experienced the matching process when they became a new resident, many would agree that they had a discussion prior to submitting their preferences about where they would rank a particular hospital and where the hospital would rank them.

CONCLUSION

In this chapter we have considered three forms of uncertainty – uncertainty about identity, interests, and inclusion. We have discussed how each form can influence the process and outcomes of team, multilateral, and marketplace negotiations. While uncertainty is often an aversive state for people, negotiators need to recognize and manage uncertainty in these three forms.

Uncertainty may exist without negotiators recognizing it and they may not anticipate its effects. For example, in intra-team negotiations, the assumption of homogeneity of perspectives and goals among team members, and, thus predictions of their actions, may be inaccurate. As a result, team members may fail to identify and align or implement team members' interests in the team's proposals. In multilateral contexts, negotiators may not know about the coalitions that exclude them. When that occurs, negotiators are at risk of being left out or of receiving less benefit than they otherwise might. In negotiations that occur in marketplaces, negotiators do not have immediate access to the value that the parties on the other side of the market see in matching with them. Negotiators in marketplace contexts may thus pursue deals with counterparties who are not the most willing to pay a premium for their services.

Uncertainty can be all too obvious, however, and negotiators sometimes may be overwhelmed by the uncertainty in a situation (see Van Kleef and Sinaceur, Chapter 5 this volume, for emotional responses to uncertainty and other factors). In multilateral negotiations, for example, the information gathering and processing demands for identifying possible agreements are much greater than in two-sided negotiations. When faced with more uncertainty than they know how to manage, negotiators tend to rely on heuristic processing. Negotiators who employ heuristics rather than systematic thinking often leave many value creation opportunities unrecognized and therefore unrealized (Neale and Bazerman, 1991).

Negotiators in multiparty contexts would be well served not to avoid uncertainty nor to be overwhelmed by it, but to engage in the improved processes that recognizing and dealing with it can bring. Seeking out more uncertainty than is initially apparent would serve both the individual negotiators in team contexts and their teams overall; uncovering the issues of internal disagreement before a team comes to the negotiation table is definitely in the team's interest. Recognizing that potential coalitions might not be obvious allows negotiators in multilateral contexts to anticipate and perhaps block those coalitions. And negotiators in marketplaces who recognize the dynamic nature of the uncertainty in such contexts are much better positioned to avoid the winner's curse or being left without any deal.

In conclusion, negotiators face different kinds of uncertainty in various kinds of multiparty contexts. While managing uncertainty presents challenges, and if done poorly can undermine negotiators' performance, effective management of uncertainty can facilitate negotiators' success.

REFERENCES

Abrams, D., Wetherell, M., Cochrane, S., Hogg, M.A., and Turner, J.C. (1990). Knowing what to think by knowing who you are: Self-categorization and the nature of norm formation, conformity and group polarization. *British Journal of Social Psychology*, 29, 97–119.

Allen, V.L. and Wilder, D.A. (1979). Group categorization and attribution of belief similarity. *Small Group Behavior*, 10, 73–80.

Anderson, N. and Neale, M.A. (2004). All fired up but nobody to blame. Paper presented at the Academy of Management, New Orleans, LA.

Bazerman, M.H., Mannix, E.A., and Thompson, L.L. (1988). Groups as mixed-motive negotiations. In E.J. Lawler and B. Markovsky (eds), *Advances in group decision making processes: Theory and research*, Vol. 5, JAI Press.

Borenstein, G. (2003). Intergroup conflict: Individual, group, and collective interests. *Personality and Social Psychology Review*, 7, 129–145.
Brett, J. (1991). Negotiating group decisions. *Negotiation Journal*, 7(3), 291–310.
Brewer, M.B. (1979). In-group bias in the minimal intergroup situation. A cognitive-motivational analysis. *Psychological Bulletin*, 86, 307–324.
Brewer, M.B. and Miller, N. (1996). *Intergroup relations*. Buckingham: Open University Press..
Bulow, J. and Klemperer, P. (1996). Auctions vs. negotiations. *American Economic Review*, 86, 180–194.
Cao, J. and Phillips, K.W. (2011). Team diversity and information acquisition: How homogeneous teams set themselves up to have less conflict. Working paper, Columbia Business School.
Chaiken, S., Liberman, A., and Eagly, A.H. (1989). Heuristic and systematic information processing within and beyond the persuasion context. In J. Uleman and J. Bargh (eds), *Unintended thought* (pp. 212–252). New York: Guilford.
Cobb, A. (1986). Coalition identification in organizational research. In R. Lewicki, B. Sheppard, and M. Bazerman (eds), *Research on negotiation in organizations* (Vol. 1, pp. 139–154). Greenwich, CT: JAI Press.
Curhan, J.R., Xu, H., and Elfenbein, H. (2006). What do people value when they negotiate? Mapping the domain of subjective value in negotiation. *Journal of Personality and Social Psychology*, 91(3), 493–512.
De Dreu, C.K.W. (2003). Time pressure and closing of the mind in negotiation. *Organizational Behavior and Human Decision Processes*, 91, 280–295.
Featherstone, C. and Mayefsky, E. (2010). Stability and deferred acceptance: Strategic behavior in two-sided matching. Working paper, Harvard Business School: http://www.people.hbs.edu/cfeatherstone/FeatherstoneMayefsky-2-10.pdf.
Gale, D. and Shapley, L. (1962). College admissions and the stability of marriage. *American Mathematical Monthly*, 69, 1–8.
Galinsky, A., Seiden, V., Kim, P., and Medvec, V. (2002). The dissatisfaction of having your first offer accepted: The role of counterfactual thinking in negotiations. *Personality and Social Psychology Bulletin*, 28(2), 271–283.
Gibson, C.B. and Vermeulen, F. (2003). A healthy divide: Subgroups as a stimulus for team learning behavior. *Administrative Science Quarterly*, 48, 202–217.
Gosling, J. and Mintzberg, H. (2003). The five minds of a manager. *Harvard Business Review*, 81(11), 54–63.
Halevy, N. (2008). Team negotiation: Social, epistemic, economic and psychological consequences of subgroup conflict. *Personality and Social Psychology Bulletin*, 34, 1687–1702.
Harrison, D.A. and Klein, K. (2007). What's the difference? Diversity constructs as separation, variety, or disparity in organizations. *Academy of Management Review*, 32, 1199–1228.
Hinds, P.J. and Mortensen, M. (2005). Understanding conflict in geographically distributed teams: The moderating effects of shared identity, shared context, and spontaneous communication. *Organization Science*, 16, 290–307.
Hogg, M.A. and Terry, D.J. (2000). Social identity. *Academy of Management Review*, 25, 121–140.
Janis, I. (1982). *Groupthink: Psychological studies of policy decisions and fiascoes*. New York: Houghton-Mifflin.
Jehn, K., Northcraft, G.B., and Neale, M.A. (1999). What differences make a difference. *Administrative Science Quarterly*, 44, 741–763.
Kagel, J. and Roth, A. (2000). The dynamics of reorganization in matching markets: A laboratory experiment motivated by a natural experiment. *Quarterly Journal of Economics*, 115, 201–235.
Kahneman, D. (2011). *Thinking fast and slow*. New York: Farrar, Straus, and Giroux.
Kahneman, D., Knetsch, J.L., and Thaler, R. (1990). Experimental tests of the endowment effect and the Coase Theorem. *Journal of Political Economy*, 98, 1325–1348.

Katzenbach, J.R. and Smith, D. (1993). *The wisdom of teams: Creating the high performance organization*. Boston, MA: Harvard Business School Press.

Kelley, H.H. (1966). A classroom study of the dilemmas in interpersonal negotiations. In K. Archibald (ed.), *Strategic interaction and conflict* (pp. 49–73). Berkeley, CA: University of California, Institute of International Studies.

Klemperer, P. (1998). Auctions with almost common values: the 'wallet game' and its applications. *European Economic Review*, 42, 757–769.

Klemperer, P. (2002). What really matters in auction design. *Journal of Economic Perspectives*, 16, 169–189.

Kramer, R.M. (1991). Intergroup relations and organizational dilemmas: The role of the categorization process. *Research in Organizational Behavior*, 13, 191–228.

Ku, G., Galinsky, A.D., and Murnighan, J. (2006). Starting low but ending high: A reversal of the anchoring effect in auctions. *Journal of Personality and Social Psychology*, 90(6), 975–986.

Ku, G., Malhotra, D., and Murnighan, J. (2005). Towards a competitive arousal model of decision-making: A study of auction fever in live and Internet auctions. *Organizational Behavior and Human Decision Processes*, 96(2), 89–103.

Loyd, D.L., Wang, C.S., Phillips, K.W., and Lount, R.L. (2012). Social category diversity promotes pre-meeting elaboration: The role of relationship focus. *Published online, Organization Science, July*.

Malhotra, D. (2010). The desire to win: The effects of competitive arousal on motivation and behavior. *Organizational Behavior and Human Decision Processes*, 111(2), 139–140.

Mannix, E.A. and Loewenstein, G.F. (1994). The effects of inter-firm mobility and individual versus group decision making on managerial time horizons. *Organizational Behavior and Human Decision Processes*, 59, 371–390.

Mannix, E.A. and Neale, M.A. (2005). What differences make a difference? The promise and reality of diverse teams in organizations. *Psychological Science in the Public Interest*, 6, 31–55.

Murnighan, J.K. (1978). Models of coalition behavior: Game theoretic, social psychological, and political perspectives. *Psychological Bulletin*, 85, 1130–1153.

Murnighan, J.K. (1986). Organization coalitions: Structural contingencies and the formation process. In R. Lewicki, B. Sheppard, and M. Bazerman (eds), *Research on negotiation in organizations* (Vol. 1, pp. 153–173). Greenwich, CT: JAI Press.

Murnighan, J.K. and Brass, D. (1991). Intraorganizational coalitions. In M. Bazerman, R. Lewicki, and B. Sheppard (eds), *Research on negotiation in organizations* (Vol. 1, pp. 283–306). Greenwich, CT: JAI Press.

Neale, M.A. and Bazerman, M.H. (1985). The effect of framing and negotiator overconfidence on bargainer behavior. *Academy of Management Journal*, 28, 34–49.

Neale, M.A. and Bazerman, M.H. (1991). *Cognition and rationality in negotiation*. New York: Free Press.

Neale, M.A. and Fragale, A.R. (2006). Social cognition, attribution, and perception in negotiation: The role of uncertainty in shaping negotiation processes and outcomes. In L.L. Thompson (ed.), *Frontiers in Negotiation*. New York: APA Press.

Neale, M.A. and Lys, T.Z. (2012). *Getting (more of) what you want: Integrating economic and psychological insights for competitive advantage*. Unpublished manuscript, Stanford University, Palo Alto, CA.

Northcraft, G.B. and Neale, M.A. (1987). Experts, amateurs, and real estate: An anchoring-and-adjustment perspective on property pricing. *Organizational Behavior and Human Decision Processes*, 39(1), 84–98.

Ocasio, W. (1995). The enactment of economic adversity: A reconciliation of theories of failure-induced change and threat rigidity. *Research in Organizational Behavior*, 17, 287–331.

Olekalns, M., Smith, P.L. and Walsh, T. (1996). The process of negotiating: Tactics, phases and outcomes. *Organizational Behavior and Human Decision Processes*, 67, 68–77.

Phillips, K.W. (2003). The effects of categorically based expectations on minority influence: The importance of congruence. *Society for Personality and Social Psychology*, 29, 3–13.

Phillips, K.W. and Apfelbaum, E.P. (2012). Delusions of homogeneity: Reinterpreting the effects of group diversity. In M.A. Neale and E.A. Mannix (eds), *Research on managing groups and teams*, 15, 185–207, Bingley, UK: JAI Emerald.

Phillips, K.W. and Loyd, D.L. (2006). When surface and deep level diversity meet: The effects of dissenting group members. *Organizational Behavior and Human Decision Processes*, 99, 143–160.

Phillips, K.W., Northcraft, G., and Neale, M. (2006). Surface-level diversity and information sharing: When does deep-level similarity help? *Group Processes and Intergroup Relations*, 9, 467–482.

Polzer, J.T., Mannix, E.A., and Neale, M.A. (1998). Interest alignment and coalitions in multiparty negotiation. *Academy of Management Journal*, 41, 42–54.

Raiffa, H. (1982). *The art and science of negotiation*. Cambridge, MA: Harvard University Press.

Roth, A.E. (1982). The economics of matching: Stability and incentives. *Mathematics of Operations Research*, 7, 617–628.

Roth, A.E. (1984). The evolution of the labor market for medical interns and residents: A case study in game theory. *Journal of Political Economy*, 92, 991–1017.

Roth, A.E. and Xing, X. (1994). Jumping the gun: Imperfections and institutions related to the timing of market transactions. *American Economic Review*, 84, 992–1044.

Roth, A.E. and Xing, X. (1997). Turnaround time and bottlenecks in market clearing: Decentralized matching in the market for clinical psychologists. *Journal of Political Economy*, 105, 284–320.

Simonsohn, U. and Ariely, D. (2008). When rational sellers face nonrational buyers: Evidence from herding on eBay. *Management Science*, 54(9), 1624–1637.

Sommers, S. (2006). On racial diversity and group decision making: Identifying multiple effects of racial composition on jury deliberations. *Journal of Personality and Social Psychology*, 90(4), 597–612.

Sondak, H. and Bazerman, M.H. (1989). Matching and negotiation processes in quasi-markets. *Organizational Behavior and Human Decision Processes*, 44, 261–281.

Sondak, H. and Bazerman, M.H. (1991). Power balance and the rationality of outcomes in matching markets. *Organizational Behavior and Human Decision Processes*, 50, 1–24.

Staw, B., Sandelands, L., and Dutton, J. (1981). Threat rigidity in organizational behavior: A multi-level analysis. *Administrative Science Quarterly*, 26, 501–524.

Stout, R., Cannon-Bowers, J., Salas, E., and Milanovich, D. (1999). Planning, shared mental models, and coordinated performance: An empirical link is established. *Human Factors*, 41, 61–71.

Subramanian, G. and Zeckhauser, R. (2004). For sale, but how? Auctions versus negotiations. *Negotiation*, 3–5.

Tajfel, H. (1974). Social identity and intergroup behaviour. *Social Science Information/sur les sciences sociales*, 13, 65–93.

Tajfel, H. and Turner, J.C. (1986). The social identity theory of inter-group behavior. In S. Worchel and L.W. Austin (eds), *Psychology of Intergroup Relations* (pp. 7–24). Chicago: Nelson-Hall.

Tajfel, H., Flament, C., Billig, M., and Bundy, R.P.(1971). Social categorisation and intergroup behaviour. *European Journal of Social Psychology*, 1, 169–192.

Tenbrunsel, A.E. and Wade-Benzoni, K.A. (1999). The negotiation matching process: Relationships and partner selection. *Organizational Behavior and Human Decision Processes*, 80, 252–283.

Thaler, R.H. (1988). Anomalies: The winner's curse. *Journal of Economic Perspectives*, 2, 191–202.

Thompson, L. (1991). Information exchange in negotiation. *Journal of Experimental Social Psychology*, 27, 61–179.

Thompson, L.L., Wang, J., and Gunia, B.C. (2010). Negotiation. *Annual Review of Psychology*, 61, 491–515.
Tiedens, L.Z. and Linton, S. (2001). Judgment under emotional certainty and uncertainty: The effects of specific emotions on information processing. *Journal of Personality and Social Psychology*, 81, 973–988.
Turner, J.C. (1981). The experimental social psychology of intergroup behavior. In J. Turner and H. Giles (eds), *Intergroup behavior* (pp. 66–101). Chicago: University of Chicago Press.
Turner, J.C. (1987). The analysis of social influence. In J.C. Turner, M.A. Hogg, P.J. Oakes, S.D. Reicher, and M.S. Wetherell (eds), *Rediscovering the social group: A self-categorization theory* (pp. 68–88). Oxford, UK: Blackwell.
Weary, G. and Jacobson, J.A. (1997). Causal uncertainty beliefs and diagnostic information seeking. *Journal of Personality and Social Psychology*, 73, 839–849.

PART IV

COMMUNICATION PROCESSES

12. Talking it through: communication sequences in negotiation
Wendi L. Adair and Jeffrey Loewenstein

If negotiation is like a dance (Adair and Brett, 2005; Raiffa, 1981; Young and Schlie, 2011), then negotiation research needs to study its choreography. If negotiation is like an athletic contest (Gelfand and McCusker, 2002), negotiation research needs to study its plays and engage in match analysis. To understand the amount of applause and the final scores, assessing the series of moves negotiators undertake to reach those outcomes is critical.

The moves in negotiations are acts of communication. Negotiators communicate using oral and written messages, conveyed with various postures, facial expressions, rates of speech, and tones of voice, among other concerns (Putnam and Roloff, 1992). Negotiators communicate in ways that are guided by the setting and their initial goals, yet even the most casual observations show that negotiators respond to each other, adapting and reacting to specific communications. The most developed line of research on communication sequences in negotiation is the work on negotiation strategy and tactics (For a related discussion of negotiation stages and turning points, see Druckman and Olekalns, Chapter 13 this volume). There is also work examining sequences of additional aspects of meaning communicated in negotiations, such as nonverbal communication and emotions (see also, Van Kleef and Sinaceur, Chapter 5 this volume), which may ultimately be combined with work on strategy and tactics into a comprehensive account of how negotiators talk their way from "hello" to "sign here".

In what follows, we first outline how scholars study the communication sequences that comprise the negotiation process. Then we examine findings on negotiation strategy and tactics, the primary emphasis of negotiation research on communication sequences. Next we examine findings on nonverbal communication. Finally, we consider lines of research that are opening up new kinds of sequences to explore.

STUDYING NEGOTIATION COMMUNICATION SEQUENCES

Studying the sequential process of negotiating requires content coding written correspondence, or audio and video recordings of negotiations. Scholars study sequences in naturalistic negotiations, such as labor-management negotiations or hostage crisis negotiations (Donohue et al., 1984; Giebels and Taylor, 2009; Putnam and Jones, 1982a; Putnam et al., 1990; Taylor, 2002). Applying the same methodologies in a laboratory setting that offers the precision of manipulation and the control of experimentation has been critical in isolating predictors of communication frequencies and sequences as well as the underlying causal mechanisms linking negotiation communications to outcomes.

The content analysis process (for a general overview, see Krippendorff, 2004) involves breaking the stream of communication into units for analysis. Those units might be single words, thought units, tactics, speech turns, emotional expressions, or whatever else the meaning under study indicates to be a primary building block (e.g., Bakeman and Gottman, 1986). Then those units are coded to evaluate the content negotiators are expressing. Researchers train coders to identify and differentiate units reliably, or select a computer algorithm capable of coding the units. There are many different coding schemes available; a selection of those generated specifically for the study of negotiation communication is listed in Table 12.1.

As an example, imagine that a negotiator angrily responds to a counterpart's threat by shouting, "Don't threaten me, I have plenty of other options I can turn to. I don't need you." Using a simple frequency code (e.g. Weingart et al., 1993), this statement could be unitized at the level of the thought unit (here, split at the comma) and coded as a Rejection (of the counterpart's threat) and a Threat (reference to walking away). Alternatively, using a cue-response coding scheme (e.g. Donohue, 1981; Donohue et al., 1984), this utterance would be unitized in a similar way but coded first as a Defending response to the counterpart's cue, and then as an Attacking cue that will prompt the counterpart's subsequent response. Coding across speakers, this utterance in conjunction with the counterpart's previous threat could be unitized together and coded as a Reciprocal Threat Sequence (e.g. Weingart et al., 1993). A researcher focusing on emotion might unitize emotional expressions (be they verbal or nonverbal), and code instead the tone of voice (angry, firm) or facial expressions (no smile, anger) used when the utterance was expressed (Semnani-Azad and Adair, 2011; in press). Or, as a final example, a researcher might unitize at the level of words and examine personal

Table 12.1 *Negotiation content analysis coding schemes*

Coding Scheme	Reference	Main Code Categories (#sub categories)	Application
Bargaining Process Analysis II, Revised	Putnam and Jones, 1982a	Substantive (5) Strategic (4) Persuasive (3) Task related (6) Affective (2) Procedural (1)	Content and function of bargaining
Cue-Response Negotiation Coding System	Donohue, Diez, and Hamilton, 1984	Response: Attacking (3) Defending (3) Integrating (3) Cue: Attacking (3) Defending (3) Integrating (3)	Coding sequences, give-and-take
Negotiation Behaviors in Strategy Clusters	Wiengart, Brett Olekalns, and Smith, 2007	Integrative info (5) Create value (8) Distributive info (7) Claim value (7) Push to closure (2) Process management (3)	Integrative versus distributive strategies
Culture and Negotiation Coding Scheme	Adair, Okumura, and Brett, 2001	Information (9) Substantiation (3) Offers (3) Reactions (2) Mutuality (2) Procedural (5) Clarification (1) Other (1)	East–West cross-cultural negotiation strategies
Emotion and Vocal Fluency	Semnani-Azad and Adair, in press	Pitch (1) Expressiveness (1) Volume (1) Fluency (3)	Observer global ratings of vocal dynamics
Linguistic Inquiry Word Count	Niederhoffer and Pennebaker, 2002; Taylor and Thomas, 2008	Linguistic (6) Social/Affect (4) Cognitive (7)	Computer-based text analysis of word types
Vocal Dynamics	Curhan and Pentland, 2007	Engagement (1) Mirroring (1) Emphasis (1) Activity (1)	Computer-based micro-coding of vocal cues

Table 12.1 (continued)

Coding Scheme	Reference	Main Code Categories (#sub categories)	Application
Nonverbal Negotiation Inventory	Semnani-Azad and Adair, 2011, in press	Posture (4) Head Movement (4) Hand Movement (3) Eye Gaze (3) Vocal Speech (2) Facial Expression (3)	Nonverbal cues
Interests, Rights, and Power Process Code	Brett, Shapiro, and Lytle, 1998; Tinsley, 2001	Interests (3) Rights (2) Power (2) Other categories (7)	Interests, rights, and power influence strategies
Influence in Negotiations Coding System	Giebels and Taylor, 2009	Relational (3) Content (8)	Influence in crisis negotiation context

references ("I", "me"; see, e.g., Niederhoffer and Pennebaker, 2002; Taylor and Thomas, 2008) as a measure of self-concern.

Choosing or designing a coding scheme is an important step in the research process. Some considerations are the nature of the research question, the level of analysis, whether the code is to be theory or data driven, task or relationship focused, and include verbal or nonverbal codes. Weingart et al. (2004) provide a detailed description of the process of developing a coding scheme, which also indicates concerns in the selection of an existing coding scheme. As the study of communication sequences depends on the unit comprising those sequences, the choice of a coding scheme is likely to shape the kind of sequences scholars might find.

Most negotiation-specific coding schemes focus on the negotiation-specific function of statements—tactics—and cluster them into two main types, integrative and distributive (Deutsch, 1974). Integrative tactics facilitate the exchange of information and discovery of mutually satisfactory solutions, such as providing information on preferences or priorities, noting where parties have similar concerns, and posing multi-issue offers. Distributive tactics assist negotiators in the task of claiming value for themselves, such as references to alternatives or a bottom line, threats, demands, and arguments.

Researchers are generally in agreement about what tactics serve integrative versus distributive functions, but there are two areas in particular where coding schemes vary substantially: conceptualization of offers and operationalization of influence tactics. In conceptualizing offers, the key gray area is the interpretation of single-issue offers, where one party stakes a claim on a single issue. In general, multi-issue offers, which highlight trade-off opportunities, are considered integrative (Weingart et al., 1990; Pruitt, 1983; Tutzauer and Roloff, 1988) whereas single-issue offers are considered distributive, as they often indicate that a negotiator is attempting to claim value. Thus, for example, Gunia and colleagues included "Substantiation and Single-Issue Offers" in a single code category capturing distributive strategies that were used more often when Indian and U.S. negotiators had low trust (Gunia et al., 2011); additional work on culture is discussed in this volume in Chapter 10 (by Aslani et al.) and Chapter 15 (by Crump). However, single-issue offers have also been categorized as an integrative strategy, because sequences of single-issue offers can lead negotiators to integrative solutions, either through heuristic trial-and-error (Pruitt, 1981) or as an indirect information search process when trust is low (Adair et al., 2007). As illustrated by the study of offer sequences, the function of a communication as an isolated statement may not be the same as the function of that statement within a sequence of communications (Olekalns and Weingart, 2008).

The challenge with operationalizing the communication of influence in negotiation is the sheer scope of the topic. Negotiators use influence to convince the other party to make a concession, change their limits, or revise their goals (Lax and Sebenius, 1986). To capture this distributive function of influence, many negotiation researchers have operationalized influence through power plays, such as stalling or making threats or demands (De Dreu et al., 1998; Pruitt and Lewis, 1975; Putnam and Wilson, 1989). Another operationalization of influence codes for "task-related information and logic" used to persuade the other party (Giebels et al., 2003). Other researchers have operationalized influence with tactics drawn from the social psychology of persuasion, for example measuring different forms of substantiation (e.g., good for you, good for me, good for both) (Adair et al., 2001; Putnam and Jones, 1982a), or coding for relational versus rational influence (Giebels and Taylor, 2009). Yet another approach to measuring influence codes for arguments that refer to negotiator's interests, rights, or power in a conflict setting (Brett et al., 1998; Lytle et al., 1999). Adair and colleagues have recently developed a 3 × 2 model of influence strategies in negotiation that measures interests, rights, and power arguments that are framed to appeal to negotiators' needs for information or negotiators' needs to uphold social norms (Adair et al., in press). Thus, negotiation researchers have many ways of operationalizing and measuring influence that focus on both tactics and communication.

Such coding schemes can be expanded and refined as researchers study new kinds of tactics, new versions of existing tactics, or develop sub-types of existing tactics.

Once a negotiation is coded into a collection of tactics or other building blocks, researchers can then examine when they tend to occur, how frequently they occur, and how they fit into sequences. One common approach to studying sequences is conducting a lag-sequential or log-linear analysis that examines the likelihoods of different responses occurring after a given cue (Olekalns and Smith, 2000). More complex Markov chain modeling allows researchers to examine longer chains of behaviors (Weingart et al., 1999). A third approach, proximity analysis, considers the relationships among all behaviors, capturing more of the complex interconnections among behaviors in an interaction (Taylor, 2006; Taylor and Donald, 2006). Having unitized, coded, and assessed the succession of codes across a negotiation, negotiation scholars are then in a position to provide evidence on what kinds of communication sequences occur and what outcomes they predict.

NEGOTIATION STRATEGY AND TACTICS

Scholars examining negotiation communications have long focused on integrative and distributive strategy and their associated tactics to understand the negotiation process and negotiation outcomes (Drake and Donohue, 1996; Olekalns et al., 1996; Putnam and Jones, 1982a; 1982b; Weingart, et al., 1993; Wilson and Putnam, 1990). The reason is that negotiators have both cooperative and competitive goals, which guide the selection of negotiation strategy and convey it to the other party. Cooperative goals imply using integrative tactics, with the potential to create value for all parties. Competitive goals imply using distributive tactics, with the potential for negotiators to claim value for themselves. Thus, for example, negotiators with a cooperative orientation are likely to offer priority information and ask questions and negotiators with a competitive orientation are likely to make positional statements and threats (O'Connor, 1997; Olekalns and Smith, 1999). These communication choices then influence negotiation outcomes.

In both laboratory and field settings, the use and reciprocation of integrative tactics predict agreements that create value and the use and reciprocation of distributive tactics predict agreements that fail to create value or fail to form any agreement (Olekalns and Smith, 1999, 2003; Putnam et al., 1990; Simons, 1993; Weingart et al., 1990; Weingart et al., 1996). One source of evidence for the link between strategy and outcomes is studies of tactic frequency, which examine how often negotiators use particular tactics (e.g., asking questions, providing information). The frequency of a given tactic is usually considered relative to the frequency of the other tactics used or the frequency with which a counterpart uses the same tactic. A meta-analysis of 28 frequency studies by De Dreu et al. (2000) confirmed that the frequency of integrative tactics, such as information sharing and problem-solving, predicted high joint gains and the frequency of distributive tactics, such as contending, predicted low joint gains.

Further, the meta-analysis and subsequent research show there are multiple moderators (e.g., power, social value orientation, negotiation situation type, national culture of the negotiators) that influence tactic use and the relationship between tactic use and joint gains (Giebels et al., 1998; Olekalns and Smith, 2003). For example, negotiators who are pro-social are more likely to use integrative tactics, whereas negotiators who are pro-self are more likely to use distributive tactics (e.g. Olekalns and Smith, 1999; 2003; O'Connor, 1997; see also Koning and van Dijk, Chapter 3 this volume). When negotiators are concerned with achieving their own high targets (i.e., have high resistance to yielding), these effects are particularly pronounced.

As a second example, due to norms for indirect communication and harmony maintenance, negotiators from East Asian cultures are less likely to state directly their preferences and priorities than negotiators from North American cultures (Adair et al., 2001). Instead, East Asian negotiators use sequences of offers to share and gather information that allows them to craft integrative solutions (Adair et al., 2007). Negotiators from national cultures with low trust (e.g., Russia, China) are unlikely to share information at all; their strategies are mostly distributive (Adair et al., 2004). Thus, communication tactics are a means by which negotiators exhibit and seek to attain their goals, but tactic types and frequencies are not fully indicative of eventual outcomes. The sequences in which those tactics are used also matter.

Patterns of reciprocity are common in negotiation, whereby counterparts respond-in-kind to both distributive and integrative tactics (e.g., Weingart et al., 1990; Adair, 2003). Reciprocated sequences of tactics convey information on how negotiators view their relationship with their counterpart (Giles et al., 1991). Integrative tactics such as noting mutual interests serve to generate affiliation and interdependence between negotiators, while distributive tactics such as threatening to walk away create distance between them (Taylor, 2002; Taylor and Thomas, 2008), as predicted by Donohue's (2001) Relational Order Theory. In contrast, reciprocating distributive tactics can lead to conflict spirals and impasses, unless negotiators can break out of the cycle and refocus on interests (Brett et al.,

1998). Thus, it is not just a matter of what goals negotiators have initially, or what tactics they use, but how they coordinate their communications within sequences.

Sequences of tactics also influence the negotiation process and outcomes by gradually narrowing negotiators' response options (Chartrand and Bargh, 1999; Weingart, et al., 1999). As negotiators establish regular patterns of reciprocal information exchange (an integrative tactic), it becomes less and less likely that either negotiator will switch to a distributive strategy such as making a threat (Weingart et al., 1999). Negotiators' sequences of communications tend to become systematic, self-sustaining, and difficult to change (Lytle et al., 1999).

A strategy sequence is defined by the kind of relationship between tactics, with the three main categories of sequences being reciprocal, complementary, and structural. A reciprocal strategy sequence is defined as response-in-kind: a counterpart exactly matches the focal negotiator's tactic. For example, if a focal negotiator shares priority information, the counterpart responds by sharing priority information. Reciprocal sequences indicate that negotiators are in-sync; they both have either an integrative or distributive focus, and they are both using the same type of tactic (Brett et al., 1998; Donohue, 1981; Olekalns and Smith, 2000; Putnam, 1990; Putnam and Jones, 1982a; Weingart et al., 1996).

Complementary strategy sequences are a less strict form of responding in kind. They are sequences in which negotiators use different tactics of the same strategic focus. For example, a complementary integrative sequence might consist of one negotiator sharing priority information and the other responding by noting a mutual interest. A complementary distributive sequence might consist of one negotiator offering a positional argument and the counterpart responding with a threat to walk away. Complementary sequences indicate that negotiators have the same strategic focus but perhaps different tactical repertoires (Adair and Brett, 2005; Weingart et al., 1999).

In contrast to reciprocal and complementary sequences, which mark synchronicity and tend to be self-sustaining, structural sequences occur when negotiators' integrative tactics are met with distributive tactics, or vice-versa. Structural sequences signal that negotiators' strategic foci diverge. Such sequences have also been called "transformational" because they can mark a shift between cooperative and competitive phases of a negotiation (Brett et al., 1998; Olekalns and Smith, 2000).

Strategy sequences do not have uniform effects, as shown in particular by studies of national culture. Negotiators are more likely to generate reciprocal sequences of culturally normative tactics than non-normative tactics (Adair, 2003). All forms of strategy sequences have been studied by comparing low context and high context cultures. Low context cultures are defined by a reliance on words and direct communication, whereas high context cultures rely on nonverbal gestures and subtle contextual cues to convey meaning beyond what is said in words (Hall, 1976). For example, in the context of police interrogations, contrast sequences (a form of structural sequence) consisting of intimidation followed by a rational argument were effective in eliciting confessions from direct, low context perpetrators, but not indirect, high context perpetrators. Perpetrators from high context cultures seemed to be more responsive to contrast sequences that included the relational component of active listening (Beune et al., 2011). Advances in our understanding of the nuanced communication characteristic of high context negotiators offer many promising avenues for process researchers to investigate (Adair et al., 2009; Buchan et al., 2011).

Together, the existing body of research shows several reliable predictors of how negotiators use strategies and tactics in general and in patterned sequences. The strongest evidence lies in social value orientation and national culture, leaving the field open to examine many other possible predictors of how negotiators enact strategies and sequences, such as individual differences (e.g., self-esteem) as well as contextual variables (e.g., communication medium) (see also Elfenbein, Chapter 2, and Friedman and Belkin, Chapter 14, both in this volume). As noted by De Dreu et al. (2000), there are also important moderators of the strategy-outcome link. In addition, recent work has identified consistent use of triple-interact (i.e., cue-response-cue-response) sequences that predict outcome differentially depending on the communication content (Taylor et al., 2012). Thus, there is a need for researchers to examine more comprehensive causal chains that include predictors, moderators, and partner effects to better understand the emergence and effects of negotiation strategy.

NONVERBAL EXPRESSION

Negotiation tactics are coded from verbal communication, but the course of a negotiation is also guided by expressions and sequences of nonverbal communication. Nonverbal communication is the expression and perception of non-linguistic messages that can occur with or without the simultaneous use of words (Afifi, 2007). Nonverbal communication occurs through many different cues, for example facial expression, posture, gesturing, tone of voice, or rate of speech. Because nonverbal communication is often sub-conscious and automatic (although see Kopelman et al., 2006 for strategic use of emotion), some scholars suggest it is trusted more and thus can have an even greater impact than verbal communication (Afifi,

2007). Still, negotiators clearly attend to both verbal and nonverbal communication when interpreting their counterpart's actions and attributing strategic intent.

A review of nonverbal communication suggests a seemingly endless number of forms and functions that researchers might tackle, yet negotiation researchers have focused mostly on the topics of deception and emotion (Gordon et al., 2006). One example is Morris and Keltner's (2000) analysis of the function of emotional expressions that negotiators use to achieve their goals. They developed a model of the phases (opening, positioning, problem solving, ending) through which negotiations likely proceed and the relational challenges (initiation, influence, trust and binding) likely to occur in each phase. Thus, nonverbal expressions of emotions, tied to particular functions and phases of a negotiation process, were argued to support and advance communicative moves.

There are several examples of main effect studies on nonverbal expression. For example, it has been shown that when negotiators are strangers, eye contact facilitates integrative agreements for female negotiators, who use eye contact to facilitate shared understanding, but not for male negotiators, who experience discomfort from eye contact (Swaab and Swaab, 2009). In a study linking national culture to nonverbal dominance expressions, Chinese male negotiators expressed dominance through taking up space (e.g., spreading out papers on the table) whereas Canadian male negotiators expressed dominance through leaning forward (Semnani-Azad and Adair, 2011). In another study, researchers coded nonverbal expression in just the first five minutes of negotiation and found that high activity, measured by time speaking, helped high status negotiators claim value, but linguistic mirroring helped low status negotiators claim value (Curhan and Pentland, 2007).

Recently, researchers have drawn on Osgood's Semantic Differential Model and work conducted in the communication field by Manusov and colleagues (Manusov, 2005; Osgood and Suci, 1955, Osgood and Anderson, 1957) to predict nonverbal communication in negotiation. Semnani-Azad and Adair (2011) developed a typology of nonverbal expression in negotiation categorized according to semantic meaning. They primed negotiators with one of six negotiation approaches: actively involved, passively involved, dominant, submissive, positive affect, or negative affect. They videotaped negotiators and trained objective observers to code the frequency of nonverbal behaviors exhibited by negotiators in each condition. The authors identified distinct clusters of nonverbal cues that accompany negotiators' general approach and therefore carry strategic meaning both within culture and across cultures. For example, Canadian negotiators are more likely than Chinese negotiators to vary their posture when passively involved, and Chinese negotiators are more likely than Canadian negotiators to lean forward when they feel positive affect towards their counterpart. This research makes several steps forward in our understanding of nonverbal communication in negotiation by connecting nonverbal cues with specific negotiator approaches and demonstrating the moderating effect of negotiator culture.

Swaab and colleagues are also making strides in the area of nonverbal expression in negotiation by integrating theories on motivation and media richness (Swaab et al., 2012). The authors conducted a meta-analysis of negotiation research testing the presence/absence of visual channels (e.g., video-conference versus email), vocal channels (e.g., face-to-face versus computer chat), and synchronicity (e.g., face-to-face versus email). They found that having more communication channels does not always positively impact negotiation outcome, as would be predicted by theories such as communication richness (Daft and Lengel, 1986). Instead, they found that negotiating with more communication channels (e.g., visual, vocal, and synchronous communication), has a positive impact only when negotiators have a neutral orientation. Greater access to nonverbal cues through more communication channels had no effect on outcome for cooperatively oriented negotiators and a negative effect for non-cooperatively oriented negotiators. This line of research not only helps reconcile prior inconsistent findings on media richness in negotiation, but also offers many new directions for examining the interaction of negotiator approach and communication channels on nonverbal expression and meaning.

Sequences of nonverbal communication in negotiation are categorized as mimicry, mirroring, or entrainment, and represent subconscious nonverbal processes that reflect coordination and affiliation (Chartrand and Bargh, 1999; McGrath and Kelly, 1986). It has been found that nonverbal mimicry during negotiation has a significant impact on negotiation outcome, especially when it occurs in the early stages of negotiation. Maddux and colleagues illustrated that mimicry, or mirroring the nonverbal behavior of a counterpart in the negotiation context, for example pen tapping or leaning forward, improves both relational and economic outcome (Maddux et al., 2008). Swaab and colleagues report a similar effect for linguistic mimicry when negotiating on-line; mimicry improved negotiation outcome when it occurred in the first 10 minutes of negotiation, an effect that was explained through increased trust (Swaab et al., in press). Applying the concept of complementarity to nonverbal expression, Wiltermuth et al. (2012) demonstrated that negotiation partners naturally fall into dominant and submissive roles evident in nonverbal expression. When negotiators' nonverbal behavior conveys one negotiator is dominant (e.g., taking up space) and one negotiator is submissive (e.g., constricting body), this natural relational order positively impacts negotiation outcome in a cooperative context.

NEW DIRECTIONS

The research on communication sequences in negotiation that we have discussed emphasizes integrative and distributive strategies and their associated tactics, as well as patterns in strategic communication, emotional expression, and relationship development. The variables we have reviewed are related to communication form, patterns, channels, and context. In future research, these categories can be expanded and integrated, communication sequences can be studied in the context of virtual negotiation (e.g., Brett et al., 2007; also see Friedman and Belkin, Chapter 14 this volume), and across multi-round negotiations. It is also possible to consider additional kinds of meaning about which negotiators communicate and the sequences that result, and employ new methods to capture such variables as communication intent.

Capturing Communication Complexity

In new work on within-negotiator strategy sequences, Beune and colleagues (2011) examine the effectiveness of different influence strategies when paired together in different orders, such as influence-offer versus offer-influence. More generally, the idea of combining multiple tactics within a single communication turn is a far broader and important consideration. For example, one might examine the effects of pairing integrative and distributive tactics, or multiple emotional expressions, within a larger communication sequence.

The focus on combining tactics raises the prospect of studying mixed messages and their effects on the negotiation process. In research on learning, scholars have found that when simultaneous (verbal) statements and (nonverbal) gestures convey different information, it signals that individuals are noticing but not yet integrating multiple pieces of information (e.g., Goldin-Meadow et al., 1993). Verbal and nonverbal mismatches have also long been associated with low sincerity (i.e., lying; e.g., Friedman, 1979). Consequently, there are rich traditions for exploring effects of mixed messages and their influence on the negotiation process.

Researchers may also consider alternative ways of thinking about the mixing of multiple strategies. Work on strategy and tactics confronts the challenge of negotiators drawing from integrative and distributive strategy. It might benefit from other approaches to how people deploy multiple mixed strategies, as people can, for example, both cooperate and compete with each other at the same time (e.g., Van de Vliert, 1999). Rather than thinking about individuals using one strategy, work by Siegler on microgenetic methods (e.g., Siegler and Svetina, 2006) suggests that people use a collection of strategies, that new strategies may not replace but work alongside previously learned strategies, and that performance variance increases just before people discover new strategies. The microgenetic approach is centrally concerned with observing people's strategy use across attempts, so it raises the question of how negotiators' patterns of strategy and tactic use change and develop over time. Most work on communication sequences has focused on single negotiations, and so stands to gain from considering commonalities and contrasts of the same negotiators conducting multiple negotiations (see also Elfenbein, Chapter 2 this volume).

A related direction is to consider alternative approaches to conceptualizing communication sequences. For example, it is possible to conceptualize the negotiation process as a progression through a script (Schank and Abelson, 1977). Rather than assume that negotiators generate completely novel sequences, negotiators may be guided by their expectations and prior experiences about the course of a negotiation. For example, novice U.S. negotiators seem to hold fairly consistent beliefs about the basic outline of a negotiation (O'Connor and Adams, 1999). Consequently, it seems likely that more advanced negotiators would also have expectations about the negotiation process, and this may vary by national culture (Adair et al., 2009). Accordingly, in addition to considering (low-level) tactics and (high-level) strategic orientations, it might also be useful to consider (mid-level) phases that capture the gist of what negotiators' conversations are attempting to accomplish for some portion of their overall discussions (e.g., Brett et al., 1999). This proposal fits with a broader analysis of events, which are typically found to have hierarchical structures (Zacks and Tversky, 2001), enabling individuals (and presumably therefore also scholars) to consider events at a range of levels of abstraction. Scripts are not the only other way to conceptualize sequences either; it is possible to consider negotiations as a sort of routine (compare Feldman and Pentland, 2003), as dynamic planning (Sycara, 1990), as arguments (Rips, 1998), or as enacting precedent (Schauer, 1987; 2008), among other options.

Measuring More Meaning

Another direction building on existing strategy and tactic research is to separate relationship building tactics from problem solving tactics.

Although there are good reasons to associate the two kinds of tactics—relationship building provides the trust that fosters information sharing necessary for problem solving—there is also documentation that liking and social concern can foster concession-making and failure to create value (Baron, 1990; Fry et al., 1983; Jap et al., 2011). Also, forming a relationship with one's counterpart is a dissociable outcome concern from agreement terms (e.g., Curhan et al., 2006; Pinkley, 1990). There are two broader issues raised by this consideration. One is that tracing tactic sequences, such as when considering complementary sequences, can depend on the categorization of tactics. The second is that tactics may not have a one-to-one match with broader strategic goals, or put another way, strategic goals may not be mutually exclusive. It is possible that a single tactic might advance multiple strategic goals rather than just one.

A new direction for communication sequence research is to consider sequences of additional kinds of meaning. For example, Prietula and Weingart (2011) examine the sequence of offers that negotiators generate. The tactics discussed earlier abstract over the content of the offers that negotiators generate and instead just focus on the broad type of offer made (e.g., single or multiple issue). As a result, they do not capture anything specific about the progression of offers. There is prior work on concession size and timing (Hilty and Carnevale, 1993; Kwon and Weingart, 2004), but this work has mostly examined patterns in the relative sizes of the concessions as an indicator of reaching a negotiator's bottom line or reservation point, rather than as the extent and nature of parties' exploration of possible agreements. Accordingly, there has been a latent opportunity to examine where, in some conceptual space of the possible offers negotiators might generate, negotiators begin, travel, and end. This is the sort of analysis is common in Raiffa's (1981) classic text, among others, but that until Prietula and Weingart (2011) had not been used as a tool to assess empirically how negotiators progressed. They suggest that negotiators are first guided by the value of proposals and then are more influenced by the content of proposals, which implies that a coding system that just tracks one or the other kind of meaning would not be able to capture the full communication sequence negotiators are likely experiencing. Prietula and Weingart (2011) map out an approach to studying movements through an offer space for scorable games. It is open for future research to expand their general approach to the study of sequences of proposals more generally, either by first generating consensus scoring systems for them or through a qualitative evaluation process. It is also open for future research to integrate offer sequences with, for example, tactic sequences. For example, perhaps single issue offers are a distributive tactic when they focus on the same part of the offer space but an integrative tactic when they mark out different parts of the offer space.

This is just one of many possible reasons to consider linking the content of offers with the functions of negotiation tactics.

Adding to the Methods Toolbox

Most research on communication sequences in negotiation has studied naturally evolving sequences rather than trying to intervene and influence those sequences directly. Yet it is possible to influence, even experimentally manipulate, the strategies negotiators use through negotiation simulation role instructions. By manipulating the use of verbal and nonverbal communication at various points in a negotiation, researchers can make stronger claims about the causal relationships between strategy, timing, and outcome.

Negotiation communication researchers may also take advantage of existing approaches from the field of communication, such as the thought and talk method. Developed in the areas of communication and clinical psychology, this method involves participants viewing a videotape of their interaction and explaining in a continuous verbal stream what they were thinking and feeling during their discussion (Sillars et al., 2000). Thoughts can then be coded to identify speaker's intent, selective attention, interpretation and attribution tendencies, perspective taking, and so on.

Another consideration is new content analysis tools that could open up additional possibilities. For example, there is a new stream of work showing that conversational mimicry generates liking using computer automated text analysis called linguistic style matching with Pennebaker's LIWC dictionaries (Taylor and Thomas, 2008). For example, Ireland and colleagues (2011), in studying romantic couples, found that pairs who used prepositions, articles, and other function (or closed class) words in similar proportions were more likely to initiate and remain in relationships. It is possible to look at the emergence of linguistic style matching over the course of a negotiation, for example, and use it analogously to a measure of reciprocal strategy sequences.

As a second example, rather than tracking types of words in texts based on pre-existing categories, a new stream of work on computer-automated text analysis is deriving small sets of words, or topics, from the texts themselves (e.g., Blei, 2012). The possibility here is the prospect of assessing the topics negotiators are using over time as a potential basis for abstracting slightly away from any particular statement to characterize negotiation phases. But more important than any current guess, the larger point is that computer automated text analysis is a rapidly developing area and one from which negotiation research using content analysis likely stands to gain.

SUMMARY AND CONCLUSIONS

Negotiation outcomes, and effects of initial conditions and context on those outcomes, are the product of sequences of communications. These sequences are channeled by individual, situational, social, cultural and other factors, and how those factors exert their influences on negotiators' communications are important topics of research. In addition, the sequences have dynamics of their own, as, for example, reciprocation entrains one line of discussion and so makes others less likely. Thus, understanding negotiators' communications is a complex and necessary task.

Research on integrative and distributive strategy, enacted through sequences of cooperative and competitive tactics, has proven fruitful for understanding communication in negotiation. Examination of sequences of nonverbal behavior and emotions also shows patterns and demonstrates the importance of tracking more than the function of verbal statements to understand negotiation communication. In addition, we discussed new lines of work and a wide array of possibilities to explore. In short, the existing body of negotiation research shows how important communication sequences are in negotiations, and yet ample opportunity remains for new work to identify important new considerations. Integrating these into a more comprehensive account of communication sequences, one that can link antecedents and outcomes, awaits.

REFERENCES

Adair, W.L. (2003). Reciprocal information sharing and negotiation outcome in East–West negotiations. *International Journal of Conflict Management*, 14, 273–296.

Adair, W.L. and Brett, J.M. (2005). The negotiation dance: Time, culture, and behavioral sequences in negotiation. *Organization Science*, 16, 33–51.

Adair, W.L., Buchan, N., and Chen, X.P. (2009). Conceptualizing culture as communication in management and marketing research. In C. Nakata (ed.), *Beyond Hofstede: Culture frameworks for global marketing and management*. New York, NY: Macmillan Palgrave.

Adair, W.L., Okumura, T., and Brett, J.M. (2001). How negotiators get to yes: Predicting the constellation of strategies used across cultures to negotiate conflict. *Journal of Applied Psychology*, 86, 371–385.

Adair, W.L., Taylor, M.S., and Tinsley, C. (2009). Starting out on the right foot: Negotiation schemas when cultures collide. *Negotiation and Conflict Management Research*, 2, 138–163.

Adair, W.L., Weingart, L., and Brett, J. (2007). The timing and function of offers in U.S. and Japanese negotiations. *Journal of Applied Psychology*, 92, 1056–1068.

Adair, W.L., Brett, J.M., Lempereur, A., Okumura, T., Shikhirev, P., Tinsley, C., and Lytle, A. (2004). Culture and negotiation strategy. *Negotiation Journal*, 20, 87–111.

Adair, W.L., Taylor, M., Chu, J., Ethier, N., Xiong, T., Okumura, T., and Brett, J. (in press). Effective influence in negotiation: The role of culture and framing. *International Studies of Management and Organization*.

Afifi, W.A. (2007). *Nonverbal Communication*. Mahwah, NJ: Lawrence Erlbaum Associates Publishers.
Bakeman, R. and Gottman, J M. (1986). *Observing interaction: An introduction to sequential analysis*. Cambridge: Cambridge University Press.
Baron, R.A. (1990). Environmentally induced positive affect: Its impact on self-efficacy, task performance, negotiation, and conflict. *Journal of Applied Social Psychology*, 20, 368–384.
Beune, K., Giebels, E., Adair, W.L., Fennis, B.M., and Van der Zee, K.I. (2011). Strategic sequences in police interviews and the importance of order and cultural fit. *Criminal Justice and Behavior*, 38, 934–964.
Blei, D. (2012). Probabilistic topic models. *Communications of the ACM*, 55(4), 77–84.
Brett, J. F., Northcraft, G. B., and Pinkley, R. L. (1999). Stairways to heaven: An interlocking self-regulation model of negotiation. *Academy of Management Review*, 24(3), 435–451.
Brett, J.M., Shapiro, D.L., and Lytle, A.L. (1998). Breaking the bonds of reciprocity in negotiations. *Academy of Management Journal*, 41, 410–424.
Brett, J.M., Olekalns, M., Friedman, R., Goates, N., Anderson, C., and Lisco, C.C. (2007). Sticks and stones: Language, face, and online dispute resolution. *Academy of Management Journal*, 50, 85–99. doi:10.5465/AMJ.2007.24161853.
Buchan, N., Adair, W.L., and Chen, X.P. (2011). Navigating cross-cultural negotiation through effective communication. In M. Benoliel (ed.), *Negotiation Excellence: Successful Deal Making*. World Scientific Publishing.
Chartrand, T.L. and Bargh, J.A. (1999). The chameleon effect: The perception-behavior link in social interaction. *Journal of Personality and Social Psychology*, 6, 893–910.
Curhan, J.R. and Pentland, A. (2007). Thin slices of negotiation: Predicting outcomes from conversational dynamics within the first 5 minutes. *Journal of Applied Psychology*, 92, 802–811.
Curhan, J.R., Elfenbein, H.A., and Xu, H. (2006). What do people value when they negotiate? Mapping the domain of subjective value in negotiation. *Journal of Personality and Social Psychology*, 91, 493–512.
Daft, R.L. and Lengel, R. (1986). Organizational information requirements, media richness and structural design. *Management Science*, 32, 554–571.
De Dreu, C.K.W., Giebels, E., and Van de Vliert, E. (1998). Social motives and trust in integrative negotiation: The disruptive effects of punitive capability. *Journal of Applied Psychology*, 83, 408–422.
De Dreu, C.K.W., Weingart, L.R., and Kwon, S. (2000). Influence of social motives on integrative negotiation: A meta-analytical review and test of two theories. *Journal of Personality and Social Psychology*, 78, 889–905.
Deutsch, M. (1974). *Resolution of conflict*. New Haven, CT: Yale University Press.
Donohue, W.A. (1981). Development of a model of rule use in negotiation. *Communication Monographs*, 48, 106–120.
Donohue, W.A. (2001). Resolving relational paradox: The language of conflict in relationships. In W.F. Eadie and P.E. Nelson (eds), *The language of conflict resolution* (pp. 21–46). Thousand Oaks, CA: Sage.
Donohue, W.A., Diez, M.E., and Hamilton, M. (1984). Coding naturalistic negotiation interaction. *Human Communication Research*, 10, 403–425.
Drake, L.E. and Donohue, W.A. (1996). Communicative framing theory in conflict resolution. *Communication Research*, 23, 297–322.
Feldman, M.S. and Pentland, B.T. (2003). Reconceptualizing organizational routines as a source of flexibility and change. *Administrative Science Quarterly*, 48, 94–118.
Friedman, H.S. (1979). The interactive effects of facial expressions of emotion and verbal messages on perceptions of affective meaning. *Journal of Experimental Social Psychology*, 15, 453–469.
Fry, W.R., Firestone, I.J., and Williams, D.L. (1983). Negotiation process and outcome of stranger dyads and dating couples: Do lovers lose? *Basic and Applied Social Psychology*, 4, 1–16.
Gelfand, M.J. and McCusker, C. (2002). Metaphor and the cultural construction of

negotiation: A paradigm for research and practice. *Handbook of cross-cultural management*, 292–314.
Giebels, E. and Taylor, P.J. (2009). Interaction patterns in crisis negotiations: Persuasive arguments and cultural differences. *Journal of Applied Psychology*, *94*, 5–19. American Psychological Association. doi:10.1037/a0012953.
Giebels, E. De Dreu, C.K.W., and Van de Vliert, E. (1998). The alternative negotiator as the invisible third: Effects of potency information on integrative negotiation. *International Journal of Conflict Management*, *9*, 5–21.
Giebels, E., De Dreu, C.K., and Van de Vliert, E. (2003). No way out or swallow the bait of two-sided exit options in negotiation: the influence of social motives and interpersonal trust. *Group processes and intergroup relations*, *6*, 369–386.
Giles, H., Coupland, N., and Coupland, J. (1991). Accommodation theory: Communication, context, and consequence. In H. Giles, J. Coupland, and N. Coupland (eds), *Contexts of accommodation: Developments in applied sociolinguistics*, 1–68.
Goldin-Meadow, S., Alibali, M.W., and Church, R.B. (1993). Transitions in concept acquisition: Using the hand to read the mind. *Psychological Review*, *100*, 279–297.
Gordon, R.A., Druckman, D., Rozelle, R.M., and Baxter, J.C. (2006). Nonverbal behavior as communication: Approaches, issues, and research. In O. Hargie (ed.), *The Handbook of Communication Skills*. London: Routledge.
Gunia, B.C., Brett, J.M., Nandkeolyar, A.K., and Kamdar, D. (2011). Paying a price: Culture, trust, and negotiation consequences. *Journal of Applied Psychology*, *96*, 774–789. doi:10.1037/a0021986.
Hall, E.T. (1976). *Beyond culture*. New York: Doubleday.
Hilty, J.A. and Carnevale, P.J. (1993). Black-hat/white-hat strategy in bilateral negotiation. *Organizational Behavior and Human Decision Processes*, *55*, 444–469.
Ireland, M.E., Slatcher, R.B., Eastwick, P.W., Scissors, L.E., Finkel, E.J., and Pennebaker, J.W. (2011). Language style matching predicts relationship initiation and stability. *Psychological Science*, *22*, 39–44.
Jap, S., Robertson, D. C., and Hamilton, R. (2011). The dark side of rapport: Agent misbehavior face-to-face and online. *Management Science*, *57*(9), 1610–1622.
Kopelman, S., Rosette, A.S., and Thompson, L. (2006). The three faces of Eve: Strategic displays of positive, negative, and neutral emotions in negotiations. *Organizational Behavior and Human Decision Processes*, *99*(1), 81–101.
Krippendorff, K. (2004). Reliability in content analysis. *Human Communication Research*, *30*(3), 411–433.
Kwon, S. and Weingart, L.R. (2004). Unilateral concessions from the other party: Concession behavior, attributions, and negotiation judgments. *Journal of Applied Psychology*, *89*, 263–278.
Lax, D.A. and Sebenius, J.K. (1986). *The manager as negotiator: Bargaining for cooperation and competitive gain*. New York: Free Press.
Lytle, A., Brett, J.M., and Shapiro, D. (1999). The strategic use of interests, rights, and power to resolve disputes. *Negotiation Journal*, *15*, 31–52.
Maddux, W.W., Mullen, E., and Galinsky, A.D. (2008). Chameleons bake bigger pies and take bigger pieces: Strategic behavioral mimicry facilitates negotiation outcomes. *Journal of Experimental Social Psychology*, *44*, 461–468.
Manusov, V.L. (ed.) (2005). *The sourcebook of nonverbal measures: Going beyond words*. Mahwah, NJ: Lawrence Erlbaum.
McGrath, J.E. and Kelly, J.R. (1986). *Time and human interaction: Toward a social psychology of time*. New York: Guilford Press.
Morris, M.W. and Keltner, D. (2000). How emotions work: The social functions of emotional expression in negotiation. *Research in Organizational Behavior*, *22*, 1–50.
Niederhoffer, K.G. and Pennebaker, J.W. (2002). Linguistic style matching in social interaction. *Journal of Language and Social Psychology*, *21*, 337–360.
O'Connor, K. (1997). Motives and cognitions in negotiation: A theoretical integration and an empirical test. *International Journal of Conflict Management*, *8*, 114–131.

O'Connor, K. and Adams, A.A. (1999). What novices think about negotiation: A content analysis of scripts. *Negotiation Journal*, *15*, 135–147.
Olekalns, M. and Smith, P.L. (1999). Social value orientations and strategy choices in competitive negotiations. *Personality and Social Psychology Bulletin*, *25*, 657–668.
Olekalns, M. and Smith, P.L. (2000). Understanding optimal outcomes: The role of strategy sequences in competitive negotiations. *Human Communication Research*, *26*, 527–557.
Olekalns, M. and Smith, P.L. (2003). Testing the relationships among negotiators' motivational orientations, strategy choices, and outcomes. *Journal of Experimental Social Psychology*, *39*, 101–117. doi:10.1016/S0022-1031(02)00520-6.
Olekalns, M. and Weingart, L.R. (2008). Emergent negotiations: Stability and shifts in negotiation dynamics. *Negotiation and Conflict Management Research*, *1*, 135–160.
Olekalns, M., Smith, P.L., and Walsh, T. (1996). The process of negotiating: Strategies, timing and outcomes. *Organizational Behavior and Human Decision Processes*, *67*, 61–77.
Osgood, C.E. and Anderson, L. (1957). Certain relations among experienced contingencies, associative structure, and contingencies in encoded messages. *The American Journal of Psychology*, *70*, 411–420.
Osgood, C.E. and Suci, G.J. (1955). Factor analysis of meaning. *Journal of Experimental Psychology*, *50*, 325–338.
Pinkley, R.L. (1990). Dimensions of conflict frame: Disputant interpretations of conflict. *Journal of Applied Psychology*, *75*, 117.
Prietula, M.J. and Weingart, L.R. (2011). Negotiation offers and the search for agreement. *Negotiation and Conflict Management Research*, *4*, 77–109. doi:10.1111/j.1750-4716.2011.00074.
Pruitt, D.G. (1981). *Negotiation behavior*. New York: Academic Press.
Pruitt, D.G. (1983). Achieving integrative agreements. In M.H. Bazerman and R.J. Lewicki (eds), *Negotiating in organizations* (pp. 35–50). Beverly Hills: Sage.
Pruitt, D.G. and Lewis, S.A. (1975). Development of integrative solutions in bilateral negotiation. *Journal of Personality and Social Psychology*, *31*, 621–633.
Putnam, L.L. (1990). Reframing integrative and distributive bargaining: A process perspective. In B.H. Sheppard, M.H. Bazerman, and R.J. Lewicki (eds), *Research on negotiation in organizations* (pp. 3–30). Greenwich, CN: JAI Press.
Putnam, L.L. and Jones, T.S. (1982a). Reciprocity in negotiations: An analysis of bargaining interaction. *Communication Monographs*, *49*, 171–191.
Putnam, L.L. and Jones, T.S. (1982b). The role of communication in bargaining. *Human Communication Research*, *8*, 262–280.
Putnam, L.L. and Roloff, M.E. (1992). Communication perspectives on negotiation. In L.L. Putnam and M.E. Roloff (eds), *Communication and Negotiation, Sage Annual Reviews of Communication Research*, *20*, 1–17.
Putnam, L.L. and Wilson, S.R. (1989). Argumentation and bargaining strategies as discriminators of integrative outcomes. In M.A. Rahim (ed.), *Managing conflict: An interdisciplinary approach* (pp. 121–141). New York: Praeger.
Putnam, L.L., Wilson, S.R., and Turner, D.B. (1990). The evolution of policy arguments in teachers' negotiations. *Argumentation*, *4*, 129–152.
Raiffa, H. (1981). *The art and science of negotiation*. Cambridge, MA: Harvard University Press.
Rips, L.J. (1998). Reasoning and conversation. *Psychological Review*, *105*, 411–441.
Schank, R. and Abelson, R.P. (1977). *Scripts, plans, goals and understanding: An inquiry into human knowledge structures*. Hillsdale, NJ: Lawrence Erlbaum.
Schauer, F. (1987). Precedent. *Stanford Law Review*, *39*, 571–605.
Schauer, F. (2008). Why precedent in law (and elsewhere) is not totally (or even substantially) about analogy. *Perspectives on Psychological Science*, *3*, 454–460.
Semnani-Azad, Z. and Adair, W.L. (2011). Nonverbal cues associated with negotiation "styles" across cultures. Presented at the International Association of Conflict Management Conference, Istanbul, Turkey.

Semnani-Azad, Z. and Adair, W.L. (in press). Watch your tone . . . relational paralinguistic messages in negotiation: The case of the East and West. *International Studies of Management and Organization*.

Siegler, R.S. and Svetina, M. (2006). What leads children to adopt new strategies? A microgenetic/cross-sectional study of class inclusion. *Child Development*, 77, 997–1015.

Sillars, A., Roberts, L.J., Leonard, K.E., and Dun, T. (2000). Cognition during marital conflict: The relationship of thought and talk. *Journal of Social and Personal Relationships*, 17, 479–502.

Simons, T. (1993). Speech patterns and the concept of utility in cognitive maps: The case of integrative bargaining. *Academy of Management Journal*, 36, 139–156.

Swaab, R.I. and Swaab, D.F. (2009). Sex differences in the effects of visual contact and eye contact in negotiations. *Journal of Experimental Social Psychology*, 45, 129–136.

Swaab, R.S., Maddux, W.W., and Sinaceur, M. (2011). Early words that work: When and how virtual linguistic mimicry facilitates negotiation outcomes. *Journal of Experimental Social Psychology*, 47(3), 616–621.

Swaab, R.I., Galinsky, A.D., Medvec, V., and Diermeier, D.A. (2012). The communication orientation model: Explaining the diverse effects of sight, sound, and synchronicity on negotiation and group decision-making outcomes. *Personality and Social Psychology Review*, 16, 25–53.

Sycara, K.P. (1990). Negotiation planning: An AI approach. *European Journal of Operational Research*, 46, 216–234.

Taylor, P.J. (2002). A partial order scalogram analysis of communication behavior in crisis negotiation with the prediction of outcome. *The International Journal of Conflict Management*, 13, 4–37.

Taylor, P.J. (2006). A cylindrical model of communication behavior in crisis negotiations. *Human Communication Research*, 28, 7–48.

Taylor, P.J. and Donald, I. (2006). The structure of communication behavior in simulated and actual crisis negotiations. *Human Communication Research*, 30, 443–478.

Taylor, P.J. and Thomas, S. (2008). Linguistic style matching and negotiation outcome. *Negotiation and Conflict Management Research*, 1, 263–281.

Taylor, P.J., Donald, I., and Conchie, S.M. (2012). *The triple-interact as a building block of negotiation*. Paper presented at the International Association of Conflict Management Conference, Stellenbosch, South Africa.

Tinsley, C.H. (2001). How negotiators get to yes: Predicting the constellation of strategies used across cultures to negotiate conflict. *Journal of Applied Psychology*, 86, 583–593. doi:10.1037/0021-9010.86.4.583.

Tutzauer, F. and Roloff, M.E. (1988). Communication processes leading to integrative agreements: Three paths to joint benefits. *Communication Research*, 15, 360–380.

Van de Vliert, E. (1999). Cooperation and competition as partners. *European Review of Social Psychology*, 10, 231–257.

Weingart, L.R., Bennett, R.J., and Brett, J.M. (1993). The impact of consideration of issues and motivational orientation on group negotiation process and outcome. *Journal of Applied Psychology*, 78, 504–517.

Weingart, L.R., Hyder, E.B., and Prietula, M.J. (1996). Knowledge matters: The effect of tactical descriptions on negotiation behavior and outcome. *Journal of Personality and Social Psychology*, 70, 1205.

Weingart, L.R., Oleklans, M., and Smith, P.L. (2004). Quantitative coding of negotiation behavior. *International Negotiation*, 9, 441–455.

Weingart, L.R., Prietula, M.J., Hyder, E., and Genovese, C. (1999). Knowledge and the sequential processes of negotiation: A Markov chain analysis of response-in-kind. *Journal of Experimental Social Psychology*, 35, 366–393.

Weingart, L.R., Thompson, L., Bazerman, M.H., and Caroll, J.S. (1990). Tactical behavior and negotiation outcomes. *International Journal of Conflict Management*, 1, 7–31.

Wilson, S.R. and Putnam, L.L. (1990). Interaction goals in negotiation. *Communication Yearbook*, 13, 374–406.

Wiltermuth, S.S., Tiedens, L.Z., and Neale, M.A. (2012). *How Dominance Complementarity Improves Value Creation in Negotiations*. Paper presented at International Association of Conflict Management Conference, Stellenbosch, South Africa.

Young, M.A. and Schlie, E.H. (2011). The rhythm of the deal: Negotiation as a dance. *Negotiation Journal, 27*, 191–203. doi:10.1111/j.1571-9979.2011.00302.x.

Zacks, J.M. and Tversky, B. (2001). Event structure in perception and conception. *Psychological Bulletin, 127*, 3–21.

13. Punctuated negotiations: transitions, interruptions, and turning points
Daniel Druckman and Mara Olekalns

On 8 December 1987, U.S. President Ronald Reagan and Soviet General Secretary Mikhail Gorbachev signed a treaty agreeing to eliminate all nuclear delivery vehicles with ranges from 500 to 5500 kilometers. Known as the Intermediate Nuclear Forces (INF) Treaty, this was the first time that an entire category of nuclear weapons had been eliminated from the arsenals of either superpower. The Treaty was the outcome of eight years of negotiation. It occurred as a result of several key decisions made by Gorbachev. One decision, made in October 1985, was the separation of French and British forces from the U.S. systems. Another, made in February 1987, was to de-link strategic and space weapons from INF systems. A third, made in July 1987, consisted of a proposed "double zero" option that made verification easier. Each of these decisions resolved major sticking points and cleared the way for the scheduling of a summit between the leaders in Reykjavik Iceland. The summit served to speed the negotiation process toward the agreement.

These three decisions and the summit event are widely regarded as turning points that served to punctuate the negotiation process. They share several features. Each is a change from earlier events, in varying degrees of abruptness, triggered by an impasse. The changes are clear or self-evident: Observers are likely to agree that a change has occurred. Each consists of an action taken by one of the parties with consequences for both: Two consequences were progress in the negotiation and a change in the relationship between the parties. Knowing *how and when* they occur and with *what* consequences would seem essential to understanding the way a negotiation unfolds. Of particular interest are the questions: Which changes are sufficiently important to turn the talks in the direction of agreements or impasses? What accounts for the changes? These questions are the basis for research on turning points in negotiation.

The idea of turning points – regarded as critical moments during an interaction or developmental process – has captured the imagination of analysts in a variety of fields. It has been a useful concept in studies conducted from a psychoanalytic perspective (e.g., Rothstein, 1997), in analyses of communication in relationships (e.g., Hooper and Drummond,

1990) and divorce counseling (Graham, 1997), in addiction research (Schulenberg et al., 1997), in a variety of analyses of child, adolescent, and life-span development (see Cohen, 2008, for a review of these studies), and in a popular treatment of macro-level social change (see Gladwell, 2000, on tipping points).

The concept has been particularly useful in studies of negotiation processes where attempts have been made to provide more precise definitions of the concept. These studies include the retrospective analysis of cases of U.S. base rights talks (Druckman, 1986), free trade (Tomlin, 1989), international (Chasek, 1997) and domestic (Hall, 2008) environmental negotiations, nuclear arms control (Druckman et al., 1991), the conflict between the Free Aceh Movement and the Republic of Indonesia (Leary, 2004), and in comparative analyses of multilateral trade talks (Crump and Druckman, 2012) as well as other issue areas (Druckman, 2001). They also include prospective analyses of change in simulated negotiations where attempts are made to predict the occurrence of turning points from prior events inside or outside the talks (Olekalns and Smith, 2005a; Druckman et al., 2009; Druckman and Olekalns, in press). Across these studies of negotiation there seems to be agreement on the key features of turning points.

FEATURES OF TURNING POINTS

A challenge for analysts is to define concepts with sufficient precision to be useful in research. Many scholars, practitioners, and journalists have been attracted to the idea of turning points, often suggesting that it is self evident: For example, the tennis match turned on a particular point; Paul Revere's ride was a tipping point in the colonists' rebellion against the redcoats (British); the frame-breaking insight discovered in a conversation was a critical moment in his career or, from a theater exhibit in Melbourne, Australia, "*Hair* was a major turning point in Livermore's career." These examples suggest that turning points may vary in terms of the amount of change (e.g., the distinction between disturbances and turning points), the abruptness of the change, the duration of change as well as the frequency of changes in an event-history, campaign, or career. Similar features have been identified in the context of research on turning points in the course of human development by Cohen (2008). This would seem to be a good place to begin the search for elements of the concept.

Turning points are self evident to the extent that negotiators are aware of these events when they occur or in retrospect, following the talks: Did a turning point occur? If so, then, negotiator reports provide useful data, particularly when opposing negotiators' judgments agree. This feature suggests also that the event or experience has an impact in terms of salience and consequences. Salience or intensity refers to the impression made on the experiencing actors; consequences refer to the immediate and longer-term changes that occur following the event and may be construed in terms of the duration of change. The former is experiential and understood at an individual level of analysis. The latter is captured by unfolding events and understood as process dynamics. A third feature of impact is abruptness. Some turning points may be more sudden than others. This element of surprise renders these key events as departures from expectations.

These features suggest a three-part model of turning points that consists of a precipitant, a departure, and a consequence. The focal concept of a departure is defined as: *A clear and self-evident change from earlier events or patterns in the form of an impactful decision taken or insight made by one or all parties*. By recognizing the importance of impact, however, the definition may confuse the departure with its consequences. A way to avoid this consists of distinguishing between impact and type of impact: the former does not specify direction in terms of positive or negative consequences while the latter takes into account direction as escalatory (progression away from agreement) or de-escalatory (progression toward agreement). This distinction suggests a definition of consequences as: *A clear and self-evident impact of a departure in terms of the direction taken by the negotiation process. The direction includes both immediate (minimum lapsed time since the departure) and delayed impacts.*

A key to understanding turning points is to identify the events that precipitated them. These events may occur inside the negotiation as procedural or substantive changes. They may also be events occurring outside the talks, including policy and leadership changes or third-party intervention. Thus, a decision made to bring experts into deliberations is a procedural precipitant leading to a decision to convene working committees (a departure). A proposal to re-frame the issues, such as Gorbachev's proposed de-linking of types of weapons systems in the INF talks, is a substantive precipitant leading to a decision to discuss only tactical weapons (a departure). A sudden shift of policy taken by the foreign ministry of one of the negotiating parties is an external precipitant that leads to a decision to suspend the talks (a departure) with short-term escalatory consequences. To satisfy the requirements of a causal analysis, precipitants are those events that occur in close proximity to the decision which signals a departure has occurred. A question raised is: How much time is needed between the precipitant and departure? (see also Cohen, 2008, p. 7). These considerations and examples suggest the following definition of a precipi-

```
┌─────────────┐      ┌─────────────┐      ┌─────────────────┐
│ Precipitant │  ⟹  │  Departure  │  ⟹  │   Consequence   │
│ • External  │      │ • Abrupt    │      │ • Short-term    │
│ • Substantive│     │ • Non-abrupt│      │   • towards or away
│ • Procedural│      │             │      │     from agreement
│             │      │             │      │ • Long-term     │
│             │      │             │      │   • towards or away
│             │      │             │      │     from agreement
└─────────────┘      └─────────────┘      └─────────────────┘
```

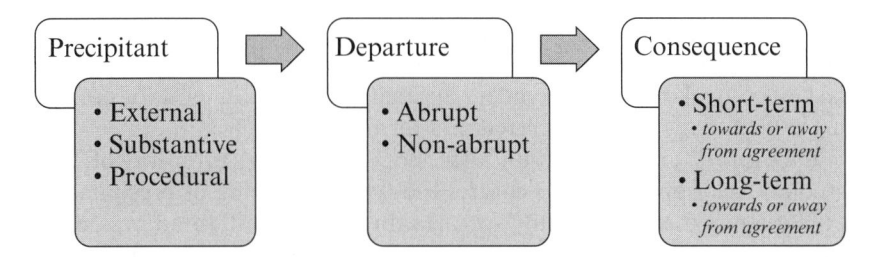

Figure 13.1 Framework for analyzing turning points

tant: *A clear and self-evident event occurring inside or outside the negotiation, causing one or more parties to make a decision that departs from earlier events or patterns.*

The three definitions provide a basis for a framework to analyze turning points. The three-part framework consists of a causal chain among precipitants, departures, and consequences. The chain is depicted in Figure 13.1.

APPROACHES TO ANALYSIS

This framework has been useful in performing analyses of processes that occur in cases and in simulations. For the case analyses, event chronologies provide the material for tracing the negotiation process by, first, identifying turning points and, second, examining events or decisions that occurred prior to and following the departure. For experiments, the turning point consists of a decision made following a manipulated precipitating event, such as a crisis, and followed by progress toward or away from agreement. For both types of studies, the three-part sequence consists of proximal events or decisions in order to bolster the argument for causation. A difference, however, is that the cases are retrospective while the experiments are designed to be prospective. Each approach has advantages and disadvantages.

A key advantage of the retrospective case study is that analyses are performed on the events that occur in actual – often high level – negotiations. The availability of archival information or access to negotiators for interviews often provide a rich dataset for capturing a variety of turning points over a long period of time. The known outcome provides the advantage of gauging the direction taken by the various turning points. It also provides an opportunity to select on the outcome for comparative analysis, for example, comparing processes for comprehensive versus partial agreements. Set against these advantages are the disadvantages of interpretive analysis for inferring causality. Opportunities for selection biases occur with regard to choosing the cases and identifying the three-part turning points sequence. Although steps can be taken to reduce these biases, the lack of control over events renders the analysis limited in terms of providing explanations for the occurrence of turning points.

Laboratory experimentation addresses some of the problems of case studies. The opportunity to control the type and timing of precipitating events strengthens arguments for causality. The question addressed by these analyses is: Can we know when a turning point occurs during the course of negotiation? This forward-looking approach facilitates developing explanatory theories. It is however offset by the disadvantages of simulated negotiations, compressed time role plays enacted usually by student negotiators, and considerations of external validity or relevance to comparable real-world negotiations. The relative strengths and weaknesses of cases and experimental analysis suggest that the approaches are complementary. Both have contributed knowledge about turning points. These contributions are discussed in the section to follow, concluding with a summary of what has been learned to date about turning points.

RESEARCH ON TURNING POINTS

Three kinds of departures have been studied in the case and laboratory research on turning points (TPs) in negotiation. These themes are used to organize the review in this section. One theme is *transitions* between negotiation stages or phases. Another theme emphasizes the importance of *interruptions* during the process. TPs are often seen to evolve from events that disrupt the process, including the occurrence of unanticipated crises. The idea of *framing*, a third theme, has been salient in recent studies. Regarded both as a strategic influence on negotiation and as a creative response to surprising developments, re-framing has been shown to turn a variety of types of negotiation processes in the direction of agreements. A fourth theme in the TP literature is *context*. Such features as the type of conflict (values, interests), the setting (domestic or international), and size of negotiation (bilateral or multilateral) have been shown to influence TPs. Each of these four themes is discussed in the sections to follow.

Stage Transitions

Negotiators do not use the same strategy throughout a negotiation. Instead, they cycle through periods of cooperation and periods of competition as they search for a mutually acceptable outcome (Olekalns and Weingart, 2008; Putnam, 1990). Despite the recognition that negotiation is a dynamic process, the mechanisms by which negotiators coordinate – implicitly or explicitly – shifts to new strategies is not well understood. Stage models provide one framework for exploring how such transitions occur. They rest on the assumption that strategic momentum is maintained through the need to complete a series of tasks. Negotiators match their strategies to the task, and switch strategies as one task is completed and another begins. Negotiators may need to pass through these stages in order to bring the process to a close with an agreement (Donohue and Roberto, 1996; Gulliver, 1979; Holmes, 1992).

Credit for introducing the stage concept is usually given to Douglas (1962). She suggested that industrial negotiation passes through three stages: establishing the bargaining range, reconnoitering the range, and precipitating the decision-making crisis. Other renditions of the concept – developed largely from dyadic negotiations – include moving from early distributive positioning to later coordination toward settlement (Morley and Stephenson, 1977; Gulliver, 1979; Pruitt, 1981; Olekalns et al., 2003; Adair and Brett, 2005), from diagnosis to defining formula to bargaining over details (Zartman and Berman, 1982), and from early debates over an agenda through searching for formulae and issue clarification to working out implementing details (Druckman, 1983). Similar stage sequences emerge in large-scale negotiations. For example, in his analysis of the negotiation phases prior to the start of the 1986 North American Free Trade talks, Tomlin (1989) showed that negotiators moved through four discrete stages: problem identification, search for options, commitment to negotiation, agreement to negotiate. A subsequent analysis of the trilateral NAFTA talks (Mexico, Canada, U.S.) again showed that prenegotiation talks pass through a series of identifiable stages (Cameron and Tomlin, 2000). Similarly, Chasek's analysis of multilateral environmental negotiations showed that the negotiations moved through five clearly identifiable stages: issue definition, statement of initial positions, drafting/ formula building, final bargaining, and ratification of the agreement. Each of these schemes include the following elements: sequential progression in chronological and conceptual time, alternating antagonistic and coordinative behavior, interconnected and overlapping stages, and recognition of transitions that signal passage from one stage to another.

The move through different stages suggests that negotiators are able to implicitly coordinate their actions, recognizing when one negotiation task is completed and a new one should be initiated. A shift in process may also be triggered by the growing recognition that impasse is likely. Consistent with this idea, Walton and McKersie's (1965) description of differentiation-before-integration implies that negotiators shift from competition to cooperation at the point where they recognize that an impasse is likely. Druckman's (1986) analysis of a 1975–76 negotiation between Spain and the United States over military base rights illustrates this point. In this negotiation, there was an initial and noticeable difference between the parties in the number of hard statements made, which led to an adjustment by the "softer" party in the direction of the other's hard behavior consequently increasing the overall level of competition. This adjustment to harder strategies triggered a crisis, the suspension of talks, which in turn led to substantive (a framework agreement) and procedural (high-level consultations) actions that presaged progress. This pattern of convergence to hard tactics followed by movement towards agreement has been shown to occur in a variety of international security negotiations (Druckman and Harris, 1990; Stoll and McAndrew, 1986). These non-linear responses occur only when a threshold is passed and, as such, may be more like a tipping point than a turning point. Like the "straws that break the camels' backs", the threshold alerts the softer negotiator to a problem that is dealt with through matching the other's tough behavior, leading to a negotiation crisis.

Although Druckman's analysis illustrates Walton and McKersie's (1965) model, it also extends that model by highlighting the role that synchronization plays in generating a turning point and moving negotiations forward. While in the case of base rights negotiations, increasingly synchronized competition led to progress, Taylor and Thomas's (2008) analysis of hostage negotiations demonstrated that synchronized cooperation may also move negotiations to agreement. Hostage negotiations were more successful when police and hostage takers matched each other's positive affect, adopted a present (rather than a past) focus, and explored alternatives. In these highly charged negotiations, actions that avoided crises moved the negotiation forward (see also, Wells et al., Chapter 18 this volume). Avoiding crises was evident as well in Tomlin's (1989) analysis of the 1986 NAFTA talks. He showed that crises were caused by the parties' taking different perspectives and holding different agenda priorities (lack of synchronization). Interestingly, by avoiding discussion of the prospective negotiation agenda, and thus staying in sync, the parties were able to make progress toward a decision to negotiate. Thus, synchronization plays a role in moving negotiations forward, although its effects are not straightforward. We return to this observation in our concluding section.

Shifts in process may also be triggered by specific events that change how negotiators approach their task. This kind of event-driven shift in strategy is evident in Cameron and Tomlin's (2000) analysis of the trilateral NAFTA talks, which showed that stage transitions were set in motion by specific procedures and resulted in the re-framing of the issues. Based on their interviews with members of the U.S. delegation to the Intermediate Range Nuclear Forces (INF) talks between the Soviet Union and the U.S. in 1987, Druckman et al. (1991) identified ten turning points in the negotiations, starting with Gorbachev's announcement to remove French and British nuclear forces from the discussion in 1985 to the announcement of an agreement in 1987. Of particular interest was the distinction made between substantive and procedural turning points. The substantive turning points were regarded as frame-breaking changes consisting of such new ideas as delinking issues and the double-zero proposal. The key procedural turning point was the preparation for the summit meeting between Gorbachev and Reagan as noted in the example provided at the beginning of the chapter. As substantive or procedural decisions, these actions could be regarded also as precipitants. This case analysis extends our understanding of stage transitions by demonstrating that they are not necessarily triggered by task completion. Instead, they are triggered by events that address either the substance or the negotiation process. The common feature is that they result in a reconceptualization of the negotiation, with a subsequent change in process. But, perhaps most important were three actions: the summit meeting as an action-forcing event, the unilateral reductions taken by Gorbachev, and Reagan's close involvement serving to galvanize the bureaucracy toward agreement. As external events, these actions could be regarded also as precipitants and are framed as such in the later research reviewed below.

Transitions are also emphasized in Druckman's (2001) temporal sequence of events from precipitants to departures to consequences. Referred to as a process trace (see Figure 13.1), the sequence makes evident the triggers and impacts of TPs (departures). Three types of international negotiations were compared in this study: security, trade and political negotiations. A key finding was that external precipitants were considerably more frequent than internal (procedures and substance) precipitants in the security cases with the reverse occurring for cases in the other areas. In most of the cases across the issue areas the departures paved the way toward agreement. The progression toward agreement was punctuated by departures, each of which can be regarded as a phase transition.

Interruptions

Phase models provide an alternative perspective on how negotiations move forward. These models are more fluid, focusing on smaller and less well defined strategic passages within negotiations. Phases are typically identified by using linguistic analyses to determine when strategic shifts have occurred in a negotiation. Research in the spirit of phase models frequently provides descriptive analyses of the "frames" that negotiators use as they move from the beginning to the end of negotiations (e.g., Putnam and Holmer, 1992). Consequently, phase models are less prescriptive in terms of specifying what generates the momentum to redirect the process from one phase to the next.

Several theoretical frameworks suggest that the necessary momentum is provided by interruptions. This perspective is grounded in the idea of sense-making, that is, individuals' attempts to interpret the events around them (Weick, 1995). The most salient pieces of information are those that stand out from an ongoing process or interaction (e.g., Baxter and Erbert, 1999; Jett and George, 2003). More recently, Ballinger and Rockmann (2010) describe the role played by anchoring events, defined as events that violate expectations. These events stand out from the flow, triggering a search for explanations, redirecting negotiators' strategies, and shaping anticipated outcomes.

Interruptions may be unintentional and alter the course of negotiations because they surprise the other party. Unexpected events, because they challenge the dominant process, create uncertainty about either the other negotiator's intentions or the ability to reach agreement. According to McGinn et al. (2004) these out-of-keeping acts challenge the dominant dynamic (the logic of the interaction) and trigger transitions to a new dynamic. The central theme in this view is that something about a specific action calls attention to the negotiation process, and transforms it (Druckman, 2004; Putnam, 2004; Stuart, 2004; Winship, 2004). Such interruptions provide motivation for the changes needed to break stalemates or, more importantly, move the talks toward lasting agreements. For example, strategies that are unexpected because they do not conform to the dominant strategic approach, appear to transform the negotiation context and affect the quality of negotiators' outcomes (Olekalns and Smith, 2000, 2003a, 2003b). The overarching theme, which we return to in our concluding section, is that actions may interrupt a negotiation because one negotiator inadvertently violates the other party's expectations.

Interruptions may also be intentional: negotiators or third parties may deliberately intervene in the negotiation process in several ways: by redirecting the negotiation back to its substantive issues, by clarifying the other party's intentions, by explicitly addressing the process, or by highlighting the need to reach agreement (Kolb, 2004). These kinds of process interruptions can successfully redirect negotiations from a distributive to an integrative phase (Olekalns et al., 2003). A different kind of interruption occurs when negotiators take timeout from the negotiation. Such temporal breaks provide negotiators with the opportunity to reassess the process so far, and, by disrupting the dynamic, enable them to restart the process anew (Kolb, 2004).

The effectiveness of such disruptions is, however, dependent on how they are used. Negotiators who use this time to ruminate further on their negotiations typically obtain poorer outcomes than those who do not. Subsequent research suggests that this may be because negotiators who ruminate may engage in competitive thinking. If, instead, they use a deliberate break to think about how to build cooperation, they improve their outcomes (Harinck and De Dreu, 2008; Druckman et al., 2004). The maximum benefits of cooperative rumination during a deliberate break are reaped if parties take a pro-social orientation to the negotiation, that is, they emphasize benefits for both parties (Harinck and De Dreu, 2011).

These findings suggest that the content of interruptions influences the negotiation process and economic outcomes. Research suggests that the type of interruption is also critical to social outcomes: interruptions have the potential to either build or erode trust. Olekalns and Smith (2005a) distinguished between interruptions that were facilitatory, and likely to move a negotiation forward, or inhibitory, and likely to hold a negotiation back. When negotiators identified interruptions as creating a positive impression or made a positive change in the negotiation, they also reported higher levels of cognitive trust in the other party. When negotiators identified interruptions that triggered negative impressions, they reported lower levels of cognitive trust. These authors also demonstrated a virtuous cycle in relation to affective trust: when affective trust was high at the start of negotiations, individuals reported more facilitating interruptions (positive impressions), which in turn increased affective trust at the end of the negotiation (for more on trust, see Lewicki and Polin, Chapter 7 this volume). This virtuous cycle may be strengthened as the number of cooperatively-motivated parties to a negotiation increases (Druckman et al., 2009).

The internal interruptions discussed above were created by the actions of the negotiators themselves. Interruptions may also be external, as was demonstrated on our review of case studies. In an experimental extension of the case analyses discussed above, Druckman et al. (2009) showed that when external interruptions changed negotiators' thoughts about what was possible, they were less likely to anticipate agreement. Negotiators' interpretations of external interruptions are sensitive to trust. An inhibitory event stimulated movement to agreement when trust was high. However, when negotiators reported low cognitive trust in the other party, they were more likely to revise their thoughts of what was possible following an inhibitory interruption than following a facilitating interruption; this reassessment of what is possible did not, however, affect negotiators willingness to move towards agreement (Druckman et al., 2009).

Framing

Interpretations of interruptions are also sensitive to salient features of the negotiating environment. Impacts of each of three primed features on decisions following an interruption were explored in an experiment by Druckman and Olekalns (in press). Referred to as motivational frames, these features consisted of power, shared identity, and transaction costs. The decision choices were to withdraw from the talks, to continue negotiating, or to reframe the issues. The re-framing choice was considered to be a departure. When an interruption was interpreted through a power frame, negotiators were less willing to continue the negotiation and more willing to reframe the issues. The same event, interpreted through a transaction cost frame, has the opposite impact. These different frames also affect the role that trust plays in responses to interruptions: when negotiators report low trust in the other party, they are more likely to reframe the negotiation when transaction costs are salient, but to search for immediate settlement when shared identity or power is salient. When trust is high, they are more likely to continue negotiations when the shared identity is salient, but to reframe the negotiation when power is salient (Druckman and Olekalns, in press). Thus, high transaction costs produced a departure when trust was low; power led to a departure when trust was high.

Framing is emphasized as well in two case studies by Putnam and her colleagues. In these studies, framing is regarded as a precipitant rather than a departure. Putnam and Shoemaker (2007) structure an analysis of negotiation stages in the Edwards Aquifer environmental conflict in terms of turning points. Focusing primarily on the way that the media framed the issues, the authors described a process that moved from early escalation to later de-escalation. A key insight is that the media were influence agents participating in a de-escalation process in several ways: shifting the naming of the disputes, altering blaming patterns, introducing multiple explanations, and casting the federal government as a common enemy. Overlooked in many other TP studies, the framing performed by the media is often an external precipitant that can trigger key changes within the negotiation.

Further analyses of the precipitating effects of media framing were conducted by Putnam and Fuller (2010). Focusing on the 2007–08 conflict between the Writers' Guild of America (WGA) and the Alliance of Motion Picture and Television Producers (AMPTP), these authors identified six TPs that defined time periods but were not considered as departures. Careful coding of precipitants and consequences allowed them to use these parts of TP framework (Druckman, 2001) to depict the unfolding negotiation process. An interesting finding is that procedural precipitants (shifts in membership on the union team, interim agreements with independent producers) played a dominant role in the talks. However, they also discovered that strategies combining external and procedural factors precipitated change. Considered by them as a fourth type of precipitant, strategies add other types of communication by influence agents to the framework. More generally, the authors emphasize the importance of depicting the way messages are framed for particular audiences, which they refer to as discursive representation. It would be interesting to explore the distinction between strategic frames that lead to departures and those that do not produce that result.

The precipitating effects of framing are emphasized as well in Leary's (2004) analysis of dialogues about the conflict in Aceh, Indonesia. Several frame changes in particular proved to be crucial to progress. One was the framing of the proximity talks as a workshop, which justified the presence of outside experts. Another was to construe it as a learning experience. A third was a suggestion that the free Aceh Movement (GAM) become a political party. Although not effective in preventing future violence in Aceh, the new ideas that emerged were considered as "frame-breaking insights" that altered the relational context for the discussions. (See also London, 1988 for a similar idea with regard to decisions about career change.)

Context

Turning points have been analysed in other contexts. Three features of the context within which negotiation occurs are the primary source of conflict between the parties, domestic or international negotiations, and multilateral negotiation. Key studies in each of these settings are reviewed in this section.

Sources of conflict

Sources of conflict, distinguishing among interests, understanding, and values, provide additional insights into the turning points sequence from precipitants through consequences (Druckman, 2005). The 34 negotiations used in the earlier study by Druckman (2001) were categorized by the predominant type of issue at stake. For the conflicts of interest, which occurred most frequently in cases of negotiations over matters of arms control and disarmament, the typical sequence took the form shown in Figure 13.2.

For the conflicts of understanding (referred to also as cognitive conflicts), which occurred most frequently in negotiations over international trade, the typical sequence took the form displayed in Figure 13.3.

344 *Handbook of research on negotiation*

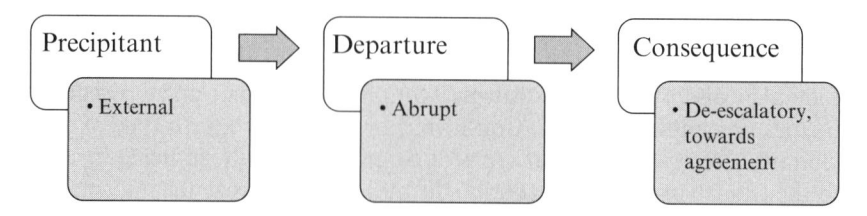

```
[Precipitant          ]  ⟹  [Departure          ]  ⟹  [Consequence         ]
  • External                   • Abrupt                  • De-escalatory,
                                                           towards
                                                           agreement
```

Figure 13.2 Turning point sequence for conflicts of interest

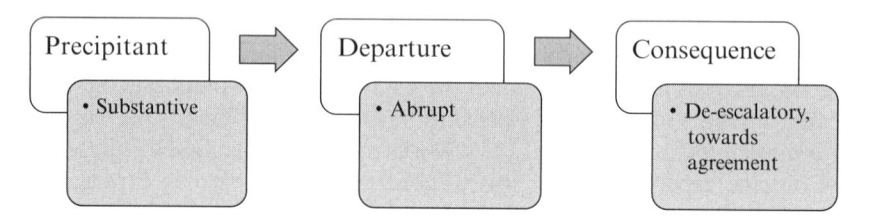

```
[Precipitant          ]  ⟹  [Departure          ]  ⟹  [Consequence         ]
  • Substantive                • Abrupt                  • De-escalatory,
                                                           towards
                                                           agreement
```

Figure 13.3 Turning point sequences for cognitive conflicts

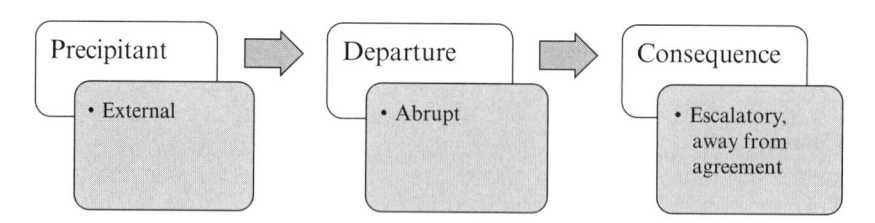

```
[Precipitant          ]  ⟹  [Departure          ]  ⟹  [Consequence         ]
  • External                   • Abrupt                  • Escalatory,
                                                           away from
                                                           agreement
```

Figure 13.4 Turning point sequence for value-based conflicts

Conflicts over values were the primary source of conflict in negotiations over political issues including those involving the environment. A typical sequence is shown in Figure 13.4.

The external precipitants that produced departures in value conflicts consisted of third party involvement. These interveners had little success in producing agreements, a finding that coincides with experiments on value conflict (e.g., Druckman et al., 1988; Harinck and Van Kleef, in press). The abrupt departures that occurred in these cases often consisted of rejections of mediator suggestions, leading to escalations. In contrast, the abrupt or non-abrupt departures that occurred in conflicts over interests or understanding moved the talks in the direction of agreement. Thus, departures can lead in either direction depending, at least in part, on the kinds of issues being negotiated.

Domestic and international contexts
In the 29 domestic environmental cases analyzed by Hall (2008), neutral third parties were instrumental in creating procedures that precipitated departures during the early phases of the negotiations. The parties themselves had more influence over the substantive decisions that precipitated agreements during the later phases. This pattern contrasts with the pattern discovered by Chasek (1997) in her analyses of 11 international environmental cases. In those cases, substantive precipitants occurred early and frequently without the help of third parties. This difference may have been due to the domestic versus international contexts: Unlike domestic disputes, international environmental talks are managed with prescribed procedures, thereby allowing more time for the parties to focus their attention on substance early in the talks; procedures come into play primarily with regard to ratification processes that follow the negotiations.

Another domestic versus international comparison, performed by Druckman (2001), showed differences in patterns of escalatory and de-escalatory consequences of departures. Unlike the international cases, repeated escalations occurred in 11 cases of negotiation between the mechanics' union (International Association of Mechanics and Aerospace Workers [IAM]) and Trans World Airlines (TWA). The differences were attributed to the institutional context within which the domestic talks were conducted. Both parties had incentives to prolong the talks: strike threats are the primary union tool to influence the company; for companies, prolonging the talks is a bargaining strategy for reducing the attractiveness of alternatives to workers. These prerogatives do not have a counterpart in the international system.

Multilateral negotiations
The turning points framework was applied in Crump and Druckman's (2012) analyses of the long chronologies of events on intellectual property issues discussed at the multilateral Uruguay round of the General Agreement on Trade and Tariiffs (GATT) and at the World Trade Organization (WTO) Doha Ministerial. This comparative analysis of two matched multilateral cases highlighted differences between cases with different outcomes on the same set of issues. More substantive precipitants and escalation consequences occurred in the stalled WTO process and more external or procedural precipitants with de-escalatory consequences occurred in the settled GATT talks.

The analysis highlighted the concepts of reframing, legitimacy, and coalitions: Reframing was regarded as a substantive precipitant, perceived legitimacy was the result of achieving the new frame (a departure), and managing coalitions was the glue that connected precipitants to departures and consequences. The work done by managing coalitions in the WTO served to reduce complexity and the need for external interventions. The prominence of new ideas (substantive precipitants) generated within the process was helpful but did not resolve the impasse. More generally, the bridge created in this study between organizational processes and negotiation decisions extends the applicability of the TP framework to global conferences. Another concept, contributed by Dougherty's (2006) turning points analysis of social movements and relevant to multilateral negotiations, is critical mass. As a networked group with a shared goal, these negotiators set in motion the sequence that extends from precipitating actions through consequences. A critical mass adds connection and size as features of effective managing coalitions.

The studies on context introduce macro-level factors into the TP framework. The different patterns obtained in analyses of domestic and international negotiations calls attention to the importance of larger structures and norms surrounding negotiation processes. The organizing role played by managing coalitions in global trade conferences highlights a social process that moves a complex negotiation toward agreement. The idea of a critical mass from the literature on social movements helps to explain how these transitions may occur. It also suggests that there is a connection between Gladwell's (2000) macro-level concept of tipping points and the turning points that are studied in negotiation.

TURNING TO THE FUTURE

In our discussion of turning points in the negotiation process, we identified several theoretical frameworks that both offer further insights into the ways in which discrete events propel negotiations forward, and open new avenues for research. These frameworks helped us to interpret findings from case analyses and experimental work. We now return to these frameworks to identify ways in which existing research and theory about turning points could be expanded. Finally, we consider how we might further increase our understanding of turning points by considering two new variables: negotiator resilience and temporal spillover.

Being 'In Sync'

In our discussion of stage transitions, we identified synchronization as a key mechanism in precipitating departures that have the consequence of moving negotiations forward. The first example that we gave was of linguistic synchronicity, that is, a convergence in the language and strategies used by negotiators. According to interpersonal adaption theory, a communication pattern in which the linguistic styles of two individuals converge serves to reduce social distance, confirm a shared perspective, and assist in the development of trust (Burgoon et al., 1995; Giles et al., 1991).

There are two important insights to be gained from the analyses that we described earlier. The first insight is that it is the occurrence of linguistic convergence, rather than the tone of that convergence, that assists negotiators to reach agreement: convergence to both hard, competitive and cooperative behavior appear equally likely to assist agreement. The hard competitive convergence often produces impasses that have been found to precipitate turning points that move the talks forward. The softer cooperative convergence, which occurs less frequently, moves the talks toward agreement when trust rather than exploitation is sustained. A foundation of trust enables negotiators to withstand competitive convergence, such as that observed in the base rights negotiations. We speculate that the trust that accrues from convergence may also enhance the credibility of cooperative convergence in the more adversarial hostage negotiations. In both cases, it provides the relational base from which agreement can be built. The second, related, insight is that the negotiating context determines whether competitive convergence that triggers a crisis, or cooperative convergence that inhibits a crisis, will be effective in moving negotiations forward.

Together, these insights suggest that we need to link patterns of convergence to interpersonal processes (trust) and context, in order to understand the role of linguistic synchronization in moving negotiations forward. Drawing on Putnam's work, we also showed that frame convergence plays an important role in moving negotiations to agreement. It is thus not just the synchronization of communication that facilitates or impedes momentum in negotiations, but also the synchronization of perspectives. This finding fits with research demonstrating that individuals strive to be "in sync" with one another in terms of goals (Adair and Brett, 2005; Blount and Janicik, 2000, 2001; McGinn and Keros, 2003). Being in sync increases the likelihood of reaching agreement (Brodt and Dietz, 1999; Drake and Donohue, 1996) as well as enhancing trust, satisfaction and negotiators' willingness to engage in future interactions (Burgoon et al., 1995; Giles et al., 1991; Pinkley and Northcraft, 1994; Olekalns and Smith, 2005b).

Although frame convergence clearly leads to progress in negotiation, our discussion of linguistic convergence suggests that we need to provide a more nuanced account of how the drive to be in sync triggers stage transitions. Such accounts may benefit from considering both the intentional and unintentional ways in which individuals align their representations, as well as the nonverbal levels at which an alignment may take place (e.g., Garrod and Pickering, 2009; Pickering and Garrod, 2006). They may also benefit from considering novel strategies for understanding others' perceptives, such as the position exchange process described by Gillespie and Richardson (2011). These new theories imply that convergence occurs at several levels. Although we have focused on convergence of frames, convergence can also occur at "lower" levels of cognition, that is in both verbal and nonverbal communication. Paralleling our discussion of linguistic convergence, we also suggest that to fully understand the convergence process, it is necessary to consider the content of frames within specific contexts. This will help to ascertain whether convergence is likely to inhibit or facilitate stage transitions.

Expectancy Violations

A second theme in our discussion of turning points is that events move negotiations forward because they violate negotiators' expectations of how the other party will behave. These expectations can be established in a variety of ways: through direct past experience with a negotiator, through indirect knowledge via a negotiators' reputation, through the rapid formation of first impressions (thin slicing; Curhan and Pentland, 2007), or derived from broad-based societal stereotypes (e.g., gender, culture, profession; McKnight et al., 1998). However negotiators form expectations, these expectations then create a behavioral baseline against which opponents' actual behavior is assessed (Burgoon et al., 1995; Forgas, 1998; Hilty and Carnevale, 1992; White and Burgoon, 2001).

In our discussion of interruptions, we highlighted the importance of events or actions that "stand out from the crowd." Any action that violates a negotiator's expectations about how the other party will behave or how the negotiation will unfold increases in salience. It is then interpreted and evaluated against the behavioral baseline that negotiators have set. Departures from baseline can be either better than expected (positive violations) or worse than expected (negative violations). Research shows that a switch from cooperative to competitive behavior (negative violation) elicits higher levels of competition and more negative emotions from the other party than a switch from competition to cooperation (a positive violation; Druckman and Bonoma, 1976; Hilty and Carnevale, 1992; Olekalns et al., 2005a).

Expectancy violation theory suggests that the same action, as an interruption to the negotiation process, may have quite different consequences depending on whether it is perceived as a positive or a negative violation. As we highlighted in the section on frames, the lens through which a crisis is interpreted (transaction costs, dependence, shared identity) affects what negotiators choose to do next. From an expectancy violation perspective, these different reactions result from the different behavioral baselines against which the crisis in assessed. It is plausible that each frame creates a different set of behavioral expectations, consequently shaping whether the same event is interpreted as a positive or negative violation.

An unexplored question is whether expectancy violations are an "all-or-none" phenomenon. By this, we mean whether a single expectancy violating event is sufficient to trigger a turning point. Two lines of research suggest that there may be different patterns in how such events accumulate. First, McGinn et al. (2004) discovered that out-of keeping acts (expectancy violations) may serve the useful function of triggering transitions that reframe the negotiation. They showed that a key distinguishing feature among transitions is the extent to which they are abrupt (surprises) or gradual. Second, trust theory suggests that while individuals react quickly to violations that call competence into question, they require a greater accumulation of evidence before they revise impressions of shared identity (Lewicki and Weithoff, 2000). A third, and related, issue is the scale of expectancy violating events. While Ballinger and Rockmann (2010) argue that violations need to be substantial in order to trigger transitions, it is possible that small violations accumulated over time may also trigger process transitions. Together, these findings suggest that to better understand turning points we need to learn how individuals accumulate evidence of expectancy violations, as well as how critical thresholds for a transition are set. In exploring these issues, it is important to also consider whether the violations are positive or negative.

Negotiator Resilience

Many of the actions that disrupt the negotiation process, or create the preconditions for a transition to a new stage, are likely to challenge negotiators' beliefs about the possibility of an agreement. Such crises call into question the other party's intentions, and require a leap of faith to continue with the negotiation. Researchers are yet to consider the conditions under which negotiators are willing to make this leap. However, McGinn and Keros' (2003) characterization of negotiations as an improvisational process suggests that negotiators who are resilient, that is, who can recover from unexpected and potentially damaging events (Powley, 2009), will be better able to recover from crises.

Behavioral flexibility and adaptability, defined as skills to be open to the present moment and to adapt their behaviors as needed (Bond et al., 2008), are central characteristics of resilience. These skills enable individuals to recognize how best to respond to an adverse event, and to change their behaviors in a way that helps them respond creatively and constructively to those events (Mancini and Bonnano, 2009). We believe that negotiators who are resilient are more likely to use crises as opportunities to redirect the negotiation to a more constructive process. The more that negotiators perceive a crisis as an opportunity, the more likely that a turning point will follow. Resilient negotiators are oriented toward action and are willing to take risks. Negotiators who do not display resilience are more likely to regard a crisis as a threat, and consequently it is less likely that a turning point will follow. These negotiators are risk-averse, often preferring outside interventions to help move the talks forward. Although resilience is often represented as a risk propensity, it is likely that negotiators' resilience can be influenced by external factors such as decision frames, regulatory focus and tolerance for ambiguity.

Continuing our focus on how the negotiating context affects the interpretation of adverse events, we suggest that the negotiation context itself may affect negotiators resilience. For example, negotiating context influences willingness to take risks. Risk-seeking in the form of new ideas or procedures has been found to occur more often in less sensitive issue areas such as trade or environmental negotiations. Risk-aversion is preferred in more sensitive areas such as security negotiations where negotiators wait for third parties to suggest approaches for moving forward (Druckman, 2001). We therefore propose that initial resilience can be amplified or attenuated by the external conditions that impact the negotiation.

Continuing our focus on interpersonal processes, we also propose that the quality of the underlying relationship with the other negotiator, specifically the extent to which negotiators trust the other party (Payne and Clarke, 2003; Pratt and Dirks, 2007), will also increase or decrease negotiators' resilience. The relationship between trust and resilience is likely a complex one: trust theory implies that negotiators' resilience in the face of adverse events may be affected by the kind of trust that characterizes their relationship with other parties. When negotiators believe that they have shared values, they are likely to require more evidence that a negative violation has occurred but also less likely to recover from that violation. Conversely, when trust is built on a cost-benefit analysis (cognitive trust), violations are more readily discerned but also have less impact (Lewicki and Wiethoff, 2000).

Temporal Horizons and Spillover

Typically, analyses of turning points have focused on events that occur within a negotiation. However, many of our negotiations are one in a series of several with the same negotiator. Negotiation researchers show both that negotiators' reputations (O'Connor et al., 2005; Tinsley et al., 2002) and their experiences from previous negotiations (Keenan and Carnevale, 1989) spill over to affect how subsequent negotiations unfold. It is therefore reasonable to conclude that the accumulation of critical events, and how they are managed within a negotiation, will spill over to shape future negotiations among the same parties. Whether negotiators choose to persist with a dysfunctional process or to switch to a more constructive process, whether they decide to reframe the issues and adopt a completely new approach, or whether they choose to withdraw from the current negotiation will cast a shadow over future negotiations. Yet little is understood about how the experiences in one negotiation, in particular how moments of adversity and transition are managed, influence the ongoing negotiation process or how they shape future negotiations.

Returning to our earlier discussion, we note that central components of resilience are openness to learning and skill in incorporating adverse experiences into behavioral scripts that guide future learning. Resilience researchers argue that individuals who put adverse events into context and learn from them are also better able to deal with adversity in the future (Mancini and Bonnano, 2009). This belief implies that negotiators who do not find constructive responses to adverse events in the moment, but use those events to build a more flexible behavioral repertoire, should establish a stronger foundation for subsequent negotiations. If we accept this proposition, then we also need to understand what kinds of responses position negotiators to bounce back from adverse events, and to strengthen relationships going forward. This understanding could well serve to enhance negotiator resilience through training.

CONCLUSION

The four themes discussed in this chapter can be regarded as partial theories. Each refers to a particular aspect of the negotiation process. Turning points can be understood in relation to each of these parts. But, the parts can also be regarded along a process timeline. Out-of-sync moves lead to impasses that may violate expectations. Negotiators must persevere in the face of these violations, often reframing the issues (a turning point) in order to move the talks forward. A longer-term consequence of these reactions is that they may spill over to future negotiations. This sequence, which highlights precipitants, departures, and consequences, is captured in Figure 13.5. The idea of resilience, introduced in the previous section, weaves it's way through these stages. Whether negotiators perceive an

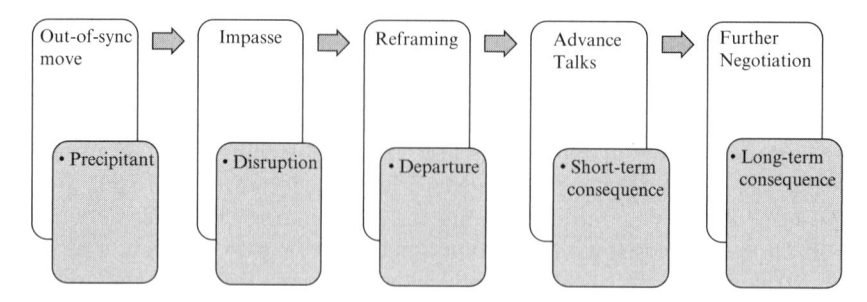

Figure 13.5 An expanded model of turning point sequences

expectancy violation as a crisis, and how they subsequently respond to those violations, is closely tied to their resilience. We thus return full cycle to the turning points framework discussed at the beginning of this chapter, but add the ideas of flexibility and adaptability as underlying mechanisms that determine negotiators' willingness to take a leap of faith and continue their negotiations.

REFERENCES

Adair, W. and Brett, J. (2005). The negotiation dance: Time, culture and behavioral sequences in negotiation. *Organization Science*, 16, 33–51.
Ballinger, G.A. and Rockmann, K.W. (2010). Chutes versus ladders: Anchoring events and a punctuated equilibrium perspective on social exchange relationships. *Academy of Management Review*, 35, 373–391.
Baxter, L.A. and Erbert, L.A. (1999). Perceptions of dialectical contradiction in turning points of development in heterosexual romantic relationships. *Journal of Social and Personal Relationships*, 16, 547–569.
Blount, S. and Janicik, G.A. (2000). Getting and staying in-pace: The "in-synch" preference and its implications for work groups. In H. Sondak (ed.), *Toward Phenomenology of Groups and Group Membership. Research on Managing Groups and Teams*, Vol. 4 (pp. 235–266). New York, NY: Elsevier Science.
Blount, S. and Janicik, G.A. (2001). When plans change: Examining how people evaluate timing changes in work organizations. *Academy of Management Review*, 26, 566–585.
Bond, F.W., Flaxman, P.E., and Bunce, D. (2008). The influence of psychological flexibility on work redesign: Mediated moderation of a work reorganization intervention, *Journal of Applied Psychology*, 93, 645–654.
Brodt, S.E. and Dietz, L.E. (1999). Shared information and information sharing: Understanding negotiation as collective construal. *Research on Negotiation in Organizations*, 7, 263–283.
Burgoon, J.K., Stern, L.A., and Dillman, L. (1995). *Interpersonal Adaptation: Dyadic Interaction Patterns*. Cambridge, MA: Cambridge University Press.
Cameron, M. and Tomlin, B.W. (2000). *The Making of NAFTA: How the Deal was Done*. Ithaca NY: Cornell University Press.
Chasek, P. (1997). A comparative analysis of multilateral environmental negotiations. *Group Decision and Negotiation*, 6, 437–461.

Cohen, P. (ed.) (2008). *Applied Data Analytic Techniques for Turning Points Research*. New York: Routledge.
Crump, L. and Druckman, D. (2012). Turning points in multilateral trade negotiations on intellectual property. *International Negotiation, 17*, 9–35.
Curhan, J. and Pentland, A. (2007). Thin slices of negotiation: Predicting outcomes from conversational dynamics within the first 5 minutes. *Journal of Applied Psychology, 92*, 802–811.
Donohue, W.A. and Roberto, A.J. (1996). An empirical examination of three models of integrative and distributive bargaining. *International Journal of Conflict Management, 7*, 209–229.
Dougherty, J. (2006). *The Critical Mass of Social Change: Northern Ireland Integrated Education*. Unpublished doctoral dissertation, George Mason University.
Douglas, A. (1962). *Industrial Peacemaking*. New York: Columbia University Press.
Drake, L.E. and Donohue, W.A. (1996). Communicative framing theory in conflict resolution. *Communication Research, 23*, 297–322.
Druckman, D. (1983). Social psychology and international negotiations: Processes and influences. In R.F. Kidd and M.J. Saks (eds), Advances in applied social psychology, Vol. 2 (pp. 51–81), Hillsdale, NJ: Lawrence Erlbaum.
Druckman, D. (1986). Stages, turning points and crises: Negotiating military base rights, Spain and the United States. *Journal of Conflict Resolution, 30*, 327–360.
Druckman, D. (2001). Turning points in international negotiations: A comparative analysis, *Journal of Conflict Resolution, 45*, 519–544.
Druckman, D. (2004). Departures in negotiation: Extensions and new directions. *Negotiation Journal, 20*, 185–204.
Druckman, D. (2005). *Doing Research: Methods of Inquiry for Conflict Analysis*. Thousand Oaks, CA: Sage.
Druckman, D. and Bonoma, T.V. (1976). Determinants of bargaining behavior in a bilateral monopoly situation II: Opponent's concession rate and attraction. *Behavioral Science, 21*, 252–262.
Druckman, D. and Harris, R. (1990). Alternative models of responsiveness in international negotiation. *Journal of Conflict Resolution, 34*, 234–251.
Druckman, D. and Olekalns, M. (2011). Turning points in negotiation. *Negotiation and Conflict Management Research, 4*, 1–7.
Druckman, D. and Olekalns, M. (in press). Motivational primes, trust and negotiators' reactions to a crisis. *Journal of Conflict Resolution*.
Druckman, D., Broome, B., and Korper, S. (1988). Value differences and conflict resolution: Facilitation or delinking? *Journal of Conflict Resolution, 32*, 489–510.
Druckman, D., Druckman, J.N., and Arai, T. (2004). E-Mediation: Evaluating the impacts of an electronic mediator on negotiating behavior. *Group Decision and Negotiation, 13*, 481–511.
Druckman, D., Husbands, J.L., and Johnson, K. (1991). Turning points in the INF negotiations. *Negotiation Journal, 7*, 89–108.
Druckman, D., Olekalns, M., and Smith, P. (2009). Interpretive filters: Social cognition and the impact of turning points in negotiation. *Negotiation Journal, 25*, 13–40.
Forgas, J.P. (1998). On feeling good and getting your way: Mood effects on negotiator cognition and bargaining strategies. *Journal of Personality and Social Psychology, 74*, 565–577.
Garrod, S. and Pickering, M.J. (2009). Joint action, alignment, and dialog. *Topics in Cognitive Science, 1*, 292–304.
Giles, H., Coupland, J., and Coupland, N. (1991). *Language: Contexts and Consequences*. Milton Keynes, UK: Open University Press.
Gillespie, A. and Richardson, B. (2011). Exchanging social positions: Enhancing perspective taking within a cooperative problem solving task. *European Journal of Social Psychology, 41*, 608–616.
Gladwell, M. (2000). *The Tipping Point*. Boston, MA: Little, Brown.

Graham, E.E. (1997). Turning points and commitment in post-divorce relationships. *Communication Monographs*, 64(4), 350–368.
Gulliver, P.H. (1979). *Disputes and Negotiations: A Cross-Cultural Approach*. Orlando, FL: Academic Press.
Hall, W. (2008). *Turning Points in Environmental Negotiation: Dynamics, Roles, and Case Related Factors*. Unpublished doctoral dissertation, George Mason University.
Harinck, F. and De Dreu, C.K.W. (2008). Take a break! or not? The impact of mindsets during breaks on negotiation processes and outcomes. *Journal of Experimental Social Psychology*, 44, 397–404.
Harinck, F. and De Dreu, C.K.W. (2011). When does taking a break help in negotiations? The influence of breaks and social motivation on negotiation processes and outcomes. *Negotiation and Conflict Management Research*, 4, 33–46.
Harinck, F. and Van Kleef, G.A. (in press). Be hard on the interests and soft on the values: Conflict issue moderates the effects of anger in negotiations. *British Journal of Social Psychology*.
Hilty, J. and Carnevale, P.J. (1992). Black-hat/white-hat strategy in bilateral negotiation. *Organizational Behaviour and Human Decision Processes*, 55, 444–469.
Holmes, M.E. (1992). Phase structures in negotiation. In L.L. Putnam and M.E. Roloff (eds), *Communication and Negotiation* (pp. 83–105). Newbury Park, CA: Sage.
Hooper, R. and Drummond K. (1990). Emergent goals at a relational turning point: The case of Gordon and Denise. *Journal of Language and Social Psychology*, 9, 39–65.
Jett, Q.R. and George, J.M. (2003). Work interrupted: A closer look at the role of interruptions in organizational life. *Academy of Management Review*, 28, 494–507.
Keenan, P.A. and Carnevale, P.J. (1989). Positive effects of within-group cooperation on between-group negotiation. *Journal of Applied Social Psychology*, 19, 977–992.
Kolb, D. (2004). Staying in the game or changing it: An analysis of moves and turns in negotiation. *Negotiation Journal*, 20, 253–267.
Leary, K. (2004). Critical moments as relational moments: The Centre for Humanitarian Dialogue and the conflict in Aceh, Indonesia. *Negotiation Journal*, 20, 311–338.
London, M. (1988). *Developing Managers*. San Francisco: Jossey-Bass.
Lewicki, R. and Wiethoff, C. (2000). Trust, trust development, and trust repair. In M. Deutsch and P.T. Coleman (eds), *The Handbook of Conflict Resolution: Theory and Practice* (pp 86–107). San Francisco: Jossey-Bass/Pfeiffer.
Mancinci, D. and Bonnano, G.A. (2009). Predictors and parameters of resilience to loss: Toward an individual differences model. *Journal of Personality*, 77, 1–27.
McGinn, K.L. and Keros, A.T. (2003). It take two: Improvisations in negotiations. *Administrative Science Quarterly*, 47, 442–473.
McGinn, K., Lingo, E., and Ciano, K. (2004). Transitions through out-of-keeping acts. *Negotiation Journal*, 20, 171–184.
McKnight, D.H., Cummings, L.L., and Chervany, N.L. (1998). Initial trust formation in new organizational relationships. *Academy of Management Review*, 23, 473–490.
Morley, I. and Stephenson, G. (1977). *The Social Psychology of Bargaining*. London: George Allen and Unwin.
O'Connor, K.M., Arnold, J.A., and Burris, E.R. (2005). Negotiators' bargaining histories and their effects on future negotiation performance. *Journal of Applied Psychology*, 90, 350–362.
Olekalns, M. and Smith, P.L. (2000). Negotiating optimal outcomes: The role of strategic sequences in competitive negotiations. *Human Communication Research*, 24, 528–556.
Olekalns, M. and Smith, P.L (2003a). Social motives in negotiation: The relationship between dyad composition, negotiation processes and outcomes. *International Journal of Conflict Management*, 14, 233–254.
Olekalns, M. and Smith, P.L. (2003b). Testing the relationships among negotiators' motivational orientations, strategy choices and outcomes. *Journal of Experimental Social Psychology*, 39, 101–117.
Olekalns, M. and Smith, P. (2005a). Moments in time: Metacognition, trust and outcomes in negotiation. *Personality and Social Psychology Bulletin*, 31, 1696–1707.

Olekalns, M. and Smith, P. (2005b). Cognitive representations of negotiation. *Australian Journal of Management*, 30, 57–76.
Olekalns, M. and Weingart, L. (2008). Emergent negotiations: Stability and shifts in process dynamics. *Negotiation and Conflict Management Research*, 1, 135–160.
Olekalns, M., Brett, J.M., and Weingart, L. (2003). Phases, transitions and interruptions: The processes that shape agreement in multi-party negotiations. *International Journal of Conflict Management*, 14, 191–211.
Olekalns, M., Roberts, C., Probst, T., Smith, O., and Carnevale, P. (2005). The impact of message frame on negotiators' social judgments, moods and behavior. *International Journal of Conflict Management*, 16, 379–402.
Payne, R.L. and Clark, M. (2003). The process of trusting: Its relevance to vulnerability and resilience in traumatic situations. In D. Paton, J.M. Violanti, and L.M. Smith (eds), *Promoting Capabilities to Manage Posttraumatic Stress: Perspectives on Resilience* (pp. 152–169). Springfield, IL: Charles C. Thomas.
Pickering, M.J. and Garrod, S. (2006). Alignment as the basis for successful communication. *Research on Language and Computation*. DOI 10.1007/s11168-006-9004-0.
Pinkley, R.L. and Northcraft, G.B. (1994). Conflict frames of reference: Implications for dispute processes and outcomes. *Academy of Management Journal*, 37, 193–205.
Powley, E. (2009). Reclaiming resilience and safety: Resilience activation in the critical period of crisis. *Human Relations*, 62, 1289–1326.
Pratt, M.G. and Dirks, K.T. (2007). Rebuilding trust and restoring positive relationships: A commitment-based view of trust. In J.E. Dutton and B.R. Ragins (eds), *Exploring positive relationships at work: Building a theoretical and research foundation* (pp. 117–136). New Jersey: Lawrence Erlbaum Associates.
Pruitt, D.G. (1981). *Negotiation Behavior*. New York: Academic Press.
Putnam, L.L. (1990). Reframing integrative and distributive bargaining: A process perspective. *Research on Negotiation in Organizations*, 2, 3–30.
Putnam, L.L. (2004). Transformations and critical moments in negotiation. *Negotiation Journal*, 20, 275–296.
Putnam, L.L. and Fuller, R. (2010). *Negotiation and corporate campaigns: The case of the 2007–2008 writers' strike*. Paper presented at the annual meeting of the National Communication Association, San Francisco, CA, November.
Putnam, L.L. and Holmer, M. (1992). Framing and reframing in negotiations. In L.L. Putnam and M.E. Roloff (eds), *Communication and Negotiation*. Newbury Park: Sage Publications (pp. 128–155).
Putnam, L.L. and Shoemaker, M. (2007). Changes in conflict framing in the news coverage of an environmental conflict. *Journal of Dispute Resolution*, 1, 167–175.
Rothstein, A. (1997). Turning points in psychoanalysis. *Journal of the American Psychoanalytic Association*, 45, 1271–1284.
Schulenberg, J., Wadsworth, K.N., O'Malley, P.M., Bachman, J.G., and Johnston, L.D. (1997). Adolescent risk factors for binge drinking during the transition to young adulthood: Variable and pattern-centered approaches to change. In G.A. Marlatt and G.R. Van den Bos (eds), *Addictive Behaviors: Readings on Etiology, Prevention, and Treatment*. Washington DC: American Psychological Association.
Stoll, R.J. and McAndrew, W. (1986). Negotiating strategic arms control, 1969–79: Modeling the bargaining process. *Journal of Conflict Resolution*, 30, 315–326.
Stuart, H.W. Jr. (2004). Surprise moves in negotiation. *Negotiation Journal*, 20, 239–252.
Taylor, P.J. and Thomas, S. (2008). Linguistic style matching and negotiation outcome. *Negotiation and Conflict Management Research*, 1, 263–281.
Tinsley, C.H., O'Connor, K.M., and Sullivan, B.H. (2002). Tough guys finish last: The perils of a distributive reputation. *Organizational Behavior and Human Decision Processes*, 88, 621–642.
Tomlin, B.W. (1989). The stages of prenegotiation: The decision to negotiate North American free trade. In J.G. Stein (ed.), *Getting to the Table*. Baltimore, MD: Johns Hopkins University Press, (pp. 18–43).

Walton, R.E and McKersie, R.B. (1965). *A Behavioral Theory of Labor Negotiations*. New York: McGraw-Hill.
Weick, K.E. (1995). *Sensemaking in Organizations*. Thousand Oaks, CA: Sage.
White, C.H. and Burgoon, J.K. (2001). Adaptation and communicative design: Patterns of interaction in truthful and deceptive conversations. *Human Communication Research, 21*, 9–37.
Winship, C. (2004). Veneers and underlayments: Critical moments and situational redefinition. *Negotiation Journal, 20*, 297–310.
Zartman, I.W. and Berman, M.R. (1982). *The Practical Negotiator*. New Haven & London: Yale University Press.

14. The costs and benefits of e-negotiations
Ray Friedman and Liuba Y. Belkin

Over the last decade there has been a growing literature on the effects of email on negotiation (e.g., Belkin et al., in press; Johnson and Cooper, 2009a; 2009b; Morris et al., 2002; Moore et al., 1999; Kurtzberg et al., 2009; Naquin et al., 2008; 2010; Rosette et al., 2012; Stuhlmacher and Citera, 2005). This research followed, and was inspired by, a generation of work on computer mediated communication (e.g., Daft and Lengel, 1986; Sproull and Keisler, 1986; Short et al., 1976; Walther, 1992). While there is now a sizeable body of knowledge on the topic of electronically mediated negotiation, competing findings and theories are emerging as well, resulting in confusion about implications of electronic communication on negotiation processes and outcomes, as well as in a lack of clear answers about the most efficient way to conduct negotiations through electronic media. This chapter reviews the existing research on communications, psychology, and negotiation, including both the traditional theoretical frameworks and a new conceptual approach, called Construal Level Theory of Psychological Distance (Trope and Liberman, 2010), while synthesizing available empirical data in terms of its implications for email negotiations. We conclude by considering several strategies for managing these contradictory recommendations, including a "contingency" approach that identifies when it is best to use face-to-face or online communications for negotiation, as well as a process of tacking back and forth – to use a sailing metaphor – between psychological distance and psychological closeness, which we label an "into the wind" strategy for managing electronically mediated negotiations.

THEORETICAL FOUNDATION

The research on email negotiations, or other forms of negotiations that are computer mediated, is predominantly grounded in theories of media richness and social presence. In their seminal work, Daft and Lengel (1986) argued that organizations primarily need to address two problems: lack of information (or uncertainty) and ambiguity of information (lack of clarity about how to act, called "equivocality"). Accordingly, the authors rated each type of communication medium in terms of its ability to address those two issues, termed a "richness" scale. They further argued that in order to reduce uncertainty, one needs to get access to clear, structured information, which can be achieved through either lean or rich media (or both), but when trying to manage equivocality, "rich" media is needed, since it allows for immediate feedback, a variety of nonverbal cues, such as tone of voice, facial expressions, postures and gestures, and, hence, a better grasp of the other party's personal information. According to Daft and Lengel's (1986) scale, face-to-face communication is the "richest" media, since it makes ambiguity and equivocality easier to manage, while text and email media is placed at the bottom of the "richness" scale.

Another prominent theory called Social Presence (Short, et al., 1976), ranked communication media in terms of their ability to incorporate social presence in communicators' interactions. According to the Social Presence scale, each medium can be ranked on a continuum based on the degree to which individuals are aware of each other's presence, with face-to-face ranked as having the highest degree of social presence and text-only media as having the lowest degree of social presence (Short et al., 1976). This theory was later applied to computer-mediated communication to explain the "cues filtered out" phenomenon of e-media, arguing that CMC is an inherently impersonal and "cold" medium that is not suitable for establishing close personal relationships. That is, due to the lack of nonverbal cues, there is limited information about the other party, which inhibits the development of personal ties (Sproull and Kiesler, 1986; Walther, 1992). Similarly, the Social Identity Model of Deindividuation Effects (SIDE Model), developed by Reicher and colleagues (1995) is based on the notion that lack of nonverbal cues, relative anonymity of the parties, and reduced presence make electronic media socially impoverished (e.g., "deindividuated") as compared to face-to-face communication channels. Finally, in his Social Information Processing (SIP) theory, Walther (1992) also built on the "cues filtered out" approach towards CMC; however, unlike other theories supporting this perspective, he maintained that meaningful relationships are also possible to establish once parties get to know each other better and get accustomed to the e-environment.

To sum up, early theories of communication focused on how objective characteristics of communication media (such as presence or absence of informational cues) affect the quality of individual communication. The main prescription resulting from those theories with respect to e-communication is to hold off on it whenever possible, unless the task is routine, suggesting that face-to-face interactions are the preferred mode of communication. An alternative to media richness, SIDE, SIP and social presence theories that has emerged recently is a construal level theory of psychological distance (Trope and Liberman, 2003; 2010), which also looks at social distance between communicators, but takes a more cognitive theoretical approach. The focus of this theory is on how actual or hypothetical distance among communication partners affects cognition and information processing and, as a result, decision-making and behavior. This theory conceptualizes psychological distance on four different dimensions of actual and/or perceived distance among individuals. Psychological distance can be rooted in temporal distance (i.e., how far or close in time the object or an event is), spatial distance (i.e., how far or close it is in space), social distance (i.e., out-group versus in-group membership or strangers versus friends), and hypotheticality (i.e., the degree to which the object or event is hypothetical, imaginary, and abstract versus real and concrete). Psychological distance from an object or an event, in any of these forms, influences individual perceptions of information relevance, and affects the mental construal and judgments about that object or event (Liberman et al., 2007; Trope and Liberman, 2003; 2010), as well as similarity predictions, emotional experiences and preferences for action (Davis et al., 2011; Milkman et al., in press; Williams and Bargh, 2008). Thus, while CMC creates social distance between the parties who are communicating, there may be some cognitive benefits to that greater distance.

Most importantly, greater social distance that occurs during CMC may enable the parties to engage in more abstract, creative problem solving since it encourages "higher level" construals. According to Trope and Liberman "higher level" construals are more abstract, general and goal-oriented depictions of the task or a situation at hand, as opposed to lower-level, detailed construals. The authors argue that higher-level construals contain fewer details about an object or an event, since irrelevant or inconsistent details are omitted from representation (or assimilated into it), but caution against perceiving high-level construals as impoverished versions of lower-level ones. As they put it: "the process of abstraction involves not only a loss of specific, idiosyncratic, and incidental information, but also ascription of new meaning deduced from stored knowledge and organized in structured representations" (Trope and Liberman, 2010, p. 441). Thus, to the degree that CMC creates social distance, it should also create abstract thinking, which may be beneficial to negotiations. While there is a loss of focus on details with more abstract thinking, there is the benefit of new knowledge creation from those more abstract processes.

In many ways, the Construal Level theory and the previous theories discussed above (Media richness, SIDE, and SIP) are similar. Each sees communication media changing individual perceptions, behaviors and interaction dynamics in important ways as one moves from face-to-face to electronic media, with face-to-face being more psychologically close and rich than electronic communications. The difference, as we will see later in this chapter, is that earlier approaches (i.e., media richness and social presence) focus primarily on costs associated with the move to electronic communications, while the latter (i.e., psychological distance) can also help scholars to identify advantages to the kind of distance created by electronic media. In the next sections, we explore theoretical and empirical results that show both positive and negative effects of media on social interactions in general, followed by a section that explores positive and negative media impact on negotiations in particular (for a summary of both cost and benefits of e-media, please refer to Table 14.1). We then look at recommendations that can be logically extrapolated from these findings for how best to manage electronically mediated negotiations.

EFFECTS OF COMPUTER MEDIATED COMMUNICATION (CMC)

Social Costs of CMC

Most of the early work on CMC, much of it done by psychologists at Carnegie Mellon University, identified negative effects of CMC on behaviors. Kiesler, Siegel and McGuire (1984) found that when people communicated online, rather than face-to-face, there were more aggressive behaviors (at the extreme, called "flaming"), which occurred due to the lack of social cues, while Kurtzberg and colleagues (Kurtzberg et al., 2005; Kurtzberg et al., 2006) found that ambiguous messages conveyed electronically (as opposed to face-to-face or paper format) are more likely to be interpreted as negative. Some recent research also supported this idea showing that as media becomes less rich, in Daft and Lengel's terms, it is not only harder to reduce equivocality, but there are also more likely to be negative attacks, conflicts and dysfunctional behavior (Goleman, 2007). Friedman and Currall (2003) examined these dynamics of CMC – and email in particular – to look at their effects on the ability of people to manage disputes. They argue that several structural properties of email make it more likely that conflicts will escalate if managed though electronic communications. First, diminished feedback due to lack of social cues makes is more likely that small disagreements are not corrected, leading to more negative interpretations of the other side's behaviors, since such disagreements occur within the context of ongoing misunderstandings. Second, the ability to write long responses in email (rather than engage in the back and forth interactions of face-to-face meetings) produces one-sided communications and little chance to adjust to the other side's views. Finally, the ability to sit in front of a computer to obsess about emails

Table 14.1 Summary of empirical findings on computer mediated communication

Features of CMC	Drawbacks	Benefits
Increase ambiguity and equivocality Lack or absence of social cues Asynchrony – lack or absence of immediate feedback Increase in psychological distance	More aggressive behavior, flaming (*Kiesler et al., 1984*) Messages are interpreted as more negative (*Kurtzberg et al., 2005; Kurtzberg et al., 2006*) Heightened conflict (*Goleman, 2007*) Less chance of conflict resolution (*Friedman and Currall, 2004*) Less satisfaction with group processes (*Ocker and Yaverbaum, 1999*) Higher self-serving bias (*Weisband and Atwater, 1999*) Increased de-individuation (*Sproull and Kiesler, 1986*) Slower and less efficient interactions (*Baltes et al., 2002; Bordia, 1997; Straus and McGrath, 1994*)	Reduction in social and cultural normative pressures (*Alexander, 2003; Bordia, 1997; Hiltz et al., 1986; Hollingshead, in press*) Greater idea generation and idea exchange within groups (*Dennis and Valacich, 1993; Galuppe et al., 1992; Valalcich et al., 1992*)

(re-writing and re-reading them) can enhance commitments to one's own position and lead to excess rumination about negative emails received. All of these conditions make it more likely that conflicts will escalate, rather than being resolved, when managed through email.

In addition, concerns that relationships are not as well protected in CMC exchanges were confirmed by a number of studies. Ocker and Yaverbaum (1999) found that although CMC groups were as effective at producing results as groups using other communication media, such as face-to-face, the participants were less satisfied with the quality of group discussions and the group interaction process. Weisband and Atwater (1999) found that self-serving biases (inflated self-ratings) were worse in CMC than face-to-face groups, while Alicke and colleagues (1995) found that self-serving bias was lower when the person being evaluated was not a subject to the de-individuation effect. In fact, according to Sproull and Kiesler (1986), CMC encourages de-individuation, as the lack of physical presence allows people to "forget" that the person with whom one interacts is a unique individual, thus "freeing" an individual from any moral or social obligations to treat one's communication partner as another human being. Hence, it appears that richer media are not just better for allowing more effective information processing, but they also reinforce adherence to social and cultural norms for proper interactions.

CMC also makes interactions slower and less efficient. Conducting experiments using three-person group meetings for a variety of tasks (i.e., idea-generation, judgment and intellective), Straus and McGrath (1994) found that there was no difference in terms of the quality of the outputs produced by the face-to-face and CMC groups on those tasks, but the groups that met face-to-face were more efficient. A summary of this literature (Bordia, 1997) reports that groups working through CMC, rather than face-to-face, tend to produce fewer remarks, take longer to complete tasks and show less understanding of co-workers involved in a task. A more recent meta-analysis of 55 studies comparing virtual to face-to-face groups also showed decreased efficiency, the need for more time to complete a task, and lower satisfaction with the process (Baltes et al., 2002).

There is also emerging evidence that the potential negative impact of CMC is affected strongly by several moderators. First, it is influenced by people's level of experience with CMC. Hollingshead and colleagues (1993) report that group performance using CMC is diminished primarily when the communication medium is very new, and group members have less experience using it. This suggests that as people become accustomed to email, instant messaging, and group chats, they will be able to avoid some of the process losses that come from CMC. Wilson and colleagues (2006) also find that trust within CMC group can be regained if there is enough repeated interaction. In addition, some tasks seem to benefit more strongly from the social cues that are stripped away with CMC. For example, negotiations and intellectual performance tasks seem very vulnerable to losses from CMC, while that is not always the case for idea-generative and decision-making tasks (Hollingshead et al., 1993). In fact, there is a stream of findings, which we review below, showing that lack of social cues and increase in social distance can enhance some group processes and help with efficient completion of a variety of tasks.

Benefits of CMC

One major benefit to the loss of social cues that comes from CMC is the reduction of social and cultural normative pressures on individuals due to an increase in social, temporal and spatial distance dimensions between communication partners. For instance, social norms can often make low status members of a group hold back their true views, and defer to those higher in status. Once the salience of power and status is stripped away in the electronic context, people can more freely contribute their ideas and observations without feeling that they are violating social norms. This makes it more likely to have greater idea generation and exchange within a group, and to promote more open sharing of alternative views. In fact, the positive impact of social cues reduction is especially evident for larger groups interacting through virtual media on creative tasks, such as brainstorming (Dennis and Valacich, 1993; Gallupe et al., 1992; Valacich et al., 1992).

In a series of experiments Dennis, Valacich and colleagues found that large (6- to 12-person) groups were more efficient in generating ideas and felt more satisfied in doing so via e-media as compared to verbal or nominal brainstorming groups. The evidence shows that electronic media can reduce production blocking, social loafing and evaluation apprehension, as well as eliminate redundancy of ideas for large groups involved in creative decision-making (Dennis and Valacich, 1993; Gallupe et al., 1992; Dennis et al., 1992). E-media seem to allow groups to engage in a more productive approach to decision-making, helping individuals to focus on generating more systematic, dispassionate, and objective ideas and ensure more equal participation of group members. In addition, it appears that electronic media may empower individuals, who are shy or otherwise uncomfortable in social situations to participate more frequently in group discussions, and allow leadership roles to emerge in a more fluid way (Alexander, 2003; Hiltz et al., 1986; Hollingshead, in press). Moreover, recent studies imply that with increases in psychological distance there is less social pressure on individuals and more chances for them to form independent opinions and attitudes. This occurs because of higher social distance and allows people to be more detached from others' influence and thus more attuned to their own values and ideas, affording higher control over one's own decision-making and attitude formation (Eyal et al., 2008; Fujita et al., 2008).

In addition to advantages of increased social distance in e-context, increase in temporal distance among e-communicators (that is, having time to react to the other party) may be beneficial as well. In particular, temporal distance may help to level out the playing field by giving members of e-teams time to search for answers and address missing knowledge/expertise without appearing unprofessional or ill-informed in front of their peers, clients, superiors or subordinates. Moreover, temporal distance should be beneficial for members of creative and decision-making teams, as having their peers' input in a written format should further eliminate the production blocking effect since there is no interruption to one's own flow of ideas and less chance to forget the partner's ideas. E-team members can always take a break and get back to the conversation with new ideas and minimal loss of information about others' suggestions and insights, unlike face-to-face partners where people have to respond immediately and a lot of potentially good ideas on either side are wasted. In addition, it is easier to build on ideas of others when the written transcript of a whole conversation is present, while in a typical face-to-face brainstorming session it is easier for some of the ideas to be ignored or omitted.

Finally, the lack of physical presence of communication partners in a virtual environment may help individuals engage in higher cognitive construals (Trope and Liberman, 2010), allowing them to arrive at more objective and rational solutions. For instance, some studies have found that higher spatial distance increases one's tendency to rely predominantly on general and abstract information when forming judgments and making decisions about events (Fujita et al., 2006; Henderson et al., 2006) leading to a more "emotion-free" and rational decision-making environment. Moreover, spatial and temporal distances may affect the emotional states of online communication partners. Recent studies show that emotional intensity and psychological distance are inversely correlated (Van Boven et al., 2010; Williams and Bargh, 2008). For example, in four experiments Williams and Bargh (2008) showed that more spatially distant events (as compared to spatially close ones) produced less emotional distress and significantly lower levels of affective judgments. Accordingly, since there is an increase in psychological distance between partners in CMC (as compared to a face-to-face mode), there should be more emotional detachment and less negative emotional antagonism if a conflict occurs among online partners.

To sum up, it appears that an increase in psychological distance among communication partners does not necessarily carry negative implications, but in fact can facilitate communication, minimize relationship conflict and aid rational decision-making by allowing people to focus on the task at hand, instead of concentrating on social status, cultural norms, emotion and relationship issues.

EFFECTS OF CMC ON NEGOTIATION

While the bulk of CMC research was initially focused on individual and group dynamics and decision-making, in the late 1990s negotiation scholars joined the study of CMC in order to understand the effects of electronic media on negotiation process and outcomes. The findings have been roughly similar to those produced by CMC research on individuals and groups, focusing mostly on negative aspects of CMC, such as less efficiency and longer time to complete negotiations (Purdue et al., 2000), but some benefits have also been identified (For a summary of findings on e-negotiations please refer to Table 14.2).

Costs of Computer Mediated Communication for Negotiation

Email clearly has a damaging effect on the quality of relationships between negotiators. For instance, Morris et al (2002) find that email negotiators had a harder time building rapport than face-to-face negotiators. Much of this problem comes from the fact that email negotiators conveyed to each other less personal information, and asked fewer questions. Similarly, Naquin and Paulson (2003) found that even before negotiations begin, when it is expected that individuals would negotiate online, there is less trust in the other party than in a face-to-face situation. The lower levels of trust persisted in their experiment throughout the negotiations, as well as afterwards, with online negotiators expressing less interest in future interactions with the other party than when they negotiated face-to-face.

The choice of the communication medium also affects negotiation moves and tactics. Galin and colleagues (2007) documented greater use of distributive and value-claiming (i.e., "hard" tactics) in e-negotiations than in face-to-face negotiations, such as use of threats, demanding offers, and intimidation, and Giordano et al (2007) report higher levels of forcing behavior, and greater tensions. Similarly, and Johnson and Cooper (2009a) found that negotiations conducted by instant messaging (versus over the phone) were associated with reductions in concessionary behavior, reduced communication of positive affect, as well as less

Table 14.2 Summary of findings of effects of CMC on negotiations

	Drawbacks	Benefits
Negotiation Process	Harder to coordinate among team members, takes longer (Baltes et al., 2002; Galin et al., 2007; Paulus et al., 1996; Purdue et al., 2000) Less collaboration/cooperation, less trust and rapport (Morris et al., 2002; Naquin and Paulson, 2003; Purdue et al., 2000) Less dialog/information exchanged (Friedman and Currall, 2004; McGinn and Keros, 2002; McGinn et al., 2003; Morris et al., 2002) More deception/less honest behavior (Naquin et al., 2010; Citera et al., 2005) Less reciprocity – concessions made by the first mover are often not reciprocated by the 2nd mover (Johnson and Cooper, 2009a) Conflict escalation and inhibition of conflict resolution (Friedman and Currall, 2003; Friedman et al., 2004) Females are more hostile through CMC than FTF (Stuhlmacher et al., 2007) Extreme opening offers (Johnson and Cooper, 2009b)	Can lower conflict due to lower reciprocity and decrease of forcing behavior (Dorado et al., 2002) Status and power are reduced (Barsness and Bhappu, 2004) Less emotional intensity (Williams and Bargh, 2008; Williams et al., forthcoming) Females have easier time expressing negative emotions (Scuhlmacher et al., 2007) Less rapport can be an effective protection against unethical behaviors (people do not let their guard down and are not taken advantage of) (Jap et al., 2011) Physical distance can increase the frequency of pareto-efficient agreements (Henderson, 2011) Temporal distance increases integrative agreements (Henderson et al., 2006) CMC highlights self-interest; thus, may be more beneficial for collectivists in terms of individual gains (Rosette et al., 2012)
Negotiation Outcomes	Less integrative agreements and higher likelihood of impasse (Moore et al., 1999; Morris et al., 2002; Johnson and Cooper, 2009a) Lower individual gains from expressing positive emotions (Belkin et al., in press)	Higher individual gains (at least short term from aggressive behavior) (Stuhlmacher and Citera, 2005) Can achieve slightly more integrative agreements and more equal outcome distribution and equality of participation (Bordia, 1997; Croson, 1999; Henderson, 2011)

chance for reaching an agreement in negotiations. Johnson and Cooper (2009b) observe that the normal process of reciprocating concessions does not happen as consistently during e-negotiations, putting a first mover at a disadvantage in e-negotiations. It is not surprising, then, that e-negotiators are seen as less credible than face-to-face negotiators (Citera et al., 2005) – both in the eyes of the other party and in one's own eyes.

In addition, as the relationship is weakened by using electronic media, so too are moral boundaries. Citera et al (2005) found that e-negotiators were more likely than face-to-face negotiators to advocate using dishonesty in the future, Rockman and Northcraft (2008) saw that e-negotiators were more deceptive and engaged less in truth telling than face-to-face negotiators and Naquin and colleagues (2010) found that e-negotiators are more likely to lie than those who interact via pen and paper, and feel more justified in doing so. This further supports the idea that perhaps due to lack of social presence and the de-individuation effect, the use of electronic media may not only relax social norms, but also ethical norms, and encourage dysfunctional behavior.

E-negotiations are also known to exacerbate cultural differences. Barsness and Bhappu (2004) argue that cultural differences on various dimensions, such as individualism-collectivism, can lead to different negotiating styles. In a face-to-face context negotiators are able to get social cues about these differences, leading to some adjustment between the parties. However, when negotiating electronically, those opportunities to adjust are taken away, making the impact of cultural differences on the negotiation process more salient. The authors caution that the tendency of e-context to enhance self-interest in negotiations may lead individualists to act even in a more self-serving manner than usual, although it may also help collectivists by injecting a bit more self-interest into an other-focused way of negotiating. Some of these expectations were confirmed in an empirical study by Rosette et al (2012), who found that use of e-negotiations shifted the behaviors of Chinese negotiators more than those of U.S. negotiators, since the loss of social cues and resulting greater aggressiveness that comes from e-negotiating was more apparent on that medium than the typical negotiating style for Chinese negotiators.

The impact on outcomes produced by e-negotiation is complicated and subtle. Morris et al (2002) found that overall joint gains were not different comparing e-negotiations to face-to-face negotiations, but they did find that these outcomes were more vulnerable to actions that caused breaches of trust from contentious tactics. The lower levels of rapport engendered in e-negotiations cause any breaches of process to have a greater impact on outcomes. They also speculated that the real effect of e-negotiations may be from higher rates of impasse, as was shown in Moore et al (1999), rather than actual lower joint gains. Higher impasse rates for electronic contexts were also found by Johnson and Cooper (2009a), who compared Instant Messaging (IM) negotiations and telephone negotiations.

Similar to the CMC literature, the extent of electronic media effects on negotiations is largely dependent on the level of experience with e-negotiations. Some studies confirm that when people get used to a mode of communication, differences between face-to-face and other media (IM, email, video conferencing) tend to disappear (van der Kleij et al., 2005; van der Kleij et al., 2009). In addition, generational effects could play a role with the level of comfort with a particular media. For instance, studies show that older adults, as compared to the younger generation (18–39), have less experience, and more anxiety and hold less positive attitudes towards computer use (Czaja et al., 2006). Moreover, research shows that younger generations may actually feel more comfortable with computer-mediated communication than with face-to-face interactions (Thayer and Ray, 2006). Accordingly, it is possible that CMC negotiations may be more beneficial for younger adults, while for the older generation comfort with CMC negotiations may gradually improve with more experience and frequency of use.

Implications for Practice

The main recommendation made by negotiation scholars who identify the downside of electronic negotiations is to insert back into e-negotiations elements of the face-to-face context that were lost. Moore and colleagues (1999) showed that holding "getting to know you" sessions helped email negotiators from different social groups (in this case universities) to reach agreements as often as other pairs. Similarly, Morris and colleagues (2002) observed that having "schmoozing" sessions before electronic interactions reduced the liability of email negotiations. McGinn and Keros (2002) also found that media effects were eliminated when negotiations occurred with friends (rather than strangers), suggesting that developing relationships can inoculate negotiators from the losses that occur in email negotiations. As Nadler and Shestowsky (2006) explained, negotiators need to minimize the effects of de-individuation by making sure that negotiators see their partners as identifiable human beings, rather than abstract or faceless others. Feng et al. (2004) advise e-negotiators to show more empathy to their partners, while others (Wallace, 1999; Walther and Bunz, 2005) suggest that frequent message exchange can help e-negotiators build trust and reduce anxiety that accompanies electronic interactions. This approach is similar to the one taken by research on CMC and teams, suggesting that by building social relations CMC teams may achieve better performance and higher satisfaction (Lin et al., 2008). A more extreme approach is expressed by Friedman and Currall, (2003), who advise people managing disputes to simply stay away from e-media for this type of negotiation.

A second set of recommendations is simply to adapt one's tactics, not letting the tendency of the medium to allow for more aggressive behavior to take over. Johnson and colleagues (2008) show that when e-negotiators engage in personal blaming of their opponents, it decreases the likelihood of an agreement, and even if there is a deal, it hurts the payoff for the party that initiates the flame. Moreover, even when flaming is not focused on the opponent, it still reduces the payoff for the party initiating those negative messages. The implication is clear: do not flame! In other work, Johnson and Cooper (2009b) suggest that it may be wise to not make an opening move in e-negotiations, since the other side may not actually reciprocate, due to the lack of social closeness and lower social norm adherence. Thus, while there is a potential benefit of going first in a negotiation in a face-to-face context (in order to shape the others' responses), in the e-negotiation context the better strategy might be to hold off and wait for the other party to put the number on a table first. The overall theme of these approaches is for negotiators to know the potential negative effects of e-negotiation, and avoid the kinds of dysfunctional behaviors that can occur because of them.

Lastly, the lack of social cues suggests that great care must be taken in how ideas are communicated. Given the findings with respect to increased flaming, deception and conflicts in e-media as compared to other forms of communication (Citera et al., 2005; Giordano et al., 2007; Friedman and Currall, 2003; Naquin et al., 2010, among others) one should remain polite, clear, and concise in electronic communications in order to reduce misunderstandings that can easily occur in electronic negotiations. Also, research shows that use of greetings helps build positive impressions about communication partners, fostering trust and relationship building (Sarbaugh-Thompson and Feldman, 1998). In addition, since there is a natural slant in e-communication towards interpreting ambiguous information in a more negative manner (Byron, 2008), using positively charged language to express some positive emotions might be a helpful strategy. However, one must be cautious when expressing positive emotions online as to not come across as over-excited, since it may be interpreted by the other side as a sign of weakness and encourage aggressive behavior (Belkin et al., in press). Finally, it is also a good idea to steer away from humor and sarcasm in online context. Several studies have shown that it is much harder to convey sarcasm and humor during email negotiations (Kurtzberg et al., 2009), so the use of humor might not be the best tactic to employ in the e-context, as people greatly overestimate how well they can communicate over email (Kruger et al., 2005).

BENEFITS OF SOCIAL DISTANCE FROM E-NEGOTIATIONS

Research shows that using electronic communication in negotiations can be advantageous to individual outcomes and enhance some aspects of the negotiation process. These findings parallel the arguments in the CMC literature on the benefits of increased social distance, the absence of nonverbal cues and diminished awareness of social norms. Moreover, an emergent literature in a negotiation field highlights positive effects of greater social distance afforded by e-media on outcomes and relationships in a negotiation context (Henderson, 2011; Hollingshead, in press; Jap et al., 2011; Rosette, et al., 2012; among others).

One advantage of e-negotiations is that some people may actually benefit from the greater degree of aggressiveness that comes with e-negotiation. Individuals from collectivist cultures have been predominantly exposed to and experience social norms to act in a cooperative way; for these negotiators, the lack of social norms reinforcement in e-negotiations allows them to assert their own needs more strongly (Rosette et al., 2012). Women may also benefit from the weakening of social norms. A meta-analysis of 43 studies that compared virtual negotiations with face-to-face negotiations (Stuhlmacher et al., 2007) revealed that females have an easier time expressing negative emotions and behaving in a more hostile way when communicating via email than communicating face-to-face, allowing them to obtain higher individual gains (no differences in behavior or outcomes were observed for males). The authors attribute these findings to the reduction of social cues and the increase of psychological distance between negotiating partners that occurs in online contexts. In particular, they argue that females are less concerned with adhering to gender roles as well as with the social status of their negotiating partners in online contexts (see also Stuhlmacher and Linnabery, Chapter 9 this volume). Hence, due to differences in the physical (i.e., greater spatial distance) and psychological (i.e., greater social distance) characteristics of the electronic context, some negotiators may increase individual short-term gains when negotiating electronically as opposed to face-to-face.

Another benefit of e-negotiations is that negotiators may be less susceptible to emotional manipulation by the other party. Research shows that greater social distance and lack of emotional expressions in electronic environments potentially create *less* personal and relationship conflict among negotiating partners than in face-to-face settings. Visual presence of others can induce arousal (Carnevale et al., 1981; Zajonc, 1965; Keltner and Haidt, 2001), thereby promoting forcing behavior and enhancing conflict frequency and intensity in face-to-face negotiations (Dorado et al., 2002). Thus, even though emotional perception is less accurate in a virtual environment, the overall lower incidence of emotional expressions and less emotional intensity (Williams and Bargh, 2008; Williams et al., forthcoming) through electronic media can be conducive to more integrative agreements and higher individual gains.

Much of the research showing a benefit from e-negotiation has focused on the downside of having rich, face-to-face media, since that rich media conveys emotions and social norms which may actually get in the way; but others have taken a different approach, arguing that the kind of psychological distance that comes from e-negotiations can actually boost negotiators cognitive skills. With respect to integrative agreements, studies demonstrate that greater spatial distance among negotiators can increase the frequency of Pareto-efficient agreements and allow for more equal outcome distribution among partners (Bordia, 1997; Henderson, 2011). Such effects are possibly a result of parties taking a more structured and conceptual approach to the negotiation task and using more abstract language (Fujita et al., 2006; Henderson et al., 2006). For example, sales managers negotiating over sales compensation policies might switch from talking about how much Mary or Joe are paid, and instead talk more abstractly about what behaviors are more important to the company and how to reward such behaviors. One of the most interesting and compelling findings on the benefits of increased distance to negotiations to date is a study by Henderson (2011), which shows that greater social distance among negotiators actually helps integrative agreements. For integrative negotiations, what matters is the ability to think conceptually (Barry and Friedman, 1998), which can be enhanced by psychological distance.

Finally, another advantage of greater psychological distance for e-negotiations is that social distance among e-negotiators may actually help protect them from unethical behavior of their opponents. In the previous section we reported studies that found more unethical behavior in e-negotiations, but there is also research showing that email can in fact offer protection against lying and unethical behavior. This is possibly due to the very lack of social closeness and decrease in trust that occurs online, since lack of trust may make negotiators less gullible. For instance, Schweitzer et al (2002) find that face-to-face negotiators may be more vulnerable to lies because of their stronger relationship with the other party, which makes them more likely to believe the other side, even when it actually is a lie. Similarly, Jap and colleagues (2011) observe that in negotiations where rapport was developed, negotiators may be so drawn to make a deal that they violate the needs of their own constituents and lie to the opponent. However, where there is less trust on the other side (due to using email to negotiate) this dynamic is less likely to occur. Also, even though there may be more deceptive behavior in e-negotiations, negotiators may have less ability to detect the deception leaving them (ironically) more satisfied with the outcome (Giordano et al., 2007).

Implications for Practice

Recommendations derived from this literature look very different than what is reported in the first "implications for practice" section above. One implication is that some people may want to take advantage of the lack of social norms, especially those who are disadvantaged by them: female negotiators (Stuhlmacher et al., 2007), Chinese negotiators who are looking to maximize personal outcomes (Rosette et al., 2012), those with individualistic goals (Giordano et al., 2007), and negotiation parties who want their agents to not be overly influenced by the desire to develop a relationship with the other side (Jap et al., 2011). These negotiators may sensibly choose to keep in place the social distance that comes from e-negotiations rather than trying to recreate social ties. In addition, some negotiators who are very shy or self-conscious may benefit from e-negotiations (Hollingshead, in press).

A second implication is that negotiators may want to create psychological distance in order to enhance broader conceptual thinking. Rather than trying to create social closeness, one might attempt to create distance by being farther from the other side. Even if there were an opportunity to meet face-to-face, Psychological Distance theory (Trope and Liberman, 2010) suggest that we might want to impose onto a negotiation a layer of electronic communications, so that the two sides could think more clearly and abstractly about solutions to problems. The greater the distance, the better, as long as the negotiation is of a type where abstract problem-solving is needed.

PSYCHOLOGICAL DISTANCE – USE IT OR AVOID IT?

Greater social and spatial distance among communication partners has been highlighted by the majority of past research as one of the main drawbacks of electronic media – it has been blamed for diminished negotiation outcomes, impoverished communication channels, increased aggressive and uninhibited behavior, and was found to be detrimental for interpersonal relationships. In fact, we can see from the above review that there is an overall agreement among researchers that online negotiations are less personal, less embedded in social relations, and more abstract than face-to-face negotiations. At the same time, greater social distance appears to be a major source of potential gains to electronically mediated interactions, which can be beneficial for some people and in some contexts. In addition, there may be types of negotiation for which abstract thinking is advantageous, but at the same time there are often costs associated with lack of social embeddedness. How can we think of these costs and benefits and reconcile the tension between preferences for psychological distance versus psychological closeness? One possibility is to think of contingencies. That is, are there some times when it is better to be psychologically distant, but other times when it is better to be psychologically close in online negotiation exchanges? We identify below various factors and situations where there appears to be a strong argument either for trying to compensate for the lack of social ties within e-negotiations, or for embracing the benefits of psychological distance. Another option is to think of the optimal approach to e-negotiations as a mixed strategy, moving back and forth between psychological distance and psychological closeness. In this view, neither pure approach is likely to be optimal, but rather deft use of both strategies at the same time, creating the tacking effect, is what is needed.

Contingency Approach

In this approach we frame the psychological distance-closeness dichotomy as the two ends of one continuum. The main advantage of psychological distance is that it allows more abstract and holistic thinking in negotiations while the advantage of psychological closeness is that it provides stronger relationship support and social influence. Thus, we suggest negotiators should choose whether to avoid or approach psychological distance in electronic negotiations based on the desire, capability, and need for abstract thinking versus social influence. The avoidance/approach choice can be affected by personal and situational constrains, goals, preferences and abilities. The following factors determine the importance of abstract thinking or greater social influence.

Personality
The choice between psychological distance versus closeness could be made based on a negotiator's personality characteristics, along with preferences

and skills. For instance, looking at the Big-5 personality characteristics (Costa and McCrae, 1992), individuals scoring high on extraversion may have a high need to be socially engaged and develop relationships and thus less comfortable with psychological distance. On the other hand, those scoring high on conscientiousness, which is a trait associated with deliberation and carefulness, may prefer higher psychological distance instead. In addition, people scoring high on neuroticism might benefit from greater psychological distance, as it might help them manage emotions better and reduce anxiety. Research in e-media also shows that people with low self-esteem exhibit preference for online interactions over personal exchanges (Caplan, 2005). Accordingly, it appears that people who are at a disadvantage or not comfortable with personal interactions may benefit from increases in psychological distance. Nevertheless, more analysis of the effects of personality traits specifically related to online negotiation context is needed to support the above suggestions.

Emotional intelligence and emotional regulation
Related to personality factors described above, the ability to recognize and perceive emotions in others, as well as the ability to regulate one's own emotions may influence one's choice of psychological distance and closeness. For instance, individuals that score high on emotional intelligence may be able to take more advantage of the ability to send and receive social cues in face-to-face negotiations, making the move to CMC especially costly for them. Inversely, individuals that have difficulties with emotional regulation may benefit from greater psychological distance (Williams et al., forthcoming) since they are less susceptible to making emotionally-driven mistakes in this context compared to a face-to-face context; using CMC rather than face-to-face interactions will allow them to reduce emotional intensity and think more rationally.

Social status and power
Negotiators' social status within the context of a particular negotiation interaction, along with psychological power (i.e., how one's position is perceived by the other side) can play a role in the choice between psychological distance versus closeness. Psychological distance should weaken, or even eliminate, the effects of personal power since social cues, which convey or reinforce standing and status, are not readily available online (Belkin et al., in press). Thus, the higher one's social status and/or power in a particular negotiation context, the more psychological closeness is a benefit that negotiators would want to preserve and use. Research on e-media and negotiations, as mentioned above, has demonstrated that electronic communication helps to equalize personal power and is a pref-

erable media to use for people with low power or status (Hollingshead et al., 1993; Sproull and Kiesler, 1986).

Legal environment and resources
The ability to enforce implementation of negotiation results due to the strength of the regulatory environment in a given context, or the availability of resources that can be used to ensure implementation of the terms of a deal, may also play an important role in the choice between psychological closeness or distance. Specifically, if enforceability of the deal is uncertain (for example due to laws and regulations in some contexts, like China (Clissold, 2004)), then the negotiator is more dependent on trust to ensure implementation. Where trust is important, psychological closeness is a benefit – or even a necessity. Thus, some macro conditions may affect negotiators' willingness to embrace psychological distance.

Cultural norms
Some societies are more focused on interpersonal ties as a major determinant of social influence and trust (Ferrin and Gillespie, 2010; Gunia et al., 2011; Aslani et al., Chapter 10 this volume). In such contexts, greater psychological closeness between negotiators is more important to maintain. However, in some collectivistic cultures the strength of social norms that govern interpersonal interaction may in fact constrain negotiators and limit their ability to maximize personal outcomes, producing a disadvantage from psychological closeness. Accordingly, greater psychological distance becomes a better choice in those circumstances (Rosette et al., 2012).

Informational ambiguity
Another factor that may affect the choice between psychological distance and closeness is the degree of informational ambiguity present in negotiations. In particular, if there is high informational ambiguity, negotiation success largely depends on gathering more data from the other side. In such cases the issue is less about abstract thinking, but more about open sharing of information (at least as a first step). Research suggests that people are more likely to share information when they trust the other side (Naquin and Paulson, 2003) making strong personal connections critical. In that situation, greater psychological closeness is necessary. On the other hand, if there is enough information available and the predominant goal for a negotiator is analysis of existing information, greater psychological distance and thus, a more abstract approach, could be more helpful.

Task complexity
The nature of the task negotiators will be involved with can also be a major factor in deciding whether greater psychological distance or closeness is a more efficient approach to negotiations. If the negotiation task is a complex one requiring creative solutions, multi-step methods and/or has multiple parties involved, it may be a good idea to allow for greater psychological distance that can help negotiators to adopt a more abstract and holistic approach. By psychologically distancing themselves from distractions and interruptions, negotiators will be able to better concentrate on core features of the deal, instead of being caught up in details. In addition, greater psychological distance in complex multi-party interactions can help to limit emotional burdens that come from coalitions and social ties and allow individuals to take a more abstract, and potentially more constructive, approach to negotiations.

Relationship stage
The stage of the relationship with potential negotiation partners may also affect the preference for psychological distance versus closeness strategy. In particular, if a positive relationship has been established among the partners in prior interactions, then when some degree of social influence is necessary for achieving negotiation goals there is a base of personal relations to draw upon. The current negotiations are not needed to establish those relations, and psychological distance may be acceptable. In fact, psychological distance can be advantageous – having the benefit of established trust, negotiation parties can instead concentrate on rational decision-making. By contrast, if there is no prior positive relationship established, then it may be important to develop some modicum of social ties during the negotiation process, making some degree of psychological closeness a priority.

MIXED MODEL APPROACH

An alternative approach is to make a different assumption – that all negotiations need both the trust and rapport that comes from psychological closeness, and the detachment and abstract thinking that comes from psychological distance. The problem is not to choose one or the other, but rather to shift effectively between them. The logic is similar to negotiation research that suggests that neither aggressive nor cooperative negotiation tactics are inherently good or bad, but rather each may be more beneficial when used in conjunction (Olekalns et al., 2003). Thus, we might argue that abstract thinking is more effective when done in

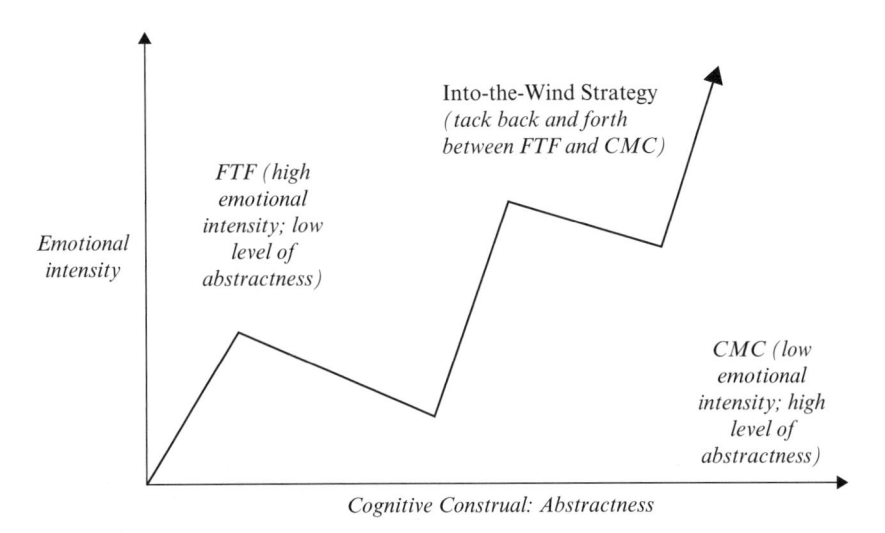

Figure 14.1   Into-the-wind strategy

the context of psychological closeness, since there is a base of trust and rapport. Inversely, it may be that psychological closeness is most helpful as a way to advance substantive ideas developed during a phase of abstract thinking. Indeed, it may be that the glow of success that comes from creative problem solving is in itself a booster of feelings of closeness and that positive affect, in turn enhances the impact of psychological closeness. In this view, it is important to not be purely close or distant, but rather to shift between times of closeness or distance, in a sense, tacking back and forth between those two states. Thus, the challenge for e-negotiators is to maintain both forms of social interaction, and know when it is time to allow one or the other approach to come to the fore. To use a sailing analogy, in order to move upwind, a sailboat cannot sail left or right exclusively, but rather has to tack back and forth, making advances in each direction. We call this the "Into the Wind" strategy (see Figure 14.1).

"Into the Wind" Strategy

Start face-to-face

As a starting point, we would argue that it is best to begin negotiations face-to-face. This is a time when relationships may not already exist, or even if relationships do exist, the contacts may not be very recent. Despite the potential cognitive benefits of abstract thinking, negotiators are not expected to jump right into problem solving when they initially meet.

378 *Handbook of research on negotiation*

They are learning to understand the other side, and decide if they can be trusted in the sense of negotiating in good faith (Lewicki et al., 1998). Since the benefits of any future information sharing depend on belief in the veracity of the information provided, it is critical to establish trust right away. Even if the first interaction does not produce trust in terms of goodwill, at least it will provide the parties with a better sense of what to expect – producing a kind of predictability trust (Mayer et al., 1995). This first stage of the negotiation process is critically dependent on the presence of strong social cues, rather than psychological distance and abstract thinking.

Move online
After the initial meeting, the challenge is to define the topics and issues to be covered in the negotiation. In this phase of negotiation, abstract thinking is more likely to be helpful. What is the broad range of issues that need to be addressed? This is a diagnostic process where the challenge is to assess what kinds of problems need to be solved to make a deal viable for both sides. Abstract thinking is likely to be helpful at this point. While there may be myriad of small concerns that could draw the focus of negotiators, it is better to get a broad view of the overall landscape to help negotiators see the big questions and issues involved and to know where to focus their efforts. A negotiator may have a particular pet concern about an issue, but focusing there could waste much of the negotiating team's time and energy. As Behfar and colleagues (2008) put it, "particularistic" strategies aimed at satisfying particular people are less helpful than "pluralistic" ones that apply to a whole group. Moving to CMC for the negotiation at this point may provide the abstractness needed to gain a broad, pluralistic view of the problems to be addressed in the negotiation.

Back to face-to-face for information sharing
Once the problems are defined, then it is incumbent on both the parties to gather the information they need to assess the situation and any options that might be proposed. Once the range of issues is known, then it is time to get more specific and find out each person's issues and concerns. Negotiators have to think "particularistically". Sharing personal information, though, does depend to some degree on trust and closeness. Several scholars (Knapp et al., 1980; Carl and Duck, 2008; Duck, 2006) have found that those who are closer tend to share more information and do so more honestly and accurately. Moreover, not only is information shared more with psychological closeness, it is also absorbed more readily. Information that is presented by those

with whom one is close is more likely to be deemed accurate, and worth acting upon.

CMC to develop solutions
With more information on hand, negotiators next need to find solutions through creative problem solving. Here, solutions are more likely when negotiators can see trade-offs between issues, so a broader, more abstract view of the problems is needed. Indeed, according to Trope and colleagues' research on psychological distance (Trope et al., 2003; 2010), if one needs to see the big picture, it is particularly beneficial to be more distant. Face-to-face contact is not needed – the issue is not trust, but the development of ideas and trade-offs among issues.

Face-to-face for final resolution
While problem-solving ideas are critical to negotiations, when it comes time to actually make a decision, psychological closeness may again be crucial. Will the other side actually do what it says? As Friedman (1993) found in the union-negotiation setting, union leaders may like the ideas of mutual gains bargaining in the abstract, but ultimately felt vulnerable if they expected the other side would take advantage of them. While in theory, each side's interests should still be protected when using integrative bargaining, the willingness to actually use that approach depended largely on trust. Thus, that final agreement depends on personal ties with the other side, and the faith one has in the other side to address inevitable unforeseen issues and contingencies.

In sum, a negotiation can best be handled with a series of back and forth moves between face-to-face and computer mediated meetings, using the benefits of each at phases of the negotiation where it is most important to either benefit from psychological closeness or from distance and abstract thinking. The phases of the negotiation may not be exactly in this order and there may be multiple moves back and forth between idea generation and information gathering, but the overall idea that negotiators can benefit from both approaches at different times still holds. This kind of tacking back and forth is what we call an "Into the Wind" approach to media strategies in negotiations.

We should also add that at times negotiators are not just managing negotiations across the table, but also managing (at the same time) negotiations with constituents – some of whom may be at a distance. In those cases, online discussions with constituents may introduce abstract thinking into a negotiating team, even as that same team is face-to-face (and psychologically close with) the other party.

CONCLUSIONS AND FUTURE RESEARCH DIRECTIONS

Three decades of research on electronic communication and negotiation produced steady, but somewhat conflicting findings. Our chapter summarized some of the main points from the field, while adding another perspective borrowed from psychology, the construal level theory of psychological distance (Trope and Lieberman, 2010), in order to explain some of the inconsistencies in e-negotiations research and help us to come up with suggestions on how to successfully manage electronic negotiations. While earlier research on e-negotiation mostly identified problems and risks due to online interactions, more recent work suggests advantages to e-communication. Therefore, the recommendations are no longer, in effect, "put face-to-face elements back into e-negotiations", but rather think through the specific advantages of psychological closeness or psychological distance and use them accordingly. That way, it is possible to identify specific contingencies that drive the choice of closeness or distance. Also, we suggest that deft use of e-media during negotiations may require not just choice of closeness or distance, but rather the deft movement between those states – a tacking back and forth. Even though these ideas are proposed in a speculative way and further research is needed to test these ideas, we suggest that this is where scholar attention should focus when considering the impact of electronic media on negotiation. Due to the prevalence of electronic media use in everyday communications and negotiations in particular, it is often no longer possible to avoid e-negotiations. We hope that this review identifies both the pitfalls and advantages of e-negotiation, and how negotiators can better manage those electronic interactions.

REFERENCES

Alexander, S.C. (2003). Leadership and social support on the Internet: A longitudinal analysis of mental and physical illness groups. *Dissertation Abstracts International Section A: Humanities and Social Sciences*.

Alicke, M.D., Klotz, M.L., Breitenbecher, D.L., Yurak, T.J., and Vredenburg, D.S. (1995). Personal contact, individuation, and the better-than-average effect. *Journal of Personality and Social Psychology*, 68, 804–825.

Baltes, B.B., Dickson, M.W., Sherman, M.P., Bauer, C.C., and LaGanke, J.S. (2002). Computer-mediated communication and group decision-making: A meta-analysis. *Organizational Behavior and Human Decision Processes*, 87, 156–179.

Barry, B. and Friedman, R. (1998). Bargainer characteristics in distributive and integrative negotiation. *Journal of Personality and Social Psychology*, 74, 345–359.

Barsness, Z.I. and Bhappu, A.D. (2004). At the crossroads of technology and culture: Social influence, information sharing, and sense-making processes during negotiations.

In M. Gelfand and J. Brett (eds), *The Handbook of Negotiation and Culture* (pp. 350–373). Stanford, CA: Stanford Business Books.

Behfar, K.J., Peterson, R.S., Mannix, E.A., and Trochim, W.M.K. (2008). The critical role of conflict resolution in teams: A close look at the links between conflict type, conflict management strategies, and team outcomes. *Journal of Applied Psychology*, 93, 170–188.

Belkin, L.Y., Kurtzberg, T.R., and Naquin, C.E. (in press). Signaling dominance in online negotiations: The role of affective tone. *Negotiation and Conflict Management Research*.

Bordia, P. (1997). Face-to-face versus computer-mediated communication: A synthesis of the experimental literature, *Journal of Business Communication*, 34, 99–120.

Byron, K. (2008). Carrying too heavy a load? The communication and miscommunication of emotion in emails, *Academy of Management Review*, 33, 309–327.

Caplan, S. (2005). A social skill account of problematic Internet use. *Journal of Communication*, 55, 721–736.

Carl, W.J. and Duck, S. (2008). How to do things with relationships . . . and how relationships do things with us. *Communications Yearbook*, 28, 1–35.

Carnevale, P.J., Pruitt, D.G., and Seilheimer, S.D. (1981). Looking and competing: Accountability and visual access in integrative bargaining. *Journal of Personality and Social Psychology*, 40, 111–120.

Citera, M., Beauregard, R., and Mitsya, T. (2005). An experimental study of credibility in e-negotiations. *Psychology and Marketing*, 22, 163–179.

Clissold, T. (2004). *Mr. China*. London: Robinson Press.

Costa Jr., P.T. and McCrae, R.R. (1992). *Revised NEO Personality Inventory (NEO-PI-R) and NEO Five-Factor Inventory (NEO-FFI) manual*. Odessa, FL: Psychological Assessment Resources.

Croson, R.T.A. (1999). Look at me when you say that: An electronic negotiation simulation. *Simulation & Gaming*, 30, 23–37.

Czaja, S.J., Charness, N., Fisk, A.D., Hertzog, C., Nair, S.N., Rogers, W.A., and Sharit, J. (2006). Factors predicting the use of technology: Findings from the Center for Research and Education on Aging and Technology Enhancement (CREATE). *Psychology and Aging*, 21, 333–352.

Daft, R.L. and Lengel, R.J. (1986). Organizational information requirements, media richness and structural design. *Management Science*, 32, 554–571.

Davis, J.I., Gross, J.J., and Ochsner, K.N. (2011). Psychological distance and emotional experience: What you see is what you get, *Emotion*, 11, 438–444.

Dennis, A.R. and Valacich, J.S. (1993). Computer brainstorms: More heads are better than one. *Journal of Applied Psychology*, 78, 531–537.

Dorado, M.A., Medina F.J., Munduate, L., Cisneros, I.F.J., and Euwema, M. (2002). Computer mediated negotiation of an escalated conflict. *Small Group Research*, 33, 509–524.

Duck, S. (2006). Hypertext in the key of G: Three types of "history" as influences on conversational structure and flow. *Communication Theory*, 12, 41–62.

Eyal, T., Liberman, N., and Trope, Y. (2008). Judging near and distant virtue and vice. *Journal of Experimental Social Psychology*, 44, 1204–1209.

Feng, J., Lazar, P.J., and Preece, J. (2004). Empathy and online interpersonal trust: A fragile relationship. *Behavior and Information Technology*, 23, 97–106.

Ferrin, D.L. and Gillespie, N. (2010). Trust differences across national-societal cultures: Much to do, or much ado about nothing? In M. Saunders, D. Skinner, G. Dietz, N. Gillespie, and R.J. Lewicki (eds), *Trust across cultures: Theory and practice* (pp. 42–86). Cambridge, UK: Cambridge University Press.

Friedman, R. (1993). Bringing mutual gains bargaining to labor negotiations: The role of trust, understanding, and control, *Human Resource Management*, 32, 435–459.

Friedman, R.A. and Currall, S.C. (2003). Conflict escalation: Dispute exacerbating elements of email communication, *Human Relations*, 56, 1325–1347.

Friedman R., Anderson C., Brett J., Olekalns M., Goates N., and Lisco C.C. (2004). The

positive and negative effects of anger on dispute resolution: evidence from electronically mediated disputes, *Journal of Applied Psychology*, 89, 369–376.
Fujita, K., Eyal, T., Chaiken, S., Trope, Y., and Liberman, N. (2008). Influencing attitudes toward near and distant objects. *Journal of Experimental Social Psychology*, 44, 562–572.
Fujita, K., Henderson, M., Eng, J., Trope, Y., and Liberman, N. (2006). Spatial distance and mental construal of social events. *Psychological Science*, 17, 278–282.
Galin, A., Gross, M., and Gosalker, G. (2007). E-negotiation versus face-to-face negotiation what has changed – if anything. *Computers in Human Behavior*, 23, 787–797.
Gallupe, R.B., Dennis, A.R., Cooper, W.H., Valacich, J.S., Nunamaker Jr., J.F., and Bastianutti, L. (1992). Electronic brainstorming and group size. *Academy of Management Journal*, 35, 350–369.
Giordano, G.A., Stoner, J.S., Brouer, R.L., and George, J.F. (2007). The influences of deception and computer-mediation on dyadic negotiations. *Journal of Computer-Mediated Communication*, 12, 362–383.
Goleman, D. (2007). Normal social restraints are weakened in cyberspace, *International Herald Tribune*, 20 February.
Gunia, B., Brett, J., Nandkeolyar, A., and Kamdar, D. (2011). Paying a price: Culture, trust, and negotiation consequences. *Journal of Applied Psychology*, 96, 774–789.
Henderson, M.D. (2011). Mere physical distance and integrative agreements: When more space improves negotiation outcomes. *Journal of Experimental Social Psychology*, 47, 7–15.
Henderson, M.D., Fujita, K., Trope, Y., and Liberman, N. (2006). Transcending the "Here": The effects of spatial distance on social judgment. *Journal of Personality and Social Psychology*, 91, 845–856.
Hiltz, S.R., Johnson, K., and Turoff, M. (1986). Experiments in group decision making: communication process and outcome in face-to-face versus computerized conferences. *Human Communication Research*, 13, 225–252.
Hollingshead, A.B. (in press). The dynamics of leader emergence in online groups. In Z. Birchmeier, B. Dietz-Uhler, and G. Stasser (eds), *Strategic Uses of Social Technology: An Interactive Perspective of Social Psychology*, Cambridge, UK: Cambridge Press.
Hollingshead, A.B., McGrath, J.E., and O'Connor, K.M. (1993). Group task performance and communication technology: A longitudinal examination of computer-mediated vs. face-to-face groups. *Small Group Research*, 24, 307–333.
Jap, S., Robertson, D.C., and Hamilton, R. (2011). The dark side of rapport. *Management Science*, 57, 1610–1622.
Johnson, N. and Cooper, R.B. (2009a). Media, affect, concession, and agreement in negotiation: IM versus telephone. *Decision Support Systems*, 46, 673–684.
Johnson, N. and Cooper, R.B. (2009b). Power, concession, and agreement in computer-mediated negotiation: An examination of first offers, *MIS Quarterly*, 33, 147–170.
Johnson, N., Cooper, R.B., and Chin, W.W. (2008). The effect of flaming on computer-mediated negotiations. *European Journal of Information Systems*, 17, 417–434.
Keltner, D. and Haidt, J. (2001). Social functions of emotions. In T. Mayne and G. Bonanno (eds), *Emotions: Current issues and future directions* (pp. 192–213). New York: Guilford Press.
Kiesler, S., Siegel, J., and McGuire, T.W. (1984). Social psychological aspects of computer-mediated communication. *American Psychologist*, 39, 1123–1134.
Knapp, M., Ellis, D.G., and Williams, B. (1980). Perceptions of communication behavior associated with relationship terms. *Communication Monographs*, 47, 262–278.
Kruger, J., Epley, N., Parker, J., and Ng, Z. (2005). Egocentrism over email: Can we communicate as well as we think? *Journal of Personality and Social Psychology*, 89, 925–936.
Kurtzberg, T.R., Belkin, L.Y., and Naquin, C.E. (2006). The effect of email on attitudes towards performance feedback, *International Journal of Organizational Analysis*, 14, 4–21.
Kurtzberg, T.R., Naquin C.E., and Belkin L.Y. (2005). Electronic performance appraisals: The effects of email communication on peer ratings in actual and simulated environments. *Organizational Behavior and Human Decision Processes*, 98, 216–226.

Kurtzberg, T.R., Naquin, C.E., and Belkin, L.Y. (2009). Overcoming the email disadvantage: Humor in online negotiations. *International Journal of Conflict Management*, 20, 377–397.

Lewicki, R.J., McAllister, D.J., and Bies, R.J. (1998). Trust and distrust: New relationships and realities. *Academy of Management Review*, 23, 513–530.

Liberman, N., Trope, Y., and Stephan, E. (2007). Psychological distance. In E.T. Higgins and A.W. Kruglanski (eds), *Social psychology: A handbook of basic principles* (pp. 353–381). New York: Guilford Press.

Lin, C., Standing, S., and Liu, Y.C. (2008). A model to develop effective virtual teams. *Decision Support Systems*, 45, 1031–1045.

Mayer, R.C., Davis, J.H., and Schoorman, F.D. (1995). An integrative model of organizational trust. *Academy of Management Review*, 20, 709–734.

McGinn, K.L. and Keros, A.T. (2002). Improvisation and the logic of exchange in socially embedded transactions. *Administrative Science Quarterly*, 47, 442–473.

McGinn, K.L., Thompson, L., and Bazerman, M.H. (2003). Dyadic processes of disclosure and reciprocity in bargaining with communication. *Journal of Behavioral Decision Making*, 16, 17–34.

Milkman, K.L., Akinola, M., and Chugh, D. (2012). Temporal distance and discrimination: An audit study in academia. *Psychological Science*, 23(7), 710–717.

Moore, D.A., Kurtzberg, T.R., Thompson, L.L., and Morris, M.W. (1999). Long and short routes to success in electronically mediated negotiations: Group affiliations and good vibrations. *Organizational Behavior and Human Decision Processes*, 77, 22–43.

Morris, M.W., Nadler, J., Kurtzberg, T.R., and Thompson, L.L. (2002). Schmooze or lose: Social friction and lubrication in email negotiations, *Group Dynamics*, 6, 89–100.

Nadler, J. and Shestowsky, D. (2006). Negotiation, information technology and the problem of the faceless other. In L. Thompson (ed.), *Negotiation theory and research*. New York: Psychology Press.

Naquin, C.E., and Paulson, G.D. (2003). Online bargaining and interpersonal trust. *Journal of Applied Psychology*, 88, 113–120.

Naquin, C.E., Kurtzberg, T.R., and Belkin, L.Y. (2008). Online communication and group cooperation in mixed motive contexts. *Social Justice Research*, 21, 470–489.

Naquin, C.E., Kurtzberg, T.R., and Belkin, L.Y. (2010). The finer points of lying online: Email versus pen-and-paper. *Journal of Applied Psychology*, 95, 387–394.

Ocker, R.J. and Yaverbaum, G.J. (1999). Asynchronous computer-mediated communication versus face–face collaboration: Results on student learning, quality and satisfaction. *Group Decision and Negotiations*, 8, 427–440.

Olekalns, M., Brett, J.M., and Weingart, L.R. (2003). Phases, transitions and interruptions: Modeling processes in multi-party negotiations. *International Journal of Conflict Management*, 14, 191–211.

Paulus, P.B., Larey, T.S., Putman, V.L., Leggett, K.L., and Roland, E.J. (1996). Social influence processes in computer brainstorming. *Basic and Applied Social Psychology*, 18, 3–14.

Purdue, J.M., Nye, P., and Balakrishnan, P.V. (2000). The impact of communication media on negotiation outcomes. *International Journal of Conflict Management*, 11, 162–187.

Reicher, S., Spears, R., and Postmes, T. (1995). A social identity model of deindividuation phenomena. In W. Stroebe and M. Hewstone (eds), *European Review of Social Psychology* (Vol. 6, pp. 161–198). Chichester: Wiley.

Rockman, K.W. and Northcraft, G.B. (2008). To be or not to be trusted: The influence of media richness on defection and deception. *Organization Behavior and Human Decision Processes*, 107, 106–122.

Rosette, A.S., Brett, J.M., Barsness, Z., and Lytle, A.L. (2012). When cultures clash electronically: The impact of email and social norms on negotiation behavior and outcomes. *Journal of Cross-Cultural Psychology*, 43, 628–643.

Sarbaugh-Thompson, M. and Feldman, M.S. (1998). Electronic mail and organizational communication: Does saying "hi" really matter? *Organization Science*, 9, 685–698.

Short, J., Williams, E., and Christie, B. (1976). *The social psychology of telecommunications.* London: John Wiley and Sons.

Sproull, L. and Kiesler, S. (1986). Reducing social context cues: Electronic mail in organizational communication. *Management Science*, 32, 1492–1512.

Straus, S.G. and McGrath, J.E. (1994). Does the medium matter? The interaction of task type and technology on group performance and member reactions. *Journal of Applied Psychology*, 79, 87–97.

Stuhlmacher, A.F. and Citera, M. (2005). Hostile behavior and profit in virtual negotiation: A meta-analysis. *Journal of Business and Psychology*, 20, 69–93.

Stuhlmacher, A.F., Citera, M., and Willis, T. (2007). Gender differences in virtual negotiation: Theory and research. *Sex Roles*, 57, 329–339.

Schweitzer, M.E., Brodt, S., and Cronson, R.T.A. (2002). Seeing and believing: Visual access and the strategic use of deception. *International Journal of Conflict Management*, 13, 258–375.

Thayer, S.E. and Ray, S. (2006). Online communication preferences across age, gender and duration of internet use. *CyberPsychology and Behavior*, 9, 432–440.

Trope, Y. and Liberman, N. (2003). Temporal construal. *Psychological Review*, 110, 403–421.

Trope, Y. and Liberman, N. (2010). Construal-level theory of psychological distance. *Psychological Review*, 117, 440–463.

Valacich, J.S., Dennis, A.R., and Nunamaker Jr., J.F. (1992). Group size and anonymity effects on computer-mediated idea generation. *Small Group Research*, 2, 49–73.

Van Boven, L., Kane, J., McGraw, A.P., and Dale, J. (2010). Feeling close: Emotional intensity reduces perceived psychological distance, *Journal of Personality and Social Psychology*, 98, 872–885.

Van der Kleij, R., Paashuis, R.M., and Schraagen, J.M.C. (2005). On the passage of time: Temporal differences in video-mediated and face-to-face interaction. *International Journal of Human-Computer Studies*, 62, 521–542.

Van der Kleij, R., Schraagen, J.M., Werkhoven, P., and De Dreu, C.K.W. (2009). How conversations change over time in face-to-face and video-mediated communication. *Small Group Research*, 40, 355–381.

Wallace, P. (1999). *The psychology of the Internet.* New York: Cambridge University Press.

Walther, J.B. (1992). Interpersonal effects in computer-mediated interaction: A relational perspective. *Communication Research*, 19, 52–90.

Walther, J.B. and Bunz, U. (2005). The rules of virtual groups: Trust, liking and performance in computer-mediated communication. *Journal of Communication*, 55, 828–846.

Weisband, S. and Atwater, L. (1999). Evaluating self and others in electronic and face-to-face groups. *Journal of Applied Psychology*, 84, 632–639.

Williams, L.E. and Bargh, J.A. (2008). Keeping one's distance: The influence of spatial distance cues on affect and evaluation. *Psychological Science*, 19, 302–308.

Williams, L., Stein, R., and Galguera, L. (forthcoming). Beyond construal: Disentangling the emotional and cognitive consequences of psychological distance. *Journal of Consumer Research*.

Wilson, J.M., Straus, S.G., and McEvily, B. (2006). All due in time: The development of trust in computer-mediated and face-to-face teams. *Organization Behavior and Human Decision Processes*, 99, 16–33.

Zajonc, R.B. (1965). Social facilitation. *Science*, 149, 269–274.

PART V

COMPLEX NEGOTIATIONS

15. International trade negotiations
Larry Crump

When examining international trade negotiations, many people may think our focus is on the buying and selling of goods in an international context—commercial transactions such as foreign oil, rice, electronics, or the many other foreign goods available in the global marketplace. This certainly is international trade, but when the academic literature examines trade negotiation the focus is on establishing the international regulatory environment that determines how goods and services are exchanged. It would be more rational to refer to this as "international trade policy negotiation" but the literature does not make this distinction.

This chapter examines that literature concerned with the negotiation or establishment (but not implementation) of the international regulatory environment for trade in goods and services. International trade embraces "free market" principles as an ideal state (Smith, 1789) and international trade negotiation is the primary tool to achieve this ideal state although sometimes we find that such negotiations purposely erect rather than dismantle trade barriers (Crump, 2006a). Nevertheless, the overall purpose of international trade negotiation is the implementation of Adam Smith's grand vision—trade liberalization.

International trade negotiations include a range of players or parties. Trade ministries or departments within national governments (trade diplomats and ambassadors) are primary actors, although at times the prime minister or president's office plays a critical role in such negotiations. National governments form bilateral, regional, and global economic associations. Global associations are guided primarily by two international organizations: the General Agreement on Tariffs and Trade (GATT, 1947–1994) and the World Trade Organization (WTO, 1995–present), which grew out of GATT and assumed its responsibilities for trade liberalization (WTO, 1994a). All these parties receive significant attention in this chapter.

International commerce offers opportunities and threats to the well-being of a national economy. Governments create trade barriers to protect inefficient economic sectors within their borders and seek to remove trade barriers in countries with markets that could be exploited. Natural endowments in production (natural resource, capital, etc.) are important but secondary to analytical resources when it comes to studying the economic and political aspects of the game and the strategic resources required to act on such analysis. Negotiating an international trade regime to maximize national gain and minimize loss is wealth enhancing.

This chapter examines the international negotiation dynamics that emerge from this economic and political environment. Significant literature exists within economics, political science, international relation, and related fields, but such literature asks questions that are fundamentally unrelated to an understanding of negotiation process and outcome. This chapter is concerned with a much smaller literature that identifies variables and examines the dynamics that establish international trade negotiation processes and outcomes.

The purpose of this chapter is to develop a research agenda that assists in moving the international negotiation field forward. It is surprising that so few negotiation researchers and scholars examine international trade negotiation (Crump and Odell, 2008). First, a simple international trade negotiation case is examined to introduce fundamental issues within this field. Second, this chapter reviews negotiation research that examines bilateral and regional trade negotiations. Third, global trade negotiations are investigated through a review of the multilateral conference literature. The chapter concludes with observations on the development of a research agenda devoted to international trade negotiation, while recommendations for future research are included throughout this chapter.

UNITED STATES–SINGAPORE TRADE NEGOTIATIONS: AN ILLUSTRATIVE CASE

Singapore Prime Minister Goh Chok Tong and U.S. President Bill Clinton announced their intentions to negotiate a trade treaty—which eventually became the United States–Singapore Free Trade Agreement (USSFTA)—at the Asia Pacific Economic Cooperation (APEC) Leaders' Summit in Brunei in November 2000 after a late-night game of golf.

Singapore's delegation was led by Professor Tommy Koh, with many Singaporean negotiators coming from the Trade Division of the Ministry of Trade and Industry (MTI). The U.S. delegation was led by Ralph F. Ives, with many U.S. negotiators coming from the Office of the U.S. Trade Representative (USTR). There were 40 to 50 negotiators or trade diplomats on each side during the course of this bilateral negotiation. Each team organized its negotiators into 21 working groups, or one group per treaty chapter. The two sides held 11 rounds of discussion (a round is normally conducted over one week) with the first round held in December 2000. There was a pause in negotiations from February to May 2001, as

President Clinton retired and President George W. Bush assumed office. The final round was held in November 2002. Most of the 11 rounds were held in London.

Among the many issues discussed and agreed, a number offered real challenges. From the beginning, the United States insisted that goods be divided into non-textile and textile products. In textile negotiations, the United States forced Singapore to adopt rules restricting where yarn can be sourced (USSFTA, Chapter 5), demonstrating that "free" trade negotiations are sometimes also about developing trade barriers. In goods, Singapore had no tariffs on almost all goods and so the United States matched this approach but negotiated over when U.S. tariffs would be removed for defined categories of goods (USSFTA, Chapter 2). Singapore sought to eliminate tariffs early and the United States sought to delay tariff elimination. Negotiations over goods are not easily separated from negotiations involving rules of origin (USSFTA, Chapter 3). Singapore initially sought to persuade the United States to accept a "value-added system" for rules of origin, but agreed to U.S. demands to adopt a "change in tariff classification system"—two different systems for establishing the country where a good is manufactured (thus making that good eligible or ineligible for specific trade benefits under a specific trade treaty).

In services (USSFTA, Chapter 8), the United States insisted on a negative list template (services listed in a treaty are specifically excluded from trade). Singapore resisted, but eventually agreed after extensive interagency consultation. In telecommunications (USSFTA, Chapter 9), Singapore and the United States created a state-of-the-art agreement between two open-market economies. In electronic commerce (USSFTA, Chapter 14), both sides sought to explore every opportunity to liberalize trade—establishing the world's first trade treaty with an electronic commerce chapter. In financial services, Singaporean liberalization was a top U.S. priority (USSFTA, Chapter 10). The United States successfully persuaded Singapore to liberalize its retail-banking sector and to phase out its wholesale bank license quota system for U.S. banks, although Singapore refused to allow U.S. banks to acquire local Singaporean banks.

The United States arrived in Singapore with a 21-page initial position on intellectual property rights (IPR). Singaporean negotiators thought the U.S. position was focused on IPR enforcement, where little enforcement exists—an approach seen to be irrelevant to Singapore. Nevertheless, much of what the United States sought is found in USSFTA (Chapter 16).

USSFTA negotiations moved toward a conclusion when U.S. trade representative Robert Zoellick and Singaporean Trade Minister George Yeo met at an APEC Ministerial Meeting in Los Cabos, Mexico in October 2002. These meetings narrowed the list of outstanding issues from 30 to five or six issues—competition policy, financial services, investment, intellectual property, and textiles. At the final round, in mid-November 2002, Yeo, Zoellick, and 10 negotiators from each side resolved all but one issue—investment and technology transfer (USSFTA, Chapter 15)—which was resolved in mid-January 2003.

President Bush notified the U.S. Congress of his intention to sign the USSFTA on January 30, and he and Singaporean Prime Minister Goh signed the 240-page treaty (800 pages when all annexes are included) at the White House on May 6, 2003. The treaty became effective on January 1, 2004 (Crump, 2006b; 2007a; Koh and Lin, 2004; USSFTA, 2003).

Regardless of form, most trade negotiations examine the issues discussed in the previous example. A bilateral negotiation between two national governments is the least complex form of international trade negotiation. We can also find bilateral negotiations that engage economic associations. Since 2000, for example, the European Union (EU), an economic and political association of 27 national governments with internal free trade and common external tariffs, and Mercosur, a customs union that includes Argentina, Brazil, Paraguay and Uruguay, have sought to conclude a trade agreement. Although fundamentally bilateral in nature, this negotiation engages two multilateral organizations in bilateral deliberations. A whole range of negotiation dynamics not observed in USSFTA emerge in this setting, as will become apparent as this chapter unfolds. Prior to this negotiation, Mercosur conducted a four-party multilateral negotiation to establish an organizational structure and a set of goals within an international trade framework. The EU, on the other hand, has been involved in this exercise for over half a century. These are just two of the many regional associations found across the globe engaged in multilateral negotiation. The largest and most complex multilateral negotiations are global—encompassing negotiations sponsored by the GATT and the WTO.

The WTO plays a controlling role in all international trade negotiations for those 159 national governments that are WTO members, as bilateral or regional trade agreements inconsistent with GATT/WTO rules is not allowed. The WTO also plays a unique role in non-WTO trade negotiations, as WTO ideology, language, international law and diplomatic culture establish the social infrastructure for almost all international trade negotiations.

Nevertheless, negotiation structure (bilateral, regional, or multilateral) also plays a substantial role in determining negotiation dynamics within international trade negotiations. The next section considers bilateral and regional negotiations, followed by an examination of multilateral conference negotiations sponsored by GATT and the WTO. In reviewing this literature, we will seek to develop a research agenda that moves the field of international negotiation forward.

BILATERAL AND REGIONAL TRADE NEGOTIATIONS

International trade negotiations exist as a kind of negotiation laboratory, especially for research grounded in networks, as the 159 WTO members (national governments) are constantly involved in multiple negotiations over the same issues (see USSFTA case) at various levels (bilateral, regional, multilateral), both concurrently and consecutively. This section examines literature on negotiation (1) linkage theory and (2) temporal theory developed via data gathered from trade negotiations. Such research primarily examines bilateral and regional trade negotiations, while the purpose of this research is not focused on explaining trade negotiation process and outcome but rather on developing negotiation theory. Nevertheless, conducting such research requires an understanding of international trade negotiation as well as of the GATT and WTO, as negotiation process and outcomes are grounded within this context.

"Linkage" is defined as the way in which one event influences or determines the process or outcome of another event. When each event is a negotiation, this constitutes "negotiation linkage" (Crump, 2006b). There is a large international relations literature that examines "issue linkage" (e.g., Davis, 2004; Haas, 1980; McGinnis, 1986; Stein, 1980), which is a negotiating device for making trades among diverse issues within a single negotiation or between separate but linked negotiations involving the same parties (Crump, 2007a). The issue-linkage literature has general relevance to negotiation research only, as international relations operate in a paradigm that is fundamentally different from the field of negotiation.

Issue linkage is just one linkage type. Watkins and Passow (1996) propose a linkage theoretical framework that includes four parts: (1) competitive links (agreement in one negotiation precludes other agreements); (2) reciprocal links (agreement must be reached in all linked negotiations for overall agreement to be possible); (3) synergistic links (enhancing negotiators' opportunities to make mutual beneficial trades); and (4) antagonistic links (diminish negotiators' opportunities to make mutual beneficial trades). Crump (2010) examines the negotiation literature to identify the most common linkage forms, including: (1) a negotiation and its best alternative or BATNA; (2) two negotiations occurring concurrently, where neither is an alternative for the other, with at least one party involved in each negotiation; (3) three-party coalition-building negotiations that evolve into two bilateral negotiations until a single bilateral agreement is reached (with the exclusion of one party) or a three-way agreement is achieved; (4) two-level games involving national governments that concurrently negotiate with their domestic constituents and internationally with other national governments; and (5) past–present linkages and present–perceived future linkages. Sondak, Neale, and Mannix consider some of these negotiation forms in great detail—especially three-party negotiations—in Chapter 11, 'Multiparty Negotiation', in this volume.

Starting initially with simple linkage relationships, it is useful to recognize that linkages occur both concurrently (at the same time) and consecutively (past–present and present–perceived future); the latter moves us into temporal theory (Crump, 2007a). In addition, it is useful to recognize that linkages can be both competitively linked and non-competitively linked. For example, a negotiation and its BATNA constitute a competitively linked negotiation, as the choice normally is between one and the other. On the other hand, Singapore need not choose between Australia and the United States in negotiating two separate bilateral trade agreements at the same time, as Singapore can (and does) have a treaty with each partner (each begun in 2000 and each signed in 2003). Competitively linked and non-competitively linked negotiations have very different dynamics (Crump, 2006b).

Role theory is relevant for concurrent linkages but not for consecutive linkages (Crump, 2007a). Watkins and Passow's (1996) theoretical framework (introduced previously) is grounded in role theory and based on Wager's (1972) concept of the link-pin party and linked parties. The link-pin party plays the role of creating linkages, as it conducts two or more discrete negotiations, while each party that negotiates with the link-pin party is a linked party (i.e., parties indirectly linked to each other through their separate interaction with the link-pin party). Watkins and Passow (1996) demonstrate that linkage theory is relevant to competitively linked negotiations and Crump (2006b) demonstrates that such theory is equally relevant to non-competitively linked negotiations. This research stream shows that each role presents parties with differing strategic choices—especially related to position coordination, concession management, and opportunities for cooperative action.

Concurrent Linkage and Role Theory

This section examines how linked parties and a link-pin party manage the challenges and opportunities inherent in their role to gain strategic advantage and to minimize disadvantage in a negotiation. In examining this question, Crump (2010) investigated four concurrently linked bilateral trade negotiations: United States–Singapore, Australia–Singapore, United States–Chile, and EU–Chile.

Crump (2010) concludes that an opportunity for one role often can represent a challenge for the other role through the following role-based typology: (1) burden sharing—two linked parties pushing the link-pin party in the same direction (e.g., United States and Australia each pushing Singapore in the same direction on trade in services), which can contribute to link-pin party compromises; (2) free riding—simple awareness of another linked party's interests, motives, and goals may allow for goal achievement without spending resources, resulting in a link-pin party making concessions that they would not normally offer (e.g., EU gains financial service benefits from Chile due to Chile's concessions to the United States); (3) outcome bundling—a strategy that allows a link-pin party to protect information about their zone of possible agreement, resulting in a link-pin party gaining more or losing less (e.g., Singapore agreeing to give Australia the same banking rules that it planned to offer to the United States); (4) solution migration—the link-pin party transfers solutions from one linked negotiation to the other (e.g., Singapore transferring eCommerce knowledge from the United States to Australia); (5) benchmarking—issues, agendas, positions, and concessions presented in one negotiation serve as a reference point in a linked negotiation (either role can utilize benchmarking for strategic advantage). The study concludes that, overall, a link-pin party has fewer opportunities and more challenges compared with a linked party (Crump, 2010, pp. 21–22).

Role-based linkage research should remain focused on concurrent linkage dynamics. Future research should seek to confirm, refute, and/or expand upon the findings summarized here, and aim to develop greater understanding of linkage structure and the dynamics operating within that structure. How might one role gain control or minimize the other role's control over a specific linkage strategy? Do other role-based strategies exist within concurrent linkages? Structural factors (the conditions that create two roles) have been found to be a necessary but not sufficient condition to establish linked dynamics, while contextual factors appear to establish the degree of linkage dynamics (Crump, 2010). How do structural and contextual factors interact to produce linkage dynamics? What contextual factors are most or least potent in creating linkage dynamics?

Some of these research questions could be examined in laboratory settings, as there is sufficient linkage knowledge to move beyond theory building to theory testing. For example, linked parties may be more likely to perceive the other as a competitor when similarities exist along significant demographic dimensions (e.g., the United States and the EU in their separate negotiations with Chile). Such variables can be isolated in a laboratory to provide greater understanding. Future research could manipulate power relations between linked parties and/or power relations between linked and link-pin parties and competitiveness (party non-competitive or competitive attitudes), while controlling contextual variables such as ethnic, social, political, and/or economic characteristics to identify the relative importance of these variables in managing strategic opportunities and challenges. Such research may further identify linked strategic opportunities/challenges.

Concurrent Linkage between Levels

This section seeks to identify and understand the dynamics that appear when examining negotiation linkages between three levels: bilateral, regional, and multilateral.

We can use linkage theory to adopt a network perspective. In so doing, a single negotiation can be seen as embedded in a constellation of negotiations, with each focused on the same issues at the same time. In this environment, we find multiple linkages occurring within levels and between three levels: bilateral, regional, and multilateral. Linkage theory is sufficiently robust to describe the relationship between a single negotiation and its context by focusing on one negotiation of analytical interest (USSFTA, for example) while defining all similar negotiations occurring at the same time as "relevant context" (Crump, 2011).

Crump (2011) concludes that multilateral negotiations such as those sponsored by the WTO can be superordinate to negotiations conducted at bilateral or regional levels. Data indicates that negotiations between the EU and Mercosur (Argentina, Brazil, Paraguay, and Uruguay) made progress in 2000–2001 but stalled after the successful WTO Doha Ministerial in 2001. A push to concluded EU–Mercosur negotiations followed the WTO Cancun Ministerial failure in 2003. The WTO July Package of 2004, a brief moment of WTO success, did not create an EU–Mercosur stalemate, but nor did it help bring closure. These data points indicate that EU–Mercosur was negatively linked to WTO activities from 2000 to 2004. Crump (2011) concludes that some regional negotiations serve as an alternative to WTO negotiations, so when WTO negotiations flounder some regional negotiations start up again. While not all regional negotiations are perceived as a viable alternative for a multilateral negotiation (e.g., the failed Free Trade Area of the Americas negotiations or FTAA), sometimes they are—and then negative linkage dynamics emerge as a result. What factors or forces cause one regional negotiation and not another to be perceived as an alternative to a WTO-sponsored negotiation? This is a research question that warrants further study.

On the other hand, positive linkage dynamics may emerge through competitive or opportunistic forces. The North American Free Trade Agreement or NAFTA (involving Canada, Mexico, and the United States), which was signed in 1992, and the FTAA (begun in 1994) probably inspired the EU to begin negotiations with Mercosur in 2000 through competitive forces operating between the EU and the United States. In a second example of positive linkage, it is clear that EU–Mercosur negotiations inspired EU–Chile negotiations—not through competitive force, but rather through opportunistic forces. See Crump (2011) for many other linkage examples operating between bilateral, regional, and multilateral levels.

Positive linkages and negative linkages are a two-part theoretical framework. Further research should seek greater understanding about the forces that create such linkages. Current data suggest that negative linkages may be created when one negotiation is perceived as an alternative for another negotiation, and that positive linkages emerge through competitive and opportunistic forces. Such observations need to be confirmed, refuted and/or refined. Are other forces present? Do mediating variables exist? Are forces creating positive and negative linkages structural, contextual, or both? What specific linkage techniques or strategies occur when competitive forces or opportunistic forces are present? Many research questions can be asked about linkages between bilateral, regional, and multilateral negotiations.

Consecutive Linkage and Temporal Theory

Temporal theory is explored through consecutive linkage dynamics. This section seeks to understand: (1) how negotiations from the past constrain or facilitate current negotiation process and outcome; (2) how negotiations conducted today can gain strategic advantage in a future negotiation; and (3) how parties strategically use an anticipated future negotiation in today's negotiation. Crump (2006b; 2007a) examined three bilateral trade negotiations: United States–Singapore (2000–2003), Australia–Singapore (2000–2003), and United States–Australia (2002–2004) to study such questions.

Temporal theory combined with linkage theory provides answers to these questions. Time is "a nonspatial continuum in which events occur in apparent irreversible succession from past through the present to the future" (Ancona et al., 2001, p. 513). A single event can exist in the past, present, and future (but not at the same time). We can anticipate an event, then we experience the event, and we can remember that event afterwards.

Crump (2007a) concludes that the past can have a significant impact on strategy. Prior experience may determine whether a party is more integrative or more distributive. For example, if relevant preceding links are absent, then the negotiation process may appear more collaborative or integrative, but if relevant preceding links are present, the negotiation process may appear more positional or distributive (compare United States–Singapore negotiations to United States–Australia negotiations). These two statements are hypotheses that could be tested empirically.

A negotiator may resist change initially, but the experience can cause reflection, learning, and perhaps acceptance. Such observations recognize that a party may negotiate several times over the same issue before it is prepared to change a particular position. Australia demonstrated such behavior in its negotiations over trade rules by first resisting Singapore's proposal (2000–2003), then adopting that same proposal in negotiations with the United States (2002–2004), and then promoting that proposal in negotiations with New Zealand (2008).

Shifting to the future, a party's perceived future can be used to influence decisions today—future expectations contribute to current decision-making. Singapore sought to influence Australia on telecommunications trade liberalization by pointing out that the position Singapore was advocating today would be the position that Australia would be forced to accept when Australia negotiated with the United States the following year (Crump, 2007a).

In addition to drawing the future into the present, parties also seek to control the future by established precedents today. For example, the United States included intellectual property text in its trade treaty with Singapore that had no relevance to the Singaporean situation (see the USSFTA case presented previously). When Singapore questioned the United States about this issue, it was advised that the United States understood the lack of relevance to Singapore but the United States wanted such conditions established so that it might take the USSFTA intellectual property chapter to other countries. In a second example, during U.S. negotiations with Australia, the United States sought to dismantle a nationally funded health benefit program (the Australian Pharmaceutical Benefit Scheme) not because the United States cared to gain access to the Australian market (it is relatively small), but to create a precedent that the United States might use in larger markets (Crump, 2007a). Such data suggest that precedents may be understood along two dimensions: the "self-serving" precedent and the "mutual-interest" precedent. The former serves the interest of one party only, and may lack creditability or reduced effectiveness, while the latter serves the interests of both parties, and so may gain creditability and effectiveness.

It is useful to consider the relationship between the past and the future within a negotiation paradigm. A temporal perspective complicates our understanding of negotiation process, although consecutive linkage theory provides clarity. How can we learn to balance a need for stability with a search for innovation and relevant solutions as negotiators? How can we establish a solid foundation built on the past without jeopardizing the potential for greater future gains? These general questions invite thought and the development of a specific research program that might respond effectively to the issues raised by these questions.

The presence or absence of preceding links appears to influence negotiation strategy choice (distributive or collaborative). Does this relationship have validity? Additional research should test this relationship to identify and understand primary and secondary forces and possible mediating variables that influence the relationship between preceding links and strategy choice.

As for consecutive future linkages; more research should be conducted on the nature of self-serving and mutual-interest precedents to identify factors that contribute to their use, success, and failure in negotiations. Furthermore, the self-serving precedent raises questions about "validity". If precedent validity is a creditable concern, it then follows that this concept raises ethical questions. Why does the negotiation literature offer so little knowledge about the role of precedents in negotiation process and outcome?

International trade negotiation offers a venue for the study of complex negotiation processes through temporal theory and linkage theory, but it also serves a venue to study questions that are specifically relevant to international trade negotiation dynamics.

Regional Trade Negotiation

This section considers the sparse literature on regional trade negotiations and the opportunity this represents. It is important to recognize that most regional trade associations tailor their trade agreements to fit within WTO rules, as many regional association members are also WTO members (Lindberg and Alvstam, 2012). Regionally based political and/or trade associations often sponsor trade conferences, such as the ASEAN Free Trade Area (10 nations in South-East Asia), the South Asia Free Trade Area (seven South Asia nations), the Gulf Cooperation Council (six Arab nations), the Southern African Development Community Free Trade Area (12 African nations), and the Southern Common Market or Mercosur (four Latin-American nations), among many other trade associations (WTO, 2012a).

Significant research exists on trade associations, but it is found mainly in the disciplines of economics, regional integration, economic development, and so on. Very little research on trade associations examines negotiation theory. Here is a "greenfield" area deserving of study that could contribute to further understanding of international trade negotiation process and outcomes. Initially, it would be useful to study the nature of regional trade negotiations and compare this process to GATT/WTO negotiations. Many critical negotiation issues could be examined through comparative analysis, as degrees of complexity (multilateral versus regional or mini-lateral) could be used to examine critical conference forces such as leadership, control, facilitation, procedural management, agenda-setting, decision-making, coalition formation, strategy, and a host of other variables relevant to negotiation process and outcomes (Crump, 2003).

The negotiation literature on regional trade generally is focused on two Western-based trade associations: the 27-member EU (Beach, 2005; Crump, 2011; Meerts and Cede, 2004; Pfetsch, 1999) and the three-member North American Free Trade Agreement or NAFTA (Mayer, 1998; Odell, 2006; Robert, 2000). Although little negotiation research examines the 21-member Asia Pacific Economic Cooperation or APEC, it offers an interesting point of comparison. APEC has enjoyed some successes in trade liberalization through open dialogue and consensus decision-making, and no binding commitments though peer pressure and economic/technical support are used to gain compliance (APEC, 2011; Bergsten, 1994; Morrison and Pedrosa, 2007). APEC achieved some policy innovations to promote economic integration and institutional modification via trial-and-error learning (Feinberg, 2008).

APEC and the EU could serve as a focused case comparison study—especially when examining the impact of "voluntary compliance" versus "rule-based compliance" on negotiation process and outcome. Such analysis could highlight negotiation processes that are more or less effective and/or efficient. Each type of trade association (voluntary or rule-based) would likely find value in such an analysis. A comparative analysis of this nature could assist in establishing guidance on negotiation processes and procedures in regional trade associations.

A footnote is necessary before moving on, as the trade and economic literature often refers to any treaty that is not a GATT or WTO agreement as a "regional" agreement (or sometimes a preferential or free trade agreement). Studies do note that "regional" is a meaningless term when applied to every non-GATT/WTO agreement. Consider the logic of referring to the United States–Jordan trade agreement of 2000 as a regional agreement. Nevertheless, this is standard nomenclature within economics and trade (Crump, 2006a; Crump and Maswood, 2007; Lindberg and Alvstam, 2012). In this chapter, "regional" only refers to regional associations. Negotiations involving two parties are "bilateral" and GATT/WTO-sponsored negotiations are "multilateral" conferences or multilateral negotiations.

The large majority of literature that examines international trade negotiation involves GATT- and WTO-sponsored multilateral conferences. The second half of this chapter begins with an introduction to multilateral trade conferences sponsored by GATT (1947–1994) and the WTO (1995–present) and then examines the four primary issue areas within multilateral conference diplomacy: leadership, procedures, strategy, and outcome.

MULTILATERAL CONFERENCE NEGOTIATION

Following the failed attempt to establish the International Trade Organization at the UN Conference on Trade and Employment in Havana, Cuba, a group of 23 like-minded nations concluded a second-best option: the General Agreement on Tariffs and Trade (GATT) in October 1947 (WTO, 2012b). GATT's evolution, through eight major negotiation rounds, has had a significant impact on the way in which the trade negotiation process transpired during the past 60+ years. The activities of the GATT, along with those of the World Trade Organization (WTO), which began in 1995 (WTO 1994a; 1994b), provide a foundation for our understanding of multilateral trade negotiation.

Sheer complexity is the primary characteristic of a GATT or WTO multilateral trade conference. Zartman (1994) notes that managing such complexity is a paradigm, not a theory. It is the context for theorizing, but more basically, it is a way of thinking about multilateral negotiation in order to achieve a better comprehension of the full process (Crump and Zartman, 2003). So what does this full process comprise? It begins with multiple parties, issues, and roles (Albin, 2012). Although the issues in a multilateral conference are essentially the same as the issues found in the introductory case (see USSFTA case), the number of parties and the variety of roles create negotiation dynamics that diverge radically from bilateral negotiations.

Negotiation research on a multilateral conference (MC) sponsored by an international organization (IO) generally seeks to reduce and/or manage complexity by investigating four major themes: (1) conference leadership including mediation; (2) conference procedures (e.g., agenda-building, decision-making); (3) strategy, especially coalitions but also other strategies; and (4) multilateral conference outcomes, including MC negotiation effectiveness and deadlocks. We will use the extant literature to examine these four themes.

Multilateral Conference Leadership

This section begins by considering a critical research question that examines two leadership options for IO and MC coordination. The extant literature also considers the meditational activities of MC leaders, as well as the relationship between leadership modes, roles, power bases, and MC process stages. Research questions are developed for each area.

It is important to recognize that the IO sponsors an MC. When an MC achieves its goals, the MC's administrative structure normally disbands, as an MC is an ad hoc venture, while the IO and its administrative structure continue to exist. In this sense, the MC is a temporary service and the IO is the service-delivery system.

Leadership operates at various levels and within various domains within an IO and MC. For example, the WTO Director-General is one of the most influential leadership positions within the WTO as an institution (basically the CEO of this IO). The chair of the WTO Negotiation Committee is the most influential leadership role within a WTO-sponsored MC. Although the Director-General and the chair of the Negotiation Committee are separate roles (the former serving the IO and the latter serving the MC), Odell (2005) observes that these two roles have been filled by a single person since the Uruguay Round (note that GATT and WTO leaders come and go, but when a new Director-General is appointed, that person has held the role of the Negotiation Committee chair since the 1980s). This combining of roles provides a tight linkage between the IO and the MC.

What are the advantages and disadvantages of linking the key leader for the IO and the key leader for the MC (two key leadership roles performed by a single person) so tightly? Compare this arrangement with one in which each position is filled by two separate leaders. Coordination challenges between the IO and MC are apparently reduced, but this consolidation of power could have unintended consequences related to balance of power, transparency, legitimacy, and so on. A comparative analysis across several international organizations of the IO Director-General (or IO president) and the MC chair (or presiding MC officer) could clarify the advantages and disadvantages of a power-consolidation versus power-sharing arrangement within an IO and its MC. Here is a solid research program focused on leadership alternatives that could provide guidance to all IOs that sponsor MCs.

Research examines the meditational activities of leaders who perform as chairs. Odell (2005) concludes that WTO Committee chairs have limited but significant capacity to influence the efficiency and legitimacy of negotiations, and the resulting distribution of gains and losses. Odell adopted a non-directive–directive meditational framework (from least to most directive) in documenting three tactical types: Type 1—observation, diagnosis and communication tactics; Type 2—formulation tactics; and Type 3—manipulation tactics. Tallberg (2006, 2010) concurs, and recognizes that a GATT/WTO Chair is a formal leader that utilizes agenda management and brokerage in overcoming negotiation barriers. Research conducted by Odell (2005) and Tallberg (2006; 2010) provides a foundation to build upon, although it is not just the use of a specific type of influence tactic or technique that matters: success also depends on when a tactic or technique is used in relation to the degree of directiveness.

For example, at some point a chair/mediator will want a multilateral discussion to shift from expansive deliberations to a more focused understanding of key issues. If this shift does not evolve, then the chair/mediator can use a directive tactic. Should a chair present either a "consolidated text" that integrates the issues and interests of major parties/coalitions or a "clarification text" that describes the key issues and differing positions ([normally in brackets]) of major parties/coalitions? What approach should be used and in what forum (issue-level committee meeting, ministerial meeting, etc.)? At what stage in an MC process will one intervention or the other be most effective? What is the nature of the relationship between the chair and members that will make one approach or the other more or less effective? Clearly, much more research could be conducted on this detailed example. Generally, what tactics might a chair use that are more or less effective in various phases of the negotiation process? These research questions will assist a chair in mediating diverse interests.

Leadership demonstrated by key negotiating parties (e.g., the United States, the EU, Brazil, India, China)—or indeed any negotiating party—is also an important theme within the multilateral negotiation literature. Zartman (2002) identifies leadership as critical to the management and analysis of multilateral complexity. Underdal (1994) examines two leadership modes relevant to the MC—coercive leadership and instrumental leadership—and observes that coercion may be counterproductive when diagnosing problems or developing solutions, and instrumental leadership might be ineffective in breaking informal resistance. There may be an optimal mix, or one mode may have greater salience at different stages of a negotiation. Who (what party or coalition) exercises what mode of leadership at what point in time? This question offers an analytical framework for the study of MC leadership. Growing out of this framework are research questions that could examine leadership mode, and negotiation process and outcome.

Building on this work, Sjostedt (1999, pp. 232–233) notes that, "Useful methods of influence in multilateral negotiation are likely to differ across process stages. Hence, the relative capacity of a country to perform a leadership role may likewise differ from one process stage to another". Here is a rich insight that could serve as the basis for a range of relevant studies related to leadership, power, process, and outcome. Sjostedt (1999) builds a model that identifies three power bases that support five leadership roles, which operate at three MC stages. (1) Power operates at three different layers: diplomatic competence, issue-specific power, and structural power; (2) leader roles or patterns of performance include coalition building, comprehensive issue presentation, determination of joint/common interests, process management, and process control (including trade and coercion); and (3) MC process stages include agenda-setting negotiations, formula negotiations, and endgame negotiations. Many studies could be developed through an analysis of the variables contained within this model.

It appears that the Sjostedt (1999) model and the Underdal (1994) framework hold the most promise for expanding our knowledge of MC leadership, although important questions about the relationship between mediation and leadership, and the relationship between IO and MC leadership, also require exploration.

Multilateral Conference Procedures

This section begins by examining the "controversial" nature of WTO decision-making, and recommends that research needs to confirm or refute such conclusions. The "single undertaking" rule is fundamental to the WTO process, while laboratory research could refine our understanding of negotiations that utilize this rule. MC phases are identified and research questions are proposed that might assist in an understanding of how to prepare or conduct specific phases. This section concludes by examining the development of the "concentric circle" process, and proposes a number of research questions based on this new MC procedure.

The nature of decision-making is crucial to regime management, and to balancing rights and obligations among WTO members with differing needs and priorities (Low, 2011). The WTO is built on the concept of one member (one nation), one vote, with majority rule. However, such voting rules do not really matter, as the WTO primarily uses consensus-style decision-making (Low, 2011; Narlikar, 2005; WTO, 2012d). This distinction has important implications, as developing countries—which are the majority within the WTO—are unable to use their numerical power to control WTO negotiation outcomes (i.e., proposing that an issue be voted upon by the WTO membership is not a GATT/WTO norm). Thus this is an organization that uses the consensus rule, social norms of inclusion and exclusion, and hidden threats of punishment and/or hidden rewards (from the powerful to the powerless) as techniques to control negotiations (Kahler, 1992; Narlikar and Odell, 2006; Steinberg, 2002).

Some scholars conclude that GATT/WTO consensus decision making is nothing more than organized hypocrisy—a procedural fiction that serves as a display for external audiences to help legitimize WTO outcomes (Steinberg, 2002). Reflecting on multilateralism in general, other scholars conclude that for much of the post-war era, multilateral institutions have disguised what is actually occurring: mini-lateral great power collaboration (Kahler, 1992). Is WTO decision-making just organized hypocrisy and a procedural fiction designed to allow for mini-lateral great power collaboration? This question needs to be either confirmed or refuted. Initially, a survey of trade policy decision-makers would be useful to determine whether such views are supported or rejected by an informed population.

Linked to consensus decision-making within the WTO is the "single undertaking" rule that does not allow a single part of an agreement to be adopted until the entire package is finalized and ready for adoption (Low, 2011; Wolfe, 2009). "The conduct, conclusion and entry into force of the outcome of the negotiations shall be treated as parts of a single undertaking" (WTO 2001, para. 47). The nature of the single undertaking rule is not fully understood (Wolfe, 2009; Rolland, 2010), so exploration of this concept within the WTO and within other multilateral settings would make a useful contribution to the literature. Such research could also be conducted in a laboratory setting, where a range of variables could be examined in relation to the inclusion or exclusion of a single undertaking rule. Understanding the relationship between the single undertaking rule, and the negotiation process and outcome, carries real significance.

In addition to decision-making rules, there are numerous other rules and procedures that determine or contribute to the negotiation process and outcome. An understanding of the multilateral conference negotiation process can assist in identifying relevant procedures. The phases of a WTO multilateral conference are outlined as follows:

1. Establish mandate to convene multilateral conference.
2. Adopt a negotiation agenda.
3. Devise a framework for each major agenda item.
4. Reach a modalities agreement (formulas or targets for each framework).
5. Adopt the text that will be the final agreement.

From this perspective, a multilateral trade negotiation is really a sub-set of five specific types of linked negotiations that occur in a set sequence and at different levels or within different forums within the WTO. Some useful research questions could be devised around this five-phase framework. Establishing a mandate, adopting an agenda, and adopting the text for a final agreement are all part of a larger question involving how to organize a ministerial meeting that achieves its intended purpose, as this is the venue where such decisions are made. Although these three phases occur in a WTO Ministerial, it may be that different planning approaches and different issues are required for each type of activity (mandate/agenda and adopting text), as they occur at different phases in the MC process.

This kind of comparative analysis is full of questions that would be useful to study via real cases. For example, what factors brought the GATT Uruguay Round to a successful conclusion? What factors caused the 1999 Seattle and 2003 Cancun Ministerials to fail? What factors contributed to the success of the 2001 Doha Ministerial and the modest success of the 2005 Hong Kong Ministerial? What occurred prior to and during each meeting? Research has been conducted on such questions (Crump, 2011; Odell, 2005; 2009; WTO, 1999), but definitive conclusions have not yet been established.

Odell (2009) recognizes the importance of inclusiveness and transparency in producing a successful ministerial. Getting inclusiveness and transparency "right" has been a real challenge in the WTO. Experiences in Seattle in 1999 and at Cancun in 2003 serve as painful and valuable lessons within the WTO. During the years since Seattle, the WTO has experimented with many procedures, while the "concentric circle" method (Ahnlid, 2012) may move the WTO closest to achieving its inclusive and transparency goals (WTO, 2012c), while concurrently achieving some degree of multilateral efficiency.

The WTO 2008 Ministerial meeting offered an opportunity to refine the concentric circle method—a management technique that involves meetings that are linked to successively larger groupings, and in this case delimited by three concentric circles. First, discussions at the 2008 Ministerial were conducted by the G-7 (Australia representing the Cairns Group, Brazil, China, India, Japan, the EU and the United States). G-7 discussions laid the foundation and linked to discussions conducted by some 30 participants (known as "Green Room" talks), followed by meetings of the Trade Negotiation Committee, consisting of all WTO members. This latter forum was too large for real negotiations, but was the setting for the exchange of information and decision-making in a formal setting. The G-7 negotiated first-tier issues (issues that must be solved for Doha negotiations to move forward). Second-tier issues were addressed in "Green Room" talks after first-tier issues (linked to second-tier issues) had made progress. Attached to this process were many self-formed supporting or functional groups (coalitions), which met for discussions about a range of issues that constantly fed into the process. These procedures ensured a considerable amount of trustworthiness, transparency and legitimacy, which contributed to the effectiveness of this multilateral process (Ahnlid, 2012).

The concentric circle process may represent state-of-the art multilateral procedural design. Can it only operate in the unique world of international trade, or does it have relevance to other multilateral settings? What kind of leader (the Director-General, in this case) can introduce such a complicated procedure? What are the key characteristics of a leader who advocates such methodology, as leader characteristics may determine its success or failure? Do membership characteristics play a role in its acceptance or effectiveness? What kind of planning and preparation are required to conduct this procedure effectively? First-tier and second-tier issues will be unique to a specific negotiation, but what are the specific characteristics that distinguish first- and second-tier issues? Many research questions can be developed now that this new model of multilateral decision making has been tested.

Multilateral conference procedures involve decision-making rules, as well as procedures for planning and implementing critical meetings, managing committee negotiations, and managing complex negotiation processes that seek to create a MC consensus. Multilateral conference strategies underpin many of these processes.

Multilateral Conference Strategy

This section begins by examining the fundamental nature of the coalition within a MC and the research questions that emerge from such a review. Coalition formation, stability, maintenance, and effectiveness are considered, along with relevant research questions for future study. The section concludes by considering the use of integrative and distributive strategies by coalitions operating within a MC, and the research questions that will refine an understanding of such actions further (see also Sondak, Neale, and Mannix in Chapter 11 of this volume).

Key decisions are not made by the voices of 159 members, as this environment is too complex. They are made among smaller groups and then ratified by this larger group. Many parties are part of long-established international associations (such as the EU or the G77) and/or form temporary coalitions of like-minded members. Coalitions are a fundamental part of a multilateral conference, so negotiation strategies—integrative or distributive strategies—are integrated within a coalition framework (Odell, 2006).

Knowledge based on the coalition literature is concerned with: (1) coalition-building or formation; (2) coalition stability; and (3) coalition impact or effectiveness (Dupont, 1994). Multilateral coalition formation is not a single event, but a process (Watkins and Rosegrant, 1996). Dupont (1996) identifies six planning issues in coalition building (1) assessment of costs and benefits for potential coalition members, (2) availability of resources which are best analysed in terms of power, (3) optimal coalition size, (4) leadership roles, (5) coalition cohesion, and (6) compatibility or similarity in values of potential coalition members. Watkins and Rosegrant (1996) recognize that coalitions normally emerge through persuasion and relationship-building processes, and that power is fundamental in this regard. Substantial coalition research has focused on formation and outcome when the two occur simultaneously (formation concludes the process), while insufficient research has sought to understanding coalition-building as a process—formation begins the process of working toward a goal (Crump and Susskind, 2008). A rich set of research questions could be developed here.

Coalition-builders can choose between two approaches: a bandwagon strategy, starting with the easier-to-convince parties and working toward the harder-to-convince parties; or a linchpin strategy, by approaching a highly influential party—often one that is harder to convince—first (Watkins, 2006). These strategies are not fully developed or studied in a multilateral setting, and it may be possible that other strategies exist. Further development of such knowledge would make an important contribution to the literature.

Coalition stability and maintenance constitute an ongoing dynamic process that is subject to constant change in party expectations and behaviors, and depend on contextual conditions within a negotiation (Dupont, 1996; Pridham, 1986). A coalition is more than a collection of parties; rather, it is a collection of parties seeking to achieve certain goals. Success requires the emergence or appointment of certain coalitional roles, with coalition leadership being the critical role. Party size (power relative to others), negotiation experience, and level of interest are identified as critical coalition leadership qualities (Money, 1998).

Coalition effectiveness is also poorly understood, although it is clear that effectiveness is related to stability and maintenance. The power that each coalition member brings to a joint effort is an important factor in determining coalition effectiveness, although how such power is applied to a negotiation is equally important (Drahos, 2003; 2007). Coalition design choices may assist in gaining understanding of coalition effectiveness. Will the coalition address a wide or narrow range of issues? Which and how many parties should be invited to join (how much power does each party bring to the coalition)? What will be more effective: an inclusive coalition to unify the most voices possible or a narrower issue-specific coalition that may not attract as many parties, but where the parties that do join are committed (Odell, 2007)? There are no clear answers to these questions. "If the goal is to influence the final outcome by negotiating as a unit, then the group [coalition] must be able to agree, during the end game, on how and how much to fall back from their opening positions" (Odell, 2007, p. 18).

A diverse coalition with a wide range of issues will have challenges at the endgame that will not be confronted by a less-diverse coalition with narrower, issue-specific goals. Crump and Druckman (2012) highlight the trade-off between coalition power and coalition control that is realized through the nature of coalition member diversity in a multilateral trade negotiation. Coalition effectiveness may not hinge on the relationship between power and control, but these are excellent variables to isolate and investigate initially.

Finally, the adoption of integrative strategies, distributive strategies, or a mixed strategy has been examined in multilateral negotiations involving coalitions. Distributive strategies are functional only for claiming value from others and defending against such claiming. In a multilateral conference, such tactic include opening with high demands, refusing all concessions, exaggerating one's minimum needs and true priorities, manipulating information to others' disadvantage, taking others' issues hostage, or worsening their alternative to agreement, making threats, and actually imposing penalties (Odell, 2007, p. 20).

A purely integrative strategy is a set of tactics instrumental to attaining goals that are not in fundamental conflict. Sharing information, being relatively open to exploring common problems or threats, proposing an exchange of concessions or fallbacks that might benefit more than one party, proposing a formula (especially if it equally disadvantages the proposer), reframing issues to ease impasses, and including a mediator are examples of integrative tactics in a multilateral conference (Odell, 2007, p. 20).

Integrative moves at the beginning of a negotiation may be seen to be a sign of weakness, especially when presented by a weaker party, although integrative moves after demonstrating a credible threat to block are likely to yield significantly higher gains (Narlikar and Tussie, 2004; Odell and Sell, 2006). Strictly employing distributive tactics may be effective temporarily for some developing country coalitions if the goal is only to block and force discussion on a proposal. However, there are real risks if a developing country coalition does not eventually shift to blending integrative and distributive tactics (Odell, 2007).

Most of the research on negotiation strategy (distributive-integrative) within international trade has focused on developing country coalitions. How does the fundamental nature of the coalition impact on effectiveness, based on the strategy (or mix of strategies) employed? What are the rewards and risks when a coalition uses one strategy or another exclusively if they are more powerful or less powerful? What role does timing play in implementing a mixed strategy and does the fundamental nature of the coalition have an impact on timing and negotiation effectiveness? The answers to such questions would enhance our understanding of coalition effectiveness and negotiation strategy.

Coalition effectiveness within a multilateral conference may have a relationship with conference outcome success, although success is not the only possible outcome within a multilateral conference, as demonstrated to date by the WTO Doha Development Agenda—a multilateral negotiation that has been stalled since 2008.

Multilateral Conference Outcomes

This section begins by considering multilateral conference effectiveness and outcomes. Management or building of the negotiation agenda, and the use of framing and reframing as methods to enhance multilateral effectiveness, are of special concern in building a future research agenda. This section also examines multilateral deadlocks, looking at what causes them and how such deadlocks can be broken. Further research needs to address questions in each area.

Albin (2012, p. 2) defines multilateral effectiveness as the capacity to arrive at a timely negotiated agreement, which resolves or settles important issues and is actually implemented by enough parties to achieve its goals. Touval (1989) identifies critical elements that contribute to multilateral effectiveness, including coalitions and groups, negotiation by representatives, consensus-building, flexible participants, asymmetries of interests, priorities and power, problem-solving, trust and risk, and mediation.

The relationship between multilateral effectiveness and a manageable agenda has become apparent through WTO Doha negotiations. Typically, issues become part of a trade negotiation agenda after a long process of maturation (Landau, 2000). Perhaps many parties worked for a very long time to get their issues on to the WTO Doha agenda, as the Work Program outlined at the Doha Ministerial turned out to be more of a wish-list compendium rather than a realistic negotiation agenda (Baldwin, 2006). The challenge is that there are no guidelines for what can or should be on a WTO agenda (substance) and how the agenda should be agreed upon (procedures). How can the agenda be shaped to enhance the prospects that an agreement might be reached? Critical to this objective is managing and reducing agenda complexity in ways that are procedurally just (Albin and Young, 2012). The challenge is to achieve a balance between reciprocity and fairness. In an ideal world, the WTO would consider a more limited agenda that achieved a balance of gains and concessions for all (developed and developing) members (Baldwin, 2006).

The initial challenge is not agenda-management, but agenda-building. Perhaps one solution is to clearly define what is meant by first-tier and second-tier issues (see Ahnlid, 2012 in the section on Procedures) and then limit the number of first-tier issues to five or ten within a single negotiation round. Too little research has been conducted on agenda-building in multilateral settings, and a theoretical framework needs to be developed. We have limited understanding of the relationship between agenda complexity and multilateral effectiveness.

Sometimes the seeds of an effective multilateral process are planted at the start of a negotiation. Certain strategies, such as "framing" (construction of a narrative, story or argument) or "reframing" may be more effective when begun long before the establishment of a multilateral conference. Framing and reframing (reconstruction of a narrative, story, or argument) are powerful strategies that can be key to securing a multilateral outcome. Reframing, in a multilateral context, involves five steps: (1) conceptualizing a reframed issue with strategic intent; (2) attaching this reframed issue to a negotiation agenda; (3) imposing or gaining acceptance from opponents; (4) negotiation give and take; and (5) an endgame (Crump and Druckman, 2012).

A fact may be perceived as an opportunity or a threat. A proposal can be framed as welcome or unwelcome. Intellectual property can be framed as a trade issue or a public health issue. Case data indicates that the framing or reframing of key issues has a dramatic impact on the shifting of power relations between negotiation parties (Crump, 2005; Crump and Druckman, 2012). We do not yet fully understand the relationship between framing, reframing, the shifting of power relations between negotiation parties, and negotiation outcomes. The theoretical framework for such understanding awaits development.

Perhaps the inverse of multilateral effectiveness is a multilateral deadlock—a topic of particular importance to international trade negotiation since the start of the WTO Doha Round, which has experienced repeated deadlocks during its 10-plus years. Narlikar (2010) identifies three types of deadlock—stalemate, delay, and breakdown—and defines deadlocks as extended non-agreements while parties adopt inconsistent positions and are unable or unwilling to make concessions sufficient to achieve a breakthrough due to a landmark moment in negotiation process. What causes deadlocks, and what are the solutions to a deadlock in a multilateral negotiation? These are key research questions. Often, there is a link between cause and solution: a viable solution depends on some understanding of the cause.

Research indicates that deadlocks are often grounded in structural factors such as balance of power or domestic-interest configurations (Druckman and Narlikar, 2010). In addition, deadlocks typically have multiple causal factors. For example, deadlocks can be influenced by interactions between structure and process, such as the uncertainty that is created when new powers (and cultures) become key players in trade talks. Deadlocks also occur when parties reevaluate alternatives due to changes in institutional norms or due to domestic realignment (Druckman and Narlikar, 2010). Understanding the relationship between multiple causal factors may provide insight into identifying deadlock solutions.

How can deadlocks be broken? The odds of breaking a deadlock become greater the more parties depart from strictly distributive tactics toward mixed-integrative tactics. As key parties perceive worsening outside alternatives (e.g., a deteriorating status quo), shifts to integrative strategies help to break deadlocks (Odell, 2009). Essentially, breaking deadlocks becomes possible as the status quo grows less attractive, while deadlocks become more likely or more entrenched as key parties continually face small win-sets (Young, 2010).

Leadership can play an important role in deadlocks. A lack of leadership change (established leaders remain in power) appears to contribute to deadlocks (Bercovitch and Lutmar, 2010), and political or charismatic leadership is identified as an important factor that may break deadlocks (Prantl, 2010). Third-party intervention—especially in the form of mediation (Odell, 2009) or active conciliation (Brown, 2010)—also has the potential of breaking deadlocks. The relationship between leadership, mediation, and negotiation deadlocks requires investigation.

What causes deadlocks and what are the solutions to a deadlock in a multilateral negotiation? These two issues will continue to be the two key research questions in this area. That the WTO Doha round may never arrive at a conclusion is a realistic possibility. It is possible that Doha could drift away. This outcome will not serve the interests of developing and developed countries, however, so it is hoped that social science might find an answer, as the diplomatic community has not yet succeeded in producing an effective WTO multilateral negotiation.

CONCLUSION

This chapter began by introducing the international trade negotiation field before presenting an illustrative international trade negotiation case: the United States–Singapore Free Trade Agreement negotiations (2000–2003). The chapter was organized into two primary sections, focused on bilateral and regional negotiations and multilateral conference negotiations. The first section reviewed the bilateral negotiation literature that uses international trade as a venue for the development of negotiation theory. The section included a literature review of concurrent linkages and role theory, concurrent linkages between levels, and consecutive linkages and temporal theory. It concluded by reviewing the sparse literature that examines negotiations within regional trade associations, while recognizing the opportunity offered by a field with such sparse literature.

The second half of the chapter examined multilateral negotiations sponsored by the General Agreement on Tariffs and Trade (GATT) and the World Trade Organization (WTO), focusing on multilateral conference leadership, procedures, strategies (especially coalitions), and outcomes. Throughout this review, the supporting literature was used to identify areas with potential for further study. When examined in whole, this analytical exercise has established a research agenda for the field of international trade negotiation.

Several years ago, Crump and Odell (2008) proposed the following research agenda for international trade negotiation. (1) What is the relationship between negotiation structure, strategy and process? (2) Is general negotiation theory sufficient for understanding the dynamics of interstate trade negotiations, or will additional concepts specific to this area (e.g., market variation effect) make that theory more useful? (3) Which international institutional differences affect which aspects of negotiation process—for example, do different decision rules lead parties to resort to different negotiation strategies (and if so which ones)? (4) What is the nature of negotiation linkage dynamics between informal negotiations to resolve trade disputes and formal procedures pursued through the WTO Dispute Settlement system?

The research agenda proposed by Crump and Odell (2008) is still relevant today, although it has been expanded considerably through the comprehensive review presented in the current chapter. Many negotiation research questions remain either unexplored or only partially explored. International trade negotiation is a fertile field that potentially can answer questions specifically relevant to international trade while expanding our knowledge of negotiation process and outcome.

REFERENCES

Agreement Establishing the World Trade Organization (1994). Geneva: WTO. Retrieved 22 September 2012 from http://www.wto.org/english/docs_e/legal_e/04-wto.pdf.
Ahnlid, A. (2012). Improving the effectiveness of multilateral trade negotiations: A practitioner's perspective on the 2008 WTO Ministerial Meeting. *International Negotiation*, 17(1): 65–89.
Albin, C. (2012). Improving the effectiveness of multilateral trade negotiations: A synopsis. *International Negotiation*, 17(1): 1–8.
Albin, C. and Young, A. (2012). Setting the table for success—or failure? Agenda management in the WTO. *International Negotiation*, 17(1): 37–64.
Ancona, D.G., Okhuysen, G.A., and Perlow. L.A. (2001). Taking time to integrate temporal research. *The Academy of Management Review*, 26(4): 512–529.
Asia-Pacific Economic Cooperation (APEC) (2011). *APEC Outcomes and Outlook*. Singapore: APEC.
Baldwin, R.E. (2006). Failure of the WTO Ministerial Conference at Cancun: Reasons and remedies. *The World Economy*, 29(6): 677–696.
Beach, D. (2005). *The dynamics of European integration: Why and when EU institutions matter*. Basingstoke, UK: Palgrave Macmillan.
Bercovitch, J. and Lutmar, C. (2010). Beyond negotiation deadlocks: The importance of mediation and leadership change. In A. Narlikar (ed.), *Deadlocks in multilateral negotiations: Cases and solutions* (pp. 232–253). Cambridge, UK: Cambridge University Press.
Bergsten, C.F. (1994). APEC and world trade: A force for worldwide liberalization. *Foreign Affairs*, 73(3): 20–26.
Brown, W. (2010). Talking one's way out of a strike. In A. Narlikar (ed.), *Deadlocks in multilateral negotiations* (pp. 79–95). Cambridge, UK: Cambridge University Press.
Crump, L. (2003). Multiparty negotiation and the management of complexity. *International Negotiation*, 8(2): 189–195.
Crump, L. (2005). For the sake of the team: Unity and disunity in a multiparty Major League baseball negotiation. *Negotiation Journal*, 21(3): 317–341.
Crump, L. (2006a). Global trade policy in a two-track system. *Journal of International Economic Law*, 9(2): 487–510.
Crump, L. (2006b). Competitively linked and non-competitively linked negotiations. *International Negotiation*, 11(3): 431–466.
Crump, L. (2007a). A temporal model of negotiation linkage dynamics. *Negotiation Journal*, 23(2): 117–153.
Crump, L. (2007b). Bilateral negotiations in a multilateral world. In L. Crump, and S.J. Maswood (eds), *Developing countries and global trade negotiations* (pp. 166–199). London: Routledge.
Crump, L. (2010). Strategically managing negotiation linkage dynamics. *Negotiation and Conflict Management Research*, 3(1): 3–27.
Crump, L. (2011). Negotiation process and negotiation context. *International Negotiation*, 16(2): 197–227.
Crump, L. and Druckman, D. (2012). Turning points in multilateral trade negotiations on intellectual property. *International Negotiation*, 17(1): 9–35.
Crump, L. and Maswood, S.J. (2007). *Developing countries and global trade negotiations*. New York: Routledge.
Crump, L. and Odell, J.S. (2008). Analyzing complex U.S. trade negotiations. *Negotiation Journal*, 24(3): 355–369.
Crump, L. and Susskind, L.E. (2008). Multiparty negotiation: Analysis of the literature. In L. Crump, and L.E. Susskind, *Multiparty negotiation: An introduction to theory and practice, vol. I* (pp. xxxiii–xxxix). London: Sage.
Crump, L. and Zartman, I.W. (2003). Multilateral negotiation and the management of complexity. *International Negotiation*, 8(1): 1–5.

Davis, C.L. (2004). International institutions and issue linkage: Building support for agricultural trade liberalization. *American Political Science Review*, 98(1): 153–169.
Drahos, P. (2003). When the weak bargain with the strong: Negotiations in the World Trade Organization. *International Negotiation*, 8(1): 79–109.
Drahos, P. (2007). Making and keeping negotiation gains: Lessons for the weak from negotiations over intellectual property rights and access to medicines. In L. Crump and S.J. Maswood (eds), *Developing countries and global trade negotiations* (pp. 97–121). London: Routledge.
Druckman, D. and Narlikar, A. (2010). Conclusion—case studies as evidence: Lessons learned. In A. Narlikar (ed.), *Deadlocks in multilateral negotiations* (pp. 254–279). Cambridge, UK: Cambridge University Press.
Dupont, C. (1994). Coalition theory: Using power to build cooperation. In I.W. Zartman (ed.), *International multilateral negotiation: Approaches to the management of complexity* (pp. 148–177). San Francisco, CA: Jossey-Bass.
Dupont, C. (1996). Negotiation as coalition building. *International Negotiation*, 1(1): 47–64.
Feinberg, R. (2008). Voluntary multilateralism and institutional modification: The first two decades of APEC. *The Review of International Organizations*, 3(3): 239–258.
Haas, E.B. (1980). Why collaborate? Issue-linkage and international regimes. *World Politics*, 32(3): 357–406.
Kahler, M. (1992). Multilateralism with small and large numbers. *International Organization*, 46(3): 681–708.
Koh, T. and Lin, C.L. (eds) (2004). *The United States Singapore Free Trade Agreement: Highlights and insights*. Singapore: World Scientific Publishing Co.
Landau, A. (2000). Analyzing international economic negotiations: Towards a synthesis of approaches. *International Negotiation*, 5(1): 1–19.
Lindberg, L. and Alvstam, C.G. (2012). The ambiguous role of the WTO in times of stalled multilateral negotiations and proliferating FTAs in East Asia. *International Negotiation*, 17(1): 163–187.
Low, P. (2011). *WTO decision-making for the future*. WTO Staff Working Paper ERSD-2001-05 (May). Geneva: WTO.
Mayer, F.W. (1998). *Interpreting NAFTA: The science and art of political analysis*. New York: Columbia University Press.
McGinnis, M.D. (1986). Issue linkage and the evolution of international cooperation. *Journal of Conflict Resolution*, 30(1): 141–170.
Meerts P. and Cede, F. (2004). *Negotiating European Union*. Basingstoke: Palgrave.
Money, R.B. (1998). International multilateral negotiations and social networks. *Journal of International Business Studies*, 29(4): 695–710.
Morrison, C.E. and Pedrosa, E. (2007). *An APEC trade agenda? The political economy of a free trade area of the Asia-Pacific*. Singapore: ISEAS.
Narlikar, A. (2005). *The World Trade Organization: A short introduction*. Oxford: Oxford University Press.
Narlikar, A. (2010). *Deadlocks in multilateral negotiations*. Cambridge, UK: Cambridge University Press.
Narlikar, A. and Odell, J.S. (2006). The strict distributive strategy for a bargaining coalition: The Like Minded Group in the World Trade Organization, 1998–2001. In J.S. Odell (ed.), *Negotiating trade: Developing countries in the WTO and NAFTA* (pp. 115–144). Cambridge, UK: Cambridge University Press.
Narlikar, A. and Tussie, D. (2004). The G20 at the Cancun Ministerial: Developing countries and their evolving coalitions in the WTO. *The World Economy*, 27(7): 947–966.
Odell, J.S. (2005). Chairing a WTO negotiation. *Journal of International Economic Law*, 8(2): 425–448.
Odell, J.S. (2006). *Negotiating trade: Developing countries in the WTO and NAFTA*. Cambridge, UK: Cambridge University Press.
Odell, J.S. (2007). Growing power meets frustration in Doha round's first four years. In L. Crump, and S.J. Maswood (eds), *Developing countries and global trade negotiations* (pp. 7–40). London: Routledge.

Odell, J.S. (2009). Breaking deadlocks in international institutional negotiations: The WTO, Seattle, and Doha. *International Studies Quarterly*, 53: 273–299.
Odell, J.S. and Sell, S. (2006). Reframing the issues: The WTO coalition on intellectual property and public health. In J.S. Odell (ed.), *Negotiating trade: Developing countries in the WTO and NAFTA* (pp. 85–114). Cambridge, UK: Cambridge University Press.
Pfetsch, F.R. (1999). Institutions matter: Negotiating the European Union. In P. Berton, H. Kimura, and I.W. Zartman (eds), *International negotiation: Actors, structure/process, values* (pp. 191–222). New York: St. Martin's Press.
Prantl, J. (2010). The role of informal negotiation process in breaking deadlocks: The UN Security Council. In A. Narlikar (ed.), *Deadlocks in multilateral negotiations* (pp. 188–209). Cambridge, UK: Cambridge University Press.
Pridham, G. (1986). *Coalition behavior in theory and practice: An inductive model for Western Europe*. Cambridge, UK: Cambridge University Press.
Robert, M. (2000). *Negotiating NAFTA*. Toronto: University of Toronto Press.
Rolland, S.E. (2010). Redesigning the negotiation process at the WTO. *Journal of International Economic Law*, 13(1): 65–110.
Sjostedt, G. (1999). Leadership in multilateral negotiations: Crisis or transition? In P. Berton, H. Kimura, and I.W. Zartman (eds), *International negotiation: Actors, structure/process, values* (pp. 223–251). New York: St. Martin's Press.
Smith, A. (1976 [1789]). *An inquiry into the nature and causes of the wealth of nations* (5th edn). Dunwoody, GA: Norman S. Berg.
Stein, A.A. (1980). The politics of linkage. *World Politics*, 33(1): 62–81.
Steinberg, R.H. (2002). In the shadow of law or power? Consensus-based bargaining and outcomes in the GATT/WTO. *International Organization*, 56(2): 339–374.
The General Agreement on Tariffs and Trade (1947). Geneva: GATT. Retrieved 20 August 2012, http://www.worldtradelaw.net/uragreements/gatt.pdf.
Tallberg, J. (2006). Formal leadership in multilateral negotiations: A rational institutionalist theory. *The Hague Journal of Diplomacy*, 1(2): 117–141.
Tallberg, J. (2010). The power of the chair: Formal leadership in international cooperation. *International Studies Quarterly*, 54(1): 241–265.
Touval, S. (1989). Multilateral negotiation: An analytic approach. *Negotiation Journal*, 5(2): 159–173.
Underdal, A. (1994). Leadership theory: Rediscovering the arts of management. In I.W. Zartman (ed.), *International multilateral negotiation: Approaches to the management of complexity* (pp. 178–197). San Francisco: Jossey-Bass.
USSFTA. (2003). *United States–Singapore Free Trade Agreement*. Retrieved 20 September 2012, http://www.usstr.gov.
Wager, L.W. (1972). Organizational 'link pins': Hierarchical status and communicative roles in interlevel conferences. *Human Relations*, 25(2): 307–326.
Watkins, M. (2006). *Shaping the game*. Boston, MA: Harvard Business School Press.
Watkins, M. and Passow, S. (1996). Analyzing linked systems of negotiation. *Negotiation Journal*, 12(4): 47–68.
Watkins, M. and Rosegrant, S. (1996). Sources of power in coalition building. *Negotiation Journal*, 12(1): 47–68.
Wolfe, R. (2009). The WTO single undertaking as negotiating technique and constitutive metaphor. *Journal of International Economic Law*, 12(4): 835–858.
World Trade Organization (WTO) (1994a). Agreement Establishing the World Trade Organization (1994). Geneva: WTO. Retrieved 22 September 2012 from http://www.wto.org/english/docs_e/legal_e/04-wto.pdf.
World Trade Organization (1994b). *Final Act Embodying the Results of the Uruguay Round of Multilateral Trade Negotiations*. Geneva: WTO. Retrieved 21 August 2012, http://www.wto.org/english/docs_e/legal_e/03-fa.pdf.
World Trade Organization (1999). *Briefing Note: Seattle*. Retrieved 21 August 2012, http://www.wto.org/english/thewto_e/minist_e/min99_e/english/about_e/resum03_e.htm.
World Trade Organization (2001). *WTO Doha Ministerial Declaration*. Geneva: WTO.

World Trade Organization (2012a). *Regional Trade Agreements*. Geneva: WTO. Retrieved 21 August 2012, http://www.wto.org/english/tratop_e/region_e/region_e.htm.

World Trade Organization (2012b). *Understanding the WTO: The GATT years—from Havana to Marrakesh*. Geneva: WTO. Retrieved 20 September 2012, http://www.wto.org/english/thewto_e/whatis_e/tif_e/fact4_e.htm.

World Trade Organization (2012c). *WTO Mission Statement*. Retrieved 21 August 2012, http://www.wto.org.

World Trade Organization (2012d). World Trade Organization website. Retrieved 21 August 2012, http://www.wto.org.

Young, A.R. (2010). Transatlantic intransigence in the Doha Round: Domestic politics and the difficult of compromise. In A. Narlikar (ed.), *Deadlocks in multilateral negotiations* (pp. 123–141). Cambridge, UK: Cambridge University Press.

Zartman, I.W. (1994). *International multilateral negotiation: Approaches to the management of complexity*. San Francisco: Jossey-Bass.

Zartmana, I.W. (2002). The structure of negotiation. In V.A. Kremenyuk (ed.), *International negotiation: Analysis, approaches, issues* (pp. 71–84). San Francisco: Jossey-Bass.

16. Making peace through negotiation
Kristine Höglund and Daniel Druckman

Each year around 30 armed conflicts are active around the world (Pettersson and Themnér, 2011). Some of these are likely to be settled via a more or less comprehensive peace agreement which is the result of negotiations between the main adversaries. In fact, after the end of the Cold War, the number of armed conflicts concluded by peace agreements has risen dramatically, with comprehensive peace agreements forming part of the war endings in Liberia, Bosnia-Hercegovina, Aceh (Indonesia), Bangladesh, and Guatemala, to mention only a few locations. Parallel to these developments, research on peace negotiations has burgeoned. This chapter provides an overview of research on peace negotiations, focusing primarily on negotiations conducted between states (to end international wars and armed conflicts) and within states (to end internal armed conflicts and civil wars).

Peace negotiations are defined as a process of dialogue and bargaining between adversaries aimed at reaching a joint decision to bring an end to or solve a violent conflict. Research on the initiation, process and outcome of peace negotiations has emerged as a sub-field of inquiry within peace and conflict research. It draws on general insights from negotiations that occur in other arenas, but is also concerned with the specific conditions underpinning negotiation to end violent conflict.

Peace negotiations share many of the general characteristics of the negotiation processes addressed in this book – such as the need for pre-negotiation, the critical role played by mediators, contractual agreements, and implementation problems. Like many other negotiations, the parties are generally well defined. But, peace negotiations can also be distinguished from other forms of negotiations by the types of issues that are addressed (a matter of life and death), strong ideological commitment by the parties, and the context of violence. They are also distinguished by the variety of stakeholders (including spoilers) with a stake in the outcomes and the critical role played by peacekeepers in enforcing the implementation of negotiated agreements. Further, most peace negotiations take place in private rarely involving the public in a direct way. However, the dynamics between leaders and followers, as well as the decision makers' relation to the broader public influence the onset, process and outcome of many of these negotiations. Hostage and terrorist negotiations, dealt with in Chapter 18 on crisis negotiation, are also high-stake negotiations, but differ in that they are generally analysed as isolated events and not considered part of broader conflict dynamics and sustained negotiations.

In the first part of the chapter, we review previous research related to approaches and factors used to understand the initiation, process, outcome and durability of peace negotiations. We will examine issues related to *getting the belligerents to the table*, where pre-negotiation processes and the notion of ripeness come into play. With regard to the *negotiation process*, we examine the difference between problem solving and bargaining approaches as well as the impacts of trust, mediators (both as representatives of states and as non-officials), communication and managing violence. Concerning the *implementation and durability* of negotiated settlements, the distinction between forward- and backward-looking agreements is relevant. This distinction, along with principles of distributive justice and other issues related to the content of peace agreements, and the role of third-party guarantees regarding security and compensation and peacekeeping, also impacts on the way that agreements are implemented, and their durability. Generally speaking, in the last two decades we have seen substantial progress in terms of what we know about peace negotiations. Recent developments were made possible with better data availability, and the fact that more scholars are devoting their time to the topic. However, overall there are surprisingly few coherent and robust findings in the literature. One reason is that different definitions and operationalizations are utilized to evaluate theories. In the review we address some of the general contentions and findings emerging from the research.

In the second part of this chapter we highlight current trends and research gaps in research on peace negotiations. As patterns of conflict and intervention are undergoing transformation, with new actors, agendas and norms emerging, so is the peace negotiation practice undergoing change. These changes in patterns and practice call for research along two lines. One consists of broadening the scope of the types of peace negotiations that require investigation. In particular, negotiations to address less studied forms of violent conflict, such as election-related disputes or communal conflict in which the state is not one of the key belligerents, are areas in which research on peace negotiations can make a useful contribution. Second, we discuss recent methodological trends that can be used to bring research on peace negotiations forward.

PEACE NEGOTIATIONS TO END VIOLENT CONFLICT

Armed conflict and large-scale violence eventually ends. They do so in one of three ways: (1) by a ceasefire or peace agreement, (2) by victory on the battlefield and (3) other outcomes, usually meaning that the fighting ceases without a clear victory for either party and without any settlement of the conflict issue (Pillar, 1983; Kreutz, 2010). What is notable is that negotiated peace agreements have become a more frequent way of ending conflict in the post-Cold War era, compared to the way in which conflicts ended during the Cold War. The issues at stake in armed conflict usually concern political power (government) or demands for territory (land) (Wallensteen, 2007). The underlying issues which drive these demands can be less material, such as the securing of a national, ethnic or religious identity, or obtaining justice. As a conflict progresses, new issues typically become part of the negotiation agenda, such as the conditions for a ceasefire, the release of political prisoners, disarmament and demobilization of the armed actors and security sector reform (Darby, 2001).

The research on peace negotiations has followed the general developments of peace and conflict research, which emerged as a response to the destructive effects of the two world wars and the threat of nuclear destruction during the Cold War era (Wallensteen, 2011). Early pioneers such as Quincy Wright, Lewis Fry Richardson, Pitirim Sorokin, Kenneth Boulding, Anatol Rapaport, and Johan Galtung were mainly concerned with the causes of war, conflict resolution and the conceptualization of peace. They developed a scientific approach to the study of peace and war. Emerging from different disciplines, they contributed to shaping an interdisciplinary field integrating politics, psychology, sociology, and mathematics.[1]

Research pertaining specifically to peace negotiations has become a sub-field within peace and conflict research, intersecting with research on negotiation in other areas. In terms of the type of violent conflicts that are drawing attention in the scholarly community, there has been a dramatic shift in focus away from inter-state conflict to intra-state conflict after the end of the Cold War. There is good reason for this shift, since the main bulk of contemporary armed conflict plays out between actors within a state. In fact, between 1989 and 2010, only five out of 133 armed conflicts were between states: Iraq–Kuwait (1990–1991), Ecuadaor–Peru (1995), Cameroon–Nigeria (1996), Djibouti–Eritrea (2008), Ethiopia–Eritrea (1998–2000), and the long-standing rivalry between India and Pakistan (Pettersson and Themnér, 2011). While many of the classic works on peace negotiations dealt primarily with inter-state conflict and war, most contemporary scholarship is focused on intra-state conflict and civil war, as suggested also by the works we review.

A good deal of the theoretical work has been inspired by and connected to a variety of cases of peace negotiations. Some of these ideas have been evaluated systematically with case data, including theory-driven comparative studies. In addition, quantitative research – seeking to ascertain general trends of the conditions under which peace negotiations begin and are concluded successfully – has gained prominence in the last two decades. This has been aided by the assembling of large datasets, some of which are updated on a yearly basis. Examples include the UN Peacemaker database, the Peace Accords Matrix (Notre Dame University), the Transitional Justice Peace Agreements Database (INCORE, hosted by USIP) and the Uppsala Conflict Data Program (UCDP) which are online collections. On the intervention side, there is a small number of datasets which address mediation and other forms of third-party efforts in violent conflict, most notably the International Conflict Management (ICM) data (Bercovitch, 1999), the Civil War Mediation Dataset (DeRouen et al., 2011) and the Managing Intrastate Low-intensity Conflict (MILC) dataset (Melander et al., 2009). In terms of data for case study work, research on peace negotiations is hampered by issues related to the nature of negotiations in the context of armed conflict (often occurring in secret and without any clear documentation emerging from the negotiations themselves) and from the challenges of doing field work in insecure and sometimes dangerous environments (Höglund and Öberg, 2011).

GETTING PARTIES TO THE TABLE

Negotiations over conflict contain several barriers that the parties need to overcome to reach agreement. When conflicts escalate into violence, entrapment dynamics – in which parties are locked into unrewarding behavior due to vested interests – often lead to larger wars where the parties view their own survival primarily in terms of eliminating the enemy (Mitchell, 1991b). Pervasive fear and mistrust, which develops in the course of violent conflict, discourages the commencement of negotiations (Kelman, 1997; Mitchell, 2000; Stedman, 1997). Negotiations to end civil wars or internal armed conflict contain additional complications. First, security concerns and commitment problems are aggravated by a need to disarm and agree on a new security structure. Relinquishing arms in such a context comes at the risk of being exploited by the other side, with potentially dire consequences as a result (Rothchild, 1997; Walter, 1999;

2002). Second, the asymmetrical character of these conflicts, fought by a state actor and an armed opposition group, makes issues concerning trust and legitimacy particularly urgent (King, 1997; Philipson, 2005). Mitchell has outlined several forms of asymmetries that are common in internal conflicts, for instance legal asymmetries, asymmetries in negotiation experience, and material asymmetries (Mitchell, 1991a; 1995).

The conditions addressed in previous research – especially entrapment dynamics as well as pervasive fear and mistrust in the context of violence – help us understand why it is difficult to shift to a negotiation track after sustained periods of violent conflict. Pre-negotiations have been suggested as a potential remedy and even a necessary phase to pave the way for serious negotiations (Saunders, 1985; 1999). While pre-negotiation may conceptually be seen as part of the actual process of negotiation, the term itself signals the important changes within and between the parties that need to take place before the inception of substantive negotiation over the conflict issues. Pre-negotiations serve several functions (Zartman, 1989). A first set addresses the relationship between the adversaries. Pre-negotiations give the parties an opportunity to gauge the other side's willingness to pursue negotiations, build trust and a sense of reciprocity in the exchange. Perceptions of trustworthiness change slowly and therefore peace negotiation may be preceded by several rounds of pre-negotiation (see Tomlin, 1989). In this phase, ceasefires often form part of a confidence test. In many cases, peace negotiations are hindered by the parties' unwillingness to enter peace negotiations without a ceasefire (Ikle, 1991). While the weaker side often refuses to give up arms before negotiations have yielded substantial progress, ceasefires may also be a way of showing good faith in the pre-negotiation phase and serve to alleviate the parties security concerns (Zartman, 1989). For instance, negotiations in Sri Lanka in 2002 was preceded by a bilateral ceasefire agreement, while the starting point of the peace process in Northern Ireland in 1994, was a result of a unilateral ceasefire by the Irish Republican Army, reciprocated by loyalist paramilitary groups (Höglund, 2011). Pre-negotiation meetings are important also for hammering out an agenda and framing the issues for negotiations and other stage setting activities such as deciding on a location and format for the talks (Druckman, 1993).

Second, pre-negotiations also serve functions in relation to intra-party dynamics. This phase gives the parties time to consolidate support within their own constituency. This means preparing ground for a major shift in the mobilization strategy, from a strategy aimed at gaining support for war, to a strategy to garner support for a peace deal with the enemy (Lilja, 2012). Saunders has emphasized how the process of building support for negotiations is nested in a broader process of building support for a peace process which engages not only the elite, but also citizens and civil society (Saunders, 1999). The experience from the Inter-Tajik Dialogue, which in the 1990s involved dialogue among stakeholders from civil society to support a peace negotiation among the warring parties in Tajikistan, is illustrative, since the negotiations resulted in a peace agreement in 1997. Saunders' research lays out the functions of the sustained dialogue, which was critical in providing interim goals during the peace process and for its potential in causing real changes in relationship with learning and practice as its basis.

Another central concept for understanding the initiation of peace negotiations is the notion of ripeness. Ripeness is a key lens through which the onset of peace negotiations has been researched (Zartman, 1985). Parties will find negotiation to be the most attractive option only when alternatives are not viable or considered too costly. The origins of this perception can arise from negative pressure, primarily a mutually hurting stalemate (MHS), in which the parties realize that they will not be conquered militarily and that the costs of sustaining the struggle will be unreasonably high. However, this negative pressure needs to be accompanied by a push factor, a "way out" as it has been put. Mutually enticing opportunities (MEO) is a term which has been launched to capture the conditions under which parties find an alternative to warfare which is attractive enough to provide positive pressure on the parties to seek negotiations (Ohlson, 1998; 2008; Zartman, 2000).

The concept has resonated with peace researchers. It has been shown to have explanatory value in the context of experimental studies (Coleman, 2000), and a variety of cases including the Philippines (Druckman and Green, 1995), Arab-Israeli conflict, Cyprus, India and Pakistan, South Africa, and Northern Ireland (Haass, 1990), South Africa (Lieberfeld, 1999), and Nagorno Karabakh (Mooradian and Druckman, 1999). Additional precision comes from research on how ripeness is initiated and can be nurtured within parties on the conflicts in Sri Lanka and Aceh (Lilja, 2012) and in Zimbabwe (Stedman, 1991).

Further refinement of the ripeness concept comes from Pruitt's (2007) psychological concept of readiness. Two aspects of readiness are: (a) motivation to escape the conflict and (b) optimism about the outcome of negotiation. The most important contributors to motivation are pessimism about winning, cost and risk produced or exacerbated by the conflict, and pressure from allies and other powerful third parties. Optimism often develops through secret exploratory communication between the parties, either direct or indirect through intermediaries. Bilateral motivation to escape the conflict ordinarily precedes this communication. By focusing attention on individuals and small groups of decision makers, the concept adds a motivational basis for entering or avoiding negotiation.

THE PROCESS OF NEGOTIATION

Research on the process of negotiation to reach a peace agreement has primarily been influenced by two approaches: the bargaining approach and the problem-solving approach. (Irmer and Druckman, 2009; Hopmann 1995; 2001; Wagner, 2008). The bargaining perspective is rooted in rationalist approaches that emphasize strategic interaction and cost-benefit calculation of the parties. Referred to as distributive bargaining, negotiation is portrayed as a competitive process in which parties seek to maximize their relative benefits in outcomes. It also emphasizes the importance of information about the other's positions and resolve to find out when it is time to close a deal.

The problem-solving approach underscores the need to move beyond the parties' positions to understand the underlying interests which drive the conflict dynamics (e.g., Fisher and Ury, 1981). The framing of the conflict is critical, since the parties' perceptions about the issue at stake may not reflect what the conflict is really about. Communication and information is central also in the problem-solving approach. However, from this perspective communication is needed to transform relationships, break down stereotypes and enemy images, and to change the parties' perspective on the conflict from a relative to a joint gains process. Three features of the process, relevant to peace negotiations, are highlighted in this section: trust, mediation, and managing violence.

Trust

Both the bargaining and problem-solving approach are concerned with issues of trust. However, the problems are framed in different ways. The bargaining perspective highlights the role played by security dilemmas and commitment problems in creating incentives to misrepresent information. Security dilemmas refer to situations where groups define themselves as vulnerable and take actions to enhance their own security that, in turn, undermines the security of others. Commitment problems highlight situations in which negotiators have difficulties committing to and implementing an agreement because they fear that the other side will exploit the agreement. In this context the role of signaling trust and reducing uncertainty becomes important. The problem-solving perspective is more concerned with the social-psychological aspects of trust, where confidence-building is essential for changing the relationship between the parties in conflict, for breaking down stereotypes and reshaping enemy images (Höglund and Svensson, 2006; Mitchell, 2000).

Trust was a key to the inter-state agreements negotiated to end violent conflicts studied by Irmer and Druckman (2009). They found that trust may have explained the relationship between problem solving or distributive and more or less comprehensive outcomes in these cases. Their case-by-case process tracing showed that comprehensive agreements emerged from a pattern that gravitated from calculus trust (predicting the other's behavior based on information) to identity-based trust (emphasizing shared identity) (Lewicki and Stevenson, 1997; also Lewicki and Polin, Chapter 7 this volume). Calculus-based trust was sustained in such less comprehensive agreements as Nagorno Karabakh. In contrast, identity-based trust emerged in the relatively more comprehensive agreements of Ecuador–Peru, Georgia–South Ossetia, and Mozambique. An implication is that types of trust are influenced by atmospheres conducive to either distributive bargaining or problem solving.

Trust has also been shown to serve as a filter that shapes negotiators' reactions: How they interpret and react to each other's moves is influenced by their trust in the other negotiator (Druckman et al., 2009; Olekalns and Smith, 2005). High trust can sustain a negotiation through the periods of crisis that occur often during peace negotiations. However, the decision to reach an agreement, continue negotiating, or re-frame the issues depends on both context and type of trust. Druckman and Olekalns (in press) found that negotiators were more willing to continue following a crisis when high trust is combined with a shared identity. The challenge for peace negotiators is to build trust or create affiliative bonds between adversaries. Although this challenge confronts other types of negotiations as well, it may be more difficult to achieve between hostile negotiators at war with each other. The case of the Mozambique peace talks provides what may be a rare example of trust development aided by active third-party involvement, while trust in the South African case came about as a result of a realization of the destructive effects of continued conflict, a formula for a solution which guaranteed the minorities' position in power for the interim period, and carefully nurtured relationships among key individuals in the negotiation team. The third party in the Mozambique case (the Vatican) nurtured a sense of a larger Mozambique identity for the Ranamo rebels and the Frelimo regime. In doing so, they created a vision for a future in which they could live together in a society where they shared political representation. In contrast, the parties in South Africa came together to prevent further losses, similar in some ways to the effects of hurting stalemates. The trust developed in that case could be regarded as deterrent.

Communication

The problem-solving approach emphasizes the importance of communication, dialogue, and track-two initiatives taken by both officials in government and non-officials in the private and non-profit sectors of society (e.g., Böhmelt, 2010; Kelman, 1991; 1995; 1998; Fisher 1997; 2005; Lieberfeld, 2002). A problem-solving workshops is one method within this approach used to break down mutual stereotypes, to reframe the issue in the minds of the parties, to achieve a deeper understanding of the sources of conflict, and to improve relationships in a variety of types of conflict. Referred to by Rouhana (2000) as micro-objectives, these are connected to both the workshop activities intended to accomplish them and to the macro-goals that they are intended to influence. Activities include sensitivity training, negotiation training, encouraging creative thinking about new ideas, and writing joint concept papers. Although systematic evaluations of workshop impacts are rare – often for reasons of sensitivity – related research on interventions suggest strong changes in attitudes among participants. However, it is also the case that the documented changes are usually short term. Without sustained changes, it is unlikely that Rouhana's macro goals would be achieved: These include influencing decision makers, changing the conflict climate and dynamics, and transforming the parties' relationship.

Other challenges to achieving these macro-goals include a lack of clarity about the goals themselves, a lack of theoretical connection between workshop objectives and societal effects, and the difficulties of evaluating macro-level impacts. These challenges are magnified further when we consider the logistics involved in proceeding from the design and implementation of a workshop to the documentation of impacts at micro (attitudes of workshop participants) and macro (attitudes of decision makers, populations) levels through time. Add to these challenges the meticulous attention needed to data collection and analysis, and we are left wondering about the feasibility of the research enterprise. (An approach to addressing these problems with advanced statistical techniques is offered by Druckman [2005, chapter 11].)

Another challenge for workshop practitioners is that of forging links between the pre-negotiation or parallel workshop sessions and the negotiation process. One approach to this challenge is presented by Rouhana and Kelman (1994). An advantage of conducting workshops in conjunction with negotiation is to open channels of communication among official representatives of the disputing parties. The informal meetings legitimize problem-solving activities among adversaries, gradually accustoming the public to these kinds of meetings. Through time and repeated interactions, the intensity of opposition to negotiation is reduced. Another approach comes from the research on turning points in negotiation. Workshops can also be instrumental in moving the pre-negotiation and negotiation process forward by creating turning points. Regarded as stage transitions, turning points have been shown to sustain a pre-negotiation process as it moves toward the formal negotiation. This progression is illuminated by Tomlin's (1989) analysis of the pre-negotiation process that led to the North American Free Trade talks. The agreement to negotiate culminated a sequence that included problem identification, a search for options, and a commitment to negotiation. This momentum toward negotiation was helped by avoiding a key sticking point during the pre-negotiation discussion, namely, agreement on the details of a prospective agenda for negotiation.

Mediation

Research on mediation has also been conducted within the bargaining and problem-solving perspectives. Mediation is a "mode of negotiation" in which external actors are brought to the negotiation process to assist the parties. It is generally considered a voluntary exercise, but the leverage and function of a mediator varies from being a relatively passive facilitator to actively manipulating the parties (Young, 1967; Touval and Zartman, 1985). The very involvement of a mediator (or other third-parties) changes the structure of the negotiation process, by making it – at a minimum – a triangular relationship (Touval and Zartman, 1985). Two functions of mediators in the context of peace negotiations are usually highlighted. First, they address issues related to mistrust. Second, they are able to persuade, or manipulate the parties to reach agreement, by bringing resources to the table that will change the belligerents' cost-benefit calculation (in essence their BATNA). The availability and use of resources by mediators is an important difference between peace talks and other types of negotiations. In relation to trust building as a core function of the mediator, the importance of neutral or impartial mediation has been subject to debate.[2] However, other features of mediation are also important, particularly the resources that the mediator can use as leverage. While smaller states, NGOs, and individual mediators primarily bring experience and skills to the table, more powerful states, groups of states, and international organizations may be able to provide direct incentives in the form of development aid, economic cooperation, or peacekeeping troops.

From a problem-solving approach, the argument has generally been that neutral or impartial mediators are required for building confidence by managing information between the parties and creating an atmosphere in which the parties' fears can be reduced, especially if the parties are to move beyond their positions to reach an integrative negotiation outcome (Kelman, 2005; Young 1967). In essence, mediators need to be trusted and accepted. However, the bargaining approach outlines arguments in favor of partial or biased mediators, suggesting that trust in a mediator stems from a different source. By being able to "deliver" an agreement from the party who is on their side, a mediator with a clear bias can be accepted (Carnevale and Arad, 1996; Touval and Zartman, 1985). Some evidence suggests that biased mediators will be able to credibly convey information about the parties' resolve, while impartial mediators, who primarily have an interest in any kind of agreement being reached, have incentives to exaggerate information about the parties' willingness to reach agreement. By accepting a biased mediator, a party can signal commitment to the negotiation path (Kydd, 2003; Svensson, 2007a).

Arguments for biased mediation have also been found in research based in the problem-solving approach. For instance, Wehr and Lederach (1991) have introduced the term "insider-partial" mediator, as a type of trust-based mediator who acquires legitimacy from being deeply enmeshed in the conflict context. They use the peace process in Central America in the late 1980s as an illustrative case. The Esquipulas process included a series of initiatives for the region's conflicts, where mediators from the region complemented other forms of mediation, in this sense bringing different forms of trust and leverage to the process.

Linked to issues of trust and bias in the context of peace negotiations, are the power, leverage and strategy mediators have at hand and put to use. A key distinction is made between mediators who use *directive strategies* (from a bargaining perspective), resting on the ability of the mediator to use inducement and negative sanctions or punitive measures (Favaretto, 2009; Svensson 2007b) versus *conciliatory strategies* (from a problem-solving perspective), relying primarily on facilitation and confidence-building (Azar, 1990; Azar and Moon, 1986).[3] The contingency approach brings together these ideas and partly reconciles the debates on which strategy works best (Bercovitch, 1996; Bercovitch et al., 1991; Fisher, 2007; Fisher and Keashley, 1991; Kleibor, 1996). It recognizes the importance and inter-linkages between the conflict being addressed, the type of mediator (which also influences the leverage available), and the type of strategies used by the mediator.[4] For instance, there is evidence suggesting that directive strategies, based on power mediation, may be more effective in actually getting the parties to reach an agreement, but that conciliatory strategies have a better potential at addressing the core issues underlying the conflict and for this reason create prospects for a long-term solution (Beardsley et al., 2006; Werner and Yuen, 2005).

Managing Violence

An issue of importance for the progression of peace negotiations is the extent to which the process is able to manage residual violence and spoilers. Spoilers are actors unwilling to accept the negotiations and an impending peace agreement, because peace challenges their interests and worldviews (Stedman, 1997). The concept of spoilers, as one of the key sources of risk for the failure of peace negotiations, was developed in a typology by Stedman, who distinguishes between different types of spoilers. These include: (1) whether the spoiler has signed or not signed the peace agreement (position); (2) whether there is one or several spoilers (number); (3) the goals and commitments of the spoiler (type); and (4) whether the spoiler reacts primarily to the leadership or to the followers (locus). The typology is accompanied by a set of strategies best suited to deal with different kinds of spoilers. For example, Stedman discusses inducement as a strategy that will work when spoilers have limited goals or are greedy, while more coercive strategies will be necessary when the spoilers have more comprehensive (or extreme) goals. The concept has since been used to understand intransigent actors and behavior during peace processes, and several critiques against its relevance have also been formulated (e.g., Greenhill and Major, 2006/07; Newman and Richmond, 2006; Pearlman 2009; Shedd, 2008; Stedman, 2003; Zahar, 2010). For instance, it has been argued that the motivations and commitment of actors can only be decided after they have carried out their spoiler activities, thus questioning the possibilities for identifying and managing spoilers (Zahar, 2003). Stedman has also been criticized for claiming that international actors are most suited to manage violence, while domestic actors, including the main belligerents, are often capable of counteracting spoilers (Ohlson, 1998; Zahar, 2003). However, in spite of its shortcomings, the idea of spoilers serves as an important analytical concept to draw attention to the threat of violence by opponents to peace.

Research on spoilers recognizes that there are costs involved in pursuing peace, since leaders and followers risk losing political standing, economic income and even physical security in the wake of peace: positions and security which during the war were achieved by the order of the gun. The research recognizes that there are other reasons for some actors to pursue peace negotiation, than to genuinely find a solution to the conflict. Relevant research includes work by Richmond (1998) on "devious" objectives, the role of veto-players – that is those actors who have the power to block civil war settlement (Cunningham, 2011) – and early research on peace negotiation that emphasized the side-effects of negotiations (Ikle, 1964, 45–58; Pillar, 1983, 51–52). While originally framed as a phenomenon that occurs only after peace agreements have been signed, it is widely recognized that spoilers may emerge as soon as negotiations are considered as an option.

Other scholars have chosen to focus less on actors and more on the function and management of violence during peace processes, drawing on case studies and comparison of negotiations in, for instance, Northern Ireland, Guatemala, Sri Lanka, South Africa, and Israel–Palestine (Darby 2001; 2006; Höglund 2008; Sisk 1993; 2001). While research on negotiation and violence traditionally has been analysed as separate processes, this strand of research explores how violence may arise as a result of negotiation, how violence-related issues often become part of the negotiation agenda, and how violence may under a combination of circumstances either serve as a catalyst for progress, or as a key stumbling block which needs to be overcome by the parties in the negotiation process. The South African case illustrates how violence was an omnipresent feature of the transition from Apartheid, how violence peaked around important breakthroughs in the negotiation process and how the parties were able to overcome the violence through elite pact-making which brought the moderate strands together (Sisk, 1993). Violence by a multitude of actors during the Norwegian-led peace process in Sri Lanka, which began in 2002 (Höglund, 2005), extremist violence in the Israeli-Palestinian conflict 1993–2001 (Kydd and Walter, 2002), and a negotiation between the Aquino regime and the communist New People's Army in the Philippines (Druckman and Green, 1995) show how negotiations between parties are undermined by intra-party conflict or factional violence, since this type of violence signals weakness and reduces inter-party trust.

THE IMPLEMENTATION AND DURABILITY OF PEACE AGREEMENTS

Peace agreements often specify provisions for their implementation. However, these provisions do not assure that the parties will adhere to the agreement over time. Indeed, the success of peace agreements, and of the negotiation process that preceded them, turns on the extent to which the provisions are implemented. Thus, it is important to cover the implementation stage in reviewing research on peace talks.

Several studies have addressed the relationship between the negotiation process, its outcome, and implementation. Downs and Stedman (2002) identified several factors that contribute to the successful implementation of peace agreements. Focusing on 16 peace agreements, most of which were negotiated just after the Cold War in the 1990s, they found that successful implementation occurred when (a) there were no spoilers, (b) the warring parties did not have access to disposable resources such as gems, minerals, or timber, (c) neighboring states were not hostile toward a peace agreement, and (d) a major power supported the agreement. These factors were the key elements of the conflict environment surrounding the negotiation: For example, the conducive environments surrounding the successfully-implemented Namibia, Nicaragua, El Salvador, and Guatemala agreements contrasted with the difficult environments surrounding the failed implementation of the Liberia, Somalia, Sierra Leone, and Angola agreements. These findings suggest that peacekeepers have an improved chance of success if they intervene in less difficult cases. It also suggests why many UN peace operations fail given their penchant to intervene in more difficult conflicts.

The type of negotiation process and outcome has also been shown to influence implementation. Research has, for instance, emphasized the importance of human rights provisions in peace accords (Bell, 2003); the inclusion and exclusion of key actors in peace agreements, including the role of civil society (Nilsson 2008; 2012), and the existence of power sharing among the warring parties (Hartzell and Rothchild, 1997; Hartzell and Hoddie, 2003; Jarstad and Nilsson, 2008; Mattes and Savun, 2009; Walter, 2002). A large share of this literature can be criticized on the basis that it only studies what is stipulated in the peace agreements, not what is actually implemented (Jarstad and Nilsson, 2008 being an exception).

An area of research that has produced interesting findings on durability of peace agreements relates to justice. Specifically, adherence to justice principles makes a difference. In their analyses of the Downs-Stedman dataset of 16 agreements, Druckman and Albin (2011) identified the importance of the distributive principle of equality. When equality was central (rather than peripheral) in the provisions, the agreements were more durable. Equality was also shown to mediate the relationship between the conflict environment and durability: The negative effects of difficult environments were reduced when equality principles were central in the agreements. Further analyses of the negotiation process also demonstrated the importance of equality: Adherence to principles of procedural justice principles led to more durable outcomes when equality was central in the agreements (Albin and Druckman, 2012). As a root cause of many of these civil wars, equality provisions – particularly those concerned with equal treatment and equal responsibilities during the implementation period – satisfied claims made by rebel groups. When adhered to during the implementation period, those claims, even in relatively difficult conflict environments, contributed to lasting peace.

The distinction between forward (future oriented) and backward-looking (past oriented) agreements, suggested by Zartman and Kremenyuk (2005), is also useful. The contrast between the forward-looking 1992 Mozambique peace agreement, which led to a stable agreement between the government (Frelimo) and the rebels (Renamo) and the backward-looking 1994 Nagorno–Karabakh negotiations, which produced a ceasefire but no resolution to the sources of the conflict between Armenia and Azerbaijan, illustrates this difference (Druckman and Lyons, 2005). Focusing on the secret Oslo I Accords, Donohue and Druckman (2009) showed that Palestinian public rhetoric surrounding the talks emphasized the past while Israeli public statements switched from forward to backward-looking rhetoric. Interestingly, Palestinian backward-looking public rhetoric combined with Israeli forward-looking rhetoric correlated with lack of progress in the talks. This pattern may be reflective of strategies used by non-state (Palestine) and state actors (Israel). With regard to implementation, however, the impact of these orientations may depend on the justice principle of equality. Further analyses of the 16 agreements discussed above showed that the relationship between forward versus backward-looking outcomes and durability was mediated by equality principles: Forward-looking agreements enhanced durability when equality was central in the provisions (Druckman and Albin, 2011).

A key to the relationships among procedural justice, outcomes, and durability may be trust. As discussed above, trust has been shown to moderate the relationship between processes and outcomes: Fair processes enhance the trust needed to enter into and sustain forward looking equality outcomes. To the extent that the trust established during the negotiation process is sustained through the implementation period, durable agreements lead to durable peace. One approach is by building a "trust network" of information sharing, verification, and mutual influence between rebel negotiators and their leaders (Lilja, 2012). Another is to build on the progress made through negotiation by designing new security and governance institutions. This micro-macro connection addresses Uslander's (2008) malevolent cycle of inequality, mistrust, and corruption. By sustaining the trust and equality developed between the parties, political leaders can move forward with the changes needed to increase political participation, reduce crime and corruption, and encourage nonviolent competition. Peace negotiations are then a vehicle for moving from Uslander's malevolent cycle to a benevolent cycle of equality, trust, and fair competition. Some insights about the transition process emerge from the empirical record.

A close examination of the implementation period for peace agreements reveals considerable variety among cases. The contrasting cases of Mozambique (1992), which resulted in stable agreement, and Sierra Leone (1996), which did not, show clear patterns of the justice-durability sequence: Adherence or lack of adherence to procedural justice principles in the process leading to forward or backward looking and equality or inequality outcomes culminated in durable (Mozambique) or fragile (Sierra Leone) implementations. The 1994 Rwanda agreement, on the other hand, showed that adherence to justice principles did not lead to durable agreements. The high distributive justice index combined with poor implementation reflected a false justice that served the interests of the incumbent regime but did not last. Shortly after these talks, the president died in a plane crash and the genocide unfolded. Other cases highlight a difference between settlements and resolutions. The successful implementation of the Guatemala (1997) and El Salvador (1994) peace agreements masked a deeper failure to address societal problems. The economic and social reforms stipulated in the agreement were not implemented even though the violence came to an end. Thus, the conditions that fueled the conflict remained (see Paris, 2004). Durable agreements based on equality principles may not sufficiently address the difficult issues of change needed to prevent future civil wars or revolutions. These cases call attention to the distinction between durability (adhering to the terms of the agreement) and durable peace (the sources of conflict are addressed during implementation). Further research on this distinction is needed.

At the heart of the implementation problem are issues related to commitment problems and lingering security threats from ex-combatants and spoilers (Themnér, 2011; Walter, 1999). Many peace agreements are monitored by peacekeeping operations, whose presence has been shown to contribute significantly to the durability of peace agreements (Fortna, 2004a; 2008; Walter, 2002). The operations are intended to implement the provisions of the agreement, which include a ceasefire (Fortna, 2004b). First and foremost the peacekeepers are responsible for abating and containing violence as well as disarming and demobilizing troops on both sides of the divide. But, more recently, the mandates of missions have expanded to include a variety of nontraditional goals that render peacekeepers agents of social change (Doyle and Sambanis, 2006). These goals include reintegrating former combatants into civil society, promoting and ensuring the smooth conduct of democratic elections, encouraging widespread political participation and other aspects of democratization, providing humanitarian assistance including the protection of delivery of food and medical aid, and the protection of human rights. Going further afield from their traditional missions, peacekeepers have been assisting in fulfilling various peacebuilding objectives. These include protecting civilians in everyday activities, insuring that political decisions are made according to legal rules, assisting in the provision of government services, and contributing to the transformation of attitudes and relationships to prevent the recurrence of armed conflict. This is a large agenda of activities and obligations. Thus, implementation largely turns on the effectiveness of peace operations. Modern peacekeepers are pivotal in achieving the durable peace envisioned by the agreements.

The expansion of peacekeeping activities has made performance evaluation complex. Recognizing this, Diehl and Druckman (2010) developed a multidimensional evaluation framework that includes indicators for core, nontraditional, and peacebuilding goals. The framework has been applied to the implementation of five peace agreements: Bosnia (UNPROFOR), Cambodia (UNTAC), Liberia (UNMIL), Cote d'Ivoire (UNOCI), and Timor-Leste. The results of these five applications show a mixed record of success and failure for the peacekeeping missions.

While UNPROFOR was successful in preventing the spread of violence across the country and in assuring voter registration and turnout, it was mostly unsuccessful in providing aid to the most vulnerable populations or in reducing corruption (Diehl and Druckman, 2010). While UNTAC was successful in containing the conflict it failed to end the violence. The mission succeeded in assisting in a large voter turnout for the transitional election but failed to disarm and demobilize former combatants (Whalan, 2012). UNMIL succeeded in achieving the core goals of abatement and containment but failed to provide adequate human rights protections for Liberian citizens (Farrall, 2012). UNOCI succeeded in providing election supervision but failed to disarm and demobilize former combatants (Bellamy and Williams, 2012). And, the various missions in Timor-Leste succeeded in accomplishing the core goals of abatement and containment but failed to disarm and demobilize as well as to police and control the local military (Braithwaite, 2012). These assessments make evident the difficulties often encountered during the period in which agreements are implemented. More specifically, they call attention to the considerable challenges to sustaining the peace agreements, including those where justice provisions are central and progress toward a more stable society is evident (Cambodia and Bosnia).

AREAS FOR NEW RESEARCH

To remain relevant, scholarship on peace negotiations needs to develop theory and methods of inquiry to capture changing patterns of conflict and intervention. Two types of improvements appear particularly beneficial to the study of negotiations as a means to achieve peace: (1) further theorizing about negotiations aimed at addressing forms of violent conflict, which peace and conflict research has only begun to pay attention to, and (2) to sharpen the methodological tools to analyse the onset and process of negotiation, as well as the durability of peace agreements.

BROADENING THE SCOPE: DIFFERENT FORMS OF VIOLENT CONFLICT

A first limitation in current research on peace negotiations is that it rests on assumptions about a certain type of armed conflict – an inter-state or civil war – which is to be managed or resolved. The frequency of what conventionally is considered armed conflict or war, which by definition includes the state as a key actor, has remained fairly constant over the last decade (Pettersson and Themnér, 2011). While other conflicts are not new per se, they are gaining more attention in the international arena, but without the negotiation literature providing adequate tools to analyse and address them.

A few examples serve to illustrate this point. A first type of conflict barely accounted for in the research on peace negotiations are conflicts pertaining to non-state actors; conflicts in which neither of the parties is the state. These conflicts include a range of situations, such as when rebel groups fight each other, or when less organized actors – formed along ethnic, religious or tribal lines – engage in violence against each another. The latter are commonly referred to as communal conflicts (Brosché and Elfversson, 2012). A second type of conflict relates to situations of violent electoral disputes, which often include elements of non-state conflict, but also substantial amounts of violence perpetrated by one organized actor against civilians (Höglund, 2009; Bekoe, 2012). As an example, the post-election violence in Kenya in 2008 took the form both of non-state conflict (between Luo and Kikuyu) and state-perpetrated one-sided violence against protesters. The significance of this type of violence is illustrated by the fact that in two of the seven countries that have cases under investigation in the International Criminal Court for crimes against humanity – Kenya and Ivory Coast – the violence was committed during elections.

It is unclear to what extent conventional negotiation theory used in the study of peace negotiation can contribute to an understanding of the measures required to solve conflict other than conventional armed inter-state and civil war. Both theoretical analysis and case study evidence suggests that more adequate responses and measures could be crafted and put to the test if some of the differences are recognized. For instance, an emergent literature on the microfoundations of civil war emphasizes the linkages between conflicts at the local level and the central conflict. In fact, it has been suggested that the focus on one main dividing line, the "master cleavage" serves to "simplify, streamline, and incorporate a bewildering variety of local conflicts . . . to tell a straight, compelling story out of many complex ones" (Kalyvas, 2006, 384). That a simplified conflict analysis would have negative influence on the outcomes of peace negotiations is alluded to in, for instance, the Darfur case. The 2006 Darfur Peace Agreement is posited to have broken down because of a failure to recognize that what was considered as a state-based conflict between a government and rebels, in fact consisted of three simultaneous and interlinked conflicts: "a) intergroup conflict at the grassroots level, b) a region-centred conflict over allegation of regional neglect of the central government and c) communal elite conflicts over holding political positions" (Mohamed, 2009, 8). This resulted in an agreement that in fact strengthened tensions rather than reduced them.

So, in what ways could negotiation research be improved by a better recognition of the array of conflicts that may be ongoing concurrently? Several differences have been pointed out which may have implications for conflict resolution. First, the role of the state in negotiation needs to be put in perspective (Brosché and Elfversson, 2012). The research on peace negotiations has a strong emphasis on the state as a problem solver or bargainer, and has thus failed to incorporate ideas about alternative approaches to conflict resolution. Moving beyond the state as a unit of analysis and incorporating research on methods of conflict resolution emphasized in, for instance, social anthropology, is likely to enrich the traditional peace negotiation paradigm, by allowing peace scholars to engage in arrangements with actors that have resonance and legitimacy in the societies subject to violent conflict (Mac Ginty, 2008).

Second, a main difference between state-based and non-state conflicts relates to the actors involved in conflict and their level of organization and capacity.[5] Communal conflict actors generally do not have a permanent capacity for sustained fighting. This has implications for violence patterns during the conflict, with outbreaks of violence tending to be short-lived and sporadic, but recurrent (Sundberg, 2008). An implication may be that standard measures that are negotiated as part of a peace agreement, such as programs to demobilize and reintegrate former combatants, are unable to address conflicts in which there are no formally organized actors.

A more comprehensive understanding of the diversity of violent conflict may also contribute to a better understanding of the success and failures of peace negotiations. An analysis of the main beneficiaries of a particular peace process is useful as a means to appreciate why the solutions favored by international mediators as remedies for violent conflict are sometimes deliberately manipulated or undermined. As an example, power sharing has become a cornerstone of international interventions to solve violent electoral disputes and has been utilized in Kenya and Zanzibar, to give only a few examples. While power sharing is often the only possible compromise which addresses issues concerning security dilemmas and commitment problems, it may be an inadequate means for certain conflicts. For instance, the power-sharing agreement in Zimbabwe has been interpreted as a protection for incumbents refusing to accept election results that would oust them from power (Maina, 2011). In the Ivory Coast, as noted by Piccolini (2012), negotiations have been used to take control of the peace process as well as avoid seeking a solution to the crisis and reduce the influence of the international community. In line with the contingency approach of mediation, theories on negotiation success need to be refined to consider the wide array of violent conflicts in which negotiations can play a significant role.

METHODOLOGICAL DEVELOPMENTS

The primary source for knowledge about peace processes and negotiations has been the single case study. Often collected in thematic edited books or data archives, a considerable variety of cases are available (e.g., Stedman et al., 2002; Zartman et al., 1996; see also the Pew Case Studies, 1999). The gains achieved in deep understanding of particular cases have been offset by losses in systematic comparison afforded by the use of state-of-the-art methodologies. These methods have addressed the trade-off between matters of internal and external validity, which are at the heart of systematic research in social science.

With regard to internal validity, the researcher can extend the number of cases chosen for analysis in order to perform a focused comparison. Based on the logic that underwrites laboratory experiments, this method focuses on the selection of a small number of cases. Peace agreements are chosen because they are similar in most respects: They differ only on one or a few independent variables. For example, the chosen cases may be from the same region with a similar history of conflict but differ on the use of third parties. Examples from analyses of peace agreements come from the recent studies conducted by Irmer and Druckman (2009), Druckman and Albin (2011), and Albin and Druckman (2012).

The Irmer and Druckman study compared the negotiation processes in the similar cases of Georgia–South Ossetia and Nagorno–Karabakh. They differed on whether a problem solving (Georgia–South Ossetia) or distributive bargaining (Nagorno–Karabakh) approach was used. More comprehensive outcomes were achieved in the Georgia–South Ossetia case. The Druckman and Albin study compared the durability of peace agreements obtained in two pairs of similar cases: Bosnia and Cambodia (intense conflict with more or less significant justice principles) and Guatemala and El Salvador (less intense conflicts with more or less significant justice principles). In both comparisons, durability was stronger for the case when justice principles were more central to the peace agreement. The Albin and Druckman study compared the durability of peace agreements for four cases that varied on adherence to procedural justice (PJ) principles during the process and the centrality of the equality principle in the agreement: The cases were the 2002 Sun City agreement in the DRC (high PJ, high equality), the 2000 Arusha accords in Burundi (low PJ, high equality), the 2005 Helsinki agreement in Aceh (high PJ, low equality), and the 2002 Luanda agreement in Angola (low PJ, low equality). Three of the four cases supported the hypothesis that the relationship between PJ and durability is mediated by equality outcomes. The Sun City agreement (high PJ, high equality) was moderate rather than strong on durability. (See also Lilja's [2012] analysis of two similar cases of peace processes in Sri Lanka and Aceh.)

Further evidence bearing on causal questions is provided by process tracing, referred to by George and Bennett (2005) as process verification. This is a qualitative time-series analysis that arranges events in a sequential order. Relevant questions concern trends in problem solving or distributive behaviors leading to more or less comprehensive outcomes: What are the trends in problem-solving statements (during the early, middle, or late phases) for more versus less comprehensive or durable agreements? The method is particularly useful for investigating stage transitions: Which events trigger turning points that move the talks forward to the next stage? Probing further, a search for explanatory mechanisms is sought with a strategy referred to as process induction (George and Bennett, 2005). Asking about whether trust mediates the relationship between peace negotiation processes and outcomes, Irmer and Druckman (2009) compared movement during the process from lower (mistrust) to higher (identity-based) levels of trust for cases with high and low frequencies of problem-solving statements. They showed that the development of trust accounted for the relationship between problem-solving (frequent or infrequent) and outcomes as comprehensive or partial. These methods are qualitative counterparts to quantitative time series.

A variety of statistical techniques have also been used to analyse peace negotiation processes and outcomes. Mediation attempts to get Armenia and Azerbaijan to the negotiating table were analysed with a six-year time series of events that occurred during the period leading up to and following the 1994 ceasefire talks (Mooradian and Druckman, 1999). Before and after mediation comparisons showed that each attempt was ineffective. The talks were shown to follow a brutal war and seemed intended to resolve a mutually hurting stalemate. When a large number of cases can be sampled from a known universe of negotiations, statistical techniques can reveal patterns that apply as well to other cases not sampled. For example, multi-dimensional scaling (MDS) has been used to distinguish among various negotiating objectives (Druckman et al., 1999) and to generate clusters of problem solving or distributive processes (Wagner, 2008). Regression-based mediation techniques are useful for causal analyses as demonstrated in the studies of 16 peace agreements by Druckman and Albin (2011) and Albin and Druckman (2012). With the advent of larger datasets, such the UN Peacemaker Database, the Uppsala Conflict Database (UCDP) and the International Conflict Management (ICM) data, more robust analyses will be possible, enhancing the external validity of findings. More fine-grained information on conflict and negotiation in the form of geo-coded and event data, will open new avenues for research on the dynamics of peace negotiations and their successes and failures. Further, a renewed focus within peace and conflict research on field experiments is likely to advance research on peace negotiations, by providing alternative research designs for causal inference.[6]

Methodological advances have also been made by researchers working in other philosophical traditions. Several methods that spring from the constructionist research tradition have become popular in the field of conflict resolution. An inductive approach referred to as grounded theory (Strauss and Corbin, 1990) relies primarily on the coding of in-depth interviews for making inferences about conflict processes. Interviews are also the primary source of information used to derive meaning from narratives provided by discourses given by participants in conflict or in negotiations intended to resolve disputes (Mishler, 1986). Emphasizing the importance of participation in the life of a culture – including negotiation cultures – some researchers conduct fieldwork to construct ethnographies in order to discover the "social and cultural dynamics (that) foment, perpetuate, and resolve conflict" (Nordstrom and Martin, 1992, 9). Each of these approaches may be particularly useful for understanding the cultures of violence that surround the conduct of peace negotiations.

CONCLUSION

As negotiation has become a more frequently-used tool to address violent conflict, so have studies into the onset and dynamics of negotiation, as well as the implementation of peace agreements, become part of the agenda of peace and conflict research. This chapter has reviewed some of the key issues in research on peace negotiations and has outlined promising areas for new further inquiry, including how the research can be revitalized and improved.

Two conclusions emerge from this chapter on how the research field has developed. First, a main share of current scholarship on peace negotiations pertains to intra-state conflict rather than inter-state conflict. This is understandable given that intra-state armed conflicts by far outnumber conflicts between states. Second, two main theoretical approaches, the problem-solving and bargaining approach, have dominated research on peace negotiations. While having different theoretical assumptions as starting points and implications that flow from these assumptions, in essence the two approaches are concerned with similar issues, such as trust, communication and the role and efficacy of mediation and other third-party interventions. A key to negotiation success, however, is the extent to which the parties, including third parties, manage the violence surrounding many of these attempts to make peace. The challenge for both researchers and practitioners is to find ways to reach agreements that endure the internal and external forces aimed at spoiling the progress made by negotiators. These forces are captured in our discussions of security dilemmas, commitment problems, spoilers, ripeness and hurting stalemates as well as by the distinction made between forward and backward-looking negotiation outcomes. These are also concepts that contribute more generally to the study of international negotiation.

NOTES

1. Important figures in the earlier stages of research on peace negotiations are: Curle (conflict transformation), Burton (track II), Fisher (interactive CR), Zartman (ripeness), Touval (mediation), Druckman (turning points), Mitchell (gestures of conciliation), Bercovitch (contingency theory of mediation), and Kelman (social-psychological factors).
2. The distinction between impartial and neutral mediators has been emphasized in several works, see for instance Young (1967) and Carnevale and Arad (1996).
3. Another widely used categorization of mediator roles and methods was launched by Touval and Zartman (1985). They distinguish between mediators as (1) communicators, (2) formulators, and (3) manipulators, indicating different levels of intervention.
4. Research on mediator motivation has, among other issues, characterized the driving forces behind the choice to mediate and analysed how mediator motives may influence choice of strategy (see, for example, Crocker et al., 2004; Mitchell, 1988; Touval, 2003; Höglund and Svensson, 2009).
5. Kalyvas and Balcells (2010) expose of warfare finds that external factors are fundamental to understanding how civil wars are fought. The ending of the Cold War changed the nature of warfare in significant ways.
6. For an overview of field experiments in the field of development studies, see Humphrey and Weinstein (2009).

REFERENCES

Albin, C. and Druckman D. (2012). Equality matters: Negotiating an end to civil wars. *Journal of Conflict Resolution, 56,* 155–182.
Azar, E.E. (1990). *The Management of Protracted Social Conflict: Theory and Cases.* Hampshire: Dartmouth Publishing Company.
Azar, E.E. and Moon, C.I. (1986). Managing protracted social conflicts in the Third World: Facilitation and development diplomacy. *Millennium – Journal of International Studies, 15,* 393–406.
Beardsley, K., Quinn, D.M. et al. (2006). Mediation style and crisis outcomes. *Journal of Conflict Resolution, 50,* 58–86.
Bekoe, D.A. (ed.) (2012). *Voting in Fear: Electoral Violence in Sub-Saharan Africa.* Washington, DC: United States Institute of Peace Press.
Bell, C. (2003). *Peace Agreements and Human Rights.* Oxford: Oxford University Press.
Bellamy, A.J. and Williams, P.D. (2012). Local politics and international partnerships: The UN operation in Cote d'Ivoire. *Journal of International Peacekeeping, 16,* 252–281.
Bercovitch, J. (ed.) (1996). *Resolving International Conflict: The Theory and Practice of Mediation.* Boulder, CO: Lienne Rienner.
Bercovitch, J. (1999). *International Conflict Management 1945–1995: Official Codebook for the International Conflict Management Dataset.* Christchurch, New Zealand: University of Canterbury.
Bercovitch, J. and Houston, A. (2000). Why do they do it like this? An analysis of the factors influencing mediation behaviour in International Conflicts. *Journal of Conflict Resolution, 44,* 170–202.
Bercovitch, J., Anagnoson, J.T., and Wille, D.L. (1991). Some conceptual issues and empirical trends in the study of successful mediation in international relations. *Journal of Peace Research, 28,* 7–17.
Böhmelt, T. (2010). The effectiveness of tracks of diplomacy strategies in third-party interventions. *Journal of Peace Research, 47,* 167–178.
Braithwaite, J. (2012). Evaluating the Timor-Leste peace operation. *International Journal of Peacekeeping, 16,* 282–305.
Brosché, J. and Elfversson, E. (2012). Communal conflicts, civil war and the state. *African Journal of Conflict Resolution, 12,* 33–60.
Carnevale, P.J. and Arad, S. (1996). Bias and impartiality in international mediation. In J. Bercovitch (ed). *Resolving International Conflicts: The Theory and Practice of Mediation* (pp. 39–53). London: Lynne Rienner Publishers.
Coleman, P.T. (2000). Fostering ripeness in seemingly intractable conflict: An experimental study. *The International Journal of Conflict Management, 1,* 300–317.
Crocker, C.A., Hampson, F.O., and Aall, P. (2004). *Taming Intractable Conflicts: Mediation in the Hardest Cases.* Washington, DC: United States Institute of Peace Press.
Cunningham, D.E. (2010). Blocking resolution: How external states can prolong civil war. *Journal of Peace Research, 47,* 115–127.
Cunningham, D.E. (2011). *Barriers to Peace in Civil War.* Cambridge: Cambridge University Press.
Darby, J. (2001). *The Effect of Violence on Peace Processes.* Washington, DC: United States Institute of Peace Press.
Darby, J. (2006). *Violence and Reconstruction.* South Bend, IN: University of Notre Dame Press.
DeRouen, K., Bercovitch, J. et al. (2011). Introducing the civil wars mediation (CWM) dataset. *Journal of Peace Research, 48,* 663–672.
Diehl, P.F. and Druckman, D. (2010). *Evaluating Peace Operations.* Boulder, CO: Lynne Reinner.
Donohue, W.A. and Druckman, D. (2009). Message framing surrounding the Oslo I Accords. *Journal of Conflict Resolution, 53,* 119–145.
Downs, G. and Stedman, S.J. (2002). Evaluation issues in peace implementation.

In S.J. Stedman, D. Rothchild, and E.M. Cousens (eds), *Ending Civil Wars: The Implementation of Peace Agreements* (pp. 43–69). Boulder, CO: Lynne Rienner.

Doyle, M.W. and Sambanis, N. (2006). *Making War and Building Peace: United Nations Peace Operations*. Princeton NJ: Princeton University Press.

Druckman, D. (1993). The situational levers of negotiating flexibility. *Journal of Conflict Resolution*, 37, 236–276.

Druckman, D. (2005). *Doing Research: Methods of Inquiry for Conflict Analysis*. London: Sage Publications

Druckman, D. and Albin, C. (2011). Distributive justice and the durability of peace agreements. *Review of International Studies*, 37, 1137–1168.

Druckman, D. and Green, J. (1995). *Political Stability in the Philippines: Framework and Analysis*. Monograph Series in World Affairs, 22, no. 3. Denver CO: University of Denver.

Druckman, D. and Lyons, T. (2005). Negotiating processes and post-settlement relationships: Comparing Nagorno-Karabakh with Mozambique. In I.W. Zartman and V.A. Kremenyuk (eds), *Peace versus Justice: Negotiating Forward- and Backward Looking Outcomes*. Lanham MD: Rowman and Littlefield.

Druckman, D. and Olekalns, M. (in press). Motivational primes, trust and negotiators' reactions to a crisis. *Journal of Conflict Resolution*.

Druckman, D., Olekalns, M., and Smith, P. (2009). Interpretive filters: Social cognition and the impact of turning points in negotiation, *Negotiation Journal*, 25, 13–40.

Farrall, J. (2012). Recurring dilemmas in places of recurring conflict: Evaluating UNMIL's performance during Liberia's transitional period (2003–2006). *International Journal of Peacekeeping*, 16, 306–342.

Favaretto, K. (2009). Should peacemakers take sides? Major power mediation, coercion, and bias. *American Political Science Review*, 103, 248–263.

Fisher, R.J. (1997). *Interactive Conflict Resolution*. Syracuse, NY: Syracuse University Press.

Fisher, R.J. (ed) (2005). *Paving the Way: Contributions of Interactive Conflict Resolution to Peacemaking*. Lanham MD: Lexington Books.

Fisher, R.J. (2007). Assessing the contingency model of third-party intervention in successful cases of prenegotiation. *Journal of Peace Research*, 44, 311–329.

Fisher, R.J. and Keashly, L. (1991). The potential complementary of mediation and consultation within a contingency model of third party intervention. *Journal of Peace Research*, 28, 29–42.

Fisher, R. and Ury, W.L. (1981). *Getting to Yes*. Boston, MA: Houghton Mifflin.

Fortna, V.P. (2004a). Does peacekeeping keep peace? International intervention and the duration of peace after civil war. *International Studies Quarterly*, 48, 269–292.

Fortna, V.P. (2004b). *Peace Time: Cease-Fire Agreements and the Durability of Peace*. Princeton, NJ: Princeton University Press.

Fortna, V.P. (2008). *Does Peacekeeping Work? Shaping Belligerents Choices after Civil War*. Princeton, NJ: Princeton University Press.

George, A.L. and Bennett, A. (2005). *Case Studies and Theory Development in the Social Sciences*. Cambridge, MA: The MIT Press.

Greenhill, K.M. and Major, S. (2006/07). The perils of profiling? Civil war spoilers and the collapse of intrastate peace accords. *International Security*, 31, 7–40.

Haass, R.N. (1990). *Conflicts Unending*. New Haven, CT: Yale University Press.

Hartzell, C. and Hoddie, M. (2003). Institutionalizing peace: Power sharing and post-civil war conflict management. *American Journal of Political Science*, 47, 318–332.

Hartzell, C. and Rothchild, D. (1997). Political pacts as negotiated agreements: Comparing ethnic and non-ethnic cases. *International Negotiation*, 2, 147–171.

Hopmann, P.T. (1995). Two paradigms of negotiation: Bargaining and problem solving. *The Annals of the American Academy of Political and Social Science*, 542, 24–47.

Hopmann, P.T. (2001). Bargaining and problem solving: Two perspectives on international negotiation. In C.A. Crocker, F.O. Hampson, and P. Aall (eds), *Turbulent Peace: The Challenges of Managing International Conflict* (pp. 445–468). Washington, DC: United States Institute of Peace Press.

Höglund, K. (2008). *Peace Negotiations in the Shadow of Violence*. Leiden, the Netherlands: Brill/Martinus Nijhoff.
Höglund, K. (2009). Electoral violence: Causes, concepts and consequences. *Terrorism and Political Violence*, 21, 412–427.
Höglund, K. (2011). Tactics in negotiations between states and extremists. In I.W. Zartman and G.O. Faure (eds), *Engaging Extremists: Trade-offs, Timing and Diplomacy* (pp. 221–244). Washington, DC: United States Institute of Peace Press.
Höglund, K. and Svensson, I. (2006). 'Sticking one's neck out': Reducing mistrust in Sri Lanka's peace negotiations. *Negotiation Journal*, 22, 367–387.
Höglund, K. and Svensson, I. (2009). Mediating between tigers and lions: Norwegian peace diplomacy in Sri Lanka's civil war. *Contemporary South Asia*, 17, 175–191.
Höglund, K. and Öberg, M. (eds) (2011). *Understanding Peace Research: Methods and Challenges*. London and New York: Routledge.
Humphreys, M. and Weinstein, J.M. (2009). Field experiments and the political economy of development. *Annual Review of Political Science*, 12, 367–378.
Ikle, F.C. (1964). *How Nations Negotiate*. New York: Harper & Row.
Ikle, F.C. (1991). *Every War Must End*. New York: Columbia University Press.
Irmer, C. and Druckman, D. (2009). Explaining negotiation outcomes: Process or context? *Negotiation and Conflict Management Research*, 2, 209–235.
Jarstad, A.K. and Nilsson, D. (2008). From words to deeds: The implementation of power-sharing pacts in peace accords. *Conflict Management and Peace Science*, 25, 206–223.
Kalyvas, S.N. (2006). *The Logic of Violence in Civil War*. Cambridge: Cambridge University Press.
Kalyvas, S.N. and Balcells, L. (2010). International system and technologies of rebellion: How the end of the Cold War shaped internal conflict. *American Political Science Review*, 104, 415–429.
Kelman, H.C. (1991). Interactive problem solving: The uses and limits of a therapeutic model for the resolution of international conflicts. In V. Volkan (ed.), *The Psychodynamics of International Relations Vol II* (pp. 145–160). Lexington, MA: Lexington Books.
Kelman, H.C. (1995). Contributions of an unofficial conflict resolution effort to the Israeli–Palestinian breakthrough. *Negotiation Journal*, 11, 19–27.
Kelman, H.C. (1997). Social-psychological dimensions of international conflict. In I.W. Zartman and J.L. Rasmussen (eds), *Peacemaking in International Conflict: Methods and Techniques* (pp. 191–237). Washington, DC: United States Institute of Peace Press.
Kelman, H.C. (1998). Interactive problem solving: An approach to conflict resolution and its application in the Middle East. *PS: Political Science and Politics*, 31, 190–198.
Kelman, H.C. (2005). Building trust among enemies: The central challenge for international conflict resolution. *International Journal of Intercultural Relations*, 29, 639–650.
King, C. (1997). Ending civil war. *Adelphi Paper*, 308.
Kleiboer, M. (1996). Understanding success and failure of international mediation. *Journal of Conflict Resolution*, 40, 360–389.
Kreutz, J. (2010). How and when armed conflicts end: Introducing the UCDP conflict termination dataset. *Journal of Peace Research*, 47, 243–250.
Kydd, A. (2003). Which side are you on? Bias, credibility, and mediation. *American Journal of Political Science*, 47, 597–611.
Kydd, A. and Walter, B.F. (2002). Sabotaging the peace: The politics of extremist violence. *International Organization*, 56, 263–296.
Lewicki, R. and Stevenson, M.A. (1997). *Trust development in negotiation: Proposed actions and a research agenda*. Paper presented at the conference on Trust and Business: Barriers and Bridges. Chicago, IL: DePaul University.
Lieberfeld, D. (1999). Conflict 'ripeness' revisited: The South African and Israeli/Palestinian case. *Negotiation Journal*, 15, 63–82.
Lieberfeld, D. (2002). Evaluating the contribution of track-two diplomacy to conflict termination in South Africa, 1984–90. *Journal of Peace Research*, 39, 355–372.

Lilja, J. (2012). Trust and treason: Social network structure as a source of flexibility in peace negotiations. *Negotiation and Conflict Management Research*, 5, 96–125.
Mac Ginty, R. (2008). Indigenous peace-making versus the liberal peace. *Cooperation and Conflict*, 43, 139–163.
Maina, G. (2011). Mediating to governments of unity – A conflict transformation approach. *Policy and Practice Brief, Accord, 3*.
Mattes, M. and B. Savun (2009). Fostering peace after civil war: Commitment problems and agreement design. *International Studies Quarterly*, 53, 737–759.
Melander, E., Möller, F., and Öberg. M. (2009). Managing intrastate low-intensity armed conflict 1993–2004: A new dataset. *International Interactions*, 35, 58–85.
Mishler, E.G. (1986). *Research Interviewing: Context and Narrative*. Cambridge, MA: Harvard University Press.
Mitchell, C.R. (1988). The motives for mediation. In C.R. Mitchell and K. Webb (eds), *New Approaches to International Mediation* (pp. 29–51). London: Greenwood Press.
Mitchell, C.R. (1991a). Classifying conflicts: Asymmetry and resolution. *Annals of the American Academy of Political and Social Science*, 518, 23–38.
Mitchell, C.R. (1991b). Ending conflicts and wars: Judgment, rationality and entrapment. *International Social Science Journal*, 127, 33–55.
Mitchell, C.R. (1995). Asymmetry and strategies of regional conflict reduction. In I.W. Zartman and V.A. Kremenyuk (eds), *Cooperative Security: Reducing Third World Wars* (pp. 25–57). Syracuse University Press.
Mitchell, C.R. (2000). *Gestures of Conciliation: Factors Contributing to Successful Olive Branches*. Basingstoke: Macmillan Press.
Mohamed, A.A. (2009). Evaluating the Darfur Peace Agreement: A call for an alternative approach to crisis management. *Claude Ake Memorial Paper series*. Uppsala: The Nordic Africa Institute/Department of Peace and Conflict Research.
Mooradian, M. and Druckman, D. (1999). Hurting stalemate or mediation? The conflict over Nagorno–Karabakh, 1990–95. *Journal of Peace Research*, 36, 709–727.
Newman, E. and Richmond, O. (eds) (2006). *Challenges to Peacebuilding: Managing Spoilers during Conflict Resolution*. New York: United Nations University Press.
Nilsson, D. (2008). Partial peace: Rebel groups inside and outside peace agreements. *Journal of Peace Research*, 45, 479–495.
Nilsson, D. (2012). Anchoring the peace: Civil society actors in peace accords and durable peace. *International Interactions*, 38, 243–266.
Nordstrom, C. and Martin, J.A. (eds) (1992). *The Paths to Domination, Resistance, and Terror*. Berkeley, CA: University of California Press.
Ohlson, T. (1998). *Power Politics and Peace Policies: Intra-State Conflict Resolution in Southern Africa*. Department of Peace and Conflict Research: Uppsala University.
Ohlson, T. (2008). Understanding causes of war and peace. *European Journal of International Relations*, 14, 133–160.
Olekalns, M. and Smith, P. (2005). Moments in time: Metacognition, trust and outcomes in negotiation. *Personality and Social Psychology Bulletin*, 31, 1696–1707.
Paris, R. (2004). *At War's End: Building Peace After Civil Conflict*. Cambridge, UK: Cambridge University Press.
Pearlman, W. (2009). Spoiling inside and out: Internal political contestation and the Middle East peace process. *International Security*, 33, 79–109.
Pettersson, T. and Themnér, L. (eds) (2011). *States in Armed Conflict 2010*. Department of Peace and Conflict Research, Uppsala University.
Pew Case Studies in International Affairs (1999). *The ISD Compendium of Case Study Abstracts and Indexes*. Washington, DC: Institute for the Study of Diplomacy, Edmund A. Walsh School of Foreign Service, Georgetown University.
Philipson, L. (2005). Engaging armed groups: The challenge of asymmetries. In R. Ricigliano (ed.), *Choosing to Engage: Armed Groups and Peace Processes*. London: Conciliation Resources.

Piccolino, G. (2010). *Mediation, local response and the limits of international engagement in Cote d'Ivoire.* Unpublished paper.

Pillar, P.R. (1983). *Negotiating Peace: War Termination as a Bargaining Process.* Princeton, NJ: Princeton University Press.

Pruitt, D.G. (2007). Readiness theory and the Northern Ireland conflict. *American Behavioral Scientist, 50*, 1520–1541.

Richmond, O. (1998). Devious objectives and the disputants' view of international mediation. *Journal of Peace Research, 35*, 707–722.

Rothchild, D. (1997). Ethnic bargaining and the management of intense conflict. *International Negotiation, 2*, 1–20.

Rouhana, N.N. (2000). Interactive conflict resolution: Issues in theory, methodology, and evaluation. In P.C. Stern and D. Druckman (eds), *International Conflict Resolution After the Cold War.* Washington, DC: National Academy Press.

Rouhana, N.N. and Kelman, H.C. (1994). Promoting joint thinking in international conflict: The Israeli-Palestinian continuing workshop. *Journal of Social Issues, 50*, 157–178.

Saunders, H.H. (1985). We need a larger theory of negotiation: The importance of prenegotiating phases. *International Negotiation, 1*, 249–262.

Saunders, H.H. (1999). *The Public Peace Process: A Sustained Dialogue to Transform Racial and Ethnic Conflict.* Basingstoke, UK: Palgrave.

Shedd, J. (2008). When peace agreements create spoilers: The Russo-Chechan agreement of 1996. *Civil Wars, 10*, 93–105.

Sisk, T.D. (1993). The violence-negotiation Nexus: South Africa in transition and the politics of uncertainty (pp. 67–90). *Negotiation Journal, 8*, 77–94.

Sisk, T.D. (2001). Peacemaking processes: Forestalling return to ethnic violence. In I.W. Zartman (ed.), *Preventive Negotiation: Avoiding Conflict Escalation.* Lanham, MD: Rowman and Littlefield Publishers.

Stedman, S.J. (1991). *Peacemaking in Civil War: International Mediation in Zimbabwe, 1974–80.* Boulder, CO: Lynne Rienner.

Stedman, S.J. (2003). Peace processes and the challenges of violence. In J. Darby and R. MacGinty (eds), *Contemporary Peacemaking: Conflict Violence and Peace Processes* (pp. 103–113). Basingstoke, UK: Palgrave Macmillan.

Stedman, S.J. (1997). Spoiler problems in peace processes. *International Security, 22*, 5–53.

Stedman, S.J., Rothchild, D., Cousens, E. (eds) (2002). *Ending Civil Wars: The Implementation of Peace Agreements.* Boulder, CO: Lynne Rienner.

Strauss, A. and Corbin, J. (1990). *Basics of Qualitative Research: Grounded Theory Procedures and Techniques.* Newbury Park, CA: Sage.

Sundberg, R. (2008). Collective violence 2002–2007: Global and regional trends. In L. Harbom and R. Sundberg (eds), *States in Armed Conflict 2007* (pp. 165–191). Department of Peace and Conflict Research, Uppsala University.

Svensson, I. (2007a). Bargaining, bias and peace brokers: How rebels commit to peace. *Journal of Peace Research, 44*, 177–194.

Svensson, I. (2007b). Mediation with muscle or mind? Exploring power mediators and pure mediators in civil war. *International Negotiation, 12*, 229–248.

Themnér, A. (2011). *Violence in Post-Conflict Societies: Remarginalization, Remobilizers and Relationships.* London: Routledge.

Tomlin, B. (1989). The stages of prenegotiation: The decision to negotiate North American free trade. In J.G. Stein (ed.), *Getting to the Table.* Baltimore, MD: Johns Hopkins University Press.

Touval, S. (2003). Mediation and foreign policy. *International Studies Review, 5*, 91–95.

Touval, S. and Zartman, I.W. (eds) (1985). *International Mediation in Theory and Practice.* Boulder and London: Westview Press.

Uslander, E. (2008). *Corruption, Inequality, and the Rule of Law.* Cambridge, UK: Cambridge University Press.

Wagner, L.M. (2008). *Problem-Solving and Bargaining in International Negotiations.* Leiden: Martinus Nijhoff Publishers.

Wallensteen, P. (2007). *Understanding Conflict Resolution*. London: Sage Publications.
Wallensteen, P. (2011). The origins of contemporary peace research. In K. Höglund and M. Öberg (eds), *Understanding Peace Research: Methods and Challenges* (pp. 14–32). London and New York: Routledge.
Walter, B.F. (1999). Designing transitions from civil war: Demobilization, democratization, and commitments to peace. *International Security*, 24, 127–155.
Walter, B.F. (2002). *Committing to Peace: The Successful Settlement of Civil Wars*. Princeton NJ: Princeton University Press.
Wehr, P. and Lederach, J.P. (1991). Mediating conflict in Central America. *Journal of Peace Research*, 28, 85–98.
Werner, S. and Yuen, A. (2005). Making and keeping peace. *International Organization*, 59, 261–292.
Whalan, J. (2012). Evaluating peace operations: The case of Cambodia. *International Journal of Peacekeeping*, 16, 226–251.
Young, O.R. (1967). *Intermediaries: Third Parties in International Crises*. Princeton, NJ: Princeton University Press.
Zahar, M.-J. (2003). Reframing the spoiler debate in peace processes. In J. Darby and R. MacGinty (eds), *Contemporary Peacemaking: Conflict, Violence and Peace Processes* (pp. 114–124). Basingstoke, UK: Palgrave Macmillan.
Zahar, M.-J. (2010). SRSG mediation in civil wars: Revisiting the spoiler debate. *Global Governance*, 16, 165–280.
Zartman, I.W. (1985). *Ripe For Resolution: Conflict and Intervention in Africa*. New York: Oxford University Press.
Zartman, I.W. (1989). Prenegotiation – phases and functions. In J. Gross Stein, *Getting to the Table: The Process of International Prenegotiation* (pp. 1–17). Baltimore and London: Johns Hopkins University Press.
Zartman, I.W. (2000). Ripeness: The hurting stalemate and beyond. In P.C. Stern and D. Druckman (eds), *International Conflict Resolution After the Cold War* (pp. 225–250). Washington, DC: National Academy Press.
Zartman I.W. and Kremenyuk, V.A. (eds) (2005). *Peace versus Justice: Negotiating Forward and Backward-Looking Outcomes*. Lanham, MD: Rowman and Littlefield.
Zartman, I.W., Deng, F.M., and Rothchild, D. (eds) (1996). *Sovereignty as Responsibility: Conflict Management in Africa*. Washington, DC: Brookings Institution Press.

17. Environmental disputes: negotiating over risks, values and the future
Barbara Gray and Julia Wondolleck

INTRODUCTION

Environmental negotiations embody many of the characteristics and dynamics of negotiations in other realms. They engage disputing parties representing legitimate but divergent interests in bargaining arrangements characterized by disparate power and influence, psychological framing, and the inevitable communication challenges associated with any human interactions. While similar in these regards, environmental negotiations nonetheless exhibit some notable distinctions. The nature of most environmental issues and, moreover, the public context within which these issues arise and are negotiated are markedly different from the other domains from which most negotiation theory has been developed and refined. This chapter briefly describes the distinguishing characteristics of environmental conflicts. It explains the variations observed within this field and summarizes major areas of research. It concludes with a discussion of the implications for future research and practice of environmental negotiation.

Early environmental negotiation processes drew heavily from the established norms and practices of labor management and collective bargaining (Susskind and Weinstein, 1980; Harrington, 1994). However, early theory posited that environmental cases presented novel challenges. In particular, Susskind and Weinstein (1980, p. 324) noted that "irreversible ecological effects may be involved; the nature, boundaries, participants, and costs are often indeterminate; one or more of the parties to most environmental disputes often claims to represent the broader 'public interest' (including the interests of inanimate objects, wildlife, and generations yet unborn); and implementation of private agreements is difficult". Furthermore, environmental negotiations are not uniform in origin, structure, or even purpose. Some processes are agency-initiated while others emerge organically from within communities of place or interest (Koontz et al., 2004; Wondolleck and Yaffee, 2000). Some are triggered by conflict while others arise from shared concern about a place or recognition of a common problem (Bernard and Young, 1996; Gray, 1996; Brick and Snow, 2000). Some encompass many inter-related issues and have a long time horizon, others focus on a few issues to be resolved in a limited time frame (Agranoff, 2007; Heikkila and Gerlak, 2005). Some enlist the assistance of professional third parties, while others do not benefit from formal intervention (Dukes, 2004). As Emerson et al. (2004, p.222) observed, "one of the most difficult challenges for Environmental Conflict Resolution (ECR) research is the heterogeneity of the ECR processes themselves as well as the diversity of applications and intended effects".

THE NATURE OF ENVIRONMENTAL ISSUES

The pervasiveness and intractability of environmental conflict can be explained by the core characteristics of environmental issues that distinguish these conflicts in significant ways from others that are subject to negotiated resolution. In particular, environmental issues are characterized by both scientific complexity and uncertainty, and value and ideological differences. Moreover, environmental conflicts entail highly visible public issues involving many parties and are inevitably buffeted by social and political factors. Additionally, environmental issues are embedded in a highly-structured institutional context that defines and constrains the manner in which environmental negotiations occur.

Scientific Complexity and Uncertainty

Environmental issues are scientifically complex (Ozawa, 1991; Karl et al., 2007). The physical and biological dynamics within and between geophysical and ecological systems are the subject of numerous academic disciplines. Social and economic dependencies on the natural environment add further complexity. The implications of this complexity to environmental negotiation are many. It is often difficult to bound any single environmental problem because of the invariable connections to other social and ecological systems and issues, and, while much is known about environmental issues even more is not known (e.g., whether or not fracking liquids used in natural gas drilling lead to adverse health effects). In many cases the facts are shrouded in uncertainty because the pertinent research is in dispute or has not yet been conducted. For example, at the time of the Three Mile Island nuclear disaster, little or no information was available on the health effects of exposure to low levels of radioactive krypton (Gricar and Baratta, 1983). Because of this uncertainty risks are linked to any decision, and parties weigh the likelihood and acceptability of different outcomes differently (Bacow, 1980; Slovic, 1992). This evolving complexity also introduces the strategic "use" of science in conflict and negotiation in which scientific data and theories are selectively referenced in order to serve one party's interests while simultaneously undermining the opposing party's arguments (Ozawa, 1991).

Not only are environmental issues complex and uncertain but, moreover, environmental science is rapidly advancing, sometimes challenging prior assumptions and unraveling programs and policies established in earlier times (Yaffee,1995). Rapidly advancing science necessitates adaptive learning processes and ongoing monitoring and assessment (Gunderson et al. 1995; Karl et.al., 2007). Science-intensive negotiations require contingencies and the sustained interactions of parties as the effects of their agreements become known and are revisited.

Conflicting Values and Ideologies

Another characteristic defining many environmental conflicts is that at least one of the parties (or many) holds strong values about the issues in contention stemming from differential valuation of environmental resources and/or ideological stances. They may be rooted in religious beliefs, Native American culture, and/or deeply held ecological beliefs (Eckberg and Blocker, 1996; Thompson and Gonzalez, 1997; Burton, 2002) or may be motivated by threats to one's fundamental identity (Bryan and Wondolleck, 2003; Gray, 2004). For example, Burton (2002) has detailed the fundamentally different orientations toward land and nature held by Native Americans and many other non-native groups in the U.S. The former exhibit strong reverence for nature which often translates into opposition to proposed projects on public lands and how they are managed. Some scholars have suggested that the attribution of "sacred" to features of a social context is contextually defined and that naming and language play a role in whether values are invoked in a dispute (Tetlock et al., 1996).

In writing about political conflicts, Coser (1956, p. 75) has distinguished those "that arise over the basis of consensus and those taking place within the basic consensus." In the first case, "parties believe that no common ends can be discovered so that a compromise can be reached". Value conflicts often fall into this category because strongly-held values typically provoke negotiators to adopt non-negotiable stances.

In many cases, strong reactions on both sides of a conflict are fueled by strong identifications with traditional ways of making a livelihood (e.g., through logging) versus deep-seated concerns about environmental protection. For example, in the Quincy Library Group dispute (so named because the disputants eventually met to resolve their issues at the local library in Quincy, California), environmental groups protested the long-standing, unsustainable logging practices that provided local employment. After years of contentious and sometimes violent wrangling, the parties agreed on a management plan for the forest that protected endangered species and preserved old growth forest while still sustaining the loggers' traditional livelihood (Bryan and Wondolleck, 2003). In such cases, interests and values become enmeshed as loggers and ranchers saw their identities threatened by proposed restrictions to preserve natural resources.

Intergenerational issues can challenge environmental negotiations when one party argues that the needs and concerns of future generations should be factored into agreements while others disagree. Intergenerational issues loom large in debates over climate change, for example, since future generations will bear the burden of failure to prevent the predicted environmental degradation and associated social calamity from rises in atmospheric temperature. A second value-infused issue associated with climate change and other transnational debates over natural resources involves the rights of people in the less developed world to enjoy a lifestyle equivalent to those in developed nations, an aspiration that challenges efforts to curtail deforestation and reduce greenhouse gas pollution.

Value-based conflicts have been shown to be particularly prone to escalation because they tend to arouse strong emotions among disputants. For example, Harinck and Van Kleef (2012) found that "people deem expressions of anger more unfair in value conflicts than in interest conflicts and that they are more likely to engage in retaliatory and escalatory behaviours when confronted with an angry reaction in the context of a value issue rather than an interest issue".

Public Issues Involving Multiple Parties

Most environmental issues encompass public resources (air, water, wildlife, climate, forests, minerals and fuels) with multiple, intertwined public interests inevitably at stake. Individuals value public resources differently and vary in their attitudes towards what constitutes appropriate decisions. The result is a milieu of often divergent but usually legitimate interested parties who stake claim to an issue and contest how others think it should be resolved. This public attribute has both political and social dimensions that can affect a negotiation process in profound ways. Social perceptions of risk and entitlement, values, identities, and ideologies can influence what is discussed, how and by whom in a negotiation. For example, the seemingly narrow question about whether and how the endangered gray wolf might be reintroduced to the Greater Yellowstone Ecosystem embodied old West politics, ideologies about freedom and constitutional rights, local/national tensions, divisive social identities involving ranchers and environmentalists and inevitable interest group politics (Fischer, 1995). While compensation for livestock lost due to wolf predation could easily address the central interests of affected ranchers, the social milieu within which the conflict and iterative negotiations resided caused this conflict, like many others, to spiral in unpredictable and unmanageable directions (Putnam and Wondolleck, 2003).

While "the public" is an important and legitimate influence in environmental conflicts, it is nonetheless an elusive, non-homogeneous, often ideological and partisan entity that creates a tumultuous backdrop for many negotiations. Environmental negotiations are unavoidably buffeted by shifting public perceptions and values and inevitable transitions in political administrations. These realities are magnified at this particular time in history when civic discourse is seldom civil, partisanship is rampant, and ideological stances create chasms that are difficult to bridge (Brownstein, 2007; Haidt, 2012; Leiserowitz et al., 2007). What a representative group of stakeholders may be willing to consider and accept in a negotiation, while perhaps a reasonably fair and well-informed way forward, can quickly unravel when unveiled for public view (Lurie, 2004; Bryan, 2008).

Highly-structured Institutional Context

Environmental conflicts are embedded in a highly-structured institutional context in which long-standing norms, policies and procedures constrain when, where and how negotiations may take place. Parties to an environmental dispute are not free to settle their differences in any manner they deem acceptable. Most environmental issues fall under the jurisdiction of public agencies deriving authorities from public laws and policies. This reality has multiple implications for any negotiation process. The negotiation processes are usually visible; transparency is often compelled by law and regulation, and negotiations can seldom occur behind closed doors. For example, the U.S. Federal Advisory Committee Act requires that notice of meetings, which must be conducted in public, are to be posted in the *Federal Register* at least 15 days in advance and issues other than those listed in the *Federal Register* announcement cannot be discussed during the meeting. Agreements reached in most environmental negotiations must be vetted and are often modified in public review processes required by existing law and procedure. There is a broader public interest at stake in any environmental settlement, not solely the interests of the stakeholders who might be sitting at the table. At the same time, there is significant distrust in the institutions and agencies intended to represent those public interests.

Susskind and Cruikshank (1987) emphasized in the early development of this field that environmental negotiations were best understood as "Add-a-Step" processes that supplemented but did not supplant established laws, policies and procedures. Hence, environmental negotiations are observed in policy arenas where policy dialogues help broaden and inform discussion of pressing issues and contribute to legislative and administrative policy development; in regulatory arenas where rules are developed and enforced in implementing the wide array of environmental laws passed by Congress (including the Clean Air Act, Clean Water Act, Superfund, Endangered Species Act, National Forest Management Act, National Environmental Policy Act, among others) (Wondolleck, 1988; Yaffee, 1982); and in local planning and development arenas where long-term goals and objectives are adopted and development proposals are reviewed and conditional permits issued (Innes and Booher, 1999).

The complex institutional context of environmental conflicts affects negotiation in many ways, including whether or not it can even take place. Institutional norms and procedures can also constrain who has access to negotiation processes. In the U.S., many environmental negotiations involving public agencies are subject to the Federal Advisory Committee Act (FACA) which ensures that agencies receive representative advice through the formation of formal advisory committees to discuss and resolve contentious issues. FACA has compelled negotiation in certain contexts such as negotiated rulemaking (Pritzer and Dalton, 1995) in which agencies invite multiple stakeholders to draft proposed legislation. In contrast, the institutional context can also provide opportunities for negotiation that might otherwise be lacking. Endangered species listing, habitat conservation planning, and species recovery planning under the Endangered Species Act are all highly-negotiated processes (Yaffee, 1982) wherein formal administrative procedures provide the forum, boundaries and deadlines that encourage negotiated solutions. In addition, the Administrative Procedures Act (APA) provides procedures for review and comment on agency decisions. One particularly challenging aspect of this highly-structured institutional context is that it provides numerous avenues by which a negotiated agreement might be challenged by individuals who disagree with its provisions. For example, the adequacy and suitability of environmental regulations promulgated following EPA negotiated rule-making processes have been contested in court by groups who were not party to the negotiation process (Coglianese, 1999). Notably, at the transnational level, no institutional authority exists that can regulate the behavior of individual nations' environmental actions (Susskind, 1994). Instead, any agreements reached, such as the Montreal Protocol, must be ratified by nation states.

Figure 17.1 provides a model of key aspects of environmental negotiations. It emphasizes the pervasive impact of institutional factors on how these negotiations unfold. In the next two sections we elaborate on the components of this model and how institutional forces shape the process by which environmental conflicts evolve into negotiated environmental agreements.

KEY THEMES IN ENVIRONMENTAL NEGOTIATION RESEARCH

We classify research on environmental negotiation into five overarching categories. Some scholars (those examining risk assessments and social dilemmas) focused on the choices that decision makers would make under conditions of uncertainty. This research was either primarily survey based (in the case of risk assessments) or laboratory-based (in the case of social dilemmas). Others, engaged in empirical field research, examine case examples of environmental conflicts and associated negotiation in detail. In this same vein, researchers began to devote attention to the structure and management of environmental negotiations and, in particular, the role of third party mediators. To some extent, this early case research might be labeled advocacy literature in the sense that it was structured to provide models and illuminate comparative advantages that made an argument for the application of negotiation principles in this issue domain. As the field matured, a parallel track of research eventually emerged, focused on more in-depth and theory-based examination of the dynamics of environmental conflicts and negotiations that might explain their complexity and intractability in more nuanced terms as well as provide new insights for their potential management (Susskind et al., 1999). How decisions were differentially framed by negotiators has become a focus of this line of research. Finally, critiques of environmental negotiation processes also began to appear in the literature. We review each of these five research approaches in more detail below.

Risk Perception

Differential judgments about risk are one likely cause of conflicts over environmental issues. Failure to understand and acknowledge how other stakeholders perceive risks is also likely to heighten existing conflict. The early 1980s pioneered work on defining and measuring the general public's perceptions of risk (Fischoff et al., 1981). Some of this work focused on developing a survey to assess attributes of perceived risk of nuclear

Institutional Factors

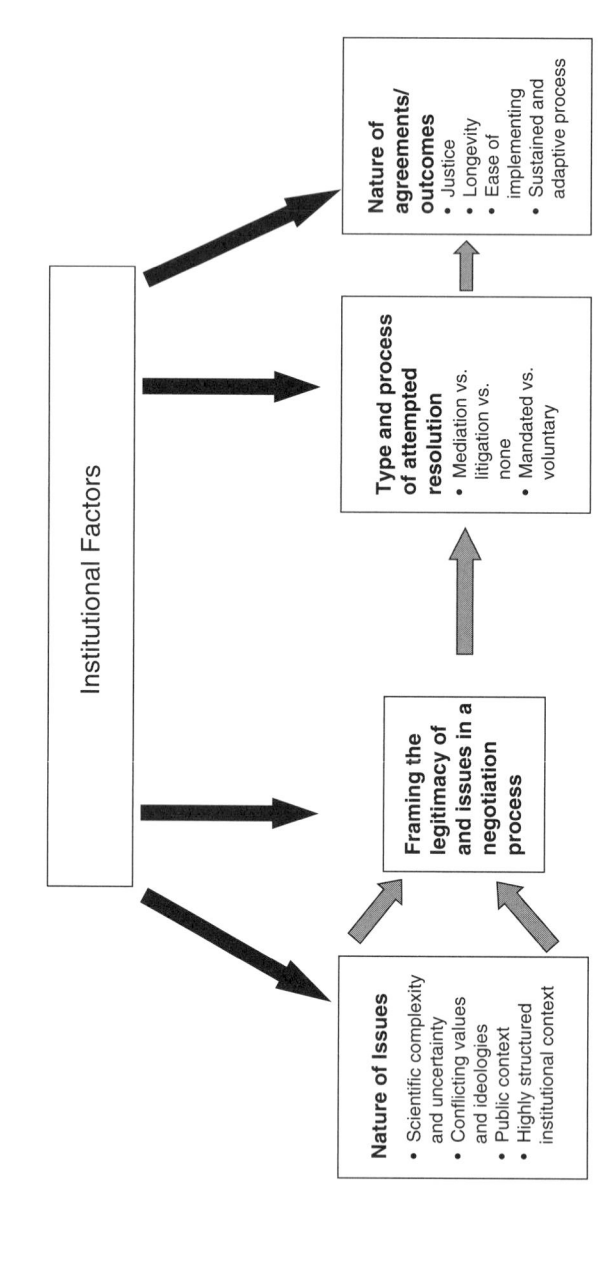

Nature of Issues
- Scientific complexity and uncertainty
- Conflicting values and ideologies
- Public context
- Highly structured institutional context

Framing the legitimacy of and issues in a negotiation process

Type and process of attempted resolution
- Mediation vs. litigation vs. none
- Mandated vs. voluntary

Nature of agreements/outcomes
- Justice
- Longevity
- Ease of implementing
- Sustained and adaptive process

Figure 17.1 Factors shaping the framing and outcomes of environmental negotiations

power (compare Thomas et al., 1980). One of the most important contributions of this work was the finding that "risk is inherently subjective" (Slovic, 1992, p. 121), and technical and lay populations used different bases for assessing it. For example, Baird (1986) identified several factors that influenced informal risk estimates and risk tolerance among the lay populations: judgments of relative benefits of a hazard, the voluntariness of individuals' exposure to the risks, their acceptance or denial of vulnerability and their familiarity with the hazard. Supporters of nuclear power saw few environmental risks and, instead, framed the issues in terms of economic and technical benefits while opponents focused almost exclusively on environmental risks and their negative psychological outcomes (Otway et al., 1978). Additionally, policy makers routinely failed to take these psychological outcomes into account in making decisions (Thomas et al., 1980) and wrote off public attitudes as uneducated and uninformed (Dietz et al., 1989) and even irrational (Wildavsky and Dake, 1990).

As research continued, additional dimensions of risk were identified including: how to define risks, which population is at risk, whether the risks were framed as gains or losses, how public decision makers should frame or structure policy problems and how to weight or value the different dimensions considered in risk acceptability decisions (e.g., economic versus health outcomes and questions about fairness in how risks were distributed in communities) (Vaughan and Seifert, 1992). The degree of uncertainty and the degree to which a risk evokes perceptions of dread, controllability, and catastrophe were also added to the list (Slovic, 1992).

In the early 1990s researchers began to develop methods for comparing these different components of risk. One approach, the contingent value (CV) method, assumed that people held hidden preferences for environmental goods (Hoevenagel, 1994), and that these could be teased out using surveys that asked individuals to declare a dollar value they would place on the quantity, quality and access to various environmental outcomes (Gregory et al., 1993). For example, in one study, respondents were willing to pay more money to reduce health risks than to reduce risks from war (Fischer et al., 1991). In another, researchers tested whether offering $5,000 in compensation would reduce opposition to a proposed repository for nuclear waste (Kunreuther et al., 1990). They found that support for the facility was related to its perceived risk to oneself, to future generations, to the perceived benefits and to the respondents' trust in government. Other researchers (Van Liere and Dunlap, 1980, mentioned above) also found that age, education and political ideology were related to environmental concerns.

This work evolved into multi-attribute utility methods (MAUT) based on the assumption that if people could make choices among their preferences, then they could assign utilities to represent them (von Winterfeldt and Edwards, 1986; Keeney and Raifa, 1993). These utilities were then combined into summary measures that discriminated among preferred outcomes. Although some policy makers found the MAUT technique useful for learning about public values toward risks, the approach also had limitations because some respondents found it difficult, and even distasteful, to assign a quantitative index to their value preferences (Hilgartner, 1985). MAUT and CV methods, however, have been criticized for several reasons: (1) priming effects – encouraging respondents to construct and quantify values that they might not hold; (2) the results could not be aggregated to large populations, and (3) failure to capture the social, cultural and institutional issues that formed the foundation for risk assessment.

To capture the social and cultural factors that shaped risk perceptions, some researchers argued that risks were not only influenced by individual values and experiences but also by cultural biases held by groups or organizations that served to amplify or attenuate the risks that were perceived by their members (Kasperson et al., 2003). While "biases" may be a loaded word in that it implies that some perceptions are "correct" while others are distorted, this research highlighted the importance of understanding how social processes and collectively institutionalized memory (Barthel, 1996) and beliefs can shape individuals' views on environmental risks. Overall, the risk perception literature has made it clear that parties in environmental conflicts view the risks associated through very different lenses, which helps to explain both their complexity and frequent intractability.

Social Dilemmas and Common Pool Resources

Two objective types of environmental problems that often prove intractable are social dilemmas and commons. A "social dilemma is a situation in which the interests of the collective and its individual members clash" (Suleman et al., 2004, p. ii). Researchers in this tradition classify disputants according to whether they have a pro-self or pro-social orientation. Those with the latter orientation are shown to exhibit more cooperative behavior than those of the former. Social dilemma theorists also classify dispute outcomes as either "take-some" or "give-some" games to differentiate how the decisions are defined. In take-some games group members can only take a fixed amount of a resource so that collectively the group does not take more than is available. In give-some games members receive payoffs based on the level of total contributions to a common pool (Rutte et al., 1987, p. 103). A recent compendium on social dilemmas research (Biel et al., 2008) reports new research directions that stress staggered decision making and the importance of social interaction in promoting cooperation.

The commons is a particular type of social dilemma in which a common pool resource has the potential to be over-utilized when individual users take only their own needs into account. This overutilization has come to be referred to as "the tragedy of the commons" because the overutilization eventually leads to depletion of the resource. Economic models for preventing such tragedies require an overarching centralized form of governance (Hardin, 1998) or localized communal solutions characterized by trust and reciprocity (Bryan, 2004; Ostrom et al., 1999).

Social constructionist theories of commons have also been proposed (Pettenger, 2007; Ansari et al., 2013) that adopt the view that commons are enacted when they are framed as such by those using the resources. From this perspective, problems over usage of commons can only be addressed when the users begin to define their over usage as a problem, acknowledge their complicity in constructing it as such and take collective responsibility for creating a governance structure to regulate use (Ansari et al., 2013). Typically, this requires one or more parties to reframe how they are viewing the problem or their preferred solution.

Overall, social dilemmas research has identified several factors that enhance the potential for cooperation in environmental negotiations including a social value orientation (Balliet et al., 2009), social norms (Bid and Thogersen, 2007), a common understanding (van Dijk et al., 2009) and face-to-face communication (Balliet, 2010) (see also Konig and van Dijk, Chapter 3 this volume).

Negotiation Processes, Structure and Management

Considerable research on environmental negotiations has been case-based, focused on negotiation process structure and management (Bingham, 1986; Cormick, 1980; Crowfoot and Wondolleck, 1990; Wondolleck, 1988; Yaffee, 1994). Case studies have probed the antecedent conditions that make a conflict ripe for negotiation in this context, the motivations or incentives that compel engagement and the elements and stages of a process that enable effective negotiation (Susskind and Cruikshank, 1987). Early high-profile environmental negotiations were mediated, in particular Storm King (Talbot, 1983), Snoqualmie Dam (Cormick, 1980), and the National Coal Policy Project (Hay and Gray, 1985), prompting attention to the varied roles of mediators and the stages and particular dynamics of mediated processes (Bingham, 1986; Carpenter, 1999; Carpenter and Kennedy, 1988; Daniels and Walker, 2001; Dukes et.al., 2000; Gray, 1989; Moore, 1996; Susskind, 1999).

Not surprisingly given the extraordinary scientific complexity of environmental issues, attention has also been paid to the particular structure and dynamics of science-intensive data negotiation processes (Adler et.al., 2000; Ozawa, 1991). More recently, attention has been given to more emergent processes that blend the principles of interest-based bargaining and those of adaptive management and long-range planning (Bernard and Young, 1996; Brick and Snow, 2000; Koontz et.al., 2004; Weber, 2003; Wondolleck and Yaffee, 2000) to both identify the conditions under which these processes emerge and the ways in which they are managed and, moreover, sustained. In addition to providing detailed insights about the evolution of environmental negotiations, including the theoretical and practical obstacles and methods used to overcome them, this line of research facilitated the refinement of the practice of mediation.

Research on Representation

Research on representation in negotiations has investigated some of the issues that arise when one person tries to speak on behalf of a group at the negotiating table. Groups may select specific individuals to serve as their negotiators for several reasons. Negotiators may have specific expertise and knowledge or a suitable temperament (Mnookin and Susskind, 1999). Representatives may also be chosen for strategic advantage or because a single negotiator can best represent the group (who themselves may be divided) (Pruitt and Carnevale, 1993). Because there are often many groups with a stake in environmental negotiations, representation is often needed to generate a manageable size group for the negotiations.

Serving as a representative places an individual in a boundary spanning role in which they typically have discretion to act as they deem appropriate at the negotiating table and yet must also be accountable to the group they are representing (De Dreu et al., 2007; Druckman, 1994; Pruitt and Carnevale, 1993). Thus, representatives must consider the preferences and tactics of both their fellow negotiators at the table and their back home constituents (Jones and Worschel, 1992). However, because they learn new information during the negotiation and may be inclined to shift their stance in the face of it, if they veer too far from the wishes of their constituents, they may be labeled as traitors to their cause. Putnam (1988) refers to this need to deal with both groups as "the two table problem" in which representatives must negotiate at two different levels: the main table and with their back-home constituents. These differential allegiances are complicated further when members of the representative's constituency disagree. Even a small contingent of hawkish members within the constituency, can pressure the negotiator to take a strong stand in the main negotiations (Steinel et al., 2009).

The factors noted above have clear consequences for the design of representation within multiparty processes for environmental conflicts. In seating representatives, it becomes necessary to consider exactly who the parties are who should be included in the negotiations. Ideally, each stakeholder group that has something at stake in the conflict should have a voice at the negotiating table. Often, however, parties are unwilling to sit down with others they have been battling in public forums or the courts because they believe that they are fanatics or untrustworthy (Thompson and Gonzalez, 1997). Nonetheless, participation by all groups who have the potential to block an agreement is important to forestall subsequent challenges to any agreement that is reached (Gray, 1989). In some cases, this number can be daunting in terms of managing an effective negotiating process. When third parties are involved as mediators, they will often work with stakeholders to streamline overall participation while ensuring that each group believes someone is championing their views at the negotiating table. Non-participants can also be seated as "observers" so that the process remains as transparent as possible to constituents. Additionally, having too hawkish a representative can scuttle negotiations or may cause a caucus to change their representative precisely because that party was alienating his counterparts at the table (Hay and Gray, 1985). Moreover, since many environmental conflicts are *issue-driven*, not *party-driven*, who should stand for a particular concern is not always clear. These issue-driven conflicts invert the traditional stakeholder-focus that drives the initial development of a negotiation process. Rather than asking "who are the parties and what do they care about?" many environmental conflicts beg the question "what are the issues that demand attention and who can speak to these issues in an informed and credible manner?" The composition of the latter process is different from the former, and may lead to different outcomes because representatives may not have the same degree of passion about the issues as they do when distinct parties are in conflict.

All in all, achieving sufficient representation is not a simple task. Seemingly aligned parties can differ. It is not unusual for the decisions of representatives of environmental or industry groups, or public agencies for that matter (Lurie, 2004) to be questioned by seemingly aligned but uninvolved parties. For example, forest products industry representatives in the Quincy Library Group negotiations were under significant pressure from industry associations to defy commitments they had made at the table (Bryan, 2008). Even when representation issues are settled and interest groups are generally aligned, they may still assess their Best Alternatives to a Negotiated Agreement (BATNAs) differently or differ with respect to ideologies and organizational considerations such as whether or not to join a collaborative negotiation (McCloskey, 2000).

Framing

Researchers have also tried to understand why environmental negotiations are so intractable by studying the way the various stakeholders frame the issues in these conflicts. This research emphasizes the differential perceptions or frames through which disputants size up the issues (Vaughan and Siefert, 1992; Lewicki et al., 2003; Brummans et al., 2008; Ansari et al., 2012). Framing is an interpretive process in which we make sense of our world. Often surfacing in the way we name or label a dispute, frames reflect the issues we judge to be salient in a dispute and the way we prefer to deal with these issues (Tannen, 1979; Vaughan and Siefert, 1992; Gray, 2003). They are both individual and collective interpretations that evolve from our past experiences and are reapplied or invoked in our current interactions to interpret what is happening.

Benford and Snow (2000) explored the role of framing in social movement organizing. They identified three kinds of frames: diagnostic (interpretations of what is at stake in the dispute); prognostic (perspectives on how the issue or problem should be solved); and mobilization frames (strategies for raising constituents' awareness about the issues). For example, in his own research, Benford (1993) identified differences in how radicals, liberals and moderates framed their view about nuclear disarmament. Radicals viewed the nuclear threat as a symptom of global systemic problems such as hegemony and greed whereas moderates, who were at the other end of the spectrum, attributed the problem to technological developments. In the Benford and Snow (2000) framework, diagnostic frames pose issues as problems that are in need of ameliorative action. They are also constructed in a way that assigns blame for the problem, typically identifying a "culprit" and framing the potential social movement recruit as a "victim" to induce them to take up the cause.

Others studying framing of environmental disputes have introduced a typology of frame types that disputants relied on to make sense of their situations and themselves (Lewicki, et al., 2003; Gray, 2004; Brummans et al., 2008). They found that disputants not only framed themselves (identity frames) and their opponents (characterization frames), they also framed types of power available to and utilized by themselves and others and how they believed the disputes should be resolved if they could be (conflict management frames). The latter are similar to prognostic frames (Benford and Snow, 2000). Some disputants held that power trumped all else and sought to explain their own helplessness as a consequence of their counterparts' power advantage. For example, a citizen's group who had lost their battle to prevent the construction of an incinerator to clean up a superfund site because they feared possible air pollution from the site, expressed concerns about black helicopters watching over them (implying that they were under surveillance from the federal government) (Hanke et al., 2003). Strong oppositional stances were usually associated with perceived threats to the group's identity with members of these groups often framing themselves as "victims" of other stakeholders' actions (Lewicki et al., 2003). Their preferred conflict management frame was protest rather than negotiation whereas disputants in other conflicts adopted more optimistic frames about how the disputes could be resolved (Brummans et al., 2008). Overall, framing research holds promise both for generating deeper understanding of how disputants make sense of the situation and each other, but also for proposing possible interventions that may improve their ability to understand and communicate with each other (Gray, 2006).

Critiques of Extant Practices

Research on environmental conflicts has also focused on the actual practice of conducting such negotiations. With over 30 years of experience with consensus-based collaborative processes to resolve environmental conflicts (with or without the assistance of a third party), there are now countless case studies chronicling these events and several more systematic attempts to evaluate the utility of such processes for promoting agreements and, moreover, solving environmental problems. While such research generally extols the value of consensus-based processes (assuming they adhere to accepted normative practices), other researchers have criticized these processes on multiple grounds including that they undermine the advocacy work of environmentalists from more important lobbying work and run counter to democratic processes of government (McCloskey, 2000), do not save decision makers time as promised in ADR's promotional literature, and fail to meet several other widely tauted benefits such as building trust and producing decisions of improved quality (Coglianese, 1997).

Criteria for evaluating environmental negotiation processes have been proposed (Conley and Moote, 2003; Innes, 1999). Some researchers advocate that such criteria be used systematically to objectify evaluation processes across settings. However, as Conley and Moote (2003) note, judgments of a given case against the criteria still entail subjective decisions by the evaluator(s) making cross-case comparisons problematic.

> Even evaluators who agreed to use a standard set of criteria would likely weight them differently and thus come up with very different evaluations of the

same case. How do we weigh capacity building against results on the ground? Economic efficiency against equity issues? Short-term results against long-term precedents? (Conley and Moote, 2003, p. 376)

At one level, the fundamental meaning of what constitutes collaboration is at stake (Gray, 2000). That is, should an enhancement of trust among the parties be considered a "success" even if, in the end, no agreement is reached? Is reaching agreement a satisfactory outcome even if it is never implemented? Innes (1999, p. 639) notes that "an agreement may be reached but the process could be regarded as a failure".

Two challenging issues pertaining to evaluation include representation and level of agreement among participants. As noted earlier, the issue of representation (or lack of it by certain groups) can forestall a collaborative effort if those parties have the ability to block any agreements that are reached (e.g., by challenging a decision legally or promoting the passage of nullifying legislation). Additionally, the quality of the agreement may suffer if stakeholders with relevant information are left out of the negotiations. "For example, a regional transit-planning effort in the San Francisco area that did not include representation of the inner city poor, failed to provide service that would link these residents to jobs in the suburbs" (Innes, 1999, p. 641). Ideally, all relevant stakeholders with an interest in the issue should be represented at the negotiating table, but many efforts do not meet this standard. The level of agreement among those who do participate is also a challenging issue since consensus requires that all agree to live with whatever agreement is developed (even if it is not their preferred solution). Despite ground rules specifying full consensus or no decision, in the end, some agreements are struck despite one or two holdouts. How should such cases be evaluated when, for example, 22 of 23 seated parties come to agreement despite an initial press for consensus? Does this constitute a failed collaboration? Or if some stakeholders refuse to join the deliberations, should a consensus among the rest be deemed a success?

Conley and Moote (2003) point out other reasons that objective comparison of cases may prove problematic. For example, they note differences between collaborative and community-based processes with representation being an important criterion for the former, but not necessarily for the latter since involvement and empowerment of less advantaged stakeholders may be paramount in community-based efforts. Similarly, decisions about a specific environmental issue may be settled through a single, one-time negotiation, whereas collaborative watershed management decision making may require ongoing decision making over many years (Wondolleck and Yaffee, 2000). Evaluation may show little progress because positive results cannot reasonably be expected for many years. Collaborative ecosystem-scale management processes proceed through stages and what might legitimately and realistically be evaluated at one stage is different from at other stages (Yaffee, 2011).

Additionally, because consensus processes do not carry the force of law, process criteria become increasingly important for effectiveness. "When process criteria are met, stakeholders who have not achieved their goals may still support an agreement because they feel their voices were heard and their interests were incorporated as much as possible" (Innes, 1999, p. 641). Still, simple surveys of participants' views of the process can be misleading if negotiators were misled or brought unrealistic expectations about what could be accomplished to the table (Innes, 1999). Research has shown that important process criteria include such issues as whether the principles of civil discourse were followed, high quality information was utilized, a commitment to collaborate was evident among the parties who challenged assumptions and reached new understanding of the issues, concerted efforts were made to find creative agreements, back-home constituents support the agreement, trust among negotiators was enhanced through transparency of motives and adherence to agreed upon ground rules, negotiators did not feel coerced and mediators were perceived as fair (Wondolleck, 2010; Gray, 1989; Innes, 1999).

Evaluating the process, however, is insufficient, if the outcomes are not also critiqued. Innes (1999) identifies a long list of outcome measures that could be assessed. Although not all may be appropriate for a given dispute, two seem particularly important: all parties are satisfied with the agreement and it is considered just. As more experience with environmental negotiation is accumulated, however, greater variation in the applications and processes are evolving (Emerson et al., 2004) making a one-size fits all approach to assessing the success of environmental negotiations even less likely (Fleischer, 2008).

Some scholars have offered explicit critiques of the use of consensus-based processes for resolving environmental conflicts. For example, some of the early critiques questioned whether parties could realistically overcome their adversarial tendencies and whether a level playing field could be established. Concerns were raised about the loss of precedent-setting associated with ADR processes and charged the proponents of ADR, many of whom were mediators, with conflicts of interest (Amy, 1983; Rabe, 1988). More recently, Coglianese (1997, p. 1276) did an extensive review of negotiated rulemaking processes and concluded that "in comparison with overall regulatory activity, then, the number of negotiated rulemakings is miniscule". Within EPA, the agency that enacted negotiated rule making most frequently, there is conflicting evidence as to the staff's beliefs about the utility of the procedure (Kerwin and Langbein, 1995; Polkinghorn, 1995), and Coglianese (1997) found little evidence that the promises of ADR for swifter and better quality decisions were realized. EDR outcomes have also been challenged with the arguments such that they constitute diluted compromises with few environmental protection results (Coglianese, 1997), they compromise the mandates of federal agencies (McCloskey, 2000) or that subsequent information renders agreements flawed (Innes, 1999). Perhaps McCloskey's (2000) greatest concern is that the will of a few might subvert the preferences of the majority.

EMERGING THEMES AND FUTURE RESEARCH

We have explained the nature of environmental conflicts, have considered the contexts within which such conflicts erupt and the wide body of research and practice that has arisen to understand them. We have explored consensus-based and mediated processes that have been employed to try to overcome negotiation impasses and foster common ground solutions. Now we turn our attention to areas for several emerging themes and promising areas for future research on environmental negotiations.

For many reasons already noted, environmental conflicts are prone to intractability. Intractable conflicts are "intense, frustrating, and complex, with no readily conceivable solutions" (Putnam and Wondolleck, 2003, p. 37). Intractability means that the parties involved in the negotiations are unable to reach an agreement about how to deal with the issue or issues at hand. Intractability is a perceptual problem because, for whatever reason, the disputants either do not agree that a problem exists, define the problem differently, agree on the problem but not on a reasonable solution (e.g., because of value-based differences) or possibly no solution acceptable to all parties is identifiable at the time.

Thus, future research on the causes of such impasses and how to overcome them is warranted. While many intractable disputes persist that way for decades or even longer and can be especially contentious (Lewicki et al., 2003), they are not necessarily permanently unresolvable. Because they are rooted in people's perceptions and because natural conditions as well as technical capabilities can change over time, the nature of the issues and people's perceptions of them may also shift (Wondolleck, 2009). New information may emerge, new issues may arise, power dynamics may shift, and/or new players may come on the scene – any of these can cause the disputants to reappraise the stakes or realize new options (Ansari et al., 2013). Researchers should examine individual, group and institutional roadblocks to negotiation as well as mechanisms that may promote favorable shifts toward agreements.

A second area deserving careful research concerns the value of mandated negotiations for addressing environmental conflicts. Several emerging themes related to mandated negotiations deserve further investigation. While voluntary engagement is a central tenet embedded in negotiation theory, not all environmental negotiation processes are voluntary (Wondolleck, 2010), and some mandated negotiations have advanced the use of consensus-based processes. Therefore, researchers should examine the potential benefits and liabilities of mandated process compared to voluntary negotiations (Rodriguez et al., 2007). In terms of liabilities, management of many environmental and natural resource issues resides in a political and organizational context that can resist negotiation. Whether it is agencies protecting turf and maintaining control (Bardach, 1998), or parties firmly-rooted in an adversarial mindset (Golann, 1989), situations exist where parties may resist negotiation even if by all objective measures their interests would be better served by so doing (Katz, 1993; SPIDR, 1991). For example, in mandated negotiations, the parties may collaborate "in name only" just to appear to satisfy the regulatory requirement. Also, local relevance and ownership may be absent (Taylor and Schweitzer, 2005) and thereby reduce the parties' overall commitment to collaborate. Parties may also feel constrained to negotiate within narrower parameters. Nabatchi (2007, p. 647) details a long list of reasons why public managers in the U.S. Environmental Protection Agency readily dismiss collaboration, including "inertia, fear of losing control and incurring oversight, and lack of knowledge, resources, high-level support, and incentives ... pervasive litigation mentality, fear of looking weak, the perception that ADR is a passing fad, lack of experience, negative experiences, perverse incentives, lack of settlement authority, and concerns about confidentiality". Questions about whether the agency is able to exert greater power over the decision in mandated negotiations compared to voluntary ones should also be examined.

Mandating collaboration is sometimes necessary for logistical reasons as well. Even if parties are willing to negotiate, the reach and magnitude of some environmental issues often extends beyond existing institutional opportunities that might accommodate voluntary engagement. Without a ready forum and with many parties to involve, negotiation can be logistically precluded unless imposed by mandate. For example, at least four mandated collaborative processes have been conducted by the USDA Forest Service alone (Cheng, 2006), and the Clean Air Act statutorily mandates the U.S. EPA to resolve selected disputes involving tribes and the states through negotiation processes (Van de Wetering and McKinney,

2006). Although the federal Negotiated Rulemaking Act (1990) does not mandate the use of consensus-based processes, during the 1990s Congress did mandate the use of negotiated rule-making in at least 75 regulatory contexts (Coglianese, 1997). Research showing when and if mandate leads to lasting agreements would be beneficial as would identification of best practices for use when with mandated negotiations.

A third promising area for future research on environmental negotiations would be to investigate agreements and non-agreements with respect to their perceived distributive and procedural justice. Since research identifies a primary rationale for utilizing mediated processes is their enhanced fairness (Bush, 1996), and perceived justice is associated with lasting agreements in other contexts (Conlon and Fasolo, 1990; Pruitt and Carnevale, 1993; Welsh, 2001; Hollander-Blumhoff and Tyler, 2008), systematic evaluation of environmental negotiations in terms of both distributive and procedural justice makes sense and may shed light on failure to reach agreement as well. For example, the durability of agreements after civil wars was increased when the distributive justice principle of equality was enacted, and procedural justice was highly correlated with equality in terms of equal treatment and equal shares (Albin and Druckman, 2012).

A fourth area for research concerns how to cope with the increasingly contentious political context within the U.S. (Manheim, 2009). Regulations to protect the natural environment ushered into U.S. policy in the early 1970s are gradually being eroded or languishing on the books because of diminishing funds for enforcement (Capiello and Plushnick-Masti, 2012), and new conflicts such as the Keystone XL Pipeline, drilling in the Arctic National Wildlife Refuge, and action on climate change remain unresolved. Unfortunately, this increasingly political environment is creating a disconnect between the available processes for conflict resolution (whether they be democratic lawmaking or alternative consensus processes) and politics writ large. With gridlock at an all-time high, the need for civil negotiation processes only increases along with the imperative to learn how such processes might be introduced, structured and managed.

A sixth area deserving further research stems from the sustained and adaptive nature of many environmental issues. This necessitates the design of more emergent processes that blend the principles of interest-based bargaining and those of adaptive management and long-range planning (Bernard and Young, 1996; Brick and Snow, 2000; Koontz et.al., 2004; Weber, 2003; Wondolleck and Yaffee, 2000). Research is needed to both identify the conditions under which these processes emerge and the ways in which they can be effectively managed over time. This means finding ways to sustain the engagement of multiple stakeholders in ongoing evaluation and dialogue about the effectiveness of agreements reached and future changes to the ecosystem.

Finally, we need to understand how increasing scope and scale of environmental issues affects negotiations about them. Environmental problems are ubiquitous. Local, regional and national players around the globe are facing off in political contexts and they themselves are becoming increasingly polarized (Fischer and Hajer, 1999); the potential for intractability at the transnational negotiating table is increasing (see also Crump, Chapter 15 this volume on international negotiations). Such current environmental conflicts range from the "Cod Wars" over offshore fishing rights in Iceland to deforestation in Africa to rising tides in the Pacific Islands. And political conflicts in Afghanistan, Iraq, and all over Africa, are ravaging the natural environment even as they leave civil societies in disarray and other similar conflicts loom large (Wier and Virana, 2011) – raising questions about whether and how the natural environment will be managed and cared for going forward. The UNEP's Disasters and Conflicts Subprogramme reports that it has intervened in conflicts in over forty countries since 1999 (UNEP, 2011).

At the transnational level, global action to forestall climate change has all but stalled (Ansari et al., 2013; Climate Change Challenge, 2010) and is facing challenges in the U.S. but also in jurisdictions around the world (Murgatroyd, 2010). These factors only heighten the need for transnational processes that transcend national political wrangling (Djelic and Quack, 2008; Ansari et al., 2013). With China now creating the largest carbon footprint, and the North/South divide over environmental protection versus economic growth ever widening, research on constructing legitimate and effective transnational dispute resolution processes is critical.

REFERENCES

Abdalla, C., Becker, J.C., Cook-Huffman, C., Gray, B., Hanke, R., and Welsh, N. (2002). Community conflicts over intensive livestock operations: How and why do such conflicts escalate? *Drake Journal of Agricultural Law, 7*(1), 7–42.

Adler, P.S., Barrett, R.C., Bean, M.C., Birkhoff, J.E., Ozawa, C.P., and Rudin, E.B. (2000). *Managing scientific and technical information in environmental cases: Principles and practices for mediators and facilitators.* Washington, DC: RESOLVE.

Agranoff, R. (2007). *Managing within networks: Adding value to public organizations.* Washington, DC: Georgetown University Press.

Albin, C. and Druckman, D. (2012). Equality matters: Negotiating an end to civil wars. *Journal of Conflict Resolution, 56*, 155–182.

Amy, D.J. (1983). The politics of environmental mediation. *Ecology Law Quarterly, 11*(1), 1–19.

Ansari, S., Wijen, F., and Gray, B. (2013). Constructing a climate change logic: An

institutional perspective on the "Tragedy of the commons". *Organization Science*, online version accessed at: http://dx.doi.org/10.1287/orsc.1120.0799.
Bacow, L.S. (1980). The technical and judgmental dimensions of impact assessment. *Environmental Impact Assessment Review*, *1*, 109–120.
Bacow, L.S. and Wheeler, M. (1984). *Environmental dispute resolution*. New York: Plenum.
Baird, B.N.R. (1986). Tolerance for environmental health risks: The influence of knowledge, benefits, voluntariness, and environmental attitudes. *Risk Analysis*, Wiley On-line library DOI: 10.1111/j.1539-6924.1986.tb00955.x.
Balliet, D. (2010). Communication and cooperation in social dilemmas: A meta analytic review. *Journal of Conflict Resolution*, *54*(1), 39–57.
Balliet, D., Parks, C., and Joireman, I. (2009). Social value orientation and cooperation in social dilemmas: A meta-analysis. *Group Processes and Intergroup Relations*, *12*(4), 533–547.
Bardach, E. (1998). *Getting agencies to work together: The practice and theory of managerial craftsmanship*. Washington, DC: Brookings Institution.
Barthel, D. (1996). *Historic preservation: Collective memory and historical identity*. New Brunswick, NJ: Rutgers University Press.
Benford, R.D. (1993). You could be the hundredth monkey: Collective action frames and vocabularies of motive within the nuclear disarmament movement. *Sociological Quarterly*, *34*, 195–216.
Benford, R.D. and Snow, D.A. (2000). Framing processes and social movements: An overview and assessment. *Annual Review of Sociology*, *26*, 611–639.
Bernard, T. and Young, J.M. (1996). *The ecology of hope: Communities collaborate for sustainability*. Gabriola Island, BC: New Society Publishers.
Bid, A. and Thogersen, J. (2007). Activation of social norms in social dilemmas: A review of the evidence and reflections on the implication for environmental behavior. *Journal of Economic Psychology*, *28*(1), 93–112.
Biel, A., Eek, D., Garling, T., and Gustafson, M. (eds) (2008). *New issues and paradigms in research on social dilemmas*. New York: Springer.
Bingham, G. (1986). *Resolving environmental disputes: A decade of experience*. Washington, DC: Conservation Foundation.
Brick, P. and Snow, D. (eds) (2000). *Across the great divide: Exploration in collaborative conservation and the American West*. Washington, DC: Island Press.
Brownstein, R. (2007). *The second Civil War: How extreme partisanship has paralyzed Washington and polarized America*. New York: Penguin.
Brummans, B.H.J.M., Putnam, L.L., Gray, B., Hanke, R., Lewicki, R.J., and Wiethoff, C. (2008). Making sense of intractable multiparty conflict: A study of framing in four environmental disputes. *Communication Monographs*, *75*(1), 25–51.
Bryan, T. (2004). Tragedy averted: The promise of collaboration. *Society and Natural Resources*, *17*, 881–896.
Bryan, T. (2008). *Aligning identity: Social identity and changing context in community-based environmental conflict*. Unpublished doctoral dissertation, School of Natural Resources and Environment, The University of Michigan, Ann Arbor, MI.
Bryan, T. and Wondolleck, J. (2003). When irresolvable becomes resolvable: The Quincy Library Group conflict. In R. Lewicki, B. Gray, and M. Elliott (eds), *Making sense of intractable environmental conflict* (pp. 63–90). Washington, DC: Island Press.
Buckle, L.G. and Thomas-Buckle, S.R. (1986). Placing environmental mediation in context: Lessons from "failed" mediations. *Environmental Impact Assessment Review*, *6*, 55–70.
Burton, L. (2002). *Worship and wilderness: Culture, religion and law in public lands and resource management*. Madison, WI: University of Wisconsin Press.
Bush, R.A.B. (1996). "What Do We Need a Mediator For?": Mediation's "Value-added" for Negotiators. *Ohio State Journal on Dispute Resolution*, *12*, 1–36.
Capiello, D. and Plushnick-Masti, R. (2012). Analysis: EPA oil statistics contradict enforcement talk in politics. *Centre Daily Times*, 31 May, A6.
Carpenter, S. (1999). Choosing appropriate consensus building techniques and strategies.

In L. Susskind, S. McKearnan, and J. Thomas-Larmer (eds), *The consensus building handbook: A comprehensive guide to reaching agreement* (pp. 61–98). Thousand Oaks, CA: Sage.
Carpenter, S.L. and Kennedy, W.J.D. (1988). *Managing public disputes: A practical guide to handling conflict and reaching agreements.* San Francisco, CA: Jossey-Bass.
Cheng, A.A. (2006). Build it and they will come? Mandating collaboration in public lands planning and management. *Natural Resources Journal, 46,* 841–858.
Climate Change Challenge (2010). Accessed from http://www.climatechangechallenge.org/News/Copenhagen%20News/Climate_change_action_has_stalled.htm.
Coggins, G.C. (1998). Regulating federal natural resources: A summary case against devolved collaboration. *Ecology Law Quarterly, 25*(4), 602–610.
Coglianese, C. (1997). Assessing consensus: The promise and performance of negotiated rule-making. *Duke Law Journal, 46*(6), 1255–1340.
Coglianese, C. (1999). The limits of consensus. *Environment, 41*(3), 28–33.
Conley, A. and Moote, M.A. (2003). Evaluating collaborative natural resource management. *Society and Natural Resources, 16,* 371–386.
Conlon, D. and Fasolo, P. (1990). Influence of speed of third-party intervention and outcome on negotiator and constituent fairness judgment. *Academy of Management Journal, 33*(4), 833–846.
Cormick, G. (1980). The "theory" and practice of environmental mediation. *The Environmental Professional, 2,* 24–33.
Coser, L. (1956). *The functions of social conflict.* New York: Free Press.
Crowfoot, J.E. and Wondolleck, J.M. (1990). *Environmental disputes: Community involvement in conflict resolution.* Washington, DC: Island Press.
Daniels, S. and Walker, G. (2001). *Working through environmental conflict: The collaborative learning approach.* Westport, CT: Praeger.
De Dreu, C.K.W., Beersma, B., Steinel, W., and Van Kleef, G.A. (2007). The psychology of negotiation: Principles and basic processes. In A.W. Kruglanski and E.T. Higgins (eds), *Handbook of basic principles in social psychology* (2nd edn, pp. 608–629). New York: Guilford.
Dietz, T., Stern, P.C., and Rycroft, R.W. (1989). Definitions of conflict and the legitimation of resources: The case of environmental risk. *Sociological Forum, 4*(1), 47–70.
Djelic, M-L. and Quack, S. (2008). Institutions and transnationalization. In R. Greenwood, C. Oliver, K. Sahlin, and R. Suddaby (eds), *The Sage handbook of organizational institutionalism* (pp. 299–324). London: Sage.
Dolin, E.J. (2004). *Political waters: The long dirty, contentious, incredibly expensive but eventually triumphant history of Boston Harbor: A unique environmental success story.* Massachusetts: University of Massachusetts Press.
Druckman, D. (1994). Determinants of compromising behavior in negotiation: A meta-analysis. *Journal of Conflict Resolution, 38,* 507–556.
Dukes, E.F., Piscolish, M.A., and Stephens, J.B. (2000). *Reaching for higher ground in conflict resolution.* San Francisco: Jossey-Bass.
Dukes, E.F. (2004). What we know about environmental conflict resolution: An analysis based on research. *Conflict Resolution Quarterly, 22,* 191–220.
Eckberg, D.L. and Blocker, T.J. (1996). Christianity, environmentalism, and the theoretical problem of fundamentalism. *Journal for the Scientific Study of Religion, 35*(4), 343–355.
Emerson, K., O'Leary, R., and Bingham, L.B. (2004). Commentary: Comment on Frank Dukes's What we know about environmental conflict resolution. *Conflict Resolution Quarterly, 22*(1–2), 221–231.
Fischer, F. and Hajer, M.A. (1999). *Living with nature: Environmental politics as cultural discourse.* Oxford: Oxford University Press.
Fischer, G.W., Morgan, M.G., Fischoff, B., Nair, I., Lave, L.B. (1991). What risks are people concerned about? *Risk Analysis, 11,* 303–314.
Fischer, H. (1995). *Wolf wars – The remarkable inside story of the restoration of wolves to Yellowstone.* Helena, MT: Falcon Press Publishing.

Fischhoff, B., Lichtenstein, S., Slovic, P., Derby, S.L., and Keeney, R.L. (1981). *Acceptable risk*. New York: Cambridge University Press.
Fleischer, J. (2008). One size does not fit all: Differentiating ADR processes. *South Texas Law Review*, 49, Summer.
Golann, D. (1989). Making ADR mandatory: The constitutional issues. *Oregon Law Review*, 68, 487–568.
Gottlieb, R. (1993). *Forcing the spring: The transformation of the American environmental movement*. Washington, DC: Island Press.
Gray, B. (1989). *Collaborating: Finding common ground for multiparty problems*. San Francisco: Jossey-Bass.
Gray, B. (1996). Cross-sector partners: Collaborative alliances among business, government and communities. In C. Huxham (ed.), *Creating collaborative advantage* (pp. 58–79). London: Sage.
Gray, B. (2000). Assessing interorganizational collaboration: Multiple conceptions and multiple methods. In D. Faulkner and M. De Rond (eds), *Cooperative strategy: Economic, business, and organizational issues* (pp. 243–260). Oxford: Oxford University Press.
Gray, B. (2003). Freeze framing: The timeless dialogue of intractability surrounding the Voyageurs National Park. In R.J. Lewicki, B. Gray, and M. Elliott (eds), *Making sense of intractable environmental conflicts: Concepts and cases* (pp. 91–126). Washington, DC: Island Press.
Gray, B. (2004). Strong opposition: Frame-based resistance to collaboration. *Journal of Community and Applied Social Psychology*, 14(3), 166–176.
Gray, B. (2006). Frame-based interventions for promoting understanding in multiparty conflicts. In T. Gössling, L. Oerlemans, and R. Jansen (eds), *Inside Networks* (pp. 223–250). Cheltenham, UK and Northampton, MA, USA: Edward Elgar Publishing.
Gregory, R., Lichtenstein, S., and Slovic, P. (1993). Valuing environmental resources: A constructive approach. *Journal of Risk and Uncertainty*, 7, 177–197.
Gricar, B.G. and Baratta, A.J. (1983). Bridging the information gap at Three Mile Island: Radiation monitoring by citizens. *Journal of Applied Behavioral Science*, 19(1), 35–48.
Gunderson, L.H., Hollings, C.C. and Light, S.S. (1995). *Barriers and bridges to the renewal of ecosystems and institutions*. New York: Columbia University Press.
Haidt, J. (2012). *The righteous mind: Why good people are divided by politics and religion*. New York: Pantheon Books.
Harinck, F. and Van Kleef, G. (2012). Be hard on the interests and soft on the values: Conflict issues moderate the effects of anger in negotiations. *British Journal of Social Psychology*, 51, 741–752.
Harrington, C. (1994). Howard Bellman: Using "bundles of input" to negotiate an environmental dispute. In Kolb, D. and Associates, *When Talk Works: Profiles of Mediators* (pp. 105–147). San Francisco: Jossey-Bass.
Heikkila, T. and Gerlak, A.K. (2005). The formation of large-scale collaborative resource management institutions: Clarifying the roles of stakeholders, science, and institutions. *Policy Studies Journal*, 33(4), 583–612.
Hanke, R., Rosenberg, A., and Gray, B. (2003). The story of Drake Chemical: A burning issue. In R. Lewicki, B. Gray, and M. Elliott (eds), *Making sense of intractable environmental conflict: Concepts and cases* (pp. 275–302). Washington, DC: Island Press.
Hardin, G. (1998). Extensions of "The tragedy of the commons". *Science*, 280(5364), 682–683.
Hay, T.M. and Gray, B. (1985). The National Coal Policy Project: An interactive approach to corporate social responsiveness. In L.E. Preston (ed.), *Research in Corporate Social Performance and Policy*, Vol. 7 (pp. 191–212). Greenwich, CT: JAI Press.
Hilgartner, S. (1985). The political language of risk: Defining occupational health. In D. Nelkin (ed.), *The language of risk* (pp. 25–66). Beverly Hills, CA: Sage.
Hoevenagel, R. (1994). *The contingent value method: Scope and validity*. Ph.D. Dissertation. Vrije Universiteit, Amsterdam.
Hollander-Blumhoff, R. and Tyler, T. (2008). Procedural justice in negotiations: Procedural

justice, outcome acceptance and integrative potential. *Law and Social Inquiry*, *33*(2), 473–500.
Innes, J.E. (1999). Evaluating consensus building. In L. Susskind, S. McKearnan, and J. Thomas-Larmer (eds), *The consensus building handbook: A comprehensive guide to reaching agreement* (pp. 631–675), Thousand Oaks, CA: Sage.
Innes, J.E. and Booher, D.E. (1999). Consensus building and complex adaptive systems: A framework for evaluating collaborative planning. *American Planning Association Journal*, *65*(4), 413–423.
Jones, J. and Worschel, S. (1992). Representatives in negotiation: Internal variables that affect external negotiations. *Basic and Applied Social Psychology*, *13*, 323–336.
Karl, H.A., Susskind, L.E., and Wallace, K.H. (2007). A dialogue, not a diatribe: Effective integration of science and policy through joint fact finding. *Environment*, *49*(1), 20–34.
Kasperson, J.X., Kasperson, R.E., Pidgeon, N., and Slovic, P. (2003). The social amplification of risk: Assessing fifteen years of research and theory. In N. Pidgeon, R.E. Kasperson, and P. Slovic (eds), *The social amplification of risk* (pp. 14–36). Cambridge, UK: Cambridge University Press.
Katz, L.V. (1993). Compulsory alternative dispute resolution and voluntarism: Two-headed monster or two sides of the coin? *Journal of Dispute Resolution*, *1993*(1), 1–55.
Kaufman, S. and Gray, B. (2003). Retrospective and prospective frame elicitation. In R. O'Leary and L.B. Bingham (eds), *The promise and performance of environmental conflict resolution* (pp. 129–147). Washington, DC: Resources for the future.
Keeney, R. and Raifa, H. (1993). *Decisions with multiple objectives: Preferences and value tradeoffs*. Cambridge: Cambridge University Press.
Kenney, D.S. and Lord, W.B. (1999). *Analysis of institutional innovation in the natural resources and environmental realm*. Boulder, CO: Natural Resources Law Center, University of Colorado.
Kerwin, C. and Langbein, L. (1995). *An evaluation of negotiated rulemaking at the Environmental Protection Agency: Phase I*. Report prepared for Administrative Conference of the United States (ACUS).
Koontz, T., Steelman, T., Carmin, J., Smith Korfmacher, K., Moseley, K., and Thomas, C. (2004). *Collaborative environmental management: What role for government?* Washington, DC: Resources for the Future.
Kunreuther, H., Easterling, D.V., Desvousges, W., and Slovic, P. (1990). Public attitudes toward siting a high-level nuclear waste repository in Nevada. *Risk Analysis*, *10*, 469–484.
Leach, W.D. and Pelkey, N.W. (2001). Making watershed partnerships work: A review of the empirical literature. *Journal of Water Resources Planning and Management*, *127*(6), 378–385.
Leiserowitz, A., Maibach, E., and Rose-Renouf, C. (2007). *Global warming's six Americas*. Fairfax, VA: George Mason University's Center for Climate Change Communication.
Lewicki, R., Gray, B., and Elliott, M. (2003). *Making sense of intractable environmental conflicts*. Washington, DC: Island Press.
Lurie, S.D. (2004). *Interorganizational dynamics in large-scale integrated resources management networks: Insights from the CALFED Bay-Delta Program*. Unpublished doctoral dissertation, School of Natural Resources and Environment, University of Michigan, Ann Arbor.
Manheim, F.T. (2009). *Conflict over environmental regulations in the United States: Origins, outcomes, and comparisons with the EU and other foreign regions*. New York: Springer.
McCloskey, M. (2000). Problems using collaboration to shape environmental public policy. *Valparaiso University Law Review*, *34*(2), 423–434.
Mnookin, R.H. and Susskind, L.E. (eds) (1999). *Negotiating on Behalf of Others: Advice to Lawyers, Business Executives, Sports Agents, Diplomats, Politicians, and Everybody Else*. Thousand Oaks, CA: Sage Publications.
Moore, C. (1996). *The Mediation Process: Practical Strategies for Managing Conflict*. San Francisco, CA: Jossey-Bass.

Murgatroyd, S. (2010). Actions on climate change forestalled by political reality. *Troy Media*, 18 May.
Nabatchi, T. (2007). The institutionalization of alternative dispute resolution in the federal government. *Public Administration Review*, 67(4), 646–661.
Ostrom, E., Burger, J., Field, C., Norgaard, R., and Policansky, D. (1999). Revisiting the commons: Local lesson, global challenges. *Science*, 284, 278–282.
Otway, H.J., Maurer, D., and Thomas, K. (1978). Nuclear power: The question of public acceptance. *Futures*, 10, 109–118.
Ozawa, C. (1991). *Recasting science: Consensual procedures in public policy making*. Boulder, CO: Westview Press.
Pettenger, M. (ed.) (2007). *The social construction of climate change: Power, knowledge, norms*. Aldershot: Ashgate.
Polkinghorn, B. (1995). *The influence of regulatory negotiations on the U.S. Environmental Protection Agency as an institution*. Unpublished paper presented at the 1995 American Political Science Association meeting.
Pritzker, D.M. and Dalton, D.S. (1995). *Negotiated rulemaking sourcebook*. Washington, DC: Administrative Conference of the United States.
Pruitt, D.G. and Carnevale, P.J. (1993). *Negotiation in social conflict*. Pacific Grove, CA: Brooks/Cole.
Putnam, R. (1988). Diplomacy and domestic politics: The logic of two-level games. *International Organization*, 42(3): 427–460.
Putnam, L.L. and Wondolleck, J.M. (2003). Intractability: Definitions, dimensions and distinctions. In R.J. Lewicki, B. Gray, and M. Elliott (eds), *Making sense of intractable environmental conflicts: Frames and cases* (pp. 91–126). Washington, DC: Island Press.
Rabe, B. (1988). The politics of environmental dispute resolution. *Policy Studies Journal*, 16(3) 585–601.
Rodriguez, C., Langley, A., Beland, F., and Denis, J-L. (2007). Governance, power and mandated collaboration in an interorganizational network. *Administration and Society*, 39(2), 150–193.
Rutte, K.G., Wilke, A.M., and Messick, D.M. (1987). The effects of framing social dilemmas as give-some or take-some games. *British Journal of Social Psychology*, 26, 103–108.
Slovic, P. (1992). *Social theories of risk*. Westport, CT: Praeger.
Society of Professionals in Dispute Resolution (SPIDR) (1991). Dispute resolution as it relates to the courts: Mandated participation and settlement coercion. *Arbitration Journal, March*, 38–47.
Steinel, W., de Dreu, C.K.W., Ouwehand, E., and Ramirez-Marin, J.Y. (2009). When constituencies speak, in multiple tongues: The relative persuasiveness of hawkish minorities in representative negotiation. *Organizational Behavior and Human Decision Processes*, 109(1), 67–78.
Suleman, R., Budescu, D.V., Fischer, I., and Messick, D.M. (eds) (2004). *Contemporary psychological research on social dilemmas*. Cambridge: Cambridge University Press.
Susskind, L. (1994). *Environmental diplomacy: Negotiating more effective global agreements*. New York: Oxford University Press.
Susskind, L. (1999). An alternative to Robert's rules of order for groups, organization and ad hoc assemblies that want to operate by consensus. In L. Susskind, S. McKearnan, and J. Thomas-Larmer (eds), *The consensus building handbook: A comprehensive guide to reaching agreement* (pp. 3–60). Thousand Oaks, CA: Sage.
Susskind, L. and Cruikshank, J. (1987). *Breaking the impasse: Consensual approaches to resolving public disputes*. New York: Basic Books.
Susskind, L. and Weinstein, A. (1980). Towards a theory of environmental dispute resolution. *Boston College Environmental Affairs Law Review*, 9, 311–357.
Susskind, L., McKearnan, S., and Thomas-Larmer, J. (eds) (1999). *The consensus building handbook: A comprehensive guide to reaching agreement*. Thousand Oaks, CA: Sage.
Talbot, A.R. (1983). *Settling things: Six case studies in environmental mediation*. Washington, DC: The Conservation Foundation and the Ford Foundation.

Tannen, D. (1979). What's in a frame? Surface evidence of underlying expectations. In R. Feedle (ed.), *New dimensions in discourse processes* (pp. 137–181). Norwood, NJ: Ablex.
Taylor, B.D. and Schweitzer, L. (2005). Assessing the experience of mandated collaborative inter-jurisdictional transport planning in the United States. *Transport Policy*, *12*, 500–511.
Tetlock, P.E., Peterson, R., and Lerner, J. (1996). Revising the value pluralism model: Incorporating social content and context postulates. In C. Seligman, J. Olson, and M. Zanna (eds), *Values: Eighth annual Ontario. Symposium on personality and social psychology* (pp. 25–51). Hillsdale, NJ: Erlbaum.
Thomas, K., Swaton, E., Fishbein, M., and Otway, H.J. (1980). Nuclear energy: The accuracy of policy makers' perceptions of public beliefs. *Behavioral Science*, *25*(5), 332–344.
Thompson, L.L. and Gonzalez, R. (1997). Environmental disputes: Competition for scarce resources and clashing of values. In M.H. Bazerman, D.M. Messick, A.E. Tenbrunsel, and K.A. Wade-Benzoni (eds), *Environment, ethics and behavior* (pp. 75–103). San Francisco: New Lexington Press.
Thomson, A.M. and Perry, J.L. (2006). Collaboration processes: Inside the black box. *Public Administration Review, supplement to Vol. 66*, 20–32.
UNEP Disasters and Conflicts Subprogramme (2011). *Biannual Progress Report*. Available from http://postconflict.unep.ch/QPR/B_2011_02/.
Van de Wetering, S.B. and McKinney, M. (2006). The role of mandatory dispute resolution in federal environmental law: Lessons from the Clean Air Act. *Journal of Environmental Law and Litigation*, *21*, 1–45.
Van Dijk, E., de Kwaadsteniet, E.W., and De Cremer, D. (2009). Tacit coordination in social dilemmas: The importance of having a common understanding. *Journal of Personality and Social Psychology*, *96*(3), 665–678.
Van Liere, K.D. and Dunlap, R.E. (1980). The social bases of environmental concern: A review of hypotheses, explanations and empirical evidence. *Public Opinion Quarterly*, *44*, 181–197.
Vaughan, E. and Seifert, M. (1992). Variability in the framing of risk issues. *Journal of Social Issues*, *48*(4), 119–135.
von Winterfeldt, D. and Edwards, W. (1986). *Decision analysis and behavioral research*. Cambridge: Cambridge University Press.
Weber, E.P. (2003). *Bringing society back in: Grassroots ecosystem management, accountability, and sustainable communities*. Cambridge, MA: The MIT Press.
Welsh, N. (2001). Making deals in court-connected mediation: What's justice got to do with it? *Washington University Law Quarterly*, *79*, 787–861.
Welsh, N. and Gray, B. (2002). Searching for a sense of control: The challenge presented by community conflicts over concentrated animal feeding operations. *Penn State Environmental Law Review*, *10*, 395–420. Republished at http://www.nationalaglawcenter.org/bibliography/results/?id=50andpage=3.
Wier, T. and Virani, Z. (2001). Three linked risks for development in the Pacific Islands: Climate change, disasters and conflict. *Climate and Development*, *3*(2), 193–208.
Wildavsky, A. and Dake, K. (1990). Theories of risk perception: Who fears what and why? *Daedalus*, *119*, 41–60.
Wondolleck, J. (1985). The importance of process in resolving environmental disputes. *Environmental Impact Assessment Review*, *5*, 341–356.
Wondolleck, J.M. (1988). *Public lands conflict and resolution: Managing national forest disputes*. New York: Plenum.
Wondolleck, J. (2010). A crack in the foundation? Revisiting ECR's voluntary tenet. *Conflict Resolution Quarterly*, *27*(3), 321–343.
Wondolleck, J.M. (2009). Old growth: Evolution of an intractable conflict. In T. Spies and S. Duncan (eds), *Old growth in a new world: A Pacific Northwest icon reexamined*. Washington, DC: Island Press.
Wondolleck, J.M. and Yaffee, S.L. (2000). *Making collaboration work: Lessons from innovation in natural resource management*. Washington, DC: Island Press.

Yaffee, S.L. (1982). *Prohibitive policy: Implementing the Federal Endangered Species Act*. Cambridge, MA: The MIT Press.

Yaffee, S.L. (1994). *The wisdom of the spotted owl: Policy lessons for a new century*. Washington, DC: Island Press.

Yaffee, S.L. (1995). Lessons about leadership from the history of the spotted owl controversy. *Natural Resources Journal*, 35(2), 381–412.

Yaffee, S.L. (2011). Collaborative strategies for managing animal migrations: Insights from the history of ecosystem-based management. *Environmental Law*, 41(2), 655–679.

18. Crisis negotiation: from suicide to terrorism intervention
Simon Wells, Paul J. Taylor and Ellen Giebels

TERRORISM AND CRISIS NEGOTIATION

At 2:30am on a Thursday morning you accompany the police to a small housing estate in north London where a man is standing on his third-floor balcony. He has a nylon rope around his neck that is attached securely to a washing line hook. He is leaning on the metal fence that separates the balcony from the drop below such that, if he falls or jumps, it is likely that he will decapitate. The man sees you approaching and acknowledges this by asking, "what the f--- do you want?" By this stage of the Handbook you will have read a great deal about negotiation. So, putting what you have read into practice, what would you say or do? Working out your BATNA or calling your favorite professor of negotiation is not an option here; you probably have about 30 seconds before it's too late.

In this chapter we follow the story of the two police officers who attended this incident. We use their story as a lens to explore what research over the last 25 years has taught us about negotiating crises, ranging from interventions to stop a suicide through to negotiations to stop terrorism. These interactions are typically characterized by a set of features that set them apart from traditional business negotiations or the interactions of students in experiments. As Taylor and Donohue (2006, p. 667) note, crisis negotiations are "not embedded in the traditional dynamics of normative thinking and good faith, but on the extreme dynamics of emotional arousal and anxiety. The negotiators must listen carefully, resist the temptation to react defensively, and work to build trust and cooperation." The need for the negotiators to think quickly and manage a set of high stakes can be stressful and challenging.

We examine the story of the two police officers at four time periods during the incident. This allows us to capture different aspects of the dynamics that shape an unfolding crisis. Figure 18.1 presents these periods along a timeline. Immediately apparent from this timeline is the importance of the first few minutes of interaction to crisis negotiation. The instant impression (e.g., first 30 seconds) and opening gambit (e.g., 5–10 minutes) of a negotiator is critical to how a crisis incident becomes framed

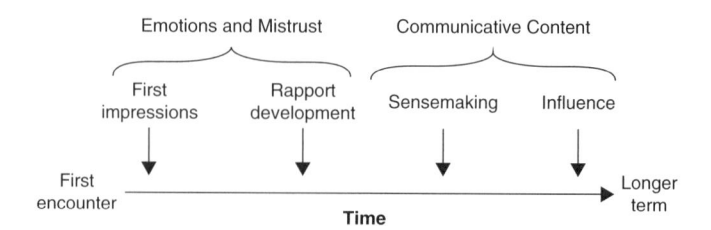

```
                Emotions and Mistrust          Communicative Content
              ⌒‾‾‾‾‾‾‾‾‾‾‾‾‾‾‾‾‾‾‾⌒       ⌒‾‾‾‾‾‾‾‾‾‾‾‾‾‾‾‾‾‾‾⌒
              First         Rapport
              impressions   development    Sensemaking   Influence
                 │             │              │             │
                 ▼             ▼              ▼             ▼
    First    ─────────────────────────────────────────────────────→  Longer
    encounter                     Time                                 term
```

Figure 18.1 A schematic overview of the interpersonal skills relevant to communicating with antagonistic individuals

and how it then unfolds. This period of the interaction is typically characterized by extreme emotions and mistrust, with perpetrators struggling for dominance and protecting their face rather than exchanging information or bargaining (Donohue et al., 1991). Sometimes, negotiations do not get past this stage. Indeed, a much cited anecdote in the literature is of the negotiation that lasted hours because the negotiator did not offer the perpetrator an opportunity to come out; the negotiation continued because the perpetrator, who has no expectation or 'script' about how the interaction should unfold, did not realize that surrendering was an option (McMains and Mullins, 2001).

A second noticeable feature of Figure 18.1, particularly in the latter time periods, is the focus on communication behaviors. This contrasts much of the negotiation literature, which has tended to focus on the impact of intrapersonal or contextual conditions on outcome rather than on the content of communication per se (Taylor and Donald, 2004; also Adair and Loewenstein, Chapter 12 this volume). While understanding the impact of 'population' variables (compare Guttman, 1992) is valuable to the development of negotiation theory, it is knowledge about content that is pertinent for practicing negotiators. When police negotiators attend an incident they have little control over who they are going to negotiate with, in terms of individual differences or experience, and little control over the nature of the bargaining space, in terms of the issues at hand and the background that has led to the crisis. They also have little influence over the setting in which the negotiations begin, since the location and timing of the incident are unilaterally set by the other side. They do, however, have control over what they are going to say. For that reason, most crisis negotiation research and training is focused on the communicative content of an interaction. In the second half of this chapter we outline conceptual frameworks that help negotiators make sense of perpetrator's dialogue, and review research that identifies the kinds of influence message that are effective at reducing cooperation.

A third important, though not unexpected feature of Figure 18.1 is the extent to which the four periods instantiate the stages of interaction proposed by phase models of negotiation. A phase model presents either a descriptive or prescriptive account of how coherent stages of communication fit together over time (Holmes, 1992). In relation to crisis negotiation, one often cited model is the Michigan State Police model, which proposes four phases of development, namely, establishing initial dialogue, building rapport, influencing, and surrender (Donohue et al., 1991; Madrigal et al., 2009). A similar, more detailed model is the Behavioral Change Staircase model developed by the FBI's Crisis Negotiation Unit (Vecchi et al., 2005). This model again emphasizes relationship development during early phases of interaction, which gives way to a focus on influencing the perpetrator's behavior in later phases. The importance of initial dialogue and building rapport map onto the first three snapshots that are presented in this chapter. The problem-solving and influence foci that characterize later phases map onto the fourth influence snapshot presented here. Thus, the principle underlying these models and the snapshots presented in this chapter are alike, and center on defusing the intense emotions of the perpetrator to achieve a calmer, more rational conversation about the issues at hand (Vecchi et al., 2005). Although these emotions may be especially present in suicide interventions and domestic disputes, which are cases often described as 'expressive' in nature, they can also be observed in more instrumental crises, such as kidnappings (Giebels and Taylor, 2009).

First Impressions

What occurred during the first few minutes of the incident in north London is a good example of why first impressions matter in crisis negotiations. The two negotiators attended the incident dressed in civilian suits and long coats. The suicidal man recognized this style of dress as typical of non-uniform police officers and yelled "no comment!" in anticipation that they were going to start questioning his intentions. One of the negotiators stood below the man, leaned on the roof of a nearby car to appear relaxed, and attempted to engage the man in dialogue. This aggravated the man and he shouted abuse at the officer for touching his car. Assessing that the man was familiar with police and unlikely to be quickly persuaded to step down, the negotiators began with a summary of what they could see, as opposed to what was being said: "My name is Dick and I work with the police to help people who may be considering killing themselves. I can see that you are three floors up, on the wrong side of the balcony, and that you have a noose around your neck. It appears to me that something has happened to you that has made you feel desperate for someone to hear what you have to say . . ."

A number of features of this opening encounter have their origins in research. For example, by communicating about what can be seen rather than inferring the likely feelings of the perpetrator, Dick is careful to avoid making assumptions or suggesting a degree of familiarity that may cause conflict (Arkowitz et al., 2008). This is consistent with a wider observation in terrorism research, which is that engagement with those promoting violence is more successful when focused on the act rather than on the underpinning ideology or motivation (Prentice et al., 2012). A negotiator can propose alternative, peaceful ways of accomplishing a goal without challenging the perpetrator's underlying belief system. Similarly, Dick selected his words carefully when conveying his reason for talking to the perpetrator, describing himself as working with the police as opposed to being from the police. Such subtle nuances in language have been shown to have a significant impact on the receiver's perceptions of the communicator (Donohue and Roberto, 1993). In this case, the negotiator hoped that it would reduce the perpetrators sense of being told what to do by an authority figure, thereby re-shaping the role dynamic to one of 'moving with' rather than 'moving against'.

The perpetrator's response was not atypical of what occurs. He responded "F—right. You bastards have stopped me seeing my kids and are going to put me away." This kind of high intensity 'face attack' is prominent in the language used by perpetrators in crises. For example, Rogan and Hammer (1995) showed that language intensity is highest in the early stages of an incident where the unfamiliar and overwhelming police response can trigger a fight or flight reaction. It also reappeared in prominence later in negotiations when parties reach the 'crunch point' where a decision has to be made (Rogan and Hammer, 1995). Their evidence mirrors that of Bilsky et al. (2005) who, using Gottschalk–Gleser's (1969) language-based hostility scale, showed that references to killing, destruction, and denial all mark periods of escalating conflict between police negotiator and perpetrator. However, critically, the increase in the occurrence of this hostile behavior was driven primarily by changes in perpetrator's dialogue. While it would be easy to respond to a perpetrator's aggression in kind, police negotiators tend to respond to such intensity in an empathic and calm manner. Indeed, such attacks are often an opportunity to learn more about the perpetrator's position, which in turn allows the police to align their dialogue with issues important to the perpetrator (we discuss how they do this in the next section).

Aside from the dialogue itself, a number of other interpersonal dynamics are occurring within this first encounter. When two strangers meet for the first time, it is inevitable that they will form initial impressions that impact on their expectations and willingness to cooperate. These impressions are made quickly (e.g., within 500 milliseconds, Willis and Todorov, 2006) and with minimal effort (Carlston and Skowronski, 2005). For example, experimental studies have shown that smell (Dematte et al., 2007), sound of voice (Ambady et al., 2000), and appearance (Willis and Todorov, 2006) each impact the way in which people perceive and react to a speaker. Such social signals may also play a role in crisis negotiations. For example, in their analysis of international aerial hijackings, Donohue and Taylor (2003) report relationships between the use of weapons and the authority's decision to act. In particular, they found a significant negative relationship between the extent to which the terrorists controlled and damaged the scene, as well as used their weapons, and the degree of capitulation by the authorities. Earlier analyses by Friedland and Merari (1992) suggest that these estimations are sensible, since they found a positive relationship between factors such as the degree to which terrorists were armed and their subsequent commitment to the act, reflecting an unwillingness to reach a peaceful resolution at all.

As well as first impressions, there is also compelling evidence that judgments of another's trustworthiness, and ensuing cooperation, is based on thin slice judgments of behavior. As Gladwell (2006) describes in his popular book, thin slicing is "the ability of our unconscious to find patterns in situations and people based on very narrow 'slices' of experience" (p. 23). Such thin slices have been shown to be predictive of later conflict in long-term relationships (Carrere and Gottman, 1999), and can be more accurate than explicit deliberations in judgments about another's intent (Albrechtsen et al., 2009). In terms of its impact on negotiation, Curhan and Pentland (2007) showed that conversational engagement, prosodic emphasis, and vocal mirroring during the first five minutes of a simulated employment negotiation predicted an average of 30 percent of the variance in negotiators' individual outcomes. The link with success is also referenced anecdotally in the crisis negotiation literature. For example, in their demonstration of the value of Verbal Interactional Analysis techniques, Fowler and DeVivo (2001) caution against the use of 'why' questions within the first five minutes of a negotiation, because it may be perceived as a challenge to the perpetrator's legitimacy.

Wilson (2000) expands on the notion of snap judgments and the expectations that these can create by discussing the role of cognitive scripts on people's behavior within a particular environment. In her examination of 160 hijacking and siege incidents, Wilson explored the nature of each incident by coding for the presence and absence of actions (e.g., use of weapons, treatment of hostages) by the terrorists and authorities. She found strong evidence of a consistency in the demands made and resources used by different terrorist groups across their attacks. These consistencies, Wilson argued, can be shown to have social or historic roots. For example, the fact that attacks perpetrated by the Japanese Red Army (JRA) are behaviorally similar to those perpetrated by the Popular Front for the Liberation of Palestine (PFLP) can be traced to the training that the JRA received from the PFLP in the 1970s.

Wilson et al. (2010) take the analysis of prior incidents one step further by showing that behavior choice depends on the type of victim targeted by the terrorists. Thus, specific kinds of attack are used for specific objectives, suggesting that a degree of planning and goal-driven behavior underlies such incidents. However, as Wilson et al. acknowledge, what is true for organized terrorist attacks may not be true for domestic hostage crises. Many perpetrators of these acts have no script to fall back on because it is the first time they find themselves in such a confrontation. In such a context, they may act according to beliefs about the accepted social roles in such contexts (Canter, 1990) and they may be responsive to the actions of others. In hostage crises, the understanding of accepted roles may come from past experience with the police or from exposure to media portrayals of negotiations. In such cases, police negotiators may play a 'pro-active' role in guiding the actions of perpetrators in the early stages (Taylor and Donohue, 2006). But they must be careful. Early aggression by the authorities can prompt reciprocal aggression and have devastating effects on the incident outcome (Taylor, 2002a).

Rapport Development

Once the first moments of the crisis negotiation are handled, negotiators must begin a more protracted interaction in which the aim is to promote calm and good rapport. One approach to achieving this, which is emphasized in the hostage negotiation literature, is active listening (Kelley, 1950; Royce, 2005). An active listener begins her or his response to the other party with a paraphrased summary of what the person has said. The Metropolitan Police Service's crisis negotiation course teaches this skill in three parts: focused listening, responsive listening, and communication encouragers. A focused listener pays close attention to the nature and content of what the perpetrator is saying in order to be able to accurately reflect back what it is they are trying to communicate. A responsive listener ensures that the perpetrator is able to say what she or he wishes without being interrupted or forced into changing content as a result of the listener's behavior. A listener using minimal encouragers will communicate positive backfeeds such as "uh-huh", "ok", and "go on" in order to demonstrate to the speaker that she or he is paying attention (Rogers, 1951).

Although active listening might appear a laborious or redundant process, it has a number of advantages. The first is that a summary can show that the other side's opinion and position is being respected. For example, Nugent's (1992; see also Nugent and Halvorson, 1995) case review showed that listening creates a positive perception on clients and led to better long-term practitioner–client relationships. Similarly, such acknowledgements have been shown to be important to reconciliation in conflict parties who do not feel listened to or understood (compare Ufkes et al., 2012). A second value of active listening is that it allows for the correction of errors in what the negotiator understands about the situation. A minor mistake is easily corrected, and the negotiator can ensure that she or he builds an accurate understanding of the other's position and thinking over time. A third advantage is that active listening can help dissipate the emotion and confrontation within the incident through a process called emotional labeling (Kennet, 2009). This technique relies on the negotiator observing the speaker's emotions, as displayed through intonation, word use, and body language, and then commenting on them. Consider the following short exchange that occurred in the London incident:

> Perpetrator: "Just get back and leave me alone"
> Negotiator: "I can't go back because you are angry"
> Perpetrator: "I am not angry I just want to be left alone."

By using a response that acknowledged a particular emotion (i.e., anger), the police negotiator learns a little more about the affective basis for the perpetrator's behavior (Van Hasselt et al., 2005).

The use of active listening is related to another apparent predictor of negotiation success, mimicry. The term mimicry refers to occasions when one person matches the speech patterns, facial expressions, postures, gestures, and mannerisms of their interlocutor (Chartrand et al., 2002; van Baaren et al., 2004; also Adair and Loewenstein (Chapter 12), and Druckman and Olekalns (Chapter 13), this volume). For example, Swaab et al. (2011) examined the outcome of online negotiations in which one party mimicked the language behavior of the other. They found that early mimicry was conducive to the mimicry of positive emotional language, which was associated with higher individual gain for the mimicker. By contrast, late mimickers tended to mimic language that was more accommodating of the other negotiator. Thus, the behavior of late mimickers served only to reduce the extent to which they protected their own interests. Taylor and Thomas' (2008) analysis of crisis negotiations showed a similar positive outcome for negotiators who were able to maintain mimicry across the interaction. They examined the degree to which police negotiators and perpetrators matched one another's language style across six periods of interaction as a function of whether the incidents ended in surrender (successful) or required tactic intervention (unsuccessful). They found that, in comparison to successful negotiations, unsuccessful negotiations were characterized by dramatic fluctuations in the degree of style matching across time, with negotiators and perpetrators periodically falling 'out of sync'. In analysing dialogue at the turn-by-turn level, Taylor and Thomas further uncovered how successful negotiators managed to maintain synchrony. Compared to their unsuccessful counterparts, the successful negotiators achieved greater coordination of turn taking, reciprocation of positive affect, and greater matching of language focused on the present rather than the past, and on alternatives rather than competition.

In recent unpublished work, Taylor and Conchie (2009) extended this finding by examining four levels of language mimicry in 18 crisis negotiations. Specifically, they measured lexical matching (i.e., common word choice), syntactic matching (i.e., common structuring of language), semantic matching (i.e., common matching of meaning) and situational matching (i.e., common framing of the situation). By examining these four levels of matching across six periods of interaction, Taylor and Conchie showed that early periods of interaction were driven by mimicry of basic lexical and syntactic form, rather than any coordination of strategic motivations or goals. The higher language levels of semantic and situational matching only came to the fore during later stages of interaction when negotiators began to deal with the substantive issues surrounding the crisis. This is some of the first evidence to suggest that cooperation emerges from a bottom-up process of synchrony as much as it does a top-down coming together of cognitive representations of the conflict and its possible solutions (compare Fusaroli et al., in press). It reinforces the importance of language choice and the behavior that techniques such as active listening promote.

Sensemaking

Over the next two hours of the north London incident, without making one suggestion as to how the man could recover his marriage or regain his job, the male took the noose off his neck, stepped inside the premises, and began talking through a door. These conversations centered not on the past but on the future, and on what options might allow the man to make his life more tolerable. This period of the interaction presented two challenges for the police negotiators. The first is that they had to work hard to make sense of the perpetrator's dialogue in order to understand his underlying motivations and goals. The second is that they had to present pertinent issues in a persuasive way in an effort to alter the perpetrator's attitudes and/or behaviors (compare Gass and Seiter, 1999). The issue of influence is considered in the next section. This section considers conceptual accounts that provide frameworks for helping negotiators make sense of the actions of the perpetrator.

A great deal of research in crisis negotiation has sought to better understand the types of goals or issues that drive crises toward and away from resolution. For example, studies using Relational Order Theory (Donohue, 2001; Donohue and Roberto, 1993) focus on how the relational dynamic between negotiators play out along dimensions of affiliation and interdependence. These studies show that crisis negotiations are characterized by a unique paradox of low affiliation but high interdependence, with both parties needing to find a way to interact with a disliked other party. Other research recognizes the importance of identity to crises and uses facework theory to better understand how utterances attack, defend and restore a person's identity or face. For example, Rogan and Hammer (1994) found that a hostage crisis ending in suicide contained more instances of the perpetrator attacking self-face than found in the other crises that they examined. Finally, some research focuses on the substantive nature of bargaining in crisis negotiation. For example, Pruitt (2006) discusses how substantive issues that are often identified by Western governments as non-negotiable may still be subject to 'negotiation' in secret backchannel talks. He showed that success in these interactions depends on the ability of both parties to manage the dissociation between the front-stage and the back-stage interactions.

According to Taylor (2002b, see also Bilsky et al., 2010; Taylor and Donald, 2004; 2007), each of these three foci of dialogue—the relational, identity, and substantive—reflects a different motivational goal or frame that will dominate interaction at any one particular time (Drake and Donohue, 1996). Each frame plays a more or less important role in the interaction depending on the current focus of each negotiator. The key for police negotiators is to align their framing of the incident with that of the perpetrator (Taylor, 2002b). For example, it is not useful to be making substantive offers when the perpetrator's primary concern is for their personal identity and the shame the incident will bring to his or her family. Equally, it is not useful to continue emphasizing trust and the need for mutual understanding when the perpetrator's concern has switched to sorting out how the incident is going to end. By focusing on an inappropriate frame, a negotiator is in danger of making the perpetrator feel misunderstood or unvalued, which may lead to further conflict spiraling and heightened emotions (Hammer and Rogan, 1997). Thus, a key skill for a police negotiator is being able to make sense of the perpetrator's dialogue and match his or her motivational goal.

Taylor (2002b) proposed making sense of these variations in language using three distinctions, which form a cylinder model. The spine of the cylinder differentiates a negotiator's overall orientation to interaction as either avoidant, competitive, or cooperative. An avoidant orientation is characterized by retractions from substantive discussion and a refusal to accept responsibility for events in the crisis (Sillars et al., 1982). This orientation may occur either because of the overwhelming nature of the situation, or because of a strategic wish to stonewall the negotiation's progress (Wang et al., 2012). A competitive orientation is expressed by behaviors that attack the other party's position (e.g., demands, threats) or credibility (e.g., personal attacks), while simultaneously restoring a personal position through positional arguing, boasting, and the rejection of compromises (Wilson and Putnam, 1990). These behaviors often form the bulk of interaction in hostage crises where the natural response to being surrounded is to push back—a phenomenon that Donohue and Taylor (2007) identify in many asymmetric negotiations and characterize as the "one-down effect". Finally, a cooperative orientation is associated with behaviors such as concessions, compliments, and messages aimed at building relationships (Donohue and Roberto, 1993). These behaviors often create a calmer, more normative discussion that leaves behind some of the unpredictability of crisis (Donohue et al., 1991).

Negotiators adopt one of these three orientations to pursue a variety of different concerns or goals. The second distinction proposed in the cylinder model characterizes these goals as driven by substantive, identity, or relational concerns. At any one point in time, a police negotiator may focus on gaining the release of hostages by using bargaining techniques such as appealing to the perpetrator's better nature and making offers of mutual exchange. This would be reflective of a substantive focus because the negotiator is using cooperative offers, concessions and information exchange to achieve an instrumental goal. By contrast, a perpetrator may use behaviors such as justifications, repeated interruptions, profanity, and insults to increase their power and personal self-worth. This behavior is less focused on an instrumental goal and more focused on attacking the police negotiator's identity while supporting self-identity. Finally, a negotiator may respond to these insults though dialogue that empathizes with the perpetrator's position and identifies points of commonality (Donohue, 2001). These messages are principally motivated by relational goals. Critically, an individual can pursue each of these motivational goals while adopting an avoidant, competitive or cooperative orientation to dialogue, creating nine communicative frames for understanding crisis interaction that form the cylinder model.

The final distinction, which was identified earlier in this chapter, is the intensity with which individuals communicate about a particular issue. The intensity of a negotiator's messages is an aspect of the interpersonal process that is easily overlooked when examining utterance content from a transcript without the original recording. High intensity dialogue includes anger and threats, profanity, obscure metaphors, and dramatic changes in paralinguistic cues that reflect a "deviat[ion] from neutrality" (Bowers, 1963). Such intensity has been found to be associated with threat conviction (Hamilton and Stewart, 1993), emotional stress (Bradac et al., 1979), and relational affect (Donohue, 2001). For example, relentlessly threatening action if a demand is not met signifies a high degree of concern for a substantive issue that is unlikely to dissipate until some form of agreement is made about the issue. Thus, language intensity focuses negotiators on one particular motivational goal, such that intensity often needs to be reduced before negotiations can move on to another issue or goal (Taylor, 2002b).

So how do police negotiators go about identifying the motivational frame of a perpetrator? One driver of their success is the use of active listening, as discussed above. However, according to Ormerod et al. (2008), they also show sensitivity to the 'status' of the interaction at any one time. Ormerod et al. found that police negotiators and perpetrators match one another's communicative goals and orientations for sustained periods, with this matching increasing over time for crises that end in the perpetrator surrendering, but decreasing over time for those that end violently. Part of this divergence in matching appeared to be due to the fact that, in successful incidents, police negotiators were more likely to switch their language style to that of the perpetrator. In the terms of Giles and Coupland's (1991) Communication Accommodation Theory, the police negotiators constantly adapt to the communication of the hostage taker in order to maintain or decrease the social distance and increase the amount of cooperation. They also varied the extent to which they talked or listened to the perpetrator at any one time. In successful resolutions, police negotiators reduced the amount they spoke by over 40 percent during transitional periods where the motivation frame of the perpetrators' speech and their own speech was not aligned. The negotiators appeared to recognize that they were no longer in sync with the perpetrator, and so held back from taking a dominate role in interaction in an attempt to retune their sense of the perpetrator's communication.

Influence Skills

Alongside listening and good communication, it is ultimately necessary for police negotiators to dissuade perpetrators from continuing their course of action. This they must do through effective influence and persuasion. There is considerable social psychological research on the contextual, personal, and message factors that define an influential message (Chaiken and Trope, 1999). Early work was grounded in the elaboration likelihood model (Petty and Wegner, 1999), and the distinction between a heuristic driven 'System 1' and rational 'System 2' level of information processing (Chen and Chaiken, 1999). It was also heavily influenced by Cialdini's (2007) identification of six principals of influence. For example, Cialdini showed that people are more likely to take a particular course of action when they believe others are also doing so; a principal referred to as social proof. Similarly, Freedman and Fraser (1966) showed that asking homeowners to display a leaflet in their window two weeks before asking them to place a billboard in their garden significantly raised the level of compliance to the billboard request; a principal referred to as commitment and consistency.

In crisis negotiation research, a number of authors have sought to identify effective influence strategies. Perhaps the most comprehensive is Slatkin (2010, p. 55), who identified 26 'stratagems' that he defined as "verbal techniques employed by a negotiator to advance the negotiations and promote a resolution". Derived from his professional experience and a review of the negotiation literature, these tactics represent concrete instances of arguments such as appealing to a higher authority, lowering expectations, the 'Yes' set (i.e., getting a used to responding in the affirmative) and good cop–bad cop. However, it is not clear which if any of the stratagems are supported by positive outcomes in previous incidents, or indeed tested in any experimental or case study analysis. The absence of such evidence is undoubtedly driven by the difficulties of obtaining for analysis sufficient transcriptions of incidents in which the stratagems were used. Equally, and perhaps more importantly, it may reflect a difficulty of isolating within an interaction the impact of one stratagem, given that even a few minutes of dialogue will contain the use of multiple tactics in a number of combinations.

One exception to the absence of empirical studies of influence comes from research by Giebels and colleagues. They have examined the use of influence in crisis negotiation using the "Table of Ten", a framework of ten influence tactics that was initially formulated from interviews with European negotiators and subsequently verified through an analysis of dialogue in Dutch and Belgian crisis negotiations (Giebels, 2002; Giebels

Table 18.1 The Table of Ten influence tactics

Tactic	Description of behavior
Being kind	All friendly, helpful behavior
Being equal	Statements aimed at something the parties have in common
Being credible	Behavior showing expertise or proving you are reliable
Emotional appeal	Playing upon the emotions of the other
Intimidation	Threatening with punishment or accusing the other personally
Imposing a restriction	Delay behavior or making something available in a limited way
Direct pressure	Exerting pressure on the other in a neutral manner by being firm
Legitimizing	Referring to what has been agreed upon in society or with others
Exchanging	Give-and-take behavior
Rational persuasion	Use persuasive arguments and logic

and Noelanders, 2004). The Table of Ten distinguishes between tactics that are primarily connected with the sender and his or her relationship with the other party (relational tactics), and tactics that are primarily connected with the content of the message and the information conveyed to the other party (content tactics). Specifically, the Table identifies three relational tactics that involve the police negotiator demonstrating empathy for the perpetrator's situation (being kind), identifying commonalities between self and perpetrator (being equal), and enhancing personal expertise and trustworthiness (being credible). It identifies seven content tactics that range from encouraging a perpetrator to rationally evaluate their position (rational persuasion), warning a perpetrator of possible consequences (intimidation), and appealing to the perpetrator's feelings and emotions as a way to engender cooperation (emotional appeals). Table 18.1 summarizes the tactics that comprise the Table of Ten. They serve as an example of the kinds of communicative codes that are examined in crisis negotiation research.

A number of studies have evaluated the relative use of these strategies and their relationship to peaceful outcomes. For example, Giebels and Noelanders (2004; see also Giebels and Taylor, 2012) found that siege, kidnap and extortion cases were dominated by instances of being kind, direct pressure, and rational persuasion. However, there were also notable differences, with extortion cases characterized by greater use of aggressive strategies such as intimidation, and sieges characterized by greater use of emotional appeals and efforts to promote credibility. Furthermore, Kamphuis et al. (2006) compared the use of influence strategies in three negotiation phases (initial encounter, problem-solving, and resolution) for relatively effective and ineffective crisis negotiations. They found that, in the initial as well as problem-solving phase of interaction, police negotiators used the strategy 'being equal' more often when they were effective. Similarly, and particularly for expressive type of incidents, the moving away strategy of 'imposing a restriction' was used less in effective than in ineffective negotiations. Finally, in the closure phase of interaction, Kamphuis et al. showed that legitimizing was positively associated with success in expressive cases, but negatively associated with success in instrumental cases. Of course, such differences require further examination. Yet they tentatively highlight the challenge that police negotiators face in selecting the most effective influence strategy at any one point in time. This is true whether it be a suicide intervention in a housing estate or a kidnapping of a wealthy businessman in the financial district.

The challenge associated with seeking the appropriate influence tactic is made clear by research on cross-cultural interactions. This research has shown how the norms and values that characterize an individual's cultural background can have a substantial effect on how they interpret messages and how they make strategic choices when negotiating. For example, Adair and Brett (2005) compared a group of negotiators from high-context cultures (e.g., Japan, Russia), whose communication is often implicit and reliant on social expectations, with a group of negotiators from low-context cultures (e.g., Germany, United States), whose communication is explicit with meaning transmitted through the message itself. They found that complementary sequences, in which both negotiators' messages are alike (e.g., both cooperative) but not identical, play a more central role for high-context communicators. Arguably, this is because the increased diversity of communication provides the flexibility needed to manage the indirect relational nature of the expected interaction.

Giebels and Taylor (2009) also examined the differences across high-context and low-context communicators but in the high-stakes context of hostage negotiation. They found that high-context hostage takers were less likely to engage in persuasive arguments or to respond to them positively, and that high-context perpetrators were more likely to reciprocate threats, particularly when they were made about self. This, they argue, is because high-context communicators expect strategic sequences to emphasize relational and identity issues over the exchange of rational arguments, such that they fail to engage in the persuasive sequences and respond negatively when the identity dynamic is challenged. The findings of Giebels and Taylor (2009) are consistent with subsequent findings of Beune et al. (2010). In the context of police interviewing, Beune et al. found that rational arguments were more effective in eliciting case-related personal information from low-context suspects than from high-context suspects. Furthermore, they showed that high-context rather than low-context suspects responded negatively to police acts of 'being kind' and 'intimidation', particularly when those messages were directed towards the social group rather than toward self.

Structural Factors

So far in this chapter we have explored the literature relating to crisis negotiations through the lens of a single case. Although many of the issues we describe are likely to be common to various forms of crisis negotiation, an interesting issue to consider is the extent to which different types of perpetrators and different types of threats change the dynamics that are encountered. They may do so, for example, by making one phase more or less salient during the unfolding interaction or by opening up new issues or phases not yet considered in this chapter.

One of the most longstanding attempts to categorize the variations observed in crisis negotiations is provided by the Federal Bureau of Investigation. They distinguish between incidents that are instrumental and incidents that are expressive (Van Hasselt et al., 2005). In instrumental crises, the nature of the interaction is far more business-like, with hostages being used by the perpetrators as 'bargaining chips' that can be traded for something that they desire. In expressive incidents, the interaction is driven by emotion and a need to counsel a perpetrator toward an alternative peaceful resolution of their crisis or predicament. Thus, while each of the four stages described above will occur across both kinds of incidents, the nature of what is important will change, as will the general communicative style of the negotiators.

An example of how the expressive versus instrumental nature of a crisis can shape an interaction is provided by Harvey-Craig et al.'s (1997) examination of UK prison sieges. They coded the occurrence and non-occurrence of 30 behaviors by perpetrators within each siege, such as the nature of the threats made, the degree of agitation and mood swings, the type of weapons used, and so on. They examined these data by identifying clusters of the kinds of behaviors that occurred within a single incident. They found that correlates of expressive prison incidents (e.g., those involving suicide threats) were not substantive demands or persuasive discussion, but physical and verbal aggression, and discussions around family issues. The sensemaking and influence that occurs in these expressive incidents is thus focused more around issues relating to self-esteem and affiliation than it is the substantive concerns of conceding to a set of demands around food and living standards.

In their analysis of terrorist negotiations, Donohue and Taylor (2003) took a different approach to the comparison of interaction types. They compared the use of tactics by terrorists and governments both as a function of contextual parameters, namely whether the incident was a hijacking or barricade-siege, and as a function of ideology, namely whether the terrorist was motivated by a nationalist-separatist, social-revolutionary, or religious fundamentalist ideology. In comparing the dynamics of incidents across these distinctions, Donohue and Taylor showed that aerial hijackings involved more overt power strategies than barricade-siege incidents, which were more likely to include aspect of bargaining for certain outcomes. Similar differences were observed across ideological background. Terrorists with a religious fundamentalist ideology typically engaged in more violence and less compromising strategies than terrorists with other ideological backgrounds.

Interestingly, Dechesne (2012) has recently shown that such 'structural' differences in the behavior and motivations of terrorist groups may be reflected, in part, in the organizational name that they choose to rally behind. For example, in comparison to nonviolent radical groups, those groups associated with violence tend to have names that refer to militancy, speak against a social reality rather than for a political change (e.g., 'liberation' versus 'fatherland'), and speak for action and combat rather than debate (e.g., 'guerrilla' versus 'congress'). Note that one factor that is not amongst these differences is a reference to Islam and Nationalism. Despite these concepts often being the focus of counter-terrorism efforts (Prentice et al., 2012), these terms are not typically associated with violent political engagement. Based on this kind of analysis, Dechesne proposes a metric— a T-value—that serves to predict the extent to which the behaviors of a terrorist group are likely to be centered on violence or aggressive dialogue.

FUTURE DIRECTIONS

There are many issues of theoretical and practical importance that are ripe for research in the crisis negotiation field. At a fundamental level, the extent to which findings from experimental research and other domains transfer to the unique context of crisis is far from understood. Indeed, issues such as an individual's long-term investment in identity and the significant consequences of failure provide compelling reasons to suspect that crisis negotiations are qualitatively different from interactions in other contexts (Donohue and Taylor, 2003). Exploring these similarities and differences will require inventive use of field data and experimental simulations. If transcripts are to be used, it will also require a significant effort on the part of the researchers to demonstrate their value and gain the trust of the police forces with whom they collaborate. However, the value of this research to developing our theoretical and practical understanding of crisis negotiation is significant. In the remainder of this section, we outline three areas where we feel contributions will have the most impact.

One area where knowledge continues to be limited is in relation to the dynamics of cross-cultural interactions. This is a particularly pressing shortcoming given the increasingly global nature of policing in the twenty-first century (Giebels, 1999). To some extent it may be possible for crisis negotiators to draw on the available experimental research on cross-cultural negotiations (e.g., Gelfand and Dyer, 2000). However, such work has two limitations. The first is that it has tended not to examine the communicative process of interaction as it occurs over time, which makes it difficult to extrapolate what if anything the negotiators did (as opposed to the contextual determinants) to influence the interaction's outcome. For example, in an analysis of act frequency, a negotiation that is characterized by relational development in the first half of the interaction and bargaining behaviors in the second half of the interaction will look identical to one in which bargaining dominates the first half and relational development dominates the second half. However, these two interactions will be very different qualitatively. Fortunately, there are now analytical techniques, such as phase analysis (Holmes, 1997), t-pattern analysis (Magnusson, 2000), and proximity coefficients (Taylor, 2006), which allow for more appropriate examination of the relationships among behaviors within an interaction sequence.

The second, perhaps more critical limitation is that research has tended to draw on comparisons of students from the US and from Asian countries. The challenges faced by the police are more wide-ranging than this, both in terms of breadth (i.e., the number of different cultures encountered) and in terms of depth (i.e., the variance within cultures, perhaps across communities). Thus, there is a significant need for more nuanced analyses of the communicative dynamic across different cultures. The recent analysis of Moroccan suspects by Beune et al. (2010) is an early example of this kind of research. It will be important for such research to strike a balance between providing more details of cultural variation on the one hand, and not regressing into a reductionist quagmire on the other. This will require the development of richer theoretical models than the dichotomous frameworks (e.g., between low- and high-context, tightness and looseness) that dominate the current literature (see Aslani et al., Chapter 10 this volume).

490 *Handbook of research on negotiation*

A second area ripe for future research is the development of our understanding of negotiator sensemaking. Almost all of the existing research on crisis negotiation has sought to understand how negotiator communication impacts on the dynamics and outcome of an interaction. Far less research has sought to gain a better understanding of how the negotiator or perpetrator understands, predicts and responds to the actions and inferred beliefs of their interlocutor. The accuracy of a negotiator's sensemaking is critical as it dictates the choice of responses in terms of how they frame their message and the tactics that they use. Consider, for example, an incident in which the police negotiator attributes a perpetrator's anger to his demands not being met rather than to his fear of being shot by the overbearing firearms team. In attempting to address the demands issue, the negotiator may use instrumentally framed communication, which is likely to be an appropriate response to somebody who has a concern about their substantive goals. However, in this scenario, such a response may jar with the perpetrator's framing of the conflict, making it less effective than if the negotiator had recognized and responded to the identity threat posed by the firearms.

The importance of studying sensemaking is demonstrated in Sillars et al.'s (2001) analysis of partners' *in vivo* thoughts during marital conflict. Sillars et al. videoed couples arguing and then replayed this recording to each partner, asking them to describe their thoughts and feelings as experienced across the interaction. Overall, spouses viewed their partner's communication in less favorable terms than their own. In particular, there was a negative correlation between the extent to which husband/wives believed they were acting in a confrontational manner; what one perceived as positive engagement the other often interpreted as confrontational. Husbands, in particular, perceived their messages as being far more cooperative than independent judges who rated their language use. Thus, interactants in conflict build opposing interpretative frameworks of what is being discussed, and it is important to begin to understand how this can impact the ability of crisis negotiators to affect a positive outcome. To attain this better understanding will likely require elaborate methodologies, such as the one used by Sillars et al., in which a negotiator's cognitions are captured alongside what she or he says.

A third area ripe for further research relates to the victims of crisis negotiation. Crisis negotiations are unique situations because human lives are used as some kind of bargaining chip in order to fulfill the demands of the perpetrators. This may involve one's own life, such as in the north London attempted suicide case, but often it also involves the lives of others who are captivated and used as leverage. Traditionally, the focus in hostage research has been on the way in which people deal with victimization, particularly in terms of dealing with its post-incident effects such as the development of a Post-Traumatic Stress Disorder (PTSD; van der Ploeg and Kleijn, 1989). Recently, Giebels et al. (2005) have argued that, because hostages and perpetrators are typically collocated during an incident, the psychological state and behavior of the hostage is likely to directly influence the process and outcomes of the negotiation. That is, whether or not hostages are being emotional, rational, quiet, or loud, is likely to have an impact on the perpetrators and their dealings with the police. Similarly, whether or not hostages decide to help or hinder the perpetrator, consider confronting them, or try to escape, all likely influences the negotiation process. In an initial effort to explore this possibility, Giebels et al. conducted semi-structured interviews with victims of siege and kidnapping incidents to draw out their experiences and their implications for crisis negotiations.

Giebels et al.'s interviewees reported both negative and positive feelings towards their captors, particularly after some time had passed. There was little evidence to suggest such positive feelings were the result of a "psychological artifact" (i.e., Stockholm syndrome); rather they resulted from normal social processes. One of Giebels et al.'s main findings regarding such processes was the remarkable difference in what victims of sieges and kidnappings experienced. While both reported feelings of helplessness and fear, the experience of uncertainty and isolation was much stronger for victims of kidnappings than for victims of sieges. In large part this was because the visible police actions and media attempts to cover the incidents led the siege victims to feel as though they were at the center of events. In contrast, kidnap victims were usually cut off from the outside world, which left them uncertain about the degree to which people were aware of the kidnapping and trying to help. This isolation also led them to report more issues around identity, especially when the kidnapping was protracted across weeks and months. These findings suggest that getting proof of life—a request by the police to see evidence that the victim is still alive—is not only important tactically but also psychologically: it may be the first sign of the outside world the victims encounter in a long time. Furthermore, the specific form may also be chosen in a way that it is able to provide moral support and reinforce the victim's identity.

CONCLUSIONS

In the end, the north London crisis was resolved peacefully. Other than one instance when an inappropriate use of humor resulted in the male going back to the balcony and place the noose around his neck, the male came out of his flat and was taken to hospital. An important factor contributing to this positive result was that the negotiators moved through the four stages identified in Figure 18.1: from the initial conscious effort to create a good first impression and set expectations about how the interaction was going to progress, to later stages where the interaction dynamic was more normative and dependent on the content of what was said. As research continues to refine our understanding of these stages, so negotiators in London and elsewhere will become better equipped to deal with crisis and those who threaten life.

REFERENCES

Adair, W.L. and Brett, J.M. (2005). The negotiation dance: Time, culture, and behavioral sequences in negotiation. *Organization Science*, *16*, 33–51.

Albrechtsen, J.S., Meissner, C.A., and Susa, K.J. (2009). Can intuition improve deception detection performance? *Journal of Experimental Social Psychology*, *45*, 1052–1055.

Ambady, N., Bernieri, F., and Richeson, J. (2000). Towards a histology of social behavior: Judgmental accuracy from thin slices of the behavioral stream. *Advances in Experimental Social Psychology*, *32*, 201–271.

Arkowitz, H., Westra, H., and Miller, W. (2008). *Motivational interviewing in the treatment of psychological problems*. New York: Guilford Press.

Beune, K., Giebels, E., and Taylor, P.J. (2010). Patterns of interaction in police interviews: The role of cultural dependency. *Criminal Justice and Behavior*, *37*, 904–925.

Bilsky, W., Tebrugge, B., and Webel-Therhorn, D. (2010). Escalation and deescalation in hostage-negotiation. In R.G. Rogan and F.J. Lanceley (eds), *Contemporary theory, research and practice of crisis and hostage negotiation* (pp. 119–140). Cresskill, NJ: Hampton Press.

Bilsky, W., Muller, J., Voss, A., and Von Groote, E. (2005). Affect assessment in crisis negotiation. An exploratory case study using two distinct indicators. *Psychology, Crime and Law*, *11*, 275–287.

Bowers, J.W. (1963). Language intensity, social introversion, and attitude change. *Speech Monographs*, *30*, 415–420.

Bradac, J.C., Bowers, J.W., and Courtwright, J.A. (1979). Three language variables in communication research: Intensity, immediacy and diversity. *Human Communication Research*, *5*, 257–269.

Canter, D. (1990). *Fires and human behaviour* (2nd edn). London: David Fulton.

Carlston, D.E. and Skowronski, J.J. (2005). Linking versus thinking: Evidence for the different associative and attributional bases of spontaneous trait transference and spontaneous trait inference. *Journal of Personality and Social Psychology*, *89*, 884–898.

Carrer, S. and Gottman, J. (1999). Predicting divorce among newlyweds from the first three minutes of a marital conflict discussion. *Family Processes*, *38*, 293–301.

Chaiken, S. and Trope, Y. (1999). *Dual processes in social psychology*. London: Guilford Press.

Chartrand, T., Cheng, C.M., and Jefferies, V.E. (2002). You're just a chameleon: The automatic nature and social significance of mimicry. In M. Jarymowicz and R.K. Ohme (eds), *Nature of automaticity*. Warsaw: IPPAN.

Chen M. and Chaiken, S. (1999). The heuristic-systematic model in its broader context. In S. Chaiken, and Y. Trope (eds), *Dual processes in social psychology*. London: Guilford Press.

Cialdini, R. (2007). *The psychology of persuasion*. New York: Collins Business Essentials.

Curhan, J.R. and Pentland, A. (2007). Thin slices of negotiation: Predicting outcomes from conversational dynamics within the first 5 minutes. *Journal of Applied Psychology, 92*, 802–811.
Dechesne, M. (2012). What's in a name? The representation of terrorism using political organization names. *Negotiation and Conflict Management Research, 5*, 269–288.
Dematte, M., Osterbauer, R., and Spence, C. (2007). Olfactory cues modulate facial attractiveness. *Chemical Senses and Medicine, 32*, 603–610.
Donohue, W.A. (2001). Resolving relational paradox: The language of conflict in relationships. In W.F. Eadie, and P.E. Nelson (eds), *The language of conflict resolution* (pp. 21–46). Thousand Oaks, CA: Sage.
Donohue, W.A. and Roberto, A.J. (1993). Relational development as negotiated order in hostage negotiation. *Human Communication Research, 20*, 175–198.
Donohue, W.A. and Taylor, P.J. (2003). Testing the role effect in terrorist negotiations. *International Negotiation, 8*, 527–547.
Donohue, W.A. and Taylor, P.J. (2007). Role effects in negotiation: The one-down phenomenon. *Negotiation Journal*, 307–331.
Donohue, W., Kaufmann, G., Smith, R., and Ramesh, C. (1991). Crisis bargaining in intense conflict situations. *International Journal of Group Tensions, 21*, 133–153.
Drake, L.E. and Donohue, W.A. (1996). Communicative framing theory in conflict resolution. *Communication Research, 23*, 297–322.
Fowler, R. and DeVivo, P.P. (2001). Analyzing police hostage negotiations with the verbal interactional analysis technique. *Journal of Police Crisis Negotiations, 1*, 83–97.
Freedman, J. and Fraser, S. (1966). Compliance without pressure: The foot-in-the-door technique. *Journal of Personality and Social Psychology, 4*, 195–203.
Friedland, N. and Merari, A. (1992). Hostage events: Descriptive profile and analysis of outcomes. *Journal of Applied Social Psychology, 22*, 134–156.
Fusaroli, R., Bahrami, B., Olsen, K., Roepstorff, A., Rees, G., Frith, C., and Tylen, K. (in press). Coming to terms: Quantifying the benefits of linguistic coordination. *Psychological Science*.
Gass, R.H. and Seiter, J.S. (1999). *Persuasion, social influence and compliance gaining*. Needham Heights, MA: Allyn and Bacon.
Gelfand, M. and Dyer, N. (2000). A cultural perspective on negotiation: Progress, pitfalls, and prospects. *Applied Psychology: An International, Review, 49*, 62–99.
Giebels, E. (1999). A comparison of crisis negotiation across Europe. In O. Adang and E. Giebels (eds), *To save lives: Proceedings of the first European conference on hostage negotiation* (pp. 17–27). Gravenhage, the Netherlands: Elsevier.
Giebels, E. (2002). Beinvloeding in gijzelingsonderhandelingen: De tafel van tien [Influencing in hostage negotiations: The table of ten]. *Nederlands Tijdschrift voor de Psychologie [Dutch Journal of Psychology], 57*, 145–154.
Giebels, E. and Noelanders, S. (2004). *Crisis negotiations: A multiparty perspective*. Veenendaal: Universal Press.
Giebels, E. and Taylor, P.J. (2009). Interaction patterns in crisis negotiations: Persuasive arguments and cultural differences. *Journal of Applied Psychology, 94*, 5–19.
Giebels, E. and Taylor, P.J. (2012). Cultural issues and communication in crisis negotiation. In M. St. Yves and P. Collins (eds), *The psychology of crisis intervention for law enforcement officers*. Montreal, Canada: Carswell.
Giebels, E., Noelanders, S.M. and Vervaeke, G. (2005). The hostage experience: Implications for negotiation strategies. *Clinical Psychology & Psychotherapy, 12*, 241–253.
Giles, H. and Coupland, N. (1991). *Language: Contexts and consequences*. Pacific Grove, CA: Brooks Cole.
Gladwell, M. (2006). *Blink: The power of thinking without thinking*. London: Penguin.
Gottschalk, L.A. and Gleser, G.C. (1969). *The measurement of psychological states through the content analysis of verbal behavior*. Berkeley, CA: University of California Press.
Guttman, L. (1992). The mapping sentence for assessing values. In H. Klages, H.J. Hippler, and W. Herbert (eds), *Werte und Wandel* (pp. 595–601). Frankfurt: Verlag.

Hamilton, N.A. and Stewart, B.L. (1993). Extending an information processing model of language intensity effects. *Communication Quarterly*, 41, 231–246.

Hammer, M.R. and Rogan, R.G. (1997). Negotiation models in crisis situations: The value of a communication-based approach. In R.G. Rogan, M.R. Hammer, and C.R. Van Zandt (eds), *Dynamic processes of crisis negotiation: Theory, research and practice* (pp. 9–23). Westport, CT: Praeger.

Harvey-Craig, A., Fisher, N.J., and Simpson, P. (1997). An explanation of the profiling of hostage incidents in HM prison services. *Issues in Criminological and Legal Psychology*, 29, 41–46.

Holmes, M.E. (1992). Phase structures in negotiation. In L.L. Putnam and M.E. Roloff (eds), Communication and negotiation (pp. 83–105). Newbury Park, CA: Sage.

Holmes, M.E. (1997). Optimal matching analysis of negotiation phase sequences in simulated and authentic hostage negotiations. *Communication Reports*, 10, 1–8.

Kamphuis, W., Giebels, E., and Noelanders, S. (2006). Effective influencing in crisis negotiations: the role of type of incident and incident phase [in Dutch]. *Nederlands Tijdschrift voor de Psychologie [Dutch Journal of Psychology]*, 21, 83–100.

Kelley, H. (1950). The warm-cold variable in first impressions of persons. *Journal of Personality*, 18, 431–439.

Kennett, R. (2009). *Crisis negotiation*. Unpublished PhD thesis at the University of Kent, Canterbury, UK.

Madrigal, D.O., Bowman, D.R., and McClain, B.U. (2009). Introducing the four-phase model of hostage negotiation. *Journal of Police Crisis Negotiation*, 9, 119–133.

Magnusson, M.S. (2000). Discovering hidden time patterns in behavior: T-patterns and their detection. *Behavior Research Methods, Instruments and Computers*, 32, 93–110.

McMains, M.J. and Mullins, W.C. (2001). *Crisis negotiations: Managing critical incidents and hostage situations in law enforcement and corrections* (2nd edn). Cincinnati, OH: Anderson Publishing.

Nugent, W. (1992). The affective impact of a clinical social worker's interviewing style: A series of single case experiments. *Research on Social Work Practice*, 2, 6–27.

Nugent, W.R. and Halvorson, H. (1995). Testing the effects of active listening. *Research on Social Work Practice*, 5, 152–175. Ormerod, T., Barrett, E., and Taylor, P.J. (2008). Investigative sensemaking in criminal contexts. In J.M. Schraagen, L.G. Militello, T. Ormerod, and R. Lipshitz (eds), *Naturalistic decision making and macrocognition* (pp. 81–102). Aldershot, UK: Ashgate.

Petty, R. and Wegner, D. (1999). The elaboration likelihood model: Current status and controversies. In S. Chaiken and Y. Trope (eds), *Dual processes in social psychology*. London: Guilford Press.

Prentice, S., Taylor, P.J., Rayson, P., and Giebels, E. (2012). Differentiating act from ideology: Evidence from messages for and against violent extremism. *Negotiation and Conflict Management Research*, 5, 289–306.

Pruitt, D.G. (2006). Negotiations with terrorists. *International Negotiation*, 11, 371–394.

Rogan, R. and Hammer, M. (1994). Crisis negotiations: A preliminary investigation of facework in naturalistic conflict. *Journal of Applied Communication Research*, 22, 216–231.

Rogan, R. and Hammer, M. (1995). Assessing message affect in crisis negotiations: An exploratory study. *Human Communication Research*, 21, 553–574.

Rogers, C. (1951). *Client-centered therapy*. Boston, MA: Houghton Mifflin.

Royce, T. (2005). The negotiator and the bomber: Analyzing the critical role of active listening in crisis negotiation. *Negotiation Journal*, 21, 5–27.

Sillars, A., Coletti, S.F., Parry, D., and Rogers M.A. (1982). Coding verbal conflict tactics: Nonverbal and perceptual correlates of the "avoidance-distributive-integrative" distinction. *Human Communication Research*, 9, 83–95.

Sillars, A., Roberts, L.J., Dun, T., and Leonard, K. (2001). Stepping into the stream of thought: Cognition during marital conflict. In A. Sillars, L.J Roberts, T. Dun, and K. Leonard (eds), *Attribution, communication behavior, and close relationships* (pp. 193–210). New York: Cambridge University Press.

Slatkin, A.A. (2010). *Communication in crisis and hostage negotiations: Practical communication techniques, stratagems, and strategies for law enforcement corrections, and emergency service personnel in managing critical incidents* (2nd edn). Springfield, IL: Charles Thomas.

Swaab, R.I., Maddux, W.W., and Sinaceur, M. (2011). Early words that work: When and how virtual linguistic mimicry facilitates negotiation outcomes. *Journal of Experimental Social Psychology, 47*, 616–621.

Taylor, P.J. (2002a). A partial order scalogram analysis of communication behavior in crisis negotiation with the prediction of outcome. *International Journal of Conflict Management, 13*, 4–37.

Taylor, P.J. (2002b). A cylindrical model of communication behavior in crisis negotiations. *Human Communication Research, 28*, 7–48.

Taylor, P.J. (2006). Proximity coefficients as a measure of interrelationships in sequences of behavior. *Behavioral Research Methods, 38*, 42–50.

Taylor, P.J. and Conchie, S.M. (2009). *How do Chameleons bake bigger pies? Dissecting the layers of behavioral alignment in negotiation.* Presentation given at the June 2009 conference of the Interactional Association of Conflict Management. Kyoto, Japan.

Taylor, P.J. and Donald, I.J. (2004). The structure of communication behavior in simulated and actual crisis negotiations. *Human Communication Research, 30*, 443–478.

Taylor, P.J. and Donald, I.J. (2007). Testing the relationship between local cue-response patterns and global dimensions of communication behavior. *British Journal of Social Psychology, 46*, 273–298.

Taylor, P.J. and Donohue, W.A. (2006). Hostage negotiation opens up. In A. Schneider and C. Honeymoon (eds), *The negotiator's fieldbook* (pp. 667–674). New York: American Bar Association Press.

Taylor, P.J. and Thomas, S. (2008). Linguistic style matching and negotiation outcome. *Negotiation and Conflict Management Research, 1*, 263–281.

Ufkes, E.G., Giebels, E., Otten, S., and Van der Zee, K.I. (2012). The effectiveness of a mediation program in symmetrical versus asymmetrical neighbor-to-neighbor conflicts. *International Journal of Conflict Management, 23*, 440–457.

van Baaren, R., Holland, R., Kawakami, K., and van Knippenberg, A. (2004). Mimicry and prosocial behavior. *Psychological Science, 15*, 71–74.

van der Ploeg, H.M. and Kleijn, W.C. (1989). Being held hostage in the Netherlands: a study of long term aftereffects. *Journal of Traumatic Stress, 2*, 153–169.

Van Hasselt, V.B., Flood, J.J., Romano, S.J., Vecchi, G.M., de Fabrique, N., et al. (2005). Hostage-taking in the context of domestic violence: Some case examples. *Journal of Family Violence, 20*, 21–27.

Vecchi, G.M., Van Hasselt, V.B., and Romano, S.J. (2005). Crisis (hostage) negotiation: Current strategies and issues in high-risk conflict resolution. *Aggression and Violent Behavior, 10*, 533–551.

Wang, Q., Fink, E.L., and Cai, D.A. (2012). The effect of conflict goals on avoidance strategies: What does not communicating communicate? *Human Communication Research, 38*, 222–252.

Wilson, S.R. and Putnam, L.L. (1990). Interaction goals in negotiation. In J. Anderson (ed.), *Communication yearbook 13* (pp. 374–406). Newbury Park, CA: Sage.

Willis, J. and Todorov, A. (2006). First impressions, making up your mind after a 100-ms exposure to a face. *Psychological Science, 17*, 592–598.

Wilson, M.A. (2000). Toward a model of terrorist behavior in hostage-taking incidents. *Journal of Conflict Resolution, 44*, 403–424.

Wilson, M.A., Scholes, A., and Brocklehurst, E. (2010). A behavioural analysis of terrorist action: The assassination and bombing campaigns of ETA between 1980 and 2007. *British Journal of Criminology, 50*, 690–707.

PART VI

CONCLUSION

19. Guiding new directions in negotiation research: a negotiation context levels framework
Wendi L. Adair and Mara Olekalns

The complexity of negotiation is often attributed to three factors: (1) parties have distinct interests, (2) parties do not have full information about their counterparts, and (3) parties are dependent on one another for agreement (Lax and Sebenius, 1986). The *Handbook of Negotiation Research* traces the roots of negotiation complexity even deeper by reviewing research that has uncovered many more sources of complexity at four levels. Factors that create uncertainty for negotiators and challenges for researchers include, but are not limited to, emotion, cognitive biases, and motivation at the level of the individual negotiator; power dynamics and trust at the level of social interaction; the impact of communication medium on verbal and nonverbal expression and strategy interpretation at the level of communication processes; and the ever-changing face of the institutional environment within which complex negotiations occur. What highlights the complexity of negotiation even further, as made salient by all of our authors, is that these factors occur simultaneously, interacting at different levels, and changing over time.

In our introductory chapter, we discussed three themes that appear across the different Handbook sections: temporal horizons, uncertainty and sense-making, and context and subjectivity. We traced the appearance of these three themes across levels of negotiation with increasing complexity: the individual, the social interaction, the communication process, and complex negotiations. We illustrated the multi-level nature of negotiation by showing that these factors play a role regardless of whether one is considering an individual negotiator, a dyad, an intra- or inter-team negotiation, or a multi-party negotiation. In our concluding chapter, we build on our observations in the Introduction to develop a multi-level conceptual framework that highlights specific new directions to advance negotiation research. We model negotiation complexity on three levels: surface- versus deep-level characteristics of the negotiator and the negotiation; proximal versus distal temporal factors; and local versus global contextual factors.

In this concluding chapter of the Handbook, we first summarize the research directions recommended by our chapter authors, focusing on questions relating to different levels of negotiator characteristics, time, and context. We then present our multi-level conceptual framework and define future directions for researchers to tackle in the coming decade.

FUTURE DIRECTIONS: RECOMMENDATIONS FROM THE EXPERTS

We asked our chapter authors to identify the most promising research questions within their subfield of negotiation, and to share their most exciting insights about where they see the field going. We hope these suggestions will stimulate research ideas for doctoral students and more seasoned researchers, insights and directions for practitioners in the field, and fruitful collaborations among these groups. Across all our chapters, authors stressed the need to broaden our questions and methods to capture the complexity of negotiation. We consider their recommendations as related to the individual, the role of time, and the broader negotiation context.

The Individual Negotiator

Several authors note that researchers have mostly studied individual factors in isolation, and recommend that future research consider how different individual factors interact to predict negotiation processes and outcomes. Koning and Van Dijk suggest that we examine interactive effects of multiple motives, for example social motivation and epistemic motivation. Lewicki and Polin call for a look into the relationship between personality factors and negotiators' propensity to trust. Adair and Lowenstein propose examining how the nonverbal cues that accompany verbal speech affect negotiator interpretation, response, and negotiation outcome.

Likewise, Van Kleef and Sinaceur note that researchers have not yet examined emotions in combination. We know from broader emotion research that while North Americans tend to experience one emotion at a time (e.g. I feel happy *or* sad), Asians can simultaneously experience seemingly paradoxical emotions (e.g. I feel both happy *and* sad) (Perunovic et al., 2007), suggesting that negotiators' national culture is another interesting variable to consider along with the experience and consequences of negotiators holding multiple emotions. Sondak and his co-authors highlight the importance of emotion as a variable for better understanding how parties in multi-party negotiations manage uncertainty.

Several chapter authors note that commonly studied social, communication and complex processes can be informed by a closer look at individual factors. For example, Druckman and Olekalns suggest that the literature on critical moments in negotiation can be advanced by a closer study of negotiator expectations, flexibility, and resilience. This idea is related to recent work developing ways to measure negotiators' chronic versus adaptive (i.e. flexible) conflict orientation (Coleman and Kugler, 2011). Friedman and Belkin question whether the benefits of e-negotiation may be stronger for negotiators who are introverted versus extraverted. And, Wells and colleagues note that in the field of crisis negotiations, personality and national culture are understudied areas.

In the chapter on negotiator power and status, the authors recommend that future research focus on within individual and within dyad microprocesses. The four-state model of power (potential power, perceived power, power tactics, and realized power) can be used to guide research on individual and dyadic power dynamics in terms of resources, perceptions, strategy and nonverbal expression (Kim et al., 2005). The dynamics of gaining, managing, and losing power can be studied as within negotiator, dyadic, or group microprocesses to enrich our understanding of the formation and maintenance of coalitions in multi-party negotiation (Polzer et al., 1998).

Several authors also note the importance of studying individual factors between negotiators, for example using actor–partner models to capture the effects of separate negotiators as well as the dyad as a whole. As noted by Overbeck and Kim, power and status are inherently social, where power "depends only on the relatively objective balance of dependence between the negotiating parties," and status must be recognized and conferred by others as it "relies on the continued consent and deference of the lower-status party". Turning to trust, Lewicki and Polin introduce the concept of trust congruence, suggesting that whether negotiators have similar or dissimilar levels of trust in each other will affect the negotiation. Finally, Wells, Taylor, and Giebels stress that sense-making as a dyadic or group social process can have critical implications for the success of a negotiation. Researchers will improve our understanding of such inherently social constructs (e.g. power, trust, and even reciprocity) by modeling both actor and partner effects when predicting negotiation outcome.

The Role of Time

The chapter on crisis negotiation shows us an extreme, real-world case of negotiating under time pressure. As the chapter opens, we meet a crisis negotiator who arrives on a suicide threat scene and has about 30 seconds to observe the situation, select a strategy, and prevent a tragedy. What can research on decision making and concession patterns in transactional negotiation tell us about how to negotiate in a high stakes, high emotion hostage or terrorist negotiation? As suggested by research on anchoring (Galinsky and Mussweiler, 2001), and thin slicing (Curhan and Pentland, 2007), "instant impressions (e.g. first 30 seconds) and opening gambits (e.g. 5–10 minutes)" are critical to how a negotiation is framed and unfolds (Wells et al., Chapter 18 this volume, p. 473). A broader temporal question posed by Adair and Loewenstein is how we can borrow from other fields in psychology, communication, or philosophy to expand our conceptualization of how negotiations develop and progress over time beyond the popular idea of negotiators enacting a script.

Many authors likewise recommend we adopt a temporal lens and study more emergent and dynamic negotiation processes. Liu and Cai suggest that researchers track the emergence of shared cognition and shared identity using multisource ratings and event history recording or diary methods that allow for temporal modeling. A field setting would allow negotiators to record ratings at multiple points across time, as well as record ratings about the self and counterparts. Van Kleef and Sinaceur also propose multi-level models to examine how negotiator affect shifts across time. Combining these ideas with the chapter on turning points, researchers might test what critical moments can alter emotions that negotiators bring with them to the table.

Effects across multi-round negotiations or "spillover" are other hot topics for future research. Adair and Loewenstein question whether strategic communication, emotional expression, and relationship development in one negotiation can impact subsequent negotiations that occur at a later point in time. Crump develops several testable questions about international trade negotiations by applying temporal theory predictions to the study of role and linkage effects across multi-round negotiations. Höglund and Druckman suggest using qualitative time series analyses to understand the progression of peace negotiations across time as well as their durability. Gray and Wondolleck also propose studying how changes in perspectives, actors, and institutions over time can move seemingly intractable conflicts towards agreement.

Turning points and critical incidents are also identified as an area worthy of future research. Lewicki and Polin ask not only what types of turning points or critical incidents cause changes in trust levels, but also how negotiators' can either proactively or reactively manage breaches of trust during a negotiation. Research on feedback loops and linkage effects should also inform our understanding of critical incidents within a broader temporal framework (e.g. Crump (Chapter 15), Druckman and Olekalns (Chapter 13), this volume).

Negotiation Context

Context is a broad construct that researchers define in many different ways. It is interesting to note that in the Individual Processes section, most authors refer to context as institutions and external environments, relating closely to the research topics addressed in the section on Complex Negotiations. In the section on Social-Psychological Processes, most chapter authors discuss the negotiation context in terms of belief systems related to ethical standards, gender roles, and cultural sources of self-worth. Both forms of context can influence and constrain negotiators' perceptions, actions, and performance, and are fertile ground for future negotiation research.

In her discussion of research on individual differences, Elfenbein suggests that negotiation researchers interested in personality must also consider the role of the situation. Personality research has shown stronger personality effects at work in weak situations, characterized by few rules and systems, than strong situations, characterized by strict rules and norms (Tett and Burnett, 2003). Similarly, negotiation researchers have found that gender effects are maximized when there is ambiguity about when and what to negotiate; and gender differences dissipate as situations become stronger (Bowles et al., 2005; Kulik and Olekalns, 2012; see also Stuhlmacher and Linnabery, Chapter 9 this volume). Both conceptually and theoretically, our field needs to identify concrete indicators of weak versus strong situations, perhaps depending on the particular institutional environment or the degree of external policies and rules.

Crossing levels, researchers might examine whether the individual level effects of negotiator personality are stronger in weak negotiation situations, for example the typical dyadic or multi-party negotiation simulations used in lab research, versus in strong situations, for example highly regulated trade negotiations (see Crump, Chapter 15 this volume) or environmental negotiations (see Gray and Wondelleck, Chapter 17 this volume). Koning and Van Dijk suggest a potential relationship between negotiators' social motivation and adherence to external rules and norms, such that the situation strength or context might moderate effects of social value orientation (SVO) on processes and outcomes. These authors also note that we may have better luck linking individual differences to outcome if we choose personality variables relevant to a particular negotiation context.

The negotiation context includes the legal and belief systems within which a negotiation occurs and impacts on negotiators' trust, ethics, fairness, justice, and deception. Distinguishing these constructs, for example answering what it means for a negotiator to behave ethically versus fairly

(Diekman et al., Chapter 8 this volume) depends on the negotiation context as well as the individual and cultural characteristics of the negotiator. For example, there is ample research evidence of national culture variation in the degree to which fairness norms (e.g. equality, equity, need) are endorsed (Fischer and Smith, 2003); and moral standards are defined as a socially shared construct, meaning they are defined differently by distinct social groups (e.g. national culture, profession, industry). Thus, models of why and when negotiators enact fairness and ethical behavior should include individual, social, and temporal factors (Volkema and Rivers, 2012).

Chapters on both gender and on culture suggest that future researchers employ a theoretical lens that accounts for the role of context in terms of belief systems and structural factors. Stuhlmacher and Linnabery propose that research on gender in negotiation use open systems theory (see Bendersky and McGinn, 2010) to generate predictions about the role of our physical and social environment, belief systems (Eagley and Wood, 2012), and negotiation context (e.g. "gendered negotiation" (Kolb and McGinn, 2009)) to predict social role congruence and subsequent negotiation behavior and performance. Aslani and colleagues propose the Honor, Dignity, Face (HDF) framework (Leung and Cohen, 2011), which uses a historical and anthropological approach to identify culture prototypes and operates at the level of cultural belief systems and human motivation, to predict strategy sequences in different negotiation settings.

Sondak, Neale, and Mannix discuss how negotiators manage uncertainty given different negotiation contexts defined by who is at the table: intra-team negotiation, inter-team negotiation, multi-party negotiation, or marketplace negotiations where not only the identity but also the number of buyers and sellers is unknown. Similar issues are discussed in a broader context in the chapters on trade, peace, and environmental negotiations, which also add the regulatory and scientific environments, parallel (linked) negotiations and ideology as variables that shape context. Another way to conceptualize negotiation context is the space within which negotiators search for agreement, as illustrated by recent research that traces patterns of offers through a problem space (Prietula and Weingart, 2011). Such methods can be used to study the interaction of verbal and nonverbal communication both within and across negotiators.

Yet another way to conceptualize negotiation context is based on the mode of communication or environment in which negotiators interact. Friedman and Belkin propose that future research test an "into the wind" strategy that involves negotiators switching between face-to-face and electronic media over time, responding to needs for cognitive complexity versus relationship building. Negotiation researchers are encouraged to test these propositions along with individual and contextual moderators. For example, the benefits of e-negotiation may be stronger for negotiators who are introverted versus extraverted but the benefits may be less evident when a negotiation task is very complex versus simple.

The broadest way to conceptualize context is represented in the complex negotiation chapters where Crump notes, most negotiations are part of a network, "embedded within a constellation of many other negotiations" (Crump, Chapter 15 this volume, p. 387). Crump notes that while our understanding of international trade negotiations has advanced significantly in the past 10 years, there are many contextual factors we still know little about, for example the relationship between informal trade dispute negotiations and formal WTO sanctioned dispute resolution procedures. Höglund and Druckman note that the literature on peace negotiations has focused almost entirely on the resolution of armed conflict where the players are governments. Researchers have failed to consider other related forms of conflict resolution such as community or electoral disputes, where neither party is a state actor and violence is not present. Gray and Wondolleck identify intractable conflict and mandated negotiation as two forms of environmental negotiation that have not been studied widely.

RECOMMENDATIONS: A NEGOTIATION CONTEXT LEVELS FRAMEWORK

Across the four *Handbook* sections, we see consistency in authors' suggestions to account for variables and processes at other levels, use experimental methods to isolate causality, and utilize multi-level methods to analyse data. It is not surprising that as our knowledge about negotiation processes grows, our research questions and methods become deeper and more complex. But there is danger in simply calling for more complexity, without a theoretical rationale to direct research questions and guide theory development. Based on the many promising themes and methods our authors have targeted for new directions, we propose a multi-level conceptual framework that highlights specific new directions to advance negotiation research.

The Negotiation Context Levels Framework (Table 19.1) suggests that new research questions address the negotiation context at and across three different levels: surface versus deep factors related to the individual negotiator and negotiation; proximal versus distal factors related to time; and local versus global factors related to the environment. Following, we define each of these levels and review the theoretical rationale for using context levels to direct future negotiation research. Using the 2 × 2 × 2

Table 19.1 Negotiation context levels framework

	Proximal		Distal	
	Surface	Deep	Surface	Deep

Local	Strategy
	Sequences
	Mimicry
	Synchronicity
	Nonverbal cues
	Face-to-face
		Emotion
		Motivation
		Physiological
		  response
		Power
			Phases
			Turning points
			Temporal
			  distance
			E-negotiation
			Linguistic
			  convergence
				Trust
				Trust repair
				Psychological
				  distance
				Frame
				  convergence
				Resilience
				Shared identity

Global	Coalitions
	Faultlines
	Multi-party
	  negotiations
	E-negotiations
	Virtual
	  negotiations
		Belief systems
		Culture
		Gender
		Status
			Spillover
			Multi-round
			  negotiations
				Laws
				Institutional
				  norms
				Policy
				Weak versus
				  strong
				  situation

framework, we identify many promising and specific new directions for researchers to tackle in the coming decades.

Surface- versus Deep-level Characteristics

The lowest level of the Negotiation Context Levels Framework considers characteristics and behaviors of the negotiator (see Table 19.1, columns 1 and 3 (surface) and columns 2 and 4 (deep)). Much of the existing research on individual negotiators as well as negotiator communication can be characterized as addressing surface- versus deep-level factors. In the organizational diversity literature, surface characteristics refer to visible diversity cues, for example ethnicity, age, or gender, while deep-level diversity refers to invisible characteristics such as education level, values, or political orientation (Harrison et al., 2002). In the negotiation context, we propose that the surface level refers to the strategy and communication in use (e.g. nonverbal cues, strategy sequences), whereas a negotiator's invisible, deep level refers to cognition and affect, such as emotion and motivation (e.g. anger, cooperativeness).

While we know a lot about negotiators' surface factors (e.g. power or strategy sequences) or deep factors (e.g. personality or trust) in isolation, we know very little about how they work together within or across negotiators (for an exception, see research on social value orientation and strategy sequences by Olekalns and Smith, 1999; 2003). In the organizational diversity literature, Phillips and Loyd (2006) show that teams with a combination of surface- and deep-level diversity are more open to dissenting opinion and new information than teams with just one form of diversity. Thus, negotiation dyads and groups with a combination of surface- and deep-level diversity might exchange more information and generate more creative solutions. Diversity researchers have also shown that there are different effects of surface- and deep-level diversity depending on diverse team members' need for cognition (Kearney et al., 2009), suggesting negotiation researchers should also examine individual level moderators.

A recent meta-analysis of nonverbal communication channels and SVO by Swaab and colleagues (2012) provides another example of the interactive effects of surface- and deep-level characteristics. The analysis shows that when more communication channels are present in a negotiation (the channels included in the meta-analysis were sight, sound, and synchronicity), neutral negotiators achieve higher quality outcomes, non-cooperative negotiators achieve poorer quality outcomes, and cooperative negotiators' outcomes are not affected (Swaab et al., 2012). Another study of surface- and deep-level factors showed differential effects of vocal paralanguage (a surface-level factor) for negotiators from East Asia versus North America (a deep-level factor) (Semnani-Azad and Adair, in press).

In recent years, negotiation researchers have begun investigating several novel deep-level negotiation characteristics. Kray and Haselhuhn (2007) have shown that negotiators who believe negotiating attributes are malleable (incremental theorists) outperform negotiators who believe negotiating attributes are fixed (entity theorists). Appelt and colleagues have brought regulatory focus to the negotiation arena, showing that buyers, who are prevention focused because they want to minimize monetary loss, and sellers, who are promotion focused because they want to maximize monetary gain, perform better when their role "fits" with their chronic dispositional or experimentally induced regulatory focus (Appelt et al., 2009, see also, Galinsky et al., 2005). We see several promising avenues for future research to examine such deep-level negotiator characteristics between negotiators and also in conjunction with surface-level strategy and communication factors.

From the literature on organizational diversity, we know that while surface-level characteristics challenge diverse teams more at early stages, it is deep-level diversity that presents more long-term and difficult challenges. When team members develop a shared identity and learn to work collaboratively, surface-level diversity becomes less striking and apparent, but deep-level value differences (for example efficiency versus quality) continue to challenge teamwork. Translating these findings to a negotiation context suggests that we should consider different and interactive effects of negotiators' surface- and deep-level characteristics over time (see below – Crossing levels: Negotiation Characteristics and Time).

Research on subgroup formation along demographic based faultlines has found that faultline groups are less likely to form a shared identity or share information and more likely to experience conflict than no-faultline groups, although these effects can be reduced by moderators such as openness to experience and shared group objectives (both deep-level characteristics) (see Thatcher and Patel, 2011 for a recent meta-analysis). These findings have implications for the role of negotiator characteristics in subgroup and alliance formation in intra-team and multi-party negotiations. For example, Olekalns et al. (2007) show that, in three-party negotiations, the negotiator who accrues the most trust also obtains the greatest share of resources.

Framing research questions in terms of negotiators' surface and deep characteristics can also offer new predictions for existing dependent measures, for example linguistic convergence, frame convergence, or physiological response. Researchers have found higher levels of the hormone oxytocin when people are trusting and altruistic, offering a physiological-based explanation for how humans regulate conflict (De Dreu et al., 2010; Zak et al., 2005). Researchers proposing that negotiators' physiological stress responses, which may arise from anxiety or expectation violation, are a key determinant of behavior in intragroup negotiation, suggest a new line of research examining the effect of negotiators' deep-level threat versus challenge responses on negotiation outcome (de Wit et al., 2011). Understanding negotiators' underlying physiology and neurocognitive bases can help us understand how variables such as trust, power, communication, and deadlines shape negotiators' actions. Importantly, this line of inquiry may give insight into underlying mechanisms and provide a unified explanation of how these social-psychological variables affect the negotiation process.

The final, deepest level to examine individual negotiators is at the neural level. Recent research on cognition and decision making has begun examining areas of the brain that are activated when people engage in decision making tasks (Sanfey, 2007). For example, Aronson and colleagues report fMRI data highlighting activity in the emotion regions of the brain, along with areas related to cognition, following the receipt of or rejection of an unfair offer (Aronson et al., 2003). McCarthy et al. (2010) have found neural evidence of cultural differences in language processing that demonstrate more deliberative processing by German negotiators than U.S. negotiators. In the future, researchers can use neuroimaging techniques to examine negotiators' reactions to surface-level characteristics, such as negotiation strategy, or deep-level characteristics, such as trust, to determine what factors elicit more emotional versus more cognitive responses.

Proximal versus Distal Temporal Factors

The second context level in our framework refers to proximal versus distal temporal horizons (see Table 19.1, columns 1 and 2 (proximal) and columns 3 and 4 (distal)). From the literature on construal level (Trope and Lieberman, 2010; reviewed in Friedman and Belkin, Chapter 14 this volume), we know that there are many ways in which we perceive people, objects, and events across space and time. People experience things perceived as distant from the self in a more abstract, holistic manner, which tends to also be more simple and concrete. Examples offered by Trope and Lieberman include seeing a "distant forest" (higher-level construal across spatial distance) that becomes "many distinct species of coniferous trees" as we move closer to it (lower-level construal with spatial closeness) or a student describing end of the term "studying" (higher-level construal with temporal distance) that becomes more specific "reviewing the textbook and quizzes" (lower level construal with temporal closeness) as the final exam approaches. Thus, people tend to use a higher, more abstract level of construal to represent people, objects, and events that are more distal (over time, space, etc.).

We propose that construal-level theory can help define future negotiation research questions by considering negotiation factors that vary in temporal proximity. Proximal characteristics of the negotiation may include a negotiator's feelings, motivations, and perceptions, as well as strategy use during a particular negotiation session. In our framework, distal refers to factors that occur either over time or across temporal distance. In other words, the study of phases, turning points, and spillover across multi-round negotiation are all investigations of distal phenomena.

Construal-level theory can be used to help with construct definition and operationalization of proximal versus distal variables. For example, trust can be operationalized with specific cooperative acts (e.g. information sharing, positive reciprocity) at the negotiation table but at a higher level of abstraction (e.g. expectations for follow-through and future cooperation) when examining longer-term negotiation outcomes. Likewise, the study of strategy frequencies or sequences represent proximal communication indicators; a more distal conceptualization of communication processes might include linguistic convergence or phase analysis as used in the context of crisis negotiations by Taylor and Thomas (2008).

Local versus Global Context

The third and most macro level of our framework is local versus global (see Table 19.1, row 1 (local) and row 2 (global)). The idea of "think globally, act locally" is a common phrase used in businesses and communities to describe the process of analysing the broader, global impact of actions we take within our immediate environment (Robertson, 1995). The term "glocalization" describes globalization strategies that take into consideration the needs and interests of local communities. In other words, local refers to spatial closeness, whereas global refers to a broader, more inclusive landscape. The variables introduced in the previous paragraphs all apply to the local level, for example factors pertaining to a focal negotiator or dyad at the negotiation table. A global lens expands our perspective to consider multiple negotiators, constituencies, institutional environments, and belief systems that guide negotiation processes and impact negotiation outcome. Importantly, many authors' recommendations to model multi-level processes, for example how the external environment impacts what goes on locally at the negotiation table, are consistent with the concept of glocalization, which specifies the simultaneous consideration of both local and global concerns.

Moving from the local to the global level brings negotiators from the visible to the unknown, from a sphere of control to a broad landscape of uncontrollable variables, and from the relatively simple to the ultimately complex. As with the previous two levels of our framework, research in general has focused on either local factors or global factors, but rarely the interaction between them. Thus, our authors recommend that characteristics of the negotiator (e.g. personality, motivation) should be studied within the broader negotiation context, for example testing how these characteristics function differently within a highly structured versus highly flexible negotiation environment. Likewise, researchers studying complex real world contexts suggest that future researchers look more closely at local factors – for example roles and characteristics of the negotiators at the table.

One area of negotiation research linking local and global factors that is quite well developed is the study of culture. We have a rich knowledge of negotiators' expectations, behaviors, motivations, and emotions within different national cultural belief systems (Brett, 2007). We propose that our understanding of how belief systems impact what goes on at the negotiation table could be developed conceptually and theoretically with the study of other belief systems (e.g. gender roles, religious beliefs, belief in a just world, political conservativism, etc.). There may be interesting individual-level or context-level variables that affect the degree to which belief systems do or do not influence individual negotiator behavior.

Another promising area for future research relating local and global factors is the study of how negotiator behavior at the table is influenced by background activity such as communication with representative constituents. Managing parties at and away from the table in the realm of labor-management negotiation has been called "the two table problem" (Putnam, 1988). But researchers of transactional negotiation have also theorized about a "shadow negotiation" represented by negotiators' information gathering, positioning, and strategizing away from the table (Kolb and Williams, 2001).

Crossing Levels

Negotiation characteristics and time
Construal-level theory can help define future research questions by considering negotiator characteristics that vary in temporal proximity. At the surface level, proximal characteristics of the negotiation itself occur at the negotiation table (e.g. strategy, sequences, nonverbal communication), while at the deep level, proximal factors refer to characteristics of the negotiator that are present at single moments in time (e.g. emotion, motivation, physiological response). Recall that in our framework, distal refers to factors that occur either over time or across temporal distance. At the surface level, distal variables include characteristics of the negotiation such as turning points, phases, and temporal distance; whereas at the deep level, distal variables are negotiator characteristics that evolve and change over time, for example trust, trust repair, and resilience.

Negotiation researchers have yet to fully examine how negotiators' surface-level characteristics, for example negotiating history, strategy in use, or leadership role, affect distal temporal factors such as spillover in a multi-round negotiation (Crump, 2010; O'Connor et al., 2005). Beyond reputation effects, how do negotiators' verbal expression and strategy choice in one negotiation affect subsequent negotiations with the same party that may have different content and structure? Deep-level negotiator characteristics may also have implications for negotiation processes over time. For example, as noted by Druckman and Olekalns, Chapter 13 this volume, a negotiator's resilience should have implications for managing challenging negotiation dynamics such as unexpected crises, and interpersonal processes such as managing trust over time. Finally, how does the role of negotiator emotion change based on whether the emotion is brought to the table or emerges over time in response to events at the table?

Negotiation characteristics and global versus local context

Environmental or contextual factors at the local level might include seating arrangements, and other physical characteristics at the surface level, and psychological mindsets at the deep level. Research by Donohue and Taylor (2003) has shown how contextual factors, for example how many guns a hostage taker has, send social signals that impact negotiation processes. Researchers have also begun examining deeper psychological factors, for example a negotiator's perceived power or self-confidence based on having the home-court advantage in a negotiation (Brown and Baer, 2011; Salacuse and Rubin, 1990).

Several chapter authors suggest that future research examine more closely characteristics of specific actors within the context of a complex negotiation landscape that includes multiple actors, constituencies, political concerns, and rigid institutional norms. Possible research questions here include: how does the absence of state actors in community negotiations impact parties' motivations and strategies used? Do negotiator culture and personality effects appear more prominently in ambiguous situations than in situations with strict norms or regulatory environments?

Time and global versus local context

Are negotiators who hold a proximal temporal perspective more likely to focus on the local context, or what is happening at the negotiation table? When negotiators have a distal temporal perspective, for example when they are involved in a multi-round negotiation and need to consider ratification of the ultimate solution at a later point in time, do they take into consideration more global contextual factors? Along these same lines, we ask whether a negotiator's temporal perspective shifts when different aspects of the negotiation context come into the foreground. Negotiation researchers have noted cultural variation in negotiators' short- versus long-term time horizon (Alon and Brett, 2007; Macduff, 2006). Researchers can test whether cultural variation in time horizons corresponds with a differential emphasis on local versus global context in negotiation communication and strategy.

Researchers can also examine construal-level theory predictions about existing models of time in negotiation. For example, Druckman and Olekalns review research on negotiation phases or stages that suggests negotiators focus on relationships, information, power, and offers at different points during a negotiation. Prior research in this area has examined local communication content, relative to the task at hand. Future research can examine whether communication content switches between local and global context at different points in a negotiation. For example, when negotiators are close to reaching agreement, they probably have a proximal temporal focus, predicting a local focus, that is, hammering out a deal. But in earlier negotiation phases, when an agreement is in the distal future, perhaps communication will illustrate more holistic, global content. Likewise, temporal disruptions, for example turning points, might shift negotiators' focus from local to global, and resolution of those turning points might shift the focus back to local context.

In the chapter on international trade, Crump suggests that future research examines the impact of a negotiation's structural factors (local context) on linkage dynamics, which refer to the effects of one negotiation on other subsequent or related negotiations (temporal factor). Friedman and Belkin's "into the wind" strategy suggests that maximizing the choice of communication media (local context) depends on the temporal phase of the negotiation, for example focus on relationship building versus problem solving. In other words, researchers can develop predictions about how the negotiation context influences temporal perspectives and also how the temporal stage within a negotiation or a negotiator's temporal perspective can influence what contextual factors are in the foreground.

Negotiation characteristics, time, and context
Despite our attempts to offer focused research questions at individual levels and across-levels of the Negotiation Context Levels Framework, in reality most negotiations involve factors at all levels simultaneously. As noted in our introduction, negotiations are extremely complex and dynamic. The consideration of all factors simultaneously may be more of a conceptual exercise or a way of thinking than true theory building or developing a realistic research design (Zartman, 1994). But researchers using a dynamical system approach might argue differently. Dynamical systems approaches attempt to explain negotiation and conflict resolution by modeling all aspects across levels simultaneously. Inherent in such approaches is the acceptance of paradox, a perspective that has also recently gained validity and interest in other areas of management research.

Dynamical systems is a theoretical approach that models "a set of interconnected elements (e.g. beliefs, feelings, and behaviors) that change and evolve in time" (Coleman et al., 2007, p. 1457). Not only do dynamical systems model the evolution of time, they also address "dynamics that define the relationships between psychological and social mechanisms within and between individuals and groups" (Coleman et al., 2007, p. 1457). Coleman and colleagues (2007) have used a dynamical systems approach to explain forces involved in intractable conflict. Although a full explanation is beyond the scope of this chapter, we offer a few examples from the realm of intractable conflict to illustrate how such systems modeling could be applied to other areas of negotiation research.

In dynamical systems, attractors are psychological or social factors that narrow the range of actors' perceptions and experiences and can lead to the perpetuation of conflict (Coleman et al., 2007). For example, negotiators with a distributive mindset may perceive a counterpart's ambiguous behaviors as distributive, reinforcing the distributive mindset and patterns of reciprocal distributive tactics that are hard to break (Brett et al., 1998). Whereas negotiation strategy researchers have uncovered a way to break the bonds of negative reciprocity by offering an interests-based proposal (Brett et al., 1998), a more holistic, dynamical systems approach would suggest that a "successful intervention . . . should aim not at pushing the person or group out of its equilibrium but rather at changing the social system in such a way that the equilibrium among forces is changed" (Coleman et al., 2007, p. 1458). In other words, it is not a change in strategy that will successfully disrupt the equilibrium of a conflict spiral but rather a change in the framing of the conflict from a distributive to an integrative problem.

A dynamical systems approach accounts for self-organization and sense-making through social categorization and the formation of in-groups, the role of positive and negative feedback loops in perpetuating or changing systematic processes that become narrow and self-reinforcing, communication with external actors, and cultural transmission of values and beliefs, all of which play a role in a system's natural movement towards coherence (a concept akin to sense-making) (Thagard, 2000; Vallacher and Nowak, 2007). And in addition to including multi-level constructs that develop and change over time, a dynamical systems model is able to account for the paradoxical co-existence of variables that help explain patterns of stability and change. For example, dynamical systems explain intractable conflict as "a paradox of stability amid change", accounting for the way that patterns of destructive conflict can become stable and self-perpetuating (Coleman et al., 2007, p. 1455).

Cross-cultural negotiation researchers have also noted the seeming paradox of constructive conflict, a method that recognizes the value of open conflict within the context of cooperative goals (Johnson et al., 1990, Tjosvold, 1986). Westerners tend to view cooperation and competition as opposites that create a paradox in need of resolution (Poole and Van de Ven, 1989). Rather than an "either-or" thinking pattern that does not consider the coexistence of both cooperation and competition, Chinese dialectical thinking allows for a "middle way" philosophy that treats cooperation and competition as a single construct – a "strategy duality" (Chen, 2008, p. 297). Based on these characteristics of conflict, Chen (2008) proposes an ambicultural or transparadoxical approach to managing conflict that allows for both cooperation and competition, reflecting not only dialectical thinking (Fang and Faure, 2011; Peng and Nisbett, 1999) but also a holistic and long-term view on managing conflict dynamics (Chen and Miller, 2010). Transparadoxical approaches to conflict help address both within-level and cross-level research questions such as how motivations and emotions shift and change over time as a function of incidents at the negotiation table and beyond.

CONCLUSION

Our concluding chapter summarizes many promising directions for future negotiation research. We have structured our review and recommendations from the simple to the complex, which leaves us ending with the most challenging research questions addressing complexity, multiple levels, and dynamic processes. But we warn researchers not to be discouraged or disheartened. The process of scholarly inquiry and knowledge building requires regular journeys to and from the simple and the complex, theory and empirics, the laboratory and the field, and many other seemingly paradoxical approaches and lenses. By reviewing the history of the study of negotiation and bringing together negotiation experts who are from different fields, study negotiation from different levels, and use diverse methods, this Handbook offers a holistic picture of the complexity of negotiation research along with a framework for guiding specific and realistic future research questions.

REFERENCES

Alon, I. and Brett, J.M. (2007). Perceptions of time and their impact on negotiations in the Arabic speaking Islamic world. *Negotiation Journal*, 23(1), 55–73.
Appelt, K.C., Zou, X., Arora, P., and Higgins, E.T. (2009). Regulatory fit in negotiation: Effects of "prevention-buyer" and "promotion-seller" fit. *Social Cognition*, 27(3), 365–384.
Aronson, J.D., Cohen, L.E., Nystrom, J.K.R., and Sanfey, A.G. (2003). The neural basis of economic decision-making in the ultimatum game (Reports). *Science*, 300(5626), 1755.
Bendersky, C. and McGinn, K.L. (2010). Open to negotiation: Phenomenological assumptions and knowledge dissemination. *Organizational Science*, 21, 781–797.
Bowles, H.R., Babcock, L., and McGinn, K.L. (2005). Constraints and triggers: Situational mechanics of gender in negotiation. *Journal of Personality and Social Psychology*, 89, 951–965.
Brett, J.M. (2007). *Negotiating globally: How to negotiate deals, resolve disputes, and make decisions across cultural boundaries*. San Francisco: Jossey-Bass.
Brett, J.M., Shapiro, D.L., and Lytle, A.L. (1998). Breaking the bonds of reciprocity in negotiations. *Academy of Management Journal*, 41, 410–424.
Brown, G. and M. Baer (2011). Location in negotiation: Is there a home field advantage? *Organizational Behavior and Human Decision Processes*, 114, 190–200.

Chen, M-J. (2008). Reconceptualizing the competition-cooperation relationship: A trans-paradox perspective. *Journal of Management Inquiry*, *17*(4), 276–281.
Chen, M-J. and Miller, D. (2010). West meets East: Toward an ambicultural approach to management. *Academy of Management Perspectives*, *24*, 17–24.
Coleman, P.T. and Kugler, K.G. (2011). Tracking adaptivity: developing a measure to assess adaptive conflict orientations in organizations (25 June). IACM 24th Annual Conference Paper. Accessed from http://ssrn.com/abstract=1872656 or http://dx.doi.org/10.2139/ssrn.1872656.
Coleman, P.T., Vallacher, R.R., Nowak, A., and Bui-Wrzosinska, L. (2007). Intractable conflict as an attractor a dynamical systems approach to conflict escalation and intractability. *American Behavioral Scientist*, *50*(11), 1454–1475.
Crump, L. (2010). Strategically managing negotiation linkage dynamics. *Negotiation and Conflict Management Research*, *3*, 3–27.
Curhan, J.R. and Pentland, A. (2007). Thin slices of negotiation: Predicting outcomes from conversational dynamics within the first 5 minutes. *Journal of Applied Psychology*, *92*, 802–811.
De Dreu, C.K., Greer, L.L., Handgraaf, M.J., Shalvi, S., Van Kleef, G.A., Baas, M., and Feith, S.W. (2010). The neuropeptide oxytocin regulates parochial altruism in intergroup conflict among humans. *Science*, *328*(5984), 1408–1411.
de Wit, F.R., Jehn, K.A., and Scheepers, D. (2011). Negotiating within groups: A psychophysiological approach. *Research on Managing Groups and Teams*, *14*, 207–238.
Donohue, W.A. and Taylor, P.J. (2003). Testing the role effect in terrorist negotiations. *International Negotiation*, *8*, 527–547.
Eagly, A.H. and Wood, W. (2012). Social role theory. In P.A.M. van Lange, A.W. Kruglanski, and E.T. Higgins (eds), *Handbook of theories in social psychology* (pp. 458–476). Thousand Oaks, CA: Sage Publications.
Fang, T. and Faure, G.O. (2011). Chinese communication characteristics: A yin yang perspective. *International Journal of Intercultural Relations*, *35*(3), 320–333.
Fischer, R. and Smith, P.B. (2003). Reward allocation and culture a meta-analysis. *Journal of Cross-Cultural Psychology*, *34*(3), 251–268.
Galinsky, A.D. and Mussweiler, T. (2001). First offers as anchors: the role of perspective-taking and negotiator focus. *Journal of Personality and Social Psychology*, *81*(4), 657.
Galinsky, A.D., Leonardelli, G.J., Okhuysen, G.A., and Mussweiler, T. (2005). Regulatory focus at the bargaining table: Promoting distributive and integrative success. *Personality and Social Psychology Bulletin*, *31*(8), 1087–1098.
Harrison, D.A., Price, K.H., Gavin, J.H., and Florey, A.T. (2002). Time, teams, and task performance: Changing effects of surface-and deep-level diversity on group functioning. *Academy of Management Journal*, 1029–1045.
Hollander-Blumoff, R. and Tyler, T.R. (2008). Procedural justice in negotiation: Procedural fairness, outcome acceptance, and integrative potential. *Law and Social Inquiry*, *33*(2), 473–500.
Johnson, D.W., Johnson, R.T., Smith, K.A., and Tjosvold, D. (1990). Pro, con, and synthesis: Training managers to engage in constructive controversy. In B. Sheppard, M. Bazerman, and R. Lewicki (eds), *Research in negotiations in organization* (pp. 139–174). Vol. 2. Greenwich, CT: JAI Press.
Kearney, E., Gebert, D., and Voelpel, S.C. (2009). When and how diversity benefits teams: The importance of team members' need for cognition. *Academy of Management Journal*, *52*(3), 581–598.
Kim, P.H., Pinkley, R.L., and Fragale, A.R. (2005). Power dynamics in negotiation. *Academy of Management Review*, *30*, 799–822.
Kolb, D. and McGinn, K. (2009). Beyond gender and negotiation to gendered negotiations. *Negotiation and Conflict Management Research*, *2*, 1–16.
Kolb, D. and Williams, J. (2001). *The shadow negotiation: How women can master the hidden agendas that determine bargaining success*. New York: Simon and Schuster.

Kray, L.J. and Haselhuhn, M.P. (2007). Implicit negotiation beliefs and performance: experimental and longitudinal evidence. *Journal of Personality and Social Psychology*, *93*(1), 49.

Kulik, C.T. and Olekalns, M. (2012). Negotiating the gender divide lessons from the negotiation and organizational behavior literatures. *Journal of Management*, *38*(4), 1387–1415.

Lax, D. and Sebenius, J. (1986). *The Manager as Negotiator*. New York: Free Press.

Leung, A.K.-Y. and Cohen, D. (2011). Within- and between-culture variation: Individual differences and the cultural logics of honor, face, and dignity cultures. *Journal of Personality and Social Psychology*, *100*, 507–526.

Lim, S.G.S. and Murnighan, J.K. (1994). Phases, deadlines, and the bargaining process. *Organizational Behavior and Human Decision Processes*, *58*(2), 153–171.

Niederhoffer, K.G. and Pennebaker, J.W. (2002). Linguistic style matching in social interaction. *Journal of Language and Social Psychology*, *21*, 337–360.

Macduff, I. (2006). Your pace or mine? Culture, time, and negotiation. *Negotiation Journal*, *22*(1), 31–45.

McCarthy, J., Scheraga, C., and Gibson, D.E. (2010). Culture, cognition and conflict: How neuroscience can help to explain cultural differences in negotiation and conflict management. In A.A. Stanton, M. Day, and I.M. Welpe (eds), *Neuroeconomics and the firm*, pp. 263–288. Cheltenham, UK and Northampton, MA, USA: Edward Elgar Publishing.

Moore, D.A. (2004). Myopic prediction, self-destructive secrecy, and the unexpected benefits of revealing final deadlines in negotiation. *Organizational Behavior and Human Decision Processes*, *94*, 125–139.

O'Connor, K.M., Arnold, J.A., and Burris, E.R. (2005). Negotiators' bargaining histories and their effects on future negotiation performance. *Journal of Applied Psychology*, *90*, 350–362.

Olekalns, M. and Smith, P.L. (1999). Social value orientations and strategy choices in competitive negotiations. *Personality and Social Psychology Bulletin*, *25*, 657–668.

Olekalns, M. and Smith, P.L. (2003). Social motives in negotiation: The relationship between dyad composition, negotiation processes and outcomes. *The International Journal of Conflict Management*, *14*, 233–254.

Olekalns, M., Lau, F., and Smith, P.L. (2007). Resolving the empty core: trust as a determinant of outcomes in three-party negotiations. *Group Decision and Negotiation*, *16*, 527–538.

Peng, K. and Nisbett, R. (1999). Culture, dialectics, and reasoning about contradiction. *American Psychologist*, *54*, 741–754.

Perunovic, W.Q.E., Heller, D., and Rafaeli, E. (2007). Within-person changes in the structure of emotion: The role of cultural identification and language. *Psychological Science*, *18*(7), 607–613.

Phillips, K.W. and Loyd, D.L. (2006). When surface and deep-level diversity collide: The effects on dissenting group members. *Organizational Behavior and Human Decision Processes*, *99*(2), 143–160.

Polzer, J.T., Mannix, E.A., and Neale, M.A. (1998). Interest alignment and coalitions in multiparty negotiation. *The Academy of Management Journal*, *41*, 42–54.

Poole, M.S. and Van de Ven, A.H. (1989). Using paradox to build management and organization theories. *Academy of Management Review*, *14*, 562–578.

Prietula, M.J. and Weingart, L.R. (2011). Negotiation offers and the search for agreement. *Negotiation and Conflict Management Research*, *4*, 77–109. doi:10.1111/j.1750-4716.2011.00074.

Putnam, R.D. (1988). Diplomacy and domestic politics: The logic of two-level games. *International Organization*, *42*, 427–460.

Robertson, R. (1995). Glocalization: Time-space and homogeneity-heterogeneity. *Global Modernities*, 25–44.

Salacuse, J.W. and Rubin, J.Z. (1990). Your place or mine? Site location and negotiation. *Negotiation Journal*, *6*(1), 5–10.

Sanfey, A.G. (2007). Social decision-making: insights from game theory and neuroscience. *Science*, *318*(5850), 598–602.

Semnani-Azad, Z. and Adair, W.L. (in press). Watch your tone . . . relational paralinguistic messages in negotiation: The case of the East and West. *International Studies of Management and Organization*.

Sillars, A., Roberts, L.J., Leonard, K.E., and Dun, T. (2000). Cognition during marital conflict: The relationship of thought and talk. *Journal of Social and Personal Relationships*, *17*, 479–502.

Swaab, R.I., Galinsky, A.D., Medvec, V., and Diermeier, D.A. (2012). The communication orientation model explaining the diverse effects of sight, sound, and synchronicity on negotiation and group decision-making outcomes. *Personality and Social Psychology Review*, *16*(1), 25–53.

Taylor, P. J. and Thomas, S. (2008). Linguistic style matching and negotiation outcome. *Negotiation and Conflict Management Research*, *1*, 263–281.

Tett, R.P. and Burnett, D.D. (2003). A personality trait-based interactionist model of job performance. *Journal of Applied Psychology*, *88*(3), 500.

Thagard, P. (2000). *Coherence in thought and action*. Cambridge, MA: The MIT Press.

Thatcher, S. and Patel, P.C. (2011). Demographic faultlines: a meta-analysis of the literature. *Journal of Applied Psychology*, *96*(6), 1119.

Tjosvold, D. (1986). Constructive controversy: A key strategy for groups. *Personnel*, April, 39–44.

Trope, Y. and Liberman, N. (2010). Construal-level theory of psychological distance. *Psychological Review*, *117*, 440–463.

Vallacher, R.R. and Nowak, A. (2007). Dynamical social psychology: Toward coherence in human experience and scientific theory. In A.W. Kruglanski and E.T. Higgins (eds), *Social psychology: Handbook of basic principles*. New York: Guilford.

Volkema, R. and Rivers, C. (2012). Beyond frogs and scorpions: A risk-based framework for understanding negotiating counterparts' ethical motivations. *Negotiation Journal*, *28*, 379–405.

Zak, P.J., Kurzban, R., and Matzner, W.T. (2005). Oxytocin is associated with human trustworthiness. *Hormones and Behavior*, *48*, 522–527.

Zartman, I.W. (1994). *International multilateral negotiation: Approaches to the management of complexity*. San Francisco: Jossey-Bass.

Index

Aaldering, H. 68
abilities
   individual differences 34–6
   trustworthiness 165
abruptness 334–5
absolute power 135
abstract thinking 359, 372, 376–7, 378
Aceh, Indonesia 343, 436
active listening 478–9
actor, focal *see* focal actor
actor–partner interaction model (APIM) 149–51
Adair, W.L. 175, 268, 315, 320–1, 486
Adam, H. 115
ADR 461–2
advocacy 229
affect 103
   gender and 229
   individual differences 27–8
   shared mental models 77, 78, 79, 84–5, 86
   see also emotions
affect–as–information model 104–5
affect infusion model (AIM) 105
affect priming models 105
affective reactions 109–11, 113–15
affiliation 29–30, 481
agency, and communion 29–30, 223
aggression 370
agreeableness 26
agricultural economies 253–4
Albin, C. 408, 429, 435–6
algorithms, matching 302
Ali ibn Ali Talib 271
Alliance of Motion Picture and Television Producers (AMPTP) 342
alliances 147–8
   see also coalitions
Allred, K.G. 107, 202
altruists 49
Amanatullah, E.T. 82, 143
ambicultural approach 514–15

American South/Southwest 253
analytic (linear) mindset 264–5, 267, 267–8, 271–2
anchoring effect 61
anchoring events 340
Anderson, C. 139, 141
Ang, S. 35
anger 116, 117, 118
   culture and negotiation strategy 265–7, 269–70
   interpersonal effects 111–12, 114–15
   intrapersonal effects 106–7
   temporal effects 120–1
   working synergistically with power 146
Angola 436
anthropological explanations of cultural differences 252–4
Anton, R.J. 239–40
anxiety 107–8
Apfelbaum, E.P. 288
apologies 182–3
Appelt, K.C. 507
appraisal theories of emotion 108
approach activation 139
appropriateness
   of emotional expression 110–11, 114–15
   of negotiation 31–2
   price negotiation 38–9
approval 142
armed conflicts *see* peace negotiations; violent conflict
Armenia–Azerbaijan peace negotiations 430, 435, 436–7
Arusha peace accords 436
Asia Pacific Economic Cooperation (APEC) 398
Asian cultures 85, 253
   see also Face culture
assertiveness 26
assumptions, suboptimal 145

attitudes
  effects of power on 138–40
  effects of status on 141–3
  gender and 229
Atwater, L. 362
Au, W.T. 107
auctions 296–9
Australia 396
authentic pride 142
autonomy 169–70
avoidant orientation 482–3
Axelrod, R. 48

Babbitt, E.F. 239
Babcock, L. 225
Bacharach, S.B. 135
backlash 228–9, 237
backward–looking peace agreements 430
Baird, B.N.R. 453
Bakan, D. 223
Ballinger, G.A. 340, 349
bandwagon strategy 406
bargaining approach to peace negotiations 422–8, 438
bargaining games 191, 210–11, 212
  ethics 204–6, 209
  fairness 193–6, 197–200
  focal actor 193–6, 204–6
  recipient 197–200, 209
Bargaining Process Analysis II, Revised 313
bargaining toughness 172
Barry, B. 178
Barsness, Z.I. 367
BATNA (best alternative to a negotiated agreement) 135–6, 141, 144, 148
Bazerman, M.H. 7
Bear, J. 226
Beersma, B. 91, 202
Begin, M. 152
behavior 313
  cultural differences 91
  effects of power on 138–40, 145
  effects of status on 141–3
  factors affecting proposer behavior 195–6
  flexibility and adaptability 349–50

gender and negotiation behaviors 225–9
behavioral approach system 139
behavioral assimilation 57
Behavioral Change Staircase model 475
behavioral decision theory 7
behavioral ethics literature 212–13
behavioral inhibition system 139
beliefs 31–3, 38–9
  implicit 32, 38–9, 204
benchmarking 393
Bendersky, C. 241
benevolence 165–6
Benford, R.D. 458
Bennett, A. 436
Bethwaite, J. 194
Beune, K. 322, 487
Bhappu, A.D. 367
Bialeschki, M.D. 238
biased mediators 426
biases 7–8, 60–3
bidders, number of 296–7, 298
big–five personality model 26–7, 374
bilateral trade negotiations 388–97
Bilsky, W. 476
Blader, S.L. 152, 197
blends of emotions 119–20
Bogaert, S. 67
Bohnet, I. 271
Boles, T.L. 205, 209
Bosnia 432, 435–6
Bowles, H.R. 228, 230, 231, 236
Brandth, B. 236
Braver, S.L. 239
breaks, temporal 340–1
Brett, J.M. 175, 486, 514
bribery 177–8
Brief, A.P. 212, 213
Brockner, J. 212
broken trust 175–84
  consequences of 178–9
  how trust can be broken 175–8
  how trust can be repaired 182–4
  reparability of 180–2
Brooks, A.W. 107–8
Brown, B.R. 3, 227
Buchan, N.R. 194
Bulow, J. 296–7
Bunker, B.B. 163, 164, 180

burden sharing 393
Burnham, T. 83
Burundi 436
Bush, G.W. 389, 390
Butler, J.K. 88

calculus–based trust 163, 180, 423
Cambodia 432, 435–6
Cameron, M. 338
Carli, L.L. 233
Carnevale, P.J. 106, 153, 202
Carson, T.L. 202–3
Caruso, D.R. 35
case study analysis 335–6
ceasefires 420
certainty 284
  see also uncertainty
Chakravarti, D. 172–3
change, emotional 119–20
characterization frames 458
Chasek, P. 337, 345
Chen, M.-J. 514–15
Chen, Y.-R. 140, 152, 197
childcare 238
China 253, 465
Cho, Y. 153
Chou, E.Y. 183
Chugh, D. 208
Cialdini, R. 484
circumplex model 27
Clenney, E.F. 147
climate change 465
  see also environmental negotiations
Clinton, B. 388, 389
Clore, G.L. 122
closure, need for 86
coalitions 123
  multilateral negotiations 293–5, 345–6, 405–8
  power and 147–8
Cobb, A. 293
coding schemes 312–16
coercive leadership 401
coercive messages 172–3
cognition 8–9, 16
  effects of power on 138–40
  effects of status on 141–3
  gender and 229
  motivated see motivated cognition
  shared see shared mental models

cognitive capacity 60
cognitive complexity 34
cognitive conflicts 343, 344
cognitive heuristics 60–2
cognitive intelligence 34
cognitive scripts 477–8
Cohen, J.R. 203
Cohen, T.R. 205, 206–7
Coleman, P.T. 513, 514
collectivism 256
  in–group and societal 262
commitment 107
  problems 422
commitment and consistency principle 484
common pool resources 451, 454–5
common value 298–9, 300–1
communal conflicts 433, 434
communication
  behaviors and crisis negotiations 474, 480–7
  channels 321, 507
  culture, mindset and 272
  development of trust 171–3
  medium 171–2, 231–2
  nonverbal see nonverbal communication
  peace negotiations 424–5
  processes 4, 12–14
  skills and shared mental models 88–9
  see also communication sequences; electronic negotiations (e–negotiations); turning points
communication accommodation theory 483
communication sequences 13, 311–31
  coding 312–16
  negotiation strategy and tactics 316–19
  nonverbal expression 319–22
  research directions 322–5
communion 29–30, 223
  unmitigated 30, 82
community–based processes 460
comparison studies 435–6
competitive arousal 298
competitive bargaining 177–8
competitive behavior 227–8
competitive convergence 347

competitive goals 316
competitive motivation/orientation 30, 50, 51, 482–3
competitively linked negotiations 392
competitors 49, 50
complementarity, postural 150–1
complementary strategy sequences 318
complex negotiations 4, 14–15, 18, 18–19
  see also crisis negotiations; environmental negotiations; peace negotiations; trade negotiations
complexity
  communication 322–3
  of negotiation 499
  scientific and environmental issues 446–7
computer–automated text analysis 325
computer mediated communication (CMC) see electronic negotiations (e–negotiations)
concentric circle method 404–5
concessions 6
Conchie, S.M. 480
conciliation 254–5, 260–3
conciliatory strategies 426
concurrent linkage 392–5
  between levels 394–5
  and role theory 392–4
confidence 31, 142, 164–5
conflict
  issues 121–2
  sources of 343–4
  violent 416, 418–19, 427–8, 433–5
  see also peace negotiations
conflict management
  cultural logics and 254–63
  mechanisms 274–5
conflict management frames 458–9
confrontation style 254–5, 258–60
Confucian ideology 253, 261
Conley, A. 459–60
conscientiousness 26–7
consecutive linkage 392, 395–7
consensus–based processes
  critiques of 459–62
  WTO decision making 402–3
consequences
  of broken trust 178–9

deception and ethics 66–7
turning points 334–5, 339, 343–4, 351–2
consistency over time, personality as 39
construal level theory of psychological distance 358–60, 380, 509
  see also psychological distance
constructive conflict 514
contending 55
content analysis 312–16, 325
context 6–7, 12–13, 18–19, 499
  factors in shared cognition and identity 77, 78, 80, 90–1
  gender and 231–5
  high and low context cultures 319, 486–7
  institutional context for environmental negotiations 449–51
  Negotiation Context Levels Framework 499, 505–15
  and negotiator resilience 350
  political 464
  research directions 503–5
  situational factors and ethics 205, 208
  situational factors and fairness 196, 197, 199–200
  social 9–12
  turning points research 336, 343–6
contingency approach to e–negotiations 373–6
contingent value (CV) method 453–4
contracts 170–1, 173, 183–4
contrast sequences 319
convergence 347–8
Cooper, R.B. 365–7, 369
cooperation 92, 164–5, 169
  gender and 227–8
cooperative convergence 347
cooperative goals 316
cooperative motivation/orientation 50, 482–3
cooperators 49
Coser, L. 447
cost–benefit analysis of computer–mediated communication 360–5
  and negotiation 365–70

Côté, S. 114–15, 117
Cote d'Ivoire 432, 433, 435
counterpart
  characteristics 207
  effects 46
  matching 299–300
Coupland, N. 483
Cramton, P.C. 203
creativity 36
credibility 168
crisis negotiations 14, 15, 18, 473–95, 501–2
  first impressions 473–4, 475–8
  influence skills 474, 484–7
  rapport development 474, 478–80
  research directions 488–91
  sensemaking 474, 480–3, 490
  structural factors 487–8
critical incidents 502
critical mass 346
Cropanzano, R. 213
Croson, R. 64, 209
cross–cultural negotiations 275, 489
cross–negotiation consistency 38
Cruikshank, J. 450
Crump, L. 345–6, 391–2, 392–3, 394, 395–6, 411
cue–response coding 312, 313
cues filtered out 358, 363
cultural intelligence 35
culture 10, 11, 18, 33, 249–82, 504
  anthropological explanations of origins 252–4
  communication sequences and 317, 318–19, 320–1
  conciliation, warmth and hospitality 255, 260–3
  confrontation style 255, 258–60
  crisis negotiations 486–7, 489
  cultural biases and environmental negotiations 454
  defining cultural prototypes 251–4
  effect on trust and negotiation transactions 174–5
  and emotional expression 115
  e–negotiations 367, 375
  and ethics 204
  high and low context cultures 486–7, 319
  intercultural negotiations 275, 489

  local and global factors 510–11
  measurement of cultural values and norms 274
  negotiation strategy and outcomes 263–73
  power and status 255, 256–7
  research directions 273–6
  sensitivity and response to insults 255, 257–8
  shared cognition and identity
    behavior and strategies 91
    motivation 85–6
Culture and Negotiation Coding Scheme 313
Curhan, J.R. 147, 153, 201–2, 477
Currall, S.C. 360–2
cylinder model 482–3

Daft, R.L. 357–8
Darfur peace agreement 434
Darwin, C. 108
datasets, large 419, 437
De Dreu, C.K.W. 30, 56, 62, 64, 65, 68, 91, 121, 197, 202, 317
deadlocks 409–10
deception 140, 202–3
  and breaking trust 176, 178–9
  e–negotiations 367
  and ethics 66–7
  marketplace negotiations 301
  motivated cognition 64–7
Dechesne, M. 488
Declerck, C.H. 67
deep characteristics 506–9
  and global vs local context 512
  and time 511
  time and local and global context 513–15
Dees, J.G. 203
de–individuation 362
delusion of homogeneity 288
demands 6
Democratic Republic of Congo (DRC) 436
demographic background 33
Dennis, A.R. 363
departures 334–5, 339, 343–4, 351–2
dependence
  interdependence 48, 166–7, 481
  theory of bargaining power 135

d'Estrée, T.P. 239
deterrence–based trust 162–3
Deutsch, F.M. 238
Deutsch, M. 3, 314
developing country coalitions 407–8
DeWall, C.N. 138
diagnostic frames 458
dictator games 193–6, 197–200
Diehl, P.F. 432
differentiation–before–integration 337–8
Dignity culture 249–50, 251, 255–6, 275–6
  anthropological explanations of origins 253–4
  conciliation, warmth and hospitality 255, 260–1
  confrontation style 255, 258–9
  negotiation strategy and outcomes 267–8
  power and status 255, 256
  sensitivity and response to insults 255, 257–8
dilemma of trust/honesty 167, 168–71
direct access information processing strategy 105
direct confrontation style 258–60
directive strategies 426
disappointment 112–13, 116
disclosure *see* information provision
discrete emotions 117–18
discursive representation 343
distal time factors 506, 509
  and global and local context 512–13
  and negotiator characteristics 511
  negotiator characteristics, local and global context and 513–15
distributive bargaining 422–8
distributive fairness 192–3, 201, 211
distributive justice 464
distributive self–efficacy 31
distributive strategies 407–8
  cultural differences and 263–73
distributive tactics 314–15, 316, 317–18
distrust 164, 165, 170–1
  see also trust
division of labor in the home 238
divorce negotiations 238–9
Doha Round 408, 409, 410
domestic contexts 345

dominance 29–30, 140–1, 320
  dominant postures 150–1
  dominant role 321–2
Donohue, W.A. 430, 473, 477, 488
Dougherty, J. 346
Douglas, A. 337
Downs, G. 428–9
Druckman, D. 338–9, 341, 342, 345–6, 410, 423, 429, 430, 432, 435–6
dual concern model 5, 30, 56
Dupont, C. 406
durability of peace settlements 417, 428–32, 432–3
Dweck, C. 32
dynamical systems approach 513–15

Eagly, A.H. 222, 223, 224
Earley, P.C. 35
economic outcomes 92–3, 229–31
economy, historical basis of 252–4
education 196
Edwards Aquifer environmental conflict 342
effectiveness
  coalitions 406–7
  multilateral conferences 408–10
egalitarian motivation 50
ego defensiveness 63
egocentric bias 8, 193
egoistic/individualist motivation/ orientation 30, 50, 51
El Salvador 431, 436
electoral disputes 433
electronic negotiations (e–negotiations) 13–14, 296, 357–84, 504–5
  benefits of social distance 370–2
  effects of computer mediated communication 360–70
  benefits 361, 363–5
  costs for negotiation 365–8
  implications for negotiation 368–70
  social costs 360–3
  gender and 231–2
  'into the wind' strategy 377–9, 504–5
  mixed model approach 376–9
  psychological distance *see* psychological distance
  research directions 380

theoretical foundation 357–60
Elfenbein, H.A. 38–9, 40
email *see* electronic negotiations (e–negotiations)
emergent processes 464–5
Emerson, K. 446
Emonds, G. 67
emotional confrontation style 258–60
emotional contagion 109
emotional intelligence 34–5, 116–17, 374
emotional labeling 479
emotional manipulation 178, 370–1
emotional regulation 117, 374
emotions 8, 9, 103–30
   coding schemes for communication 312, 313
   crisis negotiations 474, 475–80
   empirical record 106–8, 111–15
   expression of negative emotions 264, 265–7, 269–70, 272–3
   fairness and 202
   interpersonal effects 104, 108–15, 116
   intrapersonal effects 104–8, 116
   nonverbal expression of 320
   psychological distance and 364
   reactions to unfair offers 198–9
   research directions 115–23, 500
   shared cognition and identity 84–5, 86
   theoretical developments 104–6, 108–11
   and trust 172
emotions as social information (EASI) theory 109–11
empathy 67
employees 147–8
endowment effect 292–3
enduring dispositions 26–9
   see also personality
e–negotiations *see* electronic negotiations
entity theorists 32
entrapment dynamics 419, 420
Environment Protection Agency (EPA) 450, 461–2, 463
environmental forces 241
environmental negotiations 14, 15, 19, 345, 445–72

emerging themes and future research 462–5
evaluation 459–62
factors shaping framing and outcomes 451, 452
framing 451, 458–9
nature of environmental issues 446–51
   scale and scope 465
negotiation processes, structure and management 451, 455–6
representation 451, 456–8, 460
risk perception 451–4
social dilemmas and common pool resources 451, 454–5
epistemic motivation 58–60
equal split 61, 194
equality 429, 431
escalation
   of commitment 298
   of conflict 46, 345
Esquipulas peace process 426
ethically ambiguous tactics 176–8
ethically appropriate tactics 176, 177–8, 203–4
ethically inappropriate tactics 176, 177–8
ethics 11, 191–2, 202–14, 503–4
   bargaining games 204–6, 209
   deception and 66–7
   e–negotiations and 371–2
   five–factor model of negotiation tactics 32–3, 177–8
   focal actor 204–9
   gender and 239–40
   nature of 202–4
   negotiations 206–9, 209–10
   power and 139–40
   recipient 209–10
   why people desire ethics 192
ethnography 437
European Union (EU) 390, 394, 395, 398
evaluation of environmental negotiation processes 459–62
exchange–based power 135–7
expectancies 31–3, 38–9
   violations of 348–9
expectations 61

experience 33
  e–negotiations and 362, 368
experimental analysis 335–6
explanations 182
exploitation, fear of 65
expressive crises 487–8
external interruptions 341
external precipitants 334–5
extortion 485
extraversion 26

face, concern for 86
face attacks 476
Face culture 249–50, 251, 255–6, 275–6
  anthropological explanations of origins 253
  conciliation, warmth and hospitality 255, 261
  confrontation style 255, 259
  negotiation strategy and outcomes 267, 268–70
  power and status 255, 256
  sensitivity and response to insults 255, 258
face–to–face/e–negotiation combined approach 377–9
facilitating emotion 35
faculty positions 300
fair offers 193–5
  motivations for making 194–5
fairness 11, 191–202, 210–14, 503–4
  bargaining games 193–6, 197–200
  focal actor 193–7
  nature of 192–3
  negotiations 196–7, 200–2
  recipient 197–202
  why people desire fairness 192
faultline groups 508
Federal Bureau of Investigation 475, 487
Federal Register 449
Filipowicz, A. 119, 120, 122
first impressions 173
  crisis negotiations 473–4, 475–8
first–mover advantage 150–1
Fisher, R. 5, 135
fixed–pie bias 7, 31, 62
fixedness of skills 32
flextime 236
Florea, N.B. 239

Flynn, F.J. 143
focal actor 191, 192, 210–11
  bargaining games 193–6, 204–6
  ethics 204–9
  fairness 193–7
  negotiations 196–7, 206–9
Folger, R. 213
Follett, M.P. 36, 54
Forgas, J.P. 27, 106
Forsythe, R. 195
forward–looking peace agreements 430
Fragale, A.R. 144, 152
frame convergence 347–8
framing 409
  environmental negotiations 451, 458–9
  reframing 345–6, 409
  turning points 336, 342–3
Frank, R.H. 107
Fraser, S. 484
free riding 393
Free Trade Area of the Americas (FTAA) 395
Freedman, J. 484
French, J.R.P. 134
frequency code 312
frequency of tactics 316–17
Friedland, N. 477
Friedman, R. 113, 360–2, 379
Fuller, R. 342–3

G–7 404
gain frames 200
Galin, A. 365
Galinsky, A.D. 94, 139
Gelfand, M.J. 242
gender 7, 11, 33, 221–48, 504
  attitudes and perceptions 229
  composition 232–4
  and e–negotiations 231–2, 370
  gender roles and negotiation roles 222–5
  moderators, contextual factors and gender triggers 231–5
  negotiation behaviors 225–9
  power and 146, 234–5
  profit and economic outcomes 229–31
  research directions 240–3
  and shared mental models 81–2

status and 147
theoretical framework 221–5
gendered negotiation 236–40
General Agreement on Tariffs and Trade (GATT) 345, 387, 390, 399
general mental ability (g) 34
generational effects 368
geographic variation in culture 274
George, A.L. 436
Georgia–South Ossetia peace negotiations 435
Giebels, E. 89, 484–6, 486–7, 491
Giles, H. 483
Gillespie, A. 88
Gillespie, N. 162
give–some games 454
Gladwell, M. 477
global context 506, 510–11
negotiator characteristics and 512
negotiator characteristics, time and 513–15
time and 512–13
glocalization 510
Gneezy, U. 66
goals 5, 6, 29
motivational and crisis negotiations 481–2, 482–3
peacekeeping missions 431–2
power and 138
shared cognition and identity 92–3
uncertainty of interests 286–9, 292–3, 298–300
Goh Chok Tong 388, 390
Gonzalez, C. 153
goods 389
Gorbachev, M. 332, 339
Greater Yellowstone Ecosystem 448–9
greed 65
Greenberg, D. 237
Greer, L.L. 145
Greig, F. 226
Griesinger, D.W. 48–9
grounded theory 437
groups 147–8
insiders and outsiders 152–3
intra–team negotiations 285–90, 302–3
see also multiparty negotiations
groupthink 287

Guatemala 431, 436
guilt 107, 112–13
Gunia, B.C. 212, 271, 315

Hafiz 260
Halevy, N. 153, 208
Hall, W. 345
Hammer, M. 476, 481
Handgraaf, M.J.J. 199, 200
Hanke, R. 176
happiness 111, 112, 116, 117
Harinck, F. 448
harmony preservation 259
Harvey–Craig, A. 487–8
Haselhuhn, M.P. 32, 140, 146, 204, 240, 507
hedging behavior 301–2
Hegtvedt, K.A. 202
Helsinki peace agreement 436
Henderson, M.D. 371
herding economies 252–3
Hershfield, H.E. 206
heuristic information processing 60–3, 105
hidden profile tasks 287
high context cultures 319, 486–7
high value matches 300
higher level construals 359
Hirschman, A.O. 258–9
holistic mindset 264–5, 267, 269
Hollander–Blumoff, R. 193, 201, 211
Hollingshead, A.B. 362, 363
homogeneity 287–8
honesty, dilemma of 167, 168–71, 176
Honor culture 249–50, 251–2, 255–6, 274–6
anthropological explanations of origins 252–3
conciliation, warmth and hospitality 255, 262–3
confrontation style 255, 259–60
negotiation strategy and outcomes 267, 270–3
power and status 255, 256–7
sensitivity and response to insults 255, 258
hospitality 254–5, 260–3
hostage crises 338, 416–17, 478, 482, 490–1
household negotiations 238–9

hubristic pride 142
hyper–fairness 198
hypotheticality 359

idea generation 363
ideal types 255–6
identification–based trust 164, 180–1, 423
identity
  concerns in crisis negotiations 481–3
  shared *see* shared identity
  uncertainty of 285, 291–2, 296–7
identity frames 458
ideology 488
  conflicting ideologies 447–8
implementation of peace settlements 417, 428–32
implicit beliefs 32, 38–9, 204
impression management 67–8
impressions 9–10, 17, 109–10
  first 173, 473–4, 475–8
in–group collectivism 262
incidental emotions 122
inclusion, uncertainty of 289–90, 293–5, 300–2
inclusiveness 404
incompatibility bias 7–8
inconsistency of emotions 120
incremental theorists 32
indirect confrontation style 258–60
individual differences 7, 8, 18, 25–45
  abilities 34–6
  demographic and work background 33
  empirical findings 25–36
  enduring dispositions 26–9
  ethics 205, 206–7
    counterpart 207
  expectancies and beliefs 31–3, 38–9
  fairness 195–6, 196–7
  and gender 242–3
  motivational styles 29–30, 39
  questioning their importance in negotiation 36–9
  research directions 39–41, 500–1
  shared cognition and identity 81–2
  and trust 185

individual processes 4, 6–9
  see also emotions; individual differences; motivated cognition; shared mental models
individualistic (egoistic) motivation/ orientation 30, 50, 51
individualists 48, 49
industrial negotiations 337
Inesi, M.E. 139
inferential processes 109–11, 111–15
influence 133
  coding systems 314, 315–16
  power as potential for 134
  research directions 149–53
  skills and crisis negotiations 474, 484–7
  status vs power 143–4
  see also power; status
information
  asymmetries 53, 63
  misrepresentation 177–8
  shared cognition and identity 77, 78, 79
    dynamic process of development 86–7
    input 82–3
  sharing 168, 378–9
information processing 284
  EASI theory 110–11, 113–14
  heuristic 60–3, 105
  motivated cognition 47, 58–63, 69
  uncertainty of interests 288–9
information provision 47, 63–8, 69
  trust and 167, 169–70
information search 58–63
information–sharing (Q&A) strategy 175, 263–73
informational ambiguity 375
informational messages 172–3
inhibition 139
initiation of negotiation 225–6
input–process–output framework for shared mental models 77–94
insider–partial mediators 426
insiders 289–90
institutional context 449–51
instrumental crises 487–8
instrumental leadership 401

insults, response to 254–5, 257–8
integral emotions 122
integrative (cognitive) complexity 34
integrative negotiations 54–8, 371
  social motives in 55–8
integrative self–efficacy 31
integrative strategies 407–8
  cultural differences and 263–73
integrative tactics 314–15, 316, 317–18
integrity 165–6
intellectual property rights 345–6, 389, 396
intensity
  of emotional expressions 122
  of language 476, 483
intentional interruptions 340–1
intentions
  gender and 229
  reactions to unfair offers 199
  and trust violation 181
interactions, ethics and 208–9
intercultural negotiations 275, 489
interdependence 48, 166–7, 481
interest
  coding schemes 314, 315
  conflicts of 343, 344
  uncertainty of interests 286–9, 292–3, 298–300
intergenerational issues 448
Intermediate Nuclear Forces (INF) Treaty 332, 338–9
internal validity 435–6
International Association of Mechanics and Aerospace Workers (IAM) 345
international contexts 345
international organizations 399, 400
  see also General Agreement on Tariffs and Trade (GATT); World Trade Organization (WTO)
international trade negotiations see trade negotiations
interpersonal effects of emotions 104, 108–15, 116
interpersonal relationships 87
interpersonal theory 29
interruptions 336, 339–41, 351–2
inter–state conflict 418–19

Inter–Tajik Dialogue 421
'into the wind' strategy 377–9, 504–5
intractable conflicts 513–14
  environmental disputes 462–3
intrapersonal effects of emotions 104–8, 116
intra–state conflict 418–19, 438
intra–team negotiations 285–90, 302–3, 420–1
Ireland, M.E. 325
Irish Republican Army (IRA) 420
Irmer, C. 423, 435, 436
Isen, A.M. 106
Israeli–Palestinian conflict 152, 428, 430
issue linkage 391
Ives, R.F. 388
Ivory Coast 432, 433, 435

Jap, S. 372
Japan 253
Japanese Red Army (JRA) 478
job searches 300, 301–2
Johnson, N. 365–7, 369
joint gains maximization 250
justice 152
  distributive and procedural 464
  organizational 192, 211, 212–13
  peace negotiations 429, 431
  see also ethics; fairness
justifications 182

Kagel, J.H. 53
Kahneman, D. 60–1
Kalyvas, S.N. 433–4
Kammrath, L.K. 32
Kamphuis, W. 486
Karau, S.J. 222, 224
Kelley, H.H. 57
Kelman, H.C. 424–5
Keltner, D. 139, 152, 320
Kenya 433
Kern, M.C. 208
Keros, A.T. 349
Ketelaar, T. 107
kidnappings 491
Kiesler, S. 360, 362
Killian, C. 202
Kim, P.H. 136
Klemperer, P. 296–7

knowledge–based trust 163–4, 180
Koh, T. 388
Kolb, D.M. 242
Koning, L. 65, 205
Kopelman, S. 113, 115
Kray, L.J. 32, 146, 204, 223, 240, 507
Kremenyuk, V.A. 430
Krumhuber, E. 117
Ku, G. 298
Kulik, C.T. 147
Kurtzberg, T.R. 36, 360
Kvande, E. 236

labor markets 299–300, 301–2
labor mediators 224
lag–sequential analysis 316
Langan–Fox, J. 76
language
  intensity 476, 483
  linguistic convergence 347–8
  linguistic style matching 325
  nuances in crisis negotiations 476
large datasets 419, 437
LaSalle, M.M. 224, 234
Laschever, S. 225
latent coalitions 293
Lawler, E.J. 135
Lax, D. 499
leadership 400–2, 410
Leary, K. 343
Lederach, J.P. 426
legal environment 375
legitimacy 345–6
Lengel, R.J. 357–8
Leung, K. 201
level of agreement 460
Lewicki, R.J. 41, 66, 162, 163, 164, 176, 177, 180, 182, 183, 203, 204
Lewin, K. 241
lexical matching 480
Liberia 432
Liberman, N. 358–9
linchpin strategy 406
linear (analytic) mindset 264–5, 267, 267–8, 271–2
linguistic convergence 347–8
linguistic inquiry word count 313
linguistic style matching 325
linguistic synchronization 346–8
link–pin party 392–4

linkages 391–7
  concurrent 392–5
  consecutive 392, 395–7
linked parties 392–4
listening, active 478–9
Liu, L.A. 80–1, 92
Livingston, J.W. 48–9
local context 506, 510–11
  negotiator characteristics and 512
  negotiator characteristics, time and 513–15
  time and 512–13
Loewenstein, G. 87, 193
log–linear analysis 316
logrolling 55
long–term consequences 334–5, 351–2
loose cultures 174–5
loss frames 200
Lount, R.B. 173
low context cultures 319, 486–7
Luanda peace agreement 436
Luce, R.D. 250
lying 176–7
Lys, T.Z. 297

Ma, Z. 204
Machiavellianism 28
Maddux, W.W. 321
malevolent cycle 430
Malhotra, D. 167, 173, 184
malleability of skills 32
management of emotion 35
management of violence 427–8
mandated negotiations 463–4
Mannino, C.A. 238
Mannix, E.A. 144, 145, 150
marital conflict 490
marketplace negotiations 296–302, 302–3
markets 254, 256
Markov chain modeling 316
'marriage problem' 300
martyrs 49
masochists 48–9
matching 299–300, 301
  language mimicry 479–80
  unstable 301–2
maternity leave negotiations 237–8
Mathieu, J.E. 83
matrix games 227

maximizing 28–9
Maxwell, S. 201
Mayer, J.D. 35
Mayer, R.C. 162
Mazei, J. 231
McGinn, K.L. 236, 241, 340, 349
McGrath, J.E. 362
McGuire, T.W. 360
McKersie, R.B. 3, 243, 337–8
meaning 324–5
media framing 342–3
media richness 321, 357–8, 359–60
mediation
    environmental negotiations 455, 456
    peace negotiations 425–6, 437
medical students, graduating 302
mental models, shared *see* shared mental models
Merari, A. 477
Mercosur 390, 394, 395
messages 172–3
methodology
    communication sequences 325
    peace negotiations research 435–7
    personality research 37
Michigan State Police model 475
microgenetic approach 323
Middle East 253, 274
Miles, E.W. 147, 224, 228, 234
Miller, V.D. 237
mimicry 321, 479–80
mindset 264–5, 267, 270, 271–2
Mislin, A.A. 173
misrepresentation of information 177–8
mixed emotions 119–20
mixed model approach to e-negotiations 376–9
mixed–motive settings 46–7, 47–58
mixed–motive task 5
mobilization frames 458
Mohamed, A.A. 434
monitoring 169–70
moods 27–8, 103–4
Moore, D.A. 368
Moote, M.A. 459–60
Morris, M.W. 320, 365, 367
motivated cognition 8, 46–74
    information provision 47, 63–8, 69

information search and information processing 58–63
    social motives *see* social motives
motivated deception game 65
motivated information processing strategy 105
motivation
    development of shared mental models and identities 85–6
    to escape conflict 421–2
    for making fair offers 194–5
    motivational orientation 6, 85–6
    motivational styles 29–30, 39
    see also motivated cognition
motivational frames 342
Mozambique peace negotiations 423, 430, 431
multi–attribute utility methods (MAUT) 453–4
multi–dimensional scaling 437
multi–issue negotiations 54–5
multi–issue offers 315
multilateral negotiations
    environmental negotiations 337, 465
    trade negotiations 390, 394–5, 399–410
        conference outcomes 408–10
        conference procedures 402–5
        conference strategy 405–8
        leadership 400–2, 410
        turning points 345–6
        and uncertainty 290–5, 302–3
multi–level conceptual framework *see* Negotiation Context Levels Framework
multiparty negotiations 11–12, 17–18, 283–307
    environmental negotiations 448–9
    intra–team negotiations 285–90, 302–3, 420–1
    marketplace negotiations 296–302, 302–3
    multilateral negotiations *see* multilateral negotiations
    need to study emotions in 123
    power and status 147–8
    as outcomes of negotiations 152–3
multiple options 200
multiple selves 16
multiple tactics and strategies 322–3

Murnighan, J.K. 106, 173, 184, 198
mutual–interest precedents 396, 397
mutual trust principle 203
mutually enticing opportunities (MEO) 421
mutually hurting stalemate (MHS) 421

Nagorno–Karabakh peace negotiations 430, 435, 436–7
naïve realism 62–3
names of terrorist groups 488
Naquin, C.E. 205, 365
Narlikar, A. 409–10
Native Americans 447
Neale, M.A. 61, 144, 145, 150, 297
negative affect 27–8
negative emotions, expression of 264, 265–7, 269–70, 272–3
negative linkages 394–5
Negotiation Context Levels Framework 499, 505–15
  crossing levels 511–15
  local and global context 506, 510–11, 512–15
  proximal and distal temporal factors 506, 509, 511, 512–15
  surface and deep level characteristics 506–9, 511–12, 513–15
negotiation linkage 392
negotiation self–efficacy 31
negotiation strategies *see* strategies
negotiation tactics *see* tactics
negotiation training 243, 275–6
negotiatiors 4, 6–9
  research directions 500–1
  resilience 349–50, 351–2
  roles 222–5
  surface and deep level characteristics 506–9
    and local and global context 512
    and time 511
    and time and local and global context 513–15
  see also culture; emotions; gender; individual differences; motivated cognition; power; shared mental models; status; trust
Nelissen, R.M.A. 198
neuroscience 186–7, 508–9

neuroticism 27
Nixon, C.J. 206
non–competitively linked negotiations 392
non–state conflicts 433, 434
nonverbal communication 171–2
  lack of cues in electronic communication 358
  sequences 319–22
Nonverbal Negotiation Inventory 314
normative power 295
North American Free Trade Agreement (NAFTA) 337, 338–9, 395, 398, 425
North London crisis negotiation 473–87, 491–2
Northcraft, G.B. 61
Northern Ireland 420
nuclear disarmament 458
nuclear power 451–3
Nugent, W. 479
number of bidders 296–7, 298

Ocker, R.J. 362
O'Connor, K. 108
Odell, J.S. 400–1, 404, 411
offers
  fair 193–5
  reactions to unfair offers 197–200
  sequence/progression of 324–5
offers and substantiations (S&O) strategy 175, 263–73
Olekalns, M. 57–8, 147, 151, 207, 208, 341, 342
open systems perspective 241–3
openness 27
operating coalitions 293
optimism 421–2
organizational justice 192, 211, 212–13
Ormerod, T. 483
Oslo I accords 430
other
  concern for 29–30
  prosocial dyads 57–8
  prosocial motivation/orientation 30, 50–2, 56, 85
  weight assigned to others' outcomes 48–50
outcome bundling 393
outcomes

cultural differences and 263–73
e–negotiations and 366, 367–8
evaluation of environmental
  negotiation outcomes 461–2
gender and 229–31
implementation 173
  and durability of peace
    agreements 417, 428–32,
    432–3
influence as outcome 152–3
multilateral trade conferences
  408–10
shared cognition and identity 77, 78,
  92–3
social motivations and weights
  assigned to own and others'
  outcomes 48–50
suboptimal 149–50
outsiders 289–90
Overbeck, J.R. 114, 146, 147
own outcomes, weight assigned to
  48–50
oxytocin 186

parental leave 236–8
Pareto optimality 250
Passow, S. 391, 392
Paulson, G.D. 365
payment of reparations 183
peace negotiations 14–15, 19, 416–44,
  505
  gender and 239
  getting parties to the table 417,
    419–22
  implementation and durability of
    peace agreements 417, 428–32,
    432–3
  negotiation process 417, 422–8
  research directions 417, 432–7
peacekeeping operations 429, 431–2
Pearce, K.D. 238
penalties for violation 170
penance 182
Pentland, A. 477
perceived power 136–7
perceptions
  of emotion 35
  gender and 229
performance 38–9
Perry, G.M. 206

personal agency 29–30, 223
personality 7, 36–9, 503
  big–five model 26–7, 374
  enduring dispositions 26–9
  e–negotiations 373–4
  epistemic motivation and 59
  social value orientation 50–2
personality x situation (PxS)
  interactions 37
perspective exchange 88–9
phase models 339–40, 475
Philippines, The 428
Phillips, K.W. 287, 288
physical force 133
physiology 508
Pietroni, D. 112
Pillutla, M.M. 106, 173
Pinsonneault, A. 89
Plato 116
Polin, B. 182, 183
political context 464
Polzer, J.T. 294–5
Popular Front for the Liberation of
  Palestine (PFLP) 478
population density 252–4
positive affect 27–8
positive linkages 395
Postmes, T. 88
postural complementarity 150–1
potential power 136–7
power 10, 133–60, 501
  coding schemes 314, 315
  culture and 254–5, 256–7
  definitions and perspectives 134–8
  effects on cognition, attitudes and
    behavior 138–40
  e–negotiations 374–5
  and fairness 195
  framing 342
  and gender 146, 234–5
  leadership in multilateral trade
    conferences 402
  multilateral negotiations 294–5
  as outcome of negotiation 152–3
  research directions 149–53
  shared cognition and identity 89
  and status in negotiation 144–8
  status vs 143–4
power–change tactics 136–7
power distance 256

power sharing 434–5
power–use tactics 136–7
Pozzebon, M. 89
precedents 396, 397
precipitants 334–5, 339, 343–4, 351–2
pre–negotiations 420–1
prescriptive gender stereotypes 10
prestige 140–1
    see also status
pride 142
Prietula, M.J. 324
prison sieges 487–8
Prisoner's Dilemma Game (PDG) 5
private value 298–9, 300, 301
problem solving 55
    approach to peace negotiations
        422–8, 438
    e–negotiations 379
problem–solving tactics 323–4
problem–solving workshops 424–5
procedural fairness 192–3, 211
    reactions 200–2
procedural justice 464
procedural precipitants 334–5
procedural turning points 339
procedures, at multilateral trade
    conferences 402–5
process
    development of shared mental
        models and identities 84–91
    e–negotiations 365–7
    environmental negotiations 451,
        455–6
        evaluation 459–61
    gender and behavior during 227–9
    peace negotiations 417, 422–8
    suboptimal processes 149–50
process induction 436
process tracing 436
prognostic frames 458
prominent solutions 61
proof of life 491
proself dyads 57–8
proself motivation/orientation 50–2,
    56, 85
prosocial dyads 57–8
prosocial motivation/orientation 30,
    50–2, 56, 85
prospect theory 61
Provis, C. 203

proximal time factors 506, 509
    and global and local context 512–13
    and negotiator characteristics 511
    negotiator characteristics, local and
        global context and 513–15
proximity analysis 316
Pruitt, D.G. 5, 55, 56, 202, 421, 481
psychological closeness 376–9
psychological distance 358–60, 363–5,
        370–6, 380
    advantages in e–negotiations 370–2
    contingency approach 373–6
    mixed model approach 376–9
public resources 448–9
punctuated negotiations 13, 332–56
    approaches to analysis 335–6
    context 336, 343–6
    framing 336, 342–3
    interruptions 336, 339–41, 351–2
    research directions 346–51
    stage transitions 336–9
Putnam, L.L. 342–3

qualitative research 94
question and answers (Q&A) strategy
    175, 263–73
Quincy Library Group negotiations
    447–8, 457

Ragins, B.R. 234
Raiffa, H. 250, 283
Ramirez–Marin, J.Y. 268
rank–ordered preference lists 302
rapport development 474, 478–80
rational confrontation style 258–60
rationality 47–8
    misleading distinction from emotion
        115–16
Raven, B. 134
reactive devaluation 8
readiness 421–2
Reagan, R. 332, 339
real–estate agents 61
real world field settings 40
realized power 136–7
recipient 191, 192, 210
    bargaining games 197–200, 209
    ethics 209–10
    fairness 197–202
    negotiations 200–2, 209–10

reciprocal strategy sequences 318
reciprocation wariness 89–90
reciprocity 48
  patterns of 317–18
recognition of emotion 117
reflexivity 86–7
reframing 345–6, 409
regional trade negotiations 390, 394–5, 397–9
regression–based mediation 437
regret 112–13
regulation of emotion 117, 374
regulatory environment 375
regulatory focus 28
Reicher, S. 358
relational dialogue 481–3
relational messages 172–3
relational order theory 481–2
relational power 295
relational self–construal (RSC) 242–3
relationship building tactics 323–4
relationships
  agency and communion 29–30, 223
  e–negotiations and 362, 365, 368–9, 376
  ethics and 205–6, 207
  fairness and 196, 200
  peace negotiations 420
  shared cognition and identity 77, 78, 79–80
    dynamic process of development 87–90
    input 83
relative payoffs 199
relative power 135
reparation of trust 180–4
  strategies for reparation 182–4
reparations, payment of 183
repertoire of emotions 118–19
representation
  discursive 343
  environmental negotiations 451, 456–8, 460
  women as representatives 229
reputation 10, 67–8
  and status 141
  trustworthiness 168–9
research directions 500–5
  communication sequences 322–5
  context 503–5

crisis negotiations 488–91
culture 273–6
emotions 115–23, 500
e–negotiations 380
environmental negotiations 462–5
gender 240–3
individual differences 39–41
individual negotiator 500–1
peace negotiations 417, 432–7
power, status and influence 149–53
time 501–2
trade negotiations 411
trust 184–7, 501
turning points 346–51
resilience 349–50, 351–2
resources, mediation and 425–6
Richardson, B. 88
rights 314, 315
ripeness 421
risk 139
  and negotiator resilience 350
  perception and environmental negotiations 451–4
  trust and 167–8
Robinson, R.J. 32–3, 66, 176, 177–8, 204
Rockmann, K.W. 340, 349
Rodriguez Mosquera, P.M. 274
Rogan, R. 476, 481
role congruity 222, 224, 231, 235
  gender composition 232–4
role events 222
role theory 392–4
roles, social *see* social roles
Rosette, A.S. 115, 367
Ross, L. 63
Roth, N.L. 184
Rouhana, N.N. 424–5
Rousseau, D.M. 162
Rubin, J.Z. 3, 227
rule–based compliance 398
rules of origin 389
Russell, B. 133
Rwanda peace agreement 431

Sadat, A. 152
sadists 49
sado–masochists 49
salience 333–4
Salovey, P. 35

Salter, F. 146
satisficing 28–9
Saunders, H.H. 420–1
scale of environmental issues 465
Schminke, M. 213
Schwarz, N. 122
Schweitzer, M.E. 107–8, 208, 209, 371–2
scientific complexity 446–7
scope of environmental issues 465
scripts 323
  cognitive and terrorism 477–8
seating of representatives 457
Sebenius, J. 499
security dilemmas 422
self
  concern for 29–30
  multiple selves 16
  proself dyads 57–8
  proself motivation/orientation 50–2, 56, 85
  weight assigned to own outcomes 48–50
self–control 138–9
self–efficacy 31, 38–9
self–esteem 29
self–evaluation, biased 63
self–interest 47–8, 194–5, 259
self–serving precedents 396, 397
self–worth 251–2, 254–5
  sensitivity and response to insults 257–8
semantic matching 480
Semnani–Azad, Z. 320–1
sensemaking 17–18, 499
  crisis negotiations 474, 480–3, 490
sensitivity 254–5, 257–8
services 389
shadow negotiation 511
Shapiro, D.L. 162–3, 164
shared cognition *see* shared mental models
shared identity 8–9, 75–102, 285, 342, 423
  antecedents to development 81–4
  dynamic process of development 84–91
  integrative framework 77–81
shared mental models 8–9, 75–102
  antecedents to development 81–4
  dynamic process of development 84–91
  integrative framework 77–81
  outcomes of 92–3
Sheets, V.L. 239
Shirako, A. 141
Shoemaker, M. 342
Short, J. 358
short–term consequences 334–5, 351–2
Siegel, J. 360
sieges 485–6, 491
Siegler, R.S. 323
Sierra Leone 431
Sillars, A. 490
similarities 81–2
Sinaceur, M. 111–12, 114, 120, 165
Singapore 396
  trade negotiations with the US 388–91, 396
single–issue offers 315
single undertaking rule 402, 403
Sitkin, S.B. 184
situation
  epistemic motivation and 59
  factors and ethics 205, 208
  factors and fairness 196, 197, 199–200
  personality x situation (PxS) interactions 37
  see also context
situational matching 480
Sjostedt, G. 401–2
Slatkin, A.A. 484
Smith, P.L. 57–8, 151, 207, 208, 341
Snow, D.A. 458
social constructionist theories of commons 455
social context 9–12
social cues reduction 358, 363
social dilemmas 451, 454–5
social distance 13–14, 359, 364, 372–3
  benefits in e–negotiations 370–2
social–functional approaches to emotion 109–11
social identity model of deindividuation effects (SIDE model) 358, 359–60
social identity theory 76–7
social information processing (SIP) theory 358, 359–60

social interaction 12–14
  and social value orientation 51–2
  see also communication
social motives 46–7, 47–58, 60, 68–9
  and deception 64–6
  in integrative negotiations 55–8
  in negotiation 52–4
social movement organizing 458
social perception biases 7–8
social position exchange 88–9
social presence 358, 359–60
social–psychological outcomes 92–3
social–psychological processes 4, 9–12
  see also culture; ethics; fairness; gender; multiparty negotiations; power; status; trust
social referencing 110
social relations model (SRM) 38
social roles 11, 18, 221–48
  gender roles and negotiation roles 222–5
  see also gender
social value orientation (SVO) 7, 30, 31, 50–2, 53
  and ethics 67
  and fairness 195, 202
societal collectivism 262
solution migration 393
sources of conflict 343–4
South Africa 423, 428
Spain–US military base rights negotiation 338
spatial distance 359, 364, 372–3
spillover 350–1
spoilers 427–8
Sproull, L. 362
Sri Lanka 420, 428
Srivastava, J. 172–3
stage transitions 336–9
Stahelski, A.J. 57
state, role of in peace negotiations 434
statistical techniques 436–7
status 10, 133, 140–60, 501
  culture and 254–5, 256–7
  definitions and perspectives 140–1
  effects on cognition, attitudes and behavior 141–3
  e–negotiations 374–5
  as outcome of negotiation 152–3
  and power in negotiation 144–8

vs power 143–4
research directions 149–53
Stedman, S.J. 427, 428–9
Stein, J.H. 213
Steinel, W. 64, 65, 114
stereotype threat 230, 231
stereotypes 10, 61–2
Stevens, C.K. 243
Stillinger, C. 63
strategic fairness 53
strategic power 295
strategies
  communication sequences 311, 316–19
  cultural differences and 91, 263–73
  for dealing with an untrustworthy opponent 185–6
  matching 12
  mediation of peace negotiations 426
  multilateral trade conferences 405–8
  multiple mixed strategies 322–3
  social motives and 55–8
Straus, S.G. 362
stress 108
structural ambiguity 230
structural solutions 183–4
structural strategy sequences 318
structure 59
  of environmental negotiation processes 451, 455–6
  factors in crisis negotiations 487–8
  structural variables 12–13
Strudler, A. 203
Stuhlmacher, A.F. 230, 232
subjective evaluation 48
subjective value 39, 40–1, 153, 201–2
Subjective Values Inventory (SVI) 9
subjectivity 18–19, 499
submissive postures 150–1
submissive role 321–2
suboptimal assumptions and behaviors 145
suboptimal processes and outcomes 149–50
substantiation and offers (S&O) strategy 175, 263–73
substantive dialogue 481–3
substantive information processing 105
substantive precipitants 334–5
substantive turning points 339

suicide interventions 473–87, 491–2
Sun City peace agreement 436
Sundstrom, E. 234
surface characteristics 506–9
   and global and local context 512
   intra–team negotiations and surface–level similarities/differences 288–9
   and time 511
   and time and global and local context 513–15
survival 19
suspicion 164–5
Susskind, L. 445, 450
Swaab, R.I. 87, 92, 94, 321, 479, 507
synchronization 338, 346–8
syntactic matching 480

T–value 488
Table of Ten influence tactics 484–7
tactics
   communication sequences 311, 314–15, 316–19
   e–negotiations 365–7, 369
   ethical appropriateness of 176, 177–8, 203–4
   ethically ambiguous 176–8
   influence tactics 484–7
   multiple 322–3
   power–change and power–use tactics 136–7
take–some games 454
Tallberg, J. 401
Tamir, M. 116
task
   complexity and e–negotiations 376
   framing 226
   hidden profile tasks 287
   shared understanding of 82–3
   stereotypes 224
   structure 90–1
Taylor, P.J. 338, 473, 477, 479–80, 482, 486–7, 488
teams
   intra–team negotiations 285–90, 302–3
   see also groups; multiparty negotiations
teamwork 76
temporal distance 359, 364

temporal horizons 16–17, 350–1, 499
temporal theory 395–7
Tenbrunsel, A. 195
terrorist group names 488
terrorist negotiations 15, 417, 476, 477–8, 488
thin slicing 477
Thomas, S. 338, 479–80
Thompson, L. 92, 112, 193
thought and talk method 325
threats 114, 145–6, 177–8
Tiedens, L.Z. 111–12
tight cultures 174–5
time 16–17
   proximal and distal factors 506, 509
   and global and local context 512–13
   negotiator characteristics and 511
   negotiator characteristics and local and global context 513–15
   research directions 501–2
   temporal breaks 340–1
   temporal distance 359, 364
   temporal effects and emotions 120–1
   temporal horizons 16–17, 350–1, 499
   temporal theory and linkage theory 395–7
Timor–Leste 432
Tomlin, B. 337, 338, 425
Tomlinson, E.C. 173–4, 182, 183
Tompkinson, P. 194
total power 135
toughness, bargaining 172
Touval, S. 408
trade associations, regional 397–8
trade negotiations 14–15, 387–415, 505
   bilateral 388–97
   linkages 391–7
   multilateral 390, 394–5, 399–410
   regional 390, 394–5, 397–9
   research agenda 411
   turning points 345–6
   US–Singapore 388–91, 396
traditional competitive bargaining 177–8
tragedy of the commons 455
training, negotiation 243, 275–6
Trans World Airlines (TWA) 345
transaction cost frame 342

Index 539

transformational strategy sequences 318
transitions between stages 336–9
transnational negotiations *see* multilateral negotiations
transparadoxical approach 514–15
transparency 404
Triple Dominance Measure 50–1
triple–interact sequences 319
Trope, Y. 358–9
trust 10, 10–11, 16–17, 161–90
  consequences of broken trust 178–9
  crisis negotiations and mistrust 474, 475–80
  culture and 174–5, 260–1
    negotiation strategy and outcomes 264, 267, 268–9, 270–1
  development in negotiation transactions 171–4
  dilemma of 167, 168–71
  framing and 342
  how broken trust can be repaired 182–4
  how it can be broken 175–8
  interruptions and 341
  minimum level for a successful negotiation outcome 186
  mutual trust principle 203
  nature of 162–6
  peace negotiations 419–20, 422–3, 430
    mediation 425–6
  reparability of broken trust 180–2
  research directions 184–7, 501
  and resilience 350
  shared mental models and identity 88
  why it is integral to negotiation 166–8
trust congruence 11, 173–4
trustworthiness 165–6, 168–9
  strategies for dealing with an untrustworthy opponent 185–6
truth telling 176–7
  see also deception; lying
turning points 13, 332–56, 425, 502
  approaches to analysis 335–6
  context 336, 343–6

  expanded model 351–2
  features of 333–5
  framing 336, 342–3
  future research directions 346–51
  interruptions 336, 339–41, 351–2
  stage transitions 336–9
  three–part model 334–5
Tversky, A. 60–1
two table problem 456, 511
Tyler, T.R. 193, 201, 211

ultimatum bargaining games (ubgs)
  ethics 204–6, 209
  fairness 193–6, 197–200
  social motives in negotiation 52–4
uncertainty 17–18, 499, 504
  environmental issues 446–7
  of identity 285, 291–2, 296–7
  of inclusion 289–90, 293–5, 300–2
  of interests 286–9, 292–3, 298–300
  in multiparty negotiations 17–18, 283–307
Underdal, A. 401
underlying interests 5
understanding
  conflicts of 343, 344
  emotion 35
UNEP Disasters and Conflicts Subprogramme 465
unfair offers, reactions to 197–200
unintentional interruptions 340
unions 148, 379
United Nations peace operations 429, 431–2
United States (US)
  Administrative Procedures Act (APA0 450
  Clean Air Act 463
  Endangered Species Act 450
  environmental negotiations 447, 449, 450, 463–4
  EPA 450, 461–2, 463
  Federal Advisory Committee Act (FACA) 449, 450
  Negotiated Rulemaking Act 464
  Spain–US military base rights negotiations 338
  trade negotiations
    with Australia 396
    with Singapore 388–91, 396

United States–Singapore Free Trade Agreement (USSFTA) 388–91, 396
unknown pot bargaining games 195
UNMIL 432
unmitigated agency 30
unmitigated communion 30, 82
UNOCI 432
UNPROFOR 432
unstable matching 301–2
UNTAC 432
Ury, W. 5, 135
USDA Forest Service 463
Uslander, E. 430

Valacich, J.S. 363
value
  common 298–9, 300–1
  in marketplace negotiations 298–300
  private 298–9, 300, 301
  subjective 39, 40–1, 153, 201–2
value-based conflicts 344, 447–8
value claiming 144–5
Van Boven, L. 92
Van Dijk, E. 53, 195, 205–6
Van Kleef, G.A. 111, 112–13, 113–14, 114–15, 121, 145, 266, 448
Van Lange, P.A.M. 50, 51, 197
verbal accounts 182–3
verbal cues 171–2
verification 170
Vermunt, R. 195
victims of crisis negotiation 490–1
violent conflict 416, 418–19
  diversity of 433–5
  management of violence 427–8
  see also peace negotiations
virtual negotiation see electronic negotiations (e–negotiations)
vocal dynamics 313
Volkema, R.J. 204, 208, 209, 210
voluntary compliance 398

Wager, L.W. 392
Walters, A.E. 227, 228, 230
Walther, J.B. 358

Walton, R.E. 3, 243, 337–8
Wang, L. 196
warmth 254–5, 260–3
Watkins, M. 391, 392
Watson, D. 27
Weber, J.M. 168
Weber, M. 134
Wehr, P. 426
Weingart, L.R. 312, 314, 324
Weinstein, A. 445
Weisband, S. 362
Wilson, J.M. 362–3
Wilson, M.A. 477–8
Wiltermuth, S.S. 151, 321–2
winner's curse 298, 299
wolves 448–9
Wong, E.M. 140, 146
Wood, W. 222, 223
work background 33
work–life balance (WLB) 236–8
workshops, in peace negotiations 424–5
World Trade Organization (WTO) 345–6, 387, 390, 391, 394, 397, 399
  Doha Round 408, 409, 410
  leadership roles in 400–1
  multilateral conference procedures 402–5
  negotiation agenda and multilateral effectiveness 408–9
  phases of a multilateral conference 403–4
  Trade Negotiation Committee 404
worry 112–13
Writers' Guild of America (WGA) 342

Yamagishi, T. 268, 269
Yaverbaum, G.J. 362
Yeo, G. 389–90
yielding 55

Zak, P. 186
Zartman, I.W. 430
Zimbabwe 435
Zoellick, R. 389–90